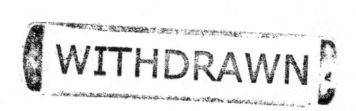

CAMBRIDGE STUDIES IN LINGUISTICS

General Editors . W. SIDNEY ALLEN . C. J. FILLMORE .
E. J. A. HENDERSON . F. W. HOUSEHOLDER . J. LYONS .
R. B. LE PAGE . F. R. PALMER AND J. L. M. TRIM

A Grammar of Yidiɲ

In this series

* Issued in hard covers and as a paperback

A GRAMMAR
OF YIDIɲ

R. M. W. DIXON

Professor of Linguistics,
Australian National University

CAMBRIDGE UNIVERSITY PRESS

CAMBRIDGE

LONDON · NEW YORK · MELBOURNE

Published by the Syndics of the Cambridge University Press
The Pitt Building, Trumpington Street, Cambridge CB2 1RP
Bentley House, 200 Euston Road, London NW1 2DB
32 East 57th Street, New York, NY 10022, USA
296 Beaconsfield Parade, Middle Park, Melbourne 3206, Australia

© Cambridge University Press 1977

Library of Congress catalogue card number: 76–27912

ISBN 0 521 21462 9

First published 1977

Printed in Great Britain at the
University Press, Cambridge

This book is dedicated to

> Dick Moses,
> Pompey Langdon,
> George Davis,
> Katie May,
> and the late Tilly Fuller,

who shared their language with me.

And to the remaining members of the
Yidiɲd̲i and Guŋgaɲd̲i tribes, who have –
through no fault of their own – lost most
of their own language and culture.

In the hope that they may be allowed
to remould their lives, and their own
society, in ways that they themselves
choose.

Contents

List of maps and plates

Preface

This is the grammar of a language originally spoken by perhaps 2000 members of the Yidiɲɟi, Guŋgaɲɟi and Maɖaɲɟi tribes, living in rain forest just to the south of the present city of Cairns, North Queensland. The writer collected some data on Yidiɲ from 1963, and worked intensively on the language from 1971 to 1975. Although there are only a handful of speakers remaining, fluent text material was obtained from Tilly Fuller (who died in 1974), Dick Moses and George Davis. The eagerness of the main informants to have their language recorded, together with their intelligence and perceptiveness, has led to a full range of data being obtained for every level of linguistic description.

Yidiɲ is quite close genetically to its northerly neighbour Dya:bugay, which is known from a short grammatical sketch by Hale (1976a); they are as similar as, say, French and Spanish. Comparison with Dya:bugay and reconstruction of aspects of proto-Yidiɲ–Dya:bugay – as well as more general reference to on-going work on comparison and reconstruction for the whole Australian language family – helps to explain many morphological alternations and irregularities in Yidiɲ.

Yidiɲ is as different from its southerly neighbour, Dyirbal (see Dixon 1972) as it is from almost any other language in Australia (while still showing typological similarities characteristic of Australian languages as a whole). Important points of grammatical difference are commented on, in small print, as are a number of interesting surface similarities (some of which may be the result of areal diffusion).

An attempt has been made roughly to separate grammatical facts (in chapters 2, 3 and 4) from theoretical interpretation (in chapter 5). A notable feature of Yidiɲ is that its grammatical categories do not fall into neat pigeon-holes. For instance, either dative or locative case may realise a certain syntactic category, and either straightforward apposition or else genitive marking can be used for inalienable possession. In each case the choice is governed by a semantic hierarchy, and operates on a 'more/less' (rather than an 'either/or') basis. Somewhat analogously,

some syntactic operations show a 'nominative–accusative' pattern (with the identification of transitive and intransitive subjects) while others work on an 'absolutive–ergative' principle (intransitive subject being identified with transitive object). Partly because of this grammatical fluidity, the 'tree structure/constituent' symbolism that is currently fashionable in grammatical description appears less than ideal for Yidiɲ.

The description is loosely based on the transformational–generative model, with a 'configurational symbolism' being used in place of the normal trees; this recognises a strict division between core elements (subject, object, main verb) and peripheral elements, the latter being subdivided into local and non-local (e.g. indirect object). The syntactic derivations which operate on these configurations are identical in form and function to conventional transformations.

The grammar also owes a good deal to the Sapirean tradition: in particular, care is taken to distinguish between the structure of words (morphology), the association of words to form phrases (phrase syntax) and the structure of sentences (sentence syntax). The syntactic description is at every stage related to semantics, paying attention to the fact that the basic task of any language is to enable meanings to be conveyed from speaker to hearer.

Ample exemplification is given for each grammatical point. About a third of the sentences quoted are from running texts, the remainder coming from material dictated by informants (only a small part was directly elicited for purposes of the point under discussion). Examples taken from the texts included at the end of the book (numbers 2, 9 and 14) are referred to by text and line number.

English glosses are kept as close as possible to those supplied by informants. For instance, *gaɲarA* is glossed 'alligator' since that was the English word always employed (despite the fact that 'crocodile' might be a scientifically more appropriate translation). Yidiɲ NPs do not obligatorily choose for definiteness or number; and one tense choice covers both 'present' and 'future'. These categories have been specified fairly arbitrarily in English translations, according to the context and/or the informant's gloss. Nothing concerning the structure of Yidiɲ should be inferred from examination of the translations.

And so, I offer this book particularly to those graduate students in American and European Universities who are sufficiently interested in out-of-the-way languages to peruse a study such as this (although not

sufficiently dedicated to undertake fieldwork themselves, and document some previously undescribed language). As you squat in your theoretical cocoons, reinterpreting data to fit universal hypotheses and generate PhDs: many happy restatements!

March 1976

Acknowledgements

Whatever value this study may have is largely due to the friendship of Dick Moses (*ḍariyi*) and the late Tilly Fuller (*buru:ɲ*), their willingness to record reminiscences and traditional stories, and generally to teach their language to the writer and answer his questions. It is impossible to overestimate the insightful and thoughtful skill that they devoted to this task. Thanks are also due for the substantial help received from Pompey Langdon (*ḍaluṟu*), George Davis (*ŋaŋgabana*), Katie May (*dugulum*), Ranji Fuller (*ḍaruga*), the late Richard Hyde (*bumiḍi*), Ida Burnett (*ɲuḍun*), the late Jack and Nellie Stewart (*mirbi, wayŋgubi*), Alec Morgan (*gaṟḍu*) and Robert Patterson (*ɲalmbi*).

The main research was undertaken in six field trips between December 1971 and December 1975, largely financed by the Australian Research Grants Council (with some supplementation from the Australian National University). Preliminary fieldwork in 1963/4, 1967 and 1970 was financed by the Australian Institute of Aboriginal Studies. The support of these bodies is gratefully acknowledged.

The Director of Aboriginal and Island Affairs, Queensland, and the various managers of Yarrabah settlement were most helpful. Particular assistance, at Yarrabah, came from Joe Rogers, Father and Mrs Brown, Stan Connolly and Sue Chinnery. The Yarrabah Council and Alf Neal provided help and encouragement in many ways.

Norman Tindale, Ken Hale, Carolyn Strachan, La Mont West Jr and Peter Sutton graciously made available their field notes and tapes on Yidiɲ. Tasaku Tsunoda searched for speakers of Guŋgay on Palm Island. Ken Hale and Helena Cassells allowed free use of their unpublished materials on Dya:bugay. John Haviland supplied material on Guugu-Yimidhirr, and fomented a number of ideas. Henry and Ruth Hershberger made available data on Gugu-Yalanji.

Sue Kesteven contributed theoretical ideas for chapter 2, and later read the whole manuscript; her insightful comments, criticisms and suggestions were most valuable. Thanks are also due, for discussion, ideas, data, references, and/or comments on sections of the manuscript, to Barry Alpher, Peter Austin, Jo Birdsell, Terry Crowley, Diana Eades,

Les Hiatt, Harold Koch, Bob Layton, Ilse Lehiste, Kenneth Pike, Geoff Pullum, Karl Rensch, Tim Shopen, Michael Silverstein, Neil Smith and Anna Wierzbicka, in addition to members of the class 'A12 – Australian Linguistics' at the ANU during 1975.

Abbreviations

+ morpheme boundary

word boundary (in chapter 2 this refers to phonological words, and in chapter 5 to grammatical words)

sentence boundary

→ in phonological rules and realisational rules

⇒ in syntactic derivations (= transformations)

> diachronic 'becoming'

/ end of intonation group (possible sentence final intonation)

C coastal dialect

T tablelands dialect

In chapter 2 we employ

S stressed syllable
U unstressed syllable
C consonant
V vowel

In chapters 3–6 we use

S subject of an intransitive verb
A subject of a transitive verb
O object of a transitive verb
Σ sentence
NP noun phrase (see 4.1.1–2)
VC verb complex (see 4.1.3)
sg singular ⎫
du dual ⎬ referring to
n-sg non-singular ⎭ pronouns

In chapter 5 we use (see 5.1.7, 5.2.1–2)

[...] to enclose the 'core' of a sentence: subject, object and main verb

: to indicate the relation between the core and syntactic peripheral elements

; to indicate the relation between the core and local peripheral elements

$+/-/\emptyset/\text{ap}$ indicate types of peripheral NP and subordinate clause (see 5.2.2, 5.3)

a, b, c, ... refer to specific NPs

V, W, ... refer to specific VCs

X, Y, Z, T, ... are variables, each referring to any non-null sequence of components

INV is a dummy verb 'involve' (see 5.4)

INCHO is a dummy verb 'become' (see 5.4.9)

CR(a, b) indicates that a and b are coreferential

M(a) refers to the case marking on a

The abbreviations '↔', '{', '//', '≠', '⌐', '←', '→', '.' and '⌐' used in 5.6 are fully explained in that section

Yidiɲ sentences are often provided with an interlinear gloss (in addition to English translation of the complete sentence). In this, lexical items are given in lower case and grammatical elements in small capitals. For the latter the following abbreviations are used:

ABL	ablative case	INTR	intransitive
ABS	absolutive case	LOC	locative case
ACC	accusative case	PRES	present-future tense
ALL	allative case		inflection
CAU	causal case	PURP	purposive case, and
CAUS	causative verbaliser		verbal inflection
COM	comitative nominal and	REDUP	reduplicated
	verbal suffixes	SUBORD	subordinate
DAT	dative case	TR	transitive
ERG	ergative case	VBLSR	verbaliser
GEN	genitive suffix	S, A, O refer to syntactic functions
IMP	imperative inflection	(and are sometimes used in
INCHO	inchoative verbaliser	glossing pronominal and
INST	instrumental case	deictic forms) – see above

Rough guide to pronunciation

Most of the discussion this book is fairly technical, and is addressed to students of linguistics. There are, however, a number of topics that may be of more general interest, to non-specialists in linguistics. The following rough guide to pronunciation is provided to assist this wider audience.

i is pronounced like the vowel in English *bit*

u is pronounced like the vowel in English *took*, but without the rounding of the lips

a is pronounced like the vowel in English *rally*

: indicates a lengthened vowel – thus *i:* is pronounced as *ii*, *u:* as *uu*, and *a:* as *aa*

b, d, l, m, n, y and *w* can be pronounced almost exactly as in English

g is pronounced as in English *gate*

r is a rolled *r*, as in Scottish pronunciation

ɽ is quite close to the English pronunciation of *r*, as in *arrow*

ɲ is like an *n* and a *y* pronounced simultaneously, similar to the nasal sound in English *onion*

ḍ is like a *d* and a *y* pronounced simultaneously, sharper than the English *j* sound in *judge*; *ḍ* does not have the friction of English *j*, but is a stop consonant, like *b, d* and *g*

ŋ occurs only at the end of a syllable in English; it is the single sound after the vowel in *sing*. *ŋ* begins most pronouns and many other words in Yidiɲ (as in other Australian languages) and it is worth making the effort to pronounce it word-initially. One way of learning how to say *ŋayu* 'I' is to begin with *sing*, add *-ayu* to form *singayu*, and on repetition gradually omit the *si-*, thus *singayu, singayu, singayu, ngayu, ngayu*.

I The language and its speakers

1.1 Linguistic type

Yidiɲ is a fairly typical Australian language (see Dixon 1972: 1–21 for a brief account of some of the recurring features of languages of the continent). It is basically agglutinative and almost exclusively suffixing. The norm word order appears to be 'subject–object–verb', but considerable deviation from this is possible.

Its phonology accords with the normal Australian pattern: there are no sibilants or fricatives, and no distinction of voicing. The sixteen segmental phonemes comprise four stop-nasal series (bilabial, apico-alveolar, lamino-palatal and dorso-velar), one lateral, two rhotics, two semi-vowels and three vowels. Vowel length is phonologically significant but (apart from a set of exceptions involving only a dozen lexical items) no roots involve long vowels. Length is introduced through some morphological processes (of affixation) and through a number of rather sweeping phonological processes. The latter operate to satisfy certain stress targets: a word should, if possible, contain a whole number of disyllabic units (either all of the type 'stressed–unstressed' or else all of the type 'unstressed–stressed'). If it does have an odd number of syllables then the extra syllable must be unstressed.

There are clearly defined classes of noun, adjective, locational qualifier, time qualifier, (first and second person) pronoun, deictic, verb, adverb, particle and interjection. In addition to singular and non-singular forms of pronouns there is a dual in the first (but not the second) person. Definite deictics – which also have some of the functions of third person pronouns in other languages – do not vary for number but involve a three-term spatial system: the third term – complementing 'here' and 'there' – is 'invisible' in the tablelands dialect, but 'far and visible' in the coastal dialect.

There is a system of ten cases for nouns, adjectives, pronouns and deictics; locational and time qualifiers take a limited selection from these inflections. There are ten stem-forming affixes that can precede case inflections with nouns and adjectives; these include 'genitive' (which

can take any further case inflection), and 'comitative', which has a strikingly wide semantic range.

Verbs show a two-term tense system (past versus non-past). Derivational affixes optionally mark 'motion aspect' – that is, whether the action is done during or after 'coming' or 'going'. There are three conjugations, characterised by 'linking morphemes' (between stem and affix) *-n-*, *-l-* and *-ṟ-* respectively; whereas the first two conjugations appear to be open, less than twenty members are known for the *-ṟ-*class. Subclasses of 'transitive' and 'intransitive' verb correlate statistically with, but do not coincide with, the conjugations.

There are three types of subordinate clause (each marked by a special verbal inflection) that correspond to the three kinds of peripheral syntactic NP (marked by dative, purposive and causal cases), which in turn parallel the three kinds of local NP (locative, allative and ablative). The functions of these subordinate clauses correspond to those of 'relative clauses' and 'complements' in other languages.

Yidiɲ has wide derivational possibilities – for deriving transitive and intransitive verbs from nouns and adjectives, deriving transitive from intransitive verbs, and so on. The verbal affix *-:ḍi-n* has a wide range of syntactic and semantic effects – marking anti-passive and reflexive constructions (surface intransitives derived from deep transitives), or an event where the 'agent' does not have volitional control over the action, or an event that is incomplete and continuing.

Pronouns inflect in a nominative–accusative paradigm (one case marking both intransitive subject and transitive subject), deictics with human reference have separate cases for transitive subject, transitive object, and intransitive subject functions, whereas nouns show an absolutive–ergative pattern (here a single case combines intransitive subject and transitive object functions). There is in addition a semantic hierarchy – from human nouns, through animates to inanimates – conditioning a number of quite disparate grammatical choices in Yidiɲ.

Sentence modification is achieved partly through a set of a score or so of non-inflecting particles (marking negation, retribution, completion, reflexive, trying, and so on) and partly through half-a-dozen post-inflectional affixes that can be added to a word belonging to any part of speech (with meanings 'now', 'still', and so on).

A noun phrase will typically involve both a 'specific' and a 'generic' noun. Investigation of generic–specific co-occurrences reveals a well-defined semantic system based on the 'nature' and the 'use' of an

animal or object. There are three levels of interrogative: 'what (genus)?', or, with the genus being known, 'what (species)?', or, finally, with the species being known, 'what sort of?' (demanding, say, an adjectival description).

1.2 Dialects

The Yidiɲɖi tribe – speaking the Yidiɲ language – lived in the rain forest just south of Cairns, occupying a fair area of coastal flats (but with access to the sea only at Cairns inlet, and near the mouth of the Mulgrave River), the foothills of the range, and a tapering finger of tableland extending as far inland as Kairi (see map 1). There were five or six 'local groups', named after the type of territory with which they were associated (in terms of conception sites, and so on) and which they occupied most of the year:

> *gulgibara* (*gulgi* 'sand'; *-bara* is a productive affix 'person belonging to–' – see 3.3.6) 'sand people' – the local group associated with the (sandy) seashore, and the lower reaches of the Mulgrave River and its tributaries, where it flows through sand.

> *malanbara* (*malan* 'large flat rock') 'flat rock people' – the local group associated with the upper reaches of the Mulgrave River (and the Little Mulgrave) where the river predominantly flows through rocks.

> *walubara* (*walu* 'side of hill') 'hillside people' – living close to the *malanbara* group, in the foothills of the range, but off the main rivers.

> *gambi:ɽbara* or *bundabara* (*gambi:ɽ* 'tablelands', *bunda* 'mountain') 'tablelands people' – inhabiting the thick 'scrub' which characterises mountains on top of the tableland.

> *warginbara* (*wargin* 'forest') 'forest people' – associated with the slighly less dense 'forest' between mountain peaks in the tableland.

> *baɖabara* (*baɖa* 'grassy plain') 'grasslands people' – inhabiting the high grassy plains on the tableland (where kangaroos are most plentiful). There was a substantial area of grasslands between Yungaburra and Atherton, and Yidiɲɖi territory extended a short way into it.

Each local group had its own dialect. There are nowadays too few speakers remaining to attempt a detailed assessment of dialectal differences, but it does appear that the *gulgibara* (or 'coastal') speech was

the most divergent, and was opposed to *malanbara, walubara, gambi:ɽbara, warginbara* and *baḍabara,* which formed a second ('tablelands') dialect group. Basic lexical items were almost all identical for the coastal and tablelands varieties, but there were some minor variations of form and meaning and a few quite small grammatical divergences; these are fully documented at the appropriate place below.

The Guŋgaɲḍi tribe – speaking Guŋgay – lived on the Cape Grafton Peninsula, to the east of the Yidiɲḍi over the Murray Prior Range, and visited Green Island. There is now no one living who can speak Guŋgay, but present members of the Yidiɲḍi and Guŋgaɲḍi tribes say that it was mutually intelligible with Yidiɲ – this is confirmed by the lexical evidence available in old vocabularies (see Appendix). To the south of Yidiɲḍi in the coastal region were the Maḍaɲḍi people, speaking Maḍay (reputedly so-called because they used the form *maḍay* for 'spear'); this tribe lived around Babinda and the mouth of the Mulgrave River. There are no speakers remaining for this tongue, and no vocabularies attributed to Maḍay (although the name is mentioned in Gribble 1933: 4, 143, but with a different location: 'mouth of the Barron River' instead of 'mouth of the Mulgrave River'). A further 'language' Waɲur or Waɲuru is known from vocabularies by Tindale and by Nekes and Wurms (see Appendix) – it was reportedly spoken to the south of Babinda and around the Russell River. A speaker of Mamu (from the south) told the writer that there were two distinct tribes, Waɲur(u) and Maḍaɲḍi, but speakers of Yidiɲ scarcely recognised the name Waɲur(u). It is perhaps possible that Waɲur(u) and Maḍaɲḍi were alternative names for a single tribe (as N. B. Tindale has suggested, private communication).

There are only lexical data available for Guŋgay (around 200 words) and Waɲur (less than 100 words). The percentages of lexical items identical or almost identical between the dialects are:

Yidiɲ		
80%	Guŋgay	
78%	69%	Waɲur

These, together with the reports of present-day members of the Yidiɲḍi and Guŋgaɲḍi tribes, suggest that Yidiɲ, Guŋgay and Waɲur could have been regarded – for linguistic purposes – as mutually intelligible dialects of a single language. (If Maḍay was not an alternative name for Waɲur, it is likely that it would have been linguistically – as it is geo-

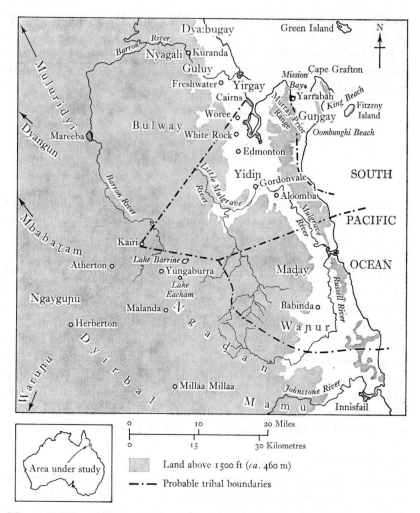

MAP 1. Yidiɲ and surrounding dialects. (Based on Roth 1910b; McConnel 1939–40; Tindale 1940; and the writer's field work. The broken line indicates approximate tribal boundaries for the peoples speaking dialects of Yidiɲ; it is not known whether Maḍay(ɲḍi) and Waɲur(u) were distinct tribes, or two names for the same group. The locations for the groups speaking the Dya:bugay language: Dya:bugay, Guluy, Yirgay, Bulway and Nyagali – are each based on a single source and have not been checked; it is possible that some of these terms may be alternate names for a single dialect/local group/tribe.)

graphically – intermediate between Yidiɲ and Waɲur, and closely similar to both of them.)

It is likely that what we can call 'the Yidiɲ language' had (at least) four main dialects; these can be schematised in approximate relative geographical positions:

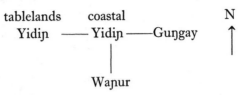

It does seem that connections between the dialects followed the lines in the diagram. For instance, there appears to have been little common to Guŋgay and Waɲur that was not also shared by coastal Yidiɲ (in fact, the limited sources reveal just one word, *ḍibi* 'hair', occurring in Guŋgay and Waɲur – and also in Dya:bugay – but not in Yidiɲ). Thus coastal Yidiɲ would have been the central dialect, maintaining communication with Guŋgay (on the promontory to the east), Waɲur (along the coast to the south) and tablelands Yidiɲ (in the mountains to the west).

It is likely that the grammar which follows would, in broad details, be applicable to the four-dialect language. But textual, grammatical and extensive lexical data have been obtainable only for coastal Yidiɲ and tablelands Yidiɲ. There is some phonotactic information on Guŋgay, but nothing is known of the eccentricities of grammatical detail which must surely have characterised the Guŋgay and Waɲur dialects.

1.3 Surrounding languages

To the north of the Yidiɲḍi were a number of tribes (or local groups) speaking what appear to have been – like Yidiɲ, Guŋgay and Waɲur – dialects of a single language: Yirgay, Guluy, Bulway, Nyagali and Dya:bugay (see map 1). As in the case of groups speaking Yidiɲ, tribal names were derived by the addition of the comitative suffix -(ɲ)ḍi – thus Yirgaɲḍi, Buluwaɲḍi, Dya:bugaɲḍi. Nowadays the name Dya:bugay (which is said to have been originally the name of the dialect spoken on the coast, towards Port Douglas) appears to be used by speakers to refer to the whole language, and Dya:bugaɲḍi to name the whole speech-community.

Dya:bugay, while clearly a separate language, is without doubt closely genetically related to Yidiɲ (and no other language belongs to

this 'sub-family'). There are close similarities in pronoun roots, in noun and verb inflectional and derivational affixes, and in some enclitics, suggesting that it should be possible to reconstruct a fair portion of proto-Dya:bugay–Yidiɲ. A 400-word sample reveals that 53% of the lexicons are identical or very similar, suggesting that the languages have been separate for a long enough period for the fraction of common vocabulary to have dropped (through separate taboo and replacement in the two languages) to the 'equilibrium level' (see Dixon 1972: 330–41).

To the south, Yidiɲ and Waɲur are contiguous with two of the dialects of the 'Dyirbal language' – Ngaḍan and Mamu. Yidiɲ and Dyirbal are – considering that they are both languages of the general Australian type – totally dissimilar in every area of grammar. Lexically, Yidiɲ has only 20% (identical or closely related) items in common with the central Dyirbal dialect, 22% with Mamu and 29% with Ngaḍan.

There appears in fact to have been considerable social contact between speakers of tablelands Yidiɲ and of Ngaḍan, who had territories of the same ecological type – forested tablelands with rivers flowing through deep ravines. For instance, Ngaḍan-speakers had the Yidiɲ-type two-moiety system, as against the four-section system of the other tribes speaking Dyirbal, and of their neighbours to the south and west (Dixon 1972: 31). Note also that the Yidiɲ method of deriving a tribal from a language name – by the productive comitative affix -(ɲ)ḍi following a consonant, -yi following a vowel (3.3.4, 4.3.1) – is used in the tribal names Ngaḍanḍi and Dyirbalḍi (the latter being an alternative to the name Dyirbalŋan), although the comitative affix in Dyirbal is -bila ~ -ba.

There appears to have been a fair amount of grammatical and phonological diffusion in the Yidiɲ–Ngaḍan area, leading to a number of points of surface similarity. For instance, both Yidiɲ and Ngaḍan have introduced contrastive vowel length rather recently, but in quite different ways (2.3.5). In Yidiɲ the penultimate syllable of a word with an odd number of syllables was stressed, then the vowel was lengthened, the length becoming distinctive when the final syllable was dropped e.g. *malánu* > *malá:nu* > *malá:n* 'right hand' (cf. *málan* 'flat rock'). In Ngaḍan a sequence of vowel-plus-liquid was replaced by a long vowel at the end of a syllable e.g. *bálgan* > *bá:gan* 'hit' (cf. *bágan* 'speared'). Contrastive length thus appears to be a regional feature shared by the Ngaḍan dialect of Dyirbal, Yidiɲ and Dya:bugay; it is missing from languages to the north of Dya:bugay (Gugu-Yalaɲḍi), to

the west of Ngaḍan (Ngayguŋu) and to the south of Yidiɲ and Ngaḍan (the remaining dialects of Dyirbal). As another instance of tablelands Yidiɲ/Ngaḍan similarity we can note that whereas Guŋgay and coastal Yidiɲ allow a final -*ŋ* in the phonetic form of words, tablelands Yidiɲ is like Ngaḍan in not allowing words to end in -*ŋ* (an underlying final -*ŋ* is realised in terms of vowel nasalisation – 2.6.3). Finally, the system of demonstratives in tablelands Yidiɲ coincides in form with those in the coastal dialect, but in meaning with the demonstratives in Ngaḍan and other Dyirbal dialects (3.7.1).

There is fuller discussion of these points, together with an account of the meanings that can be attached to the terms 'tribe' and 'language' for this region, in Dixon 1976b.

But the similarities between Yidiɲ and Ngaḍan are all at the surface level. Anyone knowing just one language would find the other quite unintelligible (many members of the two tribes had a degree of bilingualism in Yidiɲ and Ngaḍan – but this was, of course, quite another matter). The rather low lexical score between Yidiɲ and Ngaḍan – 29 % – suggests that they had been in contiguity for a relatively short time (certainly, a shorter time than that which has elapsed since Yidiɲ and Dya:bugay emerged as separate languages).

To the south-west of Yidiɲ was Ngayguŋu, an extinct and poorly documented tongue. Although Ngayguŋu had its greatest lexical similarity with Dyirbal (54 % on a 150-word comparison), it may well have been grammatically more similar to Waruŋu, its south-westerly neighbour (with which it has 47 % common vocabulary). Yidiɲ has 24 % vocabulary in common with Ngayguŋu, suggesting that there may have been a little recent borrowing; but the languages appear to have been basically quite dissimilar.

Ngayguŋu is known only from mentions by Roth (1901b, 1910b) and Sharp (1939); Tindale (1940: 157) mistakenly identifies it with Dyangun. Tilly Fuller, the writer's main informant for tablelands Yidiɲ, volunteered that her mother had told her of the Ngayguŋu language spoken around Herberton, but knew no more. Note that the tribal name is reported as Ngayguŋu-yi or Ngayguŋu-n-ḍi, again involving the comitative affix from Yidiɲ. The only linguistic materials on Ngayguŋu are unpublished – Roth compiled a 187-word list in 1898 (Mitchell Library, Sydney; uncatalogued manuscript number 216) and Tindale collected seven words in 1938 (privately making these available to the writer).

To the north-west of Yidiɲ, but perhaps not quite contiguous with it, was Mbabaɽam, a language which is on the surface highly aberrant but which can be shown to have developed from a language of normal Australian type through a number of rather drastic historical changes (Dixon 1972: 347–50 and forthcoming – b). Mbabaɽam only has around 20% likely cognates with Yidiɲ, but there are some possible grammatical similarities; more work is required to investigate the possibility of a close genetic connection between the two languages.

To the north-west of Mbabaɽam and Dya:bugay were a chain of closely related languages (or dialects?) – Wagaman, Dyangun, Muluriɖi and Gugu-Yalaɲɖi. Both lexically and grammatically these show little similarity to Yidiɲ or Dya:bugay; for instance, Yidiɲ and Muluriɖi – whose territories must have approached each other very closely just south of Mareeba – have less than 30% vocabulary in common.

1.4   Cultural background

Each Yidiɲɖi local group would spend most of the year in its own country (see 1.2); but at certain times, when a staple fruit was ready, the whole tribe would be likely to gather in one place. The advantage of a vegetationally-heterogeneous tribal territory was that in every season there was some food available in some part; coincidentally, it seems that fruit would ripen in a particular region at the time when it was climatically most pleasant to live there. Thus the coastal local groups would be likely to ascend to the tablelands – to eat yellow walnut (*gaŋgi*) and loya-cane (*mudi* and *yabulam*) – in the wet season, when the coastal flats were particularly hot, humid and insect-ridden. And the tablelands groups would come down to the coast – for Mulgrave walnut (*digil*) and quandong (*murgan*) – in the winter, avoiding some of the worst of the mountain frosts and mists.

The Yidiɲɖi had an extensive 'calendar', detailing observations of phenomena that indicated when food of a particular type was likely to be ready. Thus, when the golden flower comes out on the wattle tree (*ɖuwa:ɽ*), the carpet snake (*wuɲul*) is fat and ready to be eaten; when (inedible) white fruit appear on the *gaɽaŋgal* vine, it is time to dig for scrub-turkey eggs in the high mounds in which they are buried; when the brown pigeon (*ɖudulu*) calls out [dɔ̃ dɔ̃] it is a sign that wood grubs (*ɖambun*) will be at their most luscious; and when the small bean tree (*wuwuy*) flowers on the tableland it is time to erect stone traps or yards

in the shallow parts of tableland rivers, and catch fish when they are at their fattest.

A fair proportion of the Yidiɲɟi diet came from flesh foods – wallabies, possums, bandicoots, fish, eels, turtles and so on. But the staples were a handful of vegetables, most of which required quite complex preparation. For instance, when the tail feathers of the willy wagtail (*ḏigirḏigir*) turn white it is time to gather rickety nuts (*badil*), on the small hills in coastal country. This is roasted in the fire, its shell is cracked and it is buried in the ground overnight. The next day it is ground fine on a large flat stationary stone, by circular movements of a round grinding stone (*mugay*), then sieved through a dilly-bag, and put into the river at some rapids or a small waterfall, with water directed in a stream onto the nut by a spouting of rolled ginger-leaves. It will be left in the water overnight and can then be eaten, after a minimum of forty-eight hours preparation. Then, when the black scrub locust (*gaɲa:l*) first cries out, around Christmas time, it is a sign to ascend to the tablelands to gather black pine (*gubu:m*). This is first roasted in its shell, then the shell is broken and the kernel roasted, then the dried nuts are hung up in a dilly-bag for a short while. The nuts are chopped up, with a stone, and then ground fine, and sieved through a dilly-bag before being eaten (although this process can be shortened, and *gubu:m* eaten after only a few minutes preparation – 1.5). (And see Roth 1901b for a list of three dozen edible plants and a similar number of edible molluscs for the Guŋgaɲɟi tribe, with some details of their preparation.)

There were also signs which indicated imminent natural happenings – for instance, a cyclone. Inland tribes uniformly recognise that if they encounter sea-gulls too far from the sea, then a cyclone is approaching. When the coastal Yidiɲɟi saw the *ḏalŋgan* (a black bird, rather like a duck, with a red head) flying unusually close to the ground, to avoid the first breath of a high wind, they knew a cyclone was coming and would gather in large low huts for maximum protection from the winds. (Note that there is in Yidiɲ an appropriate verb *ɲarmbi-l* '[come down to] approach [but not reach] the ground' for describing this action by the bird – cf. 6.1.2.)

Green tree ants, *ḏilibuṛa*, were held to have medicinal properties by the Yidiɲɟi (as by neighbouring tribes) and were not included under the generic term *muɲimuɲi* 'ant' (6.2.1). The ants would be squeezed between the hands and the resultant 'milk' flavoured with clean ashes – obtained by burning wood from a blue gum tree (*gawu:l*) or a quandong (*murgan*)

or a type of tea-tree (*bagiram*) – before being drunk. Alternatively, a hardy man could effect the cure by putting the green ants directly on to his chest, and allowing them to bite him (see also Gribble 1932: 15).

The Guŋgaɲɖi and Yidiɲɖi appear to have excelled at the manufacture of mother-of-pearl fish-hooks, dilly-bags woven from loya-cane, and bark water-carriers; these were, apparently, made only by men in this region (Roth 1904, Gribble 1932: 6). Indeed, these were their major objects of trade – Gribble (1932: 31) 'remembers one trade route along the coast of north-eastern Queensland where canoes would come from the tribes in the Port Douglas district, bringing hardwood spears, and take back the cane baskets made by the Goonganjie people inhabiting Cape Grafton. The very last of these trading canoes came from the north in the year 1894'. And Roth (1910a: 18–19) gives a full account of Guŋgaɲɖi trading: 'dealing now solely with the Cape Grafton Blacks, it would appear that, prior to the institution of the Yarrabah Missionary settlement, the following list comprised the trade-articles of home production: bicornual dilly-baskets (taken or sent to Port Douglas, the Mulgrave and Barron Rivers, Mareeba and Herberton), grass-bugle necklaces (for the Mulgrave and Russell Rivers), four-pronged fish-spears (Mulgrave and Upper Russell Rivers, Johnstone River, Clump Point, etc.), straight spear-throwers without the shell-haft (for the Mulgrave, Johnstone and Russell Rivers), bent or moon-shaped spear-throwers, large fighting shields, and long single-handed swords (all for the Barron River and northwards). The imports constituting the Cape Grafton northern trade, coming mainly from the Barron River and Port Douglas, included the following: hour-glass woven-pattern dilly-bags, round-base basket dilly-bags, beeswax necklaces, straight shell-hafted spear-throwers, a variety of bamboo spear, square-cut nautilus-shell necklaces, and cockatoo top-knot head-dresses. The southern foreign trade, which used to come in either directly or indirectly from the Mulgrave River, comprised: long swords, boomerangs, shields, opossum string armlets, and the large oval-cut pearl-shell chest ornaments, the last mentioned being said to have reached the Mulgrave River via Atherton and Herberton, whither it was believed to have been brought from the Gulf country. The trading, amongst the Cape Grafton Blacks, was not carried out by any particular members of the community, the bartering being apparently personal, each one doing business on his own account.' An unusual moon-shaped woomera (*baluṛ*) was in use from Cape Grafton north to the Bloomfield River (Roth 1909: 199) and was

held to have magical properties (Gribble 1933: 7, 145; 1932: 56–7 – and see 1.8 below).

There were fighting and singing corroborees, involving several neighbourhood tribes, at regular intervals (Roth 1908). In addition to providing a regulated outlet for aggressiveness, these served for social intercourse – the exchange of news, stories and songs – and were probably used for trading. It is significant that there appears to have been little or no trading or social meetings with the Dyirbal-speaking tribes, to the south. In fact Stan Connolly, a Guŋgaɲḍi who has tried to reconstruct his tribal history, maintains that the Yidiɲ-speaking tribes lived in perpetual fear of the Mamu and Dyirbal – whom they regarded as much fiercer and more aggressive than themselves – and that the Guŋgaɲḍi (a relatively weak tribe) had a 'pact of defence' with the more dominant Yidiɲḍi, that the latter would come to their aid if they were attacked by 'the Tully mob'. Although there appears to have been some contact between the Dyirbal-speaking Ngaḍaṇḍi and the inland Yidiɲḍi – on the tablelands – there seems to have been little interchange along the coast. The writer discussed this with middle-aged Dyirbalŋan men, and they said it would explain why – in their youth – people came from a good way inland (from Ravenshoe and Herberton) to corroborees at Tully, but no one from north of Innisfail was seen there. It thus seems that Yidiɲ-speakers had major contact along the coast with those whose language was genetically closest (Dya:bugay-speakers), and little or no helpful intercourse with those whose language was most different (Dyirbal-speakers).

Young men were initiated around puberty. Circumcision was unknown on the east coast, but horizontal cicatrices (*wadir* or *muyŋga*) would be cut across the chest and stomach, after the stomach had been distended by food. Newly initiated men had to sit with their heads down (to avoid looking around the camp) in the lap of an older man. They were only allowed to leave the camp – for toiletry purposes – under supervision, and then the track had to be brushed clear of all leaves and twigs before they went along it. They were forbidden to scratch their bodies with their hands, but were provided with a small sharpened stick (*biwi*) for the purpose. By-and-by, the initiates were taken to bathe in salt-water, to wash pus from the wounds, but they now had to keep their eyes upwards, to avoid looking down into the water and annoying the rainbow-serpent. In fact, one powerful myth from this area (originating with the Ngaḍan tribe) tells how two young initiates strayed from the

camp by themselves and, trying to spear a wallaby, hit instead a flame tree, which is sacred to the rainbow-serpent. When the spear was extracted it had a grub on its point, breaking a further taboo. As a result, the rainbow-serpent punished the people by causing the sky to glow red and yellow, cracks to open in the earth, and water to pour up, engulfing the camp. This – which could pass as a plausible account of a volcanic eruption – is said to explain the volcanic crater lake, Eacham (see also Dixon 1972: 29).

The Yidiɲɟi had a considerable number of myths explaining the origin of animals and birds, of geographical formations, and so on. Unfortunately, most of these are now forgotten – and are known only by allusion – but the writer was able to collect parts of eight traditional tales. These all relate to a time in the distant past to which speakers of Yidiɲ apply the English name 'storytime' (Yidiɲ *gubi* – and note also the adjective *bulu:ɽ* 'storytime person, thing or place'); the term 'dream-time' is not used in this region and there seems to be no connection with 'dreams'.

For instance, one story tells how the rainbow (*guɖuguɖu*) originally had the only fire in the world, while the birds (who were 'storytime people') were shivering and getting sick from eating raw food. Various birds and a grasshopper tried unsuccessfully to snatch the fire away (the ways in which each was prepared for its attempt accounts for its present colouring, and other physical characteristics). Then the black satin bird (*baɖin*) – who can glide down and alight so swiftly that his arrival is not noticed – succeeded in getting the fire. The rainbow was told by the birds that he would never again have fire, but that he must now take to the water (the opposite of fire, and incompatible with it); he went to dwell in deep water-holes in the river. It is believed that these are still the abode of the rainbow and children are discouraged from bathing in deep pools for this reason (thus providing an admirable safety regu-lation). A small rainbow can often be seen in the spray of a waterfall (which are common in this region), which will invariably have a deep water-hole below it. When the rainbow (who is also believed, throughout Australia, to be able to take the form of a snake) is seen in the sky, he is thought to be travelling from one water-hole to another, or just coming out of the cold water to warm himself in the sunshine, the nearest he can get to the fire he once possessed. (There is a rather different story explaining the origin of fire, attributed to the Guŋgaɲɟi tribe by Roth 1903: 11; see also Gribble 1933: 7, 145.)

There was a complex set of beliefs surrounding the rainbow – for instance, a full rainbow in the sky can be called by the name *gamim* 'father's father', while a middle-sized rainbow can be referred to as *bimbi* 'father', and a short one as *yaba* 'brother' (in the same vein, the moon is referred to as 'mother'). But these are now largely forgotten, and the writer was only able to glean isolated fragments.

A major part of most Yidiɲ and Guŋgay myths involves the travels over the territory of storytime heroes, and the naming of places, according to something the hero saw there, or something that befell him. The most important story of this type concerns Gulɲɖaɽubay, who travelled around Cape Grafton, up the coast from near Innisfail, and all the way up the Mulgrave River – fragments of this story (dealing with places in different parts of the tribal territory) were remembered by three different informants. For instance, at one point Gulɲɖaɽubay comes to a rock on the coast (near what is now called Oombunghi Beach) opposite a small offshore island that has a freshwater spring on it (presumably the outlet for an underground freshwater stream from the mainland). The island reminds him of a child being fed by its mother through its umbilical cord and he calls it *ɲumbubu* ('new-born child'), naming the rock on the mainland *ɖibin* ('navel'). (Some place names are – like these – identical to a common noun or a verbal form, but others involve some apparently gratuitous accretion to a lexical root. The mechanics of place-name formation is discussed in 6.1.2.)

Yidiɲɖi myths clearly state that their present (coastal) territory was at one time occupied exclusively by the Guŋgaɲɖi. A man – called, in some accounts, Yidiɲ or Yidi – came by boat from the north with his people (in the story, all men) after their own country was inundated by water. It is said that at that time the Guŋgaɲɖi people spoke a different language, but the Yidiɲɖi party (which included Gulɲɖaɽubay) told them they would one day forget their own language and be able to speak only Yidiɲ.

It is currently unfashionable in anthropological circles to attribute any historical basis to traditional stories and myths. It is, however, worth noting that a theme running through all the coastal Yidiɲ myths is that the coastline was once where the barrier reef now stands (as in fact it was, some 10,000 years ago), but the sea then rose and the shore retreated to its present position. The only common noun denoting 'island' is *ɖaruway*, which also means 'small hill' – contrasting with *bunda* 'mountain, big hill'. The proper name of Fitzroy Island is *gabaɽ* 'lower arm',

so called because most of this geographical feature was submerged and only one extension remains above water. Note also that there was a place half-way between Fitzroy Island and King Beach that was called *mudaga* ('pencil cedar') after the trees which grew there; it is now completely submerged. Again, Green Island is said to have been at one time four times as big as it is now – only the north-west portion remains above water (this is, in fact, consistent with water depths around it).

Tindale and Birdsell (1941: 1, 5) report that 'in the eastern coastal and mountain region near Cairns is an area where exist several small tribes of a people characterised by a high incidence of relatively and absolutely small stature, crisp curly hair, and a tendency towards yellowish-brown skin colour...The preliminary results of blood grouping tend to substantiate the distinctness of the bloc of tribes.' They gave twelve tribes belonging to this 'Barrinean type' – six speak Dyirbal, two Dya:bugay and three Yidiɲ (Yidiɲɟi, Guŋaɲɟi and Waɲur). The final tribe is Mbabaṟam, speakers of a highly divergent language (see 1.3) which Tindale took to be symptomatic of the Barrinean languages being 'unAustralian'. In fact, the languages show striking similarities with languages spoken in other parts of the continent (by Aborigines who do not show Barrinean physical characteristics); the point worthy of note is that there is such a large linguistic difference – and such overt hostility – between the Yidiɲ–Dya:bugay speakers in the northern part of Tindale and Birdsell's bloc, and the Dyirbal speakers in the south. Note also that Dyirbal shows considerable similarities with languages on the South Queensland and New South Wales coasts, and that travellers in Dyirbal myths all come from the south (Dixon 1972, 1976b).

It is tempting to speculate that there may well have been, in the Cairns Rain Forest region, a people of a different physical type from the tribes around them, who may at one time have had their own distinctive language and culture. One would expect such an isolated block to be gradually infiltrated – perhaps by Dyirbal-speakers from the south, and by Dya:bugay/Yidiɲ-speakers from the north. This would explain the strong linguistic boundary half-way down the Barrinean bloc. It could also explain the Yidiɲ story concerning the Guŋaɲɟi tribe being the original inhabitants (the Barrinean people) and the Yidiɲɟi men coming by sea from the north (and presumably marrying Guŋaɲɟi women). Certainly, the story insists that the Guŋaɲɟi could not at that time understand Yidiɲ, whereas by this century Guŋay and Yidiɲ were without doubt mutually intelligible.

The writer was intrigued by this hypothesis, and by a comment from the main coastal Yidiɲ informant – admittedly highly prejudiced against Guŋaɲɟi (see the comments on tribal hostility at Yarrabah in 1.7) – when he volunteered that the Guŋaɲɟi were harmless and weak people 'like a midget'. As

a result of this he contacted Dr J. B. Birdsell, to see if the data from his 1938 measurements lent any support. Birdsell replied:

'Taking the two attributes of weight and stature 19 adult male Yidiɲḍi average 110.7 pounds whereas 10 adult male Guŋgaɲḍi weigh but 97.6 pounds. The range of weight in the two tribes respectively is 88–125 pounds and 78–119 pounds. Turning to stature for the same individuals, the Yidiɲḍi average 156.7 centimeters with a range of 149.4–166.8 centimeters. The Guŋgaɲḍi, on the other hand, average but 152.8 centimeters, showing a range from 139.9 centimeters to 165.9 centimeters. Although the series are not as large as would be liked, they are all we will ever have, and I am confident that the differences are of sufficient magnitude to be statistically real, and further correspond to general field impressions of the two groups.

'There is a way of doubling our universe, and that is to take the females from the two tribal groups. These are a much smaller series but the differences are of roughly similar magnitude and in the same direction. For the Yidiɲḍi seven women weighed 96.6 pounds with a range from 74 to 121 pounds while the Guŋgaɲḍi for eight women showed a mean of only 88.1 pounds with a range from 64–104 pounds. For stature the Yidiɲḍi average 147.0 centimeters, ranging from 139.0 to 152.5 centimeters. The little Guŋgaɲḍi averaged but 143.5 centimeters, with a range from 136.6–146.9 centimeters. The differences in stature match those of the males, while the differences in weight are in the right direction but slightly less.

'Since we are dealing with small breeding universes here, who numerically may never have been very large, I think there is no reason to doubt the general validity of these figures and the differences they reveal. I think your informant may have faintly exaggerated the difference between the two peoples but I don't doubt that in the curious sword duels indulged in in this area a difference of 13 pounds between males of the two groups would mean a considerable difference in endurance. (The duelling swords are heavy, made of hardwood, and slung in single alternating strokes over the head against the opponent. Strength would make a very considerable difference in the effects.)'

1.5 Moieties

The coastal Yidiɲḍi maintain that their most important story (which appears also to have been known to the Dya:bugay) concerned two 'storytime' brothers, Guyala and Damari (one version was recorded as Text 2 – pp. 513–30 below). They came into Yidiɲḍi territory, arranged all the foodstuffs that were to become the sustinence of the tribe, and ordered other aspects of daily life. Guyala was the sensible brother, who was always keen to make things easy and rational, whereas Damari was a 'silly fellow' who tried to make things as difficult as possible. They had

an argument over each type of food they were giving to the people. Guyala wanted the rickety nut, *badil* (see 1.4), to require only a short soaking in water before it was ready to eat, but Damari maintained that it should be very bitter, so that it had to be soaked for a long time (here Damari, by his persistence, won). Then Damari wanted the black pine, *gubu:m*, to require lengthy preparation but Guyala argued that it should be edible after just a few minutes roasting (in this case Guyala won). There was another argument about the mountain yam, *ḍimir*; Guyala wanted it to grow near the surface so that one would only have to pull on the vine to get it up, but Damari was intent on sinking it it deep into the earth so that it would need to be dug up with a long, pointed yam-stick (here Damari won). Guyala then named all the animals, and all the places. Damari remonstrated that only a few places need be named, each some distance from the next; but Guyala argued that names must be given to places close together so that people could easily follow a well-known sequence of names – if they were too far apart people would get lost looking for the next place on their route (here Guyala won).

Guyala and Damari had arranged to fight some people one day. But Damari got up before dawn and went in the opposite direction, running up against the prickles on a Bougainvillea tree to simulate spear wounds. Guyala, thinking Damari had already gone to the fighting ground, went there and carried on the battle by himself; then Damari appeared with his fake gashes, pretending he had been in the battle all the time (at the side, where Guyala couldn't see him). Finally, Guyala took a canoe and returned to the north, where he died; Damari – after having half of one leg bitten off by an alligator – settled down and later died near the present site of Yarrabah.

Nowadays the coastal Yidiɲḍi have two moieties – Guramiɲa and Gurabana, which are said to descend from the two brothers, Guyala and Damari, respectively. Each Yidiɲḍi person belongs to one of the moieties, and must marry someone from the other moiety; children belong to the same moiety as their father.

Gurabana (*bana* = 'water', *gura* is unknown outside these compounds) is associated with the summer, when torrential rains make living and food gathering as difficult and unpleasant as possible. Guramiɲa (*miɲa* = 'edible animal') is associated with the drier winter season, when it is possible to plan an orderly existence, and there is plenty of flesh food to be had. It is easy to see why Gurabana is connected with Damari, the silly and obtuse brother, and Guramiɲa with Guyala, the

sensible and helpful one. The totems associated with Gurabana mostly have a connection with water or monsoonal conditions – storm, rainbow, and so on; *gindaḍa* 'cassowary' is also a Gurabana totem (the writer was told that while the 'rainbow' has the status of father's father to Gurabana people, the cassowary fulfils the role of father). The Guramiɲa totems include the 'fish hawk' *guya:l* (whose name is directly related to that of the storytime brother, *guyala*), the 'eaglehawk' *biḍu:*, 'fire' *buṛi*, and so on. Each Aborigine is named after some totem of his moiety; thus Dick Moses (see 1.8) belongs to the Gurabana class and is called *ḍariyi* after the verb *ḍari-n* 'disappear, sink down, become lost', here referring to the rainbow sinking down out of the sky.

There appear, overall, to be three pairs of names for moieties within the tribes and local groups speaking dialects of Yidiɲ. Firstly, the set discussed above:

(1) *guramiɲa – gurabana*

was given by Dick Moses, informant for coastal Yidiɲ; by Sharp (1939: 268–9) for Nyagali and Dya:bugay; and by Tindale (MS notes) for Yidiɲ and Dya:bugay.

But for Guŋga:ɲḍi, Gribble (1897b: 84) gives:

(2) *guragulu – gurabana*

and these are also the terms in Sharp (1939) for Guŋgay, Yidiɲ and Yirgay and collected by Tindale (MS notes) for Guŋgay. (In a later publication Gribble, 1933: 144, mentions all three moiety names, and is plainly confused by them.)

Finally, Tilly Fuller, Katie May, Pompey Langdon and George Davis – representing various local groups of tablelands Yidiɲḍi – and Mollie Raymond – the main informant for Ngaḍan – told the writer that in the tablelands region the moieties were:

(3) *guramiɲa – guragulu*.

Some (and maybe all) of the totems for (3) Guramiɲa correspond to those for (1) Guramiɲa; it has not been possible to check (1) Gurabana against (3) Guragulu. Note that the legend of Damari and Guyala is not known (except at second-hand) to tablelands Yidiɲḍi, although they do call the fish-hawk *guya:l*. (*damari* is in fact the name for 'centipede' in the Dyalŋuy 'avoidance' style of tablelands Yidiɲ – see 1.6.) It is said that when initiation was carried out at Baguṛgu, near Lake Eacham, the Guramiɲa men would be thrown to the right, and the Guragulu youths to the left.

There is little doubt that the Guŋgaɲḍi tribe – and probably also the Yidiɲḍi – were occasional cannibals. It is worth mentioning that the main tablelands informant, Tilly Fuller, insisted that Guragulu were permitted to kill and eat men, whereas Guramiɲa (her own moiety) were not. This could not be checked and the writer is rather doubtful of its truth.

At first, the writer wondered if one of the three moiety pairs might be an error. But each of the pairs is confirmed by sufficient sources for there to be no doubt that there were these three arrangements – involving every combination of two out of the three terms: Guramiɲa, Gurabana, Guragulu. Geographically, (1) intercedes between (2) and (3) so that we have, drawing a line from Kairi to Cape Grafton:

EAST	*guragulu – gurabana*	Guŋgay
CENTRE	*guramiɲa – gurabana*	Coastal Yidiɲ (and Dya:bugay?)
WEST	*guramiɲa – guragulu*	Tablelands Yidiɲ, and Ngaḍan

This is, at first sight, confusing. Thus a coastal Yidiɲḍi Guramiɲa person would, if he chose a spouse from the west, have to select a Guragulu. But it would be a coastal Yidiɲḍi Gurabana who would marry a Guragulu from the east. And if a tablelands Yidiɲḍi Guragulu married a Guŋgaɲḍi, he would presumably have to marry a Guragulu!

Whereas *miɲa* 'animal' and *bana* 'water' are amongst the commonest nouns in Yidiɲ, there is no form *gulu*. But *gulu* does appear in Dyirbal, as the negative particle 'not'. This might conceivably supply the solution to our puzzle. We could suppose that *gulu* functions here as a negative – in the west it marks the opposite to the positively specified *miɲa*, and in the east the opposite to the positively specified *bana*; it is only in the centre that both poles receive a positive identification. However, this is a highly speculative solution (put forward in the spirit of looking for SOME clue to what seems an unexpected and counter-intuitive arrangement of terms) which would require more concrete supporting evidence before it could be accepted with confidence.

Note that all the tribes to the south and west (including all other Dyirbal-speaking tribes) have a four-section system (Dixon 1972: 31). Sharp (1939: 442) implies that at least Dyirbal, Mamu and Ngaḍan have both moiety and section names. The writer's fieldwork indicates that this is not the case; Dyirbal and Mamu had four section names (and knew nothing of moieties) whereas Ngaḍan had simply the moieties Guramiɲa and Guragulu, and did not use any section names. Unfortunately – despite several tries – it has not been possible to ascertain which section was allowed to marry which moiety in, say, a Mamu–Ngaḍan cross-tribal union.

1.6 'Mother-in-law language'

It appears that, like the Dyirbal-speaking tribes to the south, each member of the Yidiɲɖi and related tribes had at his disposal two separate 'languages' or styles: a Dyalŋuy or 'mother-in-law' avoidance language, which was used in the presence of certain taboo relatives, and an every-day language, which was used in all other circumstances.

The Dyirbal-speaking tribes called the everyday language Guwal or Ngirma and the avoidance style Dyalŋuy, so that one had to talk of Giramay Guwal and Giramay Dyalŋuy, and so on. But no term corresponding to guwal/ŋirma was encountered for the Yidiɲɖi – one either spoke just Yidiɲ (that is, the everyday style) or else Dyalŋuy.

The Dyalŋuy style dropped out of use among the Yidiɲɖi many years ago and is almost forgotten now. The writer was able to elicit almost 200 words from two speakers of the tablelands dialect, but this involved considerable effort of memory, over a period of three years, on the part of the informants (all items were carefully checked between them). It would seem that Yidiɲɖi Dyalŋuy is organised along much the same lines as Dyirbal Dyalŋuy (Dixon 1971, 1972). Thus it has the same phonology and grammar (affixes, particles, pronouns and grammatical items like 'what') as the everyday style, but a completely different lexicon. And there are many-to-one correspondences between everyday and avoidance vocabularies, with the result that Dyalŋuy must have had many fewer dictionary items than everyday Yidiɲ. For instance, where Yidiɲ has two specific nouns *binduba* 'crayfish' and *ɖungi* 'freshwater shrimp', Dyalŋuy has a single noun, *wuɽuɲ*, covering both species. A detailed discussion is in 6.3.

Although a Dyalŋuy item is always different from the corresponding form in (everyday) Yidiɲ, it sometimes coincides with a word in, for instance, Dyirbal everyday language (see Dixon 1972: 33). Informants are, of course, aware of this and there is a tendency to over-generalise. In any elicitation of avoidance vocabulary in this area care must be taken to check that each item given is in fact Dyalŋuy and not JUST the everyday language item from the next tribe (since these do not, by any means, always coincide).

It was impossible to ascertain the exact circumstances under which it was obligatory to use Dyalŋuy. Comments were 'with mother-in-law, father-in-law, and certain cousins' and (for a female ego) 'with son-in-law or uncle'. This certainly suggests a pattern of usage similar to that for Dyirbal Dyalŋuy (Dixon 1972: 32).

Comparing the available data on Dyalŋuy vocabulary for the Yidiɲɖi tribe with that for three dialects of the Dyirbal language we get the following lexical identity scores (leaving aside Dyalŋuy–everyday language correspondences, and counting just Dyalŋuy–Dyalŋuy which coincide or are very similar in form):

Dyirbal dialect
56% Mamu dialect ⎫ of the Dyirbal language
45% 64% Ngaɖan dialect ⎬
29% 39% 51% Yidiɲɖi

It is instructive to compare these with the lexical scores between the everyday styles:

Dyirbal dialect
87% Mamu dialect ⎫ of the Dyirbal language
62% 70% Ngaɖan dialect ⎬
20% 22% 29% Yidiɲ

We see that the Yidiɲɖi Dyalŋuy is relatively close to the Dyirbal Dyalŋuys, whereas Yidiɲ everyday style is quite different from the Dyirbal everyday variety.

These figures suggest that the Dyalŋuy 'avoidance style' vocabularies increased to their present size relatively recently, after the proto-Dyirbal language had split into the various modern dialects, and after Ngaɖan had come into contact with Yidiɲ (see also Dixon 1972: 345–7).

Dick Moses, main informant for coastal Yidiɲ, who had not himself had the opportunity to learn the Dyalŋuy style (but was fully aware of its existence, and the conditions for its use) maintained that there was originally a separate tribe called Dyalŋuy, which lived around Aloomba (between Yidiɲ and Maɖay). This is a fascinating idea and opens up the possibility that these could have been the original Barrinean people (according to Tindale and Birdsell's hypothesis – 1.4), words from whose language were taken over by the invaders for a special social speech-style. (It might be thought that some support for this is given by the vocabulary percentages above. But note that the Dyirbal dialect and Yidiɲɖi score 29% in Dyalŋuy vocabulary as against 20% in everyday vocabulary. The difference is probably not sufficient to provide adequate support for the idea that the Dyalŋuys of Dyirbal and Yidiɲɖi were both based on a 'third language'. It is more likely that Dyalŋuy lexicons increased to their present size – as a sort of areal linguistic feature – partly through borrowing of avoidance vocabulary between tribes.)

However, there is no mention of a Dyalŋuy tribe in the literature (every

other tribe listed above is reported by one or more of Gribble, Roth, McConnell, Sharp, Tindale) and every other present-day Yidiɲɖi the writer questioned denied knowledge of any such tribe. Regrettably, it seems unlikely that there is any truth to Dick Moses's claim.

1.7   Recent history

The Yidiɲɖi tribe came into contact with Europeans with the establishment of Cairns, in 1876, and the settlement of the Atherton tablelands the following year. Within a decade almost all their tribal lands had been invaded – there were cattle, as well as two sugar plantations (each with its own mill) on the plains, matched by gold-diggers in the hills. The tribe did not take kindly to these incursions, and appear to have put up a strong resistance. Bolton (1963: 61–2) reports that 'the Mulgrave goldfield, deep in the rain-forests behind Cairns, attracted during 1879 and 1880 a few bold spirits, who, for the sake of gold worth £1 a day, could tolerate conditions in which, while one man was digging, his mate would have to stand over him with a loaded revolver to prevent the natives from stealing their tools'.

The Guŋgaɲɖi, cut off by the high Murray Prior range from Cairns and the Mulgrave, were left alone for a while. Then, in 1892, the Rev. John B. Gribble arrived at what is now called Mission Bay, on the north side of Cape Grafton, to found a mission there. In 1880 Gribble had begun the Warangesda Mission on the Murrumbidgee River; in 1885 he moved to the Gascoyne River in northern West Australia but attempts to establish a mission there failed. Gribble then founded a station at Brewarrina on the Darling River for the Aborigines Protection Society of New South Wales, before turning to North Queensland (Gribble 1930, 1932, 1933). But his health was failing and within six months he left for the south (dying there the next year); John Gribble's place at Yarrabah – as the mission was called – was taken by his son Ernest R. Gribble, then a catechist in training for the priesthood.

Gribble soon had many of the Guŋgaɲɖi living at Yarrabah, partly due to the cooperation of Minminiy (or 'King John' Barlow, as Gribble dubbed him – Gribble 1930: 68ff.). Minminiy did not himself live at Yarrabah but visited the mission about once a week, and appears to have assisted Gribble in keeping discipline. He was given a special uniform, with brown ribbon on it, which was apparently considered greatly superior to the brass plate normally issued to a European-appointed 'king'. As Gribble (1930: 77) reports it 'at the public meeting at which

John was formally appointed King of Yarrabah, he made a speech as follows: "Now, you people, I am your king; not a jump-up king like them blackfellows that got a brass plate on their neck, but a proper fellow king. I have got a lot of people to look after. And when you have any trouble with anybody, leave it to me, I am your king. When your wife growl, do not hit her, but leave it to me. When anything go wrong, leave it to me, and I will leave it to Mr Gribble". John was a regular communicant, two of his [original three] wives had married other men, and it was a treat to see the old man take his proper seat in Church at the daily services, resplendent in his uniform, or as with great dignity he took his place as President of the Yarrabah Court.'

Gribble appears to have been remarkably ill-suited to overseeing the integration of an Aboriginal tribe into European-dominated Australia. For instance, he appears to have had virtually no understanding of Aboriginal culture or social ethic. He certainly learned nothing of the language – filling in a vocabulary questionnaire for the *Australasian Anthropological Journal* in 1897, Gribble (1897a: 17) gave for 'to live' the form *gobo*, which is in fact 'leaf', and for 'to know' he quotes *gnudju,* which is actually the negative particle (*ɲuɖu* 'no, not' is one of the commonest words in Guŋgay and if Gribble had had even a smattering of the tongue must have recognised it). Gribble left Yarrabah, for health reasons, in 1909; there is no evidence that any of his successors were much better equipped for the task there.

It is said that the Board of Missions would not allow Gribble to return to Yarrabah, once he had recovered (although it has not been possible to check this). In 1913 he went, like his father, to West Australia to establish the Forrest River Mission. Biskup (1973: 128–9) comments on this period 'Gribble was very much the son of his father: headstrong, self-righteous and authoritarian, with a permanent chip on his shoulder and a tendency to blame others for his or the mission's misfortunes... he thought nothing of knocking down an aborigine who did something to displease him, or of "arresting" aborigines caught killing the mission cattle'. Biskup also records how 'in 1927 the Australian Board of Missions asked A. P. Elkin, who was about to leave for the Kimberleys as the Australian National Research Council's first Research Fellow, to report confidentially on Gribble's administration of the mission. Elkin's report amounted to an unqualified condemnation of the superintendent. He found that Gribble's relationship with his staff was a most unhappy one and that there was little trust between the superintendent and other missionaries. Staff living quarters were appalling and the food, consisting mainly of porridge, salted meat, and half-rotten bread, "not quite what

one would like even missionaries to have". Gribble's relations with the aborigines were equally strained. Parents who refused to part with their children had their rations stopped. Compound children were kept under constant supervision. On reaching adolescence they were married in complete disregard of tribal custom. Young men who refused to marry were lined up for work with adolescent boys. Family life was discouraged. Couples were allowed to spend the nights together, but in daytime the wives were kept in the "ladies' compound" – little wonder the mission was known in nearby Wyndham as Gribble's stud farm.' There is no confidential record of how Yarrabah was run in its early years, but it is likely that it was not too different from this picture of Gribble's administration at Forrest River.

In the first decades of this century the mission appears to have made some progress in establishing a European-type culture among the Guŋgaɲɖi, and the many members of the Yidiɲɖi and other inland tribes who were progressively 'sent to Yarrabah'. There were at one time a dozen small 'villages' scattered over the considerable area of the Aboriginal Reserve – there was a good deal of agriculture (at various times: paspalum grass, cotton, peanuts and bananas as well as potatoes, turnips and other staples) in addition to dairying and later poultry farming.

There are reports (for instance, Rowland 1960: 99) that the mission diet was not adequate, but there does appear to have been a measure of self-sufficiency, with some of the people surely having a little pride and satisfaction from organising their own lives and growing their own crops. People from outlying villages would come into the main settlement on Sundays for the (compulsory) church service.

However, the situation has greatly deteriorated since the last war. There are now about one thousand people at Yarrabah, all living in the central town – but there is no trace of any agricultural endeavour. There is, in fact, very little work available at Yarrabah. Typically, a group of new houses may be built and painted by white workmen from Cairns (who tendered for a government contract), with Aborigines perhaps being used to help dig the foundations. The settlement staff is almost entirely European and although the Aboriginal Council is consulted on some matters, all major decisions and organisational details are arranged by the white manager. Some men go over during the week to work at cane farms on the Mulgrave, but a great number of people at Yarrabah subsist largely on social security benefits; there is little chance for self-respect, or pride in any kind of achievement.

But if Yarrabah appears to have failed – by all social standards – as

PLATE 1   Dick Moses (*ḍariyi*), principal informant for the coastal dialect (Yarrabah, August 1973).

PLATE 2 Tilly Fuller (*buruːɲ*), left, and her sister Katie May (*duguluŋ*), speakers of the tablelands dialect (Aloomba, January 1972).

PLATE 3   From left: Dick Moses, Robert Patterson (*ɲalmbi*) of the Guŋgaɲɖi tribe, and Pompey Langdon (*ɖaluɻu*), a table-lands Yidiɲɖi (Yarrabah, August 1975).

PLATE 4   Illustration from the *Annual Report of the Chief Protector of Aboriginals* [Queensland] *for the year 1909* (Brisbane: Government Printer, 1910): 'Wedding of Albert, Prince of Yarrabah' (Albert was the son of *minminiy* – see 1.7).

a European community, it has done worse as an Aboriginal society. Children were taken away from their parents and placed in dormitories (between the ages of ten and about sixteen) where tribes were deliberately mixed, and they were laughed at for speaking their own language. Of the present population of Yarrabah only one Yidiɲḍi man – Dick Moses, *ḍariyi*, principal informant for this study – can speak his own language fluently; and this is simply because he was brought up at Woree, on the outskirts of Cairns, and did not come into the mission until his mid-teens. (During his early years on the mission, Moses is said to have been a 'hard case', who would not go to school or obey mission rules. It is probably because of this that he today retains his own language and culture.) Although there must be three hundred people at Yarrabah who reckon to belong to the Guŋgaɲḍi tribe, there is no one who knows as many as a hundred words of that language.

Despite being monolingual in English, the children speak only an attenuated version (but it is certainly a less rich variety of English, and not a separate 'pidgin' or 'creole'). The blame for this can fairly be placed on the early missionaries. As Gribble (1930: 99) himself put it 'in the early days of our work pidgin English was used by us all, and a beastly gibberish it was. As time passed, I determined that it should cease, and good English be used; and, strange to say, the people seemed to find it easier to avoid than the staff, who had got so accustomed to its use that they found it extremely difficult to avoid addressing in pidgin English every black they met.'

It is, in fact, instructive to compare Yarrabah with Hopevale Mission, just north of Cooktown, which was founded the same year. The Lutheran Pastor Schwarz – who founded Hopevale in 1886 and ran it until he was interned as an alien in 1939 – learned the language and wrote a grammar of it. The people at Hopeville still speak Guugu-Yimidhirr; and what is more, their English seems to be of a higher standard than that at Yarrabah. Hopevale provides a fair (but perhaps not a good) example of successful mingling of European and Aboriginal civilisations; the people have retained many of their tribal beliefs and values whilst living an essentially European-style life. The contrast with Yarrabah is striking.

Most young people at Yarrabah know as little of their environment as might a child brought up in the middle of Brisbane. The writer was told that many children do not know the (European, or Yidiɲ/Guŋgay) names of most of the trees growing in the reserve, still less how to prepare their fruit (see 1.4). They know little or nothing of their traditional tribal law, beliefs and legends: moiety-determined marriage died

out long ago, and most people today would probably not know that there were such groupings as moieties. The writer was told that the dormitory system had effectively eliminated contact between generations, so that parents had no chance to instruct their children in legends, language and customs. (But nothing has really replaced the old tribal beliefs. Church attendance ceased to be compulsory when Yarrabah became a Queensland government settlement about 1960; by 1970 a good Sunday might see twenty people attending a service.)

At a guess, about a third of the people at Yarrabah are Guŋgaɲɖi; a third may be Yidiɲɖi with the remainder coming from the Cairns hinterland or more distant parts of the state. Most people do still identify themselves as either Guŋgaɲɖi or Yidiɲɖi and there is today quite fierce hostility between the two tribes. When land rights are discussed the Guŋgaɲɖi sometimes insist that the Yarrabah Reserve is their traditional land and the Yidiɲɖi are interlopers; the Yidiɲɖi reply that King Alfred (Minminiy's son) had clearly said before he died that anyone who was born at Yarrabah (whatever tribe his parents were) belonged equally to the territory. In fact, tribal rivalry is the main positive feature of the dispirited, purposeless nature of life at Yarrabah in the 1970s.

There has been some slight improvement in the last three or four years – a bakery was opened in 1974, and is managed entirely by Aborigines (in contrast, Aborigines have no place in the general running of the settlement, this being entirely the province of white administrators appointed by the Department of Aboriginal and Island Affairs in Brisbane). In 1973 newspapers were brought over from Cairns each day for sale on the settlement. There is now a settlement bus, run by Aborigines, and an Aboriginal-owned taxi. But these are small advances towards what should be the eventual goal – a community run by Aborigines (with the sort of internal authority structure that characterised tribal life but which has totally disappeared over the past eighty years, another result of the dormitory system), providing useful and satisfying occupation for its members, and achieving a degree of self-sufficiency, and with it self-respect.

Those Yidiɲɖi who avoided being sent to Yarrabah fared both worse and better. There were the usual shootings by European settlers, and people outside Yarrabah probably had less overall chance of survival than those in the mission. But the tablelands Yidiɲɖi who did survive have today a much better life than their brothers in the settlement. They speak good English; and most of them have steady jobs and live in

cleaner conditions and better houses than is normal at Yarrabah. And, what is more, they know more about their environment and about their tribal customs and beliefs.

There was closer white settlement in Yidiɲɟi territory than in that of neighbouring tribes. The last Yidiɲɟi men to be initiated were in fact put through the ritual with other tribes. Thus Dick Moses, of the *gulgibara* local group, was initiated with the Dya:bugay-speaking Guluy, at Freshwater, and Pompey Langdon (of the *malanbara*) with the Dyirbal-speaking Ngaɖan, at Malanda. The last group of Yidiɲɟi who still lived something approaching a traditional life, and spoke their own language amongst themselves (while, at the same time, working as labourers for white settlers) lived at Goldsborough, in the foothills, until about 1934.

1.8 Sources for this study

There are many more members of the Yidiɲɟi and Guŋgaɲɟi tribes living at Yarrabah than outside it. But, of the dozen or so speakers or partial speakers of Yidiɲ the writer worked with during the last twelve years, all but two were living freely in Edmonton, Gordonvale, Aloomba, Kairi, Atherton or other towns.

The first Yidiɲ speakers to be encountered were also probably the most fluent: Jack Stewart (*mirbi*) and his wife Nellie (*wayŋgubi*) recorded three hours of Yidiɲ vocabulary at Lake Barrine in November 1963 (they had originally been contacted by W. C. Wentworth, M.H.R. who reported their whereabouts to the Australian Institute of Aboriginal Studies). Several further attempts were made to work with the Stewarts during the next nine months (when the writer was almost exclusively concerned with a depth investigation of Dyirbal) but each time they were either unavailable or too ill to work. Then, in 1967, when Jack Stewart again could not be located, his brother-in-law Alec Morgan (*gaɽɖu*) gave some grammatical information on Yidiɲ, and a few words in Dyalŋuy. By 1970, when the writer began intensive work on Yidiɲ, Jack and Nellie Stewart had died and Alec Morgan was totally senile and of no further use as an informant.

The data on tablelands Yidiɲ in this grammar were largely given, between 1971 and 1973, by Tilly Fuller (*buru:ɲ*). She was born and brought up at Kairi and spoke fluent Yidiɲ, recounting myths and legends and giving a detailed account of daily life in tribal times. Tilly Fuller remembered a good deal of Dyalŋuy (and also understood a fair amount of the Ngaɖan dialect of Dyirbal). Her sister Katie May

(*dugulum*) and step-son Ranji Fuller (*ḍaruga*) found it difficult not to mix English words and phrases into their Yidiɲ but were most helpful in translating Tilly Fuller's texts, and explaining grammatical and semantic points. Although she had had a more 'tribal' upbringing than any other Yidiɲḍi encountered, Tilly Fuller's father was English (from York) and she had been married to an Englishman (from Cambridge) – as she put it, with typical frankness 'I was having his baby so he did the right thing and married me'. In 1973 she was in hospital, and it was only possible to do a little work with her. Tilly Fuller died in October 1974, aged around 75. Some grammatical points which emerged from texts that she gave cannot now be clarified or extended (for instance, 're-duplicated aspect' – 3.8.6) since there is no one living who can match Tilly Fuller's knowledge of the tablelands dialect.

The only other informant who could give any words in the Dyalŋuy style was Pompey Langdon (*ḍaluṟu*), a speaker of tablelands Yidiɲ who lived at Blackfellow Creek, near Edmonton (and moved to Yarrabah in 1975). An initiated full-blood, Pompey Langdon is now aged over 80 and is not as mentally alert as Tilly Fuller or Dick Moses; he could not give texts but it was possible to check some lexical and simple grammatical points with him.

The youngest (and perhaps the only literate) speaker of Yidiɲ is George Davis (*ŋaŋgabana*). Born about 1919, he was brought up by his grandfather at Goldsborough – spoke Yidiɲ and drank opium with him and learned a good deal of tribal lore and belief. On his grandfather's death he went to school (at the age of fifteen or sixteen) and is today a contract timbercutter. In terms of his home, his way of living and general background knowledge and articulateness, George Davis could not be distinguished from his white neighbours in Atherton (and is the only one of the thirty or forty informants the writer has worked with in North Queensland whose living conditions resemble those typical of Europeans). Yet he retains a firm knowledge of tablelands Yidiɲ and of traditional stories and life-style (although, of course, much less rich than that of Tilly Fuller). George Davis's work in the bush makes him frequently inaccessible, but the writer was able to talk with him around Christmas 1974, and again in 1975, recording one legend and benefiting greatly from his clear and revealing explanation of lexical differences, and the complexities of mythic interpretation.

The main informant for this study was Dick Moses (*ḍariyi*) a full-blood born about 1898 into the *gulgibara* local group and now living at

Yarrabah. Moses assisted the writer on six field trips, between 1970 and 1975, working patiently for five or six hours each day recounting myths and autobiographical stories, correcting transcriptions, checking and counterchecking lexical forms and meanings, and patiently providing examples of grammatical points, leading the way to generalisations that revealed the underlying structure of the language. (Until her death, most difficult grammatical points were counterchecked with Tilly Fuller.) Moses also knows some Dya:bugay but was careful to keep this separate from Yidiɲ. Indeed, he is so concerned to keep his Yidiɲ pure and free from outside influence that Moses has eliminated what were certainly established English loan words. (Thus, in place of *mudaga* 'motor car' and *biligan* 'billy can', he uses *dundalay* and *gunbu:l* which he says were originally the Dyalŋuy terms for these items; Moses only knew two or three other Dyalŋuy words. Unfortunately neither Tilly Fuller nor Pompey Langdon – the major informants for Dyalŋuy – recognised these as Dyalŋuy words; but it is possible that there were substantial differences between coastal and tablelands Dyalŋuys, as there were between the Dyalŋuy styles of, say, Dyirbal and Mamu – see 1.6 above.) The only other informants for coastal Yidiɲ were Richard Hyde (*bumiḍi*) of Yarrabah (died in 1974) who mixed English words and grammar into every Yidiɲ sentence, and Dick Moses's sister Ida Burnett (*ɲuḍun*) of White Rock, who tended to mix Yidiɲ with Dya:bugay and did not respond directly to specific inquiries.

The writer never heard Yidiɲ spoken spontaneously. This description is based on monologue texts and on Dick Moses and Tilly Fuller's systematic attempts to teach the writer to speak their language (in terms, for instance, of 'giving the right response' – see 3.1.3). The grammar is thus less complete than that for Dyirbal (Dixon 1972), a language which is still actively spoken and for which there would now be thirty or forty informants as fluent (although not necessarily so patient or thoughtful) as Dick Moses. And whereas it is possible to record twenty or more traditional Dyirbalŋan myths (each from several different informants), Dick Moses knew only parts of six or seven (and no one else at Yarrabah knew any others).

Guŋgaɲḍi myths have virtually disappeared. The writer read to Dick Moses and Robert Patterson (*ɲalmbi*) – a Guŋgaɲḍi who remembers a little of the olden times and is extremely keen to reconstruct more – Gribble's (1932: 56–7) short account of the story of 'Goonyah'. Moses then embellished this outline (and changed it a little: Gribble says that the Great Spirit Balore

caused the sea to rise against Goonyah, whereas Moses has Guɲa stand up Baluɽ – the sacred curved woomera – in the prow of his boat to calm the waves) and recorded it for the writer as a text in Yidiɲ. The story – recorded by Gribble around 1900, published by him in 1932 and re-told to the Guŋgaɲɖi in 1973 after they had quite forgotten it – is now spreading at Yarrabah, and in May 1974 Dick Moses recorded it in Yidiɲ and in English for a visiting team of film-makers from Sydney. (Moses does, on the tape, say 'you see, old Gribble, he got that in a paper...he been put that down...that's the way I been to get them out of that book, you see' but the significance of this aside might well be lost on some future anthropo-historian.) Thus is a folk tradition, which had died, on the way to being partly reestablished.

2 Phonology

Yidiɲ has a number of phonological rules of wide application, that operate on the forms of inflected words – inserting and deleting vowel length, and deleting a final syllable or final consonant – to ensure that the surface forms of words meet the stress targets of the language. These are discussed in detail in the present chapter; they are a necessary prerequisite to understanding the morphology, in chapter 3.

But consideration of the phonological processes must refer to aspects of the morphology – the alternate forms of affixes (and the conditions under which each occurs) indicate the nature and application of the phonological rules. Critical decisions in the phonology depend upon the form of certain morphological combinations, and so on.

The ideal way to understand Yidiɲ is to learn something of the phonology, then a little morphology, then some more phonology, and so on – gradually building up a picture of both levels of description (and ensuring both the phonological prerequisites for understanding each aspect of the morphology, and the morphological prerequisites for justifying and exemplifying each phonological rule and constraint). The writer follows this scheme in classroom presentation of Yidiɲ; but it would plainly be an inappropriate arrangement for a reference grammar.

Where sections of this chapter involve heavy use of morphological results, cross-references are given to chapter 3. Ideally, the reader should first go through chapter 2 – to gain a general picture of the phonological rules presented there – and then study chapter 3 (and perhaps chapter 4) before returning to a more detailed consideration of the present chapter, concentrating this time on the morphological justification for our phonological generalisations.

2.1 Segmental phonology

2.1.1 Phonemes and their realisations. Yidiɲ requires only sixteen segmental phonemes (the smallest inventory for any Australian language). These comprise:

four stop–nasal series, best described (as is usually the case for Australian languages – Dixon 1970c) in terms of active articulator:

	stop	nasal
labial	*b*	*m*
apical	*d*	*n*
laminal	*ḓ*	*ɲ*
dorsal	*g*	*ŋ*

an apical lateral – *l*
a trilled apical rhotic – *r*
an apical-postalveolar (retroflex) rhotic continuant – *ɻ*
two semi-vowels:
    laminal – *y*
  and labio-dorsal – *w*
and three vowels:
    open – *a*
    close front – *i*
  and close back – *u*

Each vowel has both a long and a short variety (2.2).

The stops and nasals involve identical articulatory localisation. In *d* and *n* the tip of the tongue is placed against the alveolar ridge, whereas *ḓ* and *ɲ* require a fair section of the tongue blade to make contact with the hard palate and the alveolar ridge; *g* and *ŋ* involve a portion of the back of the tongue touching the soft palate.

Stops are almost always voiced. Partly voiced allophones are sometimes encountered word-initially (most commonly, the word begins an intonation group); words cannot end in a stop. It is, in fact, normal for the glottis to be vibrating throughout the articulation of a Yidiɲ word; thus, in one sense, 'voiced' is (for this language) the unmarked value of the phonetic opposition 'voiced/voiceless'.

The dorsal stop /g/ has secondary labialisation in, for instance, [*g*ʷ*uyŋgan*] 'female spirit; grasshopper sp.', [*g*ʷ*uygal*], 'bandicoot; eel', [*g*ʷ*uyŋgilbi*] 'Moreton Bay tree' and [*g*ʷ*uyu*] 'tree vine sp.'; this appears to be conditioned by the following /*u*-*ŋg*/ or /*u*-*u*/. (In fact /*guyu*/ has been heard pronounced as [*g*ʷ*iyɔ*].) The laminal stop /ḓ/ can (particularly in the tablelands dialect) be weakened to semi-vowel [*y*], predominantly within the verbal derivational affix -:*ḓi-n* (see 2.6.4). Apical /*d*/ is sometimes realised as a tap [*ɾ*], particularly when it is the second occurrence of /*d*/ within a short space in a word. Thus /*bindada*/

is normally pronounced [*bindada*] but has been heard as [*bindaɾa*]; and in text 14, line 6 /*wawa:ldaŋga:daŋ*/ is said as [*wawa:ldaŋga:ɾã*]. There is no noteworthy allophonic variation for the bilabial stop /*b*/.

There is a tendency for final /*ŋ*/, /*ɲ*/ or /*n*/ to be elided, the preceding vowel being nasalised and sometimes slightly lengthened. In the case of final /*ŋ*/ this has developed into a specific realisational rule, within the tablelands dialect (2.6.3). The sequence /*aŋa*/ may be pronounced as a very long [*ã::*] – again, particularly in the tablelands dialect, and predominantly when /*ŋa*/ is the verbal comitative affix (2.6.4).

The lateral /*l*/ normally has a fairly dark (velarised) articulation, particularly after *u*. (In word-final position after *u* it is sometimes difficult to distinguish between /*l*/ and the retroflex continuant /*ɽ*/.)

The most difficult phonological distinction, for a non-native speaker of Yidiɲ, is undoubtedly that between the two rhotics. /*r*/ is an apico-alveolar trill – sometimes reducing to a single tap – and exhibits little phonetic variation. The unmarked pronounciation of /*ɽ*/ is as an apico-postalveolar grooved continuant; however it can be realised as a post-alveolar trill, typically at the end of a stressed syllable (in the tablelands dialect there seems to be a fair chance of encountering a trilled /*ɽ*/ in any position). It appears, in fact, that the crucial distinction lies in /*ɽ*/ being articulated further back in the mouth than /*r*/. Whereas /*r*/ involves the tip of the tongue against the alveolar ridge, the tongue appears to be retracted for /*ɽ*/, producing either a continuant – that is almost retroflex in quality – or else a trill that vibrates against the back of the alveolar ridge.

We have already noted that /*d*/ may be realised as [*ɾ*]. With clusters such as /*rd*/ it is particularly hard to distinguish the segments – a clear trill-plus-stop may be recognisable at one occurrence of, say, /*báɽumbárdu*/ 'wattle tree grub-ERG' but on repetition it may be heard as [*báɽumbárdu*] or [*báɽumbáru*] or simply as [*báɽumbáɾu*]; that is, since /*r*/ may reduce to a tap and /*d*/ may be realised as a tap, a single tap may simultaneously realise both underlying segments. Trilled /*ɽ*/ and a following /*d*/ may merge in similar fashion.

And note that a [*d*] has been heard inserted between /*ɽ*/ and /*n*/. Dick Moses clearly said, and confirmed [*buruḍuɽdni*] for /*buruḍuɽni*/ 'pademelon wallaby-GEN'.

The vowels show relatively little allophonic variation. The main point of note is that (as in many Australian languages) the close back vowel /*u*/ involves – on visual evidence – no significant lip rounding. Yet Yidiɲ /*u*/ is aurally much closer to the rounded [*u*] of, say, British

English, than it is to the corresponding unrounded close back vowel [ɯ] in Australian English. One can only guess that some other articulatory effect may be employed to produce a /u/ that is – on auditory grounds – maximally different from /i/, but does not involve lip rounding.

Articulation of the close vowels normally diverges little from cardinal [i] and [u]. Slightly more open varieties are encountered in word-final long vowels, but the lowering is no further than [e] and [o] – thus /yawu:/ 'grass sp.' is heard as [yawo:] (whereas /margu/ 'grey possum', with a short final vowel, would be no lower than [margɔ]), and /yiri:/ 'slatey stone' as [yirɪ:] or maybe [yire:].

This tendency of long high vowels to be slightly lowered goes against Lehiste's (1970: 30–3) measurements for a number of European languages, in which 'long vowels are characterized by more extreme values – positions further removed from the center...'

/u/ may be lowered when following a laminal, particularly the semi-vowel /y/ – thus /guyu/, [guyɔ]. /a/ varies over IPA [a], [ɑ] and [æ]; it is never raised as high as [ɛ] or [ɔ], even before /y/. An underlying vowel-plus-(non-labial) nasal sequence may be realised as a nasalised vowel in word-final position – see 2.6.3.

There is a class of (about eighty) nominals whose absolutive (zero-inflection) forms are disyllabic but which appear to have a trisyllabic root with oblique cases – for instance, ḍambu:l 'two-ABS', ḍambula+ŋgu 'two-ERG'. We set up roots with a final vowel morphophoneme (written with a capital letter – ḍambulA) that triggers the 'final syllable deletion rule' when no affix follows (2.3.4) and which is rewritten as a normal vowel phoneme in all other circumstances. Vowels emanating from these morphophonemes (A, I and U) can have normal pronunciation [a], [i] and [u]; but there is sometimes a tendency to centralise them, each approaching [ə] so closely that in normal speech they can be difficult to distinguish (and the help of the informant has to be sought, in pronouncing the word with a more 'cardinal' vowel allophone). A vowel /u/, inserted in the oblique inflection of a certain class of genitives, can be reduced to [ə] in the same way – 2.3.3. This behaviour of segments corresponding to root morphophonemes (and the genitive /u/) contrasts strongly with segments represented simply as a, i or u in underlying root and affix forms – the latter can never be centralised in this way. There is further discussion of this point in 2.3.4.

Yidiɲ differs from many other Australian languages (e.g. Dixon 1972: 278) in NOT PERMITTING the phonetic elision of /y/ before /i/ or /w/ before /u/ at the beginning of words. (The language and tribal names have been recorded

by earlier investigators as Idin, Idindji – Tindale 1974: 168. This is simply a mishearing – they can NOT be pronounced [*idiɲ*] or [*idi:ɲɖi*].

2.1.2. Phonotactics. A root in Yidiɲ has phonological structure:

$$C_1V_1C_2V_2(C_2V_2)^n(C_3) \quad \text{where} \quad n \geqslant 0$$

Here V_1 and V_2 each represent a single vowel and C_1 and C_3 a single consonant; C_2 can be a sequence of one, two or three consonants.

That is, a Yidiɲ root has at least two syllables, each of which involves a single vowel segment. It begins in a single consonant and can end in a vowel or a single consonant.

There are phonetic monosyllables, involving very long vowels [*i:*] and [*u:*]; these are taken to be phonological disyllables, involving sequences /*iyi*/ and /*uwu*/ respectively. The vowel in such a form is in fact considerably longer than a phonological long vowel (2.2), and it does alternate with vowel–semi-vowel–vowel sequences – thus [*mi:ɽ*] ~ [*miyiɽ*] 'the wind connected with a thunder-storm'. Forms in this class – for instance /*buwum*/, [*bu:m*] 'a vine' (coastal dialect only) and /*wuwuy*/, [*wu:y*] 'a small bean tree' (tablelands dialect only) – inflect in the pattern of even-syllabled (not odd-syllabled) roots. (See also the discussion of [*ɖa:*] at the end of 2.4.)

The possibilities at the structural positions are:

V_1 can be any short vowel – *a, i* or *u*.

V_2 can be any short vowel *a, i* or *u*, or a long vowel *a:, i:* or *u:* (the latter subject to certain constraints on the number of syllables in the word, and the position of the syllable in the word – 2.2).

C_1 can be any stop, nasal or semi-vowel (*b, d, ɖ, g; m, n, ɲ, ŋ; w, or y*).

One word in the writer's corpus begins with *l* – the onomatopoeic *lululumba-l* 'rock a baby to sleep, singing "*lu-lu-lu-lu-...*"'. It is worth noting that Dyirbal, which also prohibits initial *l*'s, allows no exception here – it has verbal root *yululumba-l* with the same meaning.

C_3 can be the lateral, either rhotic, the laminal semi-vowel or any nasal except dorsal *ŋ* (*l; r, ɽ; y; m, n* or *ɲ*).

C_2 can be:

  (i) any consonant

  (ii) any homorganic nasal–stop cluster (*mb, nd, ɲɖ,* or *ŋg*)

  (iii) a lateral or rhotic followed by any non-apical nasal, or stop, or homorganic nasal–stop sequence, or *w* (*l, r* or *ɽ* followed by *b, ɖ, g, m, ɲ, ŋ, mb, ɲɖ, ŋg* or *w*)

(iv) the laminal semi-vowel followed by a non-apical, non-laminal nasal, or stop, or homorganic nasal–stop sequence, or *w* (*y* followed by *b*, *g*, *m*, *ŋ*, *mb*, *ŋg* or *w*)

(v) the apical nasal followed by a non-apical stop (*n* followed by *b*, *ḍ* or *g*) or

(vi) the lateral followed by one of (v) (*l* followed by *nb*, *nḍ* or *ng*).

Of the possible clusters covered by these general rules only /*lng*/ and /*ṛɲ*/ have not been encountered; it is assumed that these are 'accidental gaps'. Only one example is known of each of /*lnb*/, /*rɲ*/, /*lɲ*/, /*ṛw*/ and /*ṛɲḍ*/ – these are the Yidiɲ forms *dulnbilay* 'white cedar tree' and *burɲa* 'heart', and the Dyalŋuy roots *mulɲari* 'blanket', *duṛwu* 'leaf' and *biṛɲḍali-n* 'run'. (It should be noted that the writer's Yidiɲ and Dyalŋuy lexicon only contains about 1,800 items; and that *ɲ* is – with *n* – the least frequent syllable-initial segment – 2.1.3.)

There are four clusters which are exceptions to our general rules for C_2. One or two occurrences of each of /*ln*/, /*nŋ*/, /*nm*/ and /*ɲb*/ are known: the adjective *bulna* 'impure, indistinct, poorly defined', the verb *manŋa-n* 'be frightened' and three Dyalŋuy forms – noun *ŋunŋun* 'breast', number adjective *ɲunmul* 'one' and noun *bulaɲbay* 'man'. There is also *gaṛna* 'black cockatoo' in coastal Yidiɲ, involving the cluster /*ṛn*/ – note that the corresponding form in the tablelands dialect is *gaṛana* (and see 2.6.2).

It is assumed that /*yɲ*/, /*yḍ*/ and /*yɲḍ*/ are systematic gaps in Yidiɲ – that is, the laminal semi-vowel cannot, within a morpheme, be followed by a laminal nasal or stop; these clusters do occur in Dyirbal, a language which otherwise has very similar phonotactic possibilities (Dixon 1972: 272–4).

Disyllabic affixes conform exactly to the phonotactic possibilities described for roots. Monosyllabic suffixes show a few eccentricities – thus, one ergative allomorph is *-ŋgu* (a form very common in Australian languages) and the dative inflection is *-nda* (although this may be a recent reduction from *-*ŋunda* – 2.3.2, 3.3.2); in addition, there are four or so monosyllabic allomorphs beginning with *l* and one with *ṛ*. The consonant cluster possibilities at morpheme boundaries are very much wider than those described for an intramorphemic cluster (C_2) – we can, effectively, have any C_3 followed by any C_1; and trisyllabic sequences /*yɲḍ*/ and so on are encountered with ergative and locative case inflections. (Roots that are inherently reduplicated allow C_3C_1 possibilities at the reduplication boundary, even though it is here intra-

morphemic. Thus *buṛimbuṛim* 'a red bird sp.' and *dugulduɡul* 'tree sp.' – note that there are no roots *buṛim, dugul*. See also 2.4.)

Inflected words differ in one important respect from roots – they can end in the dorsal nasal *ŋ*. This is supplied as the non-past inflection with verbs of the *-n-* conjugation. And it is a reduced form of ergative *-ŋgu*, and of the imperative form of transitive verbaliser *-ŋa* and verbal comitative *-ŋa*, in each case when the affix is added to a stem which ends in a vowel and has an even number of syllables (2.3.2, 2.3.3). The status of final *ŋ* in various dialects of Yidiɲ is discussed in 2.6.3.

There is one further constraint on word structure: *i(:)y* can occur only when immediately followed by a vowel (that is, *i* or *i:* can be followed by a syllable-initial, but not a syllable-final, *y*). Thus we have *giyi* 'don't', *biyal* 'a ripple', *ḍiyuya* 'catbird' but no word ending in *-i(:)y*, or with *-i(:)y-* followed by a consonant.

Loan words appear to fit into the regular phonotactic pattern with one exception – they can begin with *l* (for instance *landima-l* 'teach' from English 'learnt him').

It is in most cases easy to decide on syllable boundaries in Yidiɲ. If a single consonant comes between two vowels the boundary precedes it (V.CV); if a diconsonantal cluster occurs intervocalically then the syllable boundary falls in the middle of it (VC.CV). There is, however, no clear way of dealing with the occasional cluster of three consonants (noting that words cannot begin or end in more than a single consonant). Thus in *guyŋgan* 'spirit of a woman', the *-y-* plainly belongs to the first syllable and the *-g-* to the second one, but reasons can be advanced for assigning *-ŋ-* in either direction. (Compare with *dulnbilay* 'white cedar'; here the choice of *-n-* depends both on the preceding segment – we cannot get *-ynC-* – and on the following one – *-Cnd-* is also impermissible.)

Much of the discussion of this chapter refers to the number of syllables in a word or morpheme. There is a one-to-one relation between syllables and vowels so that there is never any question about the NUMBER of syllables in any form. And the fact that we choose not to commit ourselves to the place of a syllable boundary within a triconsonantal cluster is here quite irrelevant.

2.1.3 Probabilities of occurrence. Relative probabilities of occurrence were calculated for initial (C_1) and final (C_3 or V_2) segments. The count was based on the writer's Yidiɲ dictionary, leaving aside Dyalŋuy

and loan items (a total of about 1,600 roots). Initial probabilities cover all parts of speech; figures for final segment do not cover verbs (for which roots, as set up, all end in a vowel) or roots with a final morphophoneme A, I or U (2.3.4).

	root initial	root final
b	0.17 ⎫	
d	0.08 ⎪	
$ḍ$	0.15 ⎬ 0.63	
g	0.23 ⎭	
m	0.11 ⎫	0.04 ⎫
n	0.015 ⎬ 0.20	0.14 ⎬ 0.20
$ṇ$	0.025 ⎪	0.02 ⎭
$ŋ$	0.05 ⎭	
l		0.15 ⎫
r		0.04 ⎬ 0.26
$ṛ$		0.07 ⎭
w	0.12 ⎬ 0.17	
y	0.05 ⎭	0.10
a		0.21 ⎫
i		0.11 ⎬ 0.44
u		0.12 ⎭

Relative probabilities for vowels in V_1 position were calculated separately for nouns, adjectives and verbs; there was no significant difference. Overall probabilities at V_1 are:

$$a \quad 0.41 \qquad i \quad 0.20 \qquad u \quad 0.39$$

Probabilities differ somewhat for the vowel in the second syllable of a noun or adjective:

$$a \quad 0.47 \qquad i \quad 0.23 \qquad u \quad 0.30$$

It will be seen that the later a vowel is in the word, the less chance there is that it will be u. This is confirmed by examination of a sample of 131 trisyllabic nominal roots – the third vowel is u in only 23 (0.175) of them. (And note that in 19 of these forms the second vowel is also u.)

The chance of a late vowel being u falls off even more markedly with verbs. The probabilities at the vowel position in the second syllable of a verb root are:

$$a \quad 0.64 \qquad i \quad 0.32 \qquad u \quad 0.04$$

Eleven of the thirteen trisyllabic verb roots in the writer's corpus have *a* as their third vowel, with the remaining two showing *i* (see 3.8.3).

2.2 Vowel length and stress

There is significant length contrast among vowels in non-initial syllables. Thus we have minimal pairs (quoting nouns in citation, = absolutive or unmarked, form):

malan	'flat rock'	*wuṟu*	'spear handle (generic)'
mala:n	'right hand'	*wuṟu:*	'(i) river; (ii) snake sp.'

Length distinguishes present and past tense for disyllabic verbal stems in the *-l-* and *-ṟ-* conjugations:

	'smell'	'cook'	'look, see'	'leave'
PRESENT	*guḍil*	*waḍul*	*wawal*	*baḍaṟ*
PAST	*guḍi:l*	*waḍu:l*	*wawa:l*	*baḍa:ṟ*

Phonetically, at least three degrees of length can be distinguished. A nasal or liquid will tend to lengthen a preceding (phonologically short) vowel – /guriɲ/, [guri·ɲ] 'good', /baṟgu/, [ba·ṟgu] 'cane-knife'. A phonologically long vowel will be longer than this – /baṟi:ɲ/, [baṟi:ɲ] 'small-leaved tree sp.'. And a vowel–semi-vowel–vowel underlying sequence may be realised as what is the longest phonetic vowel – /miyiṟ/, [mi::ṟ] 'wind connected with a thunderstorm' (2.1.2, 2.4).

A long vowel could be regarded either as a sequence of two identical short vowels, or as involving a prosody of length. The latter treatment is adopted here, since it makes for simplest morphological and phonological rule statement. For instance, one derivational affix to verb stems involves lengthening the stem-final vowel and adding *ḍi*. We have

ROOT	*guḍi-l*	*waḍu-l*	*wawa-l*
DERIVED STEM	*guḍi:ḍi-n*	*waḍu:ḍi-n*	*wawa:ḍi-n*

(The final *-n*, *-l* or *-ṟ* quoted on a verbal root or stem marks the conjugation to which it belongs.) Now if a long vowel were written /VV/, this derivational affix would have to be assigned allomorphs /iḍi-n/, /uḍi-n/ and /aḍi-n/; or else we could regard it as /Vḍi-n/ and include an 'assimilation rule' rewriting *V* with the value of the vowel preceding it. The simplest statement of the affix is just /:ḍi-n/, with the convention that a long vowel is written /V:/. (Other examples of affixes beginning with ':' are verbal aspects (2.3.5, 3.8.6) and reduced forms of various case, tense, etc. inflections (2.3.2–3, 3.3.2, 3.8.4).)

The placement of stress in Yidiɲ words depends on the presence and positioning of vowel length:

STRESS ASSIGNMENT RULE. Stress is assigned to the first syllable involving a long vowel. If there is no long vowel, it is assigned to the first syllable of the word. Further stresses are then assigned (recursively) to the syllable next but one before, and the next but one after, a stressed syllable.

In 2.3.5 we show that it is not possible to take stress as prior, and infer vowel length from stress placement.

Thus, in each Yidiɲ word syllables are alternately stressed (S) and unstressed (U). For example:

(1) *yaḍí:riɲál*   'walk about-GOING-COMIT-PRES'
(2) *wúɲabá:ḍiɲúnda*   'hunt-:ḍi-DAT SUBORD'
(3) *ḍámbuláɲalɲúnda*   'two-TR VBLSR-DAT SUBORD'

In fact, long vowels in a Yidiɲ word always occur in stressed syllables. To accommodate this, there is a restriction on the occurrence of long vowels:

CONSTRAINT 1. If two or more long vowels occur in a word, each pair must be separated by an odd number of syllables.

Each pair of long vowels in a word is in fact separated by JUST ONE syllable. We have stated the constraint in a more general form ('an odd number of syllables') since if a word were encountered in which two long vowels were separated by three (or five...) syllables it would exactly conform to the rather complex phonological patterning permitted by Yidiɲ.

For example:

(4) *magí:riɲá:ldaɲú:n*   'climb up-ASPECT-COMIT-COMING-DAT SUBORD'
(5) *ḍuŋgá:riɲá:l*   'run-GOING-COMIT-PAST'
(6) *burwá:liɲá:lna*   'jump-GOING-COMIT-PURP'

About 85 % of the words in recorded Yidiɲ texts contain an even number of syllables. These are made up of a whole number of disyllabic units, which must either be all of the type SU – as in (2), (3) – or all of the type US – as in (1), (4), (5).

If a word contains an odd number of syllables, then the number of unstressed syllables will always exceed the number of stressed syllables by one. This implies, in terms of the stress assignment rules of Yidiɲ:

CONSTRAINT 2. If a word has an odd number of syllables, then there must be a long vowel in at least one even-numbered syllable. (And, by Constraints 1 and 2, ALL long vowels in such words must occur in even-numbered syllables.)

We see that, whereas in an even-syllabled word long vowels may occur in odd-numbered syllables or in even-numbered syllables (but not in a mixture of the two), in an odd-syllabled word long vowels can occur only in even-numbered syllables (as in (6)).

Thus, there are disyllabic words with stress pattern

> SU e.g. *wáṛil* 'doorway-ABS'
> or US e.g. *wayí:l* 'red-bream-ABS'

and quadrisyllabic words with

> SUSU e.g. *gúdagáni* 'dog-GEN'
> or USUS e.g. *gulúgulú:y* 'black bream-COMIT'

but all trisyllabic words must have the stress pattern

> USU e.g. *galí:na* 'go-PURP'
> *gudá:ga* 'dog-ABS'

and all quinquesyllabics must have the pattern USUSU, as in (6); and so on.

Yidiɲ plainly prefers each word to contain a whole number of disyllabic units (all of type SU, or all of type US); in 2.3.2–4 we describe the 'final syllable deletion rule' which has wide application in all areas of the grammar and serves to derive even-syllabled surface words from underlying odd-syllabled forms. If, after all phonological rules have applied, a word is left with an odd number of syllables, then the extra syllable must be an unstressed singleton.

The nature of the dynamic processing within the brain for the programming of speech is far from being fully understood; but it seems likely that in the case of Yidiɲ the programming is in terms of disyllabic stress-units (the writer is grateful to Kenneth L. Pike for discussion of this point, following a seminar presentation of the main points of Yidiɲ phonology). In this connection it is noteworthy that when Dick Moses recorded a Yidiɲ song, he missed exactly one disyllabic unit each time he took breath – this was either a complete word (the first *buŋgu* of *búŋgu búŋgu yíɲal*), or else the first two syllables of a tri-syllabic word (*bugu* from *bugú:ba ḍúnduḷúbi ḍánaŋ*).

Lehiste (1970: 163–4) mentions that disyllabic sequences function as a

3   DGY

major phonological unit in Finnish and Estonian; there seem to be considerable similarities with Yidiɲ. She mentions that 'while monosyllabic units are
possible, as are trisyllabic units, most longer words are made up of disyllabic
units'. In Yidiɲ texts, about 85% of the words are even-syllabled. Compare
with Dyirbal where primary stress falls on the first syllable of every word and,
although there does seem to be a definite preference for stressed and unstressed syllables to alternate, there is nothing comparable to Yidiɲ's 'final
syllable reduction rule'; in Dyirbal texts about 70% of the words are even-
syllabled.

2.3   Phonological rules

2.3.1   Penultimate lengthening [Rule 1]. In most Australian languages the absolutive case (marking intransitive subject and transitive
object functions) has zero realisation. Consider typical paradigms for
Yidiɲ nouns:

	ABSOLUTIVE	PURPOSIVE
'dog'	*gudá:ga*	*gúdagágu*
'mother'	*múḍam*	*muḍá:mgu*
'loya-cane sp.'	*yabú:lam*	*yábulámgu*

If we take the absolutive forms as roots, a purposive suffix *-gu* can be
isolated, contrasting with absolutive ø. But there is an inconsistent length
variation – in the case of 'dog' and 'loya-cane' we lose the length from
the second syllable of the absolutive in forming the purposive, while for
'mother' purposive lengthens the second vowel.

Compare this with a representative verbal paradigm:

	PRESENT	PURPOSIVE
'go'	*gáliŋ*	*galí:na*
'walk up'	*maḍí:ndaŋ*	*máḍindána*

Present tense inflection is plainly *-ŋ* and purposive *-na* for verbs of this
conjugation. But if we take the verbal roots as *gali-* and *maḍi:nda-*
(simply subtracting *-ŋ* from the present tense forms) we find that the
verbal purposive adds length in the first case, and deletes it in the
second.

The alternative to stating ad hoc rules of length loss and insertion in
each individual case is to take the roots as, in all cases, not involving any
long vowels. Thus we have nominal roots *gudaga*, *muḍam* and *yabulam*;
with inflection *-gu* for purposive and ø for absolutive. Similarly, the verb
roots will be *gali-* and *maḍinda-*, with present *-ŋ* and purposive *-na*.

We now need a phonological rule which will apply to the final inflected form of each word (after all morphological processes of affixation, reduplication, and so on, have applied):

RULE I – PENULTIMATE LENGTHENING

In every word with an odd number of syllables, the penultimate vowel is lengthened.

Stress assignment follows the application of Rule 1.

Sample derivations are (with a dash indicating that the rule does not apply):

	root-ABS	root-ABS	root-PURP	root-PURP
	gudaga+ø	*muḍam+ø*	*gudaga+gu*	*muḍam+gu*
Rule 1	*guda:ga*	—	—	*muḍa:mgu*
Stress assignment	*gudá:ga*	*múḍam*	*gúdagágu*	*muḍá:mgu*

And similarly for the verbal forms.

The odd-syllabled forms just given have all had just three syllables. But with longer odd-syllabled forms we find that it is always the penultimate vowel that is lengthened. For instance:

> *gudágudá:ga*   'dog-REDUP-ABS'
> *maḍíndaŋá:lna*   'walk up-COMIT-PURP'

An even-numbered syllable earlier than the penultimate in an odd-syllabled word may, of course, already involve vowel length. Thus, from verbal root *burwa-* 'jump', aspectual affix -*:li-*, comitative affix -*ŋa-l-* and purposive inflection -*na*, we get

> *burwa:liŋalna*

and rule 1 then yields

> *burwa:liŋa:lna*

quoted as (6) above.

The penultimate syllable in an odd-syllabled word may, through the inclusion of an affix that specifies length (2.3.5), already contain a long vowel. Thus we can get

> *burwa+ :li+ŋ*   'jump-GOING-PRES'
> or   *maḍinda+ŋa+ :ḍi+ŋ*   'walk up-COMIT-:ḍi-PRES'

In this case we can (as the simplest course) allow Rule 1 to apply vacuously, to derive the surface forms *burwá:liŋ* and *maḍíndaŋá:ḍiŋ*. (For another example of the vacuous application of Rule 1, see 2.3.8.)

2.3.2   Final syllable deletion [Rule 2] – (i) affix reduction. There are something like ten suffixes in Yidiɲ which have alternate forms, one being used with stems that have an even number of syllables and another with those that have an odd number of syllables. (We will exemplify with disyllabic and trisyllabic stems; quadrisyllabics behave exactly like disyllabics, quinquesyllabics like trisyllabics, and so on.)

For instance, present, past and dative subordinate inflections are, with disyllabic and trisyllabic roots of the -*n*- conjugation:

root	*gali-* 'go'	*maḍinda-* 'walk up'
PRESENT	*galiŋ*	*maḍiːndaŋ*
PAST	*galiɲ*	*maḍindaɲu*
DATIVE SUBORDINATE	*galiɲunda*	*maḍindaɲuːn*

Present tense is -*ŋ* in each case, with the length in *maḍiːndaŋ* being inserted by Rule 1 (2.3.1). But the past tense has two allomorphs -*ːɲ* and -*ɲu*, and dative subordinate inflection is -*ɲunda* or -*ɲuːn*. We can remark that -*ːɲ* looks like a reduced form of -*ɲu*, and -*ɲuːn* of -*ɲunda*; but note that -*ɲunda*, the longer form of the subordinate inflection, occurs (on even-syllabled stems) where -*ːɲ*, the shorter form of past tense, is encountered.

All roots (bar one) in the -*l*- conjugation are even-syllabled. However, the verbal comitative affix -*ŋa-l* can be added to any intransitive -*n*- root, deriving a transitive stem which belongs to the -*l*- conjugation; we thus get *galiŋa-l* 'go with, take' and *maḍindaŋa-l* 'walk up with, make walk up'. Corresponding inflections on these stems, and the -*l*- conjugation root *wawa-l* 'see' are:

stem	*wawa-*	*galiŋa-*	*maḍindaŋa-*
PRESENT	*wawal*	*galiːŋal*	*maḍindaŋal*
PAST	*wawaːl*	*galiŋalɲu*	*maḍindaŋaːl*
DATIVE SUBORDINATE	*wawalɲunda*	*galiŋalɲuːn*	*maḍindaŋalɲunda*

We see that the non-past inflection is, for this conjugation, -*l* (length in the middle syllable of *galiːŋal* is the result of Rule 1). Again, there are alternate forms for the other two inflections -*ːl* or -*lɲu* for past tense, and -*lɲunda* or -*lɲuːn* for dative subordinate.

Let us now turn to nouns, and examine some case forms for even-syllabled stems ending in a vowel (the example here is *buɲa* 'woman'), odd-syllabled stems ending in a vowel (*gudaga* 'dog') and stems of even

and odd syllabicity ending in a consonant (*guygal* 'bandicoot', *baḍigal* 'tortoise'):

root	*buɲa*	*gudaga*	*guygal*	*baḍigal*
ABSOLUTIVE	*buɲa*	*guda:ga*	*guygal*	*baḍi:gal*
ERGATIVE	*buɲa:ŋ*	*gudagaŋgu*	*guyga:ldu*	*baḍigaldu*
GENITIVE	*buɲa:n*	*gudagani*	*guyga:lni*	*baḍigalni*

There is plainly allomorphic alternation in the genitive and ergative inflections. Genitive is *-ni* after an odd-syllabled stem ending in a vowel, or with a stem of either syllabicity ending in a consonant, but *-:n* with an even-syllabled stem ending in a vowel. Ergative is more complex – it is *-du* after a consonant (with, in fact, assimilation to a stem-final nasal or *y* – 2.3.3, 3.3.2), *-ŋgu* after an odd-syllabled vowel-final stem and *-:ŋ* after an even-syllabled stem ending in a vowel. Rule 1 will account for the long vowels in the middle syllables of *guda:ga, baḍi:gal, guyga:ldu* and *guyga:lni*.

When we carefully study these alternations of verbal and nominal inflections we see that in each case the shorter allomorph is used to create an even-syllabled word (where the longer alternative would lead to an odd-syllabled result).

We could just state the allomorphs for each inflection, referring to the number of syllables in the stem as the conditioning factor. Thus:

> PAST TENSE (for *-n-* conjugation stems)
> *-ɲu* after an odd-syllabled stem
> *-:ɲ* after an even-syllabled stem

And so on, for each of the ten suffixes which shows alternation of this type.

An alternative is to consider the shorter form as a reduced version of the longer, formed by a general phonological rule which is motivated by the 'even-syllabled' stress target of Yidiɲ. We can take the canonical forms of the verbal suffixes as:

> PAST   *-ɲu ~ -l+ɲu*
> DATIVE SUBORDINATE   *-ɲu+nda ~ -l+ɲu+nda*

(Here the *-l-* conjugation demands a linking morpheme – what we can call a 'conjugation marker' – between stem and affix, see 3.8.3. Our analysis of the dative subordinate inflection as *-ɲu+nda* is discussed in

3.8.4, 4,4. ' + ' indicates a morpheme boundary.) Underlying forms of the nominal affixes are taken as:

ERGATIVE -*ŋgu*   GENITIVE -*ni*

Then we have:

EXPECTED FORM	ACTUAL WORD
gali + *ɲu*	*gali:ɲ*
maḍinda + *ɲu* + *nda*	*maḍindaɲu:n*
wawa + *l* + *ɲu*	*wawa:l*
gali + *ŋa* + *l* + *ɲu* + *nda*	*galiŋalɲu:n*
maḍinda + *ŋa* + *l* + *ɲu*	*maḍindaŋa:l*
buɲa + *ŋgu*	*buɲa:ŋ*
buɲa + *ni*	*buɲa:n*

With *gali*- we get reduction of the past tense form (disyllabic root plus monosyllabic affix gives an odd-syllabled word, which is subject to reduction) but with the disyllabic dative subordinate affix -*ɲu* + *nda* we obtain an even-syllabled word which is not reduced. With *maḍinda*-, the past tense inflection produces an acceptable even-syllabled word, whereas -*ɲu* + *nda* forms a quinquesyllabic word, which does lose its final syllable. In the case of derived transitive stems *galiŋa*- and *maḍindaŋa*- the situation is reversed – past tense yields an even-syllabled word with *galiŋa*-, but an odd-syllabled one (which is consequently reduced) with *maḍindaŋa*-; and so on.

We thus appear to have a rule that deletes the final syllable of some odd-syllabled words, producing an even-syllabled form which meets the stress target of Yidiɲ (that each word should involve a whole number of disyllabic units, either all of the type SU, or all of the type US). And in each case where the final syllable is eliminated, the vowel of the preceding syllable is lengthened. We could, tentatively, formulate the rule:

(7) $XV_1C_1(C_2)V_2\# \rightarrow XV_1:C_1\#$

with the condition that $XV_1C_1(C_2)V_1\#$ should be odd-syllabled. In this formulation the lengthening of V_1 could be viewed as 'compensatory' qua the loss of the final syllable; we could say that it serves to mark the fact that there was, in the underlying form of the word, an additional syllable.

But note that we have already provided justification for Rule 1, which lengthens the penultimate vowel of an odd-syllabled word. In fact, the 'odd-syllabicity' structural condition on (7) is identical to that on Rule 1.

This suggests that the simplest and most revealing way of explaining a form like *gali:ɲ* is to propose an underlying form *gali+ɲu*, allow Rule 1 to apply, lengthening the penultimate vowel, and then have a further rule which deletes the final syllable (and does not affect vowel length):

(8) $XV_1:C_1(C_2)V_2\# \rightarrow XV_1:C_1\#$

with the condition that $XV_1:C_1(C_2)V_2\#$ should be odd-syllabled. Sample derivations would now be:

root + affix	*gali+ɲu*	*maḍinda+ɲu+nda*	*buɲa+ŋgu*	*buɲa+ni*
Rule 1	*gali:+ɲu*	*maḍinda+ɲu:+nda*	*buɲa:+ŋgu*	*buɲa:+ni*
Rule 2	*gali:+ɲ*	*maḍinda+ɲu:+n*	*buɲa:+ŋ*	*buɲa:+n*

It remains to investigate the conditions under which the reduction represented in (8) takes place, and the optimal formulation of this reduction rule.

Firstly, only an open final syllable can be deleted. Thus, present tense inflection is always *-ŋ* with *-n-* conjugation stems, and *-l* on to *-l-* conjugation forms; this does give some odd-syllabled words – *maḍi:ndaŋ* and *gali:ɲal*, for instance – to which Rule 1 applies, but which do not meet the structural description for Rule 2. (We have already incorporated this condition into the statement of the rule in (7) and (8).) Similarly, the imperative suffix is (for *-n-* conjugation stems) *-n*, whatever the syllabicity of the stem, and the causal subordinate inflection is always *-ɲu+m*. This produces some even-syllabled forms (*galin, maḍindaɲum*), and also some odd-syllabled words (*maḍi:ndan, gali:ɲum*), but the latter do not reduce.

We also indicated in the statement of (7) and (8) that the second component (if any) of a final consonant cluster is lost. Thus, from past forms *wawa+l+ɲu* and *maḍinda+ɲa+l+ɲu* we obtain simply *wawa:l* and *maḍindaɲa:l*; and from ergative *buɲa+ŋgu* is derived *buɲa:ŋ*. Yidiɲ does not allow word-final consonant clusters.

And a further condition on (8) is that C_1 should be one of the set of permitted word-final segments; these comprise (2.1.2) *l, r, ṛ, y, m, n, ɲ* and *ŋ* (*ŋ* can, as already mentioned, occur word-finally but not root-finally – 2.1.2, 2.6.3). Thus, ergative *-ŋgu* reduces to *-:ŋ* and genitive *-ni* to *-:n*, but purposive inflection is invariably *-gu*. We get *gudagagu*, and also *buɲa:gu*; Rule 1 operates normally but, because *g* is not permitted word-finally, Rule 2 blocks in this case.

We now only have to explain why the final syllable reduction rule operates on *buɲa:+ŋgu*, *buɲa:+ni*, to produce disyllabic *buɲa:ŋ*, *buɲa:n*, but does not eliminate the last syllable from *guyga:l+du*,

guyga:l+ni (or from *guyga:l+gu*). There are a number of possibilities open at this point: we could – to explain these particular instances – say that Rule 2 will not operate if it would produce an oblique case-form in which a root-final consonant was now word-final; and so on. But the simplest condition – that will cover cases where Rule 2 does not apply, and there is no phonological explanation – is simply 'there must be a morpheme boundary between V_1 and C_1'. This condition is satisfied for verb forms such as *gali+ɲu, wawa+l+ɲu* where the root (as set up) ends in a vowel (the V_1 of the rule) and *-l-* is identified as a distinct 'conjugation marker' morpheme (3.8.3). It is satisfied in the case of disyllabic noun roots ending in a vowel. But the morpheme boundary condition is not met for roots ending in a consonant; thus Rule 2 is blocked in the case of *guyga:l+du, guyga:l+ni* (and *muḍa:m+gu* – 2.3.1) and these remain as odd-syllabled words.

There are three exceptions to Rule 2 – cases where the final-consonant and morpheme boundary conditions are satisfied but reduction does not take place (as against the twenty or so cases where the conditions correctly specify the application or non-application of the rule). At least one of these appears to have an historical explanation – dative *-ɲunda* may have reduced to *-nda* after the final syllable deletion rule was introduced into Yidiɲ; nominal dative is not reduced (2.3.3, 3.3.2). But no other statement of conditions for Rule 2 yields less exceptions.

We can now state:

RULE 2 – FINAL SYLLABLE DELETION

$$XV_1C_1(C_2)V_2\# \rightarrow XV_1C_1\#$$

if (*a*) $XV_1C_1(C_2)V_2\#$ is an odd-syllabled word;

and (*b*) C_1 is one of the set (*l, r, ṛ, y, m, n, ɲ, ŋ*) of allowable word-final consonants

and (*c*) there is a morpheme boundary between V_1 and C_1

Here V_1 can be any (long or short) vowel.

Rule 2 cannot be ordered before Rule 1 since it destroys odd-syllabicity, which is the critical condition on Rule 1. To allow the possibility of two rules applying simultaneously would introduce unnecessary complications (at other points in the phonology). Working in terms of linear ordering, then, Rule 2 must follow Rule 1.

It will be noted that whereas in (8) we specified length on V_1 – the result of Rule 1 – we now simply write 'V_1' but allow it to be a long

vowel. It is, in fact, valid to ask whether we could not insist that V_1 be long, and as a result eliminate the need for condition (*a*). Rule 1 only lengthens the penultimate vowel of an odd-syllabled word, so might not 'V_1:' be equivalent to (and simpler than) condition (*a*)? This amounts to asking whether there is an even-syllabled word, with penultimate long vowel (also satisfying conditions (*b*) and (*c*)) from which we need to block the application of Rule 2. In fact there is not.

In 2.3.5 we show that vowel length in Yidiɲ words must either be the result of Rule 1, or else is due to one of three verbal affixes that involve length specification – derivational -*:ḍi-n*, and aspectual 'going' -*:li-n* ∼ -*:ṛi-n* ∼ -*:ri-n* and 'coming' -*:lda-n* ∼ -*:da-n* (there is in fact a small set of a dozen nominals whose roots must involve a long vowel – discussion of these is deferred until 2.3.8). The aspectual allomorphs which specify length cannot be added to an odd-syllabled stem (3.8.6–7), so that the length they specify cannot be in the penultimate syllable of an even-syllabled word. The suffix -*:ḍi-n* can be added to an odd-syllabled stem. Thus, with present tense -*ŋ* or imperative -*n* we get even-syllabled words with penultimate length – for instance, *galiŋa:ḍiŋ*, *galiŋa:ḍin*. But in these cases the final syllable is closed, and C_1 is in any case not a segment that can occur word-finally; so the phonological conditions for Rule 2 are not met.

But note that this could be regarded as an 'accidental gap'. There is no theoretical reason why a Yidiɲ even-syllabled word could not have penultimate length and meet the conditions for Rule 2. Everything else being equal, it would be most satisfactory to state Rule 2 so that it should NOT apply to such a form. Otherwise, if the language changed in such a way that forms of this type did come into being – and note that underlying /*galiŋa:ḍiŋ*/ is pronounced [*galiŋa:yɪ*] in the tablelands dialect (2.6.3–4) – but were (as we would expect) not reduced, we would have to 'reformulate' Rule 2. And in such a case we could surely not claim that speakers had modified the general phonological rules with which they operate (i.e. that the language had changed in any material way).

One reason for including criterion (*a*) – and not specifying vowel length – in the structural description of Rule 2, is that the ablative case has what appears to be a reduced form which can revealingly be explained by saying that Rule 1 does not apply (the only exception to what is, otherwise, a fully productive rule) but Rule 2 does. We then have Rule 2 operating (in this case only) on an odd-syllabled form whose penultimate vowel is not long. The relevant data are given in the next section, and further justification is provided in 2.3.8.

2.3.3   Final syllable deletion [Rule 2] – instances of (i). Rule 2 can only apply if the final morpheme in a word is monosyllabic; with a disyllabic affix the morpheme boundary condition cannot be met (consider, for instance, *digara+bara* 'beach-BELONGING TO', and see also 2.4).

It will be useful now quickly to survey all monosyllabic affixes that can occur word-finally and note the effects of Rule 2. Rule 1 applies quite freely, to every odd-syllabled word, with the single exception noted below.

NOMINAL CASES. (Noun and adjective roots take identical case inflections – for full details see 3.3.2.)

[1] ergative. *-du* after a consonant (with assimilation in place of articulation to a preceding nasal or *y*). Does not reduce – (*c*) morpheme boundary condition is not met.
     -ŋgu after a vowel; reduces regularly by Rule 2.

[2] dative. *-da* after a nasal
     -nda elsewhere. Does not reduce – an exception to Rule 2 (with a possible historical explanation – see 2.3.2. and 3.3.2).

[3] purposive *-gu*. Does not reduce – (*b*) final consonant condition is not met.

[4] locative–allative–instrumental.
     -da after a consonant (assimilates like ergative). Does not reduce – condition (*c*) not met.
     following a vowel: *-la* on an odd-syllabled stem and *-:* on an even-syllabled stem. We can take the canonical form as *-la* and suggest that this reduces by Rule 2 with, in addition, an affix-specific rule deleting final *-l* in all but five irregular items. Thus we have:

trisyllabic stem – *gudaga* 'dog'   locative – *gudagala*
regular disyllabic stem – *bulmba* 'camp'   locative – *bulmba:*
irregular disyllabic stem – *ḍugi* 'tree'   locative – *ḍugi:l*

We are here presenting an optimal explanation of the synchronic data on locative allomorphy. It is, in fact, possible that allomorph *-:* may not be diachronically related to *-la* (see 3.3.2).

[5] accusative (occurs very occasionally with nouns – 3.3.7) *-ɲa*. Reduces by Rule 2 e.g. *bimbi* 'father', accusative *bimbi:ɲ*.

[6] ablative–causal. *-mu* (e.g. *guyga:lmu* 'from a bandicoot', *baḏi-galmu* 'from a tortoise', *gudagamu* 'from a dog').

   With an even-syllabled vowel-final stem this inflection is simply *-m* (*bulmbam* 'from the camp', *ḏugim* 'from the tree', *buɲam* 'from the woman')

It is possible that the allomorph *-m* is not directly diachronically related to *-mu* (3.8.4, 3.3.2). Here, however, we are – as in the case of locative – simply attempting to explain the synchronic facts.

We could explain the *-m* allomorph by the regular operation of Rules 1 and 2, and then an ad hoc rule which deletes vowel length only when a vowel-final stem is followed by ablative case. That is:

underlying form	*buɲa + mu*
Rule 1	*buɲa: + mu*
Rule 2	*buɲa: + m*
ad hoc rule	*buɲam*

The alternative is to state an exception to Rule 1 – the rule will not apply when ablative immediately follows a vowel (note that it DOES apply when ablative is added to a consonant-final stem – *guyga:lmu*). We prefer this formulation on the principle that there is less 'cost' involved in providing an ad hoc exception to an established rule, than in setting up extra ad hoc rule. In fact we will, in 2.3.8, provide strong empirical justification for preferring the 'exception to Rule 1' alternative.

It was in view of the behaviour of the ablative inflection that we adopted the formulation of Rule 2 given in 2.3.2. Odd-syllabicity is given as a condition, rather than penultimate vowel length, so that we can derive:

underlying form	*buɲa + mu*
Rule 1	[exception – does not apply]
Rule 2	*buɲa + m*

Note that there is no other exception known to the operation of Rule 1. In fact the failure of Rule 1 to apply in this instance is only possible in view of the later obligatory application of Rule 2, to derive an even-syllabled word. Otherwise, the failure of Rule 1 would lead to the generation of an odd-syllabled word that did not meet Constraint 2 (2.2). (The only other circumstances in which Rule 1 could fail to apply and not produce a word that failed to meet the stress specification of Yidiɲ would be if there were already a long

vowel in some even-numbered syllable earlier than the penultimate. But it appears that in these cases Rule 1 always does apply.)

One remaining nominal inflection is held back to [9] below.

NOMINAL DERIVATIONS

Each nominal stem can occur in absolutive case, which has zero realisation. Thus, any monosyllabic affix deriving a nominal stem is 'at risk' to be reduced by Rule 2. [7, 8, 10, 11] can be added to a nominal stem, and derive a further nominal stem. [9] is a further inflection, but is most conveniently discussed after [8].

[7] set-inclusion *-ba* (e.g. *buɲa:ba* 'a set of people, one of whom is a woman' (see 3.3.6)). Does not reduce – (*b*) final consonant condition is not met.

[8] comitative ('with'). (See 3.3.4, 4.3.1)
    -ḍi following a consonant. Does not reduce – condition (*c*) not met.
    -yi following a vowel. Reduces regularly by Rule 2.
Thus:

root		comitative	
guygal	'bandicoot'		*guyga:lḍi*
gudaga	'dog'		*gudagayi*
buɲa	'woman'		*buɲa:y*

It was noted in 2.1.2 that in the surface form of a Yidiɲ word a syllable cannot end in *-iy* or *-i:y*. We have, in fact, a general 'syllable-final yotic deletion rule' (Rule 3) that is discussed and formally stated in 2.3.7. In the present case it merely drops the yotic from the comitative of an even-syllabled stem ending in *i*. Thus the comitative of *mayi* 'vegetable food' is derived:

root plus affix	*mayi+yi*
Rule 1	*mayi:+yi*
Rule 2	*mayi:+y*
Rule 3	*mayi:*

(It will be noted that comitative falls together will locative–allative–instrumental, only in the case of an even-syllabled stem ending in *i*.)

Now a comitative form (derived from a noun or adjective root) functions as an adjective, and takes the same case inflection as the head noun it modifies (3.3.4, 4.3.1). The forms discussed above were in fact

comitative-plus-absolutive. Non-zero cases go on to the unreduced form of a comitative, and the case can then itself be reduced by Rule 2. For instance:

root	comitative-plus-absolutive	comitative-plus-ergative
gudaga 'dog'	*gudagayi*	*gudagayi:ŋ*
buɲa 'woman'	*buɲa:y*	*buɲayiŋgu*
muḍam 'mother'	*muḍa:mḍi*	*muḍamḍiŋgu*

The appearance of *i* after the comitative *y* in *buɲayiŋgu* is support for our deriving *buɲa:y* as a reduced form of *buɲa+yi*, and generalising *-yi* as the canonical form of the comitative affix with all vowel-final stems.

[9] 'fear' inflection (see 3.3.2, 4.6.1)

This involves the addition of *-da* to the underlying form of the comitative (providing further support for *-yi* as the canonical form). For instance:

gudagayi:da	'for fear of the dog'
buɲayida	'for fear of the woman'
muḍamḍida	'for fear of mother'

It is plausible to recognise a morpheme boundary between *-ḍi/-yi* and *-da*, but apprehensional forms do not reduce, condition (*b*) on Rule 2 not being met.

[10] genitive *-ni*.

This effectively derives an adjectival stem, which takes the same case inflection as its head noun (exactly like comitative) – 3.3.3, 4.7.1. Genitive-plus-absolutive reduces regularly by Rule 2, as exemplified in 2.3.2. Just as we recognised underlying suffix forms *-ŋgu* and *-yi* for ergative *buɲa:ŋ* and comitative *buɲa:y*, so we would expect to set up underlying *buɲa+ni* for the surface form *buɲa:n*, following surface forms *gudaga+ni*, *guygal+ni*, and so on.

And we should expect the suffix-final *i* to appear before non-zero case inflections, exactly as does the *i* of the comitative. In fact the genitive of a vowel-final disyllabic root does show a trisyllabic stem before an oblique case, but its final vowel is *u*, not *i*:

root	genitive-plus-absolutive	genitive-plus-ergative	genitive-plus-dative
gudaga	*gudagani*	*gudagani:ŋ*	*gudagani:nda*
buɲa	*buɲa:n*	*buɲanuŋgu*	*buɲanunda*
guygal	*guyga:lni*	*guygalniŋgu*	*guygalninda*

An attempt at a diachronic explanation of the appearance of *u*, where *i* would be expected, in forms like *buɲanuŋgu* and *buɲanunda*, is in 3.3.3, 3.6.4.

It is worth noting that this /u/ tends to be centralised, and is often pronounced as [ʌ] or [ə] – although informants would, when the writer asked for clarification, say the word slowly with a *u* vowel; they would not accept an *i* (as in **buɲaniŋgu*). The vowel articulation in this case parallels the pronunciation of the vowels representing underlying morphophonemes *A*, *I* and *U* (2.1.1, 2.3.4).

> [11] 'another' *-bi* (3.3.6). Does not reduce – (*b*) final consonant condition is not met.

VERBAL INFLECTIONS (For full details see 3.8.4)

> [12] past tense (see examples in 2.3.2).
> *-ɲu* with *-n-* conjugation stems; reduces regularly by Rule 2.
> *-l+ɲu* with *-l-* conjugation stems; reduces regularly by Rule 2.

Note that with an *-n-* conjugation form the first segment, *ɲ*, of the tense affix is retained (being C_1 in the structural description of Rule 1) but with *-l-* conjugation forms the complete tense suffix is lost, C_1 being the conjugation marker *-l-*. Only disyllabic stems are known for the *-ɽ-* conjugation and here past tense is *-:ɽ*; it is reasonable in this case to analogise an underlying form *-ɽ+ɲu*, although there is no possibility of verifying this.

> [13] purposive *-na* ~ *-l+na* ~ *-ɽ+na*. These do not reduce, and provide a second exception to Rule 2.
>
> [14] dative subordinate *-ɲu+nda* ~ *-l+ɲu+nda* ~ *-ɽ+ɲu+nda*. Reduces regularly, by Rule 2.
>
> [15] causal subordinate *-ɲu+m* ~ *-l+ɲu+m* ~ *-ɽ+ɲu+m*. Does not reduce since the structural description for Rule 2 is not satisfied, the affix ending in a consonant.
>
> [16] 'lest' inflection *-n+ḍi* ~ *-l+ḍi* ~ *-ɽ+ḍi*. This is the third and final exception to Rule 2, since it does not reduce.

It could be pointed out that if verbal purposive and 'lest' forms did reduce then they would coincide, and would also fall together with past tense inflections in the case of the *-l-* and *-ɽ-* conjugations. Similarly, if dative case forms reduced they would coincide with genitive. But the possibility of grammatical neutralisation cannot be quoted as sufficient reason for words

involving these three affixes being exceptions to a phonological rule; we have seen that locative–allative–instrumental can coincide with comitative in forms like *mayi:* (but are quite different in other instances – *buɲa:* and *buɲa:y*, *gudagala* and *gudagayi*). However it is possible that the expectation of such neutralisation played some diachronic role in these three affixes becoming established as exceptions to Rule 2. (And note that although nominal dative *-nda* does not reduce, the verbal dative subordinate inflection *-ɲu+nda* does; it is presumed that the two *-nda*'s have a common origin. Note also that while a reduced dative would coincide with genitive, the reduced dative subordinate ending does not fall together with any other form.)

VERBAL DERIVATIONS. The only zero inflection on verbs (leaving a derivational affix in word-final position) is imperative with the *-l* conjugation. The only verbal affix which derives an *-l-* conjugation stem is:

[17] comitative allomorph *-ŋa-l* (see 2.3.2, 3.8.5 and 4.3). This does reduce, by Rule 2, in the imperative inflection. Thus we get, with verbs of different syllabicity:

root + COMITATIVE + IMPERATIVE	*gali + ŋa + ø*	*maḍinda + ŋa + ø*
Rule 1	*gali: + ŋa*	—
Rule 2	*gali: + ŋ*	—
surface form	*gali:ŋ*	*maḍindaŋa*

There is an affix of identical form which derives a transitive verbal stem from a noun or adjective:

[18] causative *-ŋa-l*. This again reduces, by Rule 2, in the imperative inflection. With a disyllabic adjective root ending in a vowel we get

	root	*mada*	'soft'
	causative + imperative	*mada:ŋ*	'make soft!'
cf.	causative + present	*mada:ŋal*	'make soft'
	causative + past	*madaŋalɲu*	'made soft'

There is, of course, no reduction with trisyllabic nominal stems, or stems ending in a consonant:

root	*gumaɽi*	'red'	*guriɲ*	'good'
caus + imp	*gumaɽiŋa*	'make red!'	*guri:ɲŋa*	'make good!'
caus + pres	*gumaɽiŋal*	'makes red'	*guri:ɲŋal*	'makes good'
caus + past	*gumaɽiŋa:l*	'made red'	*guriɲŋalɲu*	'made good'

TIME AFFIXES

> [19] -*may* and -*m* derive time adverbals from adjectives (3.7.8). They
> do not reduce since they each end in a consonant (and fail the
> structural description for Rule 2).

POST-INFLECTIONAL AFFIXES. The majority of suffixes of this type (which can occur with words of any class, and always follow inflections) are disyllabic. There are, however, two monosyllabic affixes in this class – -(*a*)*la* and -*di* (3.9.1–2) – and they DO NOT REDUCE. These affixes receive separate discussion in 2.4.

Rule 2 applies quite regularly to nouns, adjectives, verbs, deictics – in fact with every part of speech bar one: pronouns. In 3.6.3 we show that the optimal analysis of the pronoun paradigm involves regarding pronouns as falling outside the scope of Rule 2. (Note though that Rule 1 applies quite regularly with pronouns, as with all other parts of speech.)

2.3.4 Final syllable deletion [Rule 2] – (ii) root reduction. Of the

1,300 or so nominal roots (nouns, adjectives, locational and temporal forms) in the writer's dictionary of Yidiɲ, around 1,200 decline regularly, taking the forms of inflectional and derivational affixes briefly summarised in the last section. Sample paradigms are in table 2.1. The first column shows inflections on to a vowel-final stem, while the last three columns show inflections on to a stem ending in a consonant (the loss of *r* from ergative and locative of *maḍur* is discussed in 3.3.2). For all 'regular' nominals the absolutive form has the same number of syllables as the root, and all oblique forms involve just one additional syllable.

There are, however, about eighty nominals in the dictionary which have disyllabic absolutive and quadrisyllabic oblique forms (that is, the non-zero case forms involve two syllables more than the absolutive form). These are exemplified in table 2.2.

Although the absolutive forms end in a consonant, these words do not decline like regular consonant-final roots (table 2.1). In fact, in all cases but the absolutive they appear to show a trisyllabic, vowel-final root – *gindanu*, *ḍambula*, *waɲaṛi*. It remains to explain the absolutive.

In terms of a root inferred from the oblique forms, the underlying form of the absolutive should be *gindanu + ø*, and so on; but the surface form is *ginda:n*. This immediately recalls underlying *buɲa + ŋgu* from which Rules 1 and 2 derived surface form *buɲa:ŋ*, etc. Rule 1 is, of

TABLE 2.1 *Regular nominal inflections*

	'initiated man'	'hornet'	'tortoise'	'frog sp.'
ABSOLUTIVE	*mula:ri*	*biɲɖin*	*baɖi:gal*	*maɖur*
ERGATIVE	*mulariŋgu*	*biɲɖi:ndu*	*baɖigaldu*	*maɖu:du*
DATIVE	*mularinda*	*biɲɖi:nda*	*baɖigalnda*	*maɖu:rnda*
PURPOSIVE	*mularigu*	*biɲɖi:ngu*	*baɖigalgu*	*maɖu:rgu*
LOCATIVE	*mularila*	*biɲɖi:nda*	*baɖigalda*	*maɖu:da*
ABLATIVE	*mularimu*	*biɲɖi:nmu*	*baɖigalmu*	*maɖu:rmu*
COMITATIVE	*mulariyi*	*biɲɖi:nɖi*	*baɖigalɖi*	*maɖu:rɖi*
GENITIVE	*mularini*	*biɲɖi:ni*	*baɖigalni*	*maɖu:rni*

TABLE 2.2 *Morphophoneme-final nominal inflections*

	'moon'	'two'	'youth'
ABSOLUTIVE	*ginda:n*	*ɖambu:l*	*waɲa:ɽ*
ERGATIVE	*gindanuŋgu*	*ɖambulaŋgu*	*waɲaɽiŋgu*
DATIVE	*gindanunda*	*ɖambulanda*	*waɲaɽinda*
PURPOSIVE	*gindanugu*	*ɖambulagu*	*waɲaɽigu*
LOCATIVE	*gindanula*	*ɖambulala*	*waɲaɽila*
ABLATIVE	*gindanumu*	*ɖambulamu*	*waɲaɽimu*
COMITATIVE	*gindanuyi*	*ɖambulayi*	*waɲaɽiyi*
GENITIVE	*gindanuni*	*ɖambulani*	*waɲaɽini*

course, totally productive (with a single exception noted in 2.3.3) and would automatically lengthen the middle vowel of *gindanu*. We could now suggest that it is Rule 2 which reduces *ginda:nu* to *ginda:n*. Note that the conditions for Rule 2 are all met, except the morpheme boundary condition. If we were to extend Rule 2 to cover the absolutive forms in table 2.2 there would have to be a disjunctive statement of its conditioning.

The most serious difficulty is that Rule 2 does NOT reduce the absolutive forms of ALL vowel-final trisyllabic roots that meet its phonological conditions (that is, whose last intervocalic consonant can be a word-final segment). We would not, of course, expect *gudaga* 'dog', *waguɖa* 'man' or *balawa* 'black sugar ant' to reduce, since a word cannot end in a stop or *w*. But we should expect

both (*a*) *gaḍara* 'possum', *bigunu* 'shield', *wayili* 'red bream'

and   (*b*) *guḍara* 'broom', *ḍudulu* 'brown pigeon', *galgali* 'curlew'
to reduce, giving disyllabic absolutives; set (*a*) do, and follow the paradigm in table 2.2, whereas set (*b*) do not reduce and have trisyllabic absolutives, following the paradigm in the first column of table 2.1. There are in fact about 80 trisyllabic roots in set (*a*) – in each case there is a single consonant (*m*, *n*, *ɲ*, *l*, *r* or *ɽ*) between the second and third vowels in the root. Set (*b*) – those whose absolutives could be reduced by Rule 2, but are not – contains about 35 roots with a single consonant in the final intervocalic position, and about 17 with a consonant cluster in that position (for instance, *ɲabuŋga* 'a wattle tree', *gindalba* 'small lizard sp.').

It appears that there is no phonological, semantic or grammatical factor conditioning this reduction. The only straightforward solution seems to be to assign roots ending in a final morphopheneme – *A*, *I* or *U* – to those items with trisyllabic oblique roots which do form a disyllabic absolutive. Thus we have *gindanU*, *ḍambulA*, *waɲaɽI*, *gaḍarA*, *bigunU*, *wayilI*, and so on. A word-final morphophoneme will trigger Rule 2; if it is not word-final it will simply be rewritten as the appropriate vowel. Words in set (*b*) are assigned roots in the normal way – *mulari*, *guḍara*, *ḍudulu*, *galgali*, and so on.

We now have two alternatives for the third condition on Rule 2. There must either be a morpheme boundary immediately after the penultimate vowel, or the final vowel must be *A*, *I* or *U*. The full statement is:

RULE 2 – FINAL SYLLABLE DELETION

$$XV_1C_1(C_2)V_2 \,\#\, \rightarrow XV_1C_1\#$$

if (*a*) $XV_1C_1 (C_2)V_2 \,\#\,$ is an odd-syllabled word;

and (*b*) C_1 is one of the set (*l*, *r*, *ɽ*, *y*, *m*, *ɲ*, *n*, *ŋ*) of allowable word-final consonants;

and (*c*) EITHER (i) there is a morpheme boundary between V_1 and C_1

OR (ii) V_2 is *A*, *I* or *U*.

Here V_1 can be any (long or short) vowel.

Rule 2 must be ordered after Rule 1.

All roots which are set up with final *A*, *I* or *U* are odd-syllabled and have a single consonant (which is an allowable word-final segment) between V_1 and V_2. Thus the inclusion of '(C_2)' in the structural description, and conditions (*a*) and (*b*), are not strictly necessary to the statement of Rule 2 for the case of root reduction. But since these conditions must be satisfied for final syllable reduction to take place, it seems most straightforward to give one general statement of the rule, as above.

It is worthwhile comparing the possibilities at final intervocalic position in the set of morphophoneme-final roots, and in the set of roots which could reduce but don't, like *mulari* (we deal just with the non-reducing forms which have a single consonant between the final and penultimate vowels). The Yidiɲ dictionary contains (excluding Dyalŋuy forms):

	l	*r*	*ɽ*	*y*	*m*	*n*	*ɲ*	*ŋ*
reducing roots	25	11	21	–	6	15	3	–
non-reducing roots	4	11	12	5	–	1	1	–

It will be seen that there is no significance in the fact that no reduced absolutive (of the type *ginda:n*) ends in *ŋ*; there are in fact no trisyllabic roots with *ŋ* in the last intervocalic position.

Only five trisyllabic forms have *y* in the last intervocalic position, and none of them reduces. In three words, *y* follows *i* (*yuɽiya* 'saltwater snake sp.', *bibiya* 'coconut tree', *gurgiya* 'freshwater khaki bream') and if these did reduce the then-final *y* would have to be deleted by Rule 3 – 2.1.2, 2.3.3, 2.3.7. In the other two, *y* follows *u* (*ŋawuyu* 'turtle', *ɖiyuya* 'catbird') and these could reduce, as do comitative forms (2.3.3). But there are so few trisyllabic forms with *y* in the last intervocalic position, that no significance should be attached to the fact that none of them reduces.

It is worthy of note, though, that whereas *l*, *r* and *ɽ* occupy the last inter-vocalic position in both reducing and non-reducing roots, the nasals (*m*, *n* and *ɲ*) are found almost exclusively in reducing roots. In fact the only two non-reducing roots with a nasal in this position exhibit alternation: *gaɽana* 'black cockatoo' has the form *gaɽna* in the coastal dialect, and *ɲiriɲi* 'a long peppery fruit' has been heard as *ɲirɲi*. (Such alternation is, in fact, rarely encountered in the dictionary as a whole. See 2.6.2.)

Each noun and adjective occurs more frequently in the absolutive form than in all other case forms put together. Thus, in most instances of use, the 'third vowel' of the root is not pronounced – but the long second vowel of, say, *mala:n* 'right-hand' (in contrast with *malan* 'flat rock') indicates that a trisyllabic root should appear in oblique cases. For

perhaps three-quarters of the reducing trisyllabic roots the writer found it an easy matter to discover the identity of the third root vowel (and the data obtained were quite consistent). But for a quarter or so of these items there was some difficulty, due to

> either (I) fluctuation in the value of the third vowel in oblique forms,
> or (II) appearance of a centralised allophone of the third vowel.

Taking these in turn:

I. FLUCTUATION

First note that there appears to be a positive association between the second vowel and final vowel or morphophoneme in a trisyllabic root.

The figures for those reducing trisyllabic roots for which a final morphophoneme can unambiguously be assigned, are:

second vowel	final morphophoneme A	I	U
a	20	4	9
i	4	8	5
u	8	–	20

Thus, in 62% of these words the second vowel and final morphophoneme coincide (if there were no association, we should expect a figure of $33\frac{1}{3}$%).

A count of all other (non-reducing) vowel-final trisyllabic roots in Yidiɲ reveals that 44% of them have identical second and third vowels.

It appears that sometimes a speaker cannot remember the identity of the third root vowel in a reducing-absolutive form. That is, he may be familiar with the absolutive form – say *baɻi:ɲ* 'spear stick' – and know from the long second vowel that there must be a root-final vowel before non-zero cases; but he is not sure whether the root should be *baɻiɲA* or *baɻiɲI* or *baɻiɲU*.

In such cases, the third vowel will be given as

> either (i) identical to the second vowel of the root,
> or (ii) identical to the vowel of the suffix.

For instance, *gambi:ɻ* has always been given as the absolutive form 'tablelands'. Most informants gave purposive *gambiɻagu*, ablative *gambiɻamu* and locative *gambiɻala*; Dick Moses gave these forms on some occasions and on others *gambiɻimu* and *gambiɻila* – he was here supposing that the third vowel was identical with the second vowel (as it is for 62% of roots of this class).

Tendency (ii) can be exemplified with *gambinU* 'top-knot pigeon'. The absolutive is consistently *gambi:n* and one informant gave ergative *gambinuŋgu*, purposive *gambinugu*, genitive *gambinuni* (consistently employing the root *gambinu*). Another informant gave, one year, ergative *gambinuŋgu*, locative *gambinala*, comitative *gambiniyi* – where the third vowel anticipates the quality of the vowel in the suffix; the following year this informant used *gambinu-* in all oblique forms.

As will be seen from the examples, variation in the third vowel occurs only on some occasions for some informants (and then only for a handful of words). In almost every case, consistent results can be obtained by detailed checking with other informants.

Whenever there seemed, after preliminary investigation, to be an alternation between two root-final morphophonemes, the choice that differed from the second vowel of the root turned out to be correct. For instance, Dick Moses used the root *gulaɽI* 'big-leaf fig tree' during the writer's 1972 field trip, but *gulaɽA* in 1973. Checking independently with Tilly Fuller and Katie May revealed that they both used *gulaɽI*.

The only morphophoneme alternations which it has not been possible to resolve are:

[1] *gaḍulA* ∼ *gaḍulU* 'dirty (e.g. of water)' – this item appears to be confined to the coastal dialect.

[2] *wagaɽI* ∼ *wagaɽA* 'wide'. Both Dick Moses and Tilly Fuller alternated on different occasions between *i* and *a*, before suffixes involving all types of vowels. Pompey Langdon used only *a*.

[3] *gunbulA* ∼ *gunbulU* 'billy can' (said to be in the Dyalŋuy style). The third vowel was given as *a* or *u* by Dick Moses, and by Katie May; as *a* by George Davis; as as *u* by Pompey Langdon and Tilly Fuller (although Mrs Fuller gave *i* before locative *la* on one occasion). From what we have said it might be thought that *gunbulA* is the most likely correct form (where the morphophoneme differs from the second vowel of the root). But the cognate form in the Ngaḍan dialect of Dyirbal is in fact *gunbulu*.

For some forms the third vowel was, on first elicitation, always the same as the vowel in the suffix; that is:

u before ergative *-ŋgu*, ablative *-mu* and purposive *-gu*
a before locative *-la*, dative *-nda*, set-inclusion *-ba* and causative verbaliser *-ŋa-l*
i before genitive *-ni* and comitative *-yi*

For instance, *gaɲaɽA* 'European-type axe' has absolutive *gaɲa:ɽ*. One informant gave ergative *gaɲaɽuŋgu*, purposive *gaɲaɽugu*, ablative *gaɽaɽumu*,

locative *gaɲaɽala*, genitive *gaɲaɽini* and comitative *gaɲaɽiyi*, suggesting that the root be taken simply as *gaɲaɽV*, with dummy V taking on the value of the suffix vowel. But another informant consistently used *gaɲaɽa-* before all suffixes, whatever their vowel (and the following year the first informant consistently used *gaɲaɽa-*).

The only putative root-final V's which it has not been possible to resolve are:

[4] absolutive *wubu:l* 'lucky (at hunting, etc.)'. Dick Moses gave ergative *wubuluŋgu*, dative *wubulanda* and past tense verbalised form *wubulaɲa:l*, suggesting a root *wubulV*.

[5] absolutive *wurgu:l* 'pelican'. Dick Moses consistently used *wurgulV*, Pompey Langdon did not recognise the word and Tilly Fuller gave ergative *wurguluŋgu* (which would be consistent with underlying *wurgulV* or *wurgulU*).

[6] absolutive *mugi:ɽ* 'mussels'. A variety of vowels have been encountered before oblique suffixes and no clear pattern emerges (this word only occurs in the coastal dialect.)

II. CENTRALISING

A morphophoneme, *A*, *I*, or *U*, normally emerges as a clearly articulated vowel, [*a*], [*i*] or [*u*], before a non-zero affix. And the normal stress rules will, of course, apply; thus we have *gáɲaráni* 'alligator-GEN' as against *gaɲá:r* 'alligator-ABS'.

But on some occasions a morphophoneme can be articulated as a central vowel [*ə*]; there will not then be stress on that syllable. Thus, the writer has recorded 'black pine-GEN' as [*gúbumáni*], but also as [*gúbumǝni*]. This centralising is quite uncharacteristic of Yidiɲ vowels – which normally have rather extreme 'cardinal' values (2.1.1) – and is encountered only in the realisation of underlying morphophonemes, and with the *u* in the declension of a genitive based on an even-syllabled vowel-final root (2.3.3, 3.3.3).

There are three likely explanations for this centralising tendency (it is possible that all have some relevance, and the central vowels observed are the result of a combination of factors). Firstly, when an informant is unsure of the quality of the third vowel in a root it is natural that he should – while still including the correct number of syllables in each word – not commit himself to the value of the vowel. This certainly explains some occurrences of [*ə*]. Thus – as noted above – Dick Moses normally used the correct root *gambiɽA* 'tablelands' but on one occasion pronounced the third vowel as *i*; at the same session he gave the genitive as simply [*gámbiɽǝni*].

Before discussing the second reason for vowel centralisation we can

remark that many of the words which in the Yidiɲ dialects have disyllabic absolute (= citation) forms, with the second vowel long,
correspond to words with trisyllabic citation forms in the Guŋgay
dialect, or in nearby languages:

Yidiɲ	*bigu:n*	Guŋgay	*bigunu*	'shield'
	birga:l	Dya:bugay,	*birgala*	'night-hawk'
		Dyirbal		
	bini:r	Dya:bugay	*biniri*	'shell'
	wayi:l	Wargamay	*wayili*	'red bream'

In just a few instances the cognate has a final consonant:

| Yidiɲ | *yagu:ɲ* | Guŋgay | *yaguɲaŋ* | 'echidna (porcupine)' |
| | *dumbu:n* | Dya:bugay | *dumbunum* | 'scorpion' |

In almost every case the third vowel of the cognate form corresponds to
the morphophoneme that is set up for the Yidiɲ root (on the basis of
inspection of oblique forms in Yidiɲ) – thus, *bigunU*, *birgalA*, *binirI*,
wayilI, *dumbunU*, but *yaguɲU*.

It is reasonable to infer from these correspondences that what are
presently morphophoneme-final roots in Yidiɲ originally had simple trisyllabic roots, which were preserved as such in absolutive case/citation
form. And that there was a specific historical change – probably in the
quite recent past – reducing absolutive forms like *bigu:nu* and *birga:la*
to the disyllabic *bigu:n* and *birga:l*.

The Yidiɲ words must, of course, have first dropped the final consonant,
where there was one – thus *dumbu:num* > *dumbu:nu* > *dumbu:n*. Qua *yagu-
ɲaŋ*, note that Yidiɲ – unlike Guŋgay – does not allow roots to end in ŋ
(2.6.3).

Now in almost every Australian language an absolutive form (marking
intransitive subject and transitive object functions) is identical – at least
as regards segmental phonology – with the root. This is the case for
1200 of the 1300 or so nominals known for Yidiɲ. But for the 80 lexical
items discussed in this section the absolutive has been reduced to two
syllables, while a trisyllabic root is maintained elsewhere. As we have
noted, this perfectly satisfies the strongest stress target of Yidiɲ – every
word involving one of these roots (for instance, every word in table 2.2)
has an even number of syllables.

But there must be a tendency – in a way, in opposition to the stress
target – to reconcile absolutive and root forms. The next historical step

TABLE 2.3   *Absolutive-root reduction*

	absolutive	root	oblique (e.g. dative)
ORIGINAL	ḍambu:la	ḍambula	ḍambulanda
PRESENT	ḍambu:l	ḍambula	ḍambulanda
NEXT STAGE (?)	ḍambu:l	ḍambu:l	ḍambu:lnda

could be to generalise the absolutive as the root on which all oblique forms are founded. We are suggesting that from the top line in table 2.3, the present system (in the middle line) developed, and that this may in time be replaced by the lower line.

The development from *ḍambulanda* to *ḍambu:lnda* would involve elimination of the third vowel (the stress pattern would then automatically follow the normal trisyllabic prescription – 2.2). This would not be expected as a sudden step, but would be likely to involve occasional, and then progressively more frequent, unstressing and reduction/centralising of this vowel. This would fit in exactly with observed pronunciations like [*gúbuməni*]; at present they are greatly outnumbered by 'regular' pronunciations [*gúbumáni*], but these may well be the first step in a change into disyllabic-root alignment, as in the bottom line of table 2.3. Note also that very occasionally what is properly a morphophoneme-final root may be inflected as if it were a consonant-final item – thus *ginda:nḍi* 'by moon (light)' has been heard instead of *gindanuyi* (informants have sometimes corrected forms like *ginda:nḍi* on listening to the tape, but at other times they may maintain that either *gindanuyi* or *ginda:nḍi* is equally acceptable).

The final point that can be made in explanation of the central realisation of morphophonemes is the normal tendency to lower, say, *u* before *y* (2.1.1). For instance, /*gindanuyi*/ is often pronounced [*gíndanəyi*] or [*gíndaniyi*], making it impossible to hear whether *u* or *i* was intended ([*gíndanwi::*] has also been heard).

It is likely that these three tendencies assist and reinforce one another. In the case of a word which is relatively infrequent – and known mostly by its absolutive form – some speakers may be unsure of the third root vowel (point 1); then this word is likely to be one of the first candidates to be assigned a disyllabic root (point 2). And if a third root vowel (say, an original *u*) is being occasionally unstressed and reduced (point 2), it

is likely to have a particularly central and neutral quality before *y* (point 3), as in [*gíndanəyi*]. There may also be interaction between (II) CENTRALISATION and (I) FLUCTUATION. Thus, a tendency to assimilate the third vowel of /*gindanuyi*/ to suffix vowel *i*, and a tendency to lower *u* slightly before *y*, may both contribute to the observed [*gíndaniyi*].

The lower line in table 2.3 introduces roots that involve a long vowel, followed by a consonant. This would be a definite phonological change since as we have seen (at least for the nominal roots so far considered) at present no root form involves a long vowel. (In 2.3.8 we discuss twelve items which do involve a long vowel, but it then comes at the end of the root.) It seems that the language is at present flirting with a phonetic alternation that might in time lead to a reinterpretation of this kind (it would be wrong, at this stage, to say that the language had irreversibly embarked on a series of changes that would lead to root reanalysis). It is a pity that – since Yidiɲ is no longer actively spoken, and will become quite extinct within a very few years – no linguist will be able to observe the changes that would have been likely to occur.

The length of our comments on vowel fluctuation and centralisation should not obscure the fact that these are marginal effects, noticed occasionally in a minority of morphophoneme-final items. Nine-tenths or more of the time these words exactly follow the paradigm in table 2.2 (and this appears always to be the canonical pattern, to which phonetic and other divergences have to be related).

Since a relatively small number of morphophoneme-final roots are known, an exhaustive list is given below. On the right-hand side are cognates in the Guŋgay dialect, or in neighbouring languages (where known). The following abbreviations are used:

GU – Guŋgay (phonemic forms inferred in most cases from written sources – see Appendix).

DYA – Dya:bugay (material from Ken Hale, Helena Cassells, and the writer's own field work).

DYI – Dyirbal, MA – Mamu, GI – Giramay, NGA – Ngaɖan (dialects of the 'Dyirbal language' – material from the writer's field work).

WA – Wargamay (material from the writer's field work).

babalA   'bone'   [NGA *babala*]
balbaɽA (tablelands dialect) ∼ *banbaɽA*
          (coastal dialect)
          'crane'

baɳɖaɽA	'madness in head'	[DYI *baɳɖaɽ* 'stupid']
baɽiɲU	'small-leaved tree, used for spear handle'	
bigunU	'shield'	[GU *bigunu*]
bilgilI	'spur wood'	
binirI	'shell, money'	[DYA *biniri*]
birgalA	'night hawk'	[DYA, MA *birgala*]
buɖalA	'fine[ly ground]'	[MA *buɖala* 'soft (cooked)']
bulguɽU	'swamp'	
buluɽU	'storytime person, thing or place'	[DYA, DYI *buluru* 'long time ago']
dumbunU	'scorpion'	[DYA *dumbunum*]
ɖaɖirI	'seven sisters (stars); a trap'	
ɖalamU	'fresh, young (e.g. leaf)'	
ɖambulA	'two'	[GU *ɖambula*]
ɖigurU	'thunderstorm'	[MA *ɖiguru*]
ɖimurU	'large house'	[DYA, NGA *ɖimuru*]
ɖinaɽA	'root'	[DYA *ɖinara*]
ɖulɲulU	'waterfall'	
ɖuŋgumU	'worm'	[DYA *ɖuŋgum*]
ɖurinU	'leech'	
ɖuwarA	'wattle'	
gabanU	'rain'	[DYA *gaba:n*]
gabulU	'stick for carrying fish'	
gaɖarA	'brown possum'	[MA *gaɖara*, DYA *gayara*]
gaɖulA ~ U	'dirty (e.g. water)'	
gambinU	'top-knot pigeon'	
gambiɽA	'tablelands'	[DYI, MA *gambil*]
gambunU	'a type of spirit'	
gangulA	'grey wallaby'	[GU, DYA *gangula*]
gaɲalA	'black scrub locust'	
gaɲarA	'alligator'	[GU, DYA, DYI *gaɲara*]
gaɲɖilA	'crab'	[cf. place-name *gaɲɖiɽa* – 6.1.2]
gaɲaɽA	'European-type axe'	
gaɲunU	'bushes arranged as an animal trap'	
gaɽbaɽA	'mangrove tree'	[cf. place-name *gaɽbaɽa* – 6.1.2]
gawiɽI	'crescent-shaped'	
gawulA (~ U?)	'blue gum tree'	[DYA *gawula* 'gum tree sp.']

gimalA	'tree used for fire drills'	[DYA *gimala* 'fire drill']
gindanU	'moon'	[DYA *ginda:n*]
giyaɻA	'stinging nettle tree'	[DYI *giyara* 'softwood stinging tree']
gubumA	'black pine'	
guḍunU	'wind'	
gugiɲU	'flying fox'	[DYI, MA *gugi*; DYA *gugi:ɲ*]
gulanU	'walnut tree'	
gulaɻI	'big-leaved fig tree'	
gumbalA	'a stage in the development of grubs'	[GI *gumbala*]
guŋgaɻI	'north'	[GU, DYA, DYI *guŋgari*]
gurunU	'language, story, news'	[GU *guruna* or *gurunu*?]
guɻbanU	'crow'	
guyalA	'fish hawk'	[GU *guyala*]
guyirI	'calm (water)'	
guyuɻU	'storm'	[DYA *guyuru*]
maḍalA	'tree fern'	
magulA (~ *U*?)	'a root food'	[DYA *magula*]
malanU	'right hand'	[DYA *mala:n*]
malaɻA	'spider web'	[DYA *malaɻa*]
mayaɻA	'young initiated man of the gurabana moiety'	
milirI	'cramp, pins and needles'	
mindirI	'salt-water centipede'	
mudalA	'black mangrove tree; garfish'	
mugiɻV	'small mussels'	[cf. Gugu-Yalandyi *mugir*]
muṇḍurU	'plenty'	
muɻinU	'ashes'	[DYA *murini* 'ashes, hot']
ɲagilI (~ *A*?)	'warm'	[GU *ɲagila*?, MA *ɲigala* 'dry']
ɲuŋgulU	'Torres Straits pigeon'	[DYA, GU *ɲuŋgulu*]
ɲuɲurU	'initiated man'	
ɲuɻulU	'shade (of a bushy plant)'	
ɲuygunU	'whispered talk'	
wagaɻI ~ *A*	'wide'	[DYA *wagara*]
wangamU	'kidney'	[NGA *wangamu*]
waɲḍirI	'how many' (number interrogative – see 3.7.7)	
waɲaɻI	'pre-pubescent boy'	[DYA *waɲari*]

waŋgamU	'overhanging cliff'	
wayilI	'red bream'	[WA *wayili*]
wiṯulU	'a shell fish'	
wubulV	'lucky (at hunting, etc.)'	
wugamU	'firefly'	
wulmbuṯU	'leafy broom'	[DYA *wulmburu* 'leaves']
wurgulV	'pelican'	
yabuṯU	'post-pubescent girl'	[DYA *yabuṯu*]
yaguɲU	'echidna'	[GU *yaguɲaŋ*]
yangaṯA	'straight'	[NGA *yangaṯa*]
yurunU	'long time ago'	

In addition, the data collected on Dyalŋuy contains a handful of morphophoneme-final roots:

buṯuṯU	'cloud'	
ḍumalA	'straight woomera'	[MA Dyalŋuy, DYI everyday style – *ḍumala*]
manḍalA	'water'	
muɲarA	'scrub turkey'	[MA everyday style – *muɲara*]
winaṯA	'foot'	[MA Dyalŋuy – *winara*]

There is also an item that may belong to Dyalŋuy or to everyday Yidiɲ (informants vary on this):

| *gunbulA* ~ *U* | 'billy can' | [NGA everyday style – *gunbulu*] |

2.3.5 Sources of vowel length. In 2.3.1 we discussed the root and inflectional forms of 'regular' nominals – those for which all segments of the root occur in each case form. We found that for trisyllabics the absolutive form involves a long vowel (*guda:ga*, *yabu:lam*). This could be taken as the root, but then inflectional processes would become quite complex, involving various specifications of length deletion and insertion. Instead, we found it simplest to set up roots which involved no long vowels at all, and to introduce length by Rule 1 (which is – with a single exception noted in 2.3.3 – totally productive in Yidiɲ).

Then in 2.3.4 we discussed nominals which have a trisyllabic root in all oblique cases, but disyllabic absolutive form – always ending in a long vowel followed by a consonant (*ginda:n*, *ḍambu:l*, *waŋa:ṯ*). The absolutive form could have been selected as the root, but then inflectional processes would have had to delete vowel length and add a (morphologically, but not phonologically, conditioned) vowel. The simplest

scheme for these items was to take the root as trisyllabic, ending in a morphophoneme *A*, *I* or *U*, and without any vowel length. Length in absolutive forms is then again introduced by Rule 1 (and the final morphophoneme is deleted by Rule 2).

In summary, none of the roots set up for the 1280 nouns, adjectives, time words and locational words considered thus far involves any vowel length (the remaining 30 nominals will be dealt with in 2.3.7, 2.3.8).

This analysis is supported by the rule for nominal reduplication (3.3.9). Reduplication, which normally indicates plural reference, involves repetition of the first two syllables of the root. Thus (quoting absolutive forms) we have *buɲa* 'woman', *buɲabuɲa* 'lots of women' and *wagu:ɖa* 'man', *waguwagu:ɖa* 'lots of men'. If the root were *wagu:ɖa* we would expect (unless the reduplication rule were explicitly framed to exclude the repetition of vowel length) *wagu:wagu:ɖa*; but with root *waguɖa*, reduplication derives *waguwaguɖa* and Rule 1 then lengthens the penultimate vowel.

Now a syllable-final consonant will normally be reduplicated – *ɲalal* 'big', *ɲalalɲalal* 'lots of big ones'; *guɲɖi:lbay* 'tiger snake', *guɲɖil-guɲɖi:lbay* 'lots of tiger snakes'. Thus, if the absolutive *yabu:ɽ* 'young woman', *ɖambu:l* 'two' were the roots we would expect reduplicated **yabu:ɽyabu:ɽ* and **ɖambu:lɖambu:l* (or perhaps **yabuɽyabu:ɽ*, **ɖambul-ɖambu:l*). In fact the forms are *yabuyabu:ɽ* 'lots of young women', *ɖambuɖambu:l* 'two together', exactly what is predicted from roots *yabuɽU* and *ɖambulA*.

We gave details, in 2.3.2–3, of a fair number of nominal and verbal inflections which have one surface allomorph involving a long vowel – thus *-:ŋ* ~ *-ŋgu* ~ *-du* ERGATIVE, *-:n* ~ *-ni* GENITIVE, *-:ɲ* ~ *ɲu* PAST TENSE (*-n-* conjugation). *-:l* ~ *-lɲu* PAST TENSE (*-l-* conjugation), and so on. In each case the alternants are phonologically conditioned – by the number of syllables in the stem to which they are attached – and we could have provided a neat distributional statement of the allomorphy. But it was again found simplest to adopt a single canonical form (which does not involve a long vowel) for each affix, allowing vowel length again to be inserted by Rule 1 and a final syllable to be deleted by Rule 2.

Thus, no nominal root – of the set thus far considered – or verbal root, or nominal or verbal inflection involves vowel length, length being entirely the result of 'penultimate vowel lengthening' (Rule 1). It is, in fact, quite predictable that the next-to-last syllable of any odd-syllabled word will involve a long vowel and will bear stress. Strictly speaking, it

is redundant to mark length in these circumstances – we could write absolutive *mulari* instead of *mula:ri*, allowing the reader silently to apply Rule 1 to all odd-syllabled words. In fact Rule 1 would be simply a specification of phonetic realisation – rather than a phonological rule – if it were not sometimes followed by Rule 2, which excises a syllable and destroys the condition for the operation of Rule 1. Thus, although we could write either *mula:ri* or *mulari*, the length must be specified in *mala:n* (absolutive of *malanU* 'right-hand') to distinguish it from *malan* (absolutive of *malan* 'flat rock'). Since length must be specified in cases where Rule 2 follows Rule 1, it seems most consistent to mark length wherever Rule 1 applies.

It can be seen that vowel length only became phonologically significant in Yidiɲ at the time at which Rule 2 (which does not itself affect length) was introduced. It is interesting in this connection to compare Yidiɲ with Wargamay, spoken 100 miles to the south. This language has contrastive vowel length (almost certainly going back to a distant ancestor language, perhaps even to proto-Australian), in the initial syllable only. Stress goes on to a long vowel if there is one in a word (*mú:ba* 'stone fish', *gi:baɽa* 'fig tree sp.'), otherwise on the first syllable of a disyllabic word (*múɲan* 'mountain') and the middle syllable of a trisyllabic form (*gagára* 'dilly-bag'). The vowel in the stressed second syllable of a trisyllabic word tends to be (phonetically) lengthened. But length in this case is entirely predictable, and is not marked in transcription of Wargamay words; it does appear to be phonetically less pronounced and less consistent than the contrastive length in initial syllables. (For further details of Wargamay phonology, see Dixon forthcoming – a.)

Vowel length in Yidiɲ comes from two main sources:

(I) application of Rule 1
(II) inherent length in three verbal affixes

(A number of further, quite minor, sources are listed in 2.3.8.)

The following verbal suffixes specify length on the final vowel of a preceding stem:

	-n- conjugation	*-l-* conjugation	*-ɽ-* conjugation
ANTIPASSIVE, etc.	*-:ḍi-n*	*-:ḍi-n*	*-:ɽḍi-n*
'GOING' ASPECT			
normal form	[*-ŋali-n*]	*-:li-n*	*-:ɽi-n*
form before comitative	*-:ri-n*	*-:ri-n*	*-:ri-n*
'COMING' ASPECT	[*-ŋada-n*]	*-:lda-n*	*-:da-n*

('Going' and 'coming' allomorphs for the *-n-* conjugation are placed within square brackets, since they do not specify vowel length.)

The length specification in these affixes is not dependent on the number of syllables in the stem, and thus cannot be explained in terms of Rule 1. For instance, with root *wawa-l* 'see, look' we get stem *wawa:ḍi-n*; this has past tense form *wawa:ḍiɲu* and present tense *wawa:ḍiɲ*. With trisyllabic root *wuɲaba-n* 'hunt', the *-:ḍi-n* plus present tense form is *wuɲaba:ḍiɲ*. The aspectual affixes exactly parallel this. (Full details of the morphological occurrence of *-:ḍi-n* are in 3.8.5; its functions are described in 4.2. The aspectual affixes are described in 3.8.6.)

We can suppose that at some time in the not-too-distant past Yidiɲ had no length contrast at the phonological level. (A distant ancestor certainly had contrastive length in initial syllables; this is preserved in some – geographically quite widely separated – modern languages, but appears to have been lost in Yidiɲ. Thus, whereas Nyawaygi (at Ingham) has *wa:ɲal* 'boomerang' and *ba:ri-* 'to cry', Yidiɲ has simply *waɲal* and *badi-*.) We can also suppose that, like a number of modern Australian languages, Yidiɲ placed major stress on the initial syllable of an even-syllabled word, but preferred to stress even-numbered syllables in odd-syllabled words so that there was a regular alternation of stressed and unstressed syllables, and no word would both begin and end with a stressed syllable. A non-initial stressed syllable would be likely to be (phonetically) slightly lengthened.

The main historical change would have been the elision of the final unstressed syllable of odd-syllabled words under certain conditions (presumably: the present-day conditions for the operation of Rule 2). With this change, stress (with concomitant length) would have become phonologically significant for even-syllabled words.

Turning now to length in aspectual affixes, it is likely that this is in some cases the remainder from an original extra syllable. The 'going' and 'coming' aspects may have evolved from compounding and reduction of lexical roots *gali-n* 'go' and *gada-n* 'come' (for an evaluation of possible evolutionary hypotheses, see 3.8.6). We can generalise from present *-n-* conjugation allomorphs and suggest that the aspectual affixes were originally (with normal conjugation markers *-ø-*, *-l-* and *-r̪-* – see 3.8.3):

	-n- conjugation	*-l-* conjugation	*-r̪-* conjugation
'GOING'	*-ŋali-n*	*-l+ŋali-n*	*-r̪+ŋali-n*
'COMING'	*-ŋada-n*	*-l+ŋada-n*	*-r̪+ŋada-n*

There must then have been the following truncations:

$$-l + \eta ali\text{-}n > -\text{:}li\text{-}n \qquad -\underline{r} + \eta ali\text{-}n > -\text{:}\underline{r}i\text{-}n$$
$$-l + \eta ada\text{-}n > -\text{:}ldan\text{-}n \qquad -\underline{r} + \eta ada\text{-}n > -\text{:}da\text{-}n$$

In present-day Yidiɲ /uwu/ and /iyi/ can be realised as [u::] and [i::] respectively (2.1.2). And the comitative suffix -*ɲa*- has been heard as simply length on a preceding vowel (2.6.4). It is thus not implausible to suggest that -*ɲa*- could have been replaced by length on the preceding vowel (whatever its quality). Since /ɹl/ is not a permitted consonant cluster, one of these segments would have had to drop, for the -*ɹ*- conjugation GOING form. The retention of *l* but not *ɹ* before *d* parallels the situation with ergative and locative case inflections – 3.3.2.

The failure of -*ɲali-n* and -*ɲada-n* to reduce to -*:li-n* and -*:da-n* with -*n*- conjugation stems may have been at least partly due to morphotactic considerations. If this reduction had taken place, -*:li-n* or -*:da-n* would be able immediately to follow -*:ɖi-n*, giving long vowels in successive syllables, which is contrary to the stress constraints of Yidiɲ. This – and the dissimilated GOING allomorph -*:ri-n* – are illustrated and discussed further in 3.8.7.

The most difficult vowel length to explain is that in -*:ɖi-n*. We can note that this is the only (derivational or inflectional) affix which is not preceded by the conjugation marker -*l*- when attached to an -*l*- conjugation stem (3.8.2). This suggests a development -*l* + *ɖi-n* > -*:ɖi-n* (compare with the changes in neighbouring Ngaɖan, described below). We would have to account for the occurrence of length in -*:ɖi-n* when attached to -*n*- and even to -*ɹ*- conjugation stems (note that the -*ɹ*- is retained) by analogic generalisation. Certainly, -*:ɖi-n* occurs predominantly with transitive stems, and most transitive verbs do belong to the -*l*- conjugation, so this is a plausible focus from which a generalisation might spread.

It is possible that the reciprocal affix in Yidiɲ's close relative Dya:bugay may be related to Yidiɲ -*:ɖi-n*. It has the form -*ɲɖiri-n* (with -*n*- conjugation stems) ∼ -*l-ɲɖiri-n* (with -*l*- conjugation stems) – note that the conjugation marker -*l*- is retained here, and there is no vowel length.

We suggested that it was stress which first became phonologically significant (on the introduction of Rule 2) and that it would have had concomitant (phonetic) length. But length is now – through diachronic reanalysis – the critical (phonological) property, which serves to deter-

mine stress. (This does, of course, tie in with our discussion of the evolution of verb affixes *-ŋali-n > -:li-n* and *-ldi-n > -:di-n*.)

The reader may well enquire whether stress could not be taken as phonologically prior in present-day Yidiɲ and length assigned by a later (phonetic) rule; Rule 1 would then be reformulated as 'penultimate syllable stressing'.

In fact, information concerning vowel length is not inferable from stress placement. Thus, if a quadrisyllabic word has the first (and all odd-numbered) syllables stressed, the third vowel could be short – as in *gáliɲálɲu* 'go-COMIT-PAST' – or long – as in *gáliɲá:diɲ* 'go-COMIT-:di-PRES'. If we know that even-numbered syllables are stressed in a quadri-syllabic word then we can infer that either the second vowel, or the fourth vowel, or both must be long (as in *wawá:liɲú* 'see-GOING-PAST', *madíndaɲá:l* 'walk up-COMIT-PAST', *dungá:riɲá:l* 'run-GOING-COMIT-PAST') but we have no way of knowing which of these three alternatives applies. In a quinquesyllabic word we know that the fourth vowel must be long – but the second vowel may be either short (*madíndaɲá:lna* 'walk up-COMIT-PURP') or long (*dungá:riɲá:lna* 'run-GOING-COMIT-PURP'). It can be appreciated from these examples that in present-day Yidiɲ we must first state the position of any long vowels in a word, and then stress will be automatically assignable by the rule given in 2.2.

Hale (1976a: 236) in his sketch grammar of Dya:bugay mentions that 'the distribution of long vowels is of some interest vis-à-vis other Australian languages – they are extremely rare in initial syllables but highly frequent in non-initial, especially final, syllables'. It seems that vowel length in Dya:bugay follows a similar pattern to that in Yidiɲ, and may have (in part) a similar origin. (Length in the initial syllable of the language name /da:bugay/ is due to the prefix *da:*. This also occurs in Yidiɲ – 2.4, 3.4.3.)

Five of the six dialects of Dyirbal, Yidiɲ's southerly neighbour, do not show contrastive vowel length. But the sixth dialect, Ngadan, has recently introduced length by a simple change (Dixon 1972: 343):

$$\begin{bmatrix} V\left\{\begin{matrix} l \\ r \end{matrix}\right\} \\ ay \\ uy \end{bmatrix} > \begin{bmatrix} V: \\ a: \\ i: \end{bmatrix} / - \left\{\begin{matrix} C \\ \# \end{matrix}\right\}$$

Ngadan has minimal pairs such as *baga-l* 'spear', *ba:ga-l* 'hit' (*baga-l* and *balga-l* in other Dyirbal dialects).

4

The Ngaḍanḍi tribe lived on the tablelands in close proximity – and social contact – with speakers of tablelands Yidiɲ. Ngaḍan resembles Yidiɲ (particularly the tablelands dialect) in a number of surface features – see 1.3.

It appears that contrastive vowel length is a recently introduced 'areal feature' for the northern part of the Cairns Rain Forest region. We have no data on which to base a guess as to whether significant length developed first in Yidiɲ or in Ngaḍan. But it is worthwhile noting that stress appears to be independent of length in Ngaḍan. As in other Dyirbal dialects, the first syllable of each Ngaḍan word bears major stress – thus *gábu:* 'carpet snake', *ḍá:ga* 'snail', *yá:ga:* 'road' (there is in citation forms a tendency for both syllables to be stressed if the second one is long e.g. [*yá:gá:*] – compare with [*mídi*] 'small' where the second syllable would never be stressed). The shift, in Yidiɲ, from contrastive stress (with concomitant length) to contrastive length (which determines stress) may have been partly motivated by the occurrence in Ngaḍan of contrastive length.

2.3.6 Illicit length elimination [Rule 4].

According to Constraint 1 (2.2), if two or more long vowels occur in a word, each pair must be separated by an odd number of syllables. It is surely now reasonable to ask if we could not have a word which contained two (or more) long vowels – coming from different sources – which were not naturally separated by an odd number of syllables. That is, could we have length in both odd-numbered and even-numbered syllables of a word? Presumably, in the case of such a 'conflict', one length would drop and the other prevail. The interesting question here is: which, of two conflicting lengths (from different sources) would win out?

Conflict could only be possible in verbal forms, with

[A] length arising from affix -:*ḍi-n*, and from Rule 1; or

[B] length arising from a 'going' or 'coming' aspectual affix, and Rule 1; or

[C] length arising from -:*ḍi-n*, and from an aspectual affix.

We will take these one at a time and see whether, in each case, two long vowels could be in successive syllables, or could be separated by an even number of syllables.

[A] -*:ḍi-n* and Rule 1 length.

If the derivational affix -*:ḍi-n* and past tense are added to a trisyllabic stem we should, by the rules given so far, expect a word with third and fourth vowels long. For instance, from *barganda-n* 'pass by', the inflected form *barganda:ḍi:ɲ* would be expected. The form which results is *bargandaḍi:ɲ*, with the 'inherent' length on -*:ḍi-n* being lost.

This is, in fact, the form that a moment's reflection should have enabled us to predict. It is true that the surface form *barganda:ḍi:ɲ* has an even number of syllables, and that even-syllabled words can have long vowels in odd-numbered or in even-numbered syllables (but not in both). However, the underlying form was *barganda + :ḍi + ɲu*, which has an odd number of syllables. Penultimate length is introduced into this form by Rule 1 (and the final syllable is then dropped). The point to notice is that *barganda:ḍiɲu* has the third vowel long – this is at odds with Constraint 2 (2.2) which insists that in an odd-syllabled word long vowels can only occur in even-numbered syllables.

The conflict here is not between -*:ḍi-n* length and 'past tense' length, since the latter is introduced by a regular, productive rule of the language. It is rather between -*:ḍi-n* length – when this suffix is attached to an odd-syllabled stem – and the Constraints of 2.2.

There are at least two alternative ways of dealing with this situation. We could say that the ANTIPASSIVE-type suffix has two allomorphs:

> -*:ḍi-n*, following an even-syllabled stem
>
> and   -*ḍi-n*, following an odd-syllabled stem

Or, we can assign a single canonical form to the suffix, -*:ḍi-n*, and adopt:

RULE 4 – ILLICIT LENGTH ELIMINATION

> If a long vowel contravenes Constraints 1 and 2 (that is, if it occurs in an odd-numbered syllable of an odd-syllabled word) then it is shortened.

This rule is required in at least one other portion of the grammar (2.3.7) and – in keeping with our earlier policy of choosing one basic form for each root and affix and allowing length variation to be determined by general rules – we prefer the second alternative.

Rule 4 must be ordered before Rule 2 (which destroys the odd-syllabicity in terms of which Rule 4, like Rule 1, operates). There is no necessary ordering between Rules 1 and 4.

4-2

We thus have the following sample derivation:

underlying form	*barganda + :ḍi + ɲu*
Rule 4	*barganda + ḍi + ɲu*
Rule 1	*barganda + ḍi : + ɲu*
Rule 2	*barganda + ḍi : + ɲ*

There are, in fact, words on which Rule 4 must operate that do not undergo reduction by Rule 2. Thus we get *bargandaḍi:na* 'pass by-*:ḍi*-PURP' and *dunḍiɲaḍi:ɲum* 'play-COMIT-*:ḍi*-CAU SUBORD'.

Constraints 1 and 2, as originally stated in 2.2, applied to the surface forms of words. We now see that an underlying form (before Rule 2 has applied) must also conform to the surface prohibitions on long vowel placement; if it does not, Rule 4 effects normalisation.

[B] Aspectual length plus Rule 1 length.

The discussion under [A] should exactly apply to this case. However, it is very difficult to generate a word in which aspectual length conflicts with the constraints of 2.2. We would need aspect directly on to an odd-syllabled stem of the *-l-* or *-ɣ-* conjugation. But there is only one tri-syllabic root in the *-l-* conjugation (and none in the *-ɣ-* class) and this could not be obtained with an aspectual affix (trisyllabic roots occur in the *-n-* conjugation, but here aspectual affixes do not involve length specification). The only derivational affix belonging to the *-l-* conjuga-tion is comitative *-ɲa-l*; but if this is followed by an aspectual affix it will also be preceded by *-:ri-* (for instance *ḍuŋga + :ri + ɲa + :lda + ɲu* 'run-ASPECT-COMIT-COMING-PAST'). A full discussion, which involves detailed reference to verbal word structure and affixal allomorphy, is in 3.8.7.

[C] *-:ḍi-n* length plus aspectual length.

We could, in theory, get a real conflict between long vowels deriving from different types of verbal affix (and not involving Rule 1). It might be thought possible to generate, say, an even-syllabled word (that did NOT have any odd-syllabled underlying form) with length in the third and fourth syllables. But in fact it is not. The order in which affixes can occur in a verbal word, and their details of allomorphy, are such that it is impossible to generate any word in which aspectual length is separated by anything other than an odd number of syllables from *-:ḍi-n* length. A full account of this presupposes an intimate knowledge of verbal morphology, and is delayed until 3.8.7.

TABLE 2.4 *Declension of roots ending in -i, -y and -iy*

	A 'tree kangaroo'	B 'initiated man'	C 'possum sp.'	D 'catfish'	E 'black nose wallaby'
ABSOLUTIVE	*mabi*	*mula:ri*	*ḍaŋguy*	*galbi:*	*guri:li*
ERGATIVE	*mabi:ŋ*	*mulariŋgu*	*ḍaŋgu:yɲḍu*	*galbi:ɲḍu*	*guriliɲḍu*
DATIVE	*mabi:nda*	*mularinda*	*ḍaŋgu:ynda*	*galbi:nda*	*gurilinda*
PURPOSIVE	*mabi:gu*	*mularigu*	*ḍaŋgu:ygu*	*galbi:gu*	*guriligu*
LOCATIVE	*mabi:*	*mularila*	*ḍaŋgu:yɲḍa*	*galbi:ɲḍa*	*guriliɲḍa*
ABLATIVE	*mabim*	*mularimu*	*ḍaŋgu:ymu*	*galbi:mu*	*gurilimu*
COMITATIVE	*mabi:*	*mulariyi*	*ḍaŋgu:ɲḍi*	*galbi:ɲḍi*	*guriliɲḍi*
GENITIVE	*mabi:n*	*mularini*	*ḍaŋgu:yni*	*galbi:ni*	*gurilini*

2.3.7   Syllable-final yotic deletion [Rule 3]. We mentioned in 2.3.4 that of the 1,300 or so nominal forms known to the writer, around 1,200 can be assigned 'regular' disyllabic, trisyllabic or quadrisyllabic roots; each root segment occurs in every case form, as exemplified in columns A, B and C of table 2.4. A further 80 items can be assigned trisyllabic roots ending in a morphophoneme *A*, *I* or *U*, this being deleted in absolutive case. In none of these cases did we have to assign vowel length to a root.

The remaining thirty or so nominal items fall into three paradigmatic classes. Firstly, there are eleven (disyllabic and quadrisyllabic) forms whose declension is exemplified in column D of table 2.4.

In column D the absolutive form ends in *i:* (the first long vowel we have encountered ending an absolutive form). But the oblique cases are quite different from those found with an even-syllabled root ending in *i* – compare column D with column A. Elsewhere ergative, locative and comitative allomorphs involving /ɲḍ/ are found only on regular roots ending in *y*, as in column C (and they are independent of the number of syllables in the root).

We have already noted that a syllable in Yidiɲ cannot end in *-i(:)y*. A sequence *i(:)*-plus-*y* can be followed by a vowel, but not by a consonant or a word boundary. In 2.3.3 we saw that the comitative affix on to an even-syllabled root ending in *i* should, by Rules 1 and 2, generate a form with final *-i:y*; but here the final *y* is simply dropped (as in *mabi:*, column A of table 2.4).

This suggests setting up a root *galbiy*. The final *y* would condition

ergative *-ŋḍu*, and so on, but would be eliminated from surface forms whenever it remained in syllable-final position. In fact a root ending in *y* would perfectly explain why genitive and ablative do not reduce in column D, as they do in column A. The morpheme boundary condition is met in the case of *mabi + ni*, but is not satisfied for *galbiy + ni* (just as it is not for *ḍaŋguy + ni*).

The critical point is that words like 'catfish' have underlying form ending in a CONSONANT *y* and not just a vowel *i(:)*. Root-final *y* is identified as C_1 in the structural description of Rule 2 and the morpheme boundary condition (c–i) is then not met.

Recently, one or two scholars working on Australian languages have suggested that only one phoneme, /i/, need be recognised where most linguists would require both /i/ and /y/, and that /u/ can similarly be employed to cover normal /u/ and /w/ – see Blake and Breen (1971), Blake (1969) and Crowley (forthcoming). They then give a phonetic realisation rule: 'the palatal or high front vowel /i/ and the velar or high back vowel /u/ are realised as glides, [j] and [w] respectively, before *a* and before one another (*i* before *u* and *u* before *i*) when a consonant precedes...[e.g.] *ianka* 'to tell' [*janka*] (Blake and Breen 1971: 31). This does decrease by two the number of phonemes needed for description of a language but only at the expense of considerable phonotactic complication (for instance, the generalisation 'each word must begin with a consonant' is lost, and the statement of consonant cluster possibilities is likely to become quite tortuous).

A solution involving the identification of *y* with *i* and *w* with *u* may be POSSIBLE for some languages, where there is no contrast between *i:* and *iy* or *iyi* (cf. Trubetzkoy 1969: 172). But, in the case of Yidiɲ, such a treatment would make it impossible to explain – in terms of the normal conditions on Rule 2 – why *galbi:ni* has not reduced, whereas *mabi:n* has. It may be that detailed investigation of other Australian languages will uncover further phonological rules which depend on the consonantal status of *y*, contrasted with vocalic *i*, in underlying representations (irrespective of how phonetically similar their realisations may be). It would also be interesting to discover whether the recognition of /y/ and /i/ as separate phonemes has 'psychological reality' (in the sense of Sapir, 1949: 46–60) for speakers of Australian languages; whether, for instance, they would feel comfortable with an orthography using just one symbol to cover *y* and *i*.

We have suggested setting up root *galbiy*. Syllable final *-iy*, which we are permitting in the underlying representation, is not allowed in the surface form of Yidiɲ words. To obtain the occurring absolutive *galbi:*, the quite natural rule:

(9) $iy \rightarrow i: / \text{-} \#$

is required. It is natural to ask whether *iy* also becomes *i:* before a consonant (that is, whether (9) should be extended to cover all syllable-final instances). In column D of table 2.4 we get, for instance, *galbi:gu* from underlying *galbiy + gu*. The length would be naturally given by Rule 1; thus, for these forms, either $iy \rightarrow i: / $ -C (which would harmlessly reinforce the application of Rule 1) or $iy \rightarrow i / $ -C would be equally appropriate.

A phonological sequence /iyi/ is often heard as [i::] or [i:]. It is thus valid to ask whether, say, genitive [*galbi:ni*] could not have underlying /galbiyini/, rather than the /galbi:ni/ we have suggested. This would imply a root /galbiy/ for ergative, locative and comitative cases, and /galbiyi/ elsewhere. Support for a genitive form ending in /iy + ni/ – and thus for a root with final /iy/ running through all the cases in column D – comes from the allomorphs of non-zero cases on to a genitive stem.

Thus, *gadigadiy* 'very small children' inflects like *galbiy*. It has genitive-plus-absolutive *gadigadi:ni* and genitive-plus-ergative *gadigadiniŋgu*, as in

(10) *ŋaɲaɲ buṇḍa:ɲ waɲa:ldu   gadigadiniŋgu*
 1sg-o hit-PAST boomerang-ERG children-GEN-ERG
 I was hit by the children's boomerang.

It will be recalled that ergative is *-ŋgu* with an odd-syllabled and *-:ɲ* after an even-syllabled vowel-final stem. The appearance of *-ŋgu* here indicates an odd-syllabled genitive stem /gadigadini/, in preference to the even-syllabled /gadigadiyini/.

It will also be noted, from this example, that there is no length on the root-final vowel when it is no longer in a penultimate syllable. To generate /gadigadiniŋgu/ we must have:

(11) $iy \rightarrow i / $ -C

This implies that the length in forms like *galbi:gu* and *gadigadi:ni* comes (only) from Rule 1.

We can now state:

RULE 3 – SYLLABLE-FINAL YOTIC DELETION

 (i) $i(:)y \rightarrow i: / $ -#

 (ii) $\begin{bmatrix} i \\ i: \end{bmatrix} y \rightarrow \begin{bmatrix} i \\ i: \end{bmatrix} $ /-C

where C is any consonant.

 y does, of course, remain in surface form when followed by a vowel.

Rule 3 must be ordered after Rule 2. Part (i) will delete a *y* that is placed in word-final position by Rule 2 (the derivation of a reduced comitative is set out in 2.3.3). And part (ii) must not apply until after Rule 2, since the *y* is needed to block the reduction of forms like *galbiy + ni*, as described above.

Let us now turn to a further paradigmatic class of nominals, with roots having an odd number of syllables (of which only six members are known); their declension is exemplified in column E of table 2.4. We see that the case forms here differ from those on regular odd-syllabled roots ending in *i* (column B), very much as column D differed from column A. Ergative, locative and comitative forms again suggest a root ending in *-y, guriliy*. This will perfectly explain all the non-zero suffixal forms. We see that there is no vowel length in any of the quadrisyllabic words in column E – surface *gurilini* corresponds to underlying *guriliy + ni*. This gives further support to (10), *iy → i / -C*, which was initially suggested by *gadigadiniŋu* and then incorporated into Rule 3.

Rule 3 specifies that a final *iy* should become *i:*, yet the absolutive form of *guriliy* is *guri:li*, with a final short vowel. There is, however, no difficulty of explanation here. We have already recognised the need for Rule 4, which simply shortens any long vowel which happens to occur in an odd-numbered syllable of an odd-syllabled word. The derivation here would be:

root + absolutive	*guriliy + ø*
Rule 1	*guri:liy*
Rule 3	*guri:li:*
Rule 4	*guri:li*

In this case Rule 3, which lengthens the final vowel, must precede Rule 4, which eliminates this length. Rule 1 can apply at any place in the derivation.

But note that in 2.3.6 we showed that Rule 4 must precede Rule 2. We also have the necessary ordering of Rule 1 before Rule 2 (2.3.2, 2.3.5) and of Rule 2 before Rule 3 (mentioned above). These orderings can be summarised:

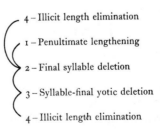

4 – Illicit length elimination

1 – Penultimate lengthening

2 – Final syllable deletion

3 – Syllable-final yotic deletion

4 – Illicit length elimination

We are here suggesting that Rule 4 applies both before and after the other phonological rules. This amounts to saying that once a word is generated by the morphological processes it is immediately checked against Constraints 1 and 2 (2.2) and any illicit length (for instance, from the affix -:*ḍi-n*, appended to an odd-syllabled stem) deleted by Rule 4. Rules 1–3 then apply to the word, after which it is again measured up against the constraints and any illicit length introduced by the rules deleted by re-application of Rule 4. We are claiming that Yidiɲ checks to see whether an underlying form adheres to surface stress/length conditions BEFORE it embarks on any further phonological tidying-up, and then has another check AFTER everything else has been seen to.

The alternative to checking against the constraints – and having Rule 4 apply – at two places in the derivation would be to specify allomorphs -:*ḍi-n* and -*ḍi-n*, conditioned by syllabicity (and similarly for aspectual affixes – 2.3.6) and/or to bring a syllabicity condition into part (ii) of Rule 3:

(i) $\begin{cases} i(:)y \to i: \mid \text{-}\# & \text{where the word is even-syllabled} \\ i(:)y \to i \mid \text{-}\# & \text{where the word is odd-syllabled} \end{cases}$

This would rewrite *galbiy* as *galbi:*, and *guri:liy* directly as *guri:li*.

It does, however, seem that a general specification like Rule 4 is preferable to ad hoc statements of this type. Given that Yidiɲ words conform to Constraints 1 and 2 it is surely natural to state a general rule 'normalising' any form that does not meet the constraints.

We have, in this section, suggested that, paralleling (disyllabic and trisyllabic) roots ending in -*ay* and -*uy*, we do have disyllabic and tri-syllabic roots ending in -*iy*. But whereas -*ay* and -*uy* roots preserve these segments in their absolute forms, -*iy* yields absolutives ending in -*i:* and -*i*.

Note that it is not necessary to set up roots with a final morphophoneme – *galbiY*, *guriliY*, and so on. The root-final segment in *galbiy*, *guriliy* appears to be exactly parallel to that in words like *ḍaŋguy* 'possum sp.' and *garaway* 'brown snail'. And Rule 3 does in any case have to deal with phonemic /y/ in the case of reduced comitatives.

The realisation of underlying /-Vŋ#/ as [-Ṽ #] in the tablelands dialect (2.6.3) is in some ways similar to the derivation of /-i:#/ from /-iy#/. But note that the ŋ-reduction rule appears to be at the phonetic level, whereas Rule 3 is plainly a phonological change (it must, for instance, precede Rule 4).

The writer's corpus contains eleven even-syllabled roots that inflect like column D of table 2.4. These comprise (absolutive form being quoted in each case):

[a] three disyllabic common nouns
   galbi: 'catfish', *diwi:* 'tree sp.', *yiri:* 'type of slatey stone'
[b] two quadrisyllabic common nouns
   giraguɲḍi: 'frog sp.', *yiŋgilibi:* 'English bee' (coastal dialect only)
yiŋgilibiy is plainly a loan word, with the final root *-iy* being chosen to produce an *-i:* in the citation form, corresponding to the vowel in the English word */bi:/*.
[c] three common nouns that involve inherent reduplication
   bili:bili: 'small hickory tree', *gadigadi:* 'very small children', *gidigidi:* 'small children'.
   The only possible cognate for any of the above forms is Dya:bugay *diwiri* 'tea-tree species', which may correspond to Yidiɲ *diwiy*. Note also that there seems to be a connection between

adjectives *gadil* 'very small'   and nouns *gadigadi:* 'very small children'
          gidil 'small'   *gidigidi:* 'small children'
The evolution of *-V:* from *-Vl* is reminiscent of the historical change which introduced long vowels into Ngaḍan (2.3.5); but note that in Ngaḍan there is no evidence that forms with underlying *-Vy* are derived from *-Vl*.
   [d] two place names (both disyllabic)
   wiḍi: 'a beach on the eastern side of Cape Grafton Peninsula'. This is named after *wiḍi* 'frog sp.' which Gulɲḍaṛubay (1.4) heard crying out on the beach. The common noun *wiḍi* has ergative *wiḍi:ŋ* and locative *wiḍi:*, whereas the place name *wiḍiy* has locative *wiḍi:ɲḍa*.
   ɲirwi: 'a coastal location'. This name is based on the adjective *ɲiwir* 'broken up' since in myth a boomerang (said to be a storytime 'boy') broke up on this spot. (There is discussion of the formation of place-names in 6.1.2.)
   [e] a common noun in Dyalŋuy – *mugi:mugi:* 'woman'.
   Note that *galbiy* (absolutive *galbi:*) reduplicates as *galbiygalbiy* (absolutive *galbi:galbi:*). Reduplication establishes a new phonological word (2.4) with a ⧣ boundary, and the rule *iy → i:/-⧣* applies here. We can follow this by suggesting that an inherently reduplicated form also involves a phonological word boundary, and set up roots *biliybiliy*, *mugiymugiy* for absolutives *bili:bili:* and *mugi:mugi:* (but note that the roots for *gadigadi:* and *gidigidi:* are simply *gadigadiy* and *gidigidiy*).
   There is a nominal */daliyi/* 'hunger, hungry'. The absolutive form is */dali:yi/*, but this is often pronounced [*dali::*] or [*dali:*] and could easily be mistaken for a form with root-final */iy/*. Case forms like purposive */daliyigu/* are again not easily distinguishable from */dali:gu/*, although four syllables are sometimes clearly heard in */daliyigu/* whereas they could never be in */galbi:gu/*. The critical case form is the ergative */daliyiŋgu/*, clearly demonstrating a tri-syllabic root. By the rules we have given, comitative should be */daliyi+yi/*; it is */dali:ɲḍi/* (and note comitative-plus-ergative *daliɲḍiŋgu*, with no vowel

length). It appears that, to avoid the tongue-twisting form /*daliyiyi*/, the root is taken as simply /*daliy*/ for comitative (only). It is in fact likely that the root is in the process of reducing from /*daliyi*/ to /*daliy*/ (one informant gave the ergative as *dali:ɲḍu* on one occasion but later corrected himself to *daliyiŋgu*, the form volunteered by all other informants.)

The corresponding form in Guŋgay was *dalaya* (supporting a Yidiɲ root *daliyi*, which would then be liable to reduce); it is *dali:r* in Dya:bugay.

Trisyllabic roots ending in -*iy*- inflecting as in column E of table 2.4 – are particularly hard to recognise, since their absolutive forms are identical to those of regular trisyllabics ending in *i* (column B). Once the ergative inflection of *guriliy* 'black nose wallaby' was noticed, a check was made of oblique case forms for all (of the two dozen or so) other *i*-final trisyllabic citation forms. This yielded one further example – *ḍumbaṟiy* 'grandchild'. There are also two Dyalŋuy nouns *ḍaṟiyiy* 'bird' and *ḍilaṟiy* 'black guana', in addition to a personal name *minminiy* (1.7) and the name of a creek *wuɲaḍiy*, declining in the same manner. *wuɲaḍiy* is based on verb *wuɲa-n* 'to drink, swallow' and affix -*:ḍi-n* (place names based on -*n*- conjugation verbal stems frequently end in -*y* – 6.1.2) but no cognates are known for any of the other five items.

2.3.8 Roots with final long vowel.
Finally, there are a dozen nominals whose absolutive form ends in *a:* or *u:*. Their declension is exemplified in columns C and D of table 2.5; regular roots – ending in *a* or *u* – are included at columns A and B for comparison.

Now we have previously encountered absolutive forms with a long vowel, but in each case we were able to justify setting up roots that involved no length – for absolutive *guda:ga* we had root *gudaga* (2.3.1), for *ḍambu:l* the root was *ḍambulA* (2.3.4), and for *galbi:* it was *galbiy* (2.3.7). However, there seems to be no way of avoiding a long vowel in the roots of *durgu:*, *galambaṟa:* and similar items.

We could experiment with a root like *durguw* (note that no surface form can end with *w* in Yidiɲ, so we would be suggesting a significant disparity between underlying and surface possibilities). But a root-final *w* would block Rule 2 (in the same way that *y* of *galbiy* did) and we would expect genitive *durgu:ni*, ergative *durgu:du* and so on. (The only way of avoiding this would be to have a rule which rewrote *uw* as *u:*, and preceded any other phonological rule. But under these conditions a -*uw* solution would be equivalent to, but more complex than, taking the root to end in -*u:*.)

We thus take the absolutive forms as roots, and acknowledge that we have just a dozen words whose roots must involve a (final) *a:* or *u:*.

TABLE 2.5   *Declension of roots ending in* u, a, u:, a:

	A 'grey possum'	B 'whale'	C 'mopoke owl'	D 'march fly'
ABSOLUTIVE	*margu*	*ŋunaŋgara*	*durgu:*	*galambaɽa:*
ERGATIVE	*margu:ŋ*	*ŋunaŋgara:ŋ*	*durgu:ŋ*	*galambaɽa:ŋ*
DATIVE	*margu:nda*	*ŋunaŋgara:nda*	*durgu:nda*	*galambaɽa:nda*
PURPOSIVE	*margu:gu*	*ŋunaŋgara:gu*	*durgu:gu*	*galambaɽa:gu*
LOCATIVE	*margu:*	*ŋunaŋgara:*	*durgu:*	*galambaɽa:*
ABLATIVE	*margum*	*ŋunaŋgaram*	*durgu:m*	*galambaɽa:m*
COMITATIVE	*margu:y*	*ŋunaŋgara:y*	*durgu:y*	*galambaɽa:y*
GENITIVE	*margu:n*	*ŋunaŋgara:n*	*durgu:n*	*galambaɽa:n*

(This does not in any way affect the argument in 2.3.7 for considering absolutive *-i:#* forms to derive from roots ending in *-iy*. There is thus a basic asymmetry – roots ending in *-ay*, *-uy*, *-iy*, *-a:*, *-u:* but not in *-i:*, and surface forms ending in *-ay*, *-uy*, *-i:*, *-a:*, *-u:* but not in *-iy*.)

Oblique case forms involve a long vowel in the penultimate syllable, and Rule 1 can be considered to apply vacuously (2.3.1). The ad hoc rule deleting locative *-l* (2.3.3) still applies, so that for this class locative coincides with absolutive.

The most interesting forms in columns C and D are ablative *durgu:m* and *galambaɽa:m*, compared to *margum* and *ŋunaŋgaram*. We mentioned in 2.3.3 that the canonical form of the ablative/causal inflection is *-mu*, but we get simply *-m* with an even-syllabled stem ending in a vowel; that is, Rule 2 has applied to excise the final syllable without the resulting form involving a long vowel. There are, as outlined in 2.3.3, two main alternative ways of dealing with this. We could say that Rule 1 applies to *margu + mu*, producing *margu: + mu*; this will then be reduced by Rule 2 to *margu: + m*, and an ad hoc rule would be required to delete the length (this rule will shorten the final vowel of an even-syllabled stem when followed by ablative case). Alternatively, we could postulate an exception to Rule 1 – it does not apply when ablative immediately follows a vowel. It seemed that there was marginally less 'cost' in accepting an ad hoc exception to an established rule, rather than in adding an extra ad hoc rule.

The second alternative is supported by forms like *durgu:m* and *galambaɽa:m* which retain the long root vowel before ablative case. If we

allowed Rule 1 to apply to *margu+mu*, the ad hoc rule which later shortened the vowel would surely be expected also to shorten the second vowel in *durgu:m* (unless the ad hoc rule were made even more special, shortening 'the final vowel of an even-syllabled stem when followed by the ablative case except where the stem is a root ending in a long vowel'!). Thus:

root + ablative	*margu+mu*	*durgu:+mu*
Rule 1	*margu:+mu*	*durgu:+mu*
Rule 2	*margu:+m*	*durgu:+m*
ad hoc rule	*margum*	**durgum*

However, if we say that *margu+mu* is an exception to Rule 1 then no length will be introduced and the root length in *durgu:* will as a matter of course go through into the ablative form:

root-ablative	*margu+mu*	*durgu:+mu*
Rule 1	[exception – does not apply]	
Rule 2	*margu+m*	*durgu:+m*

We do not, under this solution, have to distinguish at a late stage of the derivation between length introduced by Rule 1 and root length.

Rule 2 must thus be allowed to apply (in this case only) to an odd-syllabled form which does not involve a long vowel. It was in view of this that, in 2.3.2, we formulated Rule 2 with condition (a) – specifying odd-syllabicity – rather than including penultimate length in the formulaic structural description.

The full list of items encountered which demand a root ending in a long vowel is (with cognates where known):

bawu:	'backbone'	
biḍu:	'eaglehawk'	[DYA, NGA *biḍu* 'fish-hawk']
durgu:	'mopoke owl'	[DYA *durgu:*]
gaḍu:	'black tree ant'	[DYI, WA *gaḍu* 'white ant', DYA *gaḍu:* 'tree ant']
galambaɾa:	'march fly'	
gawu:	'tree sp.'	[DYA *gawula* 'gum tree sp.' may be cognate with Yidiɲ *gawu:* or *gawu:l*]
giŋa:	'vine sp.'	[may be cognate with DYI *giŋay* 'stinging bush']
wuɾu:	(i) 'river'	[DYA *wuɾu:*]
	(ii) 'snake sp.'	

yawu:	'grass sp.'	[MA Dyalŋuy *yawu*]
yibu:	'miming in dance routine'	
yulu:	'stingaree'	

Note that these all involve an even number of syllables. There is no theoretical reason why we should not have an odd-syllabled root ending in *a:* or *u:* – Rule 4 would delete the length from absolutive forms but it would occur before oblique cases (CVCVCV*:gu*, and so on). However, no root of this form has presented itself in the data collected.

In 2.3.5 we summarised the two main sources of vowel length (which between them account for at least 99 % of long vowels in Yidiɲ textual material):

[1] Rule 1
[2] verbal affixes involving inherent length
We can now add:
[3] the small set of nominal roots with inherent length.

Note that, since all roots with a final long vowel are even-syllabled, this length will always fall in an even-numbered syllable (and can never be liable to deletion by Rule 4). Root length is retained before all affixes e.g. *durgu:nula* 'owl-GEN-LOC' (3.3.3).

There are a handful of further sources of vowel length, all quite uncommon:

[4] nominal affixes *-gaɾa:* and *-ḍulu:* (3.3.7) have final long vowels. They have not been encountered followed by any further affix, and do not cohere with a preceding stem (2.4).

[5] the rather infrequent verbal affix *-:n-biḍi-n* (3.8.8) also involves length specification; it too is non-cohering.

[6] Interrogative *waɲinbara:* 'what's the matter?' (3.7.9) has a final long vowel. It does not take any further inflection.

[7] One nominal root appears to involve a medial long vowel – *waɾa:buga* 'white apple tree'. This inflects exactly like a regular even-syllabled root (for instance, *ɲunaŋgara* in column B of table 2.5) – locative is *waɾa:buga:*, ablative *waɾa:bugam*, and so on.

2.3.9 Evidence from -la ~ -ala. There is a post-inflectional affix 'now' with allomorphs (3.9.1):

| *-la* | following a vowel |
| *-ala* | following a consonant |

The forms -(*a*)*la* takes with critical roots from the discussion of the last few sections provides convincing support for the underlying forms we have set up:

absolutive form	underlying root	+(*a*)*la* form
mabi	*mabi*	*mabila*
galbi:	*galbiy*	*galbi:yala*
mula:ri	*mulari*	*mula:rila*
guri:li	*guriliy*	*guri:liyala*
durgu:	*durgu:*	*durgu:la*

-(*a*)*la* is non-cohering; the occurrence of length in these forms – and especially in *galbi:yala* – is discussed and explained in 2.4.

Note the contrast between *mabila* and *galbi:yala*, the latter form clearly indicating a consonant-final root. The contrast between *mula:rila* and *guri:liyala* is even more striking, since these words can not be distinguished in their absolutive forms. And *durgu:la* justifies our positing a root-final vowel in this case.

We noted that with an even-syllabled stem ending in *i*, locative coincides with comitative-plus-absolutive. But -(*a*)*la* forms differ. From root *mayi* 'vegetable food':

		+(*a*)*la*
locative	*mayi:*	*mayi:la*
comitative + absolutive	*mayi:*	*mayi:yala*

We suggested (2.3.3) derivations for these forms:

	locative	comitative + absolutive
underlying root + affix	*mayi + la*	*mayi + yi*
Rule 1	*mayi:la*	*mayi:yi*
Rule 2	*mayi:l*	*mayi:y*
ad hoc -*l*- deletion	*mayi:*	—
Rule 3	—	*mayi:*

The -(*a*)*la* forms provide support for the comitative-plus-absolutive derivation. It appears that the rule specifying the choice between -*la* and -*ala* must immediately precede Rule 3.

We noted in 2.1.2 that the only consonants which cannot occur as the second element of a cluster (at any position in a word) are *r*, *ɽ*, *l* and *y*. There might thus be phonotactic difficulties if we had an affix – which could follow a

consonant-final stem – beginning with one of these segments. No affix of this type begins with *r* or *ɽ*; and comitative *-yi* can only follow vowels (~ *-ɖi/C-*) as can locative *-la* (~ *-da/C-*). There are thus phonotactic reasons for the alternation *-la* ~ *-ala*. (And see the comment on *-luɲa-l* in 4.8.3.)

2.4 Grammatical and phonological words

Every language appears to have a unit that can be called '(grammatical) word'. This has considerable 'psychological reality' for its speakers: they will discuss the meanings of words, but not of parts of words; an utterance may be interrupted at a word boundary; in slow dictation a sentence will be given word-by-word or syllable-by-syllable, never morpheme-by-morpheme (see Sapir 1921: 33–5). In fact, every (or almost every) language has a word for 'word'. In each case some grammatical criteria can be given to define 'word'; the exact nature of the criteria differs from language to language.

Each grammatical word in Yidiɲ (excepting particles) has an obligatory root, and a final inflection; the latter is chosen from the set of nominal cases (if a noun, adjective, deictic, pronoun, time qualifier or locational qualifier) or from the set of verbal inflections (if a verbal stem). The main criteria for deciding whether a group of morphemes constitutes one grammatical word, or several words, are distributional in nature:

[1] fixed order of morphemes within a word.

Suppose we have a string of morphemes:

(12) *ɲuɲu wagu:ɖa wagal gimbal   ɖuŋga ɲali: na*
     that man   wife without run   going purposive
     That wifeless man should run away

We find that *gimbal* must follow *wagal*, and that *na* must follow *ɲali:* which must follow *ɖuŋga*. But that *ɲuɲu, wagu:ɖa, wagal+gimbal* and *ɖuŋga+ɲali:+na* can, potentially, be arranged in any order. This suggests that *ɲuɲu* and *wagu:ɖa* each constitutes a single word, whereas the two morphemes *wagal* and *gimbal* form one word, as do the three elements *ɖuŋga, ɲali(:)* and *na*.

[2] distribution of inflections.

Each word will have just one inflectional morpheme. We can enquire whether, in (12), *na* could be added to *ɖuŋga* as well as to *ɲali*; it can not,

so we infer that *ḍuŋga, ŋali* and *na* constitute a single word. Note the contrast between the aspectual affix *-ŋali-* 'going' in (12) and the lexical root *gali-* 'go' in:

(13) *ŋuŋu wagu:ḍa wagal+gimbal ḍuŋga:+na gali:+na*
That wifeless man should go, running

Similarly, each nominal word will have just one case inflection. Since the subject NP in (12) is in absolutive case (with zero realisation), it is impossible on this criterion to tell whether *gimbal* is an affix to *wagal* or an adjective modifying it. But this NP can be obtained in an oblique case, as in:

(14) *buɲa*   *ɲuɳḍu:+ŋ waguḍa+ŋgu wagal+gimba:l+du*
woman + ABS that + ERG man + ERG wife + WITHOUT + ERG
wawa:l
see-PAST
That wifeless man saw the woman

In (14) there is an ergative inflection following *gimbal*. We could not have the inflection following *wagal* in this instance (that is, **waga:l+du gimba:l+du* is unacceptable), indicating that *wagal+gimbal+du* constitutes a single word. We would then infer that *wagal+gimbal* should also comprise one word in (12).

Once nominal and verbal roots are recognised, in terms of these two criteria, and possible word-structures are formulated, there remains a residue of twenty or so 'particles' that (as a rule – see 4.10) take no affixes of any sort. This class of words is effectively recognised and defined on negative grounds (as lacking the defining inflectional property of nominal and verbal words), and in terms of the freedom of placement of particles in a sentence.

It also appears that in any language we can recognise a phonological unit larger than the syllable, that can conveniently be termed 'phonological word'. The exact details of the phonological criteria which serve to define 'phonological word' vary from language to language; a phonological word often contains just one major stress, or a stress pattern of a certain type. Typically, certain phonological rules will operate within phonological words, while rules of a rather different type will apply across word boundaries.

It is quite common for 'grammatical word' (set up on grammatical criteria) and 'phonological word' (justified phonologically) to coincide. This is, however, not the case in Yidiɲ. Here a grammatical word consists of a whole number of (one or more) phonological words. In fact, each of the examples quoted so far in this chapter (except for 2.3.9) has been a grammatical word that consisted of just one phonological word. It is now time to broaden our discussion to include grammatical words that involve two or more phonological units.

A root begins a phonological word. Certain suffixes cohere with the preceding root/stem and continue the same phonological word; other suffixes fail phonologically to cohere with what precedes them in the (grammatical) word, and begin a new phonological word. The crucial point here is the classification of affixes into two types:

COHERING AFFIXES – every monosyllabic inflectional or derivational affix coheres with a stem to which it is attached and continues an established phonological word.

NON-COHERING AFFIXES – every disyllabic inflectional or derivational affix, and every post-inflectional affix (whether monosyllabic or disyllabic), fails to cohere, and commences a new phonological word within the same grammatical word.

There are no affixes involving more than two syllables.

Now all the rules and constraints we have presented in this chapter apply over phonological (and not over grammatical) words. We can illustrate this – and the distinction between cohering and non-cohering affixes – by examining transitive and intransitive verbalisations of adjectives.

The transitiviser (causative) affix -*ŋa-l* (see 4.8.1) is monosyllabic and thus cohering; tense inflections also cohere. We obtain:

adjective (absolutive form)	causative verb plus past tense	
	underlying	surface
milba 'clever'	$milba + ŋa + l + ɲu$	*milbaŋalɲu* 'made clever'
gumaːɣi 'red'	$gumaɣi + ŋa + l + ɲu$	*gumaɣiŋaːl* 'made red'
gaɖuːl 'dirty'	$gaɖulA + ŋa + l + ɲu$	*gaɖulaŋaːl* 'made dirty'

Since $gumaɣi + ŋa + l + ɲu$ and $gaɖulA + ŋa + l + ɲu$ are odd-syllabled Rule 1 applies, and then Rule 2 (all its conditions being satisfied).

But the intransitiviser (inchoative) *-daga-n* (see 4.8.1) is disyllabic and non-cohering. The corresponding paradigm is:

	past inchoative	
absolutive	underlying	surface
milba	*milba+daga+ɲu*	*milbadaga:ɲ* 'became clever'
guma:ɽi	*gumaɽi+daga+ɲu*	*guma:ɽidaga:ɲ* 'became red'
gaḍu:l	*gaḍulA+daga+ɲu*	*gaḍu:ldaga:ɲ* 'became dirty'

Each of these grammatical words consists of two phonological words – firstly the root, and secondly *-daga-* plus past tense *-ɲu*. The phonological rules apply separately to each phonological word. Thus from odd-syllabled *daga+ɲu* Rules 1 and 2 derive *daga:ɲ* (irrespective of the number of syllables in the root, since this belongs to a different phonological word). And the phonological rules apply to the root elements exactly as they do in the absolutive case.

Here we had underlying forms *gumaɽi+daga+ɲu*, *gaḍulA+daga+ɲu*. If these had each constituted one phonological word, they would have been even-syllabled and no length insertion or syllable reduction would have been expected. But we have a phonological word boundary in the middle of each grammatical word – *gumaɽi#daga+ɲu, gaḍulA#daga+ɲu* – and Rules 1 and 2 thus operate separately on the two trisyllabic units in each grammatical word.

Let us now turn to affixes that derive adjectival from nominal stems. There are two interchangeable comitative ('with' or 'having') suffixes – cohering *-yi* (after a vowel) ∼ *-ḍi* (following a consonant) and non-cohering *-muḍay*; and there is the complementary privative ('without') affix, non-cohering *-gimbal*. A comitative or privative form will take the same case inflection as the head noun it modifies (see 3.3.4, 3.3.6, 4.3.1). A typical paradigm is:

root	*waɲal* 'boomerang'	*gala* 'spear'
root + *ḍi* ∼ *yi* + ABS	*waɲa:lḍi*	*gala:y*
root + *ḍi* ∼ *yi* + ERG	*waɲaldiŋgu*	*galayiŋgu*
root + *muḍay* + ABS	*waɲalmuḍay*	*galamuḍay*
root + *muḍay* + ERG	*waɲalmuḍa:yɲḍu*	*galamuḍa:yɲḍu*
root + *gimbal* + ABS	*waɲalgimbal*	*galagimbal*
root + *gimbal* + ERG	*waɲalgimba:ldu*	*galagimba:ldu*

root	*mugaṟu* 'fish net'	*bigunU* 'shield'
root + *ḍi* ~ *yi* + ABS	*mugaṟuyi*	*bigunuyi*
root + *ḍi* ~ *yi* + ERG	*mugaṟuyi:ŋ*	*bigunuyi:ŋ*
root + *muḍay* + ABS	*muga:ṟumuḍay*	*bigu:nmuḍay*
root + *muḍay* + ERG	*muga:ṟumuḍa:yɲḍu*	*bigu:nmuḍa:yɲḍu*
root + *gimbal* + ABS	*muga:ṟugimbal*	*bigu:ngimbal*
root + *gimbal* + ERG	*muga:ṟugimba:ldu*	*bigu:ngimba:ldu*

It can be seen that ergative is *-ŋgu* after a *-ḍi* ~ *-yi* comitative with an even-syllabled root, but *-:ŋ* where the root has an odd number of syllables. Each of the forms in the *-ḍi* ~ *-yi* rows is a single phonological word, and Rules 1 and 2 operate according to the syllabicity of the complete grammatical word. But with *-muḍay* and *-gimbal* forms the derivational affix begins a new phonological word; thus in *mugaṟu#gimbal + du* Rule 1 operates twice, lengthening the penultimate vowel of each phonological word, and obtains a surface form *muga:ṟugimba:ldu*.

We take our final example of the contrast between cohering and non-cohering affixes from verb morphology. We have already (2.3.2) noted paradigms involving cohering affixes with disyllabic and trisyllabic *-n*-conjugation roots:

root	*ḍuŋga-* 'run'	*ḍaḍama-* 'jump'
root + past tense	*ḍuŋga:ɲ*	*ḍaḍamaɲu*
root + comitative + past tense	*ḍuŋgaŋalɲu*	*ḍaḍamaŋa:l*

Here past tense is reduced with a disyllabic root when no derivational affix intervenes but with a trisyllabic root only following verbal comitative. Each grammatical word in this paradigm is a single phonological word, and reduction depends on the total number of syllables.

Compare this with the 'going' affix, which has the disyllabic (and non-cohering) allomorph *-ŋali-n* with *-n*- conjugation stems:

root	*ḍuŋga-*	*ḍaḍama-*
root + 'going' aspect + past tense	*ḍuŋgaŋali:ɲ*	*ḍaḍa:maŋali:ɲ*

Past tense reduces in EACH case, since *-ŋali-* begins a new phonological word (the reduction is independent of the syllabicity of the root).

The distinction between grammatical and phonological words is an important one in Yidiɲ. The discussion of morphology and syntax (in chapters 3 and 4) refers almost exclusively to grammatical words. But

the stress assignment rule and constraints 1 and 2 (2.2), and Rules 1–4 (2.3.1–8) work entirely in terms of phonological words; whenever 'word' is mentioned in one of these rules it refers to 'phonological word', and $\#$ is used to indicate the boundary between phonological words.

Lehiste (1965: 451) points out that formulae for 'quantity structures' in Finnish and Estonian (essentially based on disyllabic units) 'apply only to noncompound words. In the case of compounds and certain derivative suffixes that share many characteristics of words, the pattern starts again after a word or suffix boundary'. This seems reminiscent of the occurrence of a phonological word boundary within a grammatical word in Yidiɲ.

There appears in Yidiɲ to be a relation between 'phonological word' and the grammatical unit 'morpheme'. Each phonological word must contain just one disyllabic (or longer) morpheme – either a root or a disyllabic affix. It can also involve any number of monosyllabic (or single-consonantal) affixes (note that a single phonological word can involve at least four monomorphemic suffixes – see examples (1–6) in 2.2). We are here leaving aside the post-inflectional monosyllabic exceptions -(*a*)*la* and -*di*; these are discussed below.

The fact that a disyllabic affix must begin a new phonological word means that no phonological word is abnormally long. It does not seem, in fact, that a phonological word can involve more than seven syllables. Examples are *magi + :ri+ŋa+ :lda+ɲu+nda* 'climb up-ASPECT-COMIT-COMING-DAT SUBORD' or *maḍinda+ŋa+ :li+ɲu+nda* 'walk up-COMIT-GOING-DAT SUBORD' – both of these words have the penultimate vowel lengthened by Rule 1, and are then reduced by Rule 2, giving *magi:riŋa:ldaɲu:n* and *maḍindaŋa:liɲu:n* respectively (3.8.7).

The stress and length constraints (2.2) are adhered to very strictly within a phonological word. But it appears that any type of stress sequence is possible over a phonological word boundary. We do sometimes get a regular pattern of stressed/unstressed alternation over a whole grammatical word, as in

SU$\#$SU	*wáɲal$\#$múḍay*	'boomerang-COMIT-ABS'
or US$\#$USU	*bigú:n$\#$mudá:yɲḍu*	'shield-COMIT-ERG'

but in other cases we can obtain two successive stressed, or two successive unstressed, syllables, as in

SU$\#$USU	*wáɲal$\#$mudá:yɲḍu*	'boomerang-COMIT-ERG'
or SU$\#$US	*ḍúŋga$\#$ɲalí:ɲ*	'run-GOING-PAST'
and US$\#$SU	*bigú:n$\#$múḍay*	'shield-COMIT-ABS'
	mabí:n$\#$múḍay	'tree kangaroo-GEN-COMIT-ABS'
	durgú:$\#$múḍay	'mopoke owl-COMIT-ABS'

Pike (1964) describes how in Auca, a language of Ecuador, one stress pattern starts from the beginning of the word and another starts at the end. There are similarities and dissimilarities to the Yidiɲ example – special rules are needed in Auca to cover the meeting-place of the two stress-trains in the middle of a word, whereas in Yidiɲ there is normally no connection between the stress patterns of two phonological words that make up a single grammatical word.

We mentioned in 2.1.2 that whereas the consonant clusters that can occur within a morpheme are fairly restricted, spanning a morpheme boundary we can effectively get any word-final consonant followed by any word-initial segment. In fact, a rather wider set of possibilities is encountered across a phonological word boundary (within a grammatical word) than at a morpheme boundary within a phonological word. This is due to the fact that a number of phonological processes apply to simplify the junction of a stem with a mono-syllabic affix, whereas no changes occur at the boundary preceding a disyllabic affix. For instance, ergative *-du* assimilates in point of articulation to a pre-ceding nasal or *y*; and stem-final *ɲ* drops before genitive *-ni* or dative *-(n)da* (3.3.5). Thus, we do not happen to get clusters /md/, /ɲd/ at a morpheme boundary within a phonological word; these clusters are encountered at a morpheme boundary that is also a phonological word boundary (nominals ending in *m* and *ɲ* can be followed by *-damba* – 3.3.6). But note that a tri-consonantal cluster can occur only across a morpheme boundary within a phonological word (e.g. *gaba:y+ɲḍa* 'road-LOC', *ŋala:l+nda* 'big-DAT'), and never across a phonological word boundary.

Each Yidiɲ affix was thoroughly checked to see whether or not it 'cohered'. The main criteria are:

[a] in the case of a nominal or post-inflectional affix, check whether or not a root-final morphophoneme is realised as a vowel, or is deleted, before the affix. If the morphophoneme is deleted (by Rule 2) the affix is shown to be non-cohering – for instance, *guŋgaɽI+bara* 'tablelands-BELONGING TO' is realised as *guŋga:ɽbara*. If the morphophoneme is realised as a vowel, the following affix must be cohering – the 'fear' inflection on *gaɲarA* 'alligator' is *-yi+da* giving a surface form *gaɲa-rayi:da* (this provides part of the reason for recognising the 'fear' inflection to involve a monosyllabic increment, *-da*, to a comitative stem – 2.3.3, 3.3.2).

[b] In the case of a nominal derivational affix ending in a vowel, check whether ergative alternates between *-ŋgu* and *-:ɲ*, depending on the syllabicity of the stem (and similarly for other cases).

[c] In the case of a verbal derivational affix, check whether past tense alternates between *-ɲu* and *-:ɲ* (or *-l+ɲu* and *-:l*), depending on the syllabicity of the stem.

[d] In the case of any affix, note the stress patterning. For instance, the stress on *ŋáyu+ɲá* in line 13 of text 14 indicates that *-ɲa* is non-cohering (3.3.7). And see the discussion of *-maŋa-l* in 3.8.5.

A complete list of Yidiɲ affixes, classified as to whether or not each coheres, follows:

COHERING

NOMINAL CASES (3.3.2)

ergative *-ŋgu* ~ *-du*	ablative *-mu* ~ *-m*
locative *-la* ~ *-da*	'fear' *-yi+da* ~ *-ḍi+da*
dative *-(n)da*	accusative *-ɲa* (this is very rare –
purposive *-gu*	3.3.7)

NOMINAL DERIVATIONS (3.3.3–6)

genitive *-ni*	set-inclusion *-ba*
comitative *-yi* ~ *-ḍi*	'another' *-bi*

LOCATIONAL AND TEMPORAL SUFFIXES (3.4.2, 3.7.8, 3.5)

juxtapositional *-baɲ*	durational time *-(a)m*
point time *-(a)may*	

VERBAL INFLECTIONS (3.8.2, 3.8.4)

present *-ŋ* ~ *-l* ~ *-ṛ*	dative subordinate *-ɲu+nda* ~
past *-ɲu* ~ *-l+ɲu* ~ *-ṛ+ɲu*	*-l+ɲu+nda* ~ *-ṛ+ɲu+nda*
imperative *-n* ~ *-r*	causal subordinate *-ɲu+m* ~
purposive *-na* ~ *-l+na* ~	*-l+ɲu+m* ~ *-ṛ+ɲu+m*
-ṛ+na	'lest' *-n+ḍi* ~ *-l+ḍi* ~ *-ṛ+ḍi*

VERBAL DERIVATIONS (3.8.2, 3.8.5–6, 4.8.1)

comitative allomorph *-ŋa-l*
anti-passive etc. *-:ḍi-n* ~ *-:ṛ+ḍi-n*
'going' aspect allomorphs *-:li-n* ~ *:ṛi-n* ~ *-:ri-n*
'coming' aspect allomorphs *-:lda-n* ~ *-:da-n*
causative verbaliser (added to nominals, particles, etc.) *-ŋa-l*

NON-COHERING

NOMINAL DERIVATIONS (3.3.6–8)

comitative *-muḍay*	durative *-ḍulu:*
privative *-gimbal*	'along' *-mari*

'with a lot of' -*damba*   'up' -*waŋgi*
'belonging to' -*bara*   'down' -*ḍilŋgu*
'only, all' -*ḍamu*   'west' -*guwa*
'lots, all' -*muŋgal*   'east' -*naga*
'from' -*gaṟa:*

VERBAL DERIVATIONS (3.8.2, 3.8.5–6, 3.8.8, 4.8)

comitative allomorphs -*l*+*maŋa-l* ∼ -*ṟ*+*maŋa-l*
'going' aspect allomorph -*ŋali-n*
'coming' aspect allomorph -*ŋada-n*
'dispersed activity' - *:n*+*biḍi-n*
inchoative verbaliser -*daga-n*
incremental verbaliser -*maḍi-n*
transitive verbaliser -*luŋa-l*

All types of reduplication – which prepose the first two syllables of the root before the stem – are non-cohering, and involve a phonological word boundary at the reduplication boundary – see 3.3.9, 3.4.1, 3.8.9, 2.3.7.

We mentioned that post-inflectional affixes do not cohere, whatever their syllabicity. These are clitic-like forms, which can generally be attached to any type of word and follow an inflection (if there is one). Four of the six well-attested post-inflectional affixes are disyllabic (full details are in 3.9):

-*ŋuṟi* 'this—, like—'   -*buḍun* 'still'
-*ŋuṟu* 'for another thing'   -*waḍan* comparative

but there are two monosyllabics – -*di* 'self' and the form discussed in 2.3.9 -*la* (after vowels) ∼ -*ala* (after consonants) 'now'.

A root-final morphophoneme is deleted before these two affixes:

with root *gangulA* 'wallaby species'   we get *gangú:ldí* (not *gánguládí)
with root *bigunU* 'shield'   we get *bigú:nála* (not *bígunúla)

Compare with the nominal derivational affix -*bi* 'another' which does cohere:

with root *yabuṟU* 'young girl'   we get *yábuṟúbi* (not **yabú:ṟbí*)

Similarly, when -*di* is added to the verb *gada-n* 'come' in past tense the underlying form is *gada*+*ŋu*+*di*. This is an even-syllabled form and if it were one phonological word Rules 1 and 2 would not need to apply. But it comprises two phonological words, *gada*+*ŋu*#*di*, and the surface form is *gadá:ŋdí* (as in line 14 of text 14). Also, if -*la* ∼ -*ala*

were added to underlying *gada*+*ɲu* we would expect *gadaɲula*; the form
is in fact *gadá:ɲála*. Note that the consonant-final allomorph is used
here, indicating that the choice of -*la* or -*ala* follows the application of
Rule 2.

In 2.3.9 we described how -*ala* occurred with *galbiy* (as against -*la*
with *mabi*). There is, of course, a phonological word boundary here –
galbiy#ala. Now Rule 3 (2.3.7) specifies *iy* → *i:*/-# and this would
yield *galbi:#ala*. Note that the actual form is *galbi:yala*, suggesting a
late rule that inserts the glide *y* between *i:* and *a* (sequences of two vowels
are not permitted in Yidiɲ, even across word boundaries). We thus get
allomorph -*ala* chosen before Rule 3 operates; *y* replaced by vowel
length through the automatic operation of Rule 3; and then *y* re-
inserted by a late 'glide insertion' rule. (Rule 3 must apply, to account
for the long vowel; if we simply had -*ala* added to the root *galbiyala
would be expected.) Exactly the same argument holds for the comitative + absolutive + 'now' form *mayi:yala* (2.3.9).

-*di* and -(*a*)*la* provide the only examples of monosyllabic phonological words –
and are exceptions to the account in 2.2. Sometimes they do bear major stress
(as *gadá:ɲ#di*, *gáliɲálɲu#lá*) but on other occasions these affixes have been
heard assimilated into the stress pattern of the whole grammatical word (thus,
gadá:ɲdi, *galiɲalɲúla*). It should be noted that stress assimilation between
phonological words has only been consistently noted in the case of -*di* and
-(*a*)*la*.

There is a form -*ɲa* that may be a third monosyllabic postinflectional affix;
it appears not to cohere. The data on this form are slight, and not totally
clear – 3.3.7.

The non-coherence of these two (or three) monosyllabic affixes may
be a function of their grammatical status. They are only loosely attached
to any word in a grammatical sense, and it may be because of this that
they are considered a separate 'phonological word'.

There is, however, an alternative explanation possible in the case of
-*di*. Yidiɲ has a particle *ɲadí* with the same type of reflexive/intensive
meaning as -*di* (4.10). It is not known why *ɲadí* (which does not involve
a long vowel) has final stress. But it is undoubtedly this that has led to
its degeneration into the post-inflectional affix -*di*. (At present *ɲadí* and
-*di* are both used, in syntactic free variation, but it is likely that the affix
is gradually replacing the particle.) -*di*'s non-cohering nature may be
due to its being a recent truncation of a disyllabic form (which would not

be expected to cohere) or just to the fact that it is a recently-created affix.

Finally, Yidiɲ has just one prefix [ḍa:-]; this has quite limited occurrence – 3.4.3. It does not cohere – from root guŋgaɽI 'north' we get ḍá:guŋgá:ɽ 'northwards', and from root wurga-n 'yawn' plus past tense -ɲu we get wurgá:ɲ alternating with ḍá:wurgá:ɲ 'yawned'.

One possibility open for us to consider is that [ḍa:] has an underlying di-syllabic form /ḍawa/. It was mentioned in 2.1.2 that there are a handful of (rather uncommon) words that are normally pronounced as monosyllables involving [i:] or [u:]. We regard them as underlying disyllabics largely because they inflect on the pattern of even-syllabled stems. But we also have the particle [gi:] 'don't' and exclamation [yi:] 'yes' which take no inflections; these are assigned forms /giyi/ and /yiyi/ simply by analogy with /miyiɽ/, [mi:ɽ] and /wuwuy/, [wu:y]. The argument could be extended to [ḍa:]; but a main difficulty is the quality of the vowel. All other Yidiɲ monosyllabics involve either /iyi/ or /uwu/, realised as [i:] and [u:] respectively. (In Dyirbal /awa/ can be pronounced [a:] – Dixon 1972: 278; but the phonetic differences between Yidiɲ and Dyirbal are sufficiently great to rule out the validity of an analogical argument here.) Certainly, if [ḍa:] could be assigned a disyllabic form this would fit into our generalisation about non-cohering affixes.

Yidiɲ [ḍa:] is probably cognate with a form /ḍawa/ that occurs in many Australian languages meaning 'mouth' and sometimes 'door' (hence its optional inclusion in the verb (ḍa:)wurga-n 'to yawn' in Yidiɲ). This prefix occurs in the language name Dya:bugay; and Hall (1972: 215) reports that ḍa:w 'mouth, opening, orifice' is a prefix in Ḍa:yore, spoken 300 miles to the north-west of Yidiɲ (where it also features in the language name).

The main points of 2.2–4 were published – omitting some of the compli-cations, and with less exemplification – in Dixon (1977); that article does not contain any information or discussion that is not in the present chapter.

2.5   Other phonological processes

2.5.1   Dissimilation and double dissimilation.
In common with almost all other Australian languages, Yidiɲ shows assimilation of ergative and locative case suffixes to a stem-final nasal or yotic. It is unusual in that it also shows phonological dissimilation in a certain combination of verbal affixes.

With -*l*- conjugation roots the 'going' aspect has the form -:*li-n* (-*n* is used to show that the derived stem takes -*n*- conjugation suffixes).

Thus:

		root + 'going'
root	root + past tense	aspect + past tense
magi-l 'climb up'	*magi:l* 'climbed up'	*magi:liɲu* 'went climbing up'
burwa-l 'jump'	*burwa:l* 'jumped'	*burwa:liɲu* 'went jumping'

Now from any intransitive root (or stem) we can derive a transitive stem by adding the verbal comitative affix *-ŋa-l*. 'Going' aspect precedes comitative (for a full discussion see 3.8.6) and is in this environment realised as *-:ri-n:*

root + 'going' aspect + comitative + past tense *magi:riŋa:l*
" " " + present tense *magi:riŋal*
" " " + purposive *magi:riŋa:lna*

With an *-l-* conjugation stem, the conjugation marker *-l-* appears before all inflections save imperative (and all derivational affixes save *-:ɖi-n* – see 3.8.2). We can thus suggest that the *l* of *-:li-n* dissimilates to *r* before the *l* of *-ŋa-l* (note that comitative is the only verbal affix deriving an *-l-* conjugation stem). The dissimilation is generalised so that it applies before *-ŋa-l* in all instances (even when imperative or *-:ɖi-n* follows – 3.8.6).

The 'going' aspect is *-ŋali-n* on to an *-n-* conjugation stem and *-:ɻi-n* with a root from the *-ɻ-* conjugation, but in these cases too it becomes *-:ri-n* before comitative *-ŋa-l*.

	root + 'going' +	root + 'going' +
root	past tense	comit + past
ɖuŋga-n 'run'	*ɖuŋgaŋali:ɲ* 'went running'	*ɖuŋga:riŋa:l* 'went running with'
bayga-ɻ 'feel sore'	*bayga:ɻiɲu* 'feel sore while going'	*bayga:riŋa:l* 'make feel sore while going'

It seems that the dissimilated *-l-* conjugation allomorph of the 'going' aspect is generalised to apply to all three conjugations before comitative (otherwise we might expect the *-n-* conjugation form to be *-ŋari-n*).

It is likely that *-:li-n* is, historically, a reduced form of *-ŋali-n* (2.3.5). It may be that the unmarked *-n-* conjugation allomorph has not reduced since this would lead to length conflict (for instance – *wawa:ɖi:li-n* – 2.3.6). But there is a reduced form before comitative since there is here no chance of a length conflict. Detailed discussion of this point will be found in 3.8.6–7.

However, although the 'going' suffix is -:*ri-n* before comitative for most verbs, it does not always have this form. With some verbal roots the normal allomorph -:*li-n* still occurs before -*ŋa-l*:

root	root + 'going' + past tense	root + 'going' + comit + past
burwa-l 'jump'	*burwa:liɲu* 'went jumping'	*burwa:liŋa:l* 'went jumping with'
burgi-n 'walk about'	*burgiɲali:ɲ* 'went walkabout'	*burgi:liŋa:l* 'went walkabout with'

The set of verbs which take -:*li-n* before -*ŋa-l* is limited – it includes *warŋgi-n* 'move around', *ḍari-n* 'sink down, vanish, be submerged, drown', *gaṟba-n* 'hide', *daṟba-n* 'slip' and *wiṟa-n* 'be bent, twisted'. It seems that if the (last) consonant cluster in the root involves a rhotic then allomorph -:*li-n* is preferred over -:*ri-n*.

We could say that a rhotic simply blocks the dissimilation of aspectual *l* to *r* before -*ŋa-l*. But in this case surely we would expect the normal *n*-conjugation allomorph, -*ŋali-n*, whereas in fact we get -:*li-n*. A case can be made out for saying that -:*li-n* dissimilates to -:*ri-n* under pressure from -*ŋa-l* (and the form -:*ri-n* is then generalised to all conjugations); and that, as a second stage, -:*ri-n* dissimilates to -:*li-n* in the presence of a rhotic (of either type) in the root.

2.5.2   Nasal insertion. There are two or three scattered examples of a nasal being inserted at a morpheme boundary, and in some cases assimilating to a following stop. However, this appears to be a rather marginal and little-used phonological process in Yidiɲ (in contrast to Dyirbal, where it is quite productive – Dixon 1972: 283–6).

Thus, between a stem-final -*y* and the ergative inflection -*ḍu*, an *ɲ* can optionally be inserted; between -*y* and locative -*ḍa* or comitative -*ḍi* an *ɲ* is obligatory (see 3.3.5). There are also a few instances where *n* is inserted at a reduplication boundary, and in some cases assimilated to a following stop (e.g. from *bayga-ṟ* 'feel sore-PRES' we get *baygaṟmbaygaṟ* 'feeling very sore'). And pronouns and deictics have the basic root augmented by -*n* for many oblique case forms – 3.6, 3.7.

Whilst correcting the writer an informant once enunciated [*gílbay#dá*] very slowly and deliberately for underlying /*gilbay+nda*/ 'guana sp-DAT'; and similarly in a number of other cases. Analogously, the word /*baṟumbar*/ 'wattle tree grub' was pronounced slowly as [*báṟu#bár*]. The explanation for

this is probably that phonological words cannot begin with a consonant cluster in Yidiɲ, and if a syllable is made word-initial in slow dictation it must begin with a single consonant. (But, in the last example, [*báɽum#bár*] could have been said; this may imply that a homorganic cluster /*mb*/ is in some cases felt to be functioning as a single phonological unit.) It is unlikely that these examples are related to nasal insertion at morpheme boundaries.

2.6 Late phonetic rules

2.6.1 Stress fronting. It is acknowledged that a description of stress patterning for any language is essentially a phonological idealisation, to which the phonetic facts need not always conform. As Lehiste (1970: 150) says 'it appears probable that word-level stress is in a very real sense an abstract quality: a potential for being stressed....In other words, our knowledge of the structure of the language informs us which syllables have the potential of being stressed; we "hear" the underlying phonological form.'

Just as it is a simple matter for a native speaker of a language to recognise the phonemes, but extremely difficult to distinguish allophones, so will a native speaker always work in terms of an underlying phonological stress pattern and may be unaware of articulatory deviations from this. In some cases a phonetician, who does not know a certain language, may recognise a quite different set of stresses from that which a native speaker will perceive (although of course their judgements would be expected to coincide in most cases).

Differences between observed and underlying patterns of stressing should be describable by late phonetic rules, which have a similar status to phonetic rules specifying allophonic alternation. There appears to be just one major statement of this type needed for Yidiɲ:

STRESS FRONTING

Irrespective of long vowels, and underlying stress assignment (2.2), there is a tendency (phonetically) to stress the initial syllable of each (grammatical) word.

Thus /*ḍambu:l*/ 'two-ABS' has been heard as [*ḍambú:l*], as [*ḍámbu:l*] and as [*ḍámbú:l*]; that is, with phonetic stress on the second syllable in one instance, on the first another time, and with the two syllables pretty equally stressed in a third occurrence. To take a further example, /*gali:na*/ 'go-PURP' has been heard as [*galí:na*] and as [*gáli:na*] (but

never as [*gali:ná*]), and /*baṛa:ḍina*/ 'punch-*:ḍi*-PURP' has been heard as [*baṛá:ḍiná*] and as [*báṛa:ḍiná*].

The actual stress pattern of a word most frequently does coincide exactly with the underlying stress specification (according to 2.2), especially in learning situations (the writer was corrected if he did not conform to the underlying stress specification). Stress fronting is most apparent in texts (probably depending on sentence intonation, amongst other things). If the initial syllable is stressed, the second syllable in a word is likely to be unstressed, even though it may involve a long vowel; but in such cases the vowel length is still clearly distinguishable.

Stress fronting is presumably a recent tendency, introduced after the incorporation of Rules 1 and 2 into the phonological system of Yidiɲ.

2.6.2   Stress retraction.   There is one further stress deviation, that only concerns a handful of words. Thus *buruḍuṛ* 'pademelon (wallaby sp.)' behaves unexceptionally in all oblique cases – ergative [*búruḍúdu*], purposive [*búruḍúṛgu*], genitive [*búruḍúṛni*] and so on. But the absolutive is invariably [*bùruḍú:ṛ*], where [*burú:ḍuṛ*] would be predicted by the rules we have given.

This can be dealt with by a further phonetic specification:

STRESS RETRACTION

If the third syllable of a trisyllabic (phonological) word is closed and begins with a stop or *w*, and if the second syllable is open and begins with a lateral or rhotic, then vowel length and stress are likely to shift from second to third syllable.

We thus encounter absolutive forms [*gùṛabá:y*] 'lizard sp.', [*gàrawá:y*] 'snail sp.', [*ḍàruwá:y*] 'small hill, island'. The main preference seems to be for the stressed syllable to begin with a stop or *w* (segments that can only begin, and never end, a syllable) and for it NOT to commence with a lateral or rhotic (segments which cannot occur word-initially). But stress (and length) will not normally shift to an open final syllable – thus [*waṛá:ba*] 'creek', [*ḍará:ga*] 'step(-mother)'. And they will not normally shift from a closed second syllable – [*gurá:lŋgan*] 'curlew'. (In some cases equal stress can be heard on second and third syllables when their initial segments are as specified in the statement of the 'stress retraction rule' but the second syllable is closed – [*baṛú:mbá·r*] 'wattle tree grub', [*mirí:mbá·l*] 'yellow cockatoo feather'.)

Stress retraction appears to take precedence over stress fronting,

described in the last section. But it is still, like stress fronting, more of a tendency than a rule – strong in some words (thus [*burú:ḍuɽ*] has never been heard), but weak in others (final stress alternating or co-existing with middle syllable stress), gradually tailing off as fewer of the conditions are met.

Stress retraction can apply to a phonological word, even if it makes up only a part of a grammatical word – thus [*bùruḍú:ɽ#gímbal*] 'pademelon-PRIVATIVE'.

There are alternations of form for two lexical items, that seem to involve stress retraction. Tablelands Yidiɲ *maluway* 'spirit, shadow' corresponds to *malway* in the coastal dialect. The tablelands form satisfies all the conditions for stress retraction, so we effectively have a development [*màluwáy*] > [*málway*]. It is likely that the middle syllable of a trisyllabic form could only be open to elision when it was unstressed, and it can only be consistently unstressed when the stress retraction rule applies. A similar explanation may be valid for tablelands *guruŋga*, coastal *gurŋga* 'kookaburra' (but here, although the second syllable begins with *r* and the third one with *g*, the second syllable is closed and the final one open). (See also the discussion of *gaɽana* ~ *gaɽna* and *ɲiriɲi* ~ *ɲirɲi* in 2.3.4.) Note that a vowel could be dropped only if a permissible consonant cluster would result: lateral or rhotic, followed by (non-apical) stop or *w* is always an allowable cluster (2.1.2).

2.6.3 Final ŋ and vowel nasalisation.

It is unusual in an Australian language to have words ending in *ŋ*. For instance, none of the dialects of Dyirbal, Yidiɲ's southerly neighbour, permits roots or words to end in the dorso-velar nasal.

The Guŋgay dialect of Yidiɲ allowed both roots and words to end in *ŋ* (see Appendix). The coastal Yidiɲ dialect has no *ŋ*-final roots but morphological and phonological processes can produce words ending in *ŋ*. There are, in fact, four ways in which this can come about. Firstly, ergative *-ŋgu* is reduced to *-:ŋ* after a disyllabic root ending in a vowel e.g. *buɲa:ŋ* 'woman-ERG' (2.3.2, 2.3.3, 3.3.2). Secondly, the imperative form of the denominal transitive verbaliser reduces to *-:ŋ* under identical conditions e.g. *mada:ŋ* 'soft-CAUS-IMP', derived from *mada + ŋa + ø* (2.3.3, 4.8.1). Thirdly, the imperative form of a verbal comitative will reduce to *-:ŋ* under exactly the same conditions e.g. *gali:ŋ* 'go-COMIT-IMP', derived from *gali + ŋa + ø* (2.3.3, 3.8.5). All of these have involved the deletion of the final syllable by Rule 2, which brings an original intervocalic *ŋ* into the word-final slot. However, the fourth

example does not involve any phonological truncation – the present tense inflection of an -*n*- conjugation root is simply -*ŋ* e.g. *galiŋ* 'go-PRES'.

In the coastal dialect, word-final *ŋ* is normally quite clearly articulated – [*buɲá:ŋ*], [*madá:ŋ*], [*galí:ŋ*], [*gáliŋ*]. But the corresponding pronunciations in the tablelands dialect seldom if ever show a final *ŋ*; instead the last vowel is nasalised – [*buɳ̃á:*], [*madã́:*], [*galĩ:*], [*gálĩ*]. A linguist attempting a synchronic description of tablelands Yidiɲ – without reference to the coastal variey – might at first toy with setting up twelve vowel phonemes (long and short, nasalised and non-nasalised varieties of *a, i, u*) and constraining his phonotactic rules so that words (like roots) could not end in *ŋ*. He would, however, soon find that he needed to set up underlying forms with final *ŋ* for tablelands words (cf. Trubetzkoy 1969: 61, 122), and these would be identical to (underlying and surface) coastal forms. Thus, inflectional *ŋ* is articulated before a post-inflectional affix:

underlying form	phonetic realisation	
/galiŋ/	[galĩ]	'go-PRES'
/galiŋala/	[galiŋala]	'go-PRES-NOW'

If we took phonological forms to involve /-$\tilde{V}$ (:)/ rather than /-*V*(:)*ŋ*/ various complications would arise. Thus, a verbal form like /wawa+ :li+ŋ/ 'see-GOING-PRES' is not reduced by Rule 2 since the final syllable is closed. But surely /wawa+ :lī/ would satisfy all the conditions for Rule 2 – it would have to be listed as a further ad hoc exception to this rule. In view of all this, we take tablelands Yidiɲ to have the same underlying phonology as the coastal dialect, and to involve an additional phonetic rule: /-*V*(:)*ŋ*/ → [-$\tilde{V}$(:)], at the end of a grammatical word.

We have already noted that speakers of tablelands Yidiɲ were in close geographical and social contact with speakers of the Ngaḍan dialect of Dyirbal, and that there are a number of surface similarities between the two dialects (1.3). It may have been partly the influence of Ngaḍan that caused tablelands Yidiɲ to drop final *ŋ* from the surface realisation of words, employing vowel nasalisation effectively to mark this underlying segment.

The status of final *ŋ* in the three dialects of Yidiɲ can now be tabulated (following a W–E axis):

	tablelands	coastal	
	Yidiɲ	Yidiɲ	Guŋgay
phonological form of roots ending in *ŋ*?	no	no	YES
phonological form of words ending in *ŋ*?	YES	YES	YES
phonetic form of words ending in *ŋ*?	no	YES	YES

We see that Guŋgay treats *ŋ* exactly as it does any other nasal, but that as one goes inland the status of final *ŋ* becomes progressively restricted (until we reach Ngaḍan, which answers 'no' to all three questions).

In some languages, the replacement of vowel-plus-nasal by a nasalised vowel yields a phonologically long vowel (for instance Pope 1934: 206; and see the useful discussion in Lightner 1973). This is not the case in Yidiɲ. The second vowel of [*galĩ*] is a little longer than that in [*galiŋ*] but it is still an allophone of a phonologically short vowel (this is an instance of the general rule that a vowel in an open syllable will tend to be longer than one in a closed syllable). The contrast between /*galiŋ*/ 'go-PRES' and /*gali:ŋ*/ 'go-COMIT-IMP' is preserved in tablelands Yidiɲ as [*galĩ*] – [*galĩ:*].

Final *ŋ* has literally never been heard in tablelands Yidiɲ. Final *ɲ* is encountered, but there is a tendency to replace it, too, by vowel nasalisation. Thus /*yiŋgu:ruɲ*/ 'this way' has been heard as [*yiŋgu:rũ*] and /*ɲubi:rbiɲ*/ 'leech-ABS' as [*ɲubi:rbĩ*]. The same thing can happen with final /n/ – /*galin*/ 'go-IMP' has been heard as [*galĩ*] – but not, apparently, with *m*.

There is, as would be expected, a tendency for any vowel preceding a nasal to have some degree of nasalisation, in any dialect of Yidiɲ. In coastal Yidiɲ a final *ŋ* may sometimes scarcely be articulated, with the clue to its presence being given by nasalisation of the vowel (and the same thing has been observed with any final nasal in Dyirbal). But what is a TENDENCY – applying to all (non-labial) nasals – in the language as a whole, appears to have developed into a phonetic realisation RULE in the case of final dorso-velar nasals in the tablelands dialect.

2.6.4 Phonetic reduction. Phonetic realisation is closest to underlying phonological representation in citation forms and elicitation of sentences (where a speaker's attention is directly focused on what he is saying and HOW he is saying it). Slow monologue normally shows only slight

5   DGY

deviation, but the articulation of spontaneous conversation or quick, fluent monologue is likely to differ in many respects from the underlying forms (that is, from the written transcription that a native speaker would write down, or slowly dictate, when the recording of a fluent text is replayed). As anyone who has tried to provide an accurate phonetic transcription of his own language can attest, normal quick speech involves a considerably smaller number of (phonetic) syllables than a phonological representation would show, in addition to all manner of assimilations, lenitions and blendings.

Here we note two types of recurrent simplification that occurred in the most fluent Yidiɲ texts. Firstly, the verbal derivational affix -:ɟi-n can be heard as simply -:yi-n, occasionally in the coastal dialect and frequently in tablelands Yidiɲ.

It is likely that further comparative work will be able to show that the Yidiɲ verbal affix -:ɟi-n and nominal comitative -ɟi ~ -yi both derive from a form *-ɟiri (or *-Ḍiri – see the papers on 'The derivational affix "having"' in Dixon 1976a). Reflexes of this affix occur in many east-coast languages. Thus, Dyirbal has reflexive -yiriy (in the central Dyirbal dialect) ~ -riy (in the Mamu and Giramay dialect) – Dixon 1972: 89. And Dya:bugay (Hale 1976a) has a nominal comitative -ɟi (after consonants) ~ -:r (after vowels) – it is likely that this r derives from the second syllable of *-ɟiri (which has been lost without trace in Yidiɲ).

Now in Yidiɲ the nominal form of this affix preserves its original first syllable, -ɟi, after consonants but has lenited to -yi after vowels. This is a phonological alternation – speakers would insist that, say, 'dog-COMITATIVE' was *gudagayi*, not *gudagaɟi*. (In fact we have to recognise that the phonological form is -yi to account for its reduction by Rule 2 – 2.3.3.) But the verbal affix has phonological form -:ɟi-n in all cases, the occasional reduction to -:yi-n being a phonetic matter. That is, informants insisted that 'see-ANTIPASSIVE-PRES' was *wawa:ɟiŋ* and would not allow the writer to take it down as *wawa:yiŋ*, although it was often heard in this reduced form in fast speech.

Secondly, sequences /aɲa(:)/ or /awa(:)/ are often reduced in fluent Yidiɲ to a single long [a::], independently of morpheme and phonological word boundaries. For instance:

/wuḍá + ɲadá + :ɲ/ 'cross river-COMING-PAST' was heard as [wuḍá::dá:ɲ] in line 119 of text 2

/wawá:liɲú/ 'see-GOING-PAST' was heard as [wá::liɲú]

/wúnaɲá:lna/ 'lie down-COMIT-PURP' was heard as [wúná::lna]

The first segment of verbal comitative *-ŋa-l* is frequently lenited or lost, whatever the previous vowel. Thus, in text 2, line 31 /galiŋa:lna/ 'go-COMIT-PURP' was pronounced [galĩã:lna], with a diphthong slurring from [ĩ] to [ã].

Finally, we can remark that in speaking Yidiɲ rather more phonetic 'planning ahead' is needed than, say, in speaking Dyirbal. In Dyirbal every root and affix (bar one) is stressed on the first syllable; if a stressed syllable follows another stressed syllable, or comes at the end of a word, it loses its stress. Suppose a speaker of Dyirbal intended to say /ḍubula/ 'black pine-ABS' – this should be [ḍúbula]. But now suppose that after he had started transmitting motor commands to his articulatory organs for the first syllable, he decided to place the word in purposive case, and say /ḍubulagu/, [ḍúbulágu]. There would be little difference in the articulation of the first two syllables, but the third syllable will now be stressed and a final unstressed *-gu* added. It would be possible for him to change his intention – from /ḍubula/ to /ḍubulagu/ – after he had started to say the word, and still provide an acceptable pronunciation.

This would not, however, be possible with the corresponding Yidiɲ forms /gubú:m/ 'black pine-ABS' and /gúbumágu/ 'black pine-PURP'. The stress pattern is quite different in the two cases and each articulation would have to be planned out in advance, with no real possibility of transferring (with any success) from one to the other in mid-utterance. (The 'stress fronting' tendency in Yidiɲ would help a little – and this may be one of the reasons for the existence of the tendency – but the important point here is that the second syllable would normally be stressed in /gubu:m/, but should on no account bear stress in /gubumagu/.)

3 Morphology

The writer holds the opinion that syntax is the most central and most interesting section of the grammar of any language and is ideally presented before the welter of morphological detail (cf. Dixon 1972). However, different languages demand different strategies of description. Just as the phonological rules of Yidiɲ are a necessary prerequisite to an understanding of the morphology (and must be described first) so the morphology involves complex alternations, dependencies and orderings between derivational affixes, which suggest that it be most appropriately dealt with ahead of syntax.

3.1.1 briefly previews Yidiɲ's syntactic type, to provide some contextualisation for the discussion of morphology (from 3.2 on). 3.1.2 then mentions the semantic hierarchy in terms of which a number of rather diverse grammatical choices are made (the choices all being of a 'more/less' rather than an 'either/or' type). 3.1.3–5 describe some of the characteristic features of discourse organisation in Yidiɲ, in terms of which a number of the grammatical alternations described in Chapters 3 and 4 can better be understood and appreciated.

Note that from here on the term 'word' will normally refer to 'grammatical word'; this contrasts with the usage in Chapter 2 where 'word' indicated 'phonological word'. (A grammatical word consists of a whole number of (one or more) phonological words – 2.4.)

3.1 Preliminary remarks

3.1.1 Syntactic orientation. Nouns and adjectives in Yidiɲ have one case inflection (ergative) marking transitive subject (A) function, and a further case (absolutive, having zero realisation) for both intransitive subject (S) and transitive object (O). First and second person pronouns, on the other hand, have one form for both transitive and intransitive subject functions (A and S) and a further form for transitive object (O). Yidiɲ is thus like most other Australian languages (cf. Dixon 1972: 4f.) in having an 'absolutive–ergative' system of nominal inflection, but a 'nominative–accusative' pronoun paradigm. There are distinct forms

for all three syntactic functions – S, A and O – in the case of human deictics.

Certain syntactic processes (of subordination and coordination) demand a 'common NP' that is in S or O function in each of the sentences on which the process operates (note that these are the functions marked by the zero, absolutive, inflection in the case of nouns).

Each lexical root in Yidiɲ is strictly marked for syntactic function – it is either a noun or adjective, or a transitive verb, or an intransitive verb, etc. There are, however, a fair number of derivational processes that will change the syntactic function of a word – deriving a transitive verb from an intransitive stem, or a transitive or intransitive verb from an adjective or noun, etc. Each such syntactic derivation is clearly marked by an affix to the word.

Verbal transformations will, of course, change the case marking on NPs in a sentence. Thus, corresponding to transitive:

(15) *buɲa:ŋ wagu:ḍa wawa:l*
    woman-ERG man-NOM see-PAST

we can have intransitive:

(16) *buɲa waguḍanda wawa:ḍiɲu*
    woman-ABS man-DAT see-*:ḍi*-PAST

with essentially the same meaning: '(the) woman saw (the) man'. In (16) the verb involves the 'antipassive' derivational affix -*:ḍi-n*.

Note that NPs in Yidiɲ are not obligatorily marked for definiteness or number. The inclusion of articles, and singular or plural, in English translations is essentially arbitrary, being mainly motivated by contextual felicity. (It should not be taken to imply anything about the structure of the Yidiɲ sentences.)

Similarly we can say:

(17) *wagu:ḍa buɲa:y galiŋ*
    man-ABS woman-COMIT-ABS go-PRES
    The man is going with the woman

or, with a very similar meaning:

(18) *waguḍaŋgu buɲa gali:ŋal*
    man-ERG woman-ABS go-COMIT-PRES
    The man is taking the woman

Those affixes which have major syntactic function (syntactic cases, derivational affixes that change class membership, etc.) are in this chapter fully specified for form and morphotactic positioning, with details of their functions being deferred until chapter 4. Affixes which have more limited syntactic effect – aspectual and tense affixes on verbs, and so on – are fairly fully specified, as to both form and meaning, in the present chapter.

3.1.2 Hierarchies and grammatical choice. At a number of points in the grammar of Yidiɲ we are faced with two alternative expressions which seem to be in a relation of free variation. Thus, corresponding to the simple transitive sentence:

(19) *ŋayu balmbiɲ   wawa:l*
    I-SA grasshopper-ABS see-PAST
    I saw the grasshopper

there is a derived (intransitive) antipassive, with identical meaning:

(20) *ŋayu* $\begin{cases} \textit{balmbi:ɲḍa} \\ \text{grasshopper-LOC} \\ \textit{balmbi:nda} \\ \text{grasshopper-DAT} \end{cases}$ *wawa:ḍiɲu*
    I-SA   see-:*ḍi*-PAST

Here either dative *balmbi:nda* or locative *balmbi:ɲḍa* is equally acceptable (and would be encountered equally frequently).

But if the object of a transitive sentence has HUMAN reference, it can only occur in dative (not locative) inflection in an antipassive, as in (16). If the transitive subject is inanimate it will most frequently be found in locative case in an antipassive construction:

(21) *ŋayu walba: wawa:ḍiɲu*   I saw the stone

Dative marking is possible – and can be considered grammatical – with inanimate nouns in this function:

(22) *ŋayu walba:nda wawa:ḍiɲu*   ⟨as (21)⟩

but is rather uncommon.

It appears that the choice of dative or locative case can best be described in terms of the following diagram:

(23)

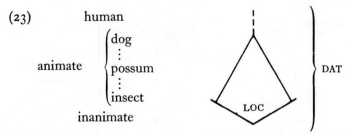

Dative can be used on any NP, whatever its reference. The use of locative increases as the hierarchy is descended. Locative is occasionally encountered with nouns referring to higher animals such as dogs (which are regarded as close to kin by the Yidiɲɖi), more frequently with lower animals, and very frequently indeed with inanimates. As one descends the hierarchy and the probability of locative increases, so that of dative case marking is proportionately reduced. It seems that dative is always POSSIBLE, but that it is progressively pushed aside by the expansion of locative, the lower one gets on the hierarchy.

Locative has occasionally been encountered on human nouns, but appears not to be grammatically acceptable with this semantic class. (The examples heard were – on playback – said by speakers to be errors, and corrected to dative.)

This explanation of the choice between locative and dative, in (23), applies to a wide range of occurrences of these cases, including some where there is no syntactic derivation involved. A full account is in 4.1.8.

There are several other grammatical choices motivated in exactly the same way as dative/locative. For instance, there are two forms of each deictic (these also fulfil the function of third person pronoun in Yidiɲ):

> ɲuɲɖu- 'that' (predominantly human reference)
> ɲuŋgu- 'that' (predominantly inanimate reference)

(and similarly for *yiɲɖu-*/*yiŋgu-* 'this' and *yuɲɖu-*/*yuŋgu-* 'that far or invisible' – 3.7.1). And there are two indefinite/interrogative forms:

waɲɖu- 'someone/who (something/what)' (predominantly human reference)

waɲi- 'something/what' (predominantly inanimate reference)

The use of these forms can be summarised:

(24)

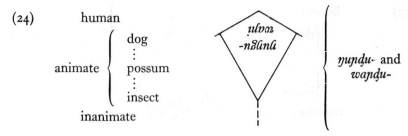

ɲuɲḍu- and *waɲḍu-* can be used to refer to any person, animal or thing. As we descend the hierarchy (beginning with the higher non-human animates) *ɲuŋgu-* and *waɲi-* become increasingly more frequent.

A hierarchical explanation appears also to be appropriate for explaining different types of instrumental inflection (4.3.2).

A similar hierarchy operates in the case of possessive constructions. Alienable possession will always involve the possessor being marked with genitive case. Inalienable possession can either be shown by genitive inflection or by simple apposition of possessor and possessed nouns. Apposition is more likely to be used the lower the possessor is on a 'human...inanimate' hierarchy, like that in (23–4). But there is an important difference here – apposition can be used for inalienable possession involving a HUMAN possessor (it is just alienable possession which is restricted to the genitive construction). A full discussion of possessives is in 4.7.

The exact placement of nouns (according to their referents) on the hierarchy is not known in any detail – this would involve answers to questions such as 'is "possum" above, below, or at the same level as "kangaroo"?', and similarly for 'moon' and 'camp', 'stick' and 'stone', and so on. An investigation of the precise articulations of the hierarchy would undoubtedly require a native speaker trained as a linguist. (Normal elicitation techniques are unsuitable for investigating whether, say, 'there is a 60% chance of using *ɲuŋgu-* in the case of a snake, but 70% for referring to a fish'!) What is known about hierarchically-motivated choice in Yidiɲ has been inferred from examination of textual occurrences, and from the preferences of a fair range of informants (which were found to be quite consistent).

3.1.3   Discourse structure. Yidiɲ shows considerable differences from its southerly neighbour Dyirbal (far more than the average differences between two contiguous languages in Australia) in grammar, phonology and lexicon. But perhaps the most striking divergence is in the struc-

turing of conversation. Dyirbal discourse is highly elliptical with maximum deletion of words that would either repeat information given in a previous sentence, or which can be inferred from the context; this applies both within a single utterance and in consecutive statement–response or question–reply involving a number of speakers. Thus a question in Dyirbal will frequently be answered by a single word. For instance,

(25) *miɲagu   ɲinda   yanuli   baŋgaybila*
     what-PURP you-SA   go-PURP   spear-COMIT-ABS
     Why are you going out with a spear?

might receive the reply:

(26) *bargangu*
     wallaby-PURP
     For wallabies

A polar question will often be answered, or a statement commented on, just with an interjection (Dixon 1972: 124): 'yes', 'no', 'that's right', 'good job', 'I don't know', etc. For instance (Dixon 1972: 391):

(27) *giyi   ɲinda   yuṛi   ḍaŋga*
     DEM-ABS   you-SA   kangaroo-ABS   eat-IMP
     'Would you [like to] eat [a piece of] this kangaroo?'

to which the reply was simply *ŋu* 'alright'. The complete question or statement sentence could be repeated, of course (thus the reply to (25) might be *ŋaḍa baŋgaybila yanuli bargangu* 'I'm going with a spear for wallabies') but more frequently just one or two words are preferred (*bargangu*, or maybe *ŋaḍa bargangu*).

In Yidiɲ, on the other hand, the normal conversational style is for a response to repeat the question that is being answered – or the statement that is being commented upon – as fully as possible:

(28) Q: *ɲundu   dugu:ṛmu   gada:ɲ*
        you-SA   house-ABL   come-PAST
        Have you just come from the house?

(29) A: (*yiyi*) *ŋayu bulmbam   gada:ɲ*
        yes   I-SA   camp-ABL   come-PAST
        (Yes), I've just come from the camp

It would not be normal to answer simply *yiyi* to a question such as (28). In fact, *ŋayu bulmbam gada:ɲ* is the main response, *yiyi* being just an optional extra which can be supplied, for emphasis, at the beginning but is more frequently omitted. In contrast to Dyirbal, Yidiɲ has very few interjections (the writer has only recorded four, whereas a comparable period of field work on Dyirbal yielded a dozen or more).

And note that Yidiɲ has a single form *ɲuḏu* functioning both as the negative imperative particle 'don't' and as an interjection 'no, nothing, no more'. Dyirbal has two separate forms, *galga* and *yimba* respectively.

The informants regarded it as their main task, in teaching Yidiɲ to the writer, to explain the construction of dialogue: 'if someone tells you so-and-so, how would you answer him back?' And, in fact, there is a considerable art to felicitous discourse in Yidiɲ. For the response must be a complete sentence, as full and informative as the original statement or question – so that a listener who heard only the response would perfectly understand it – but it must NOT simply repeat all of the lexical and grammatical elements of the original utterance. There must be some, but not too much, lexical or grammatical variation (in addition to automatic alternations such as you/I). This variation is achieved through a variety of devices. Taking these in turn:

A – INTERCHANGE OF GENERIC/SPECIFIC NOUNS

Yidiɲ has a well-articulated hierarchy of noun classification (6.2.1); an NP will often contain a specific noun and also the corresponding generic term (for instance 'animal, kangaroo' or 'vegetable, yam') – 4.1.1. This system of semantic classification is often exploited for discourse variation. Thus (29) substituted the generic *bulmba* 'camp, camping-place' for the specific *duguɽ* 'house', which it semantically subsumes.

B – USE OF SYNONYMS AND SEMI-SYNONYMS

Yidiɲ has a number of pairs of verbs which are exact synonyms. If one member of a synonym pair is employed in a statement or question, it will be normal to use the other in the response:

(30) S: *ŋanda bama   wamba:ḏiŋ*
     I-DAT person-ABS wait-:ḏi-PRES
     The person is waiting for me

(31) R: *ɲuniɲ bama:l birmibirmiŋ*
you-O person-ERG wait-REDUP-PRES
[Oh,] the person's waiting for you

The only clue to a contrast between *wamba-n* and *birmi-n* that the writer was able to obtain (using field techniques that have always revealed meaning differences in languages like Dyirbal) was that if an interlocutor used *wamba-n*, it would be felicitous to employ *birmi-n* in the reply, or vice versa. (Note two further differences between statement and response here – (30) involves a *-:ɖi-n* construction (see below); and in (31) the verb is reduplicated.)

To take another example, the verbs *burgi-n* and *yaɖi-l* appear to be completely synonymous, both meaning 'walk about i.e. leave the camp for a while with the intention of returning'. These are, again, extremely useful in the construction of felicitous dialogue. Thus:

(32) S: *ŋayu ɖaɖa magu: burgi:ŋal gaba:ɲɖa/*
I-SA baby-ABS chest-LOC walkabout-COMIT-PRES road-LOC
ŋayu galiŋalɲu / ŋanda magu: / ŋanda wurmba
I-SA go-COMIT-PAST I-DAT chest-LOC I-DAT sleep-ABS
wuna:ɲ /
lie-PAST

I walkabout along the road with the baby at [my] chest; I went with the baby; [he] was against my chest; [he] was lying asleep in my [arms]

(33) R: *ɲundu ɖaɖa yaɖiyaɖi:riŋal*
you-SA baby-ABS walkabout-REDUP-GOING-COMIT-PRES
[Oh,] you're going on a long walkabout with the baby

The original statement here involved the coordination of three sentences. The response must comprise a full sentence – with subject, object and verb – but it need not parrot the statement item-by-item. Note that the response naturally substitutes *ɲundu* 'you' for *ŋayu* 'I', retains *ɖaɖa* 'baby', and uses *yaɖi-l* in place of the synonymous *burgi-n*. Both *burgi-n* and *yaɖi-l* occur with the verbal comitative affix *-ŋa-l*, which derives a transitive from an intransitive stem. The response involves the aspectual affix *-:ri-n* 'going' which corresponds semantically to the lexical form *gali-n* 'go' in (32). Verbal reduplication in (33) indicates the respondent's understanding that the baby was taken walkabout for a considerable distance (inferred from the statement in (32) that the baby fell asleep on the journey).

There are only a handful of exact synonym pairs amongst Yidiɲ verbs

(but note that NO synonym pairs were encountered in the rather more extensive vocabulary collected for Dyirbal). It is likely that the main use of these pairs is simply to help in the synthesis of aesthetically-pleasing dialogue. Dyirbal, with its propensity for economical responses, would have little use for exact synonyms, but instead has a rich set of interjections.

When there are no true synonyms, Yidiɲ will substitute semi-synonymous items (as in the generic/specific example, (28–9)) to achieve a response that differs in some way from the original statement or question. It is not the case that one member of a synonym, or semi-synonym, pair is most appropriately used in the statement and the other in the response; either could always be encountered in either position. (But of course, one member will always be more common – of the 'wait' pair, *wamba-n* has a higher overall frequency of occurrence than *birmi-n* – and is thus more likely to occur in the first utterance of a dialogue; the less frequent alternant would then be likely to show up in the response, if one is provided.)

C – USE OF GRAMMATICAL ALTERNANTS

There are a number of grammatical alternations in Yidiɲ that are, like lexical synonyms, exploited to promote felicitous discourse. Thus, there are two equivalent nominal comitative suffixes: *-ḏi* (after consonants) ~ *-yi* (after vowels), reducing to *-:y* under specified phonological and morphological conditions (2.3.2–3), alternating with *-muḏay*, which has no allomorphic variants and undergoes no phonological reduction.

It seems that *-muḏay* is normally preferred with even-syllabled stems ending in *-i*, since here the reduction rules operating on *-yi* (e.g. *mayi+yi → mayi:y → mayi:*) produce a form that is identical to locative/allative/instrumental, and this is liable to lead to confusion. But otherwise either *-ḏi* ~ *-yi* or *-muḏay* can be used, with identical grammatical effects.

A response is likely to employ a different affix from that heard in the statement or question:

(34) S: *ŋayu ḏaḏa:y   galiŋ*
　　　 I-SA baby-COMIT-ABS go-PRES
　　　 I'm going with the baby

(35) R: *ɲundu ḏaḏamuḏay   galin*
　　　 you-SA baby-COMIT-ABS go-IMP
　　　 [Go on,] you go with the baby!

Note the imperative inflection in (35), adding a hortative element to the response.

Speakers of Yidiɲ also pay some attention to felicity within a single utterance and there is a tendency to alternate -*ḍi* ~ -*yi* and -*muḍay* when a sentence involves iteration of the nominal comitative category. Thus we can have 'someone, WITH a container, which is WITH some food or liquid' as in:

(36) *ɲuɲu   bama   gaḍaŋ / gunbuluyi*
    THAT-S person-ABS come-PRES billy-can-COMIT-ABS
    banamuḍay
    water-COMIT-ABS
    That person is coming with a billy-can full of water

or:

(37) *ɲuɲu   bama   ḍuŋga:ɲ/ bundumuḍay   badi:lḍi*
    THAT-S person-ABS run-PAST dilly-bag-COMIT-ABS nuts-COMIT-ABS
    That person ran with a dilly-bag full of nuts

Note that in (36) -*ḍi* ~ -*yi* is suffixed to the noun referring to the container and -*muḍay* to that indicating the contents, but these are reversed in (37). There does not seem to be any contrast in grammatical function here. The use of the comitative suffixes in (36–7) is motivated simply by considerations of felicity, a desire not to employ one type of comitative suffix twice in a single sentence.

The desire for felicity within a single utterance is particularly evident in the case of subordinate constructions. Where an NP is common to two clauses, a generic noun may occur in the main clause and a specific term in the subordinate clause, or vice versa. See (648–50) in 4.4.2.

In some cases an abstract nominal root occurs either with or without a comitative affix e.g. *daliyi* 'hunger/hungry'. The two sentences:

(38) *ɲayu dali:yi*

(39) *ɲayu dali:ɲḍi*

may have a slight cognitive difference (an informant explained that (38) means 'I'm hungry' as against (39) 'I'm really hungry') but it seems most likely that the contrast between (38) and (39) is largely stylistic, and is employed to facilitate more acceptable dialogue.

-*ḍi* ~ -*yi* and -*muḍay* appear to have precisely the same function,

comparable to exact synonyms in the lexicon. There are a number of other pairs of affixes which have a degree of interchangeability, comparable to lexical semi-synonyms. For instance, in 3.1.2 we mentioned dative and locative inflections, either of which can be used with a non-human noun in certain constructions. Here one alternant may be used in a statement or question and the other in a response, as in

(40) S: *ŋayu ḍana:ɲ   ɲaru   walba:*
I-SA stand-PAST on top of stone-LOC
I stood on top of the stone

(41) R: *ɲundu   ḍana:ɲ   ɲaru   walba:nda*
you-SA stand-PAST on top of stone-DAT
[Oh,] you stood on top of a stone

In an exactly analogous manner the causal/ablative possibilities -*nim* and -*mu* may be employed in felicitous alternation (4.4.4), as may – with certain verbs – nominal comitative and dative (4.3.1), and intransitive verbalisers -*maḍi-n* and -*daga-n* (4.8.2). We mentioned (3.1.2) that inalienable possession may be expressed by genitive case or through simple apposition – these can also be used as stylistic alternants (especially if the possessor is also inanimate – 4.7.3).

Note that not all hierarchically-motivated grammatical choices can be employed in this way, to ensure felicitous dialogue. We mentioned in 3.1.2 that a deictic can have the form *ɲuɲḍu-* ~ *ɲuŋgu-*, and that an indefinite/interrogative can be *waɲḍu-* ~ *waɲi-*. But if a speaker refers to some object by one of these forms, the respondent should reply using the same form (unless he is intending to correct the speaker); in this case, the alternation does not imply (semi-)synonymy or substitutability.

Finally, instances have been noted where a transitive sentence, and its antipassive congener, appear to be employed for stylistic contrast – see (31) and (30) above. The derivational affix -:*ḍi-n* can mark a wide range of syntactic and semantic effects and fulfils an important role in the grammar. But there appears sometimes to be a certain measure of substitutability (one is almost tempted to say: redundancy) between some of the alternative constructions, and this can be exploited to promote greater felicity of discourse.

3.1.4   First person orientation. The style of story narration in Yidiɲ differs radically from that of Dyirbal, and of other Australian languages with which the writer is familiar. Dyirbal narrative style is, in fact, quite

close to that of English – a narrator sets the scene and refers to the characters in the third person, being sure to quote exactly any significant dialogue between them. (The writer has never encountered a Dyirbal story – as opposed to a reminiscence – in which the narrator assumes the role of the central character.)

Dyirbal, like Yidiɲ, has no grammatical technique of indirect speech. (That is, they have no equivalents for English *that* clauses as in 'I told him that...'; both languages do have *to* complements with verbs of commanding/allowing e.g. 'I told him to...'.) In fact, the main factor distinguishing Dyirbal story-telling (and the English narrative style of speakers whose first language is Dyirbal) is the precise and lengthy reportage of direct speech, within a third person narrative. This style appears to be constant between different informants, speaking different dialects of Dyirbal.

In contrast, Yidiɲ stories typically involve the principal character serving as narrator, with the whole tale being given a 'first person' slant. There may be a few sentences at the beginning told in the third person – these set the scene and introduce the main character, who thereafter takes over the narration. If the central character changes, the narrator will shift (still remaining in the first person); the first narrator will introduce the arrival of the second character and then silently relinquish his meta-role to him.

However, if there are two simultaneous protagonists, each playing an equally important role, a third-person narrator will be continued throughout the story (and the grammatical first person will only be used with the – usually copious – direct reporting of speech by the two heroes). Most of text 2, pp. 513–30, concerns the brothers Guyala and Damari and is told in the third person. But towards the end Guyala departs and, a sentence or two later, the narrator slips into the identity of Damari.

This style of first-person narrative is common to all the Yidiɲ story-tellers encountered by the writer (and note that the two major informants belonged to different branches of the tribe, and had never had any contact with each other).

As a result, (singular and non-singular) first person pronouns are extraordinarily frequent in Yidiɲ texts (see 3.6.1). And it is sometimes difficult at first to distinguish between textual sentences that belong to the narrative, and those that are direct quotations of things said by the hero/narrator at some point in the set of events he is describing. (But see the comments in 3.1.5 on exclamatory *ɲundu*, which normally introduces a direct quotation.)

It is likely that the 'first person style' of Yidiɲ narratives has had some effect on the grammar (just as the pedantic repetition – with felicitous variation – in responses has led to some lexical and grammatical synonymy – 3.1.3). In both Yidiɲ and Dyirbal nouns follow an absolutive–ergative system of inflection while (first and second person) pronouns follow a nominative–accusative paradigm. The major condition for sentence coordination in each language is that there be a common NP which is in surface S or O function (if a noun: absolutive case) in each sentence. But Yidiɲ – unlike Dyirbal – also allows coordination of two sentences in which common NP is a pronoun in either S or A function (nominative case) – 5.1.3. Yidiɲ's narrative style leads to a preponderance of pronouns, and it is natural for one rule of syntactic identification to mirror pronominal morphology. In Dyirbal narrative nouns are far commoner than pronouns, so it is reasonable in this case for syntactic identifications squarely to reflect nominal morphology.

3.1.5 Extended use of pronouns. In addition to their normal referential functions, there are quite special uses for two pronominal forms. *ɲundu* is the second person singular subject pronoun; but the form *ɲundu* is also used as an exclamation.

Whenever, in a narrative, the first person narrator/hero comes upon something unusual he commonly prefaces a comment with *ɲundu*, translatable in this instance as 'hey', or 'well', or 'oh!'. (There will commonly be no other person involved in the scene being described, as in Text 14, line 10.)

In such exclamatory uses *ɲundu* is characterised by stress on the second syllable, coupled with high-rising intonation with a short final fall: *ɲundú*. The first syllable may be scarcely articulated, so that sometimes only *ndú* is heard. The occurrence of exclamatory *ɲundu* is frequently a vital clue that a sentence in a story is a quotation of what was said at the time, rather than being part of the narrative (3.1.4).

Exclamatory *ɲundu* and pronominal *ɲundu* should perhaps be regarded as homonyms in present-day Yidiɲ (although the exclamatory use is undoubtedly historically derived from the pronoun). They are normally phonetically and/or functionally distinguishable (although there are occasional cases where it is hard to tell which sense is intended – as in text 2, line 5). The two items *ɲundu* have been heard in sequence: *ndú ɲúndu*... 'Hey! you...'.

The other pronominal form with a non-referential use is *ŋaɖin*, first person singular genitive. When this is said with an exaggerated rising–falling intonation it conveys the speaker's sympathy for some illness or

injury of the addressee: 'I'm very sorry for you' (one informant glossed this sense of *ɳaḍin* as 'I'm sorry from the bottom of my heart').

3.2 Parts of speech

3.2.1 Grammatical criteria. For Yidiɲ the following word classes, with mutually exclusive membership, can be set up:

noun ⎫
adjective ⎬ nominal
locational qualifier
time qualifier
pronoun
deictic
verb ⎫
adverb ⎬ verbal
particle
interjection

Each root belongs to just one word class. There are a number of processes that derive a stem of a different class – forming adjectives from nouns, verbs from nominals, and so on (pronouns, deictics, particles and interjections cannot be derived).

The word classes can be distinguished in terms of semantic content, syntactic function, morphological possibilities (and, to a limited extent, phonological form). Potentiality of occurrence with derivational and inflectional affixes is the most easily observable difference and can be taken as the criterion for differentiating most pairs of word classes.

Pronoun and deictic constitute closed classes and can be simply listed; their affixes are similar to, but not in every case identical with, those on nouns and adjectives. Nominals have a well-defined system of case inflections; locational qualifiers take a limited subset of these, as do time qualifiers. Verbals have their own sets of derivational and inflectional suffixes which serve to differentiate that class. Particles can be specified on the negative grounds that they do not normally accept suffixes of any sort (save inchoative *-daga-n*, and the post-inflectional affix *-(a)la* 'now', which can occur on anything that is not an interection – 3.9.1). Interjections are set off syntactically – they occur utterance-initially, in an intonation group by themselves, and could be said to comprise a complete sentence.

Noun and adjective take identical inflections and have very similar (possibly identical) derivational possibilities; the same comments apply to verb and adverb. A major distinguishing criterion in each case is semantic content – a noun will normally refer to some object, whereas an adjective describes a quality of an object; similarly a verb refers to an action while an adverb describes, say, the way in which an action was performed. The extremes are clear enough but, especially in the case of noun and adjective, there is a threshold of uncertainty in the middle (see 3.2.2).

A noun phrase CAN involve just a noun or just an adjective (although we can note that an adjective is relatively seldom found without a noun, whereas a noun is only occasionally accompanied by an adjective). Perhaps the clearest-cut syntactic test is co-occurrence with generic nouns. For each specific noun there is normally one appropriate generic term with which it can occur – thus *ḍaŋguy* 'black and white possum' could only be found with *miɲa* '(edible) animal'. In some cases there are two possible generics – *badil* 'rickety nut' can occur with *mayi* 'vegetable food' or *ḍugi* 'tree' (or with both) – but never more. Most adjectives, on the other hand, can occur with any generic noun – we can have *miɲa ŋalal* 'large animal', *mayi ŋalal* 'large vegetable', *ḍugi ŋalal* 'large tree', *bama ŋalal* 'big person', *buɽi ŋalal* 'big fire', and so on. (The only nominals left out on this criterion are generic nouns themselves; but these form a closed set, and could be simply listed – 6.2.1.)

This 'occurrence with many generics' criterion does separate out most adjectives. But there are some adjectives which describe specifically human attributes – for instance *milba* 'clever' – which would only be likely to be found with the generic *bama* 'person'.

There is no generic/specific categorisation of verbals, and verb and adverb can only be distinguished in terms of semantic content and syntactic preferences: an adverb is seldom found without an accompanying verb (although either a verb or an adverb CAN be the sole verbal element in a sentence).

3.2.2 Semantic content. The semantic contents of the parts of speech in Yidiɲ are quite similar to those in Dyirbal (Dixon 1972: 39–41). Only points of difference from Dyirbal are noted in detail here.

The class of nouns covers all (touchable, drawable) concrete objects as well as mythical spirits, noises and language. Yidiɲ also has some abstract nouns such as 'thought', 'dream', 'heat', 'smell', 'sickness', 'promise', 'present', 'walk' (concepts which are expressed by Dyirbal

by verbs or adjectives). Some abstract nouns commonly occur with the comitative affix (which serves to derive an adjective) – *muran + ḍi* 'sickness + with' = 'sick'. Others normally co-occur with one of just two or three verbs (the noun being in some cases obligatorily incorporated into the verbal word – see 6.1.1); thus *ḍirbi* 'promise' is most often found with *budi-l* 'put down', and *biḍaṛ* 'dream' only with either *wanda-n* 'fall down' or *baḍa-l* 'bite' (in combinations of this type the verb plainly has a metaphorical sense).

Adjectives cover physical properties, physiological states, mental attitudes, value judgements, and so on (exactly like Dyirbal); numbers are regarded as a subset of the adjective class. Unlike Dyirbal, Yidiɲ also has a small subclass of quantifiers, involving 'some', 'another' (6.2.2).

There are a few nominals – referring to concepts that are dealt with by noun roots in some languages and by adjectives in others – on which the syntactic evidence in Yidiɲ is ambiguous. Thus *daliyi* 'hungry/ hunger' can either be used by itself, to describe a state (implying that the root should be taken to be an adjective) or with the comitative affix (implying a noun root) – see (38–9) above. Yidiɲ's propensity for stylistic alternations makes it impossible to decide which subclass of nominals *daliyi* properly belongs to.

Yidiɲ has a lexical set of locational qualifiers (these correspond to Dyirbal's grammatical systems of bound forms which make up 'noun markers' and 'verb markers' – Dixon 1972: 44–8, 56–7, 254–64). They indicate compass directions; up, down; behind, on top of, underneath, inside; near, far; across the river; and so on.

Time qualifiers describe temporal duration ('long' or 'short time') as well as referring to point-time in the past and future. The latter are orientated qua 'today' as point of origin. The general term 'morning' is related to 'tomorrow' and 'afternoon/evening' is derived from 'yesterday'. (This contrasts with Dyirbal which orientates time description to the point 'now' – 'earlier than now' and 'later than now'). See 6.2.3.

The pronoun class covers just first and second persons. There is a separate part of speech which includes demonstratives (these also fulfil the function of third person pronouns in other languages) and indefinite/ interrogative forms. For want of a more suitable term we refer to this class as deictics. Demonstratives (definite deictics) also specify proximity and visibility (3.7.1).

The semantic content of the verb class in Yidiɲ is similar to that in Dyirbal – covering verbs of motion, affect, giving, attention, speaking and

bodily functions. As in most (or all) Australian languages, a single word will describe something that ACTUALLY HAS or POTENTIALLY COULD HAVE a certain effect – for instance, *wawa-l* covers both 'see' and 'look' (see O'Grady 1960 and Dixon 1972: 40–1, 91–2). There are a few verbs describing mental attitudes – 'be happy', 'be jealous of' – but most concepts of this type are expressed by adjectives in Yidiɲ. Adverbals specify whether an action was performed quickly or whether it was done to all of a set of objects, and so on.

Particles mark negation, prohibition, permission, possibility, completion, appropriacy, and retribution, amongst other things; they are listed in 4.10.

3.3   Morphology of nouns and adjectives

A nominal word must involve a root and a case inflection (one choice being absolutive, which has zero realisation). Between root and inflection can come one or more derivational affixes – these include genitive (3.3.3), comitative (3.3.4), privative, 'only, all', 'lots', 'another' and so on (3.3.6). Finally, a word can be augmented by one of a set of post-inflectional affixes (3.9).

3.3.1   Case inflections – system. Inflections on nominals in Yidiɲ can be divided into local cases – those that simply indicate position 'at', or motion 'to' or 'from', a place – and syntactic cases. The latter can again be split, into 'core syntactic cases' – inflections on to the obligatory constituents of a sentence – and 'peripheral syntactic cases' – marking the optional non-local constituents.

The full set of cases is, with canonical forms:

CORE SYNTACTIC
absolutive (S and O functions) ø
ergative (A function) *-ŋgu ~ -du*

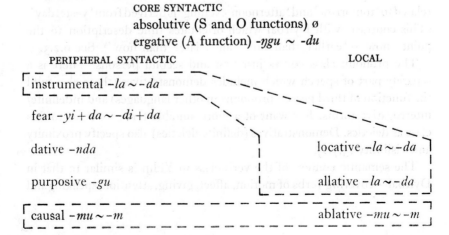

PERIPHERAL SYNTACTIC   LOCAL

instrumental *-la ~ -da*

fear *-yi + da ~ -di + da*

dative *-nda*   locative *-la ~ -da*

purposive *-gu*   allative *-la ~ -da*

causal *-mu ~ -m*   ablative *-mu ~ -m*

The broken lines indicate that locative, allative and instrumental fall together, as do causal and ablative.

We can recognise a semantic correspondence between the local and the peripheral syntactic cases. Ablative indicates simply motion from a place or object whereas causal refers to the reason for some present state (or some previous action that made the present state possible). Thus *mayi* 'vegetable food' has causal inflection in

(42) *ŋayu dubu:rḍi mayim*   I'm full up from [eating] vegetable food

and ablative inflection in

(43) *ŋayu galiŋ mayim*   I'm going (i.e. walking away) from the vegetable food

In fact (43) could have either an ablative or a causal interpretation – the latter would be 'I'm going out after [having eaten] vegetable food'.

Although nominal ablative and causal always fall together, there are separate forms for the two cases with the inanimate deictics – in this case there are different stems for peripheral and for local cases, to each of which can be added *-mu* ~ *-m* (3.7.2). This provides morphological justification for our recognising two distinct cases here.

Allative indicates motion towards some place or object; in contrast, purposive indicates that an action is directed towards some person or object to involve it in the chain of events. Compare the allative in:

(44) *ŋayu galiŋ waŋa:lda (bulmba:)*
    I'm going to (the place where) the boomerang [is]

with purposive in:

(45) *ŋayu galiŋ waŋa:lgu*
    I'm going to/for the boomerang [to do something to it, or with it]

Paralleling the ablative–causal and allative–purposive correspondences there is a clear relationship between the unmarked local case, locative, and what we will show to be the unmarked peripheral case, dative. We have already mentioned, in 3.1.2, that there is a degree of substitutability between locative and dative (conditioned by a semantic hierarchy). There is detailed discussion of these two cases in 4.1.8.

The 'fear' inflection, and its relationship to locative, is discussed in 3.3.2 and 4.6.3.

Locative and allative have the same form for nominals; there is in fact

seldom likely to be confusion since allative typically occurs with verbs of motion, and locative with verbs of rest. Note that locational qualifiers and deictics can have separate forms (3.4.1, 3.7.2), justifying our recognition of two distinct cases.

Almost all Australian languages have an instrumental case marking, and it invariably falls together either with ergative or (as here) with locative (Dixon 1972: 11). In 5.4.5 we give a deep syntactic explanation of why instrumental should coincide with locative in Yidiɲ.

For brevity the locative–allative–instrumental inflection will often be referred to simply as 'locative' below, and ablative–causal as 'ablative'.

The suffix *-ɲa* can function as an accusative case with nouns that have human reference, but it is encountered rather infrequently. A full discussion of *-ɲa* is in 3.3.7.

3.3.2   Case inflections – form.
We now take the case inflections in turn, describing the allomorphic variants and their conditioning. In 3.3.5 we give a table summarising the forms of case inflections (and genitive and comitative derivational suffixes) with all types of stem, classified in terms of syllabicity and stem-final segment.

Ample exemplification of inflections on roots ending in *-iy*, *-a:*, *-u:*, or a morphophoneme (*A*, *I* or *U*) was given in chapter 2. The examples below are chosen from the set of around 1,200 'regular' nominals.

[1] ABSOLUTIVE – marks intransitive subject and transitive object functions.

This always has zero realisation so that absolutive form coincides with the root, subject to the operation of rules 1, 2 and 3 (described in chapter 2).

[2] ERGATIVE – marks transitive subject function (with a human, animate or inanimate agent – see 4.1.5, 4.2.5). It has the forms:

(a) *-ŋgu* after a stem ending in a vowel. If the stem is even-syllabled this reduces, through the operation of rules 1 and 2, to *-:ŋ*. Thus

root *yabi*   ergative *yabi:ŋ* 'grey possum'
    baɽabaɽa   *baɽabaɽa:ŋ* 'fly sp.'
    waguɖa   *waguɖaŋgu* 'man'

(b) *-du* after a stem ending in a consonant. The *-d-* will assimilate in place of articulation to a preceding nasal. Thus (noting that no stem ends in *ŋ*):

root *ḍuḍum*	ergative *ḍuḍu:mbu* 'father's sister'
guban	*guba:ndu* 'big butterfly'
ɲubirbiɲ	*ɲubirbiɲḍu* 'leech'

When -*du* is added to an even-syllabled stem ending in a rhotic, the rhotic must drop. With an odd-syllabled stem, a stem-final rhotic may optionally be omitted (it seems that in these circumstances *r* is frequently dropped while *ṛ* is normally retained). A stem-final -*l* is never dropped before ergative -*du*. Thus:

root	ergative	
wuḍar	*wuḍa:du*	'dew, frost'
gugaṛ	*guga:du*	'large guana'
wagal	*waga:ldu*	'wife'
maŋgumbar	*maŋgumba(r)du*	'leaf grub'
buliyiṛ	*buliyi(ṛ)du*	'chicken hawk'
warabal	*warabaldu*	'flying squirrel'

And note that -*ṛ*- always drops before the aspectual suffix -*:da-n* on verbs (3.8.6).

With a stem ending in -*y*, the suffixal -*d*- assimilates to -*ḍ*-; an -*ɲ*- can optionally be inserted between stem and suffix (2.5.2) and the stem-final -*y* can optionally be deleted (with a stem ending in -*iy* the -*y* must be eliminated, by Rule 3 – 2.3.7). Thus the ergative of *gunduy* 'brown snake' has been heard as *gundu:yḍu* and as *gundu:yɲḍu*; that of *dabuy* 'brown bird sp.' as *dabu:yḍu* and as *dabu:ḍu*; that of *ḍaruy* 'bird (generic)' as *ḍaru:ɲḍu* and as *ḍaru:yɲḍu*. It has not proved possible to uncover any definite phonological conditioning for the loss or retention of *ɲ* and *y*; it is likely that all four forms would be acceptable in each instance e.g. *gundu:(y)(ɲ)ḍu*.

ɲ is MOST LIKELY if the preceding intervocalic consonant (cluster) is weak. That is, it is more frequently found when the preceding intervocalic position is filled by *r*, *ṛ*, *w* or *y* than if it is *b* or *g* (or a cluster). But this is at most a tendency, and certainly not a definite rule.

(c) There is a single irregularity: *bama* 'person' has ergative *bama:l* (*bama* inflects regularly in all other cases).

Australian languages typically have -*ŋgu* and/or -*lu* for the ergative inflection (Dixon 1972: 9–10). This suggests that *bama:l* might be reduced – by Rules 1 and 2 – from an underlying *bama+lu*. Support for this is found in Dya:bugay where *bama* is again the only nominal with an irregular ergative, here *bamalu*.

[3] LOCATIVE–ALLATIVE–INSTRUMENTAL. Locative indicates position of rest, or can be used to mark the underlying object in an antipassive construction (especially if inanimate) – see 4.2.3. Allative indicates motion towards some place or thing. A noun in instrumental case can refer to a weapon or tool with which an action is performed, or the material out of which something is made (4.1.6, 4.3.2).

The forms are:

(a) -*la* after an odd-syllabled stem ending in a vowel:
  root *gabuḍu* locative *gabuḍula* 'white clay'
(b) -*:* on to an even-syllabled stem ending in a vowel:
  root *buṛi* locative *buṛi:* 'fire'

In terms of the general phonological rules of Yidiɲ we would expect -*la* to reduce to -*:l* with an even-syllabled stem. We could put forward an ad hoc rule -*:l* → -*:* (for this case inflection only) – 2.3.3.

Note that almost all Australian languages show exact correspondence between locative and ergative allomorphs; normally the only difference is that locative ends in -*a* and ergative in -*u*. A frequent pattern (Dixon 1972: 9–11) is:

	ergative	locative
onto vowel-final disyllabic stems	-*ŋgu*	-*ŋga*
onto vowel-final trisyllabic stems	-*lu*	-*la*

Some languages have just -*ŋgu* and -*ŋga* while others show just -*lu* and -*la*. Yidiɲ is unusual in that it has ergative -*ŋgu* and locative -*la*; ergative -*lu* is the underlying form for just one noun, *bama*, and there is no surface trace at all of locative -*ŋga*. (The dialects of the Western Desert language described by Douglas 1964 and Glass and Hackett 1970 provide a complementary exception – common nouns ending in a vowel take ergative -*lu* and locative -*ŋga*.)

Suppose that originally Yidiɲ had both locative -*la* (onto odd-syllabled stems) and also -*ŋga* (onto even-syllabled forms). We would of course expect -*ŋga* to reduce to -*:ŋ*; and this is surely a likely candidate for further reduction to -*:*. Note that -*ŋ* is hardly a 'favourite' final segment in Yidiɲ (2.1.2, 2.6.3) and we do in any case have the reduced ergative -*:ŋ* (one can scarcely imagine a language welcoming the falling together of ergative and locative – yet of course this has occurred in Aranda (Strehlow 1944: 74, 202) and Wik-Munkan (data from Christine Kilham and Barbara Sayers)). In the context of Yidiɲ phonetics (2.6.3) a reduction from -*:ŋ* to -*:* is more plausible than one from -*:l* to -*:*. But, since there is nowadays no trace whatever of a locative inflection -*ŋga* in Yidiɲ (nor in Dya:bugay, whose locative inflection exactly parallels Yidiɲ's) we could scarcely put forward underlying -*ŋga* within the terms of a synchronic description.

Note also that all (or almost all) Australian languages have instrumental inflection identical either to locative, or to ergative (Dixon 1972: 11).

(c) *-da* after a stem ending in a consonant. The allomorphy here exactly parallels ergative: assimilation to a stem-final nasal; obligatory elision of a final rhotic off an even-syllabled stem and optional dropping when the stem is odd-syllabled:

root	locative	
muḍam	*muḍa:mba*	'mother'
warḍan	*warḍa:nda*	'boat'
yidiɲ	*yidi:ɲḍa*	'language name'
muygal	*muyga:lda*	'hole, trap'
dubur	*dubu:da*	'stomach'
baŋguɽ	*baŋgu:da*	'fish spear'
maŋgumbar	*maŋgumba(r)da*	'grub sp.'
guŋgambuɽ	*guŋgambu(ɽ)da*	'butterfly sp.'

It is sometimes difficult to distinguish the two segments in /-rd-/ or /-ɽd/ – for instance, they may simultaneously be realised by a flap [ɾ]; see 2.1.1. It is thus appropriate to represent [guduburu] 'stinking rat-ERG' by /gudubu(ɾ)du/. But a distinct rhotic-plus-*d* has been heard in the ergative of an odd-syllabled stem, whereas a rhotic is never audible in the even-syllabled case.

Locative *-da* assimilates to a stem-final *-y*, and the *-y* may optionally drop. There is one difference from ergative – an *-ɲ-* MUST be inserted between a *-y*-final stem and locative inflection. Thus the locative of *gabay* 'path, track,' is *gaba:(y)ɲḍa* (but never **gaba:(y)ḍa*).

(d) There are four irregular items (all are disyllabic and end in a vowel). Here locative is *-:l* (what in fact would be expected as the regular form, reduced by Rule 2 from underlying *-la*). Thus:

root *ḍugi*   locative–allative–instrumental *ḍugi:l* 'tree, wood, stick'
    ḍadu   *ḍadu:l* 'shade'
    biwi   *biwi:l* 'stick knife'
    muyubara   *muyubara:l* 'new'

These three roots are regular in all other inflections (including ergative *-:ŋ*).

The existence of these four locatives supports our hypothesis concerning the 'regular' locative with even-syllabled stems deriving from *-ŋga*. We can now suggest that locative was *-la* on all odd-syllabled stems and on these four

disyllabics, and that it was *-ŋga* elsewhere. *-ŋga* must then have reduced to *-:*, with *-la* reducing to *-:l* whenever the conditions for Rules 1 and 2 were satisfied. (The alternative hypothesis – that locative *-:* derives from *-la* – would have to incorporate some explanation of why *-l* was lost on all even-syllabled stems EXCEPT these four.)

The writer has heard locative *-:l* on two or three other words but these were all later corrected by informants to *-:*. For instance, in one text Tilly Fuller gave:

(46) *waŋal*   *gilbi:l* ... | *gaba:ɲḍa* | *ḍuluḍulu:l*
     boomerang-ABS throw-PAST road-LOC   Johnson hardwood-ALL
     ḍugi:l |
     tree-ALL

The boomerang was thrown...along the road, to the Johnson hardwood tree.

Here the specific noun *ḍuluḍulu* appears to have been given locative *-:l* by analogy with its generic superordinate *ḍugi*. In later questioning Tilly Fuller and other informants gave the allative–locative of *ḍuluḍulu* simply as *ḍuluḍulu:*.

[4] DATIVE marks 'indirect object' (with ditransitive verbs like 'give', 'take to', 'show' and 'tell', and also with simple transitive and intransitive verbs – see 4.1.6); it can also be used to mark the underlying object in an antipassive construction – 4.2.3. The forms are:

(a) *-da* after a stem ending in *-m* or *-n*; *-nda* after a stem ending in *-ɲ*, with deletion of the stem-final *-ɲ* (see 3.3.5):

root	dative	
ḍuḍum	*ḍuḍu:mda*	'father's sister'
buŋan	*buŋa:nda*	'sun'
mugiɲ	*mugi:nda*	'mouse'
buḍibiɲ	*buḍibinda*	'black and red pigeon'

(b) *-nda* elsewhere (i.e. on to stems ending in a vowel, lateral, rhotic or *y*). Stem-final *-y* is lost before dative from an odd-syllabled stem (but retained on an even-syllabled stem):

root	dative	
bimbi	*bimbi:nda*	'father'
ŋalal	*ŋala:lnda*	'big'
wadir	*wadi:rnda*	'cicatrices'
galŋgiṟ	*galŋgi:ṟnda*	'sister'
ḍaruy	*ḍaru:ynda*	'bird (generic)'
gawanday	*gawandanda*	'spirit'

Dative is the only nominal affix which is an exception to Rule 2; although all the conditions for this rule are met, dative does not reduce. Hale (1976a: 240) reports that Dya:bugay has a 'dative, benefactive' suffix which has the form -*:nda* after vowels and -*ŋunda* after consonants. If Yidiɲ -*nda* goes back to an original -*ŋunda* it might be that the reduction occurred after Rule 2 had been incorporated into the phonology; -*ŋunda* plainly would not be subject to reduction (it does not meet the morpheme boundary condition) and this might explain why -*nda* is not reduced in present-day Yidiɲ. (But note that the – probably cognate – verbal subordinate inflection -*nda* does reduce – 3.8.4.)

(c) There are two irregular datives, both on roots which show an irregular locative. Since this completes the list of case exceptions we can tabulate all the irregularities (forms within square brackets are regular):

root	ergative	locative	dative
bama	*bama:l*	[*bama:*]	[*bama:nda*] 'person'
ḍugi	[*ḍugi:ŋ*]	*ḍugi:l*	*ḍugi:l(n)da* 'tree, stick, wood'
ḍadu	[*ḍadu:ŋ*]	*ḍadu:l*	*ḍadu:l(n)da* 'shade'
biwi	[*biwi:ŋ*]	*biwi:l*	[*biwi:nda*] 'stick knife'
muyubara	[*muyubara:ŋ*]	*muyubara:l*	[*muyubara:nda*] 'new'

Note that *biwi* (which is known only in the coastal dialect) and *muyubara* have normal datives despite their irregular locatives. *ḍugi* and *ḍadu* appear to involve the addition of dative to the locative form (each has been heard with the -*n*- present, and with it omitted).

This may be taken to suggest that dative -*nda* (< *-*ŋunda*) was originally a post-inflectional affix, typically added to locative (compare with -*mari* in modern Yidiɲ – 3.3.7), and that it later became a case inflection in its own right. Certainly, these forms may add morphological backing to our recognition of a syntactic correspondence between dative (as the unmarked peripheral case) and locative (as the unmarked local case) – see 3.2.1 and 4.1.8. Note also that locative and dative inflections coincide on a stem ending in -*n* (each is just -*da*).

The words with irregular case forms are all fairly common items; and they occur most frequently in the function with irregular marking. Thus *bama* is often encountered in ergative but seldom in locative case,

whereas *ɖugi* occurs predominantly with locative inflection, and very seldom in ergative case.

[5] PURPOSIVE could also be said to mark a type of indirect object. But whereas dative indicates something or someone who is passively involved in an action (as addressee or recipient, say), purposive implies that the referent will take a major, active role in the following event (as subject or direct object). This is further discussed and exemplified in 4.1.6, 4.5.1.

There is a single form *-gu* with all types of stem. It does not reduce (since *-g* is not a possible word-final segment). Thus:

	root	purposive	
	bama	*bama:gu*	'person'
	buluba	*bulubagu*	'fighting ground'
	muɖam	*muɖa:mgu*	'mother'
	guman	*guma:ngu*	'one'
	biriɲ	*biri:ɲgu*	'salt water'
	gugal	*guga:lgu*	'fire drill'
	dubur	*dubu:rgu*	'stomach'
	ɖirgaɻ	*ɖirga:ɻgu*	'blady grass'
	gabay	*gaba:ygu*	'road, track'

[6] ABLATIVE–CAUSAL. Ablative indicates motion from a place or object; causal marks some person or thing which was the cause of a state or action referred to by the main verb. The forms are:

(a) *-mu* after trisyllabic stems ending in a vowel, and after stems ending in a consonant. After a stem ending in *-m* the inflection is simply *-u* (like most Australian languages, Yidiɲ has a general rule that if a sequence of two identical consonants is generated at a morpheme boundary, one occurrence is omitted). The suffix is normally just *-u* after an odd-syllabled stem ending in *-ɲ*, but *-mu* after an even-syllabled *ɲ*-final stem. Thus:

	root	ablative	
	ɖudulu	*ɖudulumu*	'brown pigeon'
	muygal	*muyga:lmu*	'hole, trap'
	ɲanɖar	*ɲanɖa:rmu*	'creek'
	wabaɻ	*waba:ɻmu*	'walk'
	walmbay	*walmba:ymu*	'waterfall'
	gawam	*gawa:mu*	'broken bank'

root	ablative	
biɲḍin	*biɲḍi:nmu*	'hornet'
biriɲ	*biri:ɲmu*	'salt water'
muɽuḍum	*muɽuḍumu*	'stingaree'
yaraman	*yaramanmu*	'horse'
ɲubirbiɲ	*ɲubirbiɲu*	'leech'

It appears that an -*ɲm*- cluster (which is not permitted within a root) is countenanced over a morpheme boundary that falls at the end of an even-syllabled stem, but is avoided after an odd-syllabled stem. There appear in fact to be two alternative ways of ensuring that an illicit -*ɲm*- cluster does not occur in surface structure. Either the -*m*- can be dropped (as illustrated above), or else the -*m*- is retained and stem-final -*ɲ* is reduced to -*y*; thus *ɲiḍubaymu* has been heard as the ablative of *ɲiḍubaɲ* 'small mussel'. But Rule 3 (2.3.7) must delete a -*y*- that falls between *i* and a consonant, removing all trace of stem-final -*ɲ* in these circumstances. Thus the ablative of *yiŋariɲ* 'this sort of thing' (3.7.6) was recorded as *yiŋarimu*; and *ɲubirbimu* was heard, as an alternative to *ɲubirbiɲu* (an informant insisted that either form was equally acceptable).

(b) -*m*, following an even-syllabled stem ending in a vowel. In order to relate this to an underlying -*mu*, we suggested in 2.3.3 that these forms should be regarded as exceptions to Rule 1 (which would have introduced a long vowel) but that Rule 2 does apply, deleting the final -*u*. Thus:

root	ablative		root	ablative	
bana	*banam*	'water'	*wuɽu:*	*wuɽu:m*	'river'

A special causal form -*nim*, based on the genitive stem, is discussed in 3.3.3.

The ablative–causal allomorph -*m* occurs (a) after an even-syllabled stem ending in a vowel; (b) in the form -*nim*, whatever the phonological form of the stem to which it is attached; and (c) in the causal subordinate verbal inflection -*ɲum*, again irrespective of syllabicity. In 3.8.4 we discuss the possibility that allomorph -*m* may NOT in fact be historically derived from -*mu*.

[7] FEAR marks a noun referring to 'something to be avoided' (the action referred to by the main verb being planned in order to effect this avoidance). Forms are:

(a) -*yida* following a vowel.
(b) -*ḍida* following a consonant.

Formally, the fear inflection simply involves the addition of *-da* to a comitative stem. Examples of fear forms can be obtained by simply adding *-da* to the comitatives listed in 3.3.4. The functions of this case are described in 4.1.6. and 4.6.1.

It is likely that, historically, 'fear' developed from the addition of the locative inflection to an earlier version of the comitative *-ḍir ~ -yir* (3.3.4); this would have yielded *-ḍida ~ -yida*. (Compare this with the inflection of comitatives in Waruŋu – Tsunoda, 1976.) Comitative has reduced to *-ḍi ~ -yi*, which now takes locative *-la ~ -:*. There is no feeling nowadays that fear involves the locative suffix. Thus, in modern Yidiɲ, 'fear' has to be regarded as a distinct case, which is not semantically related to comitative (despite its exact formal dependence on this suffix).

3.3.3   Genitive stems. 'Genitive' is essentially a derivational affix in Yidiɲ (as in many Australian languages) forming a stem that functions as an adjective and takes the full set of case inflections; a genitive noun or pronoun must agree in case with the 'head noun' which it qualifies. Thus, strictly speaking, we can talk of a genitive stem but only of a genitive-plus-absolutive word, a genitive-plus-ergative word, and so on.

(47) *yiɲu   guda:ga waga:lni*
THIS-ABS dog-ABS wife-GEN-ABS
This dog belongs to [my] wife

(48) *yiɲu waga:lni guda:ga wunaŋ*
This dog belonging to my wife is lying down

(49) *gudagaŋgu wagalniŋgu   ŋaɲaɲ baḍa:l*
dog-ERG   wife-GEN-ERG I-O   bite-PAST
[My] wife's dog bit me

Genitive has the canonical form *-ni*, onto stems of all phonological types. When followed by absolutive case, genitive is reduced to *-:n* (by Rules 1 and 2) with an even-syllabled stem ending in a vowel. Examples with stems ending in a vowel, lateral or rhotic are:

	genitive-plus-	
root	absolutive	
guŋgaɲḍi	*guŋgaɲḍini*	'tribal name'
bimbi	*bimbi:n*	'father'
dumbul	*dumbu:lni*	'blue-tongue lizard'
yalbur	*yalbu:rni*	'frog sp.'
gugaṟ	*guga:ṟni*	'guana sp.'
giramay	*giramayni*	'tribal name'

With a stem ending in *-n*, genitive is simply *-i* (one of the two successive tokens of the same consonant being dropped). With a stem ending in *-ɲ*, the stem-final segment drops and genitive is *-ni*. The genitive form of a stem ending in *-m* varies with its syllabicity: with an even-syllabled stem (only) the suffixal '*-n-* [may optionally be dropped. Thus:

root	genitive-plus-absolutive	
muḍam	*muḍa:m(n)i*	'mother'
biɲḍin	*biɲḍi:ni*	'hornet'
mugiɲ	*mugi:ni*	'mouse'
ḍinḍalam	*ḍinḍalamni*	'grasshopper'
yaraman	*yaramani*	'horse'
ŋiḍubaɲ	*ŋiḍubani*	'small mussel'

Dick Moses stated that *muḍa:mni* was the 'correct' form, but that *muda:mi* was an acceptable shortening. It appears not to be possible to drop the *-n-* after an odd-syllabled stem, in the coastal dialect. In the tablelands dialect, however, *-n-* is normally dropped after any *-m*-final stem: thus *muḍa:mi* and *ḍinḍalami*.

Case inflections are added quite normally to genitive stems which retain the suffixal vowel *-i* in the absolutive; they will be regularly reduced if the conditions for Rule 2 are met. Thus, from root *gunduy* 'brown snake' we get genitive stem *gunduyni* and then locative *gunduynila*:

(50) *ŋayu ɲaru ḍana:ɲ / gunduynila   muɾa:yɲḍa*
     I-SA upon stand-PAST brown snake-GEN-LOC skin-LOC
     I stood on the brown snake's skin

When genitive and ergative are added to *waguḍa* 'man' we obtain (after reduction by Rule 2) *waguḍani:y*:

(51) *ɲaɲaɲ waguḍani:y gudagaŋgu baḍa:l*
     The man's dog bit me

An example of genitive plus genitive (added to a pronoun) is given in 3.6.2.

In the case of a genitive stem which reduces in the absolutive (*bama + ni → bama:n*) we should expect oblique cases to be added to the underlying form. But, as mentioned in 2.3.3, the final vowel of the stem

is here -*u*, in place of an expected -*i*. Thus we obtain *bamanula* 'person-GEN-LOC', *bupanunda* 'woman-GEN-DAT', *ḍaḍanuŋgu* 'child-GEN-ERG', and so on:

(52) *ɲundu miɲa   ɲuɲu   wiwin | gudaganda bimbinunda*
     you-SA meat-ABS THAT-ABS give-IMP dog-DAT   father-GEN-DAT
     You give that meat to father's dog!

The occurrence of -*u*- in the inflection of just those genitives whose stem is reduced in the absolutive suggests an underlying form -*nu* in this case. It may be that genitive was once *-*nu* on all stems, and the final vowel was fronted (*$*u > i$) when it occurred word-finally. Original -*u* is preserved in forms like *bimbinunda* since the vowel of the genitive affix in this word will never appear word-finally. But any stem which has surface -*ni* in the absolutive has generalised this to all occurrences of the genitive stem (**gunduynu* becomes *gunduyni*, and by analogy **gunduynula* becomes *gunduynila*).

This hypothesis can be supported on two grounds. Firstly, we noted (2.1.3) that the later a vowel comes in a word, the less chance there is that it will be -*u*. There is thus some phonotactic pressure for a change of the type $u > i$ in a suffix. (There appears to be a general tendency for Australian languages to eliminate late or final -*u*'s. For instance, the canonical forms of the singular pronouns have in many languages changed from first person **ŋaḍu* to *ŋaḍa* and from second person *ɲundu* or *ɲindu* to *ɲunda* or *ɲinda*. In addition, past tense -*ɲu* has become -*ɲa* over a wide area of Australia. And while -*u*- occurs freely in the first syllable of verbs, most languages have few or no verb roots whose second or third vowel is -*u*-; see the data on Yidiɲ verbs in 2.1.3 and 3.8.3.) Yidiɲ does have a number of other affixes ending in -*u* – ergative -*ŋgu* ~ -*du*, purposive -*gu*, ablative -*mu* and past tense -*ɲu* – and there is no evidence that the final vowel here is in the process of change. But any change must have some beginning – if our hypothesis is true then it would appear that a general diffusional tendency to eliminate final -*u*'s (which has affected pronouns in Dyirbal, and pronouns and past tense in languages further south) may in Yidiɲ be beginning with the fronting of the genitive vowel.

Secondly, we can note that Yidiɲ's close genetic relative Dya:bugay has identical or almost identical forms for almost all nominal affixes (ergative -*ŋgu* ~ -*du*, locative -*la* ~ -: ~ -*da*, dative -*ŋunda* ~ -:*nda*, comitative -*ḍi* ~ -:*r*, and so on). Genitive is in Dya:bugay -*ŋun* following a consonant and -:*n* after a vowel. The changes *-*ŋun* > *-*ŋu* > *-*nu* form a natural chain of simplification.

Further discussion of this point is in 3.6.4.

A root ending in a long vowel (2.3.8) will retain this length before all inflectional and derivational affixes. Compare genitive-plus-locative

bamanula, from *bama* 'person', with *durgu:nula,* from *durgu:* 'mopoke owl"

(53) *ɲayu maŋga: ɖana:ɲ durgu:nula* I stood on the mopoke's nest

Genitive-plus-absolutive forms are of course phonologically parallel: *bama:n* and *durgu:n.*

There is one irregularity in the declension of genitive stems – genitive-plus-causal is always *-nim,* whatever the syllabicity of the stem to which it is added. Stems ending in a nasal trigger the normal intermorphemic boundary changes (as described above):

root	genitive-plus-causal	
bama	*bama:nim*	'person'
muɖam	*muɖa:m(n)im*	'mother'
mugiɲ	*mugi:nim*	'mouse'
guriliy	*gurilinim*	'wallaby sp.'
gudaga	*gudaganim*	'dog'
yaraman	*yaramanim*	'horse'
wagal	*waga:lnim*	'wife'
birgalA	*birgalanim*	'night hawk'

We would have predicted causal to alternate between *-m* and *-mu,* depending on syllabicity (just as ergative is *-ŋgu* ~ *-:ɲ* with a genitive stem). But here we get simply *-m,* with no alternation. (The *-m* allomorph of causal/ablative also occurs in the causal subordinate verb inflection, whatever the syllabicity – 3.8.4.)

In texts *-nim* is used for genitive-plus-causal and also genitive-plus-ablative. The writer was able to elicit a regular *-nu + mu* for genitive-plus-ablative:

(54) *ɲayu galiŋ bimbinumu* I'm going from father's [place]

The informant gave, in contrast with (54):

(55) *ɲayu galiŋ bimbi:nim* I'm going from father

But *-numu* has never been heard in texts, and *-nim* appears normally to be preferred for genitive-plus-ablative function, in addition to genitive-plus-causal.

Note that *-nim* occurs even with even-syllabled vowel-final stems, which we suggested above should have underlying genitive *-nu.* Genitive-plus-causal/ ablative may have developed from *-nu* ~ *-ni* followed by *-mu* ~ *-m,* but it now has a single form with NO allomorphic variants. It is in fact arguable whether it

6

can validly be separated into -*ni*+*m* by synchronic morphological analysis; certainly -*nim* appears to be developing towards the point where it would have to be considered a separate case inflection in its own right (just as 'fear' -*ḍida* ~ -*yida* has developed from comitative-plus-locative).

-*nim* can be used to indicate past possessor (in contrast to simple -*ni*, which indicates present ownership). See (259) below and:

(56) *ŋayu mayi   wuɲḍay   dugal / bama:nim*
     I-SA food-ABS stolen-ABS take-PRES person-GEN-ABL
     I stole food from the people

Here *bama:nim* indicates that the food USED TO BELONG to the people (but now belongs to 'me', since I have stolen it). But there is also an ablative sense here, indicating that the food was taken FROM the people who used to own it.

-*nim* forms can have causal/ablative or perfective genitive function, or both – see (669–72) in 4.4.4 and (772–5) in 4.7.2. They can fulfil the same role as normal causal NPs qua subordinate clauses – 4.4.6.

3.3.4 Comitative -ḍi ~ -yi.

There is one other derivational affix which undergoes phonological reduction – comitative -*ḍi* (following consonants) ~ -*yi* (after vowels). This forms an adjectival stem which, like genitive, takes the full range of case inflections, agreeing with the head noun it qualifies. -*ḍi* ~ -*yi* can mean 'with, accompanied by, by means of, having'; a full account of its semantic range is in 4.3.1.

-*yi* reduces, by Rule 2, when affixed to an even-syllabled root ending in a vowel. Examples of comitative on to stems of all phonological types:

root	comitative-plus-absolutive	
bama	*bama:y*	'person'
mugaṛu	*mugaṛuyi*	'fish net'
waŋal	*waŋa:lḍi*	'boomerang'
biḍir	*biḍi:rḍi*	'loya cane sp.'
baguṛ	*bagu:ṛḍi*	'sword'
muḍam	*muḍa:mḍi*	'mother'
warḍan	*warḍa:nḍi*	'raft'
yidiɲ	*yidi:ɲḍi*	'language name'
mugay	*muga:ɲḍi*	'grinding stone'

In the case of a form ending in -*y* the stem-final -*y* must be deleted and -*ɲ*- must be inserted before comitative. (The 'fear' inflection follows the same rule. Thus from root *gunduy* we get *gunduɲɖida* 'for fear of the brown snake'.)

As already noted, Rule 3 (*i:y → i:*) leads to comitative-plus-absolutive falling together with locative for even-syllabled stems ending in -*i*. The only exceptions to this neutralisation are the roots with irregular locative. For instance, we get *biwi:l* locative and *biwi:* comitative-plus-absolutive.

A comitative stem inflects quite regularly. Forms which (by Rule 2) lose the final -*i* in the absolutive case retain it before oblique inflections. For instance, from *miɲa* 'meat' we get comitative stem *miɲa+yi* which in dative case becomes *miɲayinda*:

(57) ...*ɖambu:l   gaɽba   gadigadi: ɖanaɲunda / miɲayinda*
     two-ABS   behind   children-ABS stand-SUBORD meat-COMIT-DAT
     [Uncle cut the tree for grubs whilst] the two children stood behind
     [the tree waiting] for [uncle] with the meat (grubs)

The only affix which cannot follow comitative is 'fear' (this – formally, although not in terms of synchronic morphological analysis – includes the comitative affix).

Genitive can be followed by comitative. Even-syllabled stems ending in a vowel again have -*u*- in the genitive affix:

(58) *ɲuɲu   ɖaɖa   gadaŋ   biba:y*
     THAT-S child-ABS come-PRES paper-COMIT-ABS
     buɲanuyi
     woman-GEN-COMIT-ABS
     That child is coming with the woman's paper (letter)

No example is known of genitive following comitative.

There is also a derivational affix -*muɖay* (3.3.6) which appears to have meaning and function identical to -*ɖi* ~ -*yi*; the two affixes seem always to be inter-changeable, and are used as stylistic variants (3.1.3). The main difference is in fact phonological – *muɖay* is non-cohering and undergoes no reduction.

It seems likely that -*ɖi* ~ -*yi* is a reflex of *-*ɖir(i)* ~ -*ɖir(i)*. The form -*ɖir* ~ -*ɖir* is encountered in some nearby languages (e.g. Guugu-Yimi*dhir*). Note that Dya:bugay has -*ɖi* following a consonant and -*:r* after a vowel; it is likely that both allomorphs derive from *-*ɖir* (compare with genitive -*ŋun*/C- ~ -*:n*/V-, dative -*ŋunda*/C- ~ -*:nda*/V-).

Many Australian languages show a verbal derivational affix, also going back to *-ḍiri ~ -ḍiri (-:ḍi-n in Yidiɲ probably belongs to this set). There may possibly be some diachronic deep connection with the nominal comitative (see Dixon 1976a), or else the similarity could be entirely coincidental.

Note that Rule 2 could not have applied if allomorph -ḍi occurred after a vowel (since a word cannot end in -ḍ). The reduction of -ḍi to -yi may have been partly motivated by the 'even-syllabled word' target. And once -ḍi had reduced to -yi following an even-syllabled stem ending in a vowel, it was surely reasonable for -yi to be generalised on to all vowel-final stems.

3.3.5 Review of monosyllabic nominal affixes.

We have now discussed all nominal affixes which show allomorphic variants and involve special morpheme-boundary processes. (There are two further cohering affixes, -ba and -bi; but these show no allomorphic or morphophonological complexities and are deferred until 3.3.6.)

Table 3.1 reviews the forms which the five oblique cases, and genitive and comitative derivational affixes, assume with every type of nominal stem. Stems are classified by their last segment – v indicates any final vowel (a, i or u) and V any morphophoneme (A, I or U); vowel length is always shown by ' $:$ '. A dash '-' indicates the part of the root preceding the final segment, which remains constant under all inflectional and derivational processes.

Absolutive is not shown in the table. It is identical to the stem (with vowel length being inserted by Rule 1 in appropriate cases) except for morphophoneme-final roots (2.3.4). Irregular ergative, locatives and datives were listed on page 131.

We can also summarise the odd morphophonological processes which apply at the boundary between a nominal stem and a monosyllabic affix:

(a) ASSIMILATION – ergative -du and locative -da are assimilated in place of articulation to a preceding nasal or -y.

(b) -ɲ- INSERTION. Between a stem-final -y and ergative -ḍu, locative -ḍa or comitative -ḍi, the nasal -ɲ- may be inserted and/or stem-final -y may be dropped. The possibilities vary from affix to affix:

	ergative -ḍu	locative -ḍa	comitative -ḍi
-ɲ- insertion	optional	obligatory	obligatory
-y dropping	optional	optional	obligatory

TABLE 3.1 *Summary of case inflections, genitive and comitative stems*

	ergative	locative	dative	purposive	ablative	genitive stem	comitative stem
FINAL VOWEL							
even-syllabled							
-v	-v:ŋ	-v:	-v:nda	-v:gu	-vm	-vnu-	-vyi-†
-v:	-v:ŋ	-v:	-v:nda	-v:gu	-v:m	-v:mu-	-v:yi-
odd-syllabled							
-v	-vŋgu	-vla	-vnda	-vgu	-vmu	-vni-	-vyi-
-V	-Vŋgu	-Vla	-Vnda	-Vgu	-Vmu	-Vni-	-Vyi-
FINAL NASAL							
even-syllabled							
-m	-mbu	-:mba	-:mda	-:mgu	-:mu	-m(n)i-	-mɖi-
-n	-ndu	-:nda	-:nda	-:ngu	-:nmu	-n-	-nɖi-
-ɲ	-ɲɖu	-ɲɖa	-:ɲda	-:ɲgu	-ɲmu	-ni-	-ɲɖi-
odd-syllabled							
-m	-mbu	-mba	-mda	-mgu	-mu	-mni-	-mɖi-
-n	-ndu	-nda	-nda	-ngu	-nmu	-ni-	-nɖi-
-ɲ	-ɲɖu	-ɲɖa	-nda	-ɲgu	-ɲu*	-ni-	-ɲɖi-
FINAL LIQUID							
even-syllabled							
-l	-:ldu	-:lda	-:lnda	-:lgu	-:lmu	-lni-	-lɖi-
-r	-:du	-:da	-:rnda	-:rgu	-:rmu	-rni-	-rɖi-
-ʈ	-:du	-:da	-:ʈnda	-:ʈgu	-:ʈmu	-ʈni-	-ʈɖi-
odd-syllabled							
-l	-ldu	-lda	-lnda	-lgu	-lmu	-lni-	-lɖi-
-r	-(r)du	-(r)da	-rnda	-rgu	-rmu	-rni-	-rɖi-
-ʈ	-(r)du	-(r)da	-ʈnda	-ʈgu	-ʈmu	-ʈni-	-ʈɖi-
FINAL YOTIC -y†							
even-syllabled	-(y)(ɲ)ɖu	-(y)ɲɖa	-ynda	-ygu	-ymu	-yni-	-ɲɖi-
odd-syllabled	-(y)(ɲ)ɖu	-(y)ɲɖa	-nda	-ygu	-ymu	-yni-	-ɲɖi-

Length has been added (by Rule 1) to case forms in the first five columns.
* -ɲu ~ -ymu†   † Rule 3 applies when *y* is preceded by *i* (2.3.7).

(c) NASAL DROPPING

(i) stem-final -*ɲ* drops before dative -*nda* and genitive -*ni*:

-*ɲ*+ -*nda* → -*nda*   -*ɲ*+ -*ni* → -*ni*

(ii) affix-initial -*n*- drops after final -*m*

obligatorily from dative -*nda*   -*m*+ -*nda* → -*mda*

optionally from genitive -*ni*   -*m*+ -*ni* → -*m*(*n*)*i*

(-*n*- usually drops in the tablelands dialect; and it can drop from an even-syllabled stem in the coastal dialect).

(d) SYLLABICITY-CONDITIONED ALTERNATION

(i) final -*y* drops from an odd-syllabled stem before dative -*nda*.

(ii) when ablative -*mu* is affixed to an odd-syllabled stem ending in -*ɲ* we get -*n*+ -*mu* → either -*ɲu* or -*ymu*.

(iii) a stem-final rhotic MUST drop from an even-syllabled stem, and MAY drop from an odd-syllabled stem, before ergative -*du* and locative -*da*.

See also (c–ii).

(e) IDENTICAL CONSONANT DELETION

(i) ablative -*m*+ -*mu* → -*mu*

(ii) genitive -*n*+ -*ni* → -*ni*

In many Australian languages, allomorphs of the locative case exactly parallel those of ergative, except for the final vowel. Yidiɲ shows two further differences (leaving aside irregular words, and phonological reductions):

(i) after a vowel, the canonical form of ergative is -*ŋgu* but of locative is -*la*;

(ii) -*ɲ* is optionally inserted after a stem-final -*y* when ergative follows, obligatorily when locative follows.

3.3.6   Other derivational affixes. There are eight other affixes which – like genitive and comitative – derive a nominal stem from a nominal root. All stems derived by these affixes can take the full range of nominal inflections.

[1] -*muḏay*, comitative 'with, accompanied by, by means of, having'. This affix is interchangeable with the monosyllable cohering comitative -*ḏi* ~ -*yi* (3.3.4); the two comitative suffixes can alternate, simply for stylistic felicity (3.1.3). A full discussion of the meaning and syntactic possibilities of comitatives is in 4.3.1.

[2] -*gimbal*, privative 'without'. This affix marks the lack of something:

(59) *ŋayu waŋalgimbal*   I've no boomerangs

A *-gimbal* form can restrict the reference of a noun:

(60) *ŋaɲaɲ bama:l   wagalgimba:ldu bunḍa:ɲ*
    I-SA person-ERG wife-PRIV-ERG hit-PAST
The person [man] who has no wives hit me

or simply act as a non-restrictive elaboration:

(61) *bama   ɲinaɲina:ɲ   gudaɤ | buɤigimbal*
person-ABS sit-REDUP-PAST cold-ABS fire-PRIV-ABS
The people just sat around cold, with no fire

(62) *ŋayu guman   galiŋ   bamagimbal*
    I-SA one-ABS go-PRES person-PRIV-ABS
I'm going alone, without company

One example involves *-gimbal* suffixed to *wugu* 'work', modifying a pronoun:

(63) *ɲundu dugu:da   wunawunaŋ   muguy | wugugimbal*
    you-SA house-LOC lie-REDUP-PRES all the time work-PRIV-ABS
You just lie around the house all the time, never working

A *-gimbal* form can also qualify an inanimate noun:

(64) *dunda:lay ganagayuy ḍuŋga:ɲ | bamagimbal*
    car-ABS   SELF   run-PAST person-PRIV-ABS
The car ran away by itself, with no one [inside it]

or describe some characteristics of a place:

(65) *ŋaɲḍi yiŋgu   ɲina:ɲ   yuru:n | gaḍagimba:lda*
    we-SA here-LOC sit-PAST long ago white man-PRIV-LOC
We all lived here a long time ago, when there were no white men

Here *gaḍagimba:lda* qualifies locative *yiŋgu* 'at this [place when it was] without white men, a long time ago'.

The semantic range of privative parallels that of comitative fairly well; there is further discussion in 4.3.1.

[3] *-damba* 'with a lot of –'. This suffix can not normally be used with an adjective. And it can only be used with a noun if its referent is, in the context, unpleasant and undesirable – a lot of noise, too much whistling, an uncomfortable number of bones in a fish, or

(66) *ŋayu muŋgundamba*   I have a lot of sores [on my body]

(67) *yiɲu   bulmba   ḍalgadamba*
THIS-ABS place-ABS snail-LOT OF-ABS
There are lots of snails [crawling around] in this place

(68) *muɽiɽdamba:ɲ   ŋaɲḍi:ɲ baḍa:l*
mosquito-LOT OF-ERG we-SA   bite-PAST
Lots of mosquitoes bit us

We have already noted that Yidiɲ is radically different from Dyirbal in lexicon, grammar and phonology. Few affixes are cognate. But it is remarkable on how many points the two languages show semantic similarity. For instance, Yidiɲ *-damba* is extraordinarily close to *-ginay*, in Dyirbal (Dixon 1972: 223–4).

[4] *-bara* 'something or someone pertaining to or belonging to—'. This affix is most frequently used to refer to the origin or habitat of some person or thing e.g. *ḍaruwaybara* 'person from the island'; *-bara* is always a component of local group names (1.2). A *-bara* form is often used rather like a name, to refer to a person or group of people. It can simply be affixed to a deictic in locative case (3.7.2) – see (190) and

(69) *ɲuŋgubara   /   dagul   galiŋ*
there-LOC-*bara*-ABS three-ABS go-PRES
The three people from that place are going

The term *dalubara* – based on *dalu* 'forehead' – was used to describe an ornament of little diamond-shaped shells (*ḍilɲaɽ*) 'sewn into a rope' and worn on the forehead.

-bara has been encountered suffixed to a genitive stem:

(70) *bama   gaya:lbi   galiŋ / guwal   waɲa /*
person-ABS different-ANOTHER go-PRES name-ABS who-s

gurbi   gada:ɲ   muyubara   gaḍigaḍi:nbara
PERHAPS come-PAST stranger-ABS long way-REDUP-GEN-
bara-ABS

Another person, of a different sort, is going. What is his name?
He may be a stranger [who has come] from a long way away.

Here genitive and *-bara* reinforce each other '[someone] BELONGING TO [a place/people] a long way away'.

We can, of course, also obtain genitive on to a *-bara* stem:

(71) *yiɲu   guwa gambi:ɽbara:n   buɽi   gubaŋ*
THIS-SO west tablelands-*bara*-GEN-ABS fire-ABS burn-PRES
This fire belonging to the people from the tablelands is burning at
the western [corner of the corroboree ground]

-*bara* typically occurs with *yiɲariɲ* 'this kind of thing' and *ŋuɲariɲ*
'that kind of thing' (3.7.6), again reinforcing the meaning. Thus

(72) *ɲaɲḍi:n   garu   ḍara:ldan   duguɽ /*
we-GEN-ABS by-and-by erect-COMING-IMP house-ABS
ŋuɲa:riɲbara   ɲundu ŋaɽa guriɲ   ḍara:l
THAT KIND-*bara*-ABS you-SA south good-ABS erect-PAST

[You] come and build a house for us, the same sort of good [house]
as you built [to the] south [for yourself]

(73) *bulmba: yiɲa:riɲbara   yidi:ɲḍi gurbi   ŋabi*
camp-LOC THIS SORT-*bara*-ABS name-ABS PERHAPS lots-ABS
yiŋgu   ɲinaŋ
here-LOC sit-PRES

There are probably quite a lot of these sort of Yidiɲḍi [people]
living in the camp here.

There are names for kinds of storm which involve -*bara*. Thus *guwabara*
(*guwa* 'west') will normally imply a light thunderstorm with little rain, whereas *ɲalabara* refers to a storm that rises in the east during the wet season, and
may work up to very heavy rainfall (*ɲala* is properly 'butt of a tree' but its
meaning can be extended to refer to the lower part of the continental land mass
i.e. the coast). Each of these names is a hyponym of generic *ḍigu:r* 'thunderstorm' (6.2.1).

-*bara* occurs with exactly the same meaning and function in Dyirbal
(Dixon 1972: 224–5) and in fact in most of the languages of Queensland, to
the south and west of Yidiɲ.

[5] -*ba* 'one of a group of people'. Coordination of nouns (with
human reference) within an NP is achieved through the addition of -*ba*
to each one. For instance:

(74) *waguḍaba buɲa:ba maḍi:ndaŋ*
The man and the woman are walking uphill

The use of -*ba* always implies an open conjunction; the most faithful
translation of (74) would be 'a group of people – which includes the man

and the woman – are walking uphill'. -*ba* CAN be added to a third coordinand (although this is not common). Further discussion of this affix is in 3.6.5 when we suggest that the second person non-singular pronoun *ɲunduba* may historically be based on -*ba*.

Consideration of the full range of examples suggests that the most accurate translation is 'one of a group'; under this interpretation (74) is literally 'the man – being one of a group – and the woman – being another of the group – are walking uphill'.

An NP can involve just one noun with the suffix -*ba*:

(75) *yiɲu buɲa:ba galiŋ*
     This woman and one (or more) other people (who are NOT women)
         are going

     Compare with a similar sentence involving *ḍambu:l* 'two':

(76) *yiɲu buɲa ḍambu:l galiŋ*   These two women are going

-*ba* corresponds to two suffixes in Dyirbal – *gara* 'one of a pair' and -*maŋgan* 'one of a group larger than two' (Dixon 1972: 230–1). And note – qua *ɲunduba* in Yidiɲ – that in Dyirbal third person dual and plural pronouns based on these affixes (*balagara* and *balamaŋgan*) appear to be in the process of evolution (Dixon 1972: 51–3).

   [6] -*ḍamu* 'only, all'. The restrictive meaning 'only' is exemplified by the following entreaty to a larrikin not to use the word 'cunt' in swearing:

(77) *giyi   nani:ḍin   muguy | bama:n*
     DON'T swear-:*ḍi*-IMP all the time person-GEN-ABS
         buɲaḍamu:n   ŋaɽubara
     woman-ONLY-GEN-ABS between legs-*bara*-ABS
     Don't swear all the time! ['cunt'] belongs only to women, belongs
         to between their legs (i.e. the word should only be used to
         describe a part of female anatomy, not in cursing)

Other examples include:

(78) *bama   buriburiḍamu   wuna:nbiḍi:ɲ   ŋabi*
     person-ABS old people-ONLY-ABS lie down-*biḍi*-PAST lots-ABS
     There were just lots of old people lying around [in the camp]

(79) *ḍambulanda gilbi:l | dunguḍamu | miɲa   ŋuḍu*
     two-DAT   throw-PAST head-ONLY-ABS meat-ABS NOT
     [Their uncle] only threw down the heads [of grubs] to the two
         [boys]; there was no meat on them

And see text 14.24.

In some instances -*ḍamu* appears to mean 'all and only' – see text 2.29 and:

(80) *buṇaḍamu:ŋ*   *mayi*   *ḍula:liṇu*   *mundi:may*
      woman-*ḍamu*-ERG vegetable-ABS dig-GOING-PAST yam-ABS
      All the women went to dig yams

Although their semantic extremes are far apart, it appears that -*ḍamu* and -*bi* 'another' have some degree of overlap. The writer was told that they could, in some circumstances, be used as stylistic variants. Thus a reply to

(81) *ṇundú/ yiṇu ṇabi buṇaḍamu galiŋ*
     Hey! all (and only) these women are going!

might be

(82) *ṇundú/ yiṇu buṇa:bi galiŋ*
     Yes, all the women are going

-*ḍamu* also functions, with a slightly different meaning, as a post-inflectional affix – 3.9.7.

[7] -*bi* 'another'. Examples of the use of this affix are in text 14.20, 30, 33. When used with a generic noun, such as *buṇa* 'woman', -*bi* can mean 'all' (literally 'one' and 'another' and 'another...'); it is in this sense that it can be used as a stylistic alternant of -*ḍamu*, as in (81–2). Note also:

(83) *ṇaṇaṇ buṇabiŋgu*   *ṇabi:ŋ*   *wawa:l*
     I-O   woman-*bi*-ERG lots-ERG see-PAST
     All the women saw me

Without *ṇabi:ŋ* (83) could, in a suitable context, be taken to mean 'another woman saw me'.

-*bi* is typically used to refer to geographical features; thus, corresponding to *ṇiya* 'side of the hill' we get *ṇiya:bi* 'the other side of the hill'. Note also the roots *ḍalabi* 'on the other side (of a river)' (which may be historically related to the adjective *ḍala* 'shallow') and *ḍilibugabi* 'next day' (*ḍili* 'eye', *buga* 'night').

-*bi* is often used with the quantifiers *bagil, gayal* 'another', as in (70); in this case root and affix semantically reinforce each other – see 6.2.2. -*bi* is also attested on pronouns – 3.6.2.

Dyirbal has *-bi* as a post-inflectional affix, with the meaning 'too' (the nominal derivational affix *-gabun* in Dyirbal most nearly corresponds to Yidiɲ *-bi* in meaning and function). Note also that there is a particle *ḍamu* 'just' in Dyirbal which is semantically similar to the affix *-ḍamu* in Yidiɲ. (Dixon 1972: 268, 120.)

[8] *muŋgal* 'lots, all'. This affix appears to signify quantity. It has been encountered most frequently with *waɲa* 'who' in the idiom-like *waɲamuŋgal* 'who are all those [people]?'. It can also occur with nouns, often in the response to a question that involved *waɲamuŋgal*:

(84) ⎰Q – *bama waɲamuŋgal*
     ⎱   Who are all [those] people?
     ⎰R – *bama(muŋgal) yiɲu ŋabi ɲinaŋ*
     ⎱   All these people are [just] sitting [here]

Informants would sometimes include and sometimes omit *-muŋgal* from the reply (but would never omit *ɲabi*). *bama yiɲumuŋgal ɲinaŋ*, in which *-muŋgal* is suffixed to the demonstrative, is also acceptable.

Another (non-elicited) example is:

(85) *yiɲu   guman   ɲiban | bama:l   buḍiɲ |*
     THIS-ABS one-ABS stubborn-ABS person-ERG tell-PRES
     duga:lina   buṛimuŋgal | ŋuḍu gada:ŋal
     fetch-GOING-PURP fire-LOTS-ABS NOT come-COMIT-PRES
     This [person sits] alone and stubborn. People ask [him] to fetch all
     the firewood, [but he] doesn't bring [it]

-muŋgal can be followed by a case inflection:

(86) *miɲa ŋuɲu wiwin bamamuŋga:lnda*
     Give that meat to all the people!

Its meaning appears to overlap with *-ḍamu* and they can alternate, for discourse felicity. Thus a reply to (80) could be:

(87) *ŋuɲudi   wala   buɲamuŋgal   ŋabi   ɲinaŋ*
     THAT-ABS-SELF FINISHED woman-LOTS-ABS lots-ABS sit-PRES
     It's alright, the women've finished and [they're now] all sitting
     down [back at the camp]

(The idiom *ŋuɲudi wala* is discussed in 3.9.2 and 4.10.)

Each nominal word must involve a root and a case ending (the most common case is absolutive, which has zero realisation). Between root and inflection we can have any of the derivational affixes described in this section, or comitative *-ḍi* ∼ *-yi* or genitive *-ni*.

Genitive, comitative and privative can mark a complete NP – every word in the NP will take the derivational affix. In such cases the complete NP functions very much like an adjective:

(88) *milba:n waguḍani yiŋu guda:ga*
    This dog belongs to the clever man

(89) *ŋayu galiŋ gala:y dagu:lḍi*
    I'm going out with three spears

(90) *ŋuŋu buŋa mayimuḍay ŋabimuḍay*
    That woman has a lot of vegetable food

(91) *ŋayu miŋagimbal muyŋgingimbal*
    I've no cooked meat

In contrast, *-ḍamu* is suffixed to only one word in an NP (to ANY word, it appears) – *buŋaḍamu muḍam badiŋ* or *buŋa muḍamḍamu badiŋ* are equally acceptable for 'only mother is crying', but **buŋaḍamu muḍamḍamu* is not.

-damba, -bara, -ba, -ḍamu, -bi and *-muŋgal* normally occur with nouns, and derive a stem that functions as a noun.

A word can involve more than one nominal derivational affix – we have given examples of genitive + comitative, *-bara* + genitive and genitive + *bara*. In fact, the only sequences that have been observed involve genitive and some other affix. Elicitation on this topic in Australian languages tends to be difficult and highly artificial; but it is likely that most combinations of these affixes would be semantically implausible – we could scarcely have *-damba*-plus-*bara*, or *-bara*-plus-*bi*, for instance. Where two derivational affixes can co-occur their orderings are normally semantically motivated (rather than simply following some distributional formula) – compare *-bara* + genitive with genitive-plus-*bara*, and see Dixon 1972: 232–3.

3.3.7 Further nominal affixes. Nominal derivational affixes (3.3.6) can be distinguished from post-inflectional affixes (3.9) on the following grounds:

(i) derivational affixes precede case inflections, post-inflectional affixes follow them;

(ii) nominal affixes only occur with nominal stems, whereas post-inflectional affixes can be attached to a word belonging to any part of speech.

Note however that all nominal affixes occur most frequently in NPs that are in the (unmarked) S or O functions, with zero case inflection. And some post-inflectional affixes occur predominantly on nominal words. As a result it can be difficult to determine the type of certain uncommon affixes.

It is in most cases possible to resolve any uncertainty by elicitation (although this does not always give straightforward results – for instance *-ḍamu* appears to function both as a nominal derivational affix and as a post-inflectional form).

There are four affixes whose grammatical status is still unclear to the writer. Since their major occurrences are with nominal roots it seemed most appropriate to discuss them here.

[1] *-ɲa.*

Many Australian languages have an accusative suffix, *-ɲa*, marking transitive object (O) function on pronouns and proper names. Sometimes the use of this affix can be extended to nouns with human reference, or even to any noun at all (Dixon 1970c surveys the occurrence of *-ɲa* in a fair sample of languages). Yidiɲ pronouns and deictics mark O function by the affix *-ɲ ~ -:ɲ* (note that with these word classes we never encounter the unreduced form *-ɲa*) – 3.6.2–3, 3.7.2–3.

There is in Yidiɲ an affix *-ɲa* that occurs with nominals. Of the nine occurrences in texts from the coastal dialect (told by Dick Moses) all but one were on a noun or nominal modifier in O function. Four were proper names – for instance:

(92) [*gindaḍaŋgu*] *bangilanɲa baḍa:ɽ*
    [The cassowary, a storytime 'hero'] left Bangilan there

three were kinship terms:

(93) *garu ḍuḍu:mɲa buḍi:ɲ*
    Soon [he] told his aunt

(94) *ŋali galŋa:ɲ yaymi:lna*
    We should ask uncle

and one was a temporal word that could in this instance be taken as qualifying a noun in O function (text 2.57).

It appears from these examples that *-ɲa* is an accusative case inflection in Yidiɲ; it coheres, and reduces by Rule 2. (And there is, in one case, morphophonological deletion of stem-final *-y* – *bibiyuwu:ɲa* 'Bibi-yuwuy-O' in (248) below). There are many O NPs in coastal texts

involving proper names or kin terms that show no inflection, suggesting that the use of -*ɲa* is optional. Overall, it seems that -*ɲa* is PREFERRED with proper names, and that it is POSSIBLE with kinship terms, in O function.

An affix -*ɲa* occurs in tablelands texts with what appears to be simple emphatic effect. Thus, *ŋáyuɲá* 'it's me alright' (text 14.13) and *bulmba-biɲala* (place-ANOTHER-*ɲa*-NOW) '(at) another place now' (text 14.33 – see also 14.30). This is not reduced by Rule 2 (and appears not to cohere). In elicitation of -*ɲa* forms Dick Moses was perfectly happy with this usage:

(95) *ŋayuɲa magi:l*   I DID climb up

And there was one instance in a text told in the coastal dialect:

(96) *ɲuɲuɲa guriɲ*   That'll be good

We could distinguish two quite different affixes here – accusative case -*ɲa* (in the coastal dialect) and a post-inflectional or derivational affix -*ɲa* (in both dialects). But it is not easy to draw the line between the two; informants gave no hint that there were separate affixes involved (as has consistently happened in other cases where the writer has investigated homophonous suffixes). It could be that -*ɲa* can function both as an indicator of grammatical function and as a semantic 'topic marker'.

The exact status of -*ɲa* must for the time being be left open, in the absence of sufficient data on which to base a firm judgement.

[2] -*gaɽa:*

There is an affix -*gaɽa:* that appears often to be interchangeable with the causal (but not the ablative) sense of the case inflection -*mu* ∼ -*m*. Thus:

(97) *maɳɖam wunaŋ muŋgungaɽa:*
[This] mark lies [on my skin] as the result of a sore

(98) *yiɲu muŋgun galagaɽa:*
This sore is from a spear [wound]

-*gaɽa:* can fulfil the same role as causal -*mu* ∼ -*m* qua a subordinate clause (see 4.4.6):

(99) *ŋayu dubu:rɖi* $\begin{Bmatrix} \textit{miɲagaɽa:} \\ \textit{miɲam} \end{Bmatrix}$ *buga:ɖiɲum*
I'm full up from eating meat.

There is one textual occurrence of *-gaṛa:* following a verb:

(100) *yiŋu bulmba banibani:ḍigaṛa:*
This place [is called Bandi] because of [all the people] grumbing [there]

Note that it did not prove possible to elicit further examples of verb + *gaṛa:*. *-gaṛa:* has also been given FOLLOWING the genitive-plus-ablative *-nim* – *ḍimbaṛalnimgaṛa:* '[I'm wet] from the cyclone'.

There are insufficient data to make a definite decision about the grammatical status of *-gaṛa:*. In most occurrences it appears to be a nominal affix (maybe even a case inflection) but in others it has the characteristics of a post-inflectional affix.

-gaṛa: appears not to occur – as a productive suffix – in the tablelands dialect. Stories told by tablelands informants mention two place names involving this form (*waŋalgaṛa:* and *ḍubugaṛa:*) but these are both in coastal territory.

[3] *-ḍulu:*.
This affix carries a durative meaning. It can occur on past time words, and extends the point of reference further out from the present (3.5). Only one occurrence of *-ḍulu:* with a nominal has been noted in texts:

(101) *yiŋu guriṇḍulu: wunaṇunda*
This [woman was watched] lying here alright, for a long period

Here the addition of *-ḍulu:* to the adjective *guriṇ* indicates that the woman was alright for a period of time (while she was lying convalescing, after having been rescued from the claws of an alligator).

It appears that *-ḍulu:* can be added to an adjective if it is plausible that the state referred to could have extended for a fair time. For instance:

(102) *yiŋu mayi nubaḍulu:/ guṇi gubaŋ*
This fruit is getting ripe, let it continue to be ripened [by the sun]

The informant conveyed the idea of duration by often including 'while' in the English translation he offered. Thus *yiŋu buṇa guḍalḍulu:* (*guḍal* 'pregnant') was explained 'this woman, while she's in the family way'.

-ḍulu: has not been heard used spontaneously with a non-zero case inflection. Attempts to elicit it with a case suggested that *-ḍulu:* should perhaps be regarded as a post-inflectional affix (*-ḍulu:* was obtained tacked on to *ŋala:ldu* 'big-ERG'). However, the data are at present insufficient to justify a firm decision.

[4] *-mari* 'alongside, along, through'.

This affix can either follow the locative case on a nominal, or it can go directly on to the root (and is not then followed by any further affix). Thus we can have:

(103) *ɲuɲu* $\begin{Bmatrix} gaba:ɳḍamari \\ gabaymari \end{Bmatrix}$ *galiŋ*

He is going along by the side of the road

In elicitation, informants preferred *-mari* directly on to a root (but the root + locative + *mari* alternative is fairly well attested in texts).

Compare (103) with:

(104) *ɲuɲu gaba:ɳḍa galiŋ*   He is going along on the road

(104) indicates that the subject is walking ON the road whereas (103) is likely to imply that he is walking along in the bush, parallel to and NEAR TO the road.

A sentence like

(105) *ɲuɲu galiŋ bulgu:ɽmari*

could mean either 'he's going through the swamp' or 'he's walking along by the side of the swamp'.

Further examples of *-mari* are in text 14, line 20 – 'jump THROUGH THE TREES' – and line 9 – 'hit him ACROSS THE BACK OF THE NECK'. Note also:

(106) *bana   ḍuŋga:na munum   dubu:rmu/ waɽi:mari*
water-ABS run-PURP inside-ABL stomach-ABL mouth-LOC-
                                                    THROUGH

[A woman who has been immersed in water is hung upside down and her stomach massaged] so that water will run out from the inside of [her] stomach, through [her] mouth

It is possible that *-mari*, currently a post-inflectional affix, is developing in the direction of becoming a distinct case inflection on nouns. But the data are really too slim to make this more than a guess.

3.3.8 Locational words as nominal affixes.
Yidiɲ has a fairly rich set of locational qualifiers (3.4). Just two of these –

waŋgi 'up'

and *ḍilŋgu* 'down'

can occur, not only as free forms, but also as suffixes to nouns. See (677) and:

(107) *ɲundu   banbiḍilŋgu   ɲinan*
      you-SA eyebrow-DOWN sit-IMP
      You sit with your eyes down! (Just after initiation, a young man is
          being warned not to look around the camp)

(108) *ɲundu   ḍiliwaŋgi bana: ḍuwin*
      you-SA eye-UP   water-LOC swim-IMP
      You bathe in the water with your eyes upwards! (Sometime later
          the initiate is taken to the river to wash the pus off his cicatrice
          wounds and warned not to look down in the water for fear of
          seeing and angering the rainbow-serpent)

(109) *ḍina   milma / garu   dunguḍilŋgu ḍunda:na*
      foot-ABS tie-IMP by-and-by head-DOWN hang down-PURP
      [To expel water from the stomach of a woman who has been
          immersed in water, her rescuer tells people to:] 'Tie [her] feet
          [and hang them over a branch] so that [her] head will hang
          down [and the water can be massaged out of her stomach]'

-ḍilŋgu and *-waŋgi* can only be suffixed to nouns referring to some part of an object, and then indicate the orientation of that object. They occur most frequently with body-part terms, but can describe the orientation of any material object. In fact, the meanings of body-part terms are frequently extended to apply to parts of tools and weapons. For instance, *dira* 'tooth' can refer to the cutting edge of an axe:

(110) *gana ŋayu gaɲa:ɽ   ḍara:l   diraḍilŋgu*
      TRY I-SA axe-ABS stand-PAST point-DOWN
      [Having accidentally cut my foot on an axe, next time] I tried to
          put the axe point down (i.e. embed the cutting edge in the
          ground)

and *ḍiba* 'liver' describes the front of a shield:

(111) *ɲundu   bigu:n   nambi /   ḍibaḍilŋgu*
      you-SA shield-ABS hold-IMP front-DOWN
      You hold the shield with its front downwards!

-ḍilŋgu and *-waŋgi* cannot be affixed to nouns referring to a complete object. When position rather than orientation is referred to, *ḍilŋgu* and *waŋgi* must be used as free forms:

(112) *ŋayu bigu:n nambil biḍi:ŋal waŋgi*
I'm holding the shield up properly

and not **bigu:nwaŋgi*; similarly:

(113) *ŋayu wawa:l ginda:n/ waŋgi*
I saw the moon high up [in the sky]

and not **ginda:nwaŋgi*. Similarly, *-ḍilŋgu* and *-waŋgi* cannot be suffixed to adjectives.

There is an idiom *ganawaŋgi* 'belly up'; outside this, *gana* only occurs as a particle 'try' – 4.10 (and these may well be two distinct but homophonous morphemes). *ganawaŋgi* can be used to describe a person:

(114) *ŋayu bana: walŋga:liɲu ganawaŋgi*
I went to float in the water, belly up

or, say, a canoe:

(115) *ginu munda:l/ ganawaŋgi gilbi:l/ wuna:na*
[They] pulled up the canoe, and chucked it down belly up, to lie [there until needed again]

The complement of *ganawaŋgi* is *maguḍilŋgu*, which involves the normal body-part noun *magu* 'chest'.

The morphological process of employing locational words as nominal affixes is extended, in two ways, in the tablelands dialect. Firstly, *guwa* 'west' and *naga* 'east' can operate as affixes, in addition to *ḍilŋgu* and *waŋgi*:

(116) *ḍaban wawa:l / yawu: wunaɲunda / dunguguwa*
eel-ABS see-PAST grass·LOC lie-SUBORD   head-WEST
An eel was seen lying on the grass with its head pointing to the west

Secondly, the four locational forms can also be affixed to nouns describing parts of the environment – *dangil* 'bank', *gambil* 'spur' and even *bana* 'water'. See (263) in 3.9.1 and:

(117) *ŋayu gali:ɲ muguyala gambilnaga*
I kept on going all the time now, along an easterly spur

(118) *ɲuŋgum ŋayu gali:ɲala bananaga*
From there I now went east along a river

No instances of (non-zero) case inflections have been encountered on any forms involving *-waŋgi*, *-ḍilŋgu*, *-guwa* or *-naga*, in either dialect.

3.3.9 Nominal reduplication. Reduplication of nouns and adjectives involves the first two syllables of the root being repeated before it (2.3.5):

root		reduplicated form	
buɲa	'woman'	*buɲabuɲa*	'women'
ŋalal	'big'	*ŋalalŋalal*	'lots of big [ones]'
mulari	'initiated man'	*mulamulari*	'initiated men'
ḍimurU	'house'	*ḍimuḍimurU*	'houses'
gindalba	'lizard sp.'	*gindalgindalba*	'lizards'

It seems that a syllable-final nasal which is homorganic with the following stop is not reduplicated. Thus *galambaṟa:* 'march fly', *galagalambaṟa:*. (There are no roots with a cluster of three consonants between second and third vowel.) A syllable-final consonant can be reduplicated even in an inflected form where it is lost before the inflection: thus the reduplicated locative of *ḍabiṟ* 'flat rock' is *ḍábiṟḍabí:da* 'on lots of flat rocks'. Reduplication is non-cohering – that is, the reduplicated portion forms a separate phonological word (shown by the stress marking in the last example).

A nominal in Yidiɲ is not normally specified for number (it can refer to any number of objects, according to the context). Reduplication is used, quite sparingly, specially to mark plurality:

(119) *bama:l   yabuyabuṟuŋgu   ḍuḍum   yaymi:l*
      person-ERG young girl-REDUP-ERG auntie-ABS ask-PAST
      Lots of young girls asked Auntie

Plurality can be emphasised by reduplication and also the insertion of *ŋabi* 'many':

(120) *gana ŋaɲḍi:nda ŋabi   gilbi   ŋalalŋalal*
      TRY we-DAT   lots-ABS throw-IMP big-REDUP-ABS
      Try and throw us lots of big [grubs, uncle]!

Number adjectives can be reduplicated. For instance *ḍambuḍambu:l* will indicate 'lots of two's' (cf. 4.8.2):

(121) *ɲundu:ba ɲinan   ḍambuḍambu:l*
      you all-SA sit-IMP two-REDUP-ABS
      You all sit down in pairs!

Note also:

(122) *ḏalŋgan gada:ɲ ḏabuḏabu:*
   The Dyalŋgan bird is coming [flying] low over the ground (indicating that a cyclone is approaching)

In (122) the reduplicated *ḏabuḏabu:* stresses that the bird is flying low for a considerable distance over the ground ('lots of ground'), rather than swooping down and rising up again.

And see 3.8.9 for the semantic contrast between nominal reduplication and verbal reduplication of a verbalised nominal.

Note that some nominal roots exist only in reduplicated form – thus *darŋgidarŋgi* 'old woman', *muɲimuɲi* 'ant (generic)', *ḏawaḏawa* 'scrub magpie', *guḏuguḏu* 'rainbow', *biliybiliy* 'a small hickory tree', *ḏibuḏibu* 'fancying oneself to know more than one does' (there are no forms *darŋgi*, *muɲi*, *ḏawa*, *guḏu*, *biliy* or *ḏibu*). Roots that are inherently reduplicated allow consonant clusters typical of intermorphemic juncture at the reduplication boundary (2.1.2).

3.4 Locational qualifiers

3.4.1 Case inflections. Most words referring to position and direction belong to a distinct part of speech (that we term 'locational qualifiers'). There are, however, some words describing position and rest which belong to the adjective class, and take normal nominal inflections. These two sets are contrasted in the remainder of this section.

Locational qualifiers occur only in local cases and take the following inflections:

   locative – root only
   allative – root only, or root plus *-gu*
   ablative – root plus *-mu* ~ *-m*

Ablative is identical in form and function to the corresponding nominal case. Allative *-gu* is formally identical with the syntactic case purposive on nominals.

A locational qualifier typically occurs with a nominal, with which it will agree in case. For instance, in

(123) *ŋayu dabu:lda ŋaɽa galiŋ*   I'm going south along the beach

the noun *dabul* 'beach' is in nominal locative inflection (*-da*) agreeing with the locational qualifier *ŋaɽa* 'south' (whose root form indicates locative function).

The two most frequent locational qualifiers are:

> *waŋgi* 'up'   *ḍilŋgu* 'down'

These items seldom take affixes, just the root being used for both locative and allative (the exact sense is selected by the verb). Allative forms *waŋgi:gu* and *ḍilŋgu:gu* have been encountered, but it is very much more common to encounter just *waŋgi* or *ḍilŋgu* used for allative (as well as locative). For instance, in text 2 *ḍilŋgu* has an allative sense in lines 109 and 112, and a locative sense in lines 50, 54 and 57; whereas *waŋgi* is used with allative meaning in line 38 and has a locative sense in line 37.

Some other words in this class tend to use root only and root + *gu* equally frequently for the allative. This is the case with:

> *guŋgaṛI* 'north'   *ɲaṛa* 'south'
> *guwa* 'west'   *naga* 'east'

For instance, in text 2 *guŋga:ṛ* is used as the allative in line 123 and *guŋgaṛigu* in line 115. Note that there is no choice in the case of locative – just the root must be used (thus **guŋgaṛila* and **ɲaṛa:*, with the nominal locative inflection, are impossible).

It is instructive to compare *guŋgaṛI* and *ɲaṛa* with two other words for which informants gave exactly the same glosses:

> *ḍaŋgiṛ* 'north'   *guɲin* 'south'

These inflect exactly like nominals and are probably best considered members of the adjective class. Thus locative/allative forms are *ḍaŋgi:da* and *guɲi:nda* (see text 2, line 114); informants were unhappy about using *ḍaŋgi:ṛgu* and *guɲi:ngu* (properly purposives) for the allative, and greatly preferred *ḍaŋgi:da, guɲi:nda*.

It appears that *guŋgaṛI* and *ḍaŋgiṛ* (and *ɲaṛa* and *guɲin*) are interchangeable in most contexts. Thus 'I live in the north' can be rendered equally well either by

(124) *ɲayu wunaŋ guŋga:ṛ*

or by

(125) *ɲayu wunaŋ ḍaŋgi:da*

(In the Dyalŋuy avoidance style, a single form corresponds to *guŋgaṛI* and *ḍaŋgiṛ*, and another to *ɲaṛa* and *guɲin* – 6.3.) But *guŋgaṛI/ḍaŋgiṛ* and *ɲaṛa/guɲin* are undoubtedly not exact synonyms. One informant

remarked that *guɲin* would be used to describe the southern corner of the corroboree ground (where a tribe come from *ɲaṟa* 'the south' would camp). It is likely that the difference in meaning can largely be attributed to the distinct part-of-speech membership of these words.

It is worthwhile noting that Dick Moses told the writer that *guŋga:ṟ/ɲaṟa/ guwa/naga* were the 'easy way' of giving compass directions, whereas *ḍaŋgiṟ* and *guɲin* were 'the hard way'. See also 4.8.1 and 6.3.

Locational qualifiers form ablatives in exactly the same way as nouns and adjectives – thus *waŋgim, guŋgaṟimu*, and so on (cf. *ḍaŋgi:ṟmu* etc.).

Certain nouns with strong locational reference may sometimes employ *-gu* in an allative (in addition to the normal purposive) sense, in alternation with the regular locative/allative inflection (see, for instance, *bulmba:gu* 'to the camp' in line 35 and *bulubagu* 'to the fighting ground' in line 78 of text 2). Typically, allative *-gu* is used on a noun when it co-occurs with a locational qualifier that has allative *-gu* inflection; thus:

(126) *ɲayu gali:ɲala bulmba:gu guwa:gu*
     I then went to the camp in the west.

This tendency appears to be due to analogic pressure for identical case markings to be used with locational qualifiers and with nominals having locational reference, when these co-occur in a sentence and 'agree'. (It undoubtedly involves generalisation from the identical ablatives.)

We can also compare *munu* 'inside' with *magaṟ* 'outside'. *munu* is a straightforward locational qualifier. It normally occurs with a noun (describing the enclosure which something is inside of) that is in locative case:

(127) *bana munu diwi:ɲḍa*   There is water in the Diwiy tree

(128) *garu ɲaɲḍi baḍi: munu bilan*   Soon, we must all get in the boat!

In contrast, *magaṟ* 'outside' functions as an adjective and takes normal nominal inflections. Compare:

(129) *ɲayu wunaŋ munu ḍimurula*   I'm sleeping in the hut
with
(130) *ɲayu wunaŋ maga:da*   I'm sleeping outside

Note that *munu* usually occurs with a noun in locative case whereas *magaṟ* will normally occur alone; *munu* describes something as being nside some enclos ure (and it is natural to specify the enclosure) but

magaɽ simply states 'outside ANY enclosure' (and it would not be appropriate to include a noun here). It may be this property which at least partly determines the class membership of these two words (and ensures that *magaɽ* takes a non-zero locative inflection whereas *munu* doesn't).

There are a number of locational qualifiers which behave like *munu* in normally occurring with a noun in locative or dative case (while not, of course, showing any inflection themselves). For instance, *ɲaru* 'on top of' in (40–1), (50) and:

(131) ŋayu ɲaru   burwa:l   gaɲaranda
   I-SA on top of-LOC jump-PAST alligator-DAT
   I jumped on top of the alligator

ganayir 'underneath' in:

(132) ɲundu giyi   galin   gana:yir   ḍugi:l / mayi
   you-SA DON'T go-IMP underneath-LOC tree-LOC nut-ABS
   ɲuni:nda wanda:nḍi   dungu:
   you-DAT fall-LEST-ABS head-LOC
   Don't you walk under [that coconut] tree, a nut might fall on
    your head (and hurt you)

or *biri* 'close up' in:

(133) ɲundu ŋuŋgu   ɲinan biri   gudaganda
   you-SA there-LOC sit-IMP close-LOC dog-DAT
   You sit down there close to the dog!

(The word order can be varied in all of these examples – thus *ɲaru* could occur next to *gaɲaranda* in (131) or *gana:yir* and *ḍugi:l* could be separated in (132).)

It could be suggested, from these examples, that *munu*, *ɲaru*, *ganayir* and *biri* are prepositions which govern the dative or locative case (see 3.1.2 and 4.1.8 for the factors motivating the choice between dative and locative). However, these words are morphologically identical to *guŋgaɽI*, *waŋgi* and so on, for which a 'preposition' interpretation would not be suitable. In terms of our overall description of Yidiɲ it is most appropriate to consider (128), for instance, as involving a locational qualifier (*munu*) and a noun (*baḍi*) both in locative function. Compare with (106) in which both *munu* and the noun *dubur* 'stomach' are in ablative case – and here both are marked by the same inflection, *-mu* ~ *-m*.

The point here is that while both *ɲaru* and *guŋgaṯI* can occur either alone or with a noun in locative or allative inflection, *ɲaru* is seldom encountered by itself whereas *guŋgaṯI* normally is. And while both *ɲaru* and *guŋgaṯI* can take ablative inflection, *guŋgaṯI* occurs in this form far more frequently than *ɲaru*.

These quantitative differences could in time develop into a qualitative distinction. If, say, *munu, ɲaru, ganayir* and *biri* were to be used exclusively in root form (that is, if they were to drop the *-gu* and *-mu ~ -m* inflections) it surely would then be appropriate to regard them as prepositions. This interpretation would be reinforced if *guŋgaṯI* and so on began to inflect like adjectives (following *ḍaŋgir*).

This indicates one way in which fairly concrete (lexical) words could develop into (grammatical) prepositions; the prepositions would then be likely to extend themselves, and take on more abstract functions within the grammar.

The class of locational qualifiers is fairly small and could (like pronouns and deictics) be considered a 'closed system'. (Place names, for instance, must inflect like nominals.)

The full list of locational qualifiers known is:

waŋgi 'up'	*ɲaru* 'on top'	*ganba* 'a very long way'
ḍilŋgu 'down'	*ganayir* 'underneath'	*gaḍi* 'a long way'
guŋgaṯI 'north'	*gaṯba* 'behind'	*bidi* '[at] near'
ɲaṯa 'south'	*munu* 'inside'	*biri* '[at] very near'
guwa 'west'	*murba* 'under the water'	*yalu:ga* '[motion to] close up'
naga 'east'	*guya ~ guyabay* 'across (the river)'	*gani* 'way outside the camp'
	ḍalabi 'on the other side (of the river)'	*ɲambin* 'belly down'
	gaŋgu 'on the other side (of the mountain)'	

'In front' is dealt with by the particle *ganaŋgar* – see 4.10.

Locational qualifiers commonly occur with the affix *-bara* (3.3.6); they reduplicate like nouns e.g. *guŋgaguŋga:ṯ*. Locational qualifiers can be verbalised quite freely – 4.8.1.

3.4.2 -baɲ. The affix *-baɲ* indicates that two individuals are in juxta-position; the root to which *-baɲ* is affixed marks the positional relation between them. For instance:

(134) *ɲaɲḍi wuna:ɲ ɲaru:baɲ*   We sleep on top of one another

-baɲ occurs with some (but not all) locational qualifiers. Another example is:

(135) *bama ḍambu:l ḍanaŋ gaɽbagaɽba:baɲ*
   The two men are standing behind each other (i.e. back-to-back)

It cannot occur productively with nominals. There are, however, three idiom-like words involving *-baɲ*. The most frequent involves *walmbir* 'by the side of' (in fact it could also be said that *walmbir* occurs most frequently with *-baɲ*):

(136) *ŋaɲḍi ḍambu:l ɲinaŋ walmbi:rbaɲ*
   We two sit down side-by-side

(137) *guga   ḍambu:l ḍunday   walmbi:rbaɲ   ḍina:gu*
   skin-ABS two-ABS hang down-PRES by the side-*baɲ* foot-PURP
   The two stirrups hang down either side [of a saddle] for feet [to be put into]

(*guga* 'skin, hide' is used for 'leather' and by extension for 'leather stirrups').

gulgagulgabaɲ – derived from *gulga* 'short' – is an adjective describing something as being 'shared out, a piece to every person'; for instance, *ŋuɲu miɲa gulgagulga:baɲ* 'that meat is all shared out [now]'.

The idiom-like word *ḍilibaɲ* – from *ḍili* 'eye' – indicates two people – a child, and a close relation (parent, aunt, etc.) who is looking after it:

(138) *ŋuɲu buɲa ḍambu:l ḍanaŋ/ ḍili:baɲ*
   Those two females are standing there, an adult and a closely related child

3.4.3   ḍa:-. There is a prefix *ḍa:-* which occurs with the six locational qualifiers that refer to 'up/down' and compass directions. It appears to mean 'in a – direction' Thus:

ḍa:waŋgi 'upwards'	*ḍa:ɲaɽa* 'southwards'
ḍa:ḍilŋgu 'downwards'	*ḍa:guwa* 'westwards'
ḍa:guŋga:ɽ 'northwards'	*ḍa:naga* 'eastwards'

Leaving aside noun incorporation (6.1.1) *ḍa:-* is the only prefix in Yidiɲ. It is non-cohering (and could perhaps be regarded as having underlying disyllabic form /ḍawa-/ – 2.4). No case inflections have been encountered on *ḍa:-* forms.

ḍa:- also occurs, optionally, with *wurga-n* 'yawn'. Thus, for 'I yawned' one can say either *ŋayu wurga:ɲ* or *ɲayu ḍa:wurga:ɲ*.

3.4.4 Hierarchy of locational words. Yidiɲ territory rises from the easterly seaboard to the high tableland in the west. Thus, if one is talking in terms of a distance of ten or twenty miles 'up' must be 'west' and 'down' must be 'east'. In such a context *waŋgi* is synonymous with *guwa* and *ḍilŋgu* with *naga*. (This need not of course hold for shorter distances – 'west' could well be 'downhill' over an extent of a mile or so.)

There are four main pairs of words with locational reference:

> A. *waŋgi* 'up', *ḍilŋgu* 'down'
> B. *guwa* 'west', *naga* 'east'
> C. *guŋgaṛI* 'north', *ŋaṛa* 'south'
> D. *ḍaŋgiṛ* 'northern', *guɲin* 'southern'

Sets A and B have parallel reference, as do sets C and D (but, of course, the difference between A and B is situational whereas that between C and D is grammatical).

We can recognise a hierarchy among these four pairs, on the following criteria:

(i) A, B and C are locational qualifiers and have quite different case-forms from D, which are adjectives.

(ii) A can function as affixes to body-part nouns in the coastal dialect, whereas B, C and D cannot – 3.3.8.

(iii) A and B can be affixes to body-part nouns in the tablelands dialect, but C and D can't be – 3.3.8.

(iv) A, B and C can take prefix *ḍa:-*, whereas D cannot.

(v) The inchoative verbaliser *-daga-n* can be added to the root of A, B and C, but only to the locative form of D (4.8.1).

It is clear that A are closest to being simply grammatical formatives (like, for instance, the systems of bound locational suffixes in Dyirbal – Dixon 1972: 48, 262–4) and that, as one descends the hierarchy, the forms become increasingly 'lexical'.

3.5 Time qualifiers

We can distinguish two varieties of time qualifier: those referring to some point in time, normally measured from the origin 'today' (e.g. *yurunU* 'many years ago', *ŋaḍa* 'tomorrow'); and those referring to some

time-span, without reference to any specific origin (e.g. *birgil* 'for a short while', *wayu* 'for a long time').

The first kind, which we can call 'point time qualifiers', occur in the following forms:

> simple root – 'at' a certain time
> root plus *-gu* – 'until' a certain time
> root plus *-mu* ∼ *-m* – 'since' a certain time

The affixes *-gu* and *-mu* ∼ *-m* are identical in form with nominal purposive and ablative (recurring also as allative and ablative markers with locational qualifiers).

Simple root forms can be exemplified by:

(139) *ɲaɲḍi gada:ɲ guygaguygam*   We came in the evening

See also the occurrences of the most common time qualifier *garu* 'later on, by-and-by' throughout texts 2, 9 and 14; and *yurunU* 'a long time ago' in (65) above.

'Until' and 'since' forms can be illustrated by:

(140) *ɲaɲḍi mayi baḍa:ɽ ḍilibugabigu*
>   We left the fruit [growing on the tree] until the next day [when
>   we'd go and pick it]

(141) *ɲundu:ba ɲaḍa:gu wamba:ḍin*
>   You wait until tomorrow!

(142) *ɲayu wuna:ɲ guyga:mu muguy*
>   I've been asleep all the time since yesterday

-gu can also have purposive sense when suffixed to a time word e.g. *bama ɲanda buḍi:ḍiɲu ɲaḍa:gu* 'the person told me to [do something] tomorrow'.

It appears that *-gu* can only occur on time words with future reference, and *-mu* ∼ *-m* only on those that refer to the past (sentences involving ideas like 'until yesterday' have not been obtained).

The second type of time qualifier, referring to 'duration' (examples are in text 2, lines 51 and 57) cannot occur with any case-type affix. Durational time qualifiers thus have no morphological similarity with point time words, and are included in the same word class on purely semantic grounds.

The suffixes *-(a)m* and *-(a)may* – which derive durational and point

time qualifiers, respectively, from number adjectives – are discussed in 3.7.8.

In 3.3.7 we mentioned the durational affix *-ḍulu:*. Some time qualifiers in the tablelands dialect involve this form – *baɲuḍulu:* 'a few months ago' and *ɲuriḍulu:* 'a few days ago'. There are no forms *baɲu* or *ɲuri*; but note *ɲuṛil* 'just now'. Although *baɲuḍulu:* and *ɲuriḍulu:* cannot be synchronically analysed, it is likely that they are fossilised forms which originally involved *-ḍulu:* as a productive affix.

-ḍulu: can be suffixed to some (point) time words in the tablelands dialect – *yuru:n* 'a long time ago' and *yuru:nḍulu:* 'a very long time ago'.

Time qualifiers (at least those of the durative variety) reduplicate like nominals e.g. *muguymuguyala* 'for good now' from *muguy* 'all the time'.

3.6 Pronouns

3.6.1 Reference. The class of (first and second person) pronouns has just five members. Initial elicitation suggested the following referential descriptions (citing nominative forms):

FIRST PERSON	SECOND PERSON
singular – *ŋayu*	singular – *ɲundu*
dual – *ŋali*	non-singular – *ɲundu:ba*
plural – *ŋaɲḍi*	

(We use 'plural' for reference to three or more, and 'non-singular' for two or more.)

From this it would appear that the distinction between dual and plural is made in the first, but not in the second person.

The 'first person orientation' of Yidiɲ (3.1.4) makes for the very frequent occurrence of pronouns in texts. But they are not all equally frequent – the first nine texts collected showed the following instances:

ŋayu forms – 255	*ɲundu* forms – 44
ŋali forms – 1	*ɲundu:ba* forms – 18
ŋaɲḍi forms – 131	

The main point to note is that *ŋali* forms are seldom used. In fact, *ŋaɲḍi* is frequently used to refer to two people (one of whom is the speaker). Examination of the occurrences of *ŋali* is revealing; in line 3 of text 2 we find:

(143) *gana ŋali   gali:na/ gana bulmba   numbin   / ŋaɲḍi*
    TRY   we two-SA go-PURP TRY   camp-ABS look for-IMP we-SA
    gana galin
    TRY   go-IMP
    We two should try to go. Let's try to look for a camping-site!
    We must try to go!

Here *ŋali* is used in the first clause, identifying a set of just two people;
later in the sentence (and throughout the rest of the text) *ŋaɲḍi* is used
to refer to the two people. A similar situation prevails in text 15 (another
story concerning two brothers) – *ŋali* appears twice (in the first clause
and again half-way through the text) and *ŋaɲḍi* is used a dozen times,
to refer to the pair.

    We can conclude that *ŋaɲḍi* is in fact the unmarked non-singular first
person form, exactly corresponding to second person *ɲundu:ba*; *ŋali* is a
marked 'dual' form, making a further, optional distinction within non-
singular. That is, we have (using + for the marked and − for the
unmarked member of an opposition):

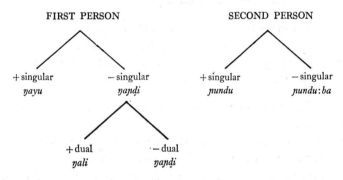

FIRST PERSON   SECOND PERSON

+ singular   − singular   + singular   − singular
 ŋayu   *ŋaɲḍi*   *ɲundu*   *ɲundu:ba*

                + dual   − dual
                 ŋali   *ŋaɲḍi*

Note that Dya:bugay has just four pronouns – singular and non-singular first
person (*ŋawu* and *ŋaɲḍi*) paralleling singular and non-singular second person
(*ɲura* and *ɲuramba*).

    ŋali is used particularly when it is desired to emphasise TWO people
(as opposed to three, etc.). This marked use of *ŋali* is exemplified in
line 26 of text 14. A man says to his son *bulmba ŋali:nala* 'the camp now
belongs to just us two' emphasising that the original third member of
the group, his brother, is now dead.

    The use of *ŋali* for the first reference to a pair, and later employment of
ŋaɲḍi, has some similarities to the use of generic/specific nouns in Yidiɲ.

Thus, a man (or group of men) may be described by *waguḍa* 'man' at first mention, but later referred to simply by *bama* 'person'.

If a second person dual requires to be specifically indicated, the number adjective *ḍambulA* is simply included with *ɲunduba*, as in (225) below and text 2.22. And note that *ɲaɲḍi ḍambu:l* has also been attested, as an alternative to *ɲali* – see (136).

Metaphorical-type uses of singular pronoun forms were mentioned in 3.1.5.

3.6.2 Paradigm. Whereas nominals have one form for S and O functions (absolutive case) and another form (ergative) for A function, pronouns have a single form (nominative) for both 'subject' functions, S and A, and a further 'marked' (accusative) form for transitive object, O. Further discussion of these differences in syntactic marking is in 4.1.4.

Pronouns also have dative, purposive and causal forms, with exactly the same functions as the corresponding nominals. The full paradigm for pronominal cases (excepting 'fear') is in table 3.2.

All pronouns form genitive and comitative stems; these again function like the corresponding nominals. They are set out in table 3.3 together with the 'fear' inflection, which has formal as well as functional parallels with nominal 'fear', again involving the addition of *-da* to the comitative stem.

The genitive-plus-absolutive forms for the first person dual and non-singular pronouns exactly follow the nominal model. The addition of *-ni* to roots *ɲali* and *ɲandi* gives underlying *ɲali + ni*, *ɲaɲḍi + ni*; Rules 1 and 2 then yield *ɲali:n* and *ɲaɲḍi:n*. The occurrence of *u* (and not *i*) as the third vowel before oblique case inflections also parallels nominal genitives. Thus:

(144) *bama   ɲaɲḍinuŋgu gudagaŋgu baḍa:l*
      person-ABS we-GEN-ERG dog-ERG   bite-PAST
      Our dog bit [that] person

The singular pronouns form idiosyncratic genitive-plus-absolutives; but before oblique cases there is again a third syllable *-nu-*. A case could be made out for *ɲaḍin* being derived from *ɲaḍi + ni*, with length being lost from the predicted *ɲaḍi:n*; on this basis we would predict the occurring stem *ɲaḍinu* before oblique cases. For the second person singular, however, the oblique stem involves the addition of a complete

TABLE 3.2   *Pronoun case paradigm*

	NOM (SA)	ACC (O)	DATIVE	PURPOSIVE	CAUSAL
1 sg	ŋayu	ɲaɲaɲ	ŋaḍu:nda[2] ~ ŋanda	ŋaḍu:ngu	ŋaḍi:nim
1 du	ŋali	ŋali:ɲ	ŋali:nda	ŋali:ngu	ŋali:nim
1 non-sg	ŋaṇḍi	ŋaṇḍi:ɲ	ŋaṇḍi:nda	ŋaṇḍi:ngu	ŋaṇḍi:nim
2 sg	ɲundu	ɲuniɲ	C ɲuni:nda[1,2] ~ ɲunda T ɲunu:nda	C ɲuni:ngu[1] T ɲunu:ngu	ɲuni:nim
2 non-sg	ɲundu:ba	ɲundu:baɲ	ɲundubanda	ɲundubangu	ɲundubanim

NOTE 1 – the second person singular dative and purposive forms are *ɲuni:nda* and *ɲuni:ngu* in the coastal dialect, but *ɲunu:nda* and *ɲunu:ngu* in the table-lands dialect.

NOTE 2 – the first person singular dative appears to have the underlying form *ŋaḍu:nda* but can be shortened to *ŋanda* (*ŋanda* is in fact a little more frequent than *ŋaḍu:nda*; the two were judged equally acceptable by informants).

The second person singular dative normally has – in the coastal dialect – the 'long' form *ɲuni:nda* (for instance, text 9, lines 3 and 22); but a shortened form *ɲunda* has been heard (as text 2, lines 34 and 105). In this case, however, informants were – in elicitation sessions – a little unhappy about the acceptability of *ɲunda*, and expressed a preference for *ɲuni:nda*.

syllable to the absolutive form. Examples of declension of singular genitives are:

(145) ŋabi   ḍaŋga   gambi: ŋaḍinula
     lots-ABS hole-ABS clothes-LOC I-GEN-LOC
     [There are] lots of holes in my clothes

(146) ɲundu   ŋuŋu   wiwin   waga:lnda ɲuninunda
     you-SA that-SO give-IMP wife-DAT you-GEN-DAT
     You give that to your wife!

No oblique forms of the 2 n-sg genitive have been observed, and attempts at elicitation on this point did not yield consistent results (see also 3.7.5).

A genitive of a genitive has been obtained: *yiŋu guda:ga ŋaḍinuni waga:lni* 'this dog belongs to my wife'.

Comitative appears to involve the regular suffixation of *-nḍi* to the nominative form except for second person singular where *-nḍi* is added

TABLE 3.3 *Genitive and comitative forms of pronouns*

	genitive + absolutive	genitive stem for oblique cases	comitative stem	fear case inflection
I sg	ŋaḍin	ŋaḍinu-	ŋaḍuṇḍi-	ŋaḍuṇḍida
I du	ŋali:n	ŋalinu-	ŋalinḍi-	ŋalinḍida
I non-sg	ŋaṇḍi:n	ŋaṇḍinu-	ŋaṇḍinḍi-	ŋaṇḍinḍida
2 sg	ɲuni	ɲuninu-	ɲuninḍi-	ɲuninḍida
2 non-sg	ɲundu:ban	?	ɲundubanḍi-	ɲundubanḍi:da

to the genitive-plus-absolutive form. Pronominal comitatives decline quite regularly; for instance

(147) *buɲa   bama:l   yulbamaŋa:l   ŋaḍuṇḍiŋgu*
   woman-ABS person-ERG sneak up-COMIT-PAST I-COMIT-ERG
   The person who had me with him sneaked up on the woman

There do not appear to be any local case forms of pronouns (but see 4.1.8). We do not even find the normal ablative/causal inflection *-mu ~ -m*; causal case on pronouns is handled by the *-nim* alternant (that appears to be historically derived from genitive-plus-ablative – 3.3.3).

It could be argued, however, that the locative–allative form of pronouns would be likely to be based on the *-n*-final stem that underlies comitative, purposive (and perhaps dative) – see below. If this were so, it would simply fall together with dative, as happens with nominals ending in *-n*. Adding to this the substitutability of locative and dative in many contexts, we should take pause before categorically asserting that pronouns in Yidiɲ have no locative–allative form; see also 4.8.3.

The nominal affix *-bi* (3.3.6) can occur with pronouns – for instance, *ɲundu:bi daliyi* 'you [must be] hungry too'.

3.6.3 Analysis. The most straightforward place to begin a morphological analysis of pronominal forms is I n-sg and I du. We can recognise:

           roots I du – *ŋali*
                    I n-sg – *ŋaṇḍi*

Most affixes have exactly the same form as with nominals (3.3.2, 3.3.3, 3.3.7):

> case inflections   nominative (SA) – ø
> accusative (O) – :ɲ (< -ɲa ?)
> dative – -nda
> causal – -nim
> derived forms   genitive + absolutive – -:n (< -ni)
> oblique genitive – -nu-

But there are two differences from nominal allomorphy. With roots *ŋali* and *ŋaɳḍi* purposive is *-ngu* (nominals have just *-gu*), and comitative (fear) is *-nḍi(da)* (in these circumstances a nominal would show *-yi(da)*).

This suggests recognising

> derived stems   1 du – *ŋalin*
> 1 n-sg – *ŋaɳḍin*

to which the following regular nominal suffixes can be added

> case inflections   purposive – -gu
> fear – -ḍida
> derived forms   comitative – -ḍi

Note that dative could be related to either the root or the derived stem (implying an analysis into *ŋali + nda*, or into *ŋalin + da*). Accusative, genitive and causal must be based on the roots *ŋali* and *ŋaɳḍi*, which also function as nominative (or 'subject') forms.

-n-final stems of this sort are required for deictics, where they are the basis for purposive *-gu*, comitatives *-ḍi* and *-muḍay*, and privative *-gimbal* – 3.7.3.

For 1 sg we could recognise stems:

> *ŋayu* – nominative
> *ŋaḍun* – for dative, purposive, comitative and fear (alternatively, dative could be based simply on *ŋaḍu*)
> *ŋaḍi* – for genitive and causal
> *ŋaɲa* – for accusative

In the case of 2 sg we need:

> *ɲundu* – nominative
> *ɲuni* – as genitive + absolutive (involving no further affix) and as the stem on which are based accusative, causal, oblique genitives (and perhaps dative)

ɲunin – for dative (as an alternative to *ɲuni*), purposive, comitative
    and fear

(*ɲunun* is the stem in the tablelands dialect on which dative and
    purposive are based)

2 sg shows one further irregularity – causal involves the addition of *-nim* to
genitive + absolutive *ɲuni* (whereas in every other case it is formed by adding
just *-m* or *-im* to the genitive + absolutive – on this basis we would have
predicted **ɲunim* in this case). In fact *ɲuni:nim* looks as if it involves two
successive tokens of genitive *-ni*! See 3.6.4.

With these stems, nominal forms of cases apply except for accusative
and genitive. Nominal accusative is *-ɲa*, reducing (by Rule 2) to *-:ɲ* after
an even-syllabled stem ending in a vowel (3.3.7). We do get 1 du *ŋali:ɲ*
and 1 n-sg *ŋaɲḍi:ɲ* but the singular pronouns are simply *ŋaɲa + ɲ* and
ɲuni + ɲ, without length. Similarly for genitive + absolutive – against the
regular *ŋali:n* and *ŋaɲḍi:n* we encounter 1 sg *ŋaḍin* with no length (2 sg
ɲuni will be discussed in the next section).

Finally, for 2 n-sg we can recognise

root *ɲunduba* – for nominative, accusative, genitive, causal
stem *ɲunduban* – for purposive, comitative and fear

This is exactly parallel to 1 du and 1 n-sg; dative could be based on
either form. But, as with the singulars, accusative and genitive are odd.
If *-ɲa* and *-ni* underlie the 1 du and 1 n-sg forms then we would expect
ɲundubaɲa and *ɲundubani*. Instead the affixes are simply *-ɲ* and *-n* (and
see 3.7.5).

We could suggest that accusative has two allomorphs with
pronouns:

-ɲa (regularly reducing by Rule 2) on 1 du, 1 n-sg
-ɲ on 1 sg, 2 sg, 2 n-sg

And similarly for allomorphs of genitive. But this obscures the really
significant point – that pronominal accusatives all end in *-ɲ* and genitive-
plus-absolutives (except 2 sg) all end in *-n*. These endings give a
regularity to the pronoun paradigm, and this must be brought out in any
morphological analysis. We should thus prefer to recognise the allomorphs as being *-:ɲ* ~ *-ɲ* and *-:n* ~ *-n*; and THEN to note that the 1 du
and 1 n-sg forms are identical with reduced forms of the corresponding
nominal affixes.

We are thus not invoking Rule 2 (with has wide application with nominals and verbals, and also with deictics) to explain any pronominal forms. Dative *-nda* is, as already mentioned, the only nominal affix which is an exception to reduction by Rule 2. We would have to admit purposive and comitative as further pronominal exceptions (the morpheme boundaries in *ŋaɲɖi+n+gu* and *ŋaɲɖi+n+ɖi* surely satisfy the condition on Rule 2) in addition to the allomorphic intricacies involved in accusative and genitive.

Considering pronouns to fall outside the scope of Rule 2 is not too unusual a step. Pronoun paradigms are notoriously irregular, standing some way apart from the regular morphological and phonological processes of a language. Note, though, that Rule 1 does apply quite regularly to all pronominal forms – compare, for example, *ŋaɲɖi* and *ŋaɲɖi:ngu* with *ɲundu:ba* and *ɲundubangu*.

3.6.4 Historical development. It remains to account for the irregularities in singular pronominal forms. These can only be explained in diachronic terms, through discussion of the development of the present-day Yidiɲ singular pronoun paradigm from a set of reconstructed forms in an ancestor language.

The remarks that follow are based on the writer's comparative study of Australian pronoun systems, and a tentative partial reconstruction. This work is so far unpublished.

It seems that an ancestor language (maybe, proto-Australian) had monosyllabic singular pronominal roots:

> 1 sg – *ŋay*   2 sg – *ɲun*

The root form alone was employed in intransitive subject (S) function; transitive subject (A) function involved the addition of ergative affix *-du*, following a consonant (with assimilation to a preceding nasal or *y*); transitive object function (O) involved the accusative affix *-ɲa*. There would also have been genitive and probably other (oblique syntactic) case forms. It appears that the *-y* of *ŋay* dropped before a laminal stop or nasal. We are thus suggesting that the ancestor language had:

	S	A	O	genitive
1 sg	*ŋay*	*ŋaɖu*	*ŋaɲa*	*ŋay* + GEN
2 sg	*ɲun*	*ɲundu*	*ɲun + ɲa*	*ɲun* + GEN

The form of the genitive suffix will be discussed below.

At a certain stage in the historical development, monosyllables were proscribed. (It is a fact that many Australian languages are like Yidiɲ in

not having any words with less than two syllables. It is also clear that these languages go back to an ancestor which showed monosyllabic pronouns, verbs and nouns – a fair sample of monosyllabic forms in each part of speech are clearly reconstructable.) Some languages added a dummy syllable -*ba* to the S forms, maintaining a distinction between A and S marking (the Giramay dialect of Dyirbal demonstrates this, although here 2 sg is based on the rather different root *ɲin* – see Dixon 1972: 243–6). Other languages, including Yidiɲ, simply generalised the A form also to cover S function.

(Some modern languages still tolerate monosyllables, and show pronoun paradigms very like that given above – see Mathew 1910: 208 and Dixon 1972: 7.)

Hale (1973: 445–6) suggests that 'there may be a tendency in the process of language acquisition to reanalyse linguistic forms in cases where there is a particular kind of disparity between underlying and surface representations'. Now if in some language all words had to involve at least two syllables, the recognition of monosyllabic roots would entail a severe disparity between underlying and surface possibilities. This leads us to suggest that the 1 sg pronoun in Yidiɲ underwent the following changes:

(1) Once the S form *ŋay* had been eliminated (along with all other monosyllabic words) *ŋay*- ceased to be recognised as the root common to 1 sg forms. Oblique forms were recreated, this time founded on the unmarked SA form *ŋaɟu*. Thus the original genitive was replaced by *ŋaɟu* + GEN. Dative, purposive and comitative involved suffixation to *ŋaɟu* + *n*.

(2) The laminal stop in nominative *ŋaɟu* (but not in any oblique form) reduced to the corresponding laminal semi-vowel, yielding *ŋayu*.

(3) By analogy with the accusative forms of the other pronouns, -*ɲ* was added to the original accusative *ŋaɲa* (< **ŋay* + *ɲa*), yielding *ŋaɲaɲ*; speakers would not at this stage perceive that *ŋaɲa* involved the accusative affix -*ɲa* since to do so would involve intuitively recognising a monosyllabic root (and these are unknown in modern Yidiɲ). *ŋaɲaɲ* thus involves two reflexes of the original accusative **-ɲa*.

Support for our suggestions concerning Yidiɲ comes from the pronoun paradigm of Dya:bugay, Yidiɲ's close genetic relative. This is (Hale 1976a: 237; adapting Hale's transcription to conform with that used for Yidiɲ):

	SA	O	possessive	dative	ablative	purposive/ allative
1 sg	*ŋawu(ŋgu)*	*ŋaɲa*	*ŋayaŋ*	*ŋayinda*	*ŋayaŋum*	*ŋayingu*
1 n-sg	*ŋaɲḍi*	*ŋaɲḍiɲ*	*ŋaɲḍin*	*ŋaɲḍinda*	*ŋaɲḍinum*	*ŋaɲḍingu*
2 sg	*ɲura*	*ɲuraɲ*	*ɲuran*	*ɲuranda*	*ɲuranum*	*ɲurangu*
2 n-sg	*ɲuramba*	*ɲurambaɲ*	*ɲuramban*	*ɲurambanda*	*ɲurambanum*	*ɲurambangu*

Note firstly that the 1 sg accusative pronoun is simply *ŋaɲa* in Dya:bugay. Although the accusative forms of other pronouns end in *-ɲ*, Dya:bugay has not generalised the final *-ɲ* to 1 sg, as has Yidiɲ.

Secondly, in the rightmost four columns the 1 sg root begins with *ŋay-*; that is, the *-ḍ-* of *ŋaḍu* has been reduced to *-y-* in oblique forms (this has happened only for the nominative form in Yidiɲ). The SA form in Dya:bugay, *ŋawu*, is a natural further development from *ŋayu*, with the semi-vowel assimilating to the following vowel (in total: *ŋaḍu > ŋayu > ŋawu*). (Hale comments that *ŋawuŋgu* and *ŋawu* are in free variation and further notes that in Dya:bugay *-ŋgu* is the ergative allomorph on a nominal which ends in a vowel.)

The development of the 2 sg pronoun in Yidiɲ would have followed similar lines. Once the original S form, *ɲun*, had been dropped (and *ɲundu* generalised to cover its function) all oblique forms were recreated. But they were based on the 2 sg genitive form *ɲuni* or its extension *ɲuni + n* (rather than on the SA form, as was the case with 1 sg). Thus, for instance, accusative simply added *-ɲ* to *ɲuni*. (This contrasts with Dya:bugay, where oblique forms of 2 sg were again formed on the SA form, here *ɲura*).

In 3.3.3 we discussed the historical development of the genitive affix in Yidiɲ. We noted that, for nominals, genitive is *-ni* before all (including zero) case inflections for a root ending in a consonant and for an odd-syllabled root ending in a vowel; but that with an even-syllabled root ending in a vowel it is *-:n* in the absolutive and *-nu* in all oblique cases.

This suggests a historical development *-*nu* > -*ni* ~ -*nu*. We suggested that *-*nu* has been replaced by -*ni* wherever the affix vowel might be word-final; in cases where the suffixal vowel can not occur word-finally (but is instead deleted by Rule 2) the form -*nu* is retained. Now the -*u*- of -*nu* occurs only when followed by a further affix.

The 2 sg pronoun provides further support for an original genitive *-*nu*. Notice that dative and purposive are based on the stem *ɲuni + n-* in the coastal dialect, but on *ɲunu + n-* in the tablelands variety (genitive + absolutive is *ɲuni* in both dialects). We can suggest that the tablelands forms preserve original genitive *ɲunu* before non-zero case inflections,

whereas coastal speakers have generalised the absolutive form *ɲuni* into all oblique cases.

We have related present-day *ɲuni* to an original monosyllabic root **ɲun-* and suffix **-nu*. (It has already been mentioned, in 3.3.3, that Dya:bugay has canonical form *-ɲun* for the genitive suffix. If Yidiɲ and Dya:bugay genitives are related we could posit changes **-ɲun > *-nu > -ni ~ -nu*. But note that this further step back – from **-nu* to **-ɲun* – is not critical for the argumentation here.) We have also suggested that all 2 sg forms excepting nominative were recreated on the base **ɲunu-* (replacing the earlier monosyllabic root **ɲun-*).

It is instructive to compare 1 sg accusative *ɲaɲaɲ* – where the final *-ɲ* has been generalised to this form, in addition to the earlier acccusative *-ɲa* – with *ɲuni*, which is the only pronominal genitive not to end in *-n*. But note that before oblique cases the genitive stem is *ɲuninu-* (not **ɲunu-*) and that the causal case is *ɲuni:nim* (not **ɲunum* or **ɲunim*).

For the 1 sg pronoun in Yidiɲ all forms bar accusative have been remodelled, taking nominative *ŋaḍu* as the founding 'root'. We would, on this basis, expect genitive stem *ŋaḍunu-* reducing to *ŋaḍu:n* in the absolutive. There are two discrepancies – second vowel is *i* not *u*, and the absolutive lacks length. *u > i* could be explained as assimilation to *ḍ-*, although we must note that this has occurred only in the genitive, *-ḍu* remaining in all other cases. But notice Dya:bugay, where there is wide variation in the second vowel of 1 sg forms – *u* is retained in nominative but changed to *i* in dative and purposive and to *a* in possessive and ablative. The occurrence of *ŋaḍin* rather than *ŋaḍi:n* is consistent with our comments that pronouns constitute the only area of the grammar where Rule 2 does not apply regularly; the main point is that genitive-plus-absolutives end in *-n* (as accusatives end in *-ɲ*) with the appearance of vowel length being confined to 1 du and 1 n-sg forms.

Note that in Dya:bugay genitive is *-ŋ* on 1 sg but *-n* with other pronouns. Compare with nominal genitive and note a pattern of similarity with other nominal suffixes in Dya:bugay

	following consonant	following vowel
genitive	*-ŋun*	*-:n*
ablative	*-ŋunum*	*-:num*
dative	*-ŋunda*	*-:nda*

It is possible (although not likely) that pronominal genitive -(:)n in Yidiɲ is, as in Dya:bugay, based on the final segment of *-ŋun, rather than on the initial *ŋ (>n); but note that this would NOT explain the form -nu of the genitive before oblique cases.

We can now summarise our internal reconstruction of the history of singular pronouns in Yidiɲ:

FIRST PERSON

	S	A	O	genitive	oblique
stage 1	ŋay	ŋaḍu	ŋaɲa	ŋay + nu	ŋay +
stage 2		ŋaḍu	ŋaɲa	ŋaḍu + nu	ŋaḍu(n) +
stage 3		ŋayu	ŋaɲaɲ	ŋaḍin ~ ŋaḍinu	ŋaḍu(n) +

SECOND PERSON

	S	A	O	genitive	oblique
stage 1	ɲun	ɲundu	ɲun + ɲa	ɲunu	ɲun +
stage 2		ɲundu	?	ɲunu	ɲunu(n) +
stage 3		ɲundu	ɲuniɲ	ɲuni ~ ɲuninu	ɲunu(n) + ~ ɲuni(n) +

If comparison with Dya:bugay is permitted, we can suggest (but not be certain of) *-ŋun as an earlier form of genitive *-nu.

Finally, there is the undoubtedly recent reduction of singular dative pronouns. The second syllable of the root (-ḍu- from ŋaḍu:nda, -ni- from ɲuni:nda) can be omitted from these frequently used forms, yielding disyllabic words. It is likely that the reduction began in the first person and is spreading to the second – we have remarked that although both ŋanda and ɲunda occur, only the former is recognised as fully grammatical.

3.6.5 ɲunduba. Almost all Australian languages have singular pronouns based on ŋay (first person) and ɲun or ɲin (second person). Almost as common is ŋali for first person dual (further marked as 'inclusive' for languages which show an inclusive/exclusive distinction). Next in number of occurrences comes second person plural ɲura. (Examples of these forms are in Dixon 1970c: 86–9 and Schmidt 1912; see also Dixon 1972: 5–9).

ɲura, which is not attested for Yidiɲ, is the 2 sg pronoun in Dya:bugay. This suggests that proto-Yidiɲ–Dya:bugay may have had the normal arrangement of second person pronouns:

	2 sg	2 n-sg
proto-Yidiɲ–Dya:bugay	ɲun(*du*)	ɲura
modern Yidiɲ	ɲundu	ɲunduba
modern Dya:bugay	ɲura	ɲuramba

The original plural form *ɲura*, has been lost in Yidiɲ and replaced by *ɲunduba*, based on the singular pronoun. In Dya:bugay *ɲura* has shifted from plural to singular reference, replacing *ɲundu*, and a new plural (based on *ɲura*) has been derived.

There are many examples, from all parts of the world, of a plural pronoun becoming the polite or formal way of referring to a single addressee, and gradually taking on singular meaning ('you' in English and 'vous' in French, for instance). Wilf Douglas (personal communication) reports that although in the Ernabella dialect of the Western Desert language 2 sg is *ɲundu* and 2 pl *ɲura*, in the Ooldean dialect *ɲura* is 2 sg with the 2 pl form, *ɲuramuga*, involving an increment to this. (He also reports that in the Warburton Ranges dialect 2 sg is *ɲundulu* and 2 pl *ɲunduluya*.) There may well have been sociolinguistic reasons for the shift of 2 pl pronoun to 2 sg reference in Ooldean and Dya:bugay, as there were in French and English.

It is clear that in Yidiɲ and Dya:bugay the 2 n-sg root is (historically) derived from 2 sg by the addition of *-ba* (with an intrusive homorganic nasal in the case of Dya:bugay). It is also clear that this *-ba* is cognate with the productive nominal affix *-ba* 'one of a group' in present-day Yidiɲ.

We mentioned in 3.3.6 that if two (human) nouns are coordinated, *-ba* must be added to each:

(148) *daŋgidaŋgi:ba   yabuɹuba   galiŋ*
    old woman-*ba*-ABS young girl-*ba*-ABS go-PRES
    An old woman (being one of a group of people) and a girl (being
        another member of the group) are going. (That is 'a woman and
        a girl are going', leaving open the question of whether they
        are going alone, or as part of a larger assemblage.)

If one of the several people involved in an action is the addressee, we would predict:

(149) *ɲundu:ba daŋgidaŋgi:ba galiŋ*
    You and an old woman are going (again leaving open the question
        of whether anyone else is also going)

and (149) – involving the 2 n-sg pronoun *ɲunduba* – is exactly what would be said here.

It will thus be seen that *ɲunduba* is literally 'a group [of people] one of which is you'. We have a choice between saying simply:

(150) *ɲundu:ba galiŋ*
    You are going with one or more other people

or specifying rather more precisely by using (149) 'you are going with one or more other people, one of whom is an old woman'. Or, if there are three (or more) people involved, we could specify more fully and say:

(151) *ɲundu:ba darŋgidarŋgi:ba yabuɽuba galiŋ*
    You are going with two or more people, one of whom is an old
    woman and one of whom is a girl

But note that, although *ɲunduba* is plainly historically derived from *ɲundu* and *-ba*, it cannot be analysed into *ɲundu + ba* in terms of a synchronic analysis of modern Yidiɲ. If *ɲunduba* did involve the productive affix *-ba* we would expect regular declension – ergative *ɲundubaŋgu*, genitive-plus-absolute *ɲundubani*, and so on (paralleling nominal-plus-*ba* forms – 3.3.6). Instead, *ɲunduba* has its own set of rather idiosyncratic case forms – 3.6.2.

ŋaɲɟi and *ŋali* function exactly like the *-ba* equivalents of *ŋayu* (note that **ŋayu:ba* is not an acceptable Yidiɲ word). The unmarked non-singular, *ŋaɲɟi*, can refer to a set of two or more than two, just like *ɲunduba* or nominal + *ba* forms. Thus:

(152) *ŋaɲɟi buɲa:ba galiŋ*
    A woman and I (and some others) are going

(153) *ŋaɲɟi buɲabaŋgu wagu:ɖa gali:ŋal*
    A woman and I (and some others) are taking a man

Note that *buɲaba* is in absolutive case (S function) in (152) but in ergative (A function) in (153): *ŋaɲɟi* is in nominative form in both instances.

(152) can be paraphrased by a construction with the nominal comitative suffix on either noun or pronoun:

(154) *ŋayu buɲa:y galiŋ*   I am going with a woman

or

(155) *buɲa ŋaɖu:nɖi galiŋ*   A woman is going with me

In all of (152–5) it is left open whether or not anyone else went with 'the woman and me'; and in fact *buɲa* could refer to one or to more than one woman. (One can, of course, include a number adjective – *ŋaɲḍi buɲa:ba ḍambulaba galiŋ* 'a group which includes me and two women is going'.)

If one wished to stress that only two people were involved, *ŋali* '[a group of] two people, one of whom is me' would be used:

(156) *ŋali waga:lba yiŋgu ɲinaŋ*
     I'm sitting here with [my] wife

ŋali is thus a particular further specification of *ŋaɲḍi*, for referring to a group which has just two members.

ŋali is only infrequently used in texts (3.6.1) and it has not been possible to survey a very wide range of occurrences. It is most frequently used in an 'inclusive' sense, for referring to speaker and addressee (see text 2, line 3) but it is clear that it can have 'exclusive' reference, to speaker and third party – as in (156). The simplest way of explicitly marking *ŋali* as exclusive is to append the *-ba* form of a deictic (3.7.5), say:

(157) *ŋali yiɲḍu:mba galiŋ* 'Me and him are going'

In contrast, an inclusive sense is indicated by apposing 1 n-sg or 1 du and 2 n-sg forms e.g. *ŋali ɲundu:ba galiŋ* 'you and I are going'. This can be translated literally as 'I, being one of a group of two, and you, being another of the group, are going'. (Here Yidiɲ differs significantly from most other Australian languages which do not have separate forms for inclusive and exclusive pronouns. The normal practice is to render the inclusive sense through appending 2 sg (NOT 2 n-sg) pronoun to 1 du or 1 pl; Dyirbal is one language behaving in this way – Dixon 1972: 63.)

We have mentioned that *ŋaḍu*, *ɲundu* and *ŋali* are found in many other Australian languages; and we have suggested an etymology for *ɲunduba*. The remaining pronoun, 1 n-sg *ŋaɲḍi*, is not in fact found outside Yidiɲ, Dya:bugay and one or two nearby languages (including Gugu-Yalandyi – see Hershberger 1964).

The origin of *ŋaɲḍi* is unknown. But we can, rather speculatively, mention that the addition of comitative *-ḍi* to monosyllabic root *ŋay* would, by the regular rules (3.3.4), yield *ŋaɲḍi* (exactly the same rules apply in Dya:bugay, yielding the same result). It could be that a sentence like:

(158) *bama ŋaɲḍi* (= *ŋay+ḍi*) *galiŋ*   A person is going with me
tended to be abbreviated to:

(159) *ŋaɲḍi galiŋ*   We are going

If this were the case it would mean that the 1 n-sg pronoun developed in quite a different way from 2 n-sg: the former would be, etymologically, 'someone, WITH ME' and the latter 'a group, ONE OF WHOM IS YOU'. (We have already noted that *ɲaɲḍi* functions like a *-ba* form, not like a comitative.) But these comments on the development of *ɲaɲḍi* are very much a guess, with no supporting evidence available. It is more likely that the similarity between *ɲaɲḍi* and *ɲay+ḍi* is simply coincidence.

3.7 Deictics – definite and indefinite/interrogative

3.7.1 Reference. Yidiɲ has a complex system of deictics. We deal in this section with the underlying semantic contrasts.

[A] DEGREE OF DISTANCE

There are three possibilities for the first syllable of a 'definite' deictic. They can be illustrated for the 'absolutive' and 'locative' forms:

yiɲu 'this'	*yiŋgu* 'here'	near speaker
ɲuɲu 'that'	*ɲuŋgu* 'there'	at a distance from speaker
yuɲu 'yon'	*yuŋgu* 'yonder'	at a considerable distance from speaker, but visible

The meanings quoted here apply for the coastal dialect (extending to the *malanbara* local group part-way up the range, whose speech seems in this instance to pattern with *gulgibara* rather than with the local groups on top of the tableland – 1.2). There are simply three degrees of distance. *yi-* forms are the most common with syntactic cases while *ɲu-* forms are more frequent for local cases. *yu-* forms are relatively rare; a typical instance is given in (160) where a traveller stands on a cliff and looks across the sea to a distant island:

(160) *yuɲu   ɲaɻa   gandagaɻa: wunaɲ*
       YON-ABS south-LOC Franklin Island lie-PRES
       'Franklin Island lies a long way off to the south'

Instances of *yuŋgu* are in coastal dialect texts 2.109 and 9.26.

The tablelands dialect has the same three definite deictic roots but here *yu-* refers to something which is not visible (but is, perhaps, audible).

It is interesting to compare the deictic systems in these two dialects of Yidiɲ with that in Dyirbal (Dixon 1972: 45):

coastal Yidiɲ		Dyirbal	
'here'	*yi-*	'here (visible)'	*yala-*
'there'	*ŋu-*	'there (visible)'	*bala-*
'yonder (visible)'	*yu-*	'invisible'	*ŋala-*

tablelands Yidiɲ

Thus, tablelands Yidiɲ has the Dyirbal semantic system associated with the coastal dialect forms.

The use of *yi-* and *ŋu-* forms in the tablelands dialect shows no appreciable differences from the coastal dialect. A good example of their contrast within a single sentence is in line 17 of text 14. Note that *yi-* and *ŋu-* (and probably also *yu-*) forms can function cataphorically and anaphorically just like English 'this' and 'that' (this can be seen from an examination of their occurrences in text 9, for instance).

There is also an idiom-like phrase *ŋuŋudi wala* 'that's alright' – see the discussion of *-di* in 3.9.1.

[B] HUMAN–INANIMATE HIERARCHY

There are in fact two forms of each definite demonstrative, whose use depends on the human-ness/animacy of the referent. They fall together in the absolutive case (quoted above) but there are distinct stems for oblique cases:

	HUMAN	INANIMATE
'this'	*yiɲḍu-*	*yiŋgu-*
'that'	*ŋuɲḍu-*	*ŋuŋgu-*
'far/invisible'	*yuɲḍu-*	*yuŋgu-*

Note that ALL definite deictics exist in three forms, with initial *yi-*, *ŋu-* or *yu-*. In the discussion below we shall simply cite *yi-* forms, but it should always be borne in mind that there are corresponding *ŋu-* and *yu-* forms.

We glossed the columns above 'human' and 'inanimate', referring to the extremes of a continuum. In fact, the use of the two forms of the definite deictic can best be explained in terms of a hierarchy (see 3.1.2):

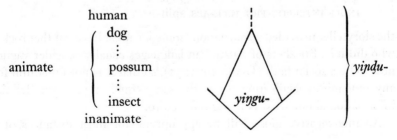

A deictic referring to a human must involve the root *yiɲɖu-*; but *yiɲɖu-* CAN be used to refer to ANYTHING, whether human or non-human, animate or non-animate. *yiŋgu-* forms are most frequently used to refer to inanimates, but can be used with animates, the likelihood of their being encountered dropping off as one ascends the hierarchy towards 'human'. *yiŋgu-* forms are not normally used to refer to (live) humans.

Thus the dative referring to a place would be most likely to be *yiŋgu:nda*; for referring to an animal it might be either *yiŋgu:nda* or *yiɲɖu:nda*; but for a person, only *yiɲɖu:nda* is allowable (see *yiɲɖu:nda bimbi:nda* 'for this father', where 'father' here refers to the Christian God – text 9.35).

Note that the inanimate form is likely to be used for referring to a human corpse - as *ɲuŋgu:gu* in text 14, line 27. A similar assignment is found in Dyirbal noun classes: all human or animate nouns belong to class 1 or class 2, but nouns referring to 'meat' (and to 'body parts') are in the 'inanimate' residue class, 4 (Dixon 1972: 306–11).

George Davis was the youngest speaker of Yidiɲ interviewed, and his command of the language was not always as good as that of people from an older generation. He had reanalysed the more/less continuum for the use of *yiɲɖu-/yiŋgu-* into a definite yes/no choice – that is, he said he would use *yiɲɖu-* only for humans and *yiŋgu-* only for inanimates, stating that neither of these forms was appropriate to refer to animals. This reanalysis has involved polarisation of the two forms, each to that end of the hierarchy at which it was most typically used, with NEITHER being allowed in the no-man's land between (in which BOTH could normally be used, with approximately equal frequency).

[C] DEFINITE versus INDEFINITE/INTERROGATIVE

In common with most or all other Australian languages, Yidiɲ has a set of forms that can have either 'indefinite' or 'interrogative' force. In fact, the most appropriate translation would normally involve BOTH notions; thus, for

(161) *waɲɖu*   *walba*   *yaŋgi:ɲ*
      INDEF/INTERROG-ERG rock-ABS split-PAST

the storyteller provided a translation 'someone must have cut that rock – who did it?'. Speakers of Australian languages usually consider vagueness to be a social fault (Dixon 1972: 30), so that it is not unnatural for any indefinite specification to, at the same time, enquire for definite information about what is being referred to.

An interrogative gloss will be appropriate for most instances of a

form like *waɲḍu*, and this can tend to obscure the 'indefinite' aspect of these words. But in some cases only the indefinite sense applies (with no overtones of interrogation); for instance – text 2.37:

(162) *bulmba   ŋanda buḍiŋ   yiŋgu:ɲ   ŋaɽa   waɲḍa*
      camp-ABS   I-DAT tell-PRES   THIS-ACC   south-LOC   INDEF-LOC
      I was told this camp was somewhere to the south

The use of an indefinite/interrogative presupposes that there IS SOMETHING (of the type that is being sought), and enquires who or what or where it is. If one has no reason to assume there is anything, it would not be appropriate to use an indefinite/interrogative. Thus, an informant said that on coming into camp one would not say *bana waɲḍa* 'where's the water' (literally 'there is some water, where is it?') but would instead use *bana ɲuḍu* 'there's no water?' If there did happen to be some water available, someone else might reply *dugubilda ḍundaŋ* 'hanging up in a water-bag'.

Authors of grammars of Australian languages have typically labelled indefinite/interrogatives as simply 'interrogatives', immediately recognising – perhaps eliciting – the 'interrogative' sense but failing to look beyond the normal confines of this Indo-European label. (The writer's grammar of Dyirbal is particularly open to the criticism, the 'indefinite' interpretation being alluded to only in a late note – Dixon 1972: 265.)

There are two indefinite/interrogatives corresponding exactly to the 'human' and 'inanimate' definite deictics (the distinction of 'degree of distance/visibility' is of course not applicable to indefinites). The oblique roots are:

	human	inanimate
indefinite/ interrogative	*waɲḍu* 'someone/who' etc.	*waɲi* 'something/what' etc.
definite	*yiɲḍu* 'this person' etc.	*yiŋgu* 'this thing' etc.

The definite deictics (*yi-*, *ŋu-* and *yu-* forms) and the indefinite/interrogatives are morphologically similar and plainly make up one word class. There appears to be no really suitable label for the class. For want of anything better, we employ 'deictic', and then talk of definite and of indefinite/interrogative deictics (the latter report the lack of deictic specification, and request it).

Exactly the same hierarchical principle of use applies to *waɲi-/waɲḍu-* as to *yiŋgu-/yiɲḍu-*. *waɲḍu-* must be used for reference to humans. Either form is possible where the referent is, say, a bird:

(163) *yiŋu maŋga* $\begin{cases} waɲḍu:n \\ waɲi:n(i) \end{cases}$

> Which [bird] does this nest belong to ? (literally, 'this nest belongs to some [bird], which one is it ?)

But where it is expected that the person answering will specify an inanimate noun, *waɲi* is preferred.

It seems that *waɲi-* may be the 'unmarked' indefinite/interrogative in the sense that it is likely to be employed when the speaker has no idea whether the thing he is asking after is human or animate or what. In these circumstances *waɲi* could be referring to a person. But it must be noted that information on this point is not totally clear.

[D] GENERIC versus SPECIFIC INTERROGATIVES

We have already noted that an NP in Yidiɲ will typically involve both a generic and a specific noun (3.1.3 – see also 4.1.1, 6.2.1). For instance:

	GENERIC	SPECIFIC
	miɲa 'edible animal'	*gangu:l* 'wallaby'
or	*mayi* 'edible vegetable'	*badil* 'rickety nut'
or	*gugu* 'noise'	*wulŋgu* 'woman's song'

There are in fact two varieties of 'inanimate' indefinite/interrogatives:

	waɲi 'what (genus)'
and	*waɲira* 'what (species), what kind of'

That is, if one has no real idea what generic term an indefinite or unknown entity should be grouped under, *waɲi* should be used. But if one does know the genus, then *waɲira* will be appropriate (and will normally be used together with the generic term). For instance, a conversation between A and B could go (with all four utterances referring to the same animal):

(164) A – *waɲi galiŋ*   What is that going [along there] ?
      B – *miɲa galiŋ*   It's an animal going [along].
      A – *waɲi:ra miɲa ḍuŋgaŋ* What sort of animal is it running
                                  along [there] ?
      B – *gangu:l wariŋ*   It's a wallaby jumping [along].

and so on. *waɲi:ra mayi* 'what kind of food' occurs in lines 40 and 44 of text 2.

waɲi- forms are four or five times more frequent than *waɲira*; *waɲi* has an irregular paradigm whereas *waɲira* appears to inflect exactly like a nominal (*waɲira* is in fact seldom encountered in oblique cases).

waɲira is not normally used to refer to humans; but an informant mentioned that *waɲira bama* is possible, and is equivalent to the more usual *waɳḍabara* 'what local group [does a person] belong to?' – see 6.2.1.

A full discussion of the semantics of generics, with further examples of *waɲira*, is in 6.2.1. A third type of interrogative, *waɳḍariɲ* 'what kind of', asking about the token of a given species type, is discussed – and contrasted with *waɲi* and *waɲira* – in 3.7.6.

[E] INDEFINITE/INTERROGATIVES versus GENERIC NOUNS

An NP in Yidiɲ can perfectly well involve just a specific, or else just a generic, noun. We could describe an event fairly precisely by:

(165) *ɲaɲaɲ ɲaḍinuŋgu bimbi:ŋ wawa:l*   My father saw me

or, at a more general level, by:

(166) *ɲaɲaɲ bama:l wawa:l*   A person saw me

The point to note here is that there is a difference in meaning between (166) and

(167) *waɳḍu ɲaɲaɲ wawa:l*   Someone (or something) saw me – who saw me?

In saying (167) the speaker admits that he does not know who saw him (and elicits clarification). But if he utters (166) it is possible that he knows who it was, but is just not naming the person at the moment. (167) is indefinite whereas (166) can be definite but underspecified. (The point to emphasise is that (166) should NOT in all cases be glossed 'SOMEONE saw me'.)

Although there is a clear distinction between generic nouns and indefinite/interrogatives in each individual Australian language, there is evidence of diachronic shift between the classes. Thus *miɲa* is a generic noun '(edible) animal' in Yidiɲ and in many other northern languages; this is surely related to the non-human indefinite/interrogative *miɲa* 'something/what' in Dyirbal and many languages to the south. In this case, a failure to recognise the 'indefinite' interpretation of 'interrogatives' would be likely to obscure the naturalness of the semantic relationship (it is by no means obvious that 'animal' and 'what' should be related).

3.7.2   Paradigm. The full paradigm for all deictic forms is given below. As already mentioned, the definite deictics have forms with initial ŋu- and yu- parallelling every yi- word cited here.

The syntactic case forms are in table 3.4. We can recall that nominals have one form for S and O functions and a separate, marked, form for A function; and that pronouns have one form for S and A functions and a further form for O. Notice that human deictics (both definite and indefinite/interrogative) have distinct forms for all three major syntactic functions – S, A and O. The inanimate indefinite/interrogative has a single form for S and O functions, exactly like a nominal. And the inanimate definite generally uses the unmarked form for O as well as S functions; but an accusative form yiŋgu:ɲ can be used – as in (162) – as alternative to yiɲu in O function only.

The point most worthy of note is that in S function (which occurs in texts more frequently than any other) the human and inanimate definites fall together; however, the indefinite/interrogatives always maintain separate forms. Thus, a sentence whose S NP consists just of a deictic:

(168) ŋuɲu wanda:ɲ   That fell

is ambiguous – it could mean 'that (person) fell (over)', or 'that (fruit) fell (off a tree)', and so on. In contrast, a dative NP would be likely to involve different forms for referring to a human, as in (169), or an inanimate, as in (170):

(169) yiɲu guda:ga ɲina:ɲ ŋuɲḍu:nda (ḍaḍa:nda) ɲaru
       This dog sat on that (child)

(170) yiɲu guda:ga ɲina:ɲ ŋuŋgu:nda (galba:nda) ɲaru
       This dog sat on that (tomahawk)

In the inanimate definite row, it will be seen that there is no ergative form based on the root yiŋgu-. Instead, yiɲḍu:ŋ is used with all types of ergatives (human, animate and inanimate):

(171) ŋuɲḍu:ŋ malga:yḍu miɲa ḍimbaŋ
       That Malgay fish [jumps up from the water and] grabs animals [flies]

(172) ɲaɲaɲ ḍugi:ŋ bunḍa:ḍiɲu/ŋuɲḍu:ŋ
       That stick hit me [= I hit myself accidentally, on the stick]

It is probably most satisfactory to say that there is no ergative (A) form of the inanimate definite deictic, and that the human definite has to be

TABLE 3.4   *Deictics – syntactic cases*

	S	O	A	DAT/INSTR	PURP	CAUSAL
DEFINITE						
human	} *yiŋu* {	*yiṇḍu:ṇ*	*yiṇḍu:ŋ*	*yiṇḍu:nda*	*yiṇḍu:ngu*	*yiṇḍu:nim*
inanimate		*yiŋu ~ yiŋgu:ṇ*	(*yiṇḍu:ŋ*)	*yiŋgu:nda*	*yiŋgu:gu*	*yiŋgu:nim* and *yiŋgu:nmu*
INDEFINITE/INTERROGATIVE						
human	*waṇa*	*waṇḍu:ṇ*	*waṇḍu*	*waṇḍu:nda*	*waṇḍu:ngu*	*waṇḍu:nim*
inanimate						
generic	*waṇi*	*waṇi*	*waṇi:ndu*	*waṇi:nda*	*waṇi:ngu*	*waṇi:nim* and *waṇi:nmu*
specific	*waṇi:ra*	*waṇi:ra*	*waṇiraŋgu*	*waṇiranda*	*waṇiragu*	*waṇiramu*

used in cases like (171–2). (What we are calling 'human' forms can of course be used whatever the reference – 3.7.1.)

There are instrumental forms for just the inanimate deictics – *waṇi:nda*, as in (173), and *yiŋgu:nda*. These coincide with dative. However, this should not be taken to imply any syntactic identification of dative and instrumental; it is simply that dative and locative coincide on stems ending in *-n* (in the next section we posit stems *waṇin-* and *yiŋgun-* here).

(173) *waṇi:nda ṇundu ḍugi gunda:l*   What did you cut the tree with?

We can note that the two human deictics lack *-mu ~ -m* causal forms – exactly as do pronouns – and have to make do with *-nim* forms (3.3.3). There are examples of a human deictic plus *-nim* co-occurring with a noun plus *-m*, as in

(174) *ṇundu   ŋuṇḍu:nim   mandim   burga:l*
   you-SA THAT-HUMAN-CAU hand-ABL pull out-PAST
   You pulled [it] out of that [person]'s hand

ŋuṇḍu:nim appears to have a normal genitive-plus-causal sense here ('that which used to belong to that [person]') whereas *mandim* can be given a purely ablative ('motion from') interpretation. But *ŋuṇḍu:nim* and *mandim* undoubtedly 'agree' in (174).

It appears in fact that *yiṇḍu:nim* and *waṇḍu:nim* from table 3.4 may have the full range of causal and ablative function normally associated with nominal *-m ~ -mu* forms. *ṇundu waṇḍu:nim gadaŋ* can mean 'who are you coming from?', with a purely local sense.

The inanimate deictics have regular causal (*-mu ~ -m*) as well as *-nim* forms. We can contrast a straight causal:

(175) *bama:l ɲaɲaɲ ḏaŋga:l | waɲi:nmu*

From (= for) what did he grumble at me? (*ḏaŋga:l* can be glossed 'jealously growl at'; here *waɲi:nmu* asks what the speaker has done, to be bawled out in this way)

with a 'perfective possessive' *-nim* form:

(176) *ɲundu ɲuɲu waɲi:nim daŋga:ɲ*

What did you take that from? (this might, say, refer to a piece of metal, with the speaker asking what inanimate thing – car or whatever – it came from)

These causal forms can be contrasted with the ablative form of the inanimate indefinite/interrogative (see table 3.7 below):

(177) *ɲundu waɲḏam ɲuɲu waɲal duga:l*

Where did you get that boomerang from?

This is the only place in the grammar of Yidiɲ where causal and ablative have quite different forms (being in fact based on 'syntactic stem' *waɲin-* and 'local stem' *waɲḏa-* respectively – see 3.7.3).

We can complete the paradigm by exemplifying the causal *-nim* form of the human indefinite/interrogative:

(178) *ɲundu waɲḏu:nim ɲuɲu waɲal duga:l*

Who did you get that boomerang from?

The purposive form of the inanimate interrogative is widely used and can often be translated as 'why' (see, for instance, lines 14, 25 of text 14 and line 57 of text 2). Compare with the purposive of the human interrogative:

(179) *yiɲu   biṟmbi:rḏi   ɲinaɲ |*
THIS-ABS jealousy-COMIT-ABS sit-PRES

    waɲḏu:ngu
    INDEF/INTERROG-HUMAN-PURP

This [person] is sitting [there] feeling jealous – concerning whom?

Here the purposive case marks the object of the jealous person's feelings – perhaps, his wife – and not, say, the rival who is making up to her.

Table 3.5 gives the genitive and comitative forms of the five deictics, together with fear inflection. Since the genitive suffix can be used to indicate the habitual camping place of an animal, or part–whole relationships for animate or inanimate things, genitives based on the inanimate deictics are quite common; for instance:

TABLE 3.5 *Deictics – genitive and comitative forms*

	genitive-plus-absolutive	genitive stem for oblique cases	comitative stem	fear inflection
DEFINITE				
human	*yiɲḍu:n*	*yiɲḍunu-*	*yiɲḍundi-*	*yiɲḍundida*
inanimate	*yiŋgu:n*	*yiŋgunu-*	*yiŋguyi-*	*yiŋguyida*
INDEFINITE/INTERROGATIVE				
human	*waɲḍu:n*	*waɲḍunu-*	*waɲḍundi-*	*waɲḍundida*
inanimate				
generic	*waɲi:n(i)*	*waɲinu-*	*waɲindi-*	*waɲindida*
specific	*waɲirani*	?	*waɲirayi-*	*waɲirayida*

(180) *yiɲu   wuɽu   yiŋgu:n   gala:n*   /
THIS-ABS handle-ABS THIS-INAN-GEN-ABS spear-GEN-ABS

ḍargi:na
embed-PURP

This handle belongs to this spear, and is to be attached to it

Genitives decline in the normal way; again the third vowel of the oblique stem is *-u-* (3.3.3, 3.6.2). In (181) *ɲuɲḍu-* is used to refer to an alligator:

(181) *garu   gaɲa:r   ɲaɲḍi baṉḍi:liŋ | bulmba:*
by-and-by alligator-ABS we-SA find-GOING-PRES camp·LOC

ɲuɲḍunula   wunaɲunda
THAT-HUMAN-GEN-LOC lie-SUBORD

By-and-by we'll go to find the alligator, who will be lying in his lair

Both *waɲi:n* and *waɲi:ni* have been recorded for the genitive + absolutive of the inanimate indefinite/interrogative; these could be related to stems *waɲi-* (with regular reduction by Rule 2) and *waɲin-* respectively – see 3.7.3. (But note that the oblique stem is *waɲinu-*.)

Comitative forms are quite regular, with *-ḍi* ~ *-yi* being added to stems *yiɲḍun-*, *yiŋgu-*, *waɲḍun-* and *waɲin-* (3.7.3). The morpheme boundary condition of Rule 2 is satisfied for the inanimate indefinite (in absolutive case) and this reduces: *yiŋgu+yi → yiŋgu:y*. Comitatives decline quite regularly, as

(182) *ɲaɲaɲ ɲuɲḍu:ŋ   waɲindiŋgu   bunḍa:ɲ*
      I-O   THAT-HUMAN-ERG   INDEF-INAN-COMIT-ERG   hit-PAST
      What did that [person] who hit me have?

Note that one sense of (182) can be paraphrased by:

(183) *ɲaɲaɲ ɲuɲḍu:ŋ waɲi:nda bunḍa:ɲ*
      What did that [person] hit me with?

where the indefinite/interrogative is in instrumental inflection.

   Fear forms involve the regular addition of -*da* to a comitative stem; for instance:

(184) *ɲayu yaɽŋga:ɲ ɲuŋguyida walbayida*
      I was frightened of those stones (lest they roll down the mountain)

   Deictic forms occur with derivational affixes -*muḍay* 'with' and -*gimbal* 'without' (3.3.6); these are shown in table 3.6   *muḍay* forms are, as usual, interchangeable with words involving the alternate comitative suffix -*ḍi* ~ -*yi*. The occurrence of -*gimbal* with *waɲḍun*- and *waɲin*- is particularly interesting in that here only the indefinite sense is relevant – *waɲḍungimbal* 'with no one' (literally 'without some one') and *waɲin-gimbal* 'with nothing' (literally 'without something'). Thus:

(185) *yiŋu guman bama gadaŋ/ waɲingimbal/ gurbi muɽay baḍa:ɽ*
      This person is coming alone, with nothing; perhaps [he] left the clothes behind

TABLE 3.6   *Deictics with derivational affixes*

		-*muḍay* 'with'	-*gimbal* 'without'
DEFINITE			
	human	*yiɲḍunmuḍay*	*yiɲḍungimbal*
	inanimate	*yiŋgumuḍay*	?
INDEFINITE/INTERROGATIVE			
	human	?	*waɲḍungimbal*
	inanimate		
	generic	*waɲinmuḍay*	*waɲingimbal*

The use of *waɲingimbal* implies that someone has nothing, when he would be expected to have something (of a certain sort); hence the inclusion of the qualifying second clause in (185).

-bara can be suffixed to the locative root *waṇḍa* or *yiŋgu* (see below). There is also an idiom *ɲuɲumbuḍun*, occurring in text 9, line 35; this is the only instance known of the form *ɲuɲum* (for *-buḍun* see 3.9.5).

The form *waɲiɲula* 'what's this' appears to be an emphatic version of *waɲi*; it has been obtained in, for instance, ergative case – *waɲiɲula:ŋ. -ɲula* is not known outside this word.

waɲamuŋgal was mentioned in discussion of the derivational affix *-muŋgal*, 3.3.6.

The inanimate indefinite/interrogative can be verbalised, giving intransitive *waɲin+daga-n* 'do what' and transitive *waɲin-ya-l* 'do what to'; details are in 4.8.1.

Finally, local cases of deictics are in table 3.7. It appears that only the inanimates take local cases (providing further evidence for the similarity between inanimate deictics and nominals – against animate deictics, which are most similar to pronouns).

Note that there is a special 'allative of direction' ('this way', 'which way'). This has the forms *yiŋgu:ruɲ/waṇḍa:ruɲ* in the coastal dialect but *yiɲa:luy/waṇḍa:luy* in tablelands Yidiɲ. It can be used with a verb of motion:

(186) *ŋaɲḍi yiŋgu:ruɲ waŋgi galiŋ*   We're going up this way

or with a verb of rest, indicating the direction in which someone is facing:

(187) *ɲundu ɲuŋgu:ruɲ ɲinan*   You sit down [facing] that way!

TABLE 3.7   *Deictics – local case forms*

	definite	indefinite/interrogative
locative	*yiŋgu*	*waṇḍa*
allative of place	*yiŋgu* (~ *yiŋgu:gu*)	*waṇḍa:l* (~ *waṇḍa:gu*)
allative of direction	C *yiŋgu:ruɲ*, T *yiɲa:luy*	C *waṇḍa:ruɲ*, T *waṇḍa:luy*
ablative	*yiŋgum*	*waṇḍam*

A directional form can be used with a noun or locational qualifier in allative case, the former specifying the direction and the latter the goal of motion:

(188) *gana ŋaɲɖi yiŋgu:ruɲ   galiŋ   bulmba:gu*
      TRY   we-SA THIS-ALL(DIRN) go-PURP home-ALL
      Let's try to go this way home!

In (188) the *-gu* inflection on *bulmba* marks allative not purposive case – this usage (which is less common than the regular nominal allative *bulmba:*) is modelled on the allative inflection for locational qualifiers – 3.4.1.

waɲɖa:ruɲ 'which way' is used in text 2, line 85; and in (220) below.

As with nominals, a single form marks locative ('where at') and allative of place ('where to') for the definite deictic. With the indefinite/interrogative, however, there are two forms – *waɲɖa* and *waɲɖa:l*. Although *waɲɖa:l* is preferred for the allative sense (as in line 19 of text 2) and *waɲɖa* for locative function (text 2, line 33 and subsequent lines) there appears to be a degree of interchangeability between these forms – *waɲɖa:l* has occasionally been encountered with what seems to be a locative sense and *waɲɖa* with allative.

There are also forms *yiŋgu:gu* and *waɲɖa:gu*, with exclusively allative meaning; these are used quite seldom, and normally accompany a locational qualifier (or a noun with locational reference) which also bears a *-gu* suffix – see 3.4.1.

Locational specification can involve both a deictic and a nominal, which must then agree in case, as in

(189) *yiŋgum   ɖugim   ŋaɲɖi guga   nada:l*
      THIS-INAN-ABL tree-ABL we-SA bark-ABS peel-PAST
      We peeled the bark off this tree

There are also forms involving the derivational affix *-bara* 'belonging to' (3.3.6) added to a locative deictic. *ɲuŋgubara* was exemplified in (69); there is also *waɲɖabara* (see also 6.2.1):

(190) *ŋaɲaɲ bama:l waɲɖabara:ŋ bunɖa:ɲ*
      Where does the person come from who hit me?

3.7.3 Analysis. The specific inanimate interrogative *waɲira* 'what kind of' inflects exactly like a trisyllabic nominal (and is in fact seldom found in oblique form); but the other four deictics have more-or-less irregular paradigms. We can suggest the following stems, underlying the forms quoted in the last section:

	definite		indefinite/interrogative	
	human	inanimate	human	inanimate
(a) absolutive (S) form	*yiɲu*	*yiɲu*	*waɲa*	*waɲi*
(b) stem for genitive				*waɲi- ~ waɲin-*
(c) stem for ergative/accusative	*yiɲḍu-*	*yiŋgu-*	*waɲḍu-*	*waɲin-*
(d) stem for other non-local suffixes	*yiɲḍun-*	*yiŋgu(n)-*	*waɲḍun-*	
(e) stem for local cases	—	*yiŋgu-*	—	*waɲḍa-*

Inanimate definite has the stem *yiŋgun-* for causal and instrumental, but *yiŋgu-* for purposive (either *yiŋgun-* or *yiŋgu-* yields the correct dative form).

To these stems we add:

(b) genitive *-ni*, causal *-nim*

(c) ergative *-ŋgu- ~ -du*, accusative *-ɲa*

(d) dative *-nda*, purposive *-gu*, causal *-mu ~ -m*, comitative *-ḍi ~ -yi*, fear *-ḍida ~ -yida*, comitative *-muḍay*, privative *-gimbal*, verbalisers *-daga-n*, *-ŋa-l*

(e) locative–allative ø (*~ -:l*), allative of place *-gu*, allative of direction *-ruɲ*, ablative *-m*

Note that Rule 2 applies quite regularly to deictics, reducing genitive, ergative and accusative on even-syllabled stems ending in a vowel.

This constitutes a major difference between deictics and pronouns; in 3.6.3 we found it simplest to exclude the class of pronouns from the domain of operation of Rule 2.

One important similarity with pronouns is the appearance of a stem augmented by final *-n*, which is the basis for causal and instrumental, and also for purposive with all deictics bar the inanimate definite. The inanimate indefinite also uses the *-n*-augmented stem for ergative; genitive alternant *waɲi:ni* would seem to involve *waɲin-* as stem, whereas *waɲi:n* is plainly based on *waɲi-*.

Dative could be based on stem (c) or stem (d) for all columns. In fact the argument for basing dative on an *-n*-final stem emanates from the 1 sg pronoun (3.6.3); here a stem without final *-n* (*ŋaḍu*) would not be needed for

any other case, and we thus prefer to relate dative *ɲaɖu:nda* to the stem *ɲaɖun*. Since everything else appears to be equal, we choose to relate dative on other pronouns, and on deictics, to an -*n*-final stem.

Our associating the stem for local cases with the inanimate column might be questioned in the case of indefinite/interrogative – here the local stem, (e), differs from the inanimate stems in rows (a–d) (it is perhaps closer to the human stems in these rows). But the inanimate syntactic-local correspondence is particularly clear in the case of definite deictics where the stem *yiŋgu* (with or without -*n*-augmentation) underlies all forms bar the absolutive. We then take the same semantic equation to apply for indefinites.

Note that the deictic locative has an entirely local sense – unlike the nominal locative it does not alternate with dative, for instance – 4.1.8, 4.2.3.

There are a number of 'gaps' qua the stem/affix combinations we have given:

   (i) there are no causal forms -*mu* ∼ -*m* for the human deictics (note that all four deictics have causals involving -*nim*);
   (ii) there is, strictly speaking, no ergative form for the inanimate definite;
   (iii) there is no accusative form for the inanimate indefinite, the absolutive form being used in O function. The inanimate definite accusative is seldom used, the unmarked absolutive being normally preferred;
   (iv) the special allative -*:l* applies only to indefinites.

We must also note one exception:

there is no ergative inflection, -*ŋgu* ∼ -*:ŋ*, with the human indefinite, the root *waɲɖu* constituting the complete A form.

The definite form of the 'allative of direction' in the tablelands dialect appears to be quite irregular. We could recognise a suffix -*luy* (or perhaps -*aluy*) from indefinite *waɲɖaluy*, but this would yield as definite stem the nonce-form *yiŋa-* or *yiŋ-*.

3.7.4 Historical development. Yidiɲ pronouns conform to the widespread Australian pattern; it was possible (in 3.6.4) to make quite detailed and confident comments on their historical development. The indefinite/interrogatives show some similarity with forms in other languages and we are able to reconstruct something of their history by analysis of the alternations within Yidiɲ. But the definite deictic roots

show little similarity with forms in any other language (even Dya:bugay has different definite forms, although the Dya:bugay interrogatives *ḏu:* 'who' and *ɲi:* 'what' are plainly related to the second syllables of the corresponding Yidiɲ forms) and we can say nothing with confidence about their development.

It is significant that the human indefinite/interrogative ergative is simply *waɲḏu*. This could be analysed as root *waɲ-* plus the regular ergative ending *-ḏu*. Present-day Yidiɲ does not, of course, tolerate monosyllabic roots. But we have already suggested an earlier stage of the language in which monosyllabic pronouns – 1 sg *ŋay* and 2 sg *ɲun* – were found; and it is plausible to couple these with monosyllabic indefinite/interrogative root *waɲ*.

The locative for *waɲ* would be predicted as *waɲḏa*; this is in fact the locative in modern Yidiɲ. These facts then suggest:

(a) Pre-Yidiɲ had a single indefinite interrogative form with the root *waɲ* used in S function, *waɲḏu* for A function and *waɲḏa* as locative.

(b) At a certain historical stage monosyllables were eliminated. Two S forms then evolved – human *waɲa* and inanimate *waɲi*.

The way in which the *waɲa/waɲi* contrast was established is not known. But note that we would have expected the O form based on monosyllabic *waɲ* to be *waɲ+ɲa = waɲa* (and the accusative suffix *-ɲa* is normally only used on a form that has human reference); if this were the origin of *waɲa* we would have to explain the shift from O to S function. Note also that the final vowel in *waɲi* is, in articulatory terms, close to the preceding consonant, *ɲ*.

(c) oblique case forms were then recreated:

(i) ergative *waɲḏu* became the basis for human syntactic cases and derived stems. Note the similarity with our postulated scheme for 1 sg pronoun – there 1 sg *ŋaḏu* re-founded all oblique cases (except, in this instance, accusative).

(ii) absolutive *waɲi* became the basis for inanimate syntactic cases and derived stems (*waɲi* being retained in O as well as S function, paralleling the ergative–absolutive paradigm for nominals);

waɲḏu and *waɲi* were augmented by *-n* before suffixes other than genitive, and accusative; this pattern of *-n*-augmentation is common to deictics and pronouns.

(iii) locative *waɲḏa* became the basis for the local cases.

There is insufficient formal parallelism between indefinites and definites to enable us to say much about the genesis of the latter. Root *yiɲḏu* could suggest

yiɲ+ḍu but here modern ergative does involve the addition of *-:ɲ*; if *yiɲḍu* were the original ergative, remodelling of forms had advanced much further than for the indefinite/interrogative. There is no further evidence for an original root *yiɲ-* (as there was for *waɲ-*).

yiŋgu could be analysed into *yiŋ-* plus purposive or ergative *-gu*. The absolutive form *yiɲu* might be thought to provide support for an original root *yiŋ-* (we could suggest that *yiɲu* is the disyllabic development of **yiŋ*, as *waɲa* and *waɲi* appear to be augmentations of **waɲ*; the quality of the final vowel of *yiɲu* could be explained by assimilation to the preceding *-ŋ*). But there is little semantic support – we would expect *yiŋgu* to function as ergative or purposive, whereas it is locative in modern Yidiɲ (and there is not even an ergative form based on *yiŋgu*!).

Reconstruction of the history of the definite deictics will have to await the discovery of cognate forms in some related language(s).

3.7.5 yiɲḍumba. In 3.6.5 we related the 2 n-sg pronoun *ɲunduba* to 2 sg *ɲundu* through the derivational affix *-ba* 'one of a group'. There is also a 'non-singular' form of the human definite deictic that appears (historically at least) to involve the nominal affix *-ba*. The following forms are attested:

> S function – *yiɲḍu:mba*
> A function – *yiɲḍumbaŋgu*
> O function – *yiɲḍu:mbaɲ*
> dative – *yiɲḍumbanda*
> purposive – *yiɲḍumbangu*
> genitive-plus-absolutive – *yiɲḍu:mban*
> comitative-plus-absolutive – *yiɲḍumbanḍi*

yiɲḍumba thus inflects just like a pronoun or deictic. Stem *yiɲḍumba* underlies S, A, O and genitive forms; ergative is the regular *-ŋgu* but accusative *-ɲ* and genitive *-n* (rather than *-ɲa* and *-ni*) are reminiscent of case endings on the 2 n-sg pronoun *ɲunduba* (3.6.3). Other forms involve the *-n*-augmented stem *yiɲḍumban-*.

Attempts at elicitation of oblique cases with the genitive of *yiɲḍumba* did not yield sure or consistent results (a similar failure occurred with *ɲunduba* – 3.6.2).

yiɲḍumba indicates a set of two or more people which includes 'this [person]'. It is often glossed by informants 'this fellow and someone else' or 'these two':

(191) *ɲundu mayi wiwin yiɲḍumbanda*
    You give some food to these two (or more) people!

yiɲḍumba differs formally from *ɲunduba* in the inclusion of a homorganic nasal
-m- between root and affix; compare with the 2 n-sg pronoun in Dya:bugay,
ɲuramba.

3.7.6 yiŋariɲ/waɲḍariɲ. There is a further set of deictic-type forms
'this/what kind of'. The full paradigm is in table 3.8. Note that these
forms inflect exactly like nominal roots with one oddity – *-l* can be added
to the locative (as in line 25 of text 9). An *-l* form occurs most frequently
with allative sense (and is thus parallel to the occurrence of *waɲḍa:l* qua
waɲḍa – 3.7.2). Derivational affixes can be added to *yiŋariɲ/waɲḍariɲ*
much as they can to any nominal – for instance, *yiŋariɲba* 'a group of
people, one of whom is this sort of person'.

There is no distinction between 'human' and 'inanimate' forms; both
yiŋariɲ and *waɲḍariɲ* can be used to refer to any sort of object. Thus, we
find human reference in:

(192) *waɲḍa:gu   yiŋa:riɲ   bama   galiɲ / ŋabi*
    WHERE-ALL THIS SORT-ABS person-ABS go-PRES lots-ABS
    gaḍa
    white man-ABS
    Where are these sort of people going? – all these white men

and inanimate reference in:

(193) *ŋayu dubu:rḍi   mayim   yiŋarimu*
    I-SA stomach-COMIT-ABS food-CAU THIS SORT-CAU
    buga:ḍiɲum
    eat-:ḍi-CAU SUBORD
    I'm full from eating this sort of food

As with all *yi*-initial deictics, there are corresponding forms beginning
with *ŋu-* and *yu-*. Semantically, *yiŋariɲ* 'this sort of thing' contrasts with
ŋuŋariɲ 'that sort of thing' – the 'this/that' distinction is shown either
deictically (by pointing) or perhaps in terms of textual anaphora.
yuŋariɲ then implies 'yet another sort of thing'. For instance:

(194) *ŋayu wunaɲ yiŋariɲḍal*
    I'll sleep on this sort [of ground]

(195) *ɲundu wunaɲ ŋuŋariɲḍal ḍabu:*
    [Whereas] you [prefer to] sleep on that sort of ground

TABLE 3.8   *Inflectional paradigm for yiɲariɲ/waɳḍariɲ*

	'this kind of'	'what kind of'
absolutive (SO)	*yiɲa:riɲ*	*waɳḍa:riɲ*
ergative (A)	*yiɲariɳḍu*	*waɳḍariɳḍu*
dative	*yiɲarinda*	*waɳḍarinda*
purposive	*yiɲariɲgu*	*waɳḍariɲgu*
causal–ablative	*yiɲarimu*	*waɳḍarimu*
locative–allative–instrumental	*yiɲariɳḍa(l)*	*waɳḍariɳḍa(l)*
fear	*yiɲariɳḍida*	*waɳḍariɳḍida*
genitive stem	*yiɲarini-*	*waɳḍarini-*
comitative stem	*yiɲariɳḍi-*	*waɳḍariɳḍi-*

(196) *ɲaḍin bimbi wunaŋ yuɲariɳḍal ḍabu:*
    [And] my father [prefers to] sleep on another sort of ground
    (i.e. on a different type of soil)

yiɲariɲ and *ɲuɲariɲ* are employed quite frequently in texts 2 and 9.
Note particularly their use in referring to different types of food – in
line 10 of text 9 *ɲuɲariɲ miɲa* 'that sort of meat' refers to the stew
served up in the early days of the mission; in line 31 *yiɲariɲ* describes
ripe bananas and suchlike (the only sort of food the white superintendent
gave the boys to eat) and in line 34 *ɲuɲariɲ mayi* refers to traditional food,
which the boys would go off into the bush to procure as soon as they
were old enough.

The occurrence of *yiɲariɲ* and *waɳḍariɲ* with the nominal affix *-bara* is
exemplified in (72–3) above.

It is instructive to compare *waɳḍariɲ* with *waɲira* and *waɲi* (3.7.1).
waɲi assumes no knowledge of the object that attention is being focused
on, and enquires about (at least) its genus. *waɲira* assumes that the genus
is known, and enquires about the species. *waɳḍariɲ* presupposes the
species but asks about the characteristics of a particular token of this
type. Thus, we might get (cf. (164)):

(197)   Question   Answer
    waɲi 'what is it?'   *miɲa* 'an [edible] animal'
    waɲi:ra miɲa 'what type   *gangu:l* 'a grey wallaby'
    of animal is it?'

waɲḍa:riɲ gangu:l 'what   *gangu:l ɲalal* 'a big grey
kind of grey wallaby   wallaby'
is it ?'

It might be appropriate to refer to *waɲḍariɲ* as indefinite/interrogative (not just 'interrogative'), following our treatment of *waɲi* and *waɲa*. However, no instance of *waɲḍariɲ* has been encountered in which the sense is simply indefinite (without any concomitant question). (But *waɲḍariɲ* has not, in fact, been encountered very frequently.)

3.7.7 waɲḍirI 'how many'. There is an interrogative number adjective *waɲḍirI* 'how many'. This is the only grammatical form demanding a root-final morphophoneme (2.3.4). It reduces, by Rule 2, in the absolutive:

(198) *waɲḍi:r*   *ɲuni:nda mayi*
HOW MANY-ABS you-DAT fruit-ABS
How many fruit have you got ?

The third vowel of the root appears before a non-zero inflection:

(199) *ɲuniɲ bama:l*   *waɲḍiriŋgu*   *wawa:l*
you-O person-ERG HOW MANY-ERG see-PAST
How many people saw you ?

The reply to (198) or (199) could involve *yarga* 'none, nothing', *ɲabi* 'many, a lot', *muɲḍuɽU* 'a great many' or a specific number adjective *guman* 'one', *ḍambulA* 'two' or *dagul* 'three'.

In one text *waɲḍirI* co-occurs with *ɲabi*:

(200) *bama waɲḍi:r ɲinaŋ ɲabi*
How many comprise the crowd sitting [here] ?

It is likely that in (200) *waɲḍi:r* is enquiring as to how many tribes the crowd of people represent.

3.7.8 Time interrogatives. The locative form of the inanimate interrogative, *waɲḍa*, normally enquires about spatial position – 'where'. But it has been encountered with a temporal sense, 'when':

(201) *ɲundu:ba yiŋgu*   *giyi*   *wayu*   /   *miɲa*   *waɲḍa*
you all-SA here-ALL DON'T long time animal-ABS 'WHEN'
garu   *ɲundu ɲuɲu*   *dugal*
by-and-by you-SA THAT-ABS catch-PRES
Don't you [sit] here too long! When are you going to catch that fish ?

There are also cases where *waɲḍa* corresponds to the 'relative pronoun' sense of 'when' in English:

(202) *garu   bama   waɲḍa   ɲalalŋalaldaga:ɲ*   /
      by-and-by person-ABS 'WHEN' big-REDUP-INCHO-PAST
      ḍuruḍurudaga:ɲ   / bama   ɲuŋgum   gunugunu
      adult man-INCHO-PAST PERSON-ABS THERE-ABL fight-ABS
      ḍara:ḍiɲu
      stand-*:ḍi*-PAST

   Later on, when the people had [grown] really big, had become
   adult men, they fought [in retribution for the crime they had
   committed as children]

Following the normal Yidiɲ pattern, *waɲḍa* can have an indefinite as well as (or instead of) an interrogative meaning; this extends to the time sense. Thus, in line 48 of text 2, *waɲḍa guygaguygam* means 'sometime in the evening'.

Informants did not use *waɲḍa* in translation of English sentences involving 'when', preferring to employ *waɲḍirimay* (see below) or to use a subordinate clause construction (4.4). *waɲḍa* is primarily a locational form (and was used exclusively as such in elicitation); but there are in texts a fair sprinkling of undoubtedly temporal uses, such as (201–2).

There are other examples of temporal use of words whose primary reference is locational. Thus *bidi* 'close by' (3.4.1) has the sense 'just now' in

(203) *yiɲu   gumba   mura:nḍidaga:ɲ*   / *bidi*
      THIS-ABS girl-ABS sickness-COMIT-INCHO-PAST 'just now'
      ɲina:ɲum
      sit-CAU SUBORD

   This girl has [suddenly] become sick, after having just now been
   sitting [here feeling alright]

Similarly *ɲuŋgum* – 'from there', ablative of the inanimate deictic – can have a time meaning 'and then' or 'from that time'; see (202) above and text 2, line 63.

ɲuŋgum exactly parallels *baɲum* 'from there, then' in Dyirbal (Dixon 1972: 115). The English narrative style of Yidiɲḍi (and some Dyirbalŋan) informants makes heavy use of 'from there' in places where 'when' would be expected.

   Dick Moses used the form *waɲḍaɲunda* 'when' in text 2, line 80, but later suggested that this was really a Dya:bugay form (Hale reports *ḍa:ɲunda* 'when'

in Dya:bugay) giving *waɲḍirimay* as the correct Yidiɲ equivalent. Compare *waɲḍaɲunda* with *yaluɲunda* 'today', a form that is attested in both coastal and tablelands dialects of Yidiɲ. (*-ɲunda* occurs as a locational affix 'some-where' in the central dialect of Dyirbal. Note that *yalu* is a Dyirbal form 'to this place', but that *-ɲunda* has not been encountered as an affix to *yalu* in Dyirbal – Dixon 1972: 57, 261.)

The most usual time interrogatives are derived from number inter-rogative *waɲḍirI* 'how many'. There are two affixes, *-may* and *-m*, which can only have time reference:

> suffix *-may* 'at — days'   giving *waɲḍirimay* 'when?'
> *-m* 'during — days'   *waɲḍirim* 'how long?'

We can literally interpret *waɲḍirimay* as 'at how many [days]' and *waɲḍirim* as 'during how many [days]'.

It was mentioned in 3.5 that time qualifiers fall into two sets – point-time and durational. *waɲḍirimay* belongs to the first set and would be appropriately answered by a point time qualifier:

(204) Q – *ɲundu waɲḍirimay gadaŋ*   When will you come?
       A – *ŋayu gadaŋ ŋaḍa*   I'll come tomorrow

(205) Q – *waɲḍirimay ɲundu garu duguɽ balgal*
       When are you going to build the house?
       A – *ŋayu wambaŋ/ ginda:n garu muyubara budi:ḍiŋ*
       I'll wait [until] by-and-by the new moon lies [in the sky]
       (i.e. until next month)

waɲḍirim belongs to the durational set, and should be answered by specification of a time-span:

(206) Q – *ɲundu waɲḍi:rim wunaŋ*   How long are you going to sleep
                                        for?
       A – *ŋayu wayu wunaŋ*   I'll sleep [for] a long time

These two time interrogatives can refer either to the future, as in (204–6), or to the past:

(207) *ɲundu:ba waɲḍirimay yiŋgu:ruɲ yiŋgu gada:ɲ*
       When did you [all] come this way here?

(208) *yiɲu buɲa waɲḍi:rim wuna:ɲ*
       How long has this woman been sleeping for?

8

The directionality of time reference in sentences like (204–8) must be deduced from the tense, any time qualifier in the sentence, and from the context. (Thus *garu* 'later on, by-and-by' in (205) underlines the future reference suggested by the non-past tense in this sentence.)

waɲḍirimay behaves like other point time qualifiers in taking the suffixes (3.5):

-*gu* 'until'
-*mu* 'since'

For instance:

(209) *ɲundu waɲḍirima:ygu galiŋ*
> Until when are you going to continue going? (This sentence was glossed by an informant as 'what time are you going to come back?')

(210) *ɲundu waɲḍirima:ymu gadaŋ*
> When did you start coming? (The informant's gloss was 'From what time you come?')

waɲḍirimaygu and *waɲḍirimaymu* thus have durational reference like *waɲḍirim*. There is a major difference: *waɲḍirim* could just be enquiring as to whether something was done for a long time or a short time (irrespective of the locus of the period), whereas *waɲḍirimaygu* and *waɲḍirimaymu* normally assume that one end-point of the time-span is the present and ask how far away (in the future or past) the other point is. *waɲḍirim* also has a sense which is identical to *waɲḍirimaygu/waɲḍirimaymu*, but it cannot explicitly distinguish between future and past as the durationals derived from *waɲḍirimay* do.

waɲḍarim, like other durational time qualifiers, cannot take -*gu* or -*mu*.

Both *waɲḍirimay* and *waɲḍirim* commonly take the comitative affix -*ḍi* – 3.3.4 (but note that -*ḍi* will not normally co-occur with suffixes -*gu*/-*mu*):

(211) *waɲḍirimḍi ɲundu ɲinaŋadaŋ*
> How many days are you going to come and sit here for? (This was the exact gloss volunteered by the informant – note the inclusion of 'how many [days]', which directly relates to the root *waɲḍirI* 'how many'.)

Affixes -*may* and -*m* can also be suffixed to number adjectives. Thus with *ḍambulA* 'two' we get

> *ḍambulamay* 'in two [days'] or 'two [days] ago'
> *ḍambulam* 'for two [days]'

ḍambulamay occurs in text 14, line 22; and in:

(212) *ŋaḍin bimbi ḍambulamay wula:ɲ*
   My father died two days ago

These forms are also commonly found with comitative *-ḍi*. Thus, an answer to (206) or (211) could be:

(213) *ŋayu wunaŋ(/ɲinaŋ) ḍambulamḍi*
   I'll stay [here] for two nights (days)

Almost all the examples of *-may* and *-m* involve *waŋḍirI* or *ḍambulA*. These affixes were elicited with *dagul* 'three' as *dagulamay, dagulam*. This suggests allomorphic alternation: *-amay, -am* after consonants; *-may, -m* after vowels. However, more examples would be needed before this could be put forward as a generalisation. It was not possible to elicit *-(a)may, -(a)m* with *ŋabi* 'many' or *guman* 'one'.

3.7.9   Other interrogatives. A further interrogative *waɲinbara:* 'what's the matter, what for?' is attested only in the coastal dialect (and occurs there fairly commonly):

(214) *buriburi yiŋu mura:nḍi wunaŋ/ waɲinbara:*
   This old man is lying sick, [I wonder] what's the matter [with him]

(215) *ɲuniɲ waŋḍu bunḍa:ɲ/ waɲinbara:*
   Someone hit you – what for?

(216) *ŋaɲaɲ waɲinbara: ŋuɲḍu:ŋ wawa:l*
   What's the matter with him looking at me all the time (= What
      is he looking at me all the time for?)

waɲinbara: does not inflect. (Note that it can not – synchronically at least – be analysed in terms of the nominal affix *-bara* 'belonging to' and locative inflection. *-bara* can in fact be added to *waŋḍa* – but not *waɲin* – and the resulting form does take case inflections – see (190).)

Finally, there is a rather infrequent form *waŋḍuluy* 'how, which way'. This is also restricted to the coastal dialect, and seems to be a separate item from tablelands *waŋḍaluy* 'in which direction' (3.7.2). A possible response to

(217) *ɲundu waŋḍu:luy ḍugi gunda:l*   How did you cut the tree?
might then be

(218) *ŋayu guriɲ gunda:l*   I cut it well (= properly)

8-2

3.8   Morphology of verbs and adverbs

3.8.1   Verbal word structure. Verbs and adverbs are morphologically identical. They are, like other parts of speech, entirely suffixing.

The prefix *ḍa:-* is attested only with *wurga-n* 'yawn' – 3.4.3. Noun incorporation could perhaps be regarded as a type of prefixation; it is dealt with in 6.1.1.

We can distinguish two kinds of verbal affix:

[1] INFLECTIONAL SUFFIXES

   (a) past tense *-ɲu ~ -l+ɲu ~ -ṛ+ɲu*
   (b) present–future (= non-past) tense *-ŋ ~ -l ~ -ṛ*
   (c) imperative *-n ~ ø ~ -r*
   (d) purposive *-na ~ -l+na ~ -ṛ+na*
   (e) dative subordinate *-ɲu+nda ~ -l+ɲu+nda ~ -ṛ+ɲu+nda*
   (f) causal subordinate *-ɲu+m ~ -l+ɲu+m ~ -ṛ+ɲu+m*
   (g) 'lest' *-n+ḍi ~ -l+ḍi ~ -ṛ+ḍi*

(a–d) occur on the verbs in a main clause; (d–g) mark the verbs of a subordinate clause. Note here that (d) has dual function – 4.5.

(a–f) cannot be followed by any further affix (except post-inflectional affixes, which can be added to a word from any part of speech, following any type of inflection). (g) takes a nominal case, agreeing with the case of the 'common NP' in the main clause – 4.6.2.

[2] DERIVATIONAL SUFFIXES

   (a) comitative *-ŋa-l ~ -l+maŋa-l ~ -ṛ+maŋa-l*
(Care should be taken to distinguish verbal comitative from nominal comitatives *-ḍi ~ -yi* and *-muḍay*. The syntactic correspondence between these suffixes – which is our justification for employing the same name – is described in 4.3.3.)

   (b) *-:ḍi-n ~ -:ṛ+ḍi-n*. This suffix has a variety of syntactic and semantic effects; most prominently, it marks a construction as 'antipassive' or 'reflexive' (4.2). There is no suitable single name and so we shall refer to this – perhaps the most important syntactic affix in Yidiɲ – simply as *-:ḍi-n*.

   (c) aspectual

     (c-i) 'going' *-ŋali-n ~ -:li-n ~ -:ṛi-n ~ -:ri-n*
     (c-ii) 'coming' *-ŋada-n ~ -:l+da-n ~ -:da-n*

A further type of 'reduplicated aspect', in the tablelands dialect only, is dealt with in 3.8.6.

There is one further derivational affix, -:n+biḏi-n. This is poorly attested, and appears only to occur with a limited set of verbs. It is dealt with in 3.8.8.

(a) and (b), unlike (c), can affect the syntactic function of stems to which they are affixed. Comitative occurs ONLY with an intransitive stem, and ALWAYS derives a transitive form. -:ḏi-n occurs PREDOMI-NANTLY with transitives, and MOST FREQUENTLY derives an intransitive stem (if it occurs with an intransitive, the resulting stem MUST BE intransitive). Aspectual suffixes, on the other hand, occur freely with stems of BOTH transitivity types, and do NOT CHANGE this transitivity. An aspectual affix will simply specify that an action was performed during or after 'going' or 'coming' – 3.8.6.

A verb in Yidiɲ must involve a root, and a final inflectional suffix – one of (1a–g) above. Between root and inflection we can, optionally, have any one, two or all three of the derivational suffixes. Aspect may occur at two positions, but no examples of a repeated comitative or -:ḏi-n have been encountered.

Derivational affixes show the following ordering possibilities:

(i)   -:ḏi-n can occur before or after comitative.

(ii)   aspect must precede comitative (aspect can follow comitative only when there is also an aspectual affix preceding it).

(iii)   aspect must follow -:ḏi-n. (Aspect can only precede -:ḏi-n when comitative intervenes. We then have, by (ii), aspect preceding comitative; and, by (i), comitative preceding -:ḏi-n.)

If a simple table of 'affix orders' were constructed we would have to allow the 'threading' of the table to loop back to account for these orderings.

It is suggested in 5.4 that the comitative suffix is the realisation of a separate 'verb' in deep structure. Partly to reflect this, we can describe the ordering of verbal suffixes through rules:

(219) (a) V → ROOT (+ -:ḏi-n) (+ ASPECT) (+ V') + INFLECTION
         (b) V' → COMITATIVE (+ :ḏi-n) (+ ASPECT)

with the proviso that comitative can only be added to an intransitive stem (effectively, to an intransitive root, or to a transitive root with -:ḏi-n in antipassive or reflexive sense – 4.2.3–4).

One constraint is necessary on (219) – ASPECT can ONLY be specified in (b) IF there is also an ASPECT choice in (a); this is discussed in 3.8.6.

We are thus regarding COMITATIVE as a type of verb root, that can be followed by the same affixes, in the same order, as a lexical root; comitative and its affixes are then 'embedded' immediately before the inflection in the 'main' verb.

(219) would generate a verb with -:ḍi-n twice, so long as comitative intervened. As already mentioned, no verb with two occurrences of -:ḍi-n has been encountered. But it is possible that this is a shortcoming of the data collected rather than a constraint on the grammar.

The full paradigm for the main verbal suffixes is given in 3.8.2. Conjugations – their membership, transitivity and phonological features – are described in 3.8.3. We then describe, in turn, the forms and functions of the inflectional, syntactic derivational and aspectual affixes. 3.8.7 provides further discussion of affix combinations and deals with the possibility of a 'length conflict' between -:ḍi and an aspectual suffix.

Affixes -daga-n and -ŋa-l, which derive verbal stems from nominal and locational forms, are dealt with at 4.8.1.

3.8.2   Paradigm. Yidiɲ has three verbal conjugations; we refer to them in terms of the 'conjugation markers' -n, -l and -ɼ.

Verb roots are set up to end in a vowel; conjugation membership is then shown by a suffixed -n, -l or -ɼ in the citation form. Each derivational affix is specified for conjugation in the same way (the conjugation membership of a derived stem is independent of that of the underlying root).

The canonical forms of verbal suffixes are in table 3.9; these are in each case to be added to a verb-final root or stem. The ways in which the inflections are reduced by Rule 2 (2.3.2) are detailed in 3.8.4.

3.8.3   Conjugations and transitivity. Each verbal root and derived stem in Yidiɲ is strictly classified as either transitive or intransitive. There are a number of syntactic tests for transitivity – only a transitive verb can occur with an ergative NP; only an intransitive stem can take the verbal comitative suffix; and so on.

There is some statistical correlation between transitivity and conjugation membership, as can be seen from the distribution of the 293 verbal roots in the writer's corpus of everyday Yidiɲ:

TABLE 3.9   *Verbal suffixes*

conjugation:	*-n*	*-l*	*-ṟ*
INFLECTIONS			
present–future	- *ŋ*	*-l*	*-ṟ*
past	- *ɲu*	*-l+ɲu*	**-ṟ+ɲu*
imperative	*-n*	- *ø*	*-r*
purposive	- *na*	*-l+na*	*-ṟ+na*
dative subordinate	- *ɲu+nda*	*-l+ɲu+nda*	*-ṟ+ɲu+nda*
causal subordinate	- *ɲu+m*	*-l+ɲu+m*	*-ṟ+ɲu+m*
'lest'	*-n+ḍi*	*-l+ḍi*	*-ṟ+ḍi*
DERIVATIONS			
comitative	- *ŋa-l*	*-l+maŋa-l*	*-ṟ+maŋa-l*
-:*ḍi-n*	-: *ḍi-n*	-: *ḍi-n*	-:*ṟ+ḍi-n*
'going' aspect			
unmarked	- *ŋali-n*	-:*li-n*	-:*ṟi-n*
before *-ŋa-l*	-: *ri-n*	-:*ri-n*	-:*ri-n*
'coming' aspect	- *ŋada-n*	-:*l+da-n*	-: *da-n*

* Postulated canonical form – this is in fact always reduced by Rule 2. See 3.8.4.

conjugation	*-n*	*-l*	*-ṟ*	total
intransitive	87	23	2	112
transitive	68	100	13	181
	155	123	15	293

Thus, 81 % of *-l* conjugation and 87 % of *-ṟ* conjugation roots are transitive; but 56 % of *-n* conjugation forms are intransitive. Note also that comitative *-ŋa-l*, which derives transitive stems, belongs to the *-l* conjugation. The major function of - :*ḍi-n* is to derive intransitive from transitive stems (in its minor functions it leaves transitivity unchanged); a - :*ḍi-n* form always belongs to the *-n* conjugation.

The corresponding figures for the corpus of verbal roots in Dyalŋuy are:

conjugation	*-n*	*-l*	*-ṟ*	total
intransitive	20	1	–	21
transitive	8	19	3	30
	28	20	3	51

yielding similar percentage figures.

But note that many Dyalŋuy verbs appear to involve a derivational affix – for instance 'bathe' is *yiraba:ḍi-n* and 'dig' *burganbaŋa-l* (*yiraba-* and *burganba-* do not occur outside these words). In fact, of the intransitive roots in Dyalŋuy ten end in -:*ḍi-n*, and amongst the transitives seven show final -*ŋa-l*.

Information on Dyalŋuy was difficult to obtain and it has not been possible rigorously to check transitivity in each case (as it was for verbs in everyday Yidiɲ); the figures above include some 'unconfirmed' assignments.

Since the -*ṟ* conjugation is so small, by comparison with the -*n* and -*l* classes, we can usefully list all its members:

Everyday Yidiɲ – Intransitive
bayga-ṟ 'feel sore, have pain'   *ḍuɲḍa-ṟ* 'wade across stream'
Everyday Yidiɲ – Transitive
baḍa-ṟ 'leave'   *gayba-ṟ* 'make body feel good'
balŋa-ṟ 'hit with a stick'   *gaymba-ṟ* 'follow, sneak up on'
banḍa-ṟ 'follow'   *ɲirḍa-ṟ* 'put sitting down'
bunḍu-ṟ '(doctor) wipe(s) off pain'   *walŋgu-ṟ* 'peep in/around'
buybu-ṟ 'blow, spit at'   *yaga-ṟ* 'hunt away'
daḍu-ṟ 'put blanket down' (T)   *yumba-ṟ* 'send message'
danda-ṟ 'rub'
Dyalŋuy style – Transitive
nayɲu-ṟ 'throw'   *ɲuɲḍu-ṟ* and *ɲuŋga-ṟ* 'smell'

Note that Dya:bugay has conjugations corresponding to Yidiɲ's -*n* and -*l* classes, but lacks a third -*ṟ* conjugation.

Just 95 % of verb roots in Yidiɲ are disyllabic. There are no monosyllabic roots at all. Of the thirteen trisyllabics all but one belong to the -*n* conjugation. Two quadrisyllabics are known, one from each of the major conjugations.

The full list of trisyllabics is:
Intransitive -*n* conjugation
bambaṟa-n 'be frightened, nervous'   *ḍaḍama-n* 'jump over'
dandaba-n 'dance around, feeling   *ḍugarba-n* 'have unsettled mind'
    lively and pugnacious'   *maḍinda-n* 'walk up'
daɲḍiri-n 'feel frisky'   *waymbala-n* 'roll'
daraba-n 'shake, rinse mouth, etc.'   *yilari-n* 'be scattered, spread about'
Transitive -*n* conjugation
barganda-n 'pass by'   *wuŋaba-n* 'look for [meat], hunt'
dandada-n '(doctor) rub(s)'
Transitive -*l* conjugation
binaŋa-l 'tell, warn'

Although *binaṛa-l* looks as if it involves comitative or causative *-ṛa-l* there is no form *binar* known in Yidiɲ. Compare *binaṛa-l* 'warn' with the derived *binaɲa-l* 'listen' (based on *bina* 'ear', through the 'causative' verbaliser *-ɲa-l* – 4.8.1).

The two quadrisyllabic roots are both transitive:

binagali-n 'forget'   *lululumba-l* 'rock baby to sleep'

lululumba-l has an onomatopoeic origin being based on the lilting '*lu-lu-lu*...' which is sung whilst rocking a child to sleep. It is the only *l*- initial word known (outside loans from English) – 2.1.2.

Only about one half of Dyalŋuy verb roots are disyllabic. There are seventeen trisyllabics and quadrisyllabics whose final syllable is -:*ḍi-n* or *-ṛa-l* and in addition seven trisyllabic roots which show no evidence of (historically) involving a derivational affix.

The probabilities for vowels in the first syllable of a verb are the same as those for the first syllable of a noun or adjective (2.1.3):

$$a \quad 0.41 \qquad i \quad 0.20 \qquad u \quad 0.39$$

But the second vowel position of a disyllabic verb root shows markedly different preferences:

$$a \quad 0.67 \qquad i \quad 0.30 \qquad u \quad 0.03$$

There is little difference between the two main conjugations and between transitivity classes qua *-a/-i* distribution (for instance, 33 % of *-n* conjugation verbs as against 28 % of *-l* conjugation roots have *-i* as second vowel).

Only seven *-u*-final roots are known in everyday Yidiɲ. Four of these are in the small *-ṛ* conjugation (listed above). The others are:

intransitive:	transitive:
ḍuyu-n '(long thing) wriggle(s)'	*ḍadu-l* 'put blanket down' (C)
	waḍu-l 'cook, burn'

There are three *-u*-final roots attested in the Dyalŋuy style – two in the *-ṛ* conjugation and:

gilḍu-l 'bite'

Examination of the allomorphs in table 3.9 reveals that almost all the forms in the middle column begin with *-l-*, those in the right-hand column have an initial *-ṛ-*, while the left-hand column lacks any corresponding segment (initial *-n-* crops up just in the 'lest' row).

There are three ways of dealing with this (cf. Householder 1971: 218ff.). Firstly, we could simply list allomorphs – purposive *-na* ~ *-lna*

~ -*ɽna*, and so on – without any attempt at further segmentation; this would, however, fail to bring out the recurrent pattern of initial *ø/-l-/-ɽ-* in the paradigm.

The second alternative would be to assign a final -*l* or -*ɽ* to the verb roots. This would certainly relate together the recurrent segments in table 3.9. But we would need to have a rule deleting – or substituting for – the final root segment for imperative, and in a few other cases. And we would either have to have an -*n* conjugation root ending in -*n*, but delete this before most inflections, or have it ending in a vowel, and then include a rule inserting -*n*- before the 'lest' suffix.

These suggestions involve segmenting say *wawa:lna* 'go-PURPOSIVE'

$$\text{into (1) } wawa + lna$$
$$\text{or into (2) } wawal + na$$

(Vowel length is, of course, inserted by Rule 1.)

The third alternative is to recognise the -*l*- as a separate morpheme, a 'conjugation marker':

$$\text{(3) } wawa + l + na$$

We would now state verb structure as

ROOT (+ CONJ. MARKER + DERIVATIONAL AFFIX)...
+ CONJ. MARKER + INFLECTION

This leads to the recognition of a single form for each inflection (except present and imperative) and for derivational -*:ḍi-n*:

past -*ɲu*	causal subordinate -*ɲu* + *m*
purposive -*na*	'lest' -*ḍi*
dative subordinate -*ɲu* + *nda*	antipassive etc. - *:ḍi-n*

We now simply have to state that conjugational marker -*ɽ*- appears before each of these suffixes, -*l*- occurs before all except antipassive -*:ḍi-n*, and -*n*- appears only before 'lest' -*ḍi*.

Comitative and aspectual suffixes involve more complex allomorphic alternation – but conjugation marker -*l*- can again be recognised, before comitative -*maɲa-l* and 'coming' -*:da-n*, and -*ɽ*- before comitative -*maɲa-l*. Further, the first syllable of the unmarked form of 'going' aspect clearly relates to the conjugation marker for the -*l* and -*ɽ* conjugations.

Present tense simply involves the conjugation markers -*l* and -*ɽ* with no further affix. For the -*n* conjugation we add -*ŋ*. Imperatives differ

from conjugation to conjugation: add *-n* in the left-hand column, use the bare root in the centre column, and add *-r* (which is phonetically close to the conjugation marker) on the right-hand side.

We choose *-n* (rather than, say, zero or *-ŋ*) as conjugation marker for the predominantly intransitive class (1) because this segment does appear in the 'conjugation marker slot' af the 'lest' row, and also functions as imperative suffix; and (2) because of the evidence from reduplication (3.8.9). Verbal reduplication repeats a disyllabic root and can also include the conjugation marker. Examples of past tense forms are:

unreduplicated	*reduplicated*
bulba:l 'ground'	*bulbalbulba:l* 'ground a lot'
baṇḍa:ɽ 'followed'	*baṇḍaɽbaṇḍa:ɽ* 'followed quickly'
buga:ɲ 'ate'	*buganbuga:ɲ* 'ate a lot/ate fast'

The statement of reduplication is plainly simplified if we set up *-n-* as conjugation marker, on a par with *-l-* and *-ɽ-*.

Note that our recognising the conjugation marker as a separate morpheme gains support from details of the application of Rule 2. Since *wawa + l + ɲu* 'see-PAST' reduces to *wawa:l*, a morpheme boundary must appear immediately before the *-l-*, to satisfy the condition on Rule 2.

Alternatively, we could say that *-l-* must be recognised as a separate morpheme – and not part of the root – IN ORDER TO JUSTIFY the morpheme boundary condition on Rule 2.

3.8.4 Inflections. Table 3.10 illustrates verbal inflections for the three conjugations and for verbs of differing syllabicity. All the inflections are phonologically cohering (2.4).

Only one trisyllabic root is known for the *-l* conjugation, and this is used in table 3.10. The comitative affix *-ŋa-l* freely derives trisyllabic *-l* stems, which inflect in exactly the same pattern (3.8.5). No trisyllabic roots are known for the *-ɽ* conjugation, nor is there any affix that derives an *-ɽ* conjugation stem.

Quadrisyllabic stems inflect exactly like disyllabics, and quinque-syllabics like trisyllabics; and so on.

Taking the inflections in turn:

[a] PRESENT/FUTURE TENSE *-ŋ ∼ -l ∼ -ɽ*

This is used for any non-past reference. It is most frequently employed for referring to the present (which can be taken to include immediate

TABLE 3.10   *Verbal inflectional paradigm*

root	gali-n 'go'	maḍinda-n 'walk up'	wawa-l 'see'	binarŋa-l 'warn'	bada-ṟ 'leave'
present–future	galiŋ	maḍi:ndaŋ	wawal	bina:rŋal	baḍaṟ
past	gali:ɲ	maḍindaɲu	wawa:l	binarŋalɲu	baḍa:ṟ
imperative	galin	maḍi:ndan	wawa	bina:rŋa	baḍar
purposive	gali:na	maḍindana	wawa:lna	binarŋalna	baḍa:ṟna
dative subord.	galiɲunda	maḍindaɲu:n	wawalɲunda	binarŋalɲu:n	baḍaṟɲunda
causal subord.	gali:ɲum	maḍindaɲum	wawa:lɲum	binarŋalɲum	baḍa:ṟɲum
'lest'+ abs.	gali:nḍi	maḍindanḍi	wawa:lḍi	binarŋalḍi	baḍa:ṟḍi

past and immediate future) and we normally term it just 'present' in textual glossing. But it can also be used for prediction about the future, contrasting here with purposive which details future obligation or necessity (4.5.2). Non-past and past are nicely contrasted in:

(220) waɲḍa:ruɲ   garu   ŋayu magil   /
    WHERE-ALL DIRN by-and-by I-SA climb up-PRES/FUT
    ŋayu wurba:ḍiɲu
    I-SA look for-PAST
    I looked to see which way I [could] climb up, by-and-by

[b] PAST TENSE *-ɲu ~ -l+ɲu ~ *-ṟ+ɲu*

-ɲu and *-l+ɲu* are set up as the canonical forms of this suffix in the two main conjugations – they are reduced, by Rule 2, to -*:ɲ* and -*:l* after even-syllabled stems. All -*ṟ* conjugation stems are disyllabic and past tense is always -*:ṟ*. We can set up underlying *-*ṟ*+*ɲu*, which is then obligatorily reduced to -*:ṟ* (that is, the conditions on Rule 2 are ALWAYS met). There is no justification for this step, other than overall symmetry and economy (we prefer to allow length to be specified by Rule 1, rather than adding to the list of affixes that have inherent length – 2.3.5, 2.3.8).

Note that subordinate inflections appear to involve the addition of *-nda* and *-m* to a form identical to past tense; and *-ɲu-* does show up in these circumstances for the -*ṟ* conjugation.

Past tense is the normal choice in narrative (although present is sometimes employed). The majority of verbs in Yidiɲ texts are in either past or present inflection; study of the occurrence of these tenses in the texts given at pages 513–39, and in examples, will indicate further details of use.

[c] IMPERATIVE *-n ~ ø ~ -r*

This is used in both positive and negative imperative constructions; a full account of the syntax of imperatives is in 4.9.

Most Australian languages have a syllabic affix for the imperative – often *-ga ~ -ya ~ -la* etc. (Dixon 1972: 15–16). Dyirbal is unusual qua Australian languages (although conforming to a general trend in languages outside the continent) in having just the root as imperative, without even a conjugation marker (Dixon 1972: 110–11). Yidiɲ is part-way between Dyirbal and the Australian norm – it uses just the root for one conjugation but adds a minimal (consonantal) suffix in the other two cases.

[d] PURPOSIVE *-na ~ -l+na ~ -r+na*

Purposive is one of the two verbal exceptions to the operation of Rule 2; although it meets all the conditions it is not reduced (there is discussion of this in 2.3.3). This inflection can occur on the verb in a main clause, in place of tense or imperative; and it can also mark a subordinate clause, paralleling *-ɲu+nda* and *-ɲu+m*. A detailed account of its meaning and function will be found in 4.5.

Most Australian languages have a purposive inflection on verbs with similar meaning to that in Yidiɲ, but the form is normally *-gu* (being identical to nominal purposive). It is valid to ask how Yidiɲ came to have the unusual form *-na* for purposive.

Compare the main verbal inflections in Dya:bugay (Hale 1976a: 238) with those in the two corresponding conjugations of Yidiɲ:

Dya:bugay			Yidiɲ	
-n	*-l*	CONJUGATION	*-n*	*-l*
-n	ø	imperative	*-n*	ø
-ɲ	*-ɲ*	past	*-ɲu*	*-l+ɲu*
-ŋ	*-l*	present ⎫	*-ŋ*	*-l*
-na	*-lna*	future ⎭		
-yŋgu	*-luŋ*	purposive	*-na*	*-l+na*

It is most plausible to suggest that the proto-system was similar to that in modern Dya:bugay, and that Yidiɲ has (i) dropped the original purposive,

(ii) shifted future -*na* to a purposive sense, and (iii) generalised present also to cover future. Common Australian purposive -*gu* is plainly part of the -*yŋgu* allomorph in Dya:bugay (and we can wonder whether -*luŋ* might be a reduction from something like -*luŋgu*).

[e] DATIVE SUBORDINATE -*ɲu* + *nda* ~ -*l* + *ɲu* + *nda* ~ -*ɽ* + *ɲu* + *nda*

When suffixed to an odd-syllabled stem this reduces regularly, by Rule 2, giving -*ɲu:n* and -*lɲu:n* (there are no odd-syllabled stems in the -*ɽ* conjugation).

A -*ɲu* + *nda* inflection marks the verb in an 'unmarked' subordinate (relative-type) clause. Full details are in 4.4.1–3.

[f] CAUSAL SUBORDINATE -*ɲu* + *m* ~ -*l* + *ɲu* + *m* ~ -*ɽ* + *ɲu* + *m*

Since it ends in a consonant, causal subordinate does not reduce. Verbs in 'perfective' subordinate clauses show this inflection – 4.4.5–7.

We demonstrate, in 4.4.6, a syntactic connection between

nominal dative -*nda* and verbal inflection -*ɲu* + *nda*

and a parallel connection between

nominal causal -*mu* ~ -*m* (and -*nim*) and verbal inflection -*ɲu* + *m*.

It is in view of this, and the formal similarity, that we choose the names 'dative subordinate' and 'causal subordinate'.

Any analysis must surely focus on the common first syllable, -*ɲu*-, in the two subordinate inflections. One way of doing this is simply to recognise a morpheme boundary in the middle of each ending – -*ɲu* + *nda* and -*ɲu* + *m*. We can then say that -*ɲu*- is the 'foundation' for subordinate verb marking, to which is added the relevant nominal inflection.

Although this -*ɲu* may well be historically related to past tense -*ɲu* (we have no evidence one way or the other) they could scarcely be equated, in a synchronic analysis.

It is in fact necessary to recognise a morpheme boundary in the middle of -*ɲu* + *nda* in order to explain its reduction by Rule 2. Note that although reduction proceeds regularly here, nominal dative -*nda* is an exception to Rule 2. We suggested (3.3.3, 2.3.2) that the non-reduction of nominal -*nda* may be explained in terms of its being a recent shortening of *-*ŋunda*. But surely the same considerations should apply to -*nda* in -*ɲu* + *nda*? It may be significant that if nominal -*nda* did reduce it would fall together with genitive -:*n*, whereas the reduced form of -*ɲu* + *nda* is quite distinct from every other verbal ending (2.3.3).

It is of course POSSIBLE that we had the following time ordering of changes: (1) *-ŋunda* reduces to *-nda* in verbal inflection; (2) Rule 2 introduced; (3) *-ŋunda* reduces to *-nda* in nominal inflection. But since we have no way at all of verifying such an ordering it is surely invalid to put forward an explanation in these terms.

The last part of causal subordinate is *-m*, whatever the syllabicity, whereas nominal causal/ablative shows *-m* after an even-syllabled and *-mu* with an odd-syllabled stem ending in a vowel. Note that *-m* is also found (again, irrespective of syllabicity) in the special genitive + causal/ablative inflection *-nim* (3.3.3).

We suggested (2.3.3, 3.3.2) that ablative–causal allomorph *-m* should perhaps be synchronically derived from canonical *-mu*. But this may not be its historical origin. Note that Dya:bugay has ablative *-mu* following a consonant but *-malim* after a vowel. It could be that Yidiɲ *-m* is a reduction from something like *-malim*. *-m* is the invariant form in *-ŋu + m* and *-nim* (following a vowel is each case) but is restricted to even-syllabled stems in regular ablative–causal inflection. This suggests that Yidiɲ may have replaced *-m* by *-mu* on an odd-syllabled stem ending in a vowel (by analogy with the post-consonantal allomorph), the better to meet its syllabicity target.

[g] 'LEST' *-n + ḍi ~ -l + ḍi ~ -ṛ + ḍi*

This does not reduce, providing the final exception to Rule 2. *-ḍi* marks the verb in a special type of subordinate clause, that normally has an NP in common with the main clause. A case ending, agreeing with that on the common NP in the matrix clause, is added to the 'lest' affix on the subordinate clause verb. Full discussion and exemplification is in 4.6.2.

3.8.5 Syntactic derivational affixes. There are two derivational affixes with syntactic effect:

[a] COMITATIVE *-ŋa-l ~ -l + maŋa-l ~ -ṛ + maŋa-l*

This occurs only with an intransitive root or stem and derives a transitive stem. It can have an 'accompanitive' meaning:

(221) *ŋayu wagal ɲina:ŋal*   I'm sitting with [my] wife

or a more 'causative' sense:

(222) *ŋaɲaɲ mayi:ŋ gamaŋalɲu*   The fruit made me vomit

(223) *bama:l ŋuɲu wanda:riŋa:l*
> A person made that [man] go and fall down (i.e. knocked him down)

A full account of the syntax and semantics of verbal comitatives is in
4.3.

Comitatives inflect exactly like -*l* conjugation roots, with the same
syllabicity-determined alternations of past and dative subordinate. We
can illustrate sample inflections on to comitatives derived from
disyllabic roots of each conjugation, and from a trisyllabic -*n*
conjugation root. (All -*ɽ* conjugation roots are disyllabic, and the only
-*l* conjugation trisyllabic root is transitive.)

root	*gali-n*	*madinda-n*
	'go'	'walk up'
comitative stem	*galiŋa-l*	*madindaŋa-l*
present	*gali:ŋal*	*madindaŋal*
past	*galiŋalɲu*	*madindaŋa:l*
imperative	*gali:ŋ*	*madindaŋa*
purposive	*galiŋalna*	*madindaŋa:lna*
dative subord.	*galiŋalɲu:n*	*madindaŋalɲunda*

root	*magi-l*	*bayga-ɽ*
	'climb up'	'feel sore'
comitative stem	*magilmaŋa-l*	*baygaɽmaŋa-l*
present	*magilmaŋal*	*baygaɽmaŋal*
past	*magilmaŋa:l*	*baygaɽmaŋa:l*
imperative	*magilmaŋa*	*baygaɽmaŋa*
purposive	*magilmaŋa:lna*	*baygaɽmaŋa:lna*
dative subord.	*magilmaŋalɲunda*	*baygaɽmaŋalɲunda*

Past tense reduces with even-syllabled stems (*madindaŋa:l, magil-
maŋa:l*) and dative subordinate with odd-syllabled forms (*galiŋalɲu:n*)
exactly as the conditions for Rule 2 are satisfied. The -*ŋa-l* allomorph
(on -*l* and -*ɽ* conjugations) coheres, as do all monosyllabic and inflectional
affixes (2.4); the *maŋa-l* allomorph is, like all other polysyllabic suffixes,
non-cohering, and commences a fresh phonological word. ('Going'
and 'coming' aspects provide further examples of morphemes with one
monosyllabic, cohering allomorph and another disyllabic, non-cohering
alternant – 3.8.6.)

It is in fact not easy to tell whether -*maŋa-l* coheres. It only occurs with
disyllabic roots and we could attribute the reduction from *magi*+*l*+*maŋa*+

l+ɲu to *magilmaŋa:l* either to the quinquesyllabicity of the whole word (if *-maŋa-l* did cohere) or to the trisyllabicity of the second phonological word *#maŋa+l+ɲu* (if *-maŋa-l* did not cohere). The only possible criterion is stress – we get *mágilmaŋá:l*, *mágilmaŋá:lna* (not **magílmaŋá:l*, **magílmaŋá:lna*) indicating that there are two phonological words in each case.

(Note that it is difficult to be sure of stress in marginal cases like this. For one thing, there is always a tendency (2.6.1) to stress an initial syllable – so that a predicted form like *magílmaŋá:l* could on occasion be heard as *mágilmaŋá:l*. For another, the stress patterns on adjacent phonological words can sometimes (2.4) be rationalised into overall stress/unstress alternation – so that a predicted *mágilmaŋá:l* could conceivably be heard as *magilmaŋá:l*). The stress patterns heard do indicate that *-maŋa-l* is non-cohering, but the evidence is – by its nature – elusive. But note that all other disyllabic affixes are non-cohering and in each other case the evidence is quite conclusive – for instance *bigunU#muḍay* 'shield-COMITATIVE-ABSOLUTIVE' is realised as *bigu:nmuḍay* (2.4), and *maḍinda#ŋali+ɲu* 'walk up-GOING-PAST' is realised as *maḍi:ndaŋali:ɲ* (3.8.6).

When an even-syllabled *-n* conjugation root, such as *gali-n* 'go', occurs with comitative and imperative (which is zero in the *-l* conjugation) we get underlying *gali+ŋa+ø*. This reduces, by Rule 2, to *gali:ŋ*. Imperatives like *maḍinda+ŋa*, *magi+l+maŋa* and *bayga+ṛ+maŋa* are not reduced, since the syllabicity condition on Rule 2 is not met. (If comitative were *-ŋa-l* with *-l-* and *-ṛ-* conjugations it should be reduced by Rule 2, the resulting form being identical to non-comitative past tense. The arrangement of allomorphs here – as elsewhere in the grammar (3.8.7) – is most convenient qua the stress and vowel length targets of Yidiɲ.)

Yidiɲ is like many other Australian languages (including Dyirbal – Dixon 1972: 85–7, 96–9, 198–9) in having (one allomorph of) comitative formally identical with an affix (here, *-ŋa-l*) which derives a transitive verbal stem from a noun or adjective. See 4.8.1.

[b] ANTIPASSIVE etc. *-:ḍi-n ~ -:ṛ+ḍi-n*

This affix has a variety of functions. In its 'antipassive' and 'reflexive' senses it occurs only with transitive forms and derives an intransitive stem. It can also occur with a transitive stem indicating that the 'agent' does not have volitional control over the action; here the resulting stem is still transitive. Finally, it can occur with transitive or intransitive stems – again leaving transitivity unchanged – marking the action as

'continuous, uncompleted'. There is lengthy discussion of these functions in 4.2.

-:*ḍi-n* stems inflect exactly like -*n* conjugation roots. Sample inflections are:

root	*buga-n*	*wuɲaba-n*
	'eat'	'hunt for'
-:*ḍi-n* stem	*buga:ḍi-n*	*wuɲaba:ḍi-n*
present	*buga:ḍiŋ*	*wuɲaba:ḍiŋ*
past	*buga:ḍiɲu*	*wuɲabaḍi:ɲ*
imperative	*buga:ḍin*	*wuɲaba:ḍin*
purposive	*buga:ḍina*	*wuɲabaḍi:na*
dative subord.	*buga:ḍiɲu:n*	*wuɲaba:ḍiɲunda*

root	*baga-l*	*baḍa-ṛ*
	'spear'	'follow'
-:*ḍi-n* stem	*baga:ḍi-n*	*baḍa:ṛḍi-n*
present	*baga:ḍiŋ*	*baḍa:ṛḍiŋ*
past	*baga:ḍiɲu*	*baḍa:ṛḍiɲu*
imperative	*baga:ḍin*	*baḍa:ṛḍin*
purposive	*baga:ḍina*	*baḍa:ṛḍina*
dative subord.	*baga:ḍiɲu:n*	*baḍa:ṛḍiɲu:n*

Vowel length in the second syllable of words like *buga:ḍiŋ* and *baga:ḍiŋ* is, of course, what would be predicted by Rule 1. We see that -:*ḍi-n* has inherent length specification from examination of even-syllabled words – for instance, present *wuɲaba:ḍiŋ* and past *buga:ḍiɲu*, *baga:ḍiɲu* etc. Note that -:*ḍi-n* length is lost in *wuɲabaḍi:ɲ* and *wuɲabaḍi:na*; this is due to the operation of Rule 4 (2.3.6) which deletes a long vowel occurring in an odd-numbered syllable of an odd-syllabled word.

All verbal affixes discussed above have had parallel occurrences of conjugation markers -*l*- and -*ṛ*-; here, for the first time, -*ṛ*- occurs but not -*l*- (with the -*l* conjugation and -*n* conjugation forms then falling together). In 2.3.5 we discussed the possible genesis of length in -:*ḍi-n*, in terms of a development like -*l*+*ḍi-n* > -:*ḍi-n*.

Note the similarity of form between the 'lest' inflection -*ḍi* and the derivational affix -:*ḍi-n*. Whether or not these affixes may have some common historical origin (and there is no evidence that they do have), they are felt to be quite distinct in present-day Yidiɲ. They can, for instance, co-occur quite freely – thus 'spear-:*ḍi*-LEST' occurs in absolutive case as *baga:ḍinḍi* and in ergative as *baga:ḍinḍi:ŋ* – examples are in 4.6.2.

-*ŋa-l* and -*:ḍi-n* can occur together, in either order. An intransitive root can take comitative -*ŋa-l*, deriving a transitive stem; if -*:ḍi-n* is added to this we would usually obtain an intransitive form. A stem like *galiŋa:ḍi-n* will inflect exactly like *wuŋaba:ḍi-n*, from the paradigm above; thus, while length appears in present *galiŋa:ḍiŋ* it is deleted by Rule 4 from past tense *galiŋaḍi:ŋ*; and so on. The syntax of comitative-plus-*:ḍi-n* is discussed in 4.3.8.

-*:ḍi-n* followed by -*ŋa-l* serves to derive a transitive stem (from an underlying transitive root, via an intermediate intransitive stem), and can put an instrumental NP into absolutive case, making it the pivot for various syntactic operations – 4.3.6. Thus *baga:ḍiŋa-l* inflects like a normal even-syllabled -*l* root. Since the length is in an even-numbered syllable it is not liable to deletion – we get present *baga:ḍiŋal*, past *baga:ḍiŋa:l*, purposive *baga:ḍiŋa:lna*, and so on.

3.8.6 Aspects – 'going' and 'coming'. There are two aspectual affixes; any verb – except *gali-n* 'go' and *gada-n* 'come' – may, optionally, make one choice from this system. Aspectual affixes have no syntactic effect, and do not alter the transitivity of the verb; they always derive a stem that takes -*n* conjugation inflections. Basic forms are:

[a] 'GOING' ASPECT -*ŋali-n* ~ -*:li-n* ~ -*:ṛi-n*
[b] 'COMING' ASPECT -*ŋada-n* ~ -*:l+da-n* ~ -*:da-n*

An aspectual affix will indicate whether an action was performed during or after 'going' or 'coming'. With a verb referring to a non-durational action, or to a position of rest ('sit', 'stand', 'lie' etc.) an aspectual specification normally implies that the actor goes/comes AND THEN performs the action referred to by the verb. Thus (text 2, lines 122 and 42):

(224) *yagalḍida: ŋayu wulaŋaliŋ ŋuŋgu*
    I'll go and die there in Yagaldyida
(225) *ŋundu:ba ḍambu:l wunaŋadan yiŋgu*
    You two come and sleep here!

Other examples are in (80), (72) and (211) above.

With a verb that refers to motion, or to a durative action, an aspectual specification can imply that the action was performed WHILST going or coming. For instance, with *ḍuŋga-n* 'run':

(226) *ŋaḍin bimbi ḍuŋgaŋaliŋ*
    My father's running away ('going running')

(227) *ɲaḍin muḍam ḍuŋgaŋadaŋ*
My mother's running here ('coming running')

But a motion/durative verb can also have the first meaning – go/come
AND THEN perform the action. Thus *bugaŋadan* 'eat-COME-IMP' could
mean 'eat while coming!' or (as in text 9, line 8) 'come and eat!'. In
line 4 of text 2 *wawa:liɲu* 'look-GOING-PAST' is used to mean 'look whilst
going' but in lines 7 and 10 of the same text it means 'go and look'.
And compare (text 2, line 35):

(228) *ɲaɲḍi bulmba:gu galiɲa:lna | bayi:lina*
    we-SA camp-ALL go-COMIT-PURP emerge-GOING-PURP
    bama:nda
    person-DAT
    We must take [the women] to the camp, [we must] go so that we
    emerge [from the bush] at the people['s camp]

with another textual example:

(229) *bana   bayi:ldaɲu*
    water-ABS emerge-COMING-PAST
    [During a volcanic eruption the ground split and] water came
    [rushing] out

   The 'origin' with respect to which 'going' and 'coming' are orientated is normally either the present position of the speaker, or the actor's
home or temporary camp, or – in a narrative – the last place mentioned.
There are a fair number of examples of aspectual affixes throughout the
texts (pages 513–39). (Note that in line 6 of text 14 the speaker uses
'going' aspect at the beginning of the sentence and 'coming' at the
end – he began by taking his present position as 'origin' but then
switched to his home.)
   The two aspects are contrasted within a single sentence, taken from a
text which describes the origin of Lake Eacham. As the water rose:

(230) *bana   ŋalal   ḍuŋgaŋali:na | bundu*
    water-ABS big-ABS run-GOING-PURP dilly-bag-ABS
    ḍuŋgaŋada:ɲ | gangu:l | ginda:ḍa |
    run-COMING-PAST grey wallaby-ABS cassowary-ABS
    buruḍu:ɽ |
    pademelon-ABS

> [The water rose and] as a result lots of water went rushing [into
> the camp]; [then] the dilly-bag, the grey wallaby, the cassowary
> and the pademelon came running [out of the camp, fleeing from
> the water]

Here the narrator took as 'origin' his location whilst he was telling the story – water WENT INTO the camp (which is nowadays fully submerged) and the people CAME OUT. (*ḏuŋga-n* 'run, move quickly' can refer to rapid movement of people or of water. Note that *bundu* 'dilly-bag' was believed – like animals and birds – to have had human form at the time of this 'storytime' myth.)

'Going' and 'coming' can be described by the lexical verbs *gali-n* and *gada-n*, or by verbal aspects, or by both simultaneously. Thus we can have, as alternatives to (226–7) with exactly the same meanings:

(231) *ŋaḏin bimbi galiŋ ḏuŋgaŋaliŋ*

(232) *ŋaḏin muḏam gadaŋ ḏuŋgaŋadaŋ*

See 4.1.3 and example (327) below. The writer has heard sentences like *ŋaḏin bimbi galiŋ ḏuŋgaŋ*, but these are less used – if one of the verbs in a verb complex is *gali-n* or *gada-n* then the other verbs in the complex will normally take the appropriate aspectual affix. In fact, the preferences for 'aspect agreement' go further. If *gali-n* or *gada-n* occurs in the main clause, then the appropriate aspect should be included in a subordinate clause, if this is semantically plausible. That is, informants preferred:

(233) *ŋayu galiŋ miɲa:gu/ miɲa duga:lina*

    I'm going for fish, going to catch fish

to

(234) *ŋayu galiŋ miɲa:gu/ miɲa duga:lna*

although both appear to be fully grammatical.

There is a strong formal similarity between lexical verbs 'go/come' and the aspectual affixes:

		'go'	'come'
lexical verb		*gali-n*	*gada-n*
aspect	*-n* conjugation	*-ŋali-n*	*-ŋada-n*
	-l conjugation	*-:li-n*	*-:lda-n*
	-r conjugation	*-:ri-n*	*-:da-n*

There are plainly two possible ways in which these forms could have evolved. The lexical verbs could have been incorporated as verbal affixes (a syntactic syntagm – verb + tense, go/come + tense – reducing to a morphological structure), with the initial *g-* softening to *ŋ-* after an *-n* conjugation stem, and the initial syllable being lost in other conjugations. Alternatively, we could

suggest that at some earlier stage of the language there was a monosyllabic verb *ga-* 'motion', without lexical differentiation between 'going' and 'coming' (exactly as we posited ancestral monosyllabic pronouns and a deictic in 3.6.4, 3.7.4); and that there were aspectual affixes with forms similar to *-li-n* and *-da-n*. It would be natural, as monosyllabic forms came no longer to be tolerated, for *ga+li-n* and *ga+da-n* to be reanalysed as disyllabic roots *gali-n* and *gada-n*. Note that there is a monosyllabic verb *ga:-*, meaning 'go' or something similar, in a number of languages from the southeast of Australia – for instance, Geytenbeek and Geytenbeek 1971: 59 (and a form *gaga-* 'go' in Wargamay, a hundred miles to the south of Yidiɲ). (We would, under this hypothesis, still need to explain the first syllable of *-ŋali-n* and *-ŋada-n*, and the presence of vowel length in *-:li-n* and *-:lda-n* etc.)

Support for the first, affix-derived-from-lexical-root, alternative is provided by Dya:bugay. Hale (1976a: 239) mentions that 'there is productive compounding of verb stems with the motion verbs *gali-* "to go" and *gara-* "to come"'. (Note that there is a regular correspondence between Dya:bugay *-r-* and Yidiɲ *-d-*; for instance *bari-/badi-* 'to cry'.) An 'incremental affix' is in Dya:bugay inserted between verb root and *gali-/gara-*; this is *-y-* for *-n* conjugation roots and *-la-* for the *-l* conjugation.

Compare also with the reduplicated aspectual suffixes in tablelands Yidiɲ, described below.

In just one text that the writer recorded (told by Dick Moses in coastal Yidiɲ) there appears to be incorporation of *ɲina-n* 'sit' between verb root and inflection – for instance *ḍaŋgaḍaŋga:diɲinaɲunda* 'grumble-REDUP-:ḍi-ɲina-DAT SUBORD'. However, it did not prove possible to elicit any further forms of this nature (or to have them judged acceptable outside the context of the text). This may have been influence from Dya:bugay, which is Dick Moses's second language; although *ɲina-* incorporation is not mentioned in Hale's short sketch grammar of that language.

We can now illustrate sample inflections of aspectual stems that are based on different types of root ('going' suffixes are used here; 'coming' is exactly parallel):

root	*wiwi-n*	*maḍinda-n*
	'give'	'walk up'
aspect stem	*wiwiŋali-n*	*maḍindaŋali-n*
present	*wiwiŋaliŋ*	*maḍi:ndaŋaliŋ*
past	*wiwiŋali:ɲ*	*maḍi:ndaŋali:ɲ*
imperative	*wiwiŋalin*	*maḍi:ndaŋalin*
purposive	*wiwiŋali:na*	*maḍi:ndaŋali:na*
dative subord.	*wiwiŋaliɲunda*	*maḍi:ndaŋaliɲunda*

root	*wawa-l*	*baḍa-ṛ*
	'see'	'leave'
aspect stem	*wawa:li-n*	*baḍa:ṛi-n*
present	*wawa:liŋ*	*baḍa:ṛiŋ*
past	*wawa:liɲu*	*baḍa:ṛiɲu*
imperative	*wawa:lin*	*baḍa:ṛin*
purposive	*wawa:lina*	*baḍa:ṛina*
dative subord.	*wawa:liɲu:n*	*baḍa:ṛiɲu:n*

Aspectual affixes have occasionally been heard as *-ŋgali-n* and *-ŋgada-n* after a trisyllabic root e.g. *ḍaḍa:maŋgadaŋ* 'jump over-COMING-PRESENT'. (An allomorph with initial *-ŋg-* has never been encountered on a disyllabic root.) This might be taken as further evidence that *-ŋali-n* and *-ŋada-n* did evolve from *gali-n* and *gada-n*.

It will be seen that the monosyllabic allomorphs *-:li-n* and *-:ṛi-n* cohere, and continue an established phonological word. In contrast, non-cohering *-ŋali-n* begins a new phonological word – note that past tense is #*ŋali:ɲ* whatever the syllabicity of the root to which it is attached.

In 2.3.5 we speculated that the 'going' aspect might at one time have been *-ŋali-n* (< *-gali-n*) with all conjugations, but that *-l-ŋali-n* reduced to *-:li-n* and *-ṛ-ŋali-n* to *-:ṛi-n*. Essentially, *-ŋa-* was replaced by vowel length (2.6.4). Since *-ṛl-* is not a possible cluster, *-l-* was dropped (retaining the distinctive conjugation marker). Similar considerations apply to 'coming' forms. Here we would suppose that *-l-ŋada-n* > *-:lda-n* and *-ṛ-ŋada-n* > *-:da-n*. The dropping of *ṛ* before *d* follows the general phonotactic preferences of Yidiɲ (2.1.2) and parallels rhotic dropping before ergative and locative cases (3.3.2).

When the 'going' aspect occurs before comitative *-ŋa-l*, its form is simply *-:ri-n*, with roots of all conjugations. Thus:

root	*ḍuŋga-n*	*magi-l*	*bayga-ṛ*
	'run'	'climb up'	'feel sore'
'going' + present	*ḍuŋgaŋaliŋ*	*magi:liŋ*	*bayga:ṛiŋ*
'going' + past	*ḍuŋgaŋali:ɲ*	*magi:liɲu*	*bayga:ṛiɲu*
'going' + comitative + present	*ḍuŋga:riŋal*	*magi:riŋal*	*bayga:riŋal*
'going' + comitative + past	*ḍuŋga:riŋa:l*	*magi:riŋa:l*	*bayga:riŋa:l*

We can explain the substitution of -*:ri-n* for the normal 'going' allomorph in terms of dissimilation qua the -*l*- of comitative -*ŋa-l* (2.5.1). Note that the conjugation marker -*l*- occurs in every inflection save imperative (table 3.9), but that -*:ri-n* is generalised to occur before -*ŋa-l* in ALL inflections, including imperative. (Conjugation marker -*l*- is also dropped from -*ŋa-l* when the derivational affix -*:ḍi-n* follows, and here too -*:ri-n* is retained – see *yaḍi:riŋa:ḍiɲu* in 3.8.7.)

It seems as if the -*l*- of the -*:li-n* allomorph is dissimilated to -*r*- and this form is then generalised to apply in all conjugations before -*ŋa-l*.

However, there are certain cases in which 'going' is -*:li-n*, not -*:ri-n*, before -*ŋa-l*. This happens when *r* or *ɽ* occurs in the last consonant cluster of the root – examples were given in 2.5.1. We could say in this case EITHER that there is a second dissimilation, -*:ri-n* giving way to -*:li-n* under pressure from a root rhotic, OR that a root rhotic blocks the dissimilation of -*:li-n* to -*:ri-n* in the presence of -*ŋa-l*. (But note that in the latter case we still have to admit the -*l* conjugation allomorph being generalised to other conjugations before -*ŋa-l*; for instance, with -*n* conjugation *burgi-n* we get *burgi-ŋali-ŋ* 'walkabout-GOING-PRES' but *burgi-:li-ŋa-l* 'walkabout-GOING-COMIT-PRES'.)

Generally, 'coming' aspect behaves exactly like the 'going' variety. There is, however, an important difference in their co-occurrence with comitative -*ŋa-l*. We can first consider a sentential paradigm involving *ḍuŋga-n* 'run' with or without 'going' aspect and with or without comitative derivational affix:

(235) a   *buɲa ḍuŋga:ɲ*
                Woman ran

      b COMIT   *ḍaḍa buɲa:ŋ ḍuŋgaŋalɲu*
                Woman ran with baby

      c 'GOING' *buɲa ḍuŋgaŋali:ɲ*
                Woman ran away

      d COMIT + 'GOING' *ḍaḍa buɲa:ŋ ḍuŋga:riŋa:l*
                Woman ran away with baby

This is quite straightforward, conforming exactly to the rules we have indicated. But consider the corresponding paradigm with the 'coming' affix:

(236) c 'COMING' *buɲa ḍuŋgaŋada:ɲ*
                  Woman ran here

      d COMIT + 'COMING' *ḍaḍa buɲa:ŋ ḍuŋga:riŋa:ldaɲu*
                  Woman ran here with baby

(236d) has both -:*ri-n* before -*ŋa-l* and -:*lda-n* after it. If we describe -:*ri-n* as an allomorph of the 'going' aspect – as (235d) suggests we should – then (236d) would appear to involve BOTH 'going' AND 'coming' specifications. But 'going' and 'coming' are complementary terms in a binary semantic system, and both cannot simultaneously be specified. (A comitative verb cannot be interpreted in such a way that the subject is going in one direction and the object in another – see 4.3.7.) Furthermore, (236d) does carry just a 'coming' meaning (there is no implication at all of 'going' or 'coming and going' or anything of that sort).

It seems that -:*ri-n*, before -*ŋa-l*, is a GENERAL MARKER OF ASPECT (not just of a particular aspect choice). If we also get -:*lda-n*, following -*ŋa-l*, then the aspectual choice is marked as 'coming'. If there is no further aspect specification in the word then the unmarked 'going' aspect is to be inferred. Note that we can, in fact, have -:*li-n* after -*ŋa-l* in addition to the -:*ri-n* preceding it. That is:

(237) COMIT + 'GOING' *ḏaḏa buɲa:ŋ ḏuŋga:riɲa:liɲu*
  Woman ran away with baby

is a paraphrase of (235d), in free variation with it.

Forms with just -:*ri-n* plus -*ŋa-l*, like (235d), seem to be commoner in texts and conversation than the longer -:*ri-n* plus -*ŋa-l* plus -:*li-n* type (237). See (223) above, and lines 27, 28 of text 2. But verbs like that in (237) are likely to be preferred when attention is focused on the niceties of semantic expression, as in an informant session that has taken a pedantic turn.

The dissimilation of -:*ri-n* to -:*li-n* after a root showing a rhotic (2.5.1) takes place whether or not -:*lda-n* follows the comitative suffix. For instance *burwa:liɲa:ldaɲu* 'jump-ASPECT-COMIT-COMING-PAST' exactly parallels *ḏuŋga:-riɲa:ldaɲu*. Another example is *gaɻba:liɲa:liɲu* 'hide-ASPECT-COMIT-GOING-PAST' which involves -:*li-n* twice.

If a verb involves the comitative affix then it must – in terms of the formula given at (219) – go into a second set of affixal possibilities. We naturally have two aspect specifications – one in terms of line (a) and one from line (b), of (219). Either -:*li-n* or -:*lda-n* can follow -*ŋa-l*, in (219b), but preceding comitative in (219a) we only find -:*ri-n* (contrasting with its absence). The structure of a verb which involves both comitative and aspect can be summarised:

$$\text{ROOT} + \underset{\substack{\text{general} \\ \text{aspect} \\ \text{marker}}}{\text{-:}ri\text{-}n} + \underset{\text{comitative}}{\text{-}\eta a\text{-}l} + \left\{ \begin{array}{l} \text{\o} \sim \text{-:}li\text{-}n \\ \text{`going' aspect} \\ \text{-:}lda\text{-}n \\ \text{`coming' aspect} \end{array} \right\} + \text{INFLECTION}$$

Note that it is not normal to obtain *-:lda-n* (or *-:li-n*) following *-ŋa-l* without a *-:ri-n* preceding it, in the case of a disyllabic root.

If Yidiɲ did allow an aspect suffix after *-ŋa-l*, where *-ŋa-l* was added directly to a disyllabic root, there would be a 'length conflict' (2.3.6) and aspectual length would have to be deleted by Rule 4. For instance, *ḍuŋga+ŋa+:li+ɲu* 'run-COMIT-GOING-PAST' would then yield *ḍuŋgaŋali:ɲ*, which is in fact identical with the realisation of *ḍuŋga+ŋali+ɲu* 'run-GOING-PAST'. (With the 'coming' aspect we should theoretically get a contrast between **ḍuŋga-ŋalda:ɲ* and *ḍuŋgaŋada:ɲ* – but the inclusion or omission of *-l-* here is something that could easily be missed in rapid speech.) It is likely that these two considerations – avoidance of ambiguity, and avoidance of underlying suffixal length failing to gain surface realisation – are at least partly responsible for the evolution of the rather complex method of 'double aspect marking' for comitatives.

The discussion of *-:ri-n* above applies only to disyllabic roots taking comitative. With trisyllabic roots (or with a disyllabic root plus *-:ḍi-n*) comitative goes directly on to the root and is then followed by aspectual *-:li-n* or *-:lda-n*. It is not acceptable to insert *-:ri-n* (or any other aspectual suffix) between a trisyllabic stem and *-ŋa-l*. Thus we encounter:

(238) *buɲa:ŋ ḍaḍa maḍindaŋa:liɲu*
       Woman is going, walking up, with the baby

whereas **maḍinda:riŋalɲu* or **maḍindariŋali:ɲ* (from underlying *maḍinda+:ri+ŋa+:li+ɲu*) were judged ungrammatical.

There is no possibility of ambiguity with (i) *maḍinda+ŋa+:li+ɲu* 'walk up-COMIT-GOING-PAST', yielding *maḍindaŋa:liɲu*. Compare with (ii) *maḍinda+ŋali+ɲu* 'walk up-GOING-PAST', which yields *maḍi:ndaŋali:ɲ*. Affixal length is naturally retained in (i) without the inclusion of anything like *-:ri-n*. And, of course, both *-ŋa-l* and *-:li-n* cohere whereas *-ŋali-n* does not (2.4); although (i) and (ii) have the same number of syllables, past tense is reduced in (ii) but not in (i).

The contrast between disyllabic and trisyllabic roots with comitative and aspect reinforces our suggestion above that *-:ri-n* is introduced before *-ŋa-l*

in order to produce words that conform as closely as possible to the stress/length targets of Yidiɲ.

There is a further type of aspect – which we refer to as 'reduplicated aspect' – that occurs only in the tablelands dialect. The regular aspectual affixes, as described above, also occur quite freely in tablelands Yidiɲ. Contrasting the two varieties:

		-n conjugation	-l conjugation	-ɽ conjugation
normal	'going'	-ŋali-n	-:li-n	-:ɾi-n
	'coming'	-ŋada-n	-:lda-n	-:da-n
reduplicated	'going'	-ŋaliŋgali-n	-:liŋgali-n	-:ɾiŋgali-n
	'coming'	-ŋadaŋgada-n	-:ldaŋgada-n	-:daŋgada-n

The reduplicated aspects occur in texts given by Tilly Fuller (see line 6 of text 14) and George Davis; it has not, however, been possible to elicit much on this topic (partly owing to the death of Tilly Fuller in 1974).

Reduplicated aspects appear to mean 'going right away' or 'coming close up', as against normal unmarked 'going' and 'coming' (but it must be emphasised that it has not been possible to pursue corroborative questioning on this semantic contrast, to the extent that the writer usually deems advisable). Thus *wawa:lday* could be 'come and look' and *wawa:ldaŋga:day* would then be 'come right up and have a look'. And, in explaining the verbs used for different modes of crossing a river George Davis said:

(239) *ŋayu ḍayŋga:da ḍuɲḍa:ɾiŋga:liŋ*
I-SA rapids-LOC walk across-REDUP GOING-PRES
I walked across [the stream] at the rapids.

Here the aspectual -*ɾiŋgali-n* emphasises that at a shallow spot, referred to by *ḍayŋgaɾ*, one can actually walk right across a river.

Verbal affixes marking 'going' and 'coming' are found in some other Australian languages. See, for instance, Chadwick (1975: 33ff.) on Djingili.

3.8.7 Affix combinations. The various possible combinations of derivational affixes have all been mentioned in the last few sections. They can now conveniently be summarised, paying particular attention to the occurrence of vowel length (bearing in mind the stress and length constraints – 2.2).

[a] COMITATIVE plus ASPECT

With a disyllabic root, -*:ri-n* precedes comitative and -*:li-n* ∼ ∅ ('going') or -*:lda-n* ('coming') follows it. The length inherent in -*:ri-n* is thus always in the second syllable of the word; this satisfies the constraints whether the complete word is even-syllabled – as *magi:riɲal* 'climb up-ASPECT-COMIT-PRES' – or odd-syllabled – as *magi:riɲa:lna* 'climb up-ASPECT-COMIT-PURP'. In past tense we find length in two distinct syllables, both even-numbered – *magi:riɲa:l*. If -*:lda-n* or -*:li-n* is included after -*ɲa-l* there will be two long vowels, again separated by just one syllable – present *magi:riɲa:ldaɲ*, purposive *magi:riɲa:ldana*, past *magi:riɲa:ldaɲu*. A word in dative subordinate inflection will involve three long vowels, falling in the second, fourth and sixth syllables – *magi:riɲa:ldaɲu:n*.

Note that we cannot get Disyllabic Root + -*ɲa-l* + Aspect; nor can 'coming' aspect be expressed through just Disyllabic Root + Aspect + -*ɲa-l*.

With a trisyllabic root, comitative must be directly suffixed to the root and is followed by regular aspect -*:li-n* ∼ -*:lda-n*. Aspectual length is then in the fourth syllable of the word and always satisfies the constraints – for instance in both odd-syllabled present tense *maḍindaɲa:liɲ*, and even-syllabled past form *maḍindaɲa:liɲu*. A word in dative subordinate inflection will involve two long vowels, separated by a single syllable – *maḍindaɲa:liɲu:n*.

[b] -*:ḍi-n* plus ASPECT

Aspect must always follow -*:ḍi-n* – see (219). The -*n* conjugational aspectual allomorphs, which must be used in this case, do not involve inherent length so that there is no chance here of a conflict between long vowels in successive syllables (2.3.6). Examples of this affix combination are:

(240) *ŋaɲḍi bimbi:nda buŋgu   ḍara:ḍiŋadaŋ*
       we-SA father-DAT knee-ABS stand-*:ḍi*-COMING-PRES
       We came and knelt [praying] to [the heavenly] father

(241) *yiŋu   bama   baga:ḍiŋali:ɲ   gangulanda*
       THIS-S person-ABS spear-*:ḍi*-GOING-PAST wallaby-DAT
       This person went and speared a wallaby

(242) *ŋayu gali:ɲ   bana: gula   daraba:ḍiŋali:ɲ*
    I-SA go-PAST water-LOC body-ABS shake-*:ḍi*-GOING-PAST
    I went to the water, went and washed [my] body [in the water]

Note that aspectual *-ŋali-n/-ŋada-n* commences a new phonological word, so that the *-:ḍi-n* length could not conflict with anything later in the (grammatical) word.

We suggested in the last section that the evidence points to all 'going' allomorphs being reflexes of *-*ŋali-n*, and to 'coming' forms descending from *-*ŋada-n*. Initial *-ŋa-* has been replaced by vowel length for the *-l* and *-ɼ* conjugations, giving monosyllabic affixes that phonologically cohere with the preceding stem. In contrast, *-n* conjugation allomorphs are disyllabic and non-cohering.

Note that if we did have, say, *-:li-n* and *-:da-n* in the *-n* conjugation we would be bound to get length in two successive syllables. With a disyllabic root plus *-:ḍi-n* plus aspect, *-:ḍi-n* length would be in an even-numbered syllable and aspect length in an odd-numbered syllable; these would be reversed in the case of an odd-syllabled root. Examples would be: present tense *baga + *:ḍi* + *:li* + *ŋ*, *wuŋaba + *:ḍi* + *:li* + *ŋ* and past *baga + *:ḍi* + *:li* + *ɲu*, *wuŋaba + *:ḍi* + *:li* + *ɲu*. Here *-:ḍi-n* and aspectual length would conflict with one another, and one would plainly have to be eliminated. How could this be done? Would it be morphologically conditioned (*-:ḍi-n* length being retained and aspect length lost, or vice versa) or phonologically determined (say, length in an odd-numbered syllable always being eliminated)? In fact, a conflict between inherent long vowels is NEVER encountered in Yidiɲ. We can surely suggest (as we did in 2.3.5) that a desire to avoid such a conflict is likely to be one of the reasons why *-ŋali-n* and *ŋada-n* have not reduced in the *-n* conjugation.

[c] *-:ḍi-n* followed by COMITATIVE

This is a common combination – see 4.3.6. With a disyllabic root the length goes onto the second syllable and the constraints will always be satisfied. The three transitive trisyllabic roots known (3.8.3) can not, it seems, plausibly take these affixes – if an example did occur, length would be in the third syllable and would be deleted by Rule 4 if the resulting word were odd-syllabled. Thus, supposing *dandada-n* 'rub' to take these affixes, we would get *-:ḍi-n* length remaining in past *dandada:ḍiŋalɲu* but being lost from present *dandadaḍi:ŋal*.

[d] -*:ḍi-n* followed by COMITATIVE, plus ASPECT

A disyllabic root plus -*:ḍi-n* functions exactly like a trisyllabic root; aspect follows (and can under no circumstances precede) comitative. Verbs can thus have the structure Root plus -*:ḍi-n* + COMIT + ASPECT but never *Root + -*:ḍi-n* + ASPECT + COMIT (nor, of course, *Root + ASPECT + -*:ḍi-n* + COMIT). There can be two long vowels in the word, but they will always be separated by one syllable – the intervening -*ŋa-l*. Thus *bunḍa* + *:ḍi* + *ŋa* + *:li* + *ɲu* (cf. 4.3.6) in

(243) *ŋayu ḍugi bama:nda bunḍa:ḍiŋa:liɲu*
     I used a stick to go and hit a person

A word involving these affixes can show three long vowels – in the dative subordinate inflection: *bunḍa:ḍiŋa:liɲu:n*; but these are all in even-numbered syllables, and satisfy the constraints of 2.2.

If a trisyllabic root could occur with -*:ḍi-* plus -*ŋa-l* plus aspect plus monosyllabic inflection, both -*:ḍi-n* and aspect length would conflict with the constraints, and both would be eliminated by Rule 4. But, as explained above, such a form has never been obtained and does not seem semantically plausible.

[e] COMITATIVE followed by -*:ḍi-n*

With a disyllabic root the length supplied by -*:ḍi-n* falls in the third syllable and will be deleted, by Rule 4, whenever a monosyllabic inflection follows – examples are at (621–2) in 4.3.8 (and see 2.3.6, 3.8.5). This affix combination is quite frequent, and this is perhaps the most common instance of the application of Rule 4.

[f] COMITATIVE followed by -*:ḍi-n*, plus ASPECT

There are three possible positions for aspect – (i) before comitative, (ii) between comitative and -*:ḍi-n*, or (iii) following -*:ḍi-n*. Formula (219), for verbal word structure, does not generate (ii) and this sequence is in fact quite unacceptable. (Note that if it were permitted we would get aspectual length and -*:ḍi-n* length in successive syllables, providing an infraction of the constraints.) (i) and (iii) are both theoretically possible, with aspect being generated on cycle a or on cycle b of (219); both have been obtained, by elicitation:

(244) *ŋayu bama maga yaḍi:riŋa:ḍiɲu*
     I went walkabout in the company of [other] people

and a sentence similar to (244), with the same meaning, but having as verb *burgiṇa:ḍiṇali:ɲ* (*yaḍi-l* and *burgi-n* are seemingly exact synonyms – 3.1.3). With dative subordinate inflection we could get a further example of a word involving three long vowels; again, they would all be in even-numbered syllables – *yaḍi:riṇa:ḍiṇu:n*.

In all the examples obtained 'going' aspect (*-:ri-n*) precedes *-ŋa+:ḍi-n* whereas 'coming' aspect (*-ŋada-n*) follows. But it must be emphasised that combinations of comitative, *-:ḍi-n* and aspect have not been encountered outside direct elicitation, and the data are certainly too slender for any generalisation – of the type 'going' precedes *-ŋa-l*, 'coming' follows *-:ḍi-n* – to be at present supportable. It is possible that aspect could occur BOTH BEFORE *-ŋa-l* AND also AFTER *-:ḍi-n* (as it can both precede and follow *-ŋa-l*); information is lacking on this point.

The main point to notice about these affix combinations is that, by careful choice of allomorphy and subtle morphotactic deployment, *-:ḍi-n* and an aspectual form involving a long vowel are always separated by exactly one syllable; similarly, two aspect tokens – both involving long vowels – must be separated by a single syllable. In this way Constraint 1 – 'if two or more long vowels occur in a word, each pair must be separated by an odd number of syllables' (2.2) – is always satisfied in these cases. The devices that achieve this end are:

(i) the aspectual allomorphs that immediately follow *-:ḍi-n* do not involve long vowels (and are in fact non-cohering);

(ii) *-:ḍi-n* cannot immediately be preceded by aspect (or else it would, of course, occur next to *-:li-n* or *-:lda-n* etc.);

(iii) if *-:ḍi-n* does occur in a word with a monosyllabic aspectual allomorph, *-:ḍi-n* and aspect are separated by the comitative *-ŋa-l* – we get *-:ḍi-n* plus *-ŋa-l* plus aspect, in (d), or aspect plus *-ŋa-l* plus *-:ḍi-n*, as in (f);

(iv) if two monosyllabic aspectual affixes occur, they must be either side of *-ŋa-l*.

Thus, to complete the discussion that was opened in 2.3.6, there is NO 'conflict' (qua the general constraints of Yidiɲ phonology) between vowel lengths coming from different sources.

We can, as described in 2.3.6, have *-:ḍi-n* length appearing in an illicit syllable (an odd-numbered syllable in an odd-syllabled form) and this will then be eliminated by Rule 4. Note, though, that there is

hardly any chance of aspectual length appearing in an illicit syllable. All trisyllabic roots bar one are in the -*n* conjugation, whose aspectual forms do not show length. Trisyllabic stems can be derived through -:*ḍi-n* (again, taking length-less aspectual allomorphs) or with -*ŋa-l*. But -*ŋa-l*, on to a disyllabic root, can only be followed by aspect if it is also preceded by -:*ri-n*, ensuring that all long vowels fall in even-numbered syllables.

Aspect length could only conceivably occur on an illicit syllable in the following circumstances:

(i) if a trisyllabic root occurred with -:*ḍi-n* plus -*ŋa-l* plus aspect plus monosyllabic inflection, then both -:*ḍi-n* and aspect length would be deleted by Rule 4. But, as noted at (d) above, such a form has never been encountered and (in terms of the trisyllabic transitive roots known) would scarcely be semantically possible.

(ii) one trisyllabic root belonging to the -*l* conjugations is known – *binaɳa-l* 'tell, warn'. Here aspectual length would presumably be lost before a monosyllabic inflection – underlying *binaɳa* + :*li* + *ɲu* 'warn-GOING-PAST' yielding *binaɳali:ɲ*. But it has not proved possible to elicit *binaɳa-l* plus aspect.

Our detailed examination of affix combinations and the occurrence of long vowels must surely indicate that the development of Yidiɲ morphology has been orientated to the language's overriding phonological targets – that every long vowel should occur in a stressed syllable, and stressed and unstressed syllables should alternate in a phonological word.

3.8.8   -:n-biḍi-n. A further derivational affix, -:*n-biḍi-n*, has been encountered – in texts from both coastal and tablelands dialects – with the verb *wuna-n* 'lie down'. It appears to imply that an activity was done at a number of places that are fairly dispersed. Thus, in the coastal dialect example – quoted at (78) in 3.3.6 – *wuna:nbiḍi:ɲ* implies that the old people were lying around lazily, anywhere in the camp. Compare with the tablelands instance:

(245) *ŋaɲḍi gindanuyi   burgiɲ | miɲa:gu*
         we-SA moon-COMIT-ABS walkabout-PRES animal-DAT
         wurba:ḍiɲ | miɲam   ŋaɲḍi gadaɲ |
         look for-:ḍi-PRES animal-ABL we-SA come-PRES
         ɲinaŋadaɲ | wuna:nbiḍiɲ   wurmba
         sit-COMING-PRES lie down-:n-biḍi-PRES asleep-ABS
         wunaɲ |
         lie down-PRES

> We go walkabout by moonlight, looking for animals. We come
> home after [hunting] animals, come to stay at home, lie down
> anywhere, lie sleeping

Here *wuna:nbiḍiŋ* indicates that the group of hunters are so tired by the
time they regain their camp that they flop down anywhere to sleep, not
bothering to make up proper beds or position themselves according to
kin ties, and so forth.

It has been possible to elicit *-:n-biḍi-n* on other verbs of position –
ɲina:nbiḍi-n can refer to a number of people 'sitting about', all at
different places, or to one man who keeps on moving about, sitting at
various spots; similarly for *ḍana:nbiḍi-n* 'stand about'. *gada:nbiḍi-n* was
glossed 'come about, dilly-dallying about'.

It seems that *-:n-biḍi-n* can only occur on verbs indicating position of
rest or (with less certitude) on some verbs of motion. The most interesting occurrence was with *wanda-n* 'fall down':

(246) *yiŋu bama guman wanda:nbiḍiŋ gadaŋ/ gaba:ɲḍa*

> This person is coming [staggering and swaying] along the road,
> falling down all over the place.

This affix has only been obtained on disyllabic verbs belonging to the
-n conjugation, and then only in present and past tenses. It appears to
be non-cohering – thus *wuná:nbiḍí:ɲ, wuná:nbiḍiŋ*. Note that this affix
seems to involve inherent specification of vowel length (and this is added
to the end of the preceding phonological word!). But the data are really
so slim that it is impossible to be totally confident about this point.

A further verbal affix, *-ba-n*, occurred in conversation with Dick Moses and
appeared to have a 'continuous' meaning – *galinbaŋu* 'kept on going',
gilbilbaŋu 'threw backwards and forwards'. But later elicitation attempts
threw doubts on the authenticity of the affix (which did not appear in any
texts); it could conceivably be an intrusion from Dya:bugay (although it is
not noted in Hale's sketch grammar of Dya:bugay).

3.8.9 Verbal reduplication. Verbs reduplicate on the same formal
pattern as nominals (3.3.9) – that is, the first two syllables of the root
are repeated before it. For instance, *ḍaḍama-n* 'jump', *ḍaḍaḍaḍama-n*
'jump a lot'.

As in the case of nominals, a syllable-final nasal that is homorganic with the
following stop is not reduplicated – *maḍinda-n* 'walk up', *maḍimaḍinda-n*
'keep walking up'. There are in fact (3.8.3) only two trisyllabic verb roots

9

with a non-homorganic cluster between second and third vowels, so that a consonant at the end of the second syllable is reduplicated – thus *ɖugarba-n* 'have unsettled mind', *ɖugarɖugarba-n* 'have unsettled mind for a long period'.

A conjugation marker may optionally be reduplicated (irrespective of whether or not it is retained as part of the word-final inflection):

	unreduplicated	
present tense	*wawal*	'look'
imperative	*bugan*	'eat!'
past	*buga:ɲ*	'ate'
present	*baygaɽ*	'feel sore'

	reduplicated	
present tense	*wawawawal* or *wawalwawal*	'look thoroughly'
imperative	*bugabugan* or *buganbugan*	'eat fast!'
past	*bugabuga:ɲ* or *buganbuga:ɲ*	'ate fast'
present	*baygaɽ(m)baygaɽ*	'feel very sore'

Only a few -*ɽ* conjugation reduplicated verbs have been encountered – the conjugation marker -*ɽ*- was always included. And in two of the three instances of *bayga-ɽ* reduplication a homorganic nasal -*m*- was also inserted.

The only syllable-final inflections that do not coincide with conjugation markers are present tense -*ŋ* (in the -*n* conjugation) and imperative -*r* (in the -*ɽ* conjugation). These can be reduplicated:

	unreduplicated	
present tense	*bugaŋ*	'eats'
imperative	*banɖar*	'follow!'

	reduplicated	
present tense	*bugabugaŋ* or *bugaŋbugaŋ*	'eats fast'
imperative	*banɖarbanɖar*	'follow quickly!'

No (part of) any other inflection could be considered part of the first two syllables of a word; thus, verbal reduplication cannot repeat (part of) any other inflection; nor is vowel length reduplicated.

Semantically, reduplication indicates that an action was performed many times, or over a long period, or to a considerable degree, or was done quickly. It occurs typically with verbs such as *ɖaŋga-n* 'grumble at', *bayga-ɽ* 'feel sore' or *muri-n* 'scream' (for this see line 29 of text 2). The 'extension in time' sense is seen in:

(247) *bibiyuwuy mura:ndidaga:ɲ/ mura:ndi wunawuna:ɲ*
Bibiyuwuy became sick, he was lying [there] sick for a long time

(248) *ḍuḍu:mbu bibiyuwu:ɲa gaṛbagaṛbaɲalɲu*
Auntie always kept Bibiyuwuy hidden

(249) *yiɲu   ḍaḍa   muguy   binda:*
THIS-S baby-ABS all the time shoulder-LOC
    yaḍi:riɲa:l | *buɲa:ndu gula   guba:ɲ* |
walkabout-ASPECT-COMIT-PAST sun-ERG   body-ABS burn-PAST
ḍaḍa   gula   biɲḍula   galigaliɲalɲum
baby-ABS body-ABS weak-NOW go-REDUP-COMIT-CAU SUBORD
This child was taken out walkabout on someone's shoulder for a
long time; its body has been burnt by the sun; the child's body
is now [feeling] weak from being taken about so much

Reduplication emphasises the 'degree' of an action or state in the
following dialogue:

(250) A – *ŋayu ḍugi:l ḍaḍamaɲu*
    I [just] jumped over [that] log
    B – *waɲi:ngu ɲundu ḍaḍamaɲu*
        Why did you jump [over it]?
    A – *ŋayu dunḍidunḍi:ɲ banḍa:ḍiɲu*
        [Oh!] I was [just] feeling very lively, and [wanted to] test
        myself.
    B – *ɲundu gurbi milbadagaŋ*
        [You'd better watch out,] you might be getting too smart [for
        your own good, and might injure yourself]

Here the reduplication of *dunḍi-n* 'feel happy, gay' emphasises the
carefree, high spirits of speaker A.

Unlike most Australian languages, Yidiɲ has no morphological marking for
reciprocal verbs. When the writer asked how to say 'the two men hit each
other'

(251) *bama ḍambu:l bunḍabunḍaŋ*

was given – see 4.2.4. (Note that in Dyirbal a reciprocal verb must be reduplicated, in addition to receiving a special derivational affix – Dixon 1972: 92–3).

Although verbal and nominal reduplication in Yidiɲ involve exactly
the same phonological process, their semantic effects are quite different.
This can be seen by comparing the reduplication of a nominal, and of a

verbal form derived from it. Thus, from *ŋalal* 'big' we obtain *ŋalal-ŋalal* 'lots of big ones', reduplication simply marking plurality – see (120) in 3.3.9. But later in the text from which (120) was taken we encounter:

(252) *garu/ bama waɲḍa ŋalalŋalaldaga:ɲala*
    Later on, when the [two] people had become really big

Here reduplication of verbal *ŋalal + daga-n* 'become big' emphasises that the children referred to earlier in the story had, by this time, REALLY grown up into adult men. (The unreduplicated form *ŋalaldaga:ɲ* could have been taken to imply that they were, say, adolescents.)

This example also emphasises the verbal nature of *ŋalal + daga-n*, as opposed to nominal *ŋalal*. Note that either could make up the main 'comment' of a sentence – *bama ŋalal* 'the person is big', *bama ŋalaldagaŋ* 'the person has become big'. This point is taken up again in 5.4.8–9, 5.6.1.

3.9 Post-inflectional affixes

There is a set of about eight clitic-like suffixes; these can as a rule occur on any word (whatever its part-of-speech membership) and always follow case or tense inflections. These affixes are, irrespective of syllabicity, phonologically non-cohering (2.4).

3.9.1 -(a)la. *-la* (after a vowel) ~ *-ala* (after a consonant) 'now'. This affix is found most frequently attached to verbs, but does occur quite freely with all parts of speech.

[a] VERBS – *-(a)la* can follow any final inflection.

With present–future tense *-(a)la* often gives an 'immediate future' sense. Thus (line 107 of text 2):

(253) *ɲundu ŋuŋgu ḍanan/ ŋayu galiŋala bulmba:gu*
    You stand there, I'll go at once to the camp

Further examples of present plus *-(a)la* will be found throughout text 14. Note that with a verb stem belonging to the *-l* conjugation, whose last root vowel is *a*, we get the phonologically repetitive string *-alala*:

(254) *ŋayu ḍaḍa ŋuŋgu:gu gali:ŋalala*
    I'll take the child there now

In narration -(*a*)*la* is often used on past tense to mean 'this is what happened next'. See (118), (126), line 24 of text 14 and:

(255) *ŋayu waɾŋgi:ɲala*   *gada:ɲ*
     I-SA do all around-PAST-NOW come-PAST
     I came, now moving by a circuitous route

And compare with (252).

Note that -(*a*)*la* is, like all post-inflectional affixes, added to a word after all phonological processes have applied (2.4). Thus we get -*ala* onto a reduced past but -*la* with an unreduced form (e.g. *maḍindaɲula* 'walk up-PAST-NOW').

With an imperative verb -(*a*)*la* serves to reinforce the urgency of the command – for instance line 29 of text 14.

-(*a*)*la* can also occur after a verbal inflection which marks a subordinate clause:

(256) *ḍaḍa*   *ŋuŋu bibiyuwuy ŋamu:ɾay bayi:l*   /
     child-ABS that-S name-ABS smell-ABS emerge-PAST
         madala   / *wunaɲunda*
     soft-ABS-NOW lie-DAT SUBORD
         buludagaɲundala
     rotten-INTR VBLSR-DAT SUBORD-NOW
     A smell came out of [the corpse of] the baby Bibiyuwuy; it was
         soft now; it had been lying [for a while] and was now turning
         rotten

[b] PRONOUNS AND DEICTICS – -(*a*)*la* often implies 'it's my (or your, or his/her) turn':

(257) *ɲundu buga:ɲ/ ŋayula buga:na*
     You've eaten, now I must eat

[c] ADJECTIVES – here the affix normally indicates that a certain object has just entered into a particular state. See *biɲḍula* in (249), *madala* in (256) and:

(258) *ŋayu ḍugi*   *wawa:l wuwuy*   *gamu*   / *ŋaɲḍi*
     I-SA   tree-ABS see-PAST bean tree-ABS flower-ABS we-SA
         miɲa:gu gali:na/ miɲa   dirgulala
     fish-PURP go-PURP fish-ABS fat-ABS-NOW
     I saw the flowers [out] on the bean tree, and so went for fish. Fish
         will be fat [and ready to eat] now (cf. 1.4)

Further examples are in line 34 of text 9, and lines 25, 27 of text 14.

[d] NOUNS – if -(a)la is used with a noun in absolutive case it may indicate that someone or something has attained a certain form, referred to by that noun. See (847) below.

-(a)la can occur after any oblique case form of a noun, adjective or pronoun. It is particularly common after genitives:

(259) *ɲuɲu   waɲal   bimbi:nim   / ɲayu wawa:l*
    THAT-ABS boomerang-ABS father-GEN-ABL I-SA see-PAST
    galigaliɲalɲum   / ɲuɲu   waɲal
    go-REDUP-COMIT-CAU SUBORD THAT-ABS boomerang-ABS
    galɲa:nala
    uncle-GEN-ABS-NOW

That boomerang used to belong to father – I used to see him taking it around [with him]; now that boomerang belongs to uncle

An example of -(a)la following purposive is:

(260) *ɲaɲḍi maḍi:ndaŋ bunda: galiŋ/ gubumagula*
[When the black locust sings out] we go walking up the mountain [to the tablelands] for black pine now

Note the formal similarity between post-inflectional -(a)la and the locative allomorph -la. The latter only occurs with odd-syllabled stems ending in a vowel and, unlike -(a)la, is phonologically cohering. There is thus a potential contrast: *gúdagála* 'dog-LOC' as against *gudá:galá* 'dog-ABS-NOW'; but it is in practice sometimes difficult to distinguish the two affixes in these circumstances. ('dog-ABS-NOW' CAN be pronounced *gúdagála* – see 2.4 and 2.6.1).

[e] TIME WORDS – an example was given at (117) above.

[f] LOCATIONAL WORDS – -(a)la occurs frequently on all types of locationals and locational deictics e.g.

(261) *wira ginda:n waŋgila dalbalala wunaŋ*
The moon is lying high up [in the sky] now

(262) *ɲayu yiŋgula wulaŋada:ɲ*
I've come to die right here

(263) *ɲuŋgum ɲayu gali:ɲ/ banaguwala*
From there I went, now [going] west along the river

Compare (263) with (118) above.

Note that -(a)la is not normally encountered on more than one word in an NP. Thus in

(264) *gana ŋayu yiŋgu bura:yṇḍala wuna:na*
   I'd better try to sleep here in [this] cave

both *yiŋgu* 'here-LOC' and *bura:yṇḍa* 'cave-LOC' are in locative case, but only the latter bears *-(a)la*. (Note however (261), in which both *waŋgi* 'up' and *dalbal* 'reaching up' take the post-inflectional suffix.)

[g] PARTICLES – *-(a)la* can also occur quite freely with particles:

(265) *ŋayu ŋuḍula gana biba:ḍina*
   I tried not to look back now [at my old home, since I now had a
   new camp]

-(a)la is quite common in coastal Yidiɲ, but is consistently more frequent in the texts collected in tablelands Yidiɲ. It is said that *-(a)la* was used much more in Guŋgay than in coastal Yidiɲ (and was in fact a characteristic feature of Guŋgay).

3.9.2 -di. This affix has an intensive or reflexive meaning, corresponding quite closely to English 'self' forms. It is found most frequently with pronouns or deictics:

(266) *ŋayudi mura:nḍi*   I myself am sick

(267) *ŋayudi bina:ŋal mayi*   I'm thinking about vegetable food

Without the *-di* (267) would mean 'I'm listening to vegetable food (e.g. to the noise of fruit falling)'. With *-di* marking its subject *binaŋa-l* 'listen' takes on the meaning 'listen to oneself' = 'think'. (Compare with Dyirbal where the reflexive form of *ŋamba-n* 'listen' is used for 'think', but in this case reflexive is derived by a verbal affix similar to *-:ḍi-n* in Yidiɲ – Dixon 1972: 41, 89.)

(268) *ŋuŋudi bini:r ɲuni:nda wiwi:ɲ*
   [On first coming into the mission Dick Moses was paid with a
   paper docket and asked where the (coin) money was. He was
   told:] 'That IS money you've been given'

-di can also occur with nouns; it is added to a proper name in:

(269) *minmi:nidi ŋuŋu ḍanaŋ*   Its Minminiy standing there

Dick Moses told a story of how (when a boy) he and a friend illicitly dug up some mission potatoes one night. A white supervisor found them and asked what they were doing. The boys stood silent because, as Moses said:

(270) *ɳaɳḍi mayidi ḍula:l baŋga:mu*
      We'd certainly been digging the potatoes

Here, the inclusion of *-di* on the first word of the NP *mayi baŋgamu* emphasises that it WAS potatoes they were digging (and they had no chance of hiding anything).

Note that *-di* – like *-(a)la* and other post-inflectional affixes – will only normally be affixed to one word in an NP, as in (268–70). This contrasts with case inflections, which must be added to each word in an NP, and with genitive, comitative and privative derivational affixes, which can also be affixed to each word in an NP (3.3.6).

-di can also be affixed to adjectives and then indicates 'certainly, really, very' (compare *-waḍan* – 3.9.6). Thus a reply to

(271) *buɲa ɲuŋu guḍu:nḍi ɳala:lḍi*
      That woman has a big bottom

might be

(272) *yiyi/guḍun ɳalaldi*
      Yes, [her] bottom is certainly big.

The particle *wala* 'ceased' (4.10) frequently occurs with adjective-plus-*di*, and serves to emphasise the judgement:

(273) *gaɲa:r ɳalaldi wala*
      [This] alligator is certainly a big one

When *-di* is affixed to *guriɲ* 'good' it is normally accompanied by *wala*: *guriɲdi wala* '[it]'s certainly alright' is a common idiom-like expression. Even more frequent is *ɲuŋudi wala* '[it]'s alright', which may optionally be augmented by *guriɲ* – see (87) in 3.3.6, text 9, line 29 and text 2, line 77.

-di also occurs, though less frequently, with verbs. Thus in

(274) *bulmba duɲuɽ ḍanaŋdi ɳabi yiŋu*
      There is a lot of noise present at this place

the verb *ḍanaŋ* 'stand' plus *-di* indicates that the noise is certainly present ('standing') at the place.

The noise is inalienably possessed by the place – hence the apposition of *bulmba* 'place' and *duɲuɽ* 'noise', both in absolute case. See 4.7.3.

In text 14, line 14, Tilly Fuller said *ɳayu gada:ɲdi*, but on playback preferred *ɳayudi gada:ɲ* (*ɳayu gada:ɲdi* is perfectly grammatical but in this context *ɳayudi gada:ɲ* appears to be more appropriate.)

-di has been encountered several times with *ɲuḍu*, but in each case it seems that the form is functioning as an interjection 'no' (4.12) rather than as the particle 'not' (4.10).

There is a particle *ɲadí* (with stress on a short non-initial syllable – a unique exception to the stress assignment rule of 2.2), that has exactly the same meaning and form as *-di*. It is likely that the affix – which is much commoner than *ɲadí* in the texts collected – is a recent shortening of the particle. See 4.10.

3.9.3 -ŋuɻi. This affix has different effects according as it is added to a pronoun or deictic, or to a noun.

[a] with a pronoun or deictic, *-ŋuɻi* is a (semantic) topicaliser 'this is the one'. See (693) and:

(275) *ŋaɲaɲɲuɻi ɲundu:ba bunḍaɲadan/.../ŋayuŋuɻi bunḍa:ɲ/*
I'm the one you must come and hit...I'm the one who killed [the old man]

(276) *ɲundu:baɲuɻi mayi ŋabi bugaŋ*
[I thought] you were the fellows who were eating all the vegetable food

(277) *yiɲuŋuɻi (ḍugi) ŋayu gunda:l*
This is the (tree) I cut down

yiɲuŋuɻi in (277) has a directly deictic sense; this sentence might be said when pointing out the tree to someone.

[b] when affixed to a noun, *-ŋuɻi* means 'like'. Thus, in explaining to the writer what type of insect *guɻuŋga* refers to, the informant said:

(278) *guɻu:ŋga wawa:l/ mindilŋuɻi gambaɲunda*
'Guɻuŋga' is seen crawling about like a tick

Note also:

(279) *bama gada:ɲ/ gulbul waŋga:ḍiɲu:n/ bundaŋuɻi*
The people came [to high land] as the waves rose like a mountain

(280) *yiŋu wagu:ḍa ɲinaŋ/ buɲaŋuɻi*
This man sitting [here] is like a woman

Compare (280) with (281), in which *-ŋuɻi* is affixed to the demonstrative *yiŋu* and thus bears sense (a):

(281) *yiŋuŋuɻi buɲa ɲinaŋ*
This is the woman, sitting [here]

(Note that the word order is rearrangeable in both (280) and (281).)

-*ɲuṟi* can occur freely with genitive forms. Thus we can have either:

(282) *bama ɲuɲu ɲinaŋ/ ɲumbaṟ gangu:lɲuṟi*
    That person sitting [here] has a face like a wallaby

or

(283) *ɲuɲu bama:n ɲumbaṟ wunaŋ/ gangulaniɲuṟi*
    That face of the person lying [there] is like [the face] of a wallaby

See 4.7.3 for discussion of the use of 'genitive construction' or 'appositional construction' for inalienable possession.

The genitive form of a pronoun can select sense (a) of -*ɲuṟi* – *ŋaḏinɲuṟi* '[I thought] it was yours' – or else, like a nominal, sense (b):

(284) *ŋaḏin ḏaḏa/ ŋayu wawa:l/ ŋaḏinɲuṟi ɲumbaṟ gula guman*
    I see my son – his face is like mine and his body is one [with mine] (i.e. he resembles me in face and build)

Only one example has been gathered of -*ɲuṟi* following an oblique nominal case. Describing the first plane seen in Cairns, Dick Moses said

(285) *garu wawa:lna ḏabu:ɲuṟi galiɲunda*
    [When the plane flew low overhead, it] looked as if it would soon be going along the ground

It is likely that speakers of Yidiɲ perceive -*ɲuṟi* as a semantically non-disjunctive suffix (rather than two homophonous forms). A pronoun or deictic refers to some specific individual whereas a noun describes a class of objects; thus sense (b) 'it is like one of this class' collapses to sense (a) 'it is this' with pronouns and deictics. (Note that the genitive pronoun has to be used for 'he is like me', as in (284).)

(285) could in fact be interpreted qua sense (a) – 'THIS IS the ground it seemed likely to go along' – or (b) – 'it WAS LIKE going along the ground'. When -*ɲuṟi* is suffixed to an adjective an interpretation qua sense (a) or sense (b) is again possible – see line 33 of text 9:

(286) *mayi binaŋ guriɲɲuṟi*   We thought the food was good

-*ɲuṟi* has been encountered suffixed to a verb – *ŋayu wamba:ḏiɲuɲuṟi* 'I waited [for him, while he had his turn]' but does not appear to be productive with this part of speech.

3.9.4 -ŋuɽu-. *-ɲuɽu* 'for another thing' has a contrastive role, marking a referent (of whichever part of speech it is attached to) of a different type. *-ɲuɽu* often carries the implication of things being encountered or happening 'in turn', one after another.

In a myth, a storytime hero comes upon a gathering of tribes. He passes the Yidiɲḍi camp, then the Ngaḍanḍi group, and then the Dya:bugay camp:

(287) *bulmba ḍa:bugay yiɲuɲuɽu ɲinaŋ*
     This next camp is the Dya:bugay [people] sitting [here]

Compare with:

(288) *ḍaḍa ŋaḍin yiŋu bana: wuɲawuɲa:ḍiɲuɲuɽu biri:ɲḍa*
     This son of mine drowned in salt water, it being his turn [to die] (the informant offered the translation 'his time having come')

-ɲuɽu has not been encountered with first or second person pronouns, but it does occur with deictics, (287), verbs, (288), and nominals. With an adjective *-ɲuɽu* indicates a state recently achieved (and contrasting with a previous state):

(289) *bana ḍuda:ɲ ḍilŋgu/ wuna:ɲ guriɲɲuɽu*
     The water went down and now [for a change] lay there peacefully [after a period of high seas and rising water]

Onto a noun, *-ɲuɽu* is close in meaning to the nominal derivational affix *-bi* (3.3.6). The two suffixes can in fact be used as stylistic variants in discourse. Thus, a command:

(290) *ɲundu waŋalɲuɽu gali:ɲ* You take another boomerang!

might elicit the response:

(291) *ŋayu waŋa:lbi gali:ŋal* I'll take another boomerang

The contrastive, listing use of *-ɲuɽu* shows up well in (292) where the informant was explaining the meaning of *wigi-l* 'be made satiated and sick by [eating] too much food of different kinds':

(292) *ŋayu mayi ŋabi buga:ɲ/ miɲa mugu/ miɲa ŋayu buga:ɲɲuɽu/ ŋayu dubu:rḍi ɲinaŋ/ ŋaɲaɲ miɲa:ŋ wigil*
     I ate a lot of vegetable food; then [I] couldn't help [going on to] meat. I then ate meat as well. [Now] I'm sitting feeling full; and the meat (on top of the vegetable food) is making me feel ill

Here -*ɲuɽu* is effectively suffixed to the clause *ŋayu miɲa buga:ɲ*, indicating that the speaker went on to meat after having filled himself up with vegetables. (The Yidiɲɟi believe that one should not normally combine *mayi* and *miɲa* in one meal.)

3.9.5 -buḍun. -*buḍun* 'still' can be affixed to a verb:

(293) *gaɲa:r galiŋbuḍun*
    The alligator is still going [down the river]

or to an adjective (note that in (295) -*buḍun* co-occurs with -*ɲuɽu*; compare with (289) above):

(294) *gana ŋaɲḍi daliyibuḍun ɲinaŋ*
    We're trying to sit [here], but we're still very hungry

(295) *guyiriŋal bana/ guriɲbuḍunŋuɽu*
    [The magic woomera] made the water calm, so that it was still alright (in contrast to its former turbulent state)

or to a deictic:

(296) *ŋuŋubuḍun ŋayu gilbil/ dungu bugan*
    [Two boys have complained to their uncle that he is keeping the meaty parts of grubs for himself and throwing down just the grub-heads to them. Uncle replies:] 'That's all I can throw [to you] – eat the heads!'

or to a noun, in any case inflection – for instance, ergative:

(297) *buriburi:ŋbuḍun mula:ri gali:ŋal*
    The old people still take the newly-initiated man [clearing a path for him in the bush when he goes to defecate] (i.e. his cicatrices are not yet healed sufficiently for him to be allowed to go out by himself.)

or a locational word – see line 57 of text 2. -*buḍun* is not attested with particles.

There is also what appears to be an idiom *ŋuŋumbuḍun* 'and then the same thing' (e.g. line 35 of text 9); it appears that *ŋuŋum* does not appear outside this compound – 3.7.2.

3.9.6 -waḍan. The main function of this affix is to effect the comparison of adjectives:

(298) *ŋayu ŋalal/ yiɲu bagil ŋalalwaḍan*
    I'm big but this other [man] is bigger [than me]

When the writer enquired how to say 'molasses is sweeter than honey' he was given:

(299) *mala:ḍi   wigilwigilwaḍan / banga   ŋuḍu gana*
     molasses-ABS sweet-REDUP-*waḍan* honey-ABS NOT TRY
     biɲḍu
     innocuous-ABS
     Molasses is very sweet, honey isn't – it is only mild[ly sweet]

And when 'my son is cleverer than your son' was asked:

(300) *ŋaḍin   ḍaḍa   milbawaḍan / ɲuni   ŋuḍu*
     I-GEN-ABS child-ABS clever-*waḍan* you-GEN-ABS NOT
     milbadaga:ɲ
     clever-INCHO-PAST
     My son is cleverer (at hunting, etc.), yours never became clever (at it)

The inchoative verbaliser *-daga-n* is discussed in 4.8.1.

As Sapir has emphasised (1949: 122) judgements of grading must precede absolute descriptions. Thus, 'this man is big' can only follow from 'this man is bigger than the norm' or 'this man is bigger than most other men in the community' etc. It appears that the comparative sense of *-waḍan* is primary. But, if there is no explicit second object against which the object under focus is being compared, then *-waḍan* can be translated by something like 'very'. For instance, the first three words of (300) said in isolation could be rendered as 'my son is very clever (i.e. high on the scale of skilfulness qua the other young men in the camp)'. And:

(301) *ŋaɲaɲ bama:l ŋala:lduwaḍan wawa:l*
     The (very) big person saw me

(302) *ŋayu ŋuɲḍu:ɲ baryga:ɲ / bama   yiɲu   milbawaḍan*
     I-SA THAT-ACC praise-PAST person-ABS THIS-ABS clever-*waḍan*
     I praised that [fellow]: 'This person is certainly clever'

-waḍan does not normally occur on a noun, if this is accompanied by an adjective – **bamawaḍan ŋalal(waḍan)*. However, a noun making up an NP by itself can take *-waḍan*, which then implies a comparative judgement on some quality of the noun e.g. *wagu:ḍawaḍan* 'really a man' (or, as the informant put it, 'it's a man alright!').

-waḍan is more limited in occurrence than *-(a)la, -di, -ŋuṛi, -ŋuṛu* and

-*buḍun*, being attested only with nominals. But it is certainly post-inflectional, following all derivational affixes and case endings, as in (301) and:

(303) *ŋayu maḍi:ndaŋ   bunda: ŋala:ldawaḍan*
      I-SA walk up-PRES mountain-LOC big-LOC-*waḍan*
      I'll climb a bigger mountain

3.9.7 Summary. The five main post-inflectional affixes, listed in 3.9.1–5, can occur with nouns, adjectives, locational and time qualifiers, and deictics. All occur after verbs except -*ɲuṛi* and all after pronouns except -*ɲuṛu* and -*buḍun*. Only -(*a*)*la* occurs with particles and only -*di* with the interjection *ɲuḍu*.

A post-inflectional affix will occur on just one word in an NP, even though it may be modifying the meaning of the complete NP. In some instances – for example, (292) – a post-inflectional affix seems to be qualifying a complete sentence, but is again attached to a single word (probably, in this case, the last word in the sentence).

There are three other affixes that also show some post-inflectional characteristics. In 3.3.7 we mentioned the suffix -*ɲa* (possibly one of two homophonous affixes -*ɲa*) that has simple emphatic effect; it is non-cohering and non-reducing. -*mari* 'alongside, along, through' (3.3.7) either goes directly on to a root, or else follows locative case. Finally, -*ḍamu* 'only, all' (3.3.6) is a nominal derivational affix, but it does occur in line 77 of text 2 following a verb (with the meaning '[happens] just a bit'). In addition, the writer elicited

(304) *mayi gurḍiḍamu bana:*
      Let the vegetable get soaked in water just a bit

-*ḍamu* cannot occur productively with verbs.

4 Syntax

4.1 Simple sentences

4.1.1 Non-pronominal noun phrases. The words in a noun phrase in Yidiɲ agree, in all showing the same case inflection. It is this case ending that enables us to group the words together as members of one NP, and it is the choice of case inflection which indicates the function of the NP in the sentence.

Yet Yidiɲ does have a fairly definite preferred word order. Deviations from the norm occur, but they are not frequent. (Here Yidiɲ contrasts with its southern neighbour Dyirbal, which shows exceptionally wide word order possibilities – Dixon 1972: 59, 107–8, 291.) But since grammatical function is entirely determined by case inflections – the Yidiɲ preference for a fixed word order is best regarded as an aesthetic (or pedantic) fad, rather than a syntactic necessity – sentences showing unusual orders are generally quite grammatical, any oddity being at the level of 'style'.

A noun phrase can involve the following constituents:

[i] a specific (i.e. non-generic) noun e.g. *badil* 'rickety nut', *waɲal* 'boomerang', *ḍaḍa* 'child'. This normally functions as the 'head' of the NP.
[ii] one or more generic nouns (the twenty or so generic terms, and the semantic hierarchy they define, are given in 6.2.1). A generic will normally precede a specific noun (deviations from this ordering are encountered extremely rarely). Thus:

(305) *gana mayi   ḍimir   ḍula:lin*
     TRY   vegetable-ABS yam-ABS dig-GOING-IMP
     Go and try to dig some yams up! (text 2.53)

(306) *bama   mula:ri   wulŋga:ɲ   bana:*
     person-ABS initiated man-ABS cover-PAST water-LOC
     The initiated men were drowned by the [rising] water

It is possible to find two generic nouns co-occurring with a specific noun in an NP. They can either be at different levels of generality (both referring to the

nature of the object) as *bama buɲa yabu:ɽ* 'person, woman, pubescent girl';
or one can refer to the function and one to the nature of the object, as *wira
gala biwuɽ* 'moveable object, spear (generic), fish-spear'.

[iii] a genitive noun or pronoun, together with appropriate modifiers/
qualifiers. We can effectively have an NP embedded within an NP; the
case inflection appropriate to the matrix NP is added after the genitive
affix on each word of the embedded phrase. A genitive NP normally
precedes the specific head noun (and any generic qualifier) although it
can – in perhaps 10–12 % of the occurrences noted from texts – follow
the head. Detailed discussion and examples are in 4.7.1–3.

[iv] Genitive marking must be used for alienable possession and can
also be employed in case of an inalienable (part–whole) relationship.
There is an alternative method of indicating inalienable possession – just
appose possessor and possessed nouns, with no special marking (both
will, of course, take the case inflection appropriate to the whole NP).
In this construction it seems that the possessed ('part') noun will
normally follow the 'head' possessor noun:

(307) *ɲundu/ bama   dungu   numaŋ*
     hey!   person-ABS head-ABS move about-PRES
     Hey! that's a person's head moving about

(308) *ɖugi   gubu   gana ŋayu waŋgi wawa:lna*
     tree-ABS leaf-ABS TRY I-SA up   look-PURP
     I must try to look up at the leaves on the trees [to see what colour
        they are, when the clouds have turned yellow just before a
        volcanic eruption]

[v] An NP can, of course, involve a member of the class of adjectives
(which includes, in Yidiɲ, numeral qualifiers). Adjectives normally
follow nouns, as in lines 21, 49, 68 etc. of text 2 and in:

(309) *bama:l   ŋabi:ŋ   guru:n   gadaŋalɲu*
     person-ERG many-ERG language-ABS come-COMIT-PAST
     A lot of people brought news

Most examples of NPs with two adjectives involve one descriptive
adjective and a numeral; both will follow the noun (insufficient examples
are known to determine whether there is any relative ordering between
types of adjective). In (310) the descriptive adjective *ŋalal* 'big' occurs,
unusually, between generic and specific nouns:

(310) *bama   ŋalalŋalal   ḍuruḍuru   ŋabi   gada:ɲ*
person-ABS big-REDUP-ABS adult man-ABS many-ABS come-PAST
Many big adult people came

Only two NPs have been encountered (outside direct elicitation) which show two descriptive adjectives: *ɲuni digir guran ḍuɾi* 'your nose is long and pointed'; *ganda [galiŋalɲu] gadil gulga* '[took along] a short little yamstick'.

Only two or three examples are known of an adjective preceding the head noun; it may be significant that all of these involve numerals; for instance, an informant said *bama ḍambu:l milba* 'person two clever' but then repeated it as *ḍambu:l bama milba*.

[vi] an NP can involve one of a set of logical-type modifiers:

> *bagil* 'another token of the same type'
> *gayal* 'a token of a different type'
> *wawur* 'some of'

(a full account of their syntax and semantics is in 6.2.2).

These generally follow the noun. Note that these modifiers can – more frequently than other non-noun constituents – make up a whole NP:

(311) *ŋaɲḍi gayal   mugu   ŋaŋga:ɲ*
we-SA other-ABS PARTICLE forget-PAST

[After the mission had given us European food] we couldn't help but forget about the other sort (of food) [i.e. traditional Yidiɲ food] (text 9.34)

[vii] Finally, an NP may include a deictic, from the set discussed in 3.7.

Definite deictics seem not to have any preferred place in ordering – they precede the head noun in about half the instances collected and follow them in the other half. In fact, although a definite deictic can occur at the beginning or end of an NP, it is frequently found somewhere in the middle. For example, between possessive and head noun:

(312) *ŋaɲḍi bama:n   yiŋu   buɲa   ḍambu:l*
we-SA person-GEN-ABS this-ABS woman-ABS two-ABS
ḍuŋga:riŋa:lna
run-GOING-COMIT-PURP

We must run away with these two women who belong to the people (text 2.27)

or between a generic noun and a specific proper name:

(313) *bama   yiŋu   yidi:ɲɟi   gadaŋ*
person-ABS this-ABS 'tribe'-ABS come-PRES
This Yidiɲɟi person is coming

or between a noun and adjective:

(314) *bama   yiŋu   ŋabi   ɲinaŋ*
person-ABS this-ABS lots-ABS sit-PRES
A lot of these people are sitting [there] (text 2.8)

Indefinite/interrogative deictics have also been observed at all positions in an NP; but they do – unlike the definite variety – show a distinct preference for NP-initial (and sentence-initial) position.

It will be noted that most of the NPs exemplified in (305–14) have been in absolutive case (marking S or O function). In fact, absolutive NPs tend to convey more information than oblique constituents (syntactic rules are often used to bring a complex NP into surface S or O function). But the evidence available suggests that the possibilities we have outlined apply to all NPs; it is just that absolutive NPs – because of their pivotal role as syntactic 'topic' – tend to take up more of the available choices.

In summary, an NP can involve (with norm ordering shown on the left:

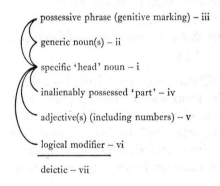

possessive phrase (genitive marking) – iii

generic noun(s) – ii

specific 'head' noun – i

inalienably possessed 'part' – iv

adjective(s) (including numbers) – v

logical modifier – vi

deictic – vii

Note that none of these can be regarded as an obligatory constituent of an NP. There is normally a specific or generic noun, but an NP can quite happily consist of just a deictic, or adjective, or deictic and adjective – in fact, of any combination of choices from i to vii.

Australian languages can be ranged along a continuum qua freedom of word order: at one extreme is Dyirbal, where words can occur in any order within a sentence and case marking is quite obligatory on each nominal item; at the

other end is Diyari (Peter Austin, personal communication) where the order of words within NPs and within VPs (and of phrases within sentences) is quite fixed, and case inflection is normally added to just the last word in an NP. Yidiɲ shows characteristics of both types – most NPs conform to norm restrictions on word order, but each word in an NP must be marked for case.

4.1.2 Pronominal noun phrases. An NP can, of course, consist of just a (first or second person) pronoun. A pronominal NP can also involve any of the items listed in i–vii of the last section. It can include a specific noun or a generic noun, or both:

(315) *ŋaɲḍi ŋabi   bama   gadigadi: gada:ɲ*
      we-SA lots-ABS person-ABS small children-ABS come-PAST
      All of us little children came

Possession can be shown by an embedded NP with genitive marking:

(316) *ɲundu ŋaḍin   ḍaḍa   wala   wula:ɲ*
      you-SA I-GEN-ABS baby-ABS PARTICLE die-PAST
      You, my baby, have passed away

(317) *ɲuni   ɲuŋu   dungu   ŋayu gunda:l*
      you-GEN-ABS that-ABS head-ABS I-SA cut-PAST
      I cut off that head of yours [said to a spirit] (text 14.19)

Inalienable possession of a 'part' can be shown by apposition, as in text 2, line 97, and

(318) *ŋaɲaɲ gurga   gunda:l*
      I-O   neck-ABS cut-PAST
      My neck was cut

A pronominal NP can include an adjective, as in (62), (315) and line 42 of text 2; or a quantifier:

(319) *ŋaɲḍi wawur yaɽŋga:ɲ*   Some of us were frightened

    An interrogative deictic can feature in a pronominal NP – as *ɲundu waɲa* 'who are you?' in line 15 of text 2. A definite deictic can also co-occur with a pronoun – *ɲundu ɲuŋu wagu:ḍa ɲinan* 'you, that man, sit down!'.

    The inclusive sense of a non-singular pronoun is brought out by the inclusion of *ɲunduba* 'a set of people, one of whom is you' with 1 n-sg *ŋaɲḍi* or 1 du *ŋali*. Similarly, the addition of a definite deictic suffixed by *-ba*, to a non-singular first person pronoun, yields an exclusive form (3.6.5).

    A pronoun will normally come first in any NP; exceptions to this rule occur, but are very rare.

A personal name can occur in an NP together with any or all of the possibilities listed in 4.1.1. The proper noun normally comes last in the NP; failing that, it occurs initially (that is, it will not intervene between other constituents). Thus, with deictic, and two common nouns:

(320) *yiɲu   bama   buɲa   bindam   gali:ɲ*
      this-ABS person-ABS woman-ABS 'name'-ABS go-PAST
      This woman Bindam went

or with a genitive pronoun and a head noun that has kinship reference:

(321) *guya:la   ŋaḍin   guŋga:ṟ yaba   gali:ɲ*
      'name'-ABS I-GEN-ABS north   brother-ABS go-PAST
      My brother Guyala has gone north (text 2.123)

It could be argued that when a personal name or a pronoun occurs with other nominal constituents we effectively have two distinct NPs in apposition, filling a single structural slot (one follows the specifications of 4.1.1, and the other consists of just a pronoun or name). Certainly the positioning of pronoun/name before or after the other constituents lends support to this suggestion.

We also find instances of an NP (or, in terms of the suggestion above, two apposed NPs) involving pronoun and personal name:

(322) *ŋayu gulɲḍaṟubay galiŋ*   I, Gulɲḍaṟubay, am going

4.1.3 Verb complexes. The verbal slot in a Yidiɲ sentence can involve two or more verbal forms, provided that these agree in surface transitivity and in final inflection. We will refer to such a syntagm as a 'verb complex'. ('Verb phrase' is normally taken to refer to a constituent involving a verb complex and a noun phrase.)

There appear to be three basic types of verbal complex:
[i] an adverb can occur with a verb. Adverbs and verbs have identical morphological possibilities, as do adjectives and nouns. An adverb provides semantic qualification to a verb, exactly as an adjective does for a noun.

Only five adverbs are known for Yidiɲ. Four are transitive:
giḍa-n 'do quickly'   *gaymbi-n* 'do to all of a set of
burɲḍi-n 'finish off, make die out'   objects'
                                        banḍa-l 'try to do, taste'
and one is intransitive: *waraŋgi-n* 'do all around'
Note that there is also an adjective *giḍa* 'quick'.

VCs involving a verb and adverb occur in (255) above and in:

(323) *bama*   *yabuyabu:ɽ*   *yagar*
     person-ABS pubescent girl-REDUP-ABS hunt away-IMP
     gaymbin
     do to all-IMP
     Hunt all the teenage girls away!

(324) [*mayi*   ] *giḍa:na*   *daŋga:na*   *banam*
     vegetable-ABS do quickly-PURP take out-PURP water-ABL
     [We must] quickly take [the vegetables] out of the water (text 2.52)

In (323–4) both verb and adverb are inherently transitive; in (255) both are inherently intransitive. If there is a difference in underlying transitivity we must either employ a comitative (transitivised) form of the intransitive member, as in

(325) *ŋayu ḍugi*   *warŋgiɲalɲu*   *gunda:l*
     I-SA tree-ABS do all round-COMIT-PAST cut-PAST
     I cut all round the [trunk of the] tree

or else we can derive a surface intransitive by affixing -:*ḍi-n* to the transitive root, as in

(326) *ŋayu gana waŋgi bunda:*   *banḍa:ḍina*
     I-SA TRY up   mountain-LOC try to do-:*ḍi*-PURP
     magi:lina
     climb up-GOING-PURP
     I must try and go climb up that mountain

See also the third line of (250) above.

Note that in both (325) and (326) it is the adverb whose transitivity is changed, to agree with that of the verb. An adverb will normally come first in a VC, although it does sometimes follow the verb, as in (323), (250).

[ii] *gali-n* 'go' or *gada-n* 'come' can co-occur with another verb which is then normally (though not invariably) marked with the appropriate 'going' or 'coming' aspectual suffix.

(327) *ŋayu garu*   *gali:ŋal*   *wiwiɲaliŋ*
     I-SA by-and-by go-COMIT-PRES give-GOING-PRES
     I'm taking [the shells] to give [to them] by-and-by

In (327) *gali:ŋal* and *wiwiɲaliŋ* effectively refer to a single event; that is, the 'going' is thought of as part of the activity of 'giving' (and this can

not easily be brought out through English translation). Note that in
(327) *gali-n* takes comitative *-ŋa-l* to agree in transitivity with *wiwi-n*;
and *wiwi-n* takes aspectual *-ŋali-n*, in semantic concord with *gali-n*.

Other examples of 'transitive verb plus *galiŋa-l*' – without, in these
cases, the verbs having an aspectual suffix – are in lines 63, 64, 115, 120
of text 2.

[iii] Finally, ANY two verbs can be placed in a single verb complex,
subject to transitivity and inflectional agreement (and to semantic
plausibility). Note that VCs of type [iii] are less frequently encountered
in texts than those of types [i] and [ii].

(328) *ŋayu ḍana:ɲ wawa:ḍiɲu* OR *ŋayu ḍanaŋalɲu wawa:l*
      I stood watching

(329) *bama:l   wagal   guman   duga:l   ḍuŋga:riŋa:l*
      person-ERG wife-ABS one-ABS grab-PAST run-GOING-COMIT-PAST
      A person grabbed one woman and ran away with her

(330) *baḍa:ɽ   guɲila   wuna:na/ bagi:ldu   garu*
      leave-PAST PARTICLE-NOW lie-PURP another-ERG by-and-by
        baḍa:lday   bugaŋadaŋ   /
        bite-COMING-PRES   eat-COMING-PRES
      [They] left [the wounded alligator] to lie [there, saying:] 'Another
      [alligator] will come along by-and-by and bite and eat [him]'

4.1.4   Syntactic marking. Much of our discussion in this chapter and
the next will be in terms of the three basic syntactic functions, which we
abbreviate:
                        S – intransitive subject
                        A – transitive subject
                        O – transitive object

Different word classes in Yidiɲ show different patterns of morphological marking for these functions. They are exemplified in table 4.1.

It will be seen, in column i, that pronouns (which must have human
reference) employ an unmarked form for S and A functions, but add the
suffix *-:ɲ ~ -ɲ* to mark a pronoun being used as transitive object. In
fact, a 'transitive event' is most likely to have a human agent, who
initiates and controls the action; this is unremarkable, and it is thus
natural that an unmarked form should be used for A function. The
marked circumstance is for speaker or addressee to be object (rather
than the object being a non-human animate, or else something in-

TABLE 4.1 *Morphological marking for syntactic function*

	i	ii	iii	iv
A	*ŋaṇḍi*	*yiṇḍu:ŋ*	(*yiṇḍu:ŋ* ?)	*bana:ŋ*
S	*ŋaṇḍi*	*yiŋu*	*yiŋu*	*bana*
O	*ŋaṇḍi:ɲ*	*yiṇḍu:ɲ*	*yiŋu ~ yiŋgu:ɲ*	*bana*
	all (first and second person) pronouns	human deictics	definite inanimate deictic	all nominals and indefinite inanimate deictic

animate) and this semantically unusual case is morphologically marked by the suffix -*:ɲ ~ -ɲ*.

The reverse applies in column iv. The majority of nouns refer to non-human entities which are typically found as object of a transitive action; there is no morphological marking for this function. It is less usual to find a non-human as transitive subject and it is thus perfectly natural that this function should be marked by a special (ergative) affix.

A detailed discussion of syntactic hierarchies, exemplified from a wide variety of languages, is in Silverstein (1976). The partial explanation given above was suggested by Silverstein's paper.

We can summarise the case suffixes employed in table 4.1:

	i	ii	iii	iv
A	ø	-*ŋgu*	(-*ŋgu*)	-*ŋgu*
S	ø	ø	ø	ø
O	-(:)*ɲ*	-(:)*ɲ*	ø ~ -(:)*ɲ*	ø

Where just O, of the three syntactic functions, is marked it is said to involve an 'accusative inflection'; 'nominative' is used as the name for the zero marking of S and A functions in such a system (column i). When just A is marked, its case inflection is termed 'ergative', and the zero marking for S and O functions in this type of system is called 'absolutive' (column iv).

Column ii plainly involves both ergative and accusative suffixes. Column iii probably has no true ergative form (*yiṇḍu:ŋ* belonging properly in column ii – 3.7.2). Since O, as well as S, can be realised as *yiŋu* in column iii this form is appropriately referred to as absolutive (paralleling the zero marking for S and O functions in column iv). But *yiŋu* also

functions as the S form in column ii, suggesting that the name absolutive be extended to cover it, too. This gives a full set of case labels:

	i	ii	iii	iv
A	NOM	ERG	(ERG)	ERG
S	NOM	ABS	ABS	ABS
O	ACC	ACC	ABS ∼ ACC	ABS

Note that an accusative-type affix -*ɲa* (which is certainly historically related to pronominal/deictic -:*ɲ* ∼ -*ɲ*) can be added to proper names and kin terms, in the coastal dialect only (3.3.7).

The extreme morphological systems (i and iv) can now be illustrated in sentences. Zero inflection on a noun marks intransitive subject function:

(331) *guda:ga gadaŋ*   The dog is coming

or transitive object function:

(332) *waguḍaŋgu guda:ga bunḍa:ɲ*   The man hit the dog

Transitive subject function demands the ergative affix -*ŋgu*:

(333) *wagu:ḍa gudagaŋgu baḍa:l*   The dog bit the man

Pronouns use the unmarked case for intransitive subject function:

(334) *ŋaɲḍi gadaŋ*   We are coming

and transitive subject function:

(335) *ŋaɲḍi ɲuniɲ bunḍaŋ*   We'll hit you

When a pronoun occurs as transitive object it is marked by the affix -(:)*ɲ*:

(336) *ɲundu ŋaɲḍi:ɲ bunḍa:ɲ*   You hit us

Sentences can, of course, mix nouns, pronouns and deictics without any possibility of confusion. Reference to table 4.1 shows that in (337) *bana:ŋ* is A and *ŋaɲḍi* O:

(337) *bana:ŋ ŋaɲḍi:ɲ ḍaḍa:l*   The (sacred) water doesn't like us

In contrast, (338) involves *ŋaɲḍi*, which can be used for A or S function, and *bana*, which can be S or O. But S cannot co-occur with A or O and so *ŋaɲḍi* must be A and *bana* O. (Alternatively, we could note that *wuɲa-n* is a transitive verb, which demands A and O NPs.)

(338) *ŋaɲḍi bana wuɲaŋ*   We'll drink the water

Indeed, as outlined in 4.1.2 an NP will often involve pronoun/deictic and nominals. Compare (315) with:

(339) *ŋaṇḍi ŋabi:ŋ   wurba:ɲ / waɲi:ra   wira*
      we-SA lots-ERG look-PAST what kind-ABS thing-ABS
      We all looked for [the thing:] 'What kind of thing is this?'

4.1.5 Syntactic types of verbs. Transitive verbs in Yidiɲ fall into two syntactico-semantic types. Firstly, the great majority of verbs in the language expect an animate (normally human) agent, who controls and regulates the action:

(340) *mayi badil buṇa:ŋ bugaŋ*   The woman is eating Badil nuts

(341) *ŋayu bana wuŋa:ɲ*   I drank some water

(342) *ŋayu gidi gilbi:l gaba:ygu*
      I threw the Gidi (tea-tree) torch away, on to the road

However, there are occasional metaphorical uses of verbs from this class, with an inanimate subject:

(343) *ŋaɲaɲ giṇa:ŋ   bugaŋ   gula*
      I-O   fever-ERG eat-PRES body-ABS
      The fever is eating my body away

(344) *bana:ŋ   bulmba   wuŋaŋ*
      water-ERG camp-ABS drink-PRES
      The water [rose up and] drowned the camp

(345) *baḍi   gilbi:l   bana:ŋ*
      boat-ABS throw-PAST water-ERG
      [Waves rose high in the sea and] the water threw the boat up

In the case of a verb that engenders physical change in the object ('hit', 'cut', 'spear' etc. – we use the term 'affect' for this semantic class), the derivational affix -*:ḍi-n* must be added to the verb whenever the A NP is inanimate. This is discussed in 4.2.5.

The second type of transitive verb can only take inanimate subjects. Its most common member is *guba-n* 'burn', whose A NP must be 'something burning' ('fire', 'flame', 'sun', etc.). Examples are at (249) and

(346) *buṛi:ŋ   ŋaɲaɲ guba:ɲ*
      fire-ERG I-O   burn-PAST
      The fire burnt me

(347) *ŋuɳḍu:ŋ   buŋa:ndu mayi   gubaŋ*
ᴛʜᴀᴛ-ᴇʀɢ sun-ᴇʀɢ fruit-ᴀʙꜱ burn-ᴘʀᴇꜱ
That sun is ripening the fruit

buɽi can refer to a burning or to an unlit fire (a pile of wood waiting to be set alight). In the latter sense *buɽi* can be O of *guba-n*, as in:

(348) *buɽi gidi:ŋ guba:ɲ*
The Gidi torch set the fire alight (literally: 'the torch burnt the fire')

Sentences of the type:

(349) *ŋuɳu buɽi gubaŋ*
That fire is burning

are not uncommon. These do not, however, demonstrate an intransitive sense of *guba-n*; (349) is simply an elliptical version of something like (348), with the ergative NP unstated (but potentially statable).

It is instructive to compare *guba-n* with *waḍu-l* 'burn, cook' – this belongs to the first syntactic type and must have a human subject. With *waḍu-l* the 'something burning' can either be in O function:

(350) *ɲundu buɽi waḍu*   You make a fire!

or in instrumental function:

(351) *ɲundu miɲa buɽi: waḍu*   You cook the meat on the fire!

Instrumental and locative cases are marked by the same inflection. There is, however, a syntactic test to distinguish them – only an instrumental NP can be placed in absolute case in a *-:ḍi + ŋa-l* construction (4.3.6); on this criterion *buɽi* is instrument, and not locative, in (351).

guba-n and *waḍu-l* appear to have identical semantic content, and to differ only in syntactic type; they are discussed and contrasted further in 4.2.5, 4.3.7.

The second type of verb, taking only inanimate subject, constitutes a very small class. *guba-n* is, in fact, the only commonly occurring member. Others are *ḍaḍa-l* whose A must be 'water' – 'water turns against some person who has broken a taboo' – and *wigi-l* whose A must be some kind of foodstuff – 'rich food makes some person feel sick' – see (337) and (292) above.

4.1.6 Syntactic extensions. To the core of any sentence – consisting of subject/object NPs and the main VC – can be added peripheral NPs, marked either by syntactic or local cases. In this section we exemplify syntactic extensions, and in the next local extensions are discussed.

Local extensions merely mark the orientation of an action – 'to', 'at' or 'from' some place or object. Syntactic extensions, on the other hand, specify additional participants or objects involved in an event, or explain cause or purpose. There is (as explained and exemplified in 3.3.1) a semantic correspondence between local and syntactic cases: ablative-to-causal (which do, in fact, have the same realisation), allative-to-purposive, and locative-to-dative. The relationship between locative and dative is particularly important to an understanding of Yidiɲ syntax, and is gone into in detail in 4.1.8.

There are five types of syntactic extension to a core sentence, each marked by a separate case inflection. Intransitive cores (consisting of S NP and intransitive VC) and transitive cores (involving A NP, O NP and transitive VC) show the same possibilities of extension.

[1] DATIVE, -*nda*, most nearly corresponds to what is called 'indirect object function' in other languages. That is, it marks the third NP with inherently ditransitive verbs such as *niba-l* 'show [something] to', *buḍi-n* 'tell [something] to', *wiwi-n* 'give [something] to' and *yumba-ṛ* 'send [a message] to'; for example (268) and

(352) *ŋaɲḍi mayi   galŋa:nda wiwi:na*
we-SA food-ABS uncle-DAT give-PURP
We must give some food to uncle

(353) *guru:n   galiɲalɲu   bama:nda yumba:ṛ*
language-ABS go-COMIT-PAST person-DAT take message-PAST
The message was taken to the people

In addition, any transitive or intransitive VC can take a dative NP, indicating something like the orientation of the action:

(354) *ŋaɲḍi ɲuŋgu   bimbi:nda buŋgu   ḍara:liɲu*
we-SA there-LOC father-DAT knee-ABS put standing-GOING-PAST
(text 9.28)
We all went and knelt there [in Church] for (the heavenly) Father

(355) *bulmba: ŋanda wiḍi   badiŋ*
place-LOC I-DAT frog-ABS cry-PRES
The frog is crying out to me in [that] place

(356) *ɲuɲu buɲa badiŋ ŋanda*
That woman is crying for me [e.g. wishing for my return, during my absence]

In (354) *buŋgu* 'knee' is the object and *ŋaɲḍi* 'we' the subject of the transitive verb *ḍara-l* 'put standing up'. Note the contrast between (355) which describes the frog crying out to me, as I pass a camping-site, and (356), telling how the woman cries out because she misses and wants me.

An adjective may take a dative NP as complement:

(357) *ɲuni:nda ŋuŋu buɲa   mundu:y*
      you-DAT that-s woman-ABS desire-COMIT-ABS
      That woman wants you (in a sexual sense)

(358) *waɲḍi:r ɲuni:nda mayi*   How many fruit have you got?

(359) *bulmba ɲalaɲ ɲuni:nda*   The place is unfamiliar to you

[2] PURPOSIVE, *-gu*, has superficial similarities of function with dative; for instance, English translations of both types of NP will frequently involve a preposition 'to' or 'for'.

But there is a crucial semantic difference between purposive and dative. Purposive marks an NP which is peripheral in the current sentence but which is expected to function as a core NP (subject or object) in a subsequent sentence. That is, the referent of a purposive NP in a given sentence is not a central participant in the action described by that sentence, but is likely to be a central participant in a further, logically connected, action.

Typical examples of purposive NPs are (179), (260) and:

(360) *ŋaɲḍi ḍaral   duŋgul   gulugulu:gu*
      we-SA set up-PRES fish-yard-ABS black bream-PURP
      We set up a fish-trap for black bream

(361) *ŋaɲḍi:ɲ bama:l   guga:l   mayi:gu*
      we-O   person-ERG call-PAST food-PURP
      The people called us for food

(362) *bugul   duga:lin   bundu:gu*
      loya vine-ABS pull-GOING-IMP dilly-bag-PURP
      Go and pull loya vines for dilly-bags

Sentences like (360–2) are likely to be extended by a verb – which bears verbal purposive inflection *-na* – describing an action for which the referent of the purposive NP is a core participant. To (361) we can add a clause with *buga-n* 'eat' and to (362) one which features *balga-l* 'make':

(363) *ŋaɲḍi:ɲ bama:l guga:l mayi:gu buga:ḍina*
      The people called us to eat food (text 9.7)

(364) *bugul duga:lin/ bundu:gu balga:lna*
　　Go and pull loya vines, to make dilly-bags [with them]

We have seen that a purposive NP introduces a new participant who
will be playing an increasingly central role as the chain of events unfolds.
In contrast, a dative NP refers to a peripheral participant who has an
entirely 'passive' role, and will not be the agent or patient of any related
action. Someone referred to by a dative NP is merely the recipient or
locus of one event, and is unlikely to play any further role in the chain
of events.

There are examples where dative and purposive appear to be interchangeable. Compare (357) where the object of *mundu:y* 'with desire
for' is in dative case, with (365) where the object of this adjective is
marked by purposive inflection:

(365) *ŋayu mundu:y ŋuɲḍu:ngu buɲa:gu*　　I want that woman

There is, however, an important semantic difference between these two
sentences. (357) indicates passive desire, with no expectation that
anything will be done about it. In contrast, we would expect (365) to be
continued by a verb indicating what the subject intended to do to the
object of his desire:

(366) *ŋayu mundu:y*　　　　*ŋuɲḍu:ngu buɲa:gu*　　　　*garu*
　　　I-SA desire-COMIT-ABS that-PURP woman-PURP by-and-by
　　　ḍuŋga:riɲa:lna
　　　run-GOING-COMIT-PURP
　　　I want to go and run away with that woman by-and-by

Note that, as these sentences occurred at different places in the corpus, (357)
has a female subject, desiring a man, whereas (365–6) deal with a man's
desire for a woman. It is significant that in Yidiɲ society a woman would not
normally do anything in these circumstances, whereas a man might well take
positive steps, as in (366). Further examples of dative/purposive contrast are
at (708–10) in 4.5.1.

Dative and purposive also have quite different syntactic roles, outside
simple sentences. Dative, but not purposive, can be used to mark a deep
O NP in a -*:ḍi-n* construction (4.2.3); purposive, but not dative, can
co-occur with a subordinate clause marked by purposive verbal inflection
-*na*, as in (363–4, 366) (and see 4.5.4); dative co-occurs, in an analogous
manner, with subordinate clauses bearing -*ɲunda* marking (4.4.6).

[3] CAUSAL NPs, marked by -*mu* ~ -*m*, indicate the reason for or cause of something referred to by the core constituents. See (42) in 3.3.1 and:

(367) *muŋgun   yiŋaːriɲ   wawal   galam*
     wound-ABS this sort-ABS see-PRES spear-CAU
     These sort of wounds can be seen [on a certain man] caused by
     spears (text 2.100)

(368) *ŋayu banḍaːɽ   gabay   galiɲunda   / waŋaːlmu*
     I-SA follow-PAST road-ABS go-DAT SUBORD boomerang-CAU
     I followed the road, resulting from the boomerang, as it went
     (i.e. the boomerang was thrown through the bush, and as it
     travelled it cut a swathe that was later used as a road)

Just as the referent of a purposive NP is likely to be a central participant in some later event, so the referent of a causal NP will have had a central role in a previous event (of which the current event is a logical consequence). Thus 'food' would have been the object of 'eat' qua (42), 'spear' would have been the subject or instrument of 'pierce' in an event previous to (367), and 'boomerang' would have been the subject of something like 'cut (a path)' for (368).

The relation between syntactic cases purposive ('in order to') and causal ('as a result of') parallels that between local cases allative ('to a place') and ablative ('from a place') – 3.3.1.

A causal NP can co-occur with a -*ɲum* subordinate clause (4.4.6), just as purposive can occur with -*na* and dative with -*ɲunda* subordinates.

[4] FEAR, -*ḍida* ~ -*yida*, markes a type of peripheral NP that can occur in any type of sentence. The referent of a fear NP is something which is to be avoided, and the verb will normally be describing or suggesting action that can be taken to bring this about. See (740–2) and:

(369) *ḍaḍa   munubuḍun   ɲinaːɲ / bamayida*
     child-ABS inside-STILL sit-PAST person-FEAR
     The child still sat inside [the hut] for fear of [being seen by] the
     people.

(370) *ŋawuːyu   dungu   bayiːldaɲu   / ḍariːɲ   ɲuɲḍunḍida*
     turtle-ABS head-ABS emerge-COMING-PAST sink-PAST that-FEAR
     The turtle's head came out [of the water], and then ducked down
     [again] frightened of something

Note also that the complement of a verb of fearing takes 'fear' inflection:

(371) *yiɲu ḍaḍa yaɽŋgaŋ/ gurilɲḍi:da*
      This child is frightened of the wallaby

Fear NPs co-occur with subordinate clauses marked by the inflection *-ḍi –* 4.6.3.

[5] INSTRUMENTAL NPs, marked by *-da ~ -la ~ -:*, refer to a weapon or tool used in some action. See (536–43) and:

(372) *ŋayu biwu:da   miɲa   ḍaban   baga:l*
      I-SA fish-spear-INST animal-ABS eel-ABS spear-PAST
      I speared an eel with a [multi-pronged] fish-spear

Or to the material out of which something is made:

(373) *ŋaɲḍi dugur   balga:l   ḍirga:da*
      we-SA house-NOM   make-PAST   blady grass-INST
      We made [thatched] a house with blady grass (text 9.18)

Instrumental differs from dative, purposive, causal and fear in that an instrumental NP can, through two syntactic transformations (marked by verbal derivational affixes *-:ḍi-n* and *-ŋa-l*) be placed in absolute case – 4.3.6.

Instrumental NPs have only been encountered in transitive simple sentences. This may just reflect on the corpus available rather than indicating a constraint on the grammar. (Dixon 1972: 93–5 mentions that instrumental NPs are very occasionally found with intransitive simple sentences in Dyirbal.)

4.1.7 Local extensions. We can recognise two distinct uses of local NPs, as they occur with verbs that explicitly refer to position, and with verbs of other types.

Verbs of position can be divided into two subsets – those that specify a 'position of rest' ('sit', 'stand', 'lie', 'put', 'leave' etc.) and those that describe 'motion' ('go', 'come', 'run', 'take', 'carry' etc.). Members of the first subset can take NPs in locative case, and those of the second set may select allative and/or ablative NPs.

With nouns and adjectives, locative and allative inflections coincide. The sense intended can be simply inferred from the semantic nature of the verb – whether it is a 'verb of rest' or a 'verb of motion'. Thus:

(374) *ɲuniɲ bulmba: baḍa:daŋ | buriburi:ŋ*
      you-O camp-LOC leave-COMING-PRES old man-ERG
      The old man brings you and leaves you in the camp

and

(375) *buɲa   ŋuɲu   gadaŋ   banam   bulmba:*
      woman-ABS that-ABS come-PRES water-ABL camp-ALL
      That woman is coming from the river to the camp

Note that there is a distinctive allative inflection on locational qualifiers
(3.4.1) and deictics (3.7.2). This provides some justification for our recognising locative and allative as distinct cases (and generalising the distinction
throughout the grammar). Instrumental also falls together with locative and
allative; syntactic reasons for recognising instrumental as a separate case are
in 4.3.2.

Any action that is not centrally concerned with 'motion' or 'rest' can
be qualified by an NP in the unmarked local case, locative. This simply
indicates the place at which the action took place:

(376) *ŋaɲaɲ ḍina   galba:ndu gunda:ḍiɲu bulmba:*
      I-O   foot-ABS axe-ERG   cut-:ḍi-PAST camp-LOC
      I accidentally cut my foot on the stone tomahawk, in the camp

An NP in local case appears to have a close syntactic connection with a VC of
'rest' or 'motion' (as shown by the selection of case by the verb). With verbs
of other types, however, there is no particular link with locative NPs – here
VC and local NP are simply constituents of the same sentence.

A local NP can consist of nominals, or of a locational qualifier (3.4), or
of a deictic (3.7.2); or it can involve any mixture of these, provided they
agree in case.

4.1.8   Dative and locative. We described, in 4.1.6, the use of dative to
mark a 'passive' beneficiary or indirect object. In the examples given
thus far – (120), (162), (352–9) – dative has occurred on nouns with
human reference.

Locative appears on the surface to be quite different; it indicates that
an action takes place at or in or on a place:

(377) *ŋayu bana: walŋga:liɲu*
      I went and floated on the water

(378) *naga ŋayu ŋanḍa:da yuŋaŋali:ɲ*
      I went and crossed the creek in the east

In (378) the locative form of *ŋaɳɖar* 'creek' indicates where the action referred to by the intransitive verb *yuŋa-n* 'cross the river' took place.

Locative can be suffixed to a noun referring to noise, meaning 'while the noise was going on':

(379) *gawa:lda ŋaɲaɲ wanda:riŋa:l*
  shout-LOC I-o fall down-GOING-COMIT-PAST
  I was taken and put down [on the ground, to have cicatrices cut]
   amidst [much] shouting

Note that in examples such as (127–9), (374), (377–9) locative is in each case added to a noun that has inanimate reference.

There are circumstances in which either dative or locative case can be used, with no difference whatsoever in meaning. 'I sat on the grasshopper' can be rendered either by:

(380) *ŋayu ɲina:ɲ balmbi:ɲɖa*

in which *balmbiɲ* 'grasshopper' shows locative inflection, or by:

(381) *ŋayu ɲina:ɲ balmbi:nda*

in which it is marked by dative case. Similarly, the locational qualifier *ɲaru* 'on top of' can be accompanied by either locative or dative case, as in:

(382) *buriburi burwal ɲaru* $\begin{cases} \textit{gaɲarala} \\ \textit{gaɲaranda} \end{cases}$
  The old man jumped on top of the alligator

In constructions like (380–2) the occurrence of dative or locative appears to be conditioned by a semantic hierarchy, described and diagrammed in 3.1.2. Dative can be used on any NP, whatever its reference. Locative occurs predominantly with inanimates, less with non-human animates, and not at all with humans. As the continuum inanimate–human is gradually ascended, so the chances of locative being used decrease, and the probability of dative increases proportionately. With nouns like *balmbiɲ* 'grasshopper' and *gaɲarA* 'alligator' either case would be about equally likely. With, say, *gulgi* 'sand' both (383) and (384) are perfectly GRAMMATICAL, but the locative (383) would be much COMMONER than dative (384):

(383) *ɲuŋu ɖaɖa burwal ɲaru gulgi:* ⎫ That child jumped on to the
(384) *ɲuŋu ɖaɖa burwal ɲaru gulgi:nda*⎬ sand

However, at the other end of the scale only dative is considered fully acceptable on a human noun:

(385) *ɲuɲu ɖaɖa burwal ɲaru buɲa:nda*
That child jumped on top of the woman

*(386) *ɲuɲu ɖaɖa burwal ɲaru buɲa:*

Sentences like (386) have very occasionally been heard, but were later corrected by informants. Thus, locative could be substituted for dative in (170) of 3.7.2, but not in (169). See also (50) in 3.3.3.

The alternation between dative and locative is frequently exploited for stylistic effect – if a question or statement uses one of these cases, the response may effect stylistic variation by employing the other. This was exemplified by (40–1) in 3.1.3.

The correspondence between locative and dative is nicely exemplified by an informant's explanation of particular uses of the generic noun *ɖaŋga* 'hole, orifice'. He mentioned that it can refer to a hole in the ground:

(387) *ɖabu: wunaŋ ɖaŋga*   '*ɖaŋga*' holes exist in the ground

or to a woman's vaginal opening:

(388) *buɲa:nda wunaŋ ɖaŋga*   '*ɖaŋga*' holes exist on a woman

Here *ɖabu* 'ground' bears locative case, but *buɲa* 'woman' shows dative (cf. 6.2.1).

Locative or dative can be used to mark an underlying O NP in a -:*ɖi-n* construction; case employment here is determined by the same semantic hierarchy – 3.1.2, 4.2.3.

Perhaps the most interesting aspect of the dative/locative association concerns inalienable (part–whole) possession. This is shown either by simple apposition, or by genitive marking (a hierarchy conditions the choice between these types of construction – 4.7.3). In the former case the nouns referring to 'whole' and to 'part' normally show different cases when in peripheral function within a simple sentence.

A body-part noun (body parts are grouped with 'inanimates' in the Yidiɲ semantic classification) is likely to take locative inflection:

(389) *guli gambaŋ dungu:*   A louse is crawling on [someone's] head

whereas in the same functional slot a human noun must take dative marking:

(390) *guli gambaŋ buɲa:nda* A louse is crawling on a woman

(389) and (390) could be alternative descriptions of the same event. More fully, we could put *dungu* and *buɲa* together,. in a relation of inalienable possession:

(391) *guli gambaŋ buɲa:nda dungu:* A louse is crawling on a woman's head

This is in fact the normal construction for a syntagm of inalienable possession in indirect object function. See (32), (132) above and

(392) *ɲundu ɲinan magu: buriburi:nda*
      You sit in the old man's lap

(393) *ḍiran manḍa:ḍiŋ bala: ŋanda*
      Tiredness fills my calves

It is possible, in a construction like (391), for part as well as whole to be in dative case:

(394) *guli gambaŋ buɲa:nda dungu:nda* ⟨= (391)⟩

But, if the possessor is human, the two nouns could not both show locative marking:

*(395) *guli gambaŋ buɲa: dungu:*

(And similarly, locative could not be substituted for dative in (390).)

In S, O or A function both words in a part–whole syntagm will be marked by the same case – 4.7.3. It is only in peripheral function that a case alternation, dative ∼ locative, occurs.

Note that the dative ∼ locative alternation only holds for nominals. Deictic locatives have an entirely local function and cannot be substituted for datives in the way that nominal locatives can (that is, *ŋuŋgu* only means 'there', never 'on that thing'). Pronouns do not show any locative form at all.

In 3.7.1 we explained how the choice between 'human' and 'inanimate' deictics was conditioned by a semantic hierarchy; we have here suggested that the choice between dative and locative is made in terms of the same hierarchy. There is no interpenetration between these two choices – if a deictic is employed, only dative case is admissible in sentences like (380–94).

The genitive suffix derives a noun that functions like an adjective and MUST take the same case inflection as the 'possessed' noun it modifies. Thus we get:

(396) *ŋayu ɲina:ɲ bamanula gala:*   I sat on the man's spear

and not **bamanunda gala:*. Other examples are at (50), (145–6) above.

It is not the case that dative and locative are substitutable – within the constraints of the semantic hierarchy – in every construction. In (377–9) no animate or human noun could be substituted (without gross change in meaning) for *bana* 'water', *ŋanḍar* 'creek' or *gawal* 'shouting'; and here dative could NOT be used in place of locative. In (353), involving *yumba-ɽ* 'take message to', the indirect object must be human, and dative is the only possible case marking. The beneficiary of *wiwi-n* 'give' can be any type of noun and this must be marked by dative case (NEVER locative) whether it is human, as in (352), or animate as in (52) from 3.3.3, or inanimate as in:

(397) *ŋayu bana wiwiŋ dundalaynda*
    I'll give the car some water (i.e. I'll put water in the car's radiator)

The morphological connection between irregular datives and locatives (3.3.2) may be related to the syntactic correspondence between these cases.

4.1.9   Order of sentential constituents. The order in which NPs (and their constituent words) occur in a sentence can be quite free. That is, if a large enough body of texts is examined, any particular word order will doubtless be found. But there are strong ordering preferences, which are adhered to in the great majority of cases; although deviations from the norm are potentially unlimited they are only taken advantage of in a minority of instances.

The order of NPs within a sentence (as of words within an NP, and overall of words within a sentence) is much more constant in Yidiɲ than in Dyirbal, for instance (Dixon 1972: 59, 107–8, 291).

The order of sentential constituents in Yidiɲ appears to be controlled by the following preferences:

(a) S, A, O and instrumental NPs should precede the verb; also (i) S, A and O should come before instrumental; and (ii) A should precede O;
(b) dative, purposive, causal, fear and local NPs should follow the verb;
(c) pronouns should come as near as possible to the beginning of the sentence.

These demands can strengthen or counter each other. Thus, a pronominal O NP is much less likely – through (c) reinforcing (a) – to be found following the verb than is a noun in O function. And whereas a non-pronominal dative NP most frequently follows the verb, a pronominal dative is found before the verb more often than after it (this could be taken as implying that preference (c) is stronger than (b)). In fact a pronominal dative will often precede a non-pronominal O NP:

(398) *ɲundu gana ŋanda guman wiwin*
  you-SA PARTICLE I-DAT one-ABS give-IMP
  You give me [just] one [shell]!

If both A and O NPs are nominals, ergative (A) will precede absolutive (O):

(399) *buɲa:ŋ bama wagu:ɖa bunɖa:ɲ* The woman hit the man

If both are pronouns, nominative (A) will precede absolutive (O):

(400) *ŋayu ɲuniɲ wawa:l* I saw you

When the A NP is a pronoun and the O NP a nominal, preference (a–ii) reinforces (c), with the A NP preceding the O constituent. If, however, A is a noun and O a pronoun, (a–ii) is in conflict with (c); both possibilities occur, but 'pronoun first' is a little commoner:

(401) *ŋaɲaɲ bama:l wawa:l* A person saw me

suggesting that preference (c) takes precedence over (a–ii).

Deictics appear to function more like nominals than like pronouns qua these ordering preferences. Interrogatives do occur initially, but they also frequently occur medially, in the slot predicted by (a–c) – see lines 15 and 17 of text 2.

 Preferences (a–c) help to explain the relative frequencies of orders observed in texts; as already noted, all ordering possibilities are encountered, but some rather seldom. (For instance, instrumental comes between A and O NPs and the verb in (183) and (351); but it occurs sentence-initially in (173), between A and O NPs in (372) and after the verb in (373). In elicitation informants always preferred instrumental to come before the verb, following core S/A/O NPs.)

 There is a tendency for all the constituents of an NP to occur together (in the order discussed in 4.1.1, 4.1.2). However, there is one frequent way in which an NP can be split – one word will occur before the verb (in the position expected by preferences (a–c)) and the remainder after the verb. Thus (258), (270), (343) above and:

(402) *ŋayu bama   wawa:ḍiɲu   ḍambu:l*
I-SA   person-ABS see-:ḍi-PAST two-ABS
I (unexpectedly) saw two people

(403) *ŋayu miɲa   bugaŋ   gangu:l*
I-SA   animal-ABS eat-PRES wallaby-ABS
I am eating wallaby

(404) *ŋayu ɲuɲu   wawa:l   munil*
I-SA   that-ABS see-PAST vine-ABS
I saw that Munil vine

(405) *bama   galiŋ ŋabi   gaḍa*
person-ABS go-PRES many-ABS white man-ABS
Lots of white men are going

Occasional examples of 'splitting' of peripheral NPs have been encountered. For instance:

(406) *miɲa:gu   yiŋu gadaŋ   ḍaba:ngu*
animal-PURP this-S come-PRES eel-PURP
This [person] is coming for eels.

Since a purposive NP normally occurs after the verb it appears here as if the first word is moved to the front of the sentence. This contrasts with (402–5) which – working in terms of the underlying ordering preferences – involve all but the first word of an S or O NP being moved to the right of the verb.

Split ergative NPs do not occur in the author's corpus (but it must be remarked that ergative NPs are typically less complex – involving fewer words – than absolutive NPs). They MAY be possible, but informants were not too happy with them.

The part of an NP which precedes the verb is normally a generic noun or a deictic, with specific noun, adjective etc. coming later in the sentence. It seems as if an event is first outlined through a general description of the participants, and then of the action; once this is completed, referential details can be filled in.

The Yidiɲ pattern of splitting NPs could be the first step in a series of historical changes that would lead to the development of pronominal prefixes to the verb. If (a) each NP had to include a pronoun or deictic, and (b) this had to be the initial element in the NP, and (c) S, O and A NPs always had one word before the verb and the rest after, then these free form pronouns and deictics would be very likely to reduce to bound prefixes. The main innovations necessary would be (i) for deictics to be included in each non-

pronominal NP, and to occur initially; (ii) for A NPs to 'split' like S and O NPs; and (iii) for splitting to be obligatory, rather than optional as at present.

(Alternatively, a single prefix could develop marking just S or O NP, with A NPs being dealt with entirely by free forms. Note, though, that Australian languages which have bound form pronominal prefixes or suffixes have one form cross-referencing S or A NP, and a second form for O NP. Certainly, the morphology of pronouns in Yidiɲ would make such a nominative–accusative cross-referencing scheme more likely than S-and-O-but-not-A incorporation.)

Locational qualifiers occur as part of a local NP and – by preference (b) – normally follow the verb. Within a local NP a locational qualifier will normally precede a noun in local inflection.

ɲaru consistently FOLLOWS a noun if a deictic is also included, but PRECEDES the noun when there is no deictic. Thus in (170) of 3.7.2 the informant gave *ɲaru galba:nda* 'on top of the axe' but *ɲuŋgu:nda galba:nda ɲaru* 'on top of that axe'. (However it is not certain that other locational qualifiers behave in similar fashion.)

There are two further types of sentential constituent – time qualifiers (3.5) and particles (4.10). Both normally occur immediately before the verb, although they are occasionally encountered earlier in the sentence or even following the verb.

Time qualifier *garu* is an exception – the preferred position for this word is at the very beginning of the sentence.

Finally, we can note that ANY nominal constituent can be deleted from a sentence in Yidiɲ; this applies even to subject and object NPs. (In this Yidiɲ differs from Dyirbal, whose sentences must include an absolutive 'topic' NP – Dixon 1972: 70.)

4.1.10 Minor sentences. Like most Australian languages, Yidiɲ has no copula (although *wuna-n* 'lie' covers some of the 'exist' functions of 'to be' in English – 6.2.4). There are thus a number of types of sentence that include no verb at all. These involve a noun in absolutive case (or a pronoun in nominative form) and a 'comment' consisting of either [i] a noun, as in

(407) *ḍugi yiɲu ḍundu*   This tree is [just] a stump

or [ii] a simple adjective, as in

(408) *mayi mamba*   The fruit is sour (text 2.68)

(409) *gurbi wira ḍangan*   This thing might be dangerous

(410) *bulmba yiɲu ḍabu madamada*
    The ground at this camping-site is soft

or [iii] an adjective formed from a noun by the addition of one of the derivational suffixes listed in 3.3.6; examples are at (42), (67), (84), (90–1) and:

(411) *yiɲu bulmba banamuḍay*
    There's water at this camping-site (i.e. a stream of drinking water
        there)

(412) *yiɲu bulmba banagimbal*
    There's no water at this camping-site

Adjectives in 'comment' function frequently bear the post-inflectional affix -(*a*)*la*, as in (258).

Some (simple and derived) adjectives may take a dative complement, very much like a verb – see (357–9) above;
or [iv] a noun bearing the post-inflectional affix -*ɲuɽi* 'like a', or an adjective bearing the post-inflectional affix -*waḍan*, which carries a comparative meaning. See examples (298–300, 302) in 3.9.6;
or [v] a possessive NP, marked by the genitive suffix, as (47), (88) and (762), (767) from 4.7.1. Note also

(413) *mayi miwuɽ ŋaḍin*   The fruit has been gathered up for me

which involves both the adjective *miwuɽ* 'gathered up' and the possessive pronoun *ŋaḍin* 'belonging to me' as comment on *mayi* 'fruit'.

A possessive phrase in comment slot is also likely to bear the post-inflectional affix -(*a*)*la*, as in (259).

The majority of Yidiɲ texts concern the travels of 'storytime heroes' who named each place they came to, basing the name on some geographical feature or on something that befell them there. There are many verb-less sentences 'naming a place'; these are often followed, as in (414), by an explanation of why that name was chosen:

(414) *bulmba yiŋu balbu:ɽu/ balbun ḍana:ɲ*
    This place [was called] Balbuɽu: the Balbun tree grew [there]

The first clause in (414) could be regarded as consisting of a single NP which involves a generic common noun *bulmba* 'place', the deictic *yiŋu*, and a proper name *balbuɽu*. But note that here the generic noun functions as 'topic' and the name is the 'comment'. (The phonological formation of place-names is discussed in 6.1.2.)

4.2   -:ḍi-n constructions

4.2.1   Transitivity distinction. We have already noted (3.1.4) that
Yidiɲ stories are highly first-person orientated. Taking into account the
identity of S and A forms for pronouns and the fact that an O NP (like
any other nominal constituent of a sentence) can be deleted, it can be
seen that it is frequently not immediately clear whether a sentence like:

(415) *ɲayu bargandaɲu*   I passed by

is transitive or intransitive. The transitivity of *barganda-n* can, of course,
be ascertained from its occurrence in other sentences. Thus

(416) *ɲayu bama buɲa bargandaɲu*   I passed the woman by

(417) *ɲaɲaɲ bama:l buɲa:ŋ bargandaɲu*   The woman passed me by

show *barganda-n* to be inherently transitive; the object NP has simply
been deleted from (415).

It might be inferred, from this discussion, that transitivity is not a
cut-and-dried matter, of much syntactic importance, in Yidiɲ (just as in
English it is sometimes difficult to decide whether some occurrence of a
verb like 'eat' is transitive or intransitive). But this would be a mistaken
impression. Every Yidiɲ verb is inherently transitive or intransitive, and
its transitivity is of the utmost importance for the syntactic operations
that can be applied to it. For instance, coordinated verbs within a VC
must agree in surface transitivity (4.1.3); and subordinate clauses must
have an S or O (but not A) NP coreferential to an NP in the main clause
(4.4–6).

Knowledge of the transitivity of a verb is often vital for the semantic
interpretation of a sentence with only one core NP stated. Consider
(418), which has nouns in absolutive case in place of the pronoun in
(415):

(418) *bama buɲa bargandaɲu*

If *barganda-n* 'pass by' were intransitive this sentence would mean 'the
woman passed by'; since it is, in fact, transitive (418) means '[someone]
passed the woman by'.

These examples have depended on choosing a Yidiɲ verb whose English
translation equivalent is ambi-transitive, with A corresponding to S. If we had
chosen an ambi-transitive verb in English for which O corresponded to S,
the noun example – corresponding to (418) – would have been semantically

constant, while the pronoun example – corresponding to (415) – would have involved inversion. ('Get up' is a verb of this type – 'X got Y up' can describe the same action as 'Y got up', quite different from that referred to in 'X got up'.) Discussion of the semantic types S ≡ A and S ≡ O is in 4.3 below (see also Dixon 1972: 296–301).

Although each verb has an inherent transitivity value, this can be changed by a syntactic process; such change is, in Yidiɲ, always morphologically marked. Thus, a transitive stem can be derived from an intransitive root by the addition of comitative *-ŋa-l* (*galiŋa-l* 'take' from *gali-n* 'go', for instance) – 4.3. And an intransitive stem can be derived from a transitive root by the addition of *-:ḍi-n*.

In fact, *-:ḍi-n* is at once the most important and the most complex derivational affix in Yidiɲ. We first survey its uses and present the conditions for its employment (4.2.2) before discussing and exemplifying the individual senses (4.2.3–7).

4.2.2   -:ḍi-n – survey of functions. First note that it is always possible to determine the function of an NP by comparing nominal and pronominal possibilities (4.1.4). For instance:

	pronoun ('I')	noun ('man')
A	*ŋayu*	*waguḍaŋgu*
S	*ŋayu*	*wagu:ḍa*
O	*ŋaɲaɲ*	*wagu:ḍa*

The functions of NPs in

(419) *ŋayu buɲa giba:l*   I scratched the woman

are ascertained to be A and O, by comparison with:

(420) *waguḍaŋgu buɲa giba:l*   The man scratched the woman

(421) *ŋayu ɲuniɲ giba:l*   I scratched you

With this criterion to guide us, we can survey the uses of *-:ḍi-n*:
[1] the most frequent and important function of this verbal suffix is to mark a derived intransitive sentence. For instance, corresponding to (420) there is:

(422) *wagu:ḍa giba:ḍiɲu buɲa:nda*   ⟨= (420)⟩

There are a number of reasons for regarding (422) as intransitive. Firstly, *wagu:ḍa* is plainly an S NP, as can be seen by comparing with the *-:ḍi-n* correspondent of (419):

(423) *ŋayu giba:ḍiɲu buɲa:nda*   ⟨= (419)⟩

In addition, *giba:ḍi-n* can be combined with an intransitive verb within a VC.

[2] *-:ḍi-n* also marks a reflexive construction, as:

(424) *wagu:ḍa giba:ḍiɲu*   The man scratched himself (on purpose)

Again the NP is in S function, the corresponding pronominal sentence being:

(425) *ŋayu giba:ḍiɲu*   I scratched myself (on purpose)

showing that (424-5) are intransitive.

[3] there are a few sentences in which *-:ḍi-n* is suffixed to an underlying transitive root and the resulting sentence is still transitive, with A NP marked by ergative case (on a nominal) and O NP by accusative (on a pronoun). For instance:

(426) *ɲaɲaɲ ginga:ŋ*   *giba:ḍiɲu*   (*ŋayu baŋgaɲunda*)
I-O   prickle-ERG scratch-:ḍi-PAST I-SA pass by-DAT SUBORD
A prickle scratched me (as I went past [a bush])

(427) *ɲuɲu buɲa*   *gaba:ɲḍa ḍana:ɲ* / *ɲuɲḍu:ŋ waguḍaŋgu*
THAT-S woman-ABS road-LOC stand-PAST THAT-A man-ERG
gunda:ḍiɲu   baŋga:lda/
cut-:ḍi-PAST axe-INST

That woman was standing in the road (in the way) and the man cut her accidentally with his axe (as he was making to cut a tree)

(428) *ɲaɲaɲ bama:l*   *ḍaŋga:ḍiŋ*   *muguy*
I-O   person-ERG grumble at-:ḍi-PRES all the time
[That] person keeps grumbling at me at all the time [telling me to work]

These three examples do not immediately appear to have any semantic common denominator; and *-ḍi-n* does not in (426-8) seem to have any syntactic effect.

[4] *-:ḍi-n* does very occasionally occur with an intransitive root, the resulting stem being again intransitive:

(429) *ɲuɲu bama gama:ḍiɲu*
That person is vomiting (the informant glossed this as 'that person been STILL retch up')

An exhaustive investigation of the occurrences of the verbal derivational affix *-:ḍi-n* suggests the following explanation for its use.

First note that S and O functions play a central role in the grammar of Yidiɲ. For instance, if a subordinate clause has an NP coreferential with some NP in the matrix clause, then this NP must be in surface S or O function in the subordinate clause; and, morphologically, absolutive case marks a nominal in either S or O function.

Now the norm case in Yidiɲ is for a transitive verb to occur in a sentence which has a (deep) A NP that is

(i)   distinct from the surface S/O NP, and

(ii) has volitional control over

(iii) a single completed or anticipated action

Any sentence that deviates from this norm will have its verb(s) marked by the derivational affix -*:ḍi-n*.

Thus -*:ḍi-n* is used

(a) in an 'antipassive' construction, like (422–3), where the deep A NP becomes surface topic (S function) and the deep O NP takes on a peripheral role, marked by dative or locative case. Condition (i) is broken, since the deep A NP becomes surface S.

(b) in a 'reflexive' construction, like (424–5). Here deep A is identical with deep O and Yidiɲ adopts the convention of including a single NP in the surface structure – this is in fact in S function. Condition (i) is again broken.

(c) if the A NP refers to something inanimate, as in (426), the agent could not be said to have volitional control over the action. Here condition (ii) is broken. (There is a semantic restriction on the class of verbs with which -*:ḍi-n* is used in this sense – see 4.2.5.)

(d) if an A NP has human reference but, as in (427), achieves some result quite accidentally, without planning or control. Here condition (ii) is again broken.

(e) if the action referred to by the verb is 'continuous', extending into the present and future, so that it cannot be viewed as a (prospective or retrospective) whole, from the vantage point of the present, as in (428–9). Here condition (iii) is broken.

(i–ii) refer to an NP in A function, and so -*:ḍi-n* in senses (a–d) is restricted to transitive verbs. (iii), however, simply refers to the duration of the action, and can apply equally well to transitive verbs, (428), or to intransitives, (429).

4.2.3–7 take (a–e) one at a time – discussing, explaining and exemplifying these uses of -*:ḍi-n*. Note that -*:ḍi-n* must always be used in cases (a–b), when an intransitive clause is derived from an underlying

transitive configuration. *-:ḍi-n* will always be used in case (c), if the verb is from a semantic set that we term 'affect'. The line between 'accident' and 'purpose' (with a human agent in each case) and that between 'discrete' and 'continuous' are hard to draw and *-:ḍi-n* will only sometimes be employed in cases (d) and (e) – it is used specially to mark an action as embarrassingly 'accidental' or as inconveniently 'continuous'.

4.2.3 Antipassives. There is a syntactic process in Yidiɲ that derives an intransitive from an underlying transitive sentence. Thus from:

(430) *waguḍaŋgu guda:ga wawa:l*   The man saw the dog

we obtain either:

(431) *wagu:ḍa wawa:ḍiɲu gudaganda* ⟨= (430)⟩

or

(432) *wagu:ḍa wawa:ḍiɲu gudagala* ⟨= (430)⟩

Absolutive replaces the ergative inflection on the deep A NP, and either dative – as in (431) – or locative – as in (432) – replaces the absolutive inflection on the deep O NP; the verb receives the derivational affix *-:ḍi-n*.

The occurrence of dative or locative on the deep O in a *-:ḍi-n* construction of this type is conditioned by the semantic hierarchy described in 3.1.2 and 4.1.8. With an inanimate noun locative is preferred, although dative is perfectly possible, as (21–2); with a (non-human) animate noun dative and locative are both acceptable and both fairly common, as (20) and (431–2); with a human noun only dative case is allowed, as (16).

Note that two nouns which are in apposition, showing a 'part–whole' (or inalienable possession) relationship, in the O NP of a simple sentence:

(433) *wagu:ḍa dungu   buɲa:ŋ   ḍina: baɾa:l*
man-ABS head-ABS woman-ERG foot-INST strike-PAST
The woman kicked the man's head

will be likely to take different cases in the corresponding *-:ḍi-n* construction. Here the human 'owner' will be in dative case while the body-part is normally placed in locative inflection (although it, too, CAN take dative):

(434) *buɲa   waguḍanda dungu: ḍina: baɾa:ḍiɲu* ⟨= (433)⟩
woman-ABS man-DAT   head-LOC foot-INST strike-*:ḍi*-PAST

Pronouns do not occur in locative case, so there is not even a morphological alternative to dative for this part of speech. Corresponding to

(435) *ŋayu ɲuniɲ wawa:l*   I saw you

we get just

(436) *ŋayu ŋanda wawa:ɖiɲu* ⟨= (435)⟩

As mentioned in 4.1.8, locative deictics have an entirely local sense, and could not function as the surface marker of a deep O NP in an antipassive construction.

In the last section we gave reasons for regarding (431–2), (434) and (436) as intransitive sentences; the absolutive noun or nominative pronoun constitutes an S NP. This process – of deriving (431–2) from (430), and so on – has in fact two syntactic effects: (1) to make the verb intransitive, and (2) to place the A NP in the unmarked case. In view of this it seems appropriate to (follow Silverstein and) refer to this type of . construction as 'antipassive' (qua 'passive', which places a deep O NP in the unmarked case).

Any type of A NP can take on surface S function in a -*:ɖi-n* construction – an inanimate example is at (393) above.

An antipassive is syntactically 'marked' – qua simple sentences like (430), (433), (435). It is used in the following typical circumstances:

[i] To derive an intransitive verb for inclusion in an intransitive VC – 4.1.3. See (326) and:

(437) *ŋayu gana:ŋgar galiŋ* / *gaṛbam   miɖi:ɖiŋala*
      I-SA IN FRONT go-PRES behind-ABL block-*:ɖi*-PRES-NOW
      galiŋ
      go-PRES
      I go in front, now [I'm] going blocking [the road against anyone coming] from behind

Note that *miɖi-l* is a transitive root, as in:

(438) *ŋayu gabay   miɖil*
      I-SA road-ABS block-PRES
      I'm blocking the road [so that no one can get by]

[ii] To put the A NP in surface S function in order to meet the syntactic requirements on coordination (5.1.3) or subordination. Suppose, for instance, that we wished to embed:

(439) *yiṇḍu:ŋ bama:l mayi ḍula:l*
These people dug up vegetables (i.e. potatoes)

as a subordinate clause within

(440) *ŋayu yiṇu bama baṇḍi:liṇu* I went and found these people

A condition on this type of embedding is that the 'common NP' (here *yiṇu bama*) should be in S or O function in each clause. This is met in the case of (440), but (439) must be antipassivised to satisfy the condition. We then get:

(441) *yiṇu bama mayi: ḍula:ḍiṇu* ⟨= (439)⟩

which can be embedded in (440), yielding:

(442) *ŋayu yiṇu bama baṇḍi:liṇu mayi: ḍula:ḍiṇu:n*
I went and found these people digging up vegetables

(The second occurrence of *yiṇu bama* is deleted, and subordinate inflection *-ṇunda* replaces tense on the verb of the bound clause. *ḍula+ :ḍi+ṇu+nda* is then reduced to *ḍula:ḍiṇu:n* through the operation of Rules 1 and 2 – 3.8.4, 2.3.1, 2.3.2.)

Where a -:*ḍi-n* construction occurs as a subordinate clause it is possible for the deep O NP to be marked by a peripheral case other than dative or locative (causal and purposive are attested). A detailed discussion of this and other aspects of subordination are in 4.4.6, 4.5.4.

[iii] Sentences in Yidiɲ should, if possible, include an absolutive or nominative NP (these constituents are only very rarely deleted). In contrast, dative/locative NPs – including those acting as surface realisation of O in a -:*ḍi-n* construction – are particularly liable to deletion. Thus, if a speaker wishes to indicate the A for some action, but prefers not to commit himself concerning the O, he can simply use a -:*ḍi-n* construction:

(443) *yiṇu buṇa buga:ḍiŋ* This woman is eating

The corresponding simple sentence:

(444) *yiṇḍu:ŋ buṇa:ŋ bugaŋ*

is decidedly awkward, having an empty (absolutive) O slot.

[iv] A -:*ḍi-n* construction may be used simply for stylistic felicity. A response may employ -:*ḍi-n* in reply to a question or statement whose verb bore no derivational affix; or, if a statement uses -:*ḍi-n* the response may avoid it – see (30–1) in 3.1.3. In discussing (430–2) informants

volunteered that these were alternatives, with identical meaning, and that they could be substituted one for another to satisfy the aesthetic demands of discourse structure.

Just as we can have an imperative version of a simple sentence, from which the subject NP can optionally be deleted (4.9):

(445) *(ɲundu) gangu:l baga*   (You) spear the wallaby!

so we can have an imperative of the corresponding antipassive:

(446) *(ɲundu) gangulala baga:ɖin*   ⟨= (445)⟩

However, informants greatly preferred the more straightforward (445), mentioning that (446) would only be likely as a response, for the sake of stylistic variation.

'Antipassive' is the commonest sense of the affix -*:ɖi-n*, accounting for more than three-quarters of its occurrences in texts. Examples will be found throughout the texts given on pages 513–39.

Some verbs in Yidiɲ exist only in *:ɖi-n* form; they are all intransitive. Examples include *ɲaŋga:ɖi-n* 'talk', *waŋga:ɖi-n* 'get up', *bani:ɖi-n* 'grumble' in (100), and *muri:ɖi-n* 'scream' in line 29 of text 2. Haviland (1972) reports that Guugu-Yimidhirr has a rather larger number of verbs that only occur in *-dhi* form (Guugu-Yimidhirr *-dhi* appears to be cognate to Yidiɲ -*:ɖi-n*, and seems to have a similar range of functions).

4.2.4 Reflexives. A transitive simple sentence must have referentially distinct A and O NPs:

(447) *ŋayu wagu:ɖa bambi:l*   I covered the man

(448) *waguɖaŋgu ɲaɲaɲ bambi:l*   The man covered me

If the agent and patient of an action described by a transitive verb are identical, then a reflexive construction must be used. There is a single S NP, describing agent/patient, and the verb bears the suffix -*:ɖi-n*:

(449) *ŋayu bambi:ɖiɲu*   I covered myself

(450) *wagu:ɖa bambi:ɖiɲu*   The man covered himself

Other examples of reflexives are at (240), (242) in 3.8.7.

Note that reflexives – like transitive simple sentences and their antipassive counterparts – assume that the agent has volitional control over the action, and that he performs it quite deliberately and purposefully ('accidental reflexives' are discussed in 4.2.5). In terms of our explanation of 4.2.2, -*:ɖi-n* in (449–50) simply marks the fact that the deep agent is realised in surface structure through an S NP.

It is interesting to compare reflexives (449–50) with the antipassive counterparts of (447–8):

(451) *ŋayu bambi:ḍiŋu waguḍanda* ⟨= (447)⟩

(452) *wagu:ḍa ŋanda bambi:ḍiŋu* ⟨= (448)⟩

The dative NP could be deleted from (451), giving a sentence identical to (449). Thus, *ŋayu bambi:ḍiŋu* is ambiguous between reflexive and antipassive readings ('I covered myself' vs 'I covered someone/something' with the patient unstated). Similarly for (452) and (450).

The ambiguity can be resolved by including particle *ganagayuy* 'self' or *ganamaṛbu* 'self' (4.10) or post-inflectional clitic *-di* 'self' (3.9.2) in the reflexive:

(453) *ŋayu ganagayuy bambi:ḍiŋu*   I covered myself

Note that both *ganagayuy* and *-di* appear (like 'self' words in English) to have intensive as well as reflexive uses; either could conceivably be included in (451–2). But it does seem that reflexive is the predominant sense – of *ganagayuy* at least – and if it were included in (453) this particle would be likely to be taken as providing disambiguation in the direction of reflexive.

We can, of course, have an imperative version of any reflexive sentence; thus:

(454) *(ɲundu) ganagayuy bambi:ḍin*   (You) cover yourself!

A *-:ḍi-n* reflexive occurs in line 53 of text 2.

Note also that ditransitive verbs such as *wiwi-n* form reflexives. Thus:

(455) *ɲuɲu   ḍambu:l wiwi:ḍiɲula | bigunuyi   ḍara:ḍiɲu*
       THAT-S two-ABS give-:*ḍi*-PAST-NOW shield-COMIT-ABS stand-:*ḍi*-PAST
       Those two gave themselves up, standing with shields [in their hands].

It was the custom in Yidiɲ society that when a man admitted some crime he would offer himself as a target for people to throw spears at, attempting to protect himself with his shield (but not running away, or retaliating by throwing spears himself). (455) describes such an invitation.

The reflexive of *wiwi-n* can also be used to describe a woman submitting to the sexual advances of a man:

(456) *ŋayu wiwi:ḍiŋu   yiɲḍu:nda waguḍanda/ ŋaɲaɲ ḍumba:lna*
       I-SA give-:*ḍi*-PAST THIS-DAT   man-DAT   I-O   swive-PURP

I gave myself to this man, for him to swive [= make love to] me

Unlike its neighbours Dya:bugay (Hale 1976a: 238) and Dyirbal (Dixon 1972: 92–3), Yidiɲ has no verbal affix marking 'reciprocal' constructions.

The reduplicated form of *bunḍa-n* 'hit' consistently behaves as a reciprocal (and is intransitive):

(457) *bama ḍambu:l bunḍabunḍaŋ*

The two people are fighting (literally 'hitting each other')

This, however, appears to be unique; the reduplicated forms of all other transitive verbs are still transitive and mean simply 'keep on doing'.

However, most of the writer's attempts to elicit reciprocal brought forth sentences of the form 'One person painted another, and then the other painted the first person, in turn' involving one of the particles *ḍaymbi*, *ḍaybaṛ* 'in turn' – see 4.10.

4.2.5 Non-animate agent. Suppose that someone accidentally steps on an axe lying on the ground and hurts himself on it. He might say, in English, 'The axe cut my foot', putting the instrument 'axe' as subject of a transitive verb. Yidiɲ uses an exactly analogous construction, but here the verb must be marked by *-:ḍi-n* to indicate an inanimate agent:

(458) *ŋaɲaɲ ḍina bayga:ldu gunda:ḍiɲu*

I-O foot-ABS axe-ERG cut-*:ḍi*-PAST

The axe cut my foot (= I cut myself, accidentally, on the axe)

The ergative and accusative inflections indicate that (458) is a normal transitive sentence – compare (458) with examples of antipassive and reflexive in the last two sections, for which *-:ḍi-n* marked a derived intransitive construction. But in (458) the referent of the A NP does not have volitional control over the action; there can be no imperative counterpart of this sentence. It is because condition (ii) of 4.2.2 is broken that the suffix *-:ḍi-n* must be included in (458).

Summarising and contrasting the three uses of *-:ḍi-n* dealt with, we can begin with 'normal' transitive sentences – which meet conditions (i–iii) of 4.2.2 – that can appropriately include an instrumental NP:

(459) *ŋayu wagu:ḍa bayga:lda gunda:l*

I cut the man with an axe

(460) *ŋaɲaɲ waguḍaŋgu bayga:lda gunda:l*

The man cut me with an axe

From these sentences we can derive antipassives, with essentially the same meaning (note that *bayga:lda* 'axe-INST' is retained without change in an antipassive):

(461) *ŋayu waguḍanda bayga:lda gunda:ḍiɲu* ⟨= (459)⟩

(462) *wagu:ḍa ŋanda bayga:lda gunda:ḍiɲu* ⟨= (460)⟩

If underlying agent and patient coincide we must have a reflexive:

(463) *ŋayu baŋga:lda gunda:ɖiɲu*
     I cut myself (on purpose) with an axe

(464) *wagu:ɖa baŋga:lda gunda:ɖiɲu*
     The man cut himself (on purpose) with an axe

Finally, we can have transitive sentences, similar to (459–60) but with an inanimate A NP which is not the 'controller' of the action:

(465) *ŋaɲaɲ baŋga:ldu gunda:ɖiɲu*
     I cut myself (accidentally) on an axe (= An axe cut me)

(466) *wagu:ɖa baŋga:ldu gunda:ɖiɲu*
     The man cut himself (accidentally) on an axe (= An axe cut him)

(463–4) imply that the actor did something to himself deliberately and on purpose. In contrast, (465–6) indicate that he did something to himself accidentally – in these examples the agent could have injured himself by standing on an axe, or letting it drop on his foot, or nicking himself in the neck when swinging the axe back.

English translations which involve a reflexive can be appropriate for (465–6), as for (463–4). But it must be emphasised that only (463–4) are reflexives in Yidiɲ – derived intransitive sentences with a single S NP. (465–6) are transitive sentences, with A and O NPs but involving a non-controlling A.

Informants would sometimes translate sentences like (465–6) by reflexives in English, but often used a transitive gloss with inanimate A. Thus the reflexive

(467) *ŋayu dungu   babalala   bunɖa:ɖiɲu*
     I-SA head-ABS bone-INST hit-:ɖi-PAST

was glossed 'I hit my head on that bone', whereas the 'inanimate A' transitive sentence:

(468) *ŋaɲaɲ dungu   babalaŋgu bunɖa:ɖiɲu*
     I-O   head-ABS bone-ERG hit-:ɖi-PAST

was translated by the informant 'That bone hit my head'. (He explained that if one walked into a butcher's shop where bones were hanging from the ceiling, and accidentally knocked one's head on a bone, (468) would be an appropriate description.)

As already mentioned, any NP can be omitted from a Yidiɲ sentence. Thus we can have shortened versions of (463) and (465):

(469) *ŋayu gunda:ɖiɲu*   I cut myself (on purpose)

(470) *ɲaɲaɲ gunda:ɖiɲu*   I cut myself (accidentally) (= Something in-
      animate cut me)

Here the different form of the pronoun, for S and O functions respectively, clearly distinguishes the two meanings. Consider, however,
shortened versions of (464) and (466):

(471) *wagu:ḍa gunda:ḍiɲu*   The man cut himself (on purpose)

(472) *wagu:ḍa gunda:ḍiɲu*   The man cut himself (accidentally)
      (= Something inanimate cut the man)

Since a noun has the same form for both S and O functions, (471) and
(472) are identical (*wagu:ḍa gunda:ḍiɲu* is in fact three-ways ambiguous,
the third possibility being a shortened form of the antipassive (462), just
as (469) could be a reduced version of either (463) or (461)). (471/2) can
only be disambiguated by including an NP indicating the weapon or tool
involved – if this is in instrumental case it indicates a true reflexive, and
if in ergative case a non-controlled transitive sentence.

We can, as mentioned above, have imperative versions of (459–64),
(469), (471) but not of (465–6), (470), (472).

The distinction between sentences like (463–4) and those like (465–6)
is an important one in Yidiɲ. For instance, text 2 describes how Guyala
and Damari are to fight against some other people on a certain day.
Damari gets up early and slinks off by himself, to avoid the fight; he
runs up against a Bougainvillea tree so that its prickles pierce his skin and
it will look as if he has been speared in battle. He rehearses what he will
say to Guyala (line 97):

(473) *ŋayu ḍuŋga:na/ ɲaɲaɲ gula   baga:ḍina*
      I-SA run-PURP I-O   body-ABS spear-:ḍi-PURP
      I had to run, and as a result my body got speared

The inclusion of the O form *ɲaɲaɲ* shows that Damari is using the
transitive 'inanimate A' construction, of the pattern shown in (465–6);
he is saying that he was speared accidentally, whilst trying to dodge
away. But in fact he had purposefully speared himself, on the Bougainvillea prickles, and should have described this by using *ŋayu* in place of
ɲaɲaɲ (employing a reflexive sentence, of the type exemplified at
(463–4)). By choosing *ɲaɲaɲ* rather than *ŋayu*, Damari is telling a lie
although it is difficult to convey this in a simple manner through
English translation.

The contrast between purposeful reflexives and non-controlled transitives ('accidental reflexives' in English translation) is further brought out by the compound verb *giḍaṛ+gunda-l* 'paint in pattern' (see 6.1.1). This is built up from a noun *giḍaṛ* 'mark' and the transitive verb *gunda-l* 'cut'. Corresponding to (469) we have the acceptable Yidiɲ sentence:

(474) *ŋayu giḍaṛ+gunda:ḍiɲu*   I painted myself up

However the sentence patterned on (470),

*(475) *ŋaɲaɲ giḍaṛ+gunda:ḍiɲu*

was judged quite unacceptable by informants, since it is impossible to get painted accidentally (if a pot of paint were spilt on one, it would not fall into an accepted pattern).

Other examples of 'inanimate A' transitive sentences with -:ḍi-n marking include (172) in 3.7.2, (376) in 4.1.7 and:

(476) *dunda:lay ḍuŋga:ŋ gaba:yɲḍa/ walba:ŋ bunḍa:ḍiɲu*
      car-ABS   run-PAST road-LOC   stone-ERG hit-:ḍi-PAST
      A car was going along the road, and a stone [rolling down the hillside] smashed into it

(477) A – *ŋaɲaɲ mandi   baga:ḍiɲu*
          I-o   hand-ABS pierce-:ḍi-PAST
          My hand was pierced

      B – *waɲi:ndu   ɲuniɲ baga:ḍiɲu*
          WHAT-ERG you-o pierce-:ḍi-PAST
          What pierced you?

Note that the inanimate interrogative *waɲi:ndu* is used in (477), emphasising the 'inanimateness' of the subject of *baga:ḍiɲu*. (If the person responding had wished to ask 'who pierced you?' he would have said *waɲḍu ɲuniɲ baga:l*, using the human interrogative *waɲḍu* and not marking the verb with -:ḍi-n.)

In 4.1.5 we distinguished two kinds of transitive verb. There is a small class, members of which MUST take an inanimate agent, and a complementary large class whose agent is normally animate (and usually human). The types can be exemplified by the 'semantic minimal pair' *guba-n* '(fire) burns' and *waḍu-l* '(person) burns/cooks'.

-:ḍi-n is only used to mark an inanimate A with verbs from the larger class, whose A NP is normally human. Thus, corresponding to the simple sentence:

(478) *bama*   *wagu:ḍa buɲa:ŋ*   *buṛi:*   *waḍu:l*
person-ABS man-ABS woman-ERG fire-INST burn-PAST
The woman burnt the man with the fire

we can have:

(479) *bama wagu:ḍa buṛi:ŋ waḍu:ḍiɲu*
The man burnt himself, accidentally, on the fire (= The fire
burnt the man)

Note that (479) appears to have exactly the same meaning as the corresponding simple sentence involving *guba-n* (cf. (346–7) above):

(480) *bama wagu:ḍa buṛi:ŋ guba:ɲ*   The fire burnt the man

Either (479) or (480) could be used, in appropriate circumstances; (480)
would normally be preferred on the grounds that it is simpler.

    guba-n, and other verbs that demand an inanimate A, cannot take
-*:ḍi-n* with the sense described in this section. A reflexive sense is like-
wise impossible; but verbs of this set do form antipassives, which are
marked in the regular way by -*:ḍi-n*. Corresponding to (480) there is:

(481) *buṛi guba:ḍiɲu bama:nda waguḍanda*   ⟨= (480)⟩

    When -*:ḍi-n* is added to *waḍu-l* it can have any of the three senses
described in this and the last two sections. *waḍu:ḍi-n* is a transitive verb
with non-controlling A in (479); it functions as a derived intransitive in
the reflexive sentence:

(482) *bama wagu:ḍa dama:ri waḍu:ḍiɲu buṛi:*
The silly man burnt himself on the fire (on purpose)

and in the antipassive version of (478):

(483) *buɲa waḍu:ḍiɲu bama:nda waguḍanda buṛi:*   ⟨= (478)⟩

A semantically based generative grammar – cf. McCawley (1968), Lakoff
(1971) – might explain these facts by suggesting that the lexical item *guba-n*
is substituted for *waḍu-l+-:ḍi-n* in the syntactic representation of a sentence
like (479), yielding (480). This lexical insertion would have to follow the
semantico-syntactic operation of recognising that A is inanimate and as a
result marking the verb by -*:ḍi-n*. If the lexical insertion were not applied,
(479) would simply result. The Dyalŋuy avoidance style (1.6) typically has one
lexical item corresponding to several distinct words in everyday Yidiɲ. There
is just one Dyalŋuy verb 'burn, cook' – *maba-l*. It is significant that informants gave *maba-l* as the Dyalŋuy correspondent of *waḍu-l* and *maba:ḍi-n*
for *guba-n*, explicitly showing that *guba-n* is precisely equivalent to *waḍu-l*
plus -*:ḍi-n* understood in the 'inanimate agent' sense.

We mentioned that -:*ḍi-n*, in the sense discussed in this section, can only be added to members of the large class of transitive verbs that expect animate subjects. It can, in fact, only be used with CERTAIN verbs from this class. -:*ḍi-n* is used to mark an inanimate agent only with a verb which describes an action which effects some physical change in the patient, and demands an instrumental NP (referring to a weapon or implement). It is this weapon or implement that becomes the A NP in a -:*ḍi-n* construction of the type just described. We use the term 'affect verbs' to refer to this semantic class, which includes 'hit', 'cut', 'split', 'spear', 'burn' and so on. (The class corresponds roughly to the semantic type 'affect' set up for verbs in Dyirbal – Dixon 1968: 331–45 and 1971.)

Verbs outside the 'affect' class seldom have an inanimate A, but if they do this can NOT be marked by verbal -:*ḍi-n*. See (343–5) in 4.1.5 and the conversation:

(484) A – *ŋaɲaɲ muni:ldu guṛi   duga:l*
          I-o   vine-ERG waist- ABS grab-PAST
          The Munil-vine grabbed me by the waist (that is, its barbs hooked onto me)

        B – *ɲundu giyi   galin   ŋuŋgu:ruɲ/ muni:ldu duga:lḍi*
          you-SA DON'T go-IMP THAT WAY vine-ERG grab-LEST-ABS
          Don't you go that way, lest the Munil-vine grab you!

Other non-affect verbs which cannot take -:*ḍi-n* in the 'inanimate A' sense include 'cover' (as in 'the bark fell off the tree and covered the person lying beneath it') and 'coil' (as in 'the vine coiled around my foot').

Note that *duga-l* could NOT bear the suffix -:*ḍi-n* in either of the sentences of (484) and still retain its transitivity. Informants insisted that *duga:ḍi-n* could only be used in a derived intransitive sentence such as the anti-passive

(485) *munil ŋanda duga:ḍiɲu* The Munil-vine grabbed me

There is thus a restriction on condition (ii) from our explanation of the use of -:*ḍi-n* in 4.2.2. The suffix will only mark a non-controlling inanimate subject with a verb from the 'affect' class. Note, however, that -:*ḍi-n* can indicate that a human A accomplished some action by chance, whatever the semantic type of the verb involved. This is discussed in the next section.

In 4.1.4 we explained the case inflections on pronouns, deictics and nominals in terms of a hierarchy 'human–animate–inanimate'; it was

noted that an A NP is most likely to have human reference, and an O NP inanimate reference. The sense of -:ɖi-n described above could be taken as marking the REVERSAL of the norm – that is, inanimate A and human O – for the class of affect verbs.

4.2.6   Chance events. There are two ways in which condition (ii) of 4.2.2 – that the A NP have volitional control over the action – may not be met. The A NP may refer to something non-animate, as described above; or, there could be a human agent, which achieves some result by pure chance.

There is a contrast between the two transitive sentences:

(486) *bama:l bana wawa:l*   The person saw the water [he was looking for]

(487) *bama:l bana wawa:ɖiɲu*   The person saw the water [unexpectedly]

(486) implies that the person was looking for, say, a stream that he knew to be somewhere around, and did find it; (487) suggests that he encountered a stream entirely by chance, when he was engaged on some other errand.

There are thus four ways of translating into Yidiɲ the English sentence 'I saw the dog'. Firstly (cf. (430–2) from 4.2.3) a 'simple sentence' and the corresponding antipassives:

(488) a. *ɲayu guda:ga wawa:l*
      b. *ɲayu wawa:ɖiɲu gudaganda*   } I looked at the dog
      c. *ɲayu wawa:ɖiɲu gudagala*

and secondly (cf. (402) in 4.1.9):

(489) *ɲayu guda:ga wawa:ɖiɲu*
      I saw the dog [when I wasn't looking for it]

An informant stressed that (489) might be used when one almost bumped into a dog, before one realised it was there.

Most of the known examples of the 'chance' sense of -:ɖi-n are on verbs of perceiving or finding:

(490) *ɲayu waɲal banɖi:ɖiɲu/ wunaɲunda*
      By chance, I found the boomerang, lying [by the roadside]

Compare with line 38 of text 2 in which *banɖi-l* (without -:ɖi-n) describes the finding of a camp that had been specifically sought in a certain locality.

However, it does seem that -:ḍi-n, with 'chance' meaning, can be suffixed to a verb of any semantic type. (427) above describes a man cutting a woman accidentally. Note also:

(491) ŋayu yiŋu   ganda   ŋuɲḍu:nda bama:nda
      I-SA THIS-ABS yamstick-ABS THAT-DAT   person-DAT
      ŋuraŋura:l   / yiŋu   yiɲḍu:ŋ baḍa:ɽḍiɲu
      show-REDUP-PAST THIS-ABS THIS-ERG leave-:ḍi-PAST
      I showed this yamstick to that person 'This [woman] has left this
      [yamstick] by mistake' (i.e. she should have taken it with her
      on her yam-collecting expedition)

(492) *gidi ŋayu gilbi:ḍiɲu*   I threw the Gidi torch away accidentally

(492) indicates that as the narrator was walking along, waving a Gidi torch
about, he suddenly lost his hold and it flew out of his hand. The informant
translated *gilbi:ḍi-n* here as 'drop' (whereas he normally gave 'chuck' for
gilbi-l).

This sense of -:ḍi-n is used quite sparingly, to draw attention to the
accidental nature of some event when this does have significance in the
context of discourse. If the fact that something was more accidental than
planned is essentially immaterial to the chain of events, then -:ḍi-n need
not be employed.

4.2.7 Continuous action. The final sense in which -:ḍi-n can be used
is quite distinct from antipassive, reflexive, 'inanimate A' and 'chance'
uses described above. It can indicate a continuous (or repeated) action,
extending into the past and future – something which cannot be viewed
as a whole by looking in either direction from the vantage point of the
present. (428) and (429) illustrated with 'keeps grumbling' and 'keeps
vomiting'; other examples include:

(493) *ŋaɲaɲ bama:l bunḍa:ḍiɲu*   The people kept on hitting me

(494) *bangilandu   bama   gaymbi:ɲ   gadaŋaḍi:ɲ*
      'Name'-ERG person-ABS   do to all-PAST come-COMIT-:ḍi-PAST
      Bangilan brought all the people with him (to a new territory he
      had chosen for his tribal group, after their previous home had
      been submerged by rising water)

In (494) the VC contains the transitive adverb *gaymbi-n* 'do to all O' and
transitive verb *gada-ŋa-l* 'come with, bring'. The inclusion of -:ḍi-n here
suggests that it took a fair time for Bangilan to bring all his people the full
distance to the new home he had found for them.

It seems that -*:ḍi-n*, in its continuous sense, can be affixed to a verb of any semantic type. For example:

(495) *ŋaṇḍi bulmba wawa:ḍiŋ*

We keep looking around the camp (mourning the fact that one of its owners has been murdered)

It thus seems quite likely that a fifth sentence could be added to the paradigm at (488–9) in the last section.

-*:ḍi-n*, in the 'continuous' sense, can sometimes completely alter the semantic character of a verb (so that a different English translation would be appropriate). From *budi-l* 'put down' we derive *budi:ḍi-n* 'own, have around', as in:

(496) *baŋgal garu   waṇḍu:nim dugal | galŋa:ŋ   ŋuṇu*

axe-ABS by-and-by WHO-CAU get-PRES uncle-ERG THAT-ABS

baŋgal   budi:ḍiŋ

axe-ABS put down-*:ḍi*-PRES

'Who can [we] get a tomahawk from?' [Two young boys ask each other] 'Uncle usually has some around' [one of them suggested]

When *buḍi-n* 'tell' bears a continuous -*:ḍi-n* it has the sense 'be called (a name)' – see line 15 of text 2.

Like the 'chance' sense discussed in the last section, -*:ḍi-n* is only used to mark a verb as continuous if there is some special significance attached to the duration of the action. Thus when Dick Moses told the story of how, when a boy, he and a friend had dug up some mission potatoes, he emphasised that, when the missionary came upon them:

(497) *ŋuṇḍu:ŋ   guman   ḍanaŋaḍi:ṇ | ŋayu guman*

THAT-ERG one-ABS stand-COMIT-*:ḍi*-PAST I-SA one-ABS

ḍanaŋaḍi:ṇ

stand-COMIT-*:ḍi*-PAST

That one [Dick Moses's friend] was standing with one [potato in his hand], and I was standing with one [in my hand]

Here the addition of -*:ḍi-n* to the comitative *ḍana-ŋa-l* 'stand with' stresses that the boys had the potatoes in their hands for a fair period, so that the white man could see quite plainly what they had been doing (and there was no point in their denying it).

Imperative inflection on a continuous -*:ḍi-n* yields an exhortation to continue something that has already been commenced:

(498) *mandi: galabuḍun   galiɲa:ḍin   ḍaba:ngu*
hand-LOC spear-ABS-STILL go-COMIT- *:ḍi*-IMP eel-PURP
Keep going, with your spear still in your hand, for eels!

A fair number of Australian languages do have a special verbal affix or combination of affixes for 'continuous imperative'. These include Yidiɲ's westerly neighbour Mbabaram (Dixon, forthcoming – b). Other languages showing this distinction are mentioned in Dixon 1972: 16.

Some verbs, referring to an action that is normally likely to be drawn out, occur almost exclusively in *-:ḍi-n* form – for instance, *wurba-n* 'search for'.

Finally, it is only in the continuous sense that *-:ḍi-n* (occasionally) occurs with intransitive verbs. See (429) and:

(499) *ŋayu bayi:ḍiɲu bama:nda*
I kept coming out [and showing myself] to the people

(500) *mayi wanda:ḍiɲu*
The fruit is falling [off the tree] now

An intransitive example of continuous imperative involves a narrator describing how he and two women jumped down some rocks and into a boat below. *bilɲḍi-n* 'jump down' is a hyponym of the generic verb *burwa-l* 'jump':

(501) *gana ŋaɲḍi giḍa   bilɲḍi:ɲ | burwa:ḍin   munu|*
TRY   we-SA quick-ABS jump down-PAST jump- *:ḍi*-IMP   INSIDE
       buɲa   ḍambu:l
woman-ABS two-ABS
We all quickly jumped down [the rocks, and I said to my companions: 'You] two women, carry on jumping into [the boat]!'

4.2.8   -:ḍi-n summary. We can summarise, in table 4.2, the five senses of *-:ḍi-n* in terms of the referent of the A NP in underlying structure, the semantic possibilities of the verb and its underlying transitivity, and whether the action was performed deliberately or not (that is, whether the agent had volitional control over it). Note that a verb cannot involve two tokens of the affix *-:ḍi-n* (3.8.1). It is possible, however, that one occurrence of *-:ḍi-n* could cover two of the senses listed here.

The uses of *-:ḍi-n* at first appeared to be quite diverse. We attempted, in 4.2.2, to relate them all to deviations from a norm. 5.5.2–3 provides

TABLE 4.2   *The five senses of verbal derivational affix* -:ḍi-n

Sense	Reference of deep A NP	verb type	underlying transitivity	does A have volitional control?	syntactic effect
a (4.2.3)	any	any	trans.	yes	derives (antipassive) intransitive sentence; deep A becomes surface S, deep O marked by dative/locative
*b (4.2.4)	animate	any (?)	trans.	yes	derives (reflexive) intransitive sentence; deep A/O becomes surface S
c (4.2.5)	inanimate	affect	trans.	—	—
d (4.2.6)	animate	any	trans.	no	—
**e (4.2.7)	—	any	any	immaterial	—

* further condition on sense (b) – A = O referentially
** further condition on sense (e) – action extends into past and future

further discussion of the semantics and syntax of -*:ḍi-n*, relating the facts in Yidiɲ to those in a number of other languages, from Australia and from other language families.

4.3 Comitative constructions

The verbal derivational affix -*ŋa-l* (~ *maŋa-l*, 3.8.5) can be suffixed only to an intransitive stem; it always derives a transitive form. But although -*ŋa-l* does – unlike -*:ḍi-n* – have an invariable syntactic effect, its range of uses is scarcely less wide than that of -*:ḍi-n*.

We mentioned in 3.1.1 that an intransitive simple sentence involving a comitative NP:

(502) *wagu:ḍa buɲa:y galiŋ*   The man is going with the woman

can effectively be paraphrased by:

(503) *waguḍaŋgu buɲa gali:ŋal* ⟨ = (502)⟩

in which the S NP has become A, the comitative NP now fills the O slot, and the verb is marked by verbal comitative -*ŋa-l*.

We can refer to this sense of -*ŋa-l* as S ≡ A, in terms of the referential identities of NPs filling the functional slots in (502) and (503). In fact, examples like (502–3) account for the great majority of -*ŋa-l* verbs in texts. But there are also constructions like:

(504) *waguḍaŋgu buɲa badi:ŋal*   The man is crying for the woman

which corresponds to intransitive:

(505) *wagu:ḍa badiŋ buɲa:nda*

S ≡ A again, but the O NP in (504) corresponds to dative – and not comitative – in (505). In fact

(506) *wagu:ḍa buɲa:y badiŋ*   The man is crying with the woman

has a quite different meaning from (504–5), implying that both the man and the woman are crying over some third person.

There is a third type of -*ŋa-l* construction, exemplified by:

(507) *ŋayu ḍugi guɲḍiɲalɲu*   I broke the stick

The corresponding intransitive sentence, from which we could suggest (507) is derived, is:

(508) *ḍugi guɲḍi:ɲ*   The stick broke

Here S ≡ O; (507) appears to be a simple causative counterpart of (506). (Although on detailed study 'causative' is not the most appropriate term here – see 4.3.7.)

-*ŋa-l* constructions also relate to instrumental NPs. It will be recalled that a simple sentence can involve an NP marked by instrumental case (which coincides formally with locative):

(509) *bama:l   ḍugi   galba:nda gunda:l*
person-ERG tree-ABS axe-INST   cut-PAST
The person cut the tree with an axe

This can be placed in antipassive form:

(510) *bama galba:nda gunda:ḍiɲu ḍugi:l*

And then a -*ŋa-l* construction can be derived from (510), which has the instrumental NP in absolutive case:

(511) *bama:l galban gunda:ḍiɲa:l ḍugi:l* ⟨= (509)⟩

(510/11) are most similar to (505/4); S becomes A and here the instrumental NP becomes O. This can be particularly useful for purposes of conjunction (5.1.3) and subordination (4.4–6); the fact that *galban* is here the 'syntactic pivot' (i.e. the NP is S/O function) can be brought out through translating (511) as 'The man used the axe to cut the tree'.

We first discuss the semantic range of comitative (4.3.1) and instrumental (4.3.2) NPs, and then (4.3.3–7) deal in turn with the various syntactic–semantic uses of -*ŋa-l* (only some of which have been previewed here).

4.3.1 Comitative NPs. The addition of the comitative affix -*ḍi* ~ -*yi* (3.3.4) to any nominal stem serves to derive a form that functions like an adjective; it will take the same case inflection as the head noun which it qualifies. Thus we can have a comitative form occurring in an A NP, taking ergative case; see (182) and

(512) *ɲaɲaɲ buɲa:ŋ wawa:l gandayiŋgu*
The woman with a yamstick saw me

An example of comitative followed by dative case is at (57) in 3.3.4.

There is a further comitative affix -*muḍay* (3.3.6) that has exactly the same syntactic and semantic properties as -*ḍi*; the two suffixes are substitutable one for the other, and are often alternated for stylistic effect (3.1.3).

Comitative can mark a complete NP (embedded within a further NP); every word in the NP will take the derivational affix, plus case inflection. An NP may mix *-ḍi* and *muḍay*:

(513) *ŋayu gada:ɲ   yiŋgumuḍay   wira:y*
     I-SA come-PAST THIS-COMIT-ABS moveable object-COMIT-ABS
       walba:y
       stone-COMIT-ABS
     I came with this piece of [gold-bearing] rock

In fact, an informant emphasised that all four alternatives:

(514) *ŋuɲu bama* $\begin{cases} \textit{mayi: ɲabi:} \\ \textit{mayi: ɲabimuḍay} \\ \textit{mayimuḍay ɲabi:} \\ \textit{mayimuḍay ɲabimuḍay} \end{cases}$ That person has a lot of food

are equally acceptable.

The nominal comitative in Yidiɲ covers a considerable semantic range. This includes:

[1] Describing some quality of a person or animal. A 'minor sentence' (3.1.10), which does not include a verb, is normal in this case.

  (a) an inherent physical characteristic – see (271) and

(515) *yiŋu wuṛgun ɲumbu:lḍi*   This teenage boy has a beard

  (b) an induced characteristic:

(516) *ŋaḍin galbin muyŋgamuḍay*
     My son has his tribal marks (cicatrices)

  (c) alienable possession – see (90) and (514).

(515) or (516) may of course function just as an NP within a verbal sentence:

(517) *ŋuŋgum ŋaɲḍi ɲinaŋ muyŋgamuḍay*
     Then we all sit [there] with our [newly acquired] tribal marks

[2] Characteristics of a place – as (411) and

(518) *bulmba   ḍira:y*
     place-ABS twig-COMIT-ABS
     There are [lots of] twigs in [this] place

[3] Referring to someone at rest
  (a) with some inanimate object – see (455)
  (b) in human company:

(519) *ŋayu ɲinaŋ waga:lḍi*   I'm sitting (= staying) with [my] wife

There is close similarity of meaning between (519), where *wagal* 'wife' is marked by comitative suffix with the S NP, and

(520) *ŋayu ɲinaŋ waga:lnda* ⟨= (519)⟩

in which it constitutes a separate peripheral NP, marked by dative case. There is, however, a basic syntactic difference between these two sentences – whereas (519) indicates accompaniment, (520) implies that the act 'I am sitting' is performed with respect to 'my wife'. (520) could be glossed 'I'm sitting next to my wife' against (519)'s 'I'm sitting with my wife'. The contrast emerges most clearly with an inanimate noun; there is considerable difference of meaning between comitative

(521) *ŋayu waŋa:lɖi ɲinaŋ*
      I'm sitting with a boomerang (e.g. holding it in my hands)

and locative

(522) *ŋayu ɲinaŋ waŋa:lda*   I'm sitting on a boomerang

Choice of locative – as in (522) – or dative (as in 520) – is conditioned by the hierarchy described in 4.1.8. (520) and (522) belong to the same syntactic type as (380–96).

Informants noted that sentences like (519) and (520) – which have very similar meanings – can be alternated to meet the requirements of stylistic felicity (3.1.3); a reply to *ɲundu ɲinan waga:lɖi* might be *ŋayu ɲinaŋ waga:lnda*. This is of course not the case for sentences which involve an inanimate noun, like (521) and (522).

[4] Referring to some inanimate object in a container. See (36–7) and

(523) *ŋaɲɖi gubu:m   ɲiɽal   bundu:y*
      we-SA black pine-ABS hang up-PRES dilly-bag-COMIT-ABS
      We hang up the black pine nut in a dilly-bag

Note that in (523) *gubu:m bundu:y* comprise the O NP – literally 'we hang "black pine in a dilly-bag" up'. A similar sense could have been obtained by placing *bundu* in locative, rather than comitative, inflection – but *bundu* would then have been syntactically bound to the verb *ɲiɽa-l*, rather than to *gubu:m*.

[5] Referring to someone in motion
    (a) with something that does not assist his movement in any way; see (513) and (89) in 3.3.6.
    (b) with something that does aid him in walking or climbing (and is effectively an 'instrument', with respect to this type of action):

(524) *ŋayu gana guwa gali:na   mandi: ḍubu:y*
  I-SA TRY west go-PURP hand-LOC walking stick-COMIT-ABS
  I tried to go west [i.e. uphill] with [the help of] a stick in my hand

  (c) in human company; see (502), (34–5), (154–5) and

(525) *bama   bangi:lan   warḍa:nda gada:ɲ*
  person-ABS 'name'-ABS canoe-LOC come-PAST
    bama:y
  person-COMIT-ABS
  Bangilan came in a canoe with [many] men

The meaning similarity between comitative and dative on a human noun, that we noted under [3b] for a verb of rest, does not hold for a verb of motion. Thus dative *ŋayu galiŋ ḍaḍa:nda* is 'I'm going for (= to) the baby' as against *ŋayu ḍaḍa:y galiŋ* 'I'm going with the baby'.

[6] Referring to something inanimate in motion, with inanimate accompaniment:

(526) *maṟun   bugal   banamuḍay   gadaŋ*
  cloud-ABS black-ABS water-COMIT-ABS come-PRES
  A black cloud full of rain is coming

[7] Referring to an instrument – see the discussion in 4.3.2.
[8] Referring to a time or season
  (a) the time AT which some event takes place, as (245) in 3.8.8 and

(527) *ŋaɲḍi gana   gunḍiŋ   yiwa:ɲḍi*
  we-SA PARTICLE return-PRES wind-COMIT-ABS
  In the wintertime we return [from the tableland to the coast]

  (b) the duration of some event

(528) *ŋayu wunaŋadaŋ   bugamuḍay   guma:nḍi*
  I-SA lie down-COMING-PRES night-COMIT-ABS one-COMIT-ABS
  I'll come and stay for one night

[9] Describing a physical or mental state – e.g. 'hungry' ('with hunger') in (39), 'jealous' ('with jealousy') in (179), 'sick' ('with sickness') in (214), and 'full of food' (literally 'with stomach') in (42) and (193).

We noted in 3.2.2 that Yidiɲ has abstract nouns for some concepts which are expressed by verbs or adjectives in many other Australian languages (including the neighbouring Dyirbal). Nouns such as *muran* 'sickness' and *biṟmbir* 'jealousy' most commonly occur with the comitative suffix, which

derives an adjectival stem. As explained in 3.1.3, the syntactic evidence does not make clear whether *daliyi* is basically a noun ('hunger') or an adjective ('hungry'); it may possibly have dual membership (which could imply that it is – diachronically – shifting from one word-class to another).

Comitatives can, like all other nominal stems, be verbalised; this is encountered particularly frequently with 'state' descriptions such as:

(529) *bibiyuwuy mura:ndidaga:n*   Bibiyuwuy became sick

The noun *mundu* appears to refer centrally to 'wind (from the lungs)', with metaphorical overtones of 'life-force'; it can also mean 'temper', 'ease' or 'desire'. For instance:

(530) *ŋayu munduyiŋgu   dugi   gundal*
       I-SA ease-COMIT-ERG tree-ABS cut-PRES
       I can easily cut that tree

An informant glossed (530) as 'I feel up to cutting that tree', and indicated that either *mundu:ŋ* 'ease-ERG' or *munduyiŋgu* could be employed in it, without change in meaning. Examples of *mundu:y* being used to indicate 'want' or 'desire' were discussed at (357) and (366) in 4.1.6.

Guugu-Yimidhirr *wawu* appears to have exactly the same meaning and function as *mundu* in Yidiɲ (Roth 1901a: 7, 21; and Haviland, personal communication). The Lutheran missionaries at Hopevale used *wawu* to translate 'the soul' (missionaries at Yarrabah never attempted to learn Yidiɲ or to translate the Bible into the language, but *mundu* could be an effective gloss for 'spirit' or 'soul'). *wawu* does have one extra sense that is not held by *mundu* – 'centre' or 'inside' (a meaning that appears to be covered by the locational qualifier *munu* in Yidiɲ).

[10] It is the custom in this region to derive a tribal name by the addition of *-di* ∼ *-yi* to the appropriate language name; the Yidiɲdi are literally '[people] with the Yidiɲ language'. This system of naming is used for all the tribes speaking Yidiɲ and Dya:bugay, for two of the six tribes speaking Dyirbal, to the south, and for Ngayguŋu, to the west of Yidiɲ (1.3).

The comitative in Yidiɲ appears to have a much wider semantic range than comparable affixes in other Australian languages. In Dyirbal, for instance, comitative *-bila* ∼ *-ba* could be used only in senses [1–3, 5a, 5c] above. A survey of the syntactic and semantic ranges of the nominal comitative affix in twenty Australian languages is in Dixon (1976a).

There is an obvious formal similarity between nominal comitative -*ḍi* and the verbal derivational affix -:*ḍi-n*. Cognate affixes occur in a number of other Australian languages – thus Guugu-Yimidhirr (Haviland, forthcoming) has nominal comitative -*ḍir* and verbal derivational suffix -*ḍi* with very similar functions to -*ḍi* and -:*ḍi-n* in Yidiɲ. It is not clear whether this similarity between nominal and verbal affixes is merely coincidental, or whether it is the reflection of an underlying syntactic connection (if not in the modern languages, then perhaps in some common ancestor language). This point is discussed in Dixon 1976a.

The privative affix -*gimbal* (3.3.6) is far less common than either comitative, but it does appear to cover essentially the same semantic range. Thus -*gimbal* can be substituted for -*ḍi*/-*muḍay* in the examples quoted under [1–6] above. To the sentences given at (91), (59–60), (412), (65) and (62) can be added:

(531) *yiɲu wuɽgun ɲumbulgimbal*   The teenage boy has no beard

Corresponding to (245) of 3.8.8 under sense [8a] 'time at' there is:

(532) *ɲaɲḍi burgiɲ ginda:ngimbal*
      We'll go walkabout on a moonless night

Privative equivalents of state descriptions (sense [9]) would not be common, but can be used when the presence of a quality in one person is contrasted with its absence in another:

(533) *ɲuɲu bama mura:nḍi/ ɲayu murangimbal*
      That person is sick, [but] I'm not sick

daliyi 'hunger/hungry' cannot occur with -*gimbal*, it seems. An informant preferred to employ the negative particle *ɲuḍu* in saying 'I'm not hungry':

(534) *ɲayu wala buga:ḍiɲu | ɲuḍu daliyi*
      I-SA STOP eat-:*ḍi*-PAST NOT hungry-ABS
      I've stopped eating, I'm not hungry [any more]

mundu 'temper, ease, desire' can occur with -*gimbal*, just as it does with -*ḍi*:

(535) *ɲayu mundugimbal ɲinaŋ | gula   gagal | ŋaḍin*
      I-SA ease-WITHOUT sit-PRES body-ABS light-ABS I-GEN-ABS
      wagal   ḍuŋga:ɲ
      wife-ABS run-PAST
      I'm sitting [here] feeling sad, my body feels light [because] my
      wife has run away [and left me]

mundugimbal can also mean 'broken-voiced', in terms of the central meaning of *mundu*, 'wind'.

The semantic range of privative does not, of course, perfectly correspond to that of comitative. There appears to be no privative equivalent of sense [8b] 'duration of an event'. And whereas we can say *ḍiligimbal* 'eye-WITHOUT' to describe someone who has his eyes half-shut, or is pretending to be asleep, it would not be normal to use a comitative with *ḍili* to refer to someone who was wide awake.

-gimbal may be used to mark some unusual event (where *-ḍi* or *muḍay* would not normally be invoked in the unmarked circumstances). Thus (64) of 3.3.6 describes a car running away by itself, *bamagimbal* 'without a person [in it]'. This involves a sense not listed above: inanimate object with[out] human accompaniment.

4.3.2 Instrumental NPs. Any sentence may involve an instrumental NP (4.1.6). This will typically refer to a weapon or tool used in some action which 'affects' the physical state of an object. Thus 'pierce with a spear' in (372), 'cut with an axe' in (459–64), 'dig with a yamstick' in lines 54, 57 of text 2, and:

(536) *ɲaɲaɲ wugul   ɲuɲḍu:ŋ   ḍugi:l   bunḍa:ɲ*
      I-o   nape-ABS THAT-ERG stick-INST hit-PAST
      That [person] hit me in the back of the neck with a stick

(537) *buriburi:ŋ   ɲuniɲ gulgi: dandaɽ*
      old man-ERG you-o sand-INST rub-PRES
      [When, as a young man, your cicatrices are cut, after they have healed over] an old man [will take you to the river and] rub sand on your [scars]

(538) *ɲaɲaɲ bama:l ɲambi:ɲ gambu:da*
      A person painted me with white clay

Note also that 'fire' is marked by instrumental case with *waḍu-l* 'burn, cook' – see (351).

Instrumental NPs are not confined to occurrence with 'affect' verbs. Line 62 of text 2 describes how animals are CAUGHT WITH A TRAP, (373) in 4.1.6 refers to a hut being THATCHED WITH BLADY GRASS and in (539) the instrumental NP involves *giḍaɽ* 'mark' and *biba* 'paper', a set collocation that refers to 'money' (or the chits used as a substitute for money, in early mission days):

(539) *ŋaɲḍi gambi   dugal   giḍa:da   biba:*
    we-SA clothes-ABS get-PRES mark-INST paper-INST
    We buy clothes with money (cf. text 9.20)

Body part nouns can occur quite freely in instrumental case. The affect verb *baṛa-l*, which refers to a short, sharp blow delivered with a rounded implement, covers both 'kick' and 'punch'. These are distinguished by the inclusion of *ḍina* 'foot' or *mandi* 'hand' in instrumental inflection. Thus (433–4) and

(540) *ŋayu bama ḍina: baṛa:l*   I kicked the person

(541) *ŋayu bama mandi: baṛa:l*   I punched the person

Dick Moses mentioned that *dungu: baṛa-l* 'butt with the head' describes a way of fighting called 'double butt', practised by Kanakas (Pacific Islanders, brought as indentured labourers to the sugar fields of North Queensland during the late nineteenth century).

Other body part instrumentals include 'bite with the mouth', 'look with one eye', 'feed with the breast' or, in a story telling how an alligator ran off with a woman, holding her close to his belly with one paw:

(542) *gaɲaraŋgu   bigu:ɲḍa   ŋaɲaɲ nambi:l*
    alligator-ERG fingernail-INST I-O   hold with hand-PAST
    'The alligator held me with his claws' (the woman exclaimed to
      her rescuers apropos of the wounds on her skin)

Comitative can sometimes be used in place of instrumental for referring to an implement; for instance, a text concerning food preparation included:

(543) *ŋaɲḍi ḍalŋgal   walba: | muga:yɲḍi*
    we-SA chop-PRES stone-INST grinding stone-COMIT-ABS
    yuŋgal
    grind-PRES
    We chop [the black pine] with a stone, and then grind it with a
      Mugay stone

Note here that instrumental is used with *ḍaŋga-l* 'chop' but comitative with *yuŋga-l* 'grind'. It seems from the limited evidence available that the use of comitative in place of instrumental depends on the natures of the object and of the action. Instrumental case would have to be used when the patient is human, as in (536–8, 540–2), or when the state of

the object is profoundly altered, as with 'chop' in (543). It is only weak instrumentals – describing a mild action on an inanimate patient – that can alternate with comitative. (The alternation may in part be conditioned by a hierarchy similar to that which motivates the choice between 'human' and 'inanimate' deictics, between dative and locative, and between different types of possessive construction – 3.1.2, 3.7.1, 4.1.8, 4.7.3.)

Where comitative is used with an instrumental sense, ergative case can optionally be added to it. There is then alternation between instrumental, comitative plus absolutive, and comitative plus ergative:

(544) *bama:l badil* $\begin{cases} muga:y\underline{n}\underline{d}a \\ muga:y\underline{n}\underline{d}i \\ mugay\underline{n}\underline{d}i\eta gu \end{cases}$ *yu\eta ga:l*

    A person ground Badil nut with a Mugay stone

See also (182) in 3.7.2.

Although instrumental inflection coincides formally with locative, there are grammatical reasons for recognising two separate cases. Thus, uses of locative that are not local in the strictest sense ('at a place') alternate with dative in the way described in 4.1.8; but dative can never be substituted for instrumental in examples like (536–42). The interrogative *wa\underline{n}\underline{d}a* 'where' corresponds to strictly local uses of locative; but the instrumental interrogative is *wa\underline{n}i:nda* – see (173) and (183) in 3.7.2. (We could regard *wa\underline{n}i:nda* as involving locative–instrumental inflection added to the syntactic stem *wa\underline{n}in-*, see 3.7.3. Instrumental coincides with dative here just as it always does with *-n*-final stems.)

The alternative to recognising two distinct cases would be to say that instrumental and locative were two 'senses' of a single case. But both can occur in the same sentence, as in antipassive:

(545) *bama:l gurili\underline{n}\underline{d}a baga:\underline{d}i\underline{n}u gala:*
    The person speared the wallaby with a spear

If we did allow the 'single case' hypothesis, sentences like (545) would constitute the ONLY exception to an empirical rule that no Yidiɲ sentence can involve two distinct NPs, each marked by the same case (from the list in 3.3.1).

4.3.3 Verbal -ŋa-l (i) comitative sense. Senses [3], [5] and [6] of the nominal comitative, listed in 4.3.1, involve an intransitive verb of position (that is, 'rest' or 'motion' – 4.1.7) whose S NP includes an

embedded comitative NP. Corresponding to each sentence of this type there is a transitive construction in which the comitative NP becomes O, S becomes A and the verb is marked by the derivational affix *-ŋa-l*. This is exemplified by (502–3); it can be summarised (with || joining identical constituents):

(i) intransitive   [NP   [NP + COMIT]]$_S$ VC
                    || || ||
   transitive   NP$_A$ NP$_O$ VC + *ŋa-l*

Taking the senses of nominal comitative one at a time:

[3] Referring to someone at rest
   (a) with some inanimate object

(546) a *ŋayu ḍanaŋ ḍugi:*   ⎫   I am standing with a stick [in
      b *ŋayu ḍugi ḍana:ŋal*   ⎭   my hand]

Note that (546b) can only refer to someone standing with a stick in his hand, or else standing with his hand on a tree (showing the tree to some other person). The corresponding Dyirbal sentence (Dixon 1972: 96) *ŋaḍa bala yugu ḍanayman* may mean 'I am standing with a stick OR under a tree OR on a block of wood'; the latter two senses have to be rendered in Yidiɲ by *ŋayu ḍanaŋ ḍugi:l*, with 'tree' in locative case.

   (b) in human company

(547) a *wagu:ḍa ɲinaŋ waga:lḍi*   ⎫   The man is sitting with [his]
      b *waguḍaŋgu wagal ɲina:ŋal* ⎭   wife

[5] Referring to someone in motion
   (a) with something that does not assist his movement. Note line 12 from text 14:

(548) *malu:way gana   gada:ɲ   gulugulu:y*   /
      spirit-ABS PARTICLE come-PAST black bream-COMIT-ABS
      gulugulu   gadaŋalɲu   gabulala
      black bream-ABS come-COMIT-PAST fish stick-LOC
      The spirit came with a black bream [for all the people to eat]; he
      brought the black bream on a Gabu:l stick

Here the first clause involves a nominal comitative, and the second clause repeats the same information using a verbal comitative construction.

   (b) with something that does assist his movement. Corresponding to (524) there is:

(549) *ŋayu ḍubu gali:ŋal mandi:*
      I'm going with a walking stick in [my] hand

(c) in human company – see (502–3) as well as (494) and (329).

[6] Referring to something inanimate in motion, with inanimate accompaniment. Parallel to (526) there is:

(550) *maɽu:ndu bana gada:ŋalala*
    The cloud is bringing rain now

Senses [1], [2], [4] and [9] of nominal comitative do not in the same way involve an intransitive verb of position, and there is no corresponding verbal comitative construction. Sense [8], however, does yield nominal/verbal comitative pairs on the same pattern as [3], [5] and [6]. The sentence

(551) *ŋayu ginda:n ɲina:ŋal*

is in fact ambiguous between [8a] and [8b] – it can mean either 'I'll sit by moonlight' or 'I'll stay for a month'.

Note that the possibility of ambiguous interpretation depends on the verb. *ŋayu ginda:n burgi:ŋal* can – like (245) – only be taken to mean 'I'll go walkabout by moonlight' since no one would go walkabout for a month. To specify the 'sit by moonlight' sense for (551) one need only add *buga:* 'night-LOC' (this restricts *ginda:n* to the meaning 'moonlight' rather than 'month').

Sense [8b] 'duration of event' is unambiguously shown by:

(552) *ɲundu waɳḍi:r buga ɲina:ŋal*
    How many nights will you stay here for?

We have already indicated the wide range of semantic and syntactic effects of verbal *-ŋa-l*. The comitative sense described in this section – deriving a transitive sentence from an intransitive, where O corresponds to a comitative NP and A to S – is far and away the most frequent; more than 80% of the textual occurrences of *-ŋa-l* fall under this heading. It is in view of this that we employ 'comitative' as the conventional name for the verbal derivational affix *-ŋa-l*. But it must be emphasised that in fact comitative is ONLY ONE of the five or six functions of *-ŋa-l*; the others are detailed in the following sections.

The comitative sense of *-ŋa-l* occurs most frequently with verbs of position, but it can probably occur with ANY intransitive stem, including derived antipassives (see 4.3.8).

Over and above these various functions, each of which has a distinctive syntactico-semantic characterisation, there is a further use of *-ŋa-l*

which is entirely dictated by considerations of discourse structure. This is to derive a transitive verbal stem which can occur in a VC with some other transitive form; examples were given in 4.1.3.

Often a verb which is in *-ŋa-l* form to satisfy the 'VC transitivity' requirement will conform to the specifications we have given above. Thus *gali:ŋal* in (327) can be paraphrased by an intransitive sentence involving *gali-n* and a nominal comitative. But in other examples the transitivity requirement demands a syntactic derivation that does not conform to the semantic guidelines we have described. Thus in one myth Dick Moses gave:

(553) *ŋayu ŋanḍar guwa banḍa:ṟ galiŋalɲu*
I-SA creek-ABS west follow-PAST go-COMIT-PAST
I went following the creek to the west.

where there is no nominal comitative

*(554) *ŋayu gali:ɲ ŋanḍa:rḍi*

and even

*(555) *ŋayu ŋanḍar galiŋalɲu*

is not, in isolation, an acceptable sentence. To express 'I went by the creek' one has to put *ŋanḍar* in locative case:

(556) *ŋayu gali:ɲ ŋanḍa:da*

That is, the object of *galiŋa-l* must be something that one takes with one; in contrast, the O NP of *banḍa-ṟ* can refer to a geographical feature. In (553) *banḍa-ṟ* is the 'head' verb in the VC, and dictates selectional requirements on NPs.

Similar comments apply to *ŋayu ḍanaŋalɲu wawa:l* 'I stood watching' in (328) of 4.1.3.

4.3.4 Verbal -ŋa-l (ii) locative sense. There are basically two ways of saying 'You talk in the Yidiɲ language!'. The noun referring to the language can be in absolutive case, within the S NP (so that it might be regarded as a type of inalienable possession – 4.7.3):

(557) *ɲundu yidiɲ ɲaŋga:ḍin*

or it could be in locative case:

(558) *ɲundu ɲaŋga:ḍin yidi:ɲḍa*

Now there is a transitive *-ŋa-l* construction corresponding to intransitive (557–8):

(559) *ɲundu yidiɲ ɲaŋga:ɖiɲa*   ⟨= (557–8)⟩

If we choose to relate (559) to (558) (although (557) could perhaps equally well have been chosen) the correspondence can be summarised:

(ii) intransitive   NP$_S$ NP+LOC   VC
                   ‖   ‖   ‖
    transitive   NP$_A$ NP$_O$ VC+*ŋa-l*

This construction is used in line 3 of text 9:

(560) *...gaɖa:ŋ*   *...buɖi:na   guru:n   ɲuni:nda/ bama:l*
    ...white man-ERG tell-PURP language-ABS you-DAT   person-ERG
    ɲaŋga:ɖiɲa:lna   guru:n
    speak-COMIT·PURP language-ABS

    [As children we were told to come into the mission] 'so that the white man could tell you stories, so that [white] people could speak to you in [their, English] language'

There is a meaning difference here between *buɖi-n* 'tell' and *ɲaŋga:ɖiɲa-l* 'speak in'. As the O of *buɖi-n*, *guru:n* refers to stories in (the English) language; as the O of *ɲaŋga:ɖiɲa-l*, *guru:n* just has general reference to this language.

    -ŋa-l constructions of this type can only be used with verbs of 'speaking'; and the locative NP in the intransitive sentence – which becomes O in the transitive *-ŋa-l* construction – must refer to some language or style of speech. Note that there are no *-ŋa-l* constructions corresponding to intransitive sentences with a normal locative NP (of the type exemplified in 4.1.7, 4.1.8). For instance, we mentioned in the last section that corresponding to (556) we can NOT have *(555).

    The intransitive verb *badi-n* 'cry' refers to a child sobbing or to a wailing style of mourning recitative. In the latter sense *badi-n* could take a locative NP referring to the speech style employed:

(561) *bama badiŋ gugulula*   OR   *bama gugu:lu badiŋ*
    The person is crying in [men's] Gugulu style

There is here a corresponding *-ŋa-l* construction:

(562) *bama:l gugu:lu badi:ŋal*   ⟨= (561)⟩

4.3.5 Verbal -ŋa-l (iii) dative and (iv) 'fear' senses. We can distinguish two kinds of intransitive verb. Firstly, those for which S NP and VC normally provide a full specification of some event – thus *ŋayu wunaŋ* 'I'm lying down', *ɲuɲu ḍaruy waymbaŋ* 'that bird is flying', *yiɲu bama burŋgal* 'this person is snoring'.

There is a second class of intransitive verbs, describing an action that is directed towards some other person or thing. Thus

(563) *yiɲu gurŋga ŋanda maŋgaŋ*
      This kookaburra is laughing at me

(564) *ɲuɲu buɲa badiɲ muŋga:nda*
      That woman is crying for [her] husband

(565) *ɲuɲu bama yulbal ɲaḍinunda waga:lnda*
      That person is sneaking up on my wife

These verbs commonly take a dative (sometimes purposive) NP, referring to some object towards which the action is orientated.

We could in fact follow Hale (1970: 759ff.) in referring to them as 'middle verbs', that obligatorily take an S and a dative NP. Cases where *badi-n*, *maŋga-n* and *yulba-n* occur without a peripheral NP could then be accounted for in terms of ellipsis.

Since these verbs effectively involve reference to two NPs we might expect to find that the corresponding verbs in other languages are in some cases transitive. In fact, in Guugu-Yimidhirr (Haviland 1972) 'laugh' can be expressed only by a transitive verb *di:ŋa-l* 'laugh at'.

There are transitive *-ŋa-l* constructions for all verbs of the 'obligatory indirect object' type. O NP corresponds to dative and again A is identical to S:

(iii) intransitive NP_S NP+DAT   VC
                     $\parallel$ $\parallel$ $\parallel$
      transitive NP_A NP_O VC+ŋa-l
as in

(566) *ŋaɲaɲ yiɲḍu:ŋ gurŋga:ŋ maŋga:ŋal* ⟨= (563)⟩
(567) *ŋuɲḍu:ŋ buɲa:ŋ muŋga badi:ŋal* ⟨= (564)⟩
(568) *ɲaḍin wagal ŋuɲḍu:ŋ bama:l yulbalmaŋal* ⟨= (565)⟩

The important point to note here is that *-ŋa-l* constructions of this 'dative' variety are only attested for intransitive verbs that refer to an action which MUST be motivated by or directed towards some 'indirect object'.

For instance, it is not possible to get *ŋayu ḍaḍa gali:ŋal* with the meaning 'I am going TO the child', corresponding to *ŋayu galiŋ ḍaḍa:nda*; a sentence like *ŋayu ḍaḍa gali:ŋal* is, as described in 4.3.3, restricted to a 'comitative' interpretation 'I am going WITH the child'.

We mentioned that when *badi-n* refers to mourning recitative – rather than to simple sobbing – it can take a locative NP referring to the language used, and that there is a corresponding *-ŋa-l* construction of the 'locative' type. There are thus two kinds of *-ŋa-l* form for:

(569)   *bama ŋanda badi:ɲ gugulula*
        The person cried for me in Gugulu style

Either the 'dative' construction:

(570)   *bama:l ŋaɲaɲ badiŋalɲu gululula*
        The person CRIED FOR me, in Gugulu style

or else 'locative'

(571)   *bama gugu:lu ŋanda badiŋalɲu*
        The person CRIED IN Gugulu style, for me

There is of course no possibility of confusion, since the O NPs are referentially quite distinct in (570) and (571).

    badi-n and *maŋga-n* do not enter into comitative *-ŋa-l* constructions (which are more-or-less restricted to verbs of position); *maŋgaŋa-l* has a unique interpretation 'laugh at'. But *yulbalmaŋa-l* can have a comitative sense; corresponding to:

(572)   *muḍam ḍaḍa:y gada:ɲ | yulba:l ŋanda*
        Mother came with the baby, and sneaked up on me

there is

(573)   *muḍa:mbu ḍaḍa gadaŋalɲu| yulbalmaŋa:l ŋanda   ⟨= (572)⟩*

The inclusion of a dative NP with *yulbalmaŋa-l* in (573) precludes a 'dative' interpretation, on the lines of (568). But (568) itself is potentially ambiguous – it could mean 'that person is sneaking up ON my wife' or 'that person is sneaking up WITH my wife (on someone else)'.

However, a verb of motion that can take *-ŋa-l* in the 'dative' sense is normally restricted to this interpretation. (568) would usually be taken as 'sneak up ON' and in fact (573) is only interpretable in the 'sneak up WITH' sense because no Yidiɲḍi adult would be likely to sneak up on a child! It seems that if, for some grammatical reason, one wished to put into absolute case the

NP referring to a person who accompanied one on a furtive expedition of this kind, a verb other than *yulba-l* would be preferred. In place of (568) one informant gave:

(574) *ɲaḍin wagal ɲuɳḍu:ɲ bama:l gamba:ɲal*
 That person is crawling with my wife

although this too is ambiguous (it could mean 'that person is crawling up to my wife', the interpretation depending entirely on the situation in which the utterance occurs). In fact *gambaɲalɲu* is preferred over *yulbamaɲa:l* in (573), although both are acceptable.

The three types of *-ɲa-l* construction discussed thus far serve to place a non-core NP in O function (taking absolutive case, if a nominal). This can be for purposes of discourse emphasis and semantic orientation, or else to facilitate syntactic coordination or subordination. Thus, in a text about how the original Yidiɲḍi invaded Guŋgaɲḍi territory and found them speaking a strange language (Guŋgay), a sick Yidiɲḍi man fears that

(575) *ɲuḍu garu   badi:ɲal   ɲaɲaɲ gaḍa*
 NOT by-and-by cry-COMIT-PRES I-O   spirit-ABS
 wunaɲunda
 lie-DAT SUBORD
 [The Guŋgaɲḍi] won't be able to mourn me [in my own language] when I'm lying as a spirit (i.e. when I'm dead)

If a subordinate clause, marked by verbal inflection *-ɲunda*, has an NP in common with the main clause, this must be in S or O function in EACH of the clauses; the *-ɲa-l* construction ensures that 'I' is here the O NP of the main clause, and secures the subordination.

Only a handful of verbs (all intransitive) are normally found with a peripheral NP in 'fear' inflection – for instance *manɲa-n*, as in *buɲa manɲa:ɲ waguḍayi:da* 'the woman was frightened of the man'. There is a special *-ɲa-l* construction for these few verbs where the A corresponds to the S NP, and the O NP to the 'fear' constituent – *buɲa:ɲ wagu:ḍa manɲaɲalɲu* 'the woman was frightened of the man'.

4.3.6 Verbal -ŋa-l (v) instrumental sense. The mechanism of co-ordination in Yidiɲ is discussed in 5.1.3. Basically, if two sentences involve the same nominal, they can only be coordinated if the nominal is in absolutive case in both. Suppose we wish to join together, say:

(576) *bama gala:y burgi:ɲ*
 A person went walkabout with a spear

(577) *bama:l   gangu:l   gala: baga:l*
   A person speared a wallaby with a spear

on the basis of the common NP *gala* 'spear'. For this to be possible, *gala* must be placed in absolutive case in both sentences. From (576) we can derive a 'comitative' *-ŋa-l* construction:

(578) *bama:l gala burgiɲalɲu*   ⟨= (576)⟩

We can first obtain the antipassive version of (577):

(579) *bama gala: baga:ɖiɲu gangulala*   ⟨= (577)⟩

and then derive a *-ŋa-l* version of (579), in which S takes on A function and the instrumental NP becomes O:

(580) *bama:l gala baga:ɖiɲa:l gangulala*   ⟨= (577)⟩

We can now coordinate (578) and (580) to obtain:

(581) *bama:l gala burgiɲalɲu/ (bama:l) baga:ɖiɲa:l gangulala*
   The person went walkabout with a spear, and speared a wallaby with it

   (580) illustrates a fourth sense of verbal *-ŋa-l*, that we can term 'instrumental':

(iv) intransitive NP_S NP + INST   VC
          || || ||
   transitive NP_A NP_O VC + *ŋa-l*

Note that the original O NP *gangu:l* – which was put into locative case by the antipassive transformation – is unaffected by the *-ŋa-l* derivation and remains in locative case in (580). A *-ŋa-l* construction could not normally be based on the locative or dative NP realising deep O in an antipassive.

   This provides further support for our recognising locative and instrumental as two distinct cases (despite their formal identity).

   Other examples of *-:ɖi + ŋa-l* 'instrumental' constructions are at (243), (511), (590) and

(582) *ɲuɲɖu:ŋ   ɖugi   mandi: bunɖa:ɖiɲa:lna   buɲa:nda*
   THAT-ERG stick-ABS hand-LOC hit-:*ɖi*-COMIT-PURP woman-DAT
   That [person] had a stick in his hand to hit the woman

The *-na* purposive inflection on the verb in (582) provides the irrealis sense – the person raised a stick to strike the woman, but did not carry through his action.

(583) *ŋayu wawa:l walba bunḍa:ḍiŋalŋunda bama:l*
  I-SA see-PAST stone-ABS hit-:ḍi-COMIT-DAT SUBORD person-ERG
  waguḍaŋgu buŋa:nda
  man-ERG woman-DAT
  I saw the stone used by the man to hit the woman

Here the instrument *walba* 'stone' has to be brought into O function to satisfy the constraints on subordinate clauses – 4.4.1.

We have already mentioned that body-parts can occur in instrumental inflection. They can be placed in surface O function within a -:*ḍi*+*ŋa-l* construction; see (590) and

(584) *gini buyal bama:l ḍumba:ḍiŋal*
  penis-ABS strong-ABS person-ERG swive-:ḍi-COMIT-PRES
  buŋa-nda
  woman-DAT
  The man will swive (copulate with) the woman with [his] strong (i.e. erect) penis

Some languages have a single morphological/syntactic marking which covers comitative and instrumental NPs (for example English 'with'). Yidiɲ comitative differs from instrumental in both form and function (for instance, only comitative can be followed by a case inflection); but it is worth noting that the two productive types of S ≡ A -*ŋa-l* derivation are based one on comitative NPs and the other on instrumentals.

Locative and dative senses of -*ŋa-l* are – by comparison with comitative and instrumental uses – relatively restricted, applying only to a small number of intransitive verbs. Note that the peripheral cases on which -*ŋa-l* can be based – dative, locative, instrumental and 'fear' – are just those that are not concerned with syntactic or local 'to' or 'from' (3.3.1).

4.3.7 Verbal -ŋa-l (vi) controlling sense. The four senses of -*ŋa-l* discussed above all belong to what we call the 'S ≡ A type'. The A NP of the -*ŋa-l* construction corresponds to the S NP in a simple sentence, with O corresponding to a peripheral NP, or to a comitative NP that is embedded within the intransitive S.

The fifth sense is quite different. Here S ≡ O, and transitive A constitutes an additional factor (not referred to in the intransitive simple sentence) which controls the action. Thus:

(v) intransitive NP$_S$ VC
              ‖ ‖
  transitive NP$_A$ NP$_O$ VC+*ŋa-l*

A gloss along the lines 'NP$_A$ made NP$_O$ do VC' is sometimes but not always appropriate. Our reasons for preferring the label 'controlling' over 'causative' are explained below.

Examples have already been provided at (222) 'the food MADE ME VOMIT', (223) 'the person MADE HIM FALL DOWN' and (507) 'I MADE THE STICK BREAK'. Others are:

(585) a *mula:ri waŋga:ḍiɲu*
        The initiated man got up

   b *buriburi:ŋ mula:ri waŋga:ḍiɲa:l*
        The old man lifted up the initiated man

(586) a *ŋayu bunḍi:l buɲa:nda*
        I collided with the woman

   b *ŋaɲaɲ bama:l bunḍilmaɲa:l buɲa:nda*
        The person (who was pulling me this way) made me collide with the woman

(587) a *ŋayu warŋgi:ɲ*
        I turned around

   b *ŋaɲaɲ guḍunuŋgu warŋgiɲalɲu*
        The wind spun me round

As in all its other senses, *-ŋa-l* can only be added to intransitive stems – here *waŋga:ḍi-n* 'rise up', *bunḍi-l* 'burst, explode, collide (with)' and the adverb *warŋgi-n* 'do all around, turn round'.

Occasionally, controlling *-ŋa-l* makes a difference to the lexical import of a verb (at least, qua English translation equivalents). Intransitive *giwa-n* means 'stirred up' as in *yiɲu bana giwaŋ* 'this water is all stirred up'. One sense of transitive *giwaŋa-l* is 'tickle (a person)', as in:

(588) *ŋayu murŋga:lda   ɲuniɲ bina   giwaŋalna | ɲundu*
        I-SA feather-INST you-O ear-ABS stirred up-COMIT-PURP you-SA
        maŋga:na
        laugh-PURP
        I'll tickle your ear with a feather so that you will laugh

A 'controller' *-ŋa-l* construction can refer to an agent dealing with some other object:

(589) a *yiɲu bulmba balaŋ*
        This house is open

   b *ŋayu yiɲu bulmba bala:ŋal*
        I'll open up the house (open the door, or make a hole in the wall)

or it can refer to an agent controlling some part of his own body. Thus in a story about an old man trying to catch an alligator, the narrator said:

(590) *gaɲaraŋgu   waṛi   balaɲalɲu | baḍa:ḍiɲa:lna*
    alligator-ERG mouth-ABS open-COMIT-PAST bite-:ḍi-COMIT-PURP
    ɲuɲḍu:nda buriburi:nda
    THAT-DAT old man-DAT

The alligator opened its mouth, to use it to bite that old man

Here the first clause corresponds to intransitive:

(591) *gaɲarani   waṛi   bala:ɲ*
    alligator-GEN-ABS mouth-ABS open-PAST

The alligator's mouth opened

under an S ≡ O -*ɲa-l* correspondence. The second clause relates to the simple sentence:

(592) *gaɲaraŋgu   ɲuɲu   buriburi   waṛi: baḍa:l*
    alligator-ERG THAT-S old man-ABS mouth-INST bite-PAST

The alligator bit the old man with its mouth

being placed in the -:*ḍi*+*ɲa*+*l* instrumental construction (described in the last section) by a -*ɲa-l* transformation of the S ≡ A variety. The net result is that *waṛi* is in absolute case (and *gaɲa:r* in ergative) in both clauses allowing a purposive subordinate construction (4.5) with deletion of repeated constituents.

Another example of an agent controlling a body part is

(593) *bama:l ɲuɲu ḍina bilaɲalɲu guga:*

A person put his foot into the stirrup

guga 'skin' is used to denote 'leather', being extended here to a stirrup made of leather.

Sentences involving *bilaɲa-l* 'put in' with an O NP that is not a body part are in line 57 of text 2 and line 10 of text 9.

Verbal suffix -*ɲa-l* may, in the S ≡ O 'controller' sense, be attached to verbs of any semantic type. There appear to be just two small classes of exceptions:

[a] Verbs which take -*ɲa-l* in the dative or locative sense (4.3.4, 4.3.5) do not form 'controlled' transitive counterparts. Thus:

(594) *bama:l ɲaɲaɲ badiɲalɲu*

can only mean 'the person cried for me', never 'the person made me cry'. The latter meaning has to be rendered by a two-clause sentence, specifying what was done to provoke the tears, say

(595) *ɲaɲaɲ bama:l ḍiṟmbiɲalɲu/ ŋayu badi:ɲ*
    The person teased me, and I cried

When asked 'made me laugh' the informant gave:

(596) *ɲaɲaɲ ɲuɲḍu:ŋ buḍi:ɲ maŋga:na*
    That [person] told me to laugh

Note that we can obtain *bama:l ɲaɲaɲ muri:ḍiɲa:l* 'the person made me cry out (by frightening me)'; *muri:ḍi-n* 'cry out' does not take an indirect object, and so can form an S ≡ O *-ɲa-l* construction.

Similarly, it seems that *ɲaŋga:ḍiɲa-l* can NOT be used for 'someone MADE someone talk' (only for 'talk IN a particular language or style', or 'talk ABOUT some person or thing').

[b] Yidiɲ has a number of pairs of verbs that have the same semantic content, but differ only in transitivity. Some of these pairs are of the type S ≡ A (e.g. I speak (to you), I tell you) but all those in the semantic class of 'position' are of type S ≡ O. They include:

ḍana-n	'stand up'	*ḍara-l*	'put standing up'
ɲina-n	'sit down'	*ɲirḍa-ṟ*	'put sitting down'
bayi-l	'come out'	*ḍaŋga-n*	'take out'

A single event could be described by either an intransitive or a transitive sentence, where S and O NPs coincide:

(597) *yiɲu ḍaḍa ḍanaŋ*
    This baby is standing up

(598) *muḍa:mbu yiɲḍu:ɲ ḍaḍa ḍaral*
    Mother is standing this baby up (i.e. holding its hand while it tries standing for the first time)

Plainly, pairs like (597/8) are exactly equivalent to (585–7a/b), and so on. That is, *ḍara-l* corresponds to what would be the 'controller' sense of *ḍanaɲa-l*.

The distribution of S ≡ O and S ≡ A intransitive/transitive pairs in the various semantic types in Yidiɲ is similar to that in Dyirbal (Dixon 1972: 296–301, 1971: 461–7). Dyirbal has one S ≡ A pair amongst 'position' verbs – 'follow'; Yidiɲ deals with 'follow' only through transitive verbs.

When an intransitive verb has a transitive congener of the type S ≡ O, then *-ɲa-l* cannot, in fact, be applied to it with the 'controlling' sense. That is, *ḍanaɲa-l* can only mean 'stand with' (in the comitative sense), never 'make stand (= put standing)'; and similarly for *ɲina-n*,

bayi-l, and so on. This is a convenient exception. We mentioned that the comitative sense of *-ŋa-l* occurs predominantly with verbs of position, and that the controlling sense can occur with verbs of all semantic types. This gives rise to the possibility of considerable ambiguity; the possibilities are reduced by the exclusion of the 'controller' sense for intransitive verbs of 'position' that have S ≡ O transitive congeners.

It is interesting to note that the *-ŋa-l* form of *bayi-l* 'come out' can only be understood in the comitative sense, since it has an S ≡ O transitive congener *daŋga-n* 'take out'. But there is no transitive correspondent of *bila-n* 'go in' and so *bilaŋa-l* can mean either 'put in', as in (593), or else 'go in with', as in

(599) *ŋayu waga:lḍi bila:ɲ dugu:da* ⎱ I went into the house with
(600) *ŋayu wagal bilaŋalɲu dugu:da* ⎰ [my] wife

In the case of the commonest verbs of motion – 'go', 'come' and maybe also 'run', 'jump' and a few others – a *-ŋa-l* construction could, when the O NP has human reference, be understood in the S ≡ O or S ≡ A sense, without any difference in meaning. For instance (cf. (502–3)):

(601) *waguḍaŋgu buɲa gadaŋalɲu*
    The man came with the woman (= The man brought the woman)

implies both

(602) *wagu:ḍa (buɲa:y) gada:ɲ*
    The man came (with the woman)

and also

(603) *buɲa gada:ɲ* The woman came

Whereas, in the case of a verb of rest, there is considerable difference between *ɲirda-ɼ* 'put [someone] sitting down' and *ɲinaŋa-l* 'sit down with [someone]'.

With an inanimate O there is no difficulty, only the S ≡ A interpretation being open. Thus:

(604) *waguḍaŋgu gala gadaŋalɲu*
    The man came with a spear (= The man brought a spear)

implies

(605) *wagu:ḍa (gala:y) gada:ɲ* The man came (with a spear)

but not

*(606) *gala gada:ɲ* The spear came

It is in view of this that we prefer the S ≡ A interpretation for (601), linking it to (602).

An inanimate NP such as *gala* cannot normally be the subject of *gada-n*. It could be argued from this that (601) is indeed syntactically – although not semantically – ambiguous, with the second reading being excluded on selectional grounds. We are here preferring the other alternative, of recognising a small class of verbs of 'motion' that cannot take *-ŋa-l* in a 'controller' sense.

The important point here is that the only way a man can 'control' a woman's coming (from point A to point B) is to COME WITH her; the semantic structuring of (601) is, in essence 'the man controls [the woman comes]'. That is, a *-ŋa-l* form in Yidiɲ can NOT mean that someone MADE someone do something by TELLING them to do it. The fifth sense of *-ŋa-l* involves control of a physical nature; just as one can only make someone fall down by pushing them, so one can only make someone travel a certain path by going with them (setting them off in a certain direction would not ensure that they arrived – it would just be 'make set off').

This can be illustrated by the *-ŋa-l* form of *ḍangi-l* 'get caught, snagged, bogged'. The only sense that can be attached to *ḍangilmaŋa-l* in a sentence like

(607) *bama:l baba:ŋ ŋaɲaɲ ḍangilmaŋa:l*
       The silly person got me bogged

is that I followed a person who went into boggy ground and got me stuck – I should have remembered that he was half-witted (*baba*, literally 'deaf') and that it could be foolish to follow him. *ḍangilmaŋa-l* can NOT mean 'he got me bogged by TELLING me to go a certain way'.

Thus the controller of an action must be WITH the person he is controlling. It was in view of this that we stressed, in 3.8.6, that (236) *ḍuŋga:riŋa:ldaɲu* could not be interpreted in such a way that 'A is going but O is coming' (or vice versa).

Examples like (222), (507), (585–7) might be taken to suggest that the S ≡ A sense of *-ŋa-l* could be described as 'causative'. The explanation just given – that it implies control by physical means, and not by words – could be held merely to specify the type of causation admitted. The description 'causative' is, however, misleading; we prefer to characterise this use of *-ŋa-l* in terms of an agent 'controlling' or even 'using' some action referred to by an intransitive verb, rather than 'causing' it. This can best be illustrated by considering the effect of *-ŋa-l* with *guba-n* 'burn'; the data here are amongst the most interesting and important

available on any aspect of Yidiɲ syntax and it will be worthwhile presenting them quite carefully.

First, recall the 'semantic minimal pair' *waḍu-l* 'burn, cook' which must take a human A, and *guba-n* 'burn, cook' whose A NP must be 'sun', 'fire' or something hot or burning (4.1.5). *waḍu-l* behaves like a normal verb of 'affect', taking an instrumental NP:

(608) *ɲayu miɲa buɽi: waḍu:l*   I cooked the meat on the fire

which is unaffected by the antipassive *-:ḍi-n* transformation (cf. (483) in 4.2.5):

(609) *ɲayu buɽi: waḍu:ḍiɲu miɲa:*   ⟨= (608)⟩

and can then be placed in absolutive case by application of *-ŋa-l* in the 'instrumental' sense (4.3.6):

(610) *ɲayu buɽi waḍu:ḍiŋa:l miɲa:*
      I used the fire to cook the meat

Alternatively, one can say:

(611) *yiŋu   gima:l   ḍugi   buɽi:gu   waḍu:ḍiŋa:lna*
      THIS-ABS firestick tree-ABS tree-ABS fire-PURP burn-:ḍi-COMIT-PURP
      This firestick tree is for making fire (i.e. lighting firewood)

Compare with (351) and (350).

From a transitive simple sentence involving *guba-n*:

(612) *buɽi:ŋ miɲa guba:ɲ*   The meat was cooked in the fire

we can form an antipassive in the normal way:

(613) *buɽi guba:ḍiɲu (miɲa:)*   The fire has cooked (the meat)

For (612-13) we quote glosses exactly as supplied by the informant.

Corresponding to (613) there is a *-ŋa-l* construction, which must be of the S ≡ O 'controlling' type:

(614) *ɲayu buɽi guba:ḍiŋa:l miɲa:*
      I used the [light of] the burning fire to [look at] the meat

Here *buɽi guba:ḍi-n* describes 'the fire burning'. The *-ŋa-l* clause which is derived from this refers to an agent – here *ɲayu* 'I' – making use of the burning fire to throw light on something. (610) can mean 'I made the fire burn' but (614) can NOT carry this interpretation.

miɲa: in (613) is the deep O of *guba-n*; this should probably not be directly related to the *miɲa:* in (614), which refers to something that the agent is interested in seeing.

In normal use *guba:ḏiɲa-l* would be likely to have an O NP which specifically referred to, say, a burning torch:

(615) gidi   maba / miɲa:gu   ḏaba:ngu guba:ḏiɲa:lna
      torch-ABS light-IMP animal-PURP eel-PURP burn-:ḏi-COMIT-PURP
      Light a Gidi torch, to use it [to look] for eels

Corresponding to *guba:ḏiɲa-l*, Dyirbal has lexical items – intransitive *ginda-y*, transitive *ginda-l* 'look with a light' (quite distinct from *ganda-y* 'fire burns', the Dyirbal equivalent of *guba-n*). To be syntactically precise *guba:ḏiɲa-l* corresponds to the instrumentive *gindalma-l* in Dyirbal (Dixon 1972: 96–9 and cf. 383–5).

It is in view of the meaning attached to (614–15) that the S ≡ O sense of *-ɲa-l* appears to be better termed 'controller' than 'causer'. The point here is that *guba-n* describes a fire or light which is burning by itself; (614–15) describe some person exploiting this for his own ends (by holding the torch in such a position that the flame throws light on a certain object). Any description of a person CAUSING A FIRE TO BURN OR COOK something must employ *waḏu-l*.

The interpretation of agent as 'controller' (rather than 'causer') is supported by

(616) a *ŋayu bugu:lda wuḏi:ɲ*   I grew up at Woree (Bugul)
     b *bimbi:ŋ ŋaɲaɲ wuḏiɲalɲu*   Father brought me up

Here father can be thought of as overseeing or controlling a boy's development (whereas he certainly does not MAKE the child grow up).

But 'controller' may not be the perfect label. A controller need not, for instance, always be human. Note (222) in 3.8.5 'THE FRUIT made me vomit' and also

(617) ŋaɲaɲ waba:du gula   baygaɽmaɲa:l
      I-O   walk-ERG body-ABS feel sore-COMIT-PAST
      The walk made my body feel sore/tired

where the A NP is the abstract noun *wabaɽ* 'a walk'.

4.3.8 -ɲa-l and -:ḏi-n. The six senses of verbal *-ɲa-l* we have discussed are summarised in table 4.3. Each of the intransitive sentences corresponds to the transitive structure in the last line, with identity holding between NPs that are in the same column. The domain of application of each sense is summarised very roughly on the right.

TABLE 4.3   *Types of -ŋa-l construction*

intransitive	(i) [NP	NP+COMIT]$_s$	VC	predominantly verbs of position
	(ii) NP$_s$	NP+LOC	VC	only verbs of speaking (NP+LOC refers to speech)
	(iii) NP$_s$	NP+DAT	VC	only verbs with 'obligatory NP+DAT'
	(iv) NP$_s$	NP+FEAR	VC	only verbs with 'obligatory NP+FEAR'
	(v) NP$_s$	NP+INST	VC	VC antipassive (-:ḍi-n version of transitive)
	(vi)	NP$_s$	VC	[a] not verbs which take sense (ii) or (iii) [b] not verbs for which there is a corresponding transitive of type S ≡ O (and not 'go', 'come' and a few other verbs of 'simple motion')
corresponding to transitive	NP$_A$ NP$_O$		VC+ŋa-l	

There is another affix -*ŋa-l*, which derives a transitive verbal stem from a noun or adjective. This is very similar to sense (vi) of verbal -*ŋa-l*; in 4.8.1 we show that the verbaliser -*ŋa-l* CAN appropriately be labelled 'causative'.

Note that Dyirbal has a verbal comitative affix, -*mal* ~ -*mbal*, which is entirely of S ≡ A syntax, corresponding roughly to the Yidiɲ 'comitative' and 'dative' senses (Dixon 1972: 96–9, 296–9). The transitive verbalising suffix in Dyirbal, -*mal* ~ -*(m)bal*, has – like its counterpart in Yidiɲ – an entirely 'causative' meaning (Dixon 1972: 85–7).

Compare the syntactic effect of -*ŋa-l* with that of the other major derivational affix -*:ḍi-n*. In its major, antipassive sense we get correspondence between:

	transitive	NP$_A$	NP$_O$		VC
and	intransitive	NP$_s$	NP+DAT/LOC		VC+:ḍi-n

-*:ḍi-n* does of course occur in a number of other senses (4.2.4–7) some of which do not affect transitivity.

We can now summarise, from a syntactic point of view, the co-occurrence of these two derivational affixes in a verbal stem.

[A] -:*ḍi-n* followed by -*ŋa-l*

Almost all examples here fall under the 'instrumental' sense of -*ŋa-l*, discussed in 4.3.6. Thus:

transitive   NP$_A$ NP$_O$ NP + INST   VC
antipassive -:*ḍi-n*:
intransitive   NP$_S$ NP + DAT/ LOC   NP + INST   VC + :*ḍi-n*
instrumental -*ŋa-l*:
transitive   NP$_A$ NP + DAT/ LOC   NP$_O$ VC + :*ḍi* + *ŋa-l*

as illustrated by (577, 579, 580).

There are, however, two examples in the writer's corpus of the comitative sense of -*ŋa-l* being added to an antipassive, according to the scheme:

transitive   [NP   NP + COMIT]$_A$ NP$_O$ VC
antipassive -:*ḍi-n*:
intransitive   [NP   NP + COMIT]$_S$ NP + DAT/LOC   VC + :*ḍi-n*
comitative -*ŋa-l*:
transitive   NP$_A$ NP$_O$ NP + DAT/LOC   VC + :*ḍi* + *ŋa-l*

Thus:

(618) a *bama:l waŋalḍiŋgu ŋaɲaɲ*
          wawa:l
       b *bama waŋa:lḍi ŋanda*   The person with a boomerang
          wawa:ḍiɲu   saw me
       c *bama:l waŋal ŋanda*
          wawa:ḍiŋa:l

(619) a *bama:l ŋaḍundiŋgu ḍugi*
          gunda:l
       b *bama ŋaḍu:nḍi gunda:ḍiɲu*   The person, who had me with
          ḍugi:l   him, cut the tree down
       c *bama:l ŋaɲaɲ gunda:ḍiŋa:l*
          ḍugi:l

The informant glossed (618c) as 'Person, he looking at me when he has boomerang' and (619c) as 'Person been take me to cut that tree down'.

guba:ḍiŋa-l, in (614–15), involves antipassive -:*ḍi-n* followed by the 'controller' sense of -*ŋa-l*. Note that no instance of -:*ḍi* + *ŋa-l* involves -:*ḍi-n* in any sense other than antipassive; and none involves the locative or dative senses of -*ŋa-l*.

[B] *-ŋa-l* followed by *-:ḍi-n*

We can classify the examples here in terms of the sense of *-ŋa-l* involved. There are no examples of 'locative' or 'instrumental' *-ŋa-l* but we do have:

(i) comitative *-ŋa-l*. This appears only to be followed by *-:ḍi-n* in the 'continuous' sense (4.2.7); examples have already been given, as (494), (497–8) and (244).

(iii) dative *-ŋa-l*. There are relatively few verbs that take *-ŋa-l* in the dative sense, and just one example is attested with a following *-:ḍi-n*. Compare (563), (566) and:

(620) *yiŋu gurŋga ŋanda maŋgaŋa:ḍiŋ*
The kookaburra is laughing at me

Note that (620) is identical with (563) except for the verb – (563) has intransitive root *maŋga-n* whereas (620) shows the derived intransitive *maŋga + ŋa + :ḍi-n*. Here *-ŋa-l* and *-:ḍi-n* appear exactly to cancel each other out. The reason for using (620) in place of (563) is unknown – it may involve some systematic syntactic–semantic difference not known to the writer, or it may simply be stylistic.

(vi) controlling *-ŋa-l*. This use has the widest possibilities and can be followed by *-:ḍi-n* in any one of several senses.

To *giwaŋa-l* 'tickle' – cf. (588) – we can add *-:ḍi-n* in the reflexive sense (4.2.4):

(621) *ŋayu ganagayuy murŋga:lda giwaŋaḍi:ɲ*
I tickled myself with a feather (on purpose)

or in the 'inanimate A' sense (4.2.5):

(622) *ŋaɲaɲ murŋga:ldu giwaŋaḍi:ɲ*
The feather tickled me (= I tickled myself on the feather, accidentally)

Finally, controlling *-ŋa-l* can be followed by antipassive *-:ḍi-n*. The derivations involved are:

intransitive		NP$_\text{S}$	VC
'controlling' *-ŋa-l*:			
transitive	NP$_\text{A}$	NP$_\text{O}$	VC + *ŋa-l*
'antipassive' *-:ḍi-n*:			
intransitive	NP$_\text{S}$	NP + DAT/LOC	VC + *ŋa* + *:ḍi-n*

This places the controlling agent in surface S function, allowing it to serve as the pivot of a subordinating construction, as in

(623) *ŋanda bambaṟaŋa:ḍiɲum* | *bama   ḍuŋga:ɲ*
      I-DAT be frightened-COMIT-*:ḍi*-CAU SUBORD person-ABS run-PAST
      After having made me frightened, the person ran away

4.4 Dative and causal subordinate clauses

There are in Yidiɲ three types of subordinate clause, with distinctive verbal inflections (3.8.4):

> dative subordinate   *-ɲunda ~ -lɲunda ~ -ṟɲunda*
> causal subordinate   *-ɲum ~ -lɲum ~ -ṟɲum*
> purposive subordinate   *-na ~ -lna ~ -ṟna*

Causal subordinate clauses show a syntactic connection with causal NPs (with case inflection *-m ~ -mu*), and purposive clauses show an exactly parallel connection with purposive NPs (case marking *-gu*). There are also grounds (partly negative) for establishing a connection between the unmarked subordinate clause (with *-ɲunda* marking) and the unmarked type of peripheral syntactic NP (showing dative inflection *-nda*).

Semantically, a *-ɲunda* clause will normally describe something that is happening concurrently with the main clause, a *-ɲum* clause will refer to a prior, completed action (that may have resulted in some state or happening described by the main clause) and a *-na* clause will detail some anticipated or intended event (which will normally follow from some action described by the main clause).

It is in view of this syntactic and semantic connection – and the morphological similarity between verbal *-ɲunda, -ɲum* and nominal *-nda*, *-m ~ -mu* – that we employ peripheral case names dative, causal and purposive for the three types of subordinate clause.

Morphological analysis suggests a segmentation *-ɲu + nda* and *-ɲu + m*; we can say that *-ɲu-* proves a 'foundation' for a subordinate verb, to which is added the relevant nominal inflection (3.8.4). It is in fact necessary to recognise a morpheme boundary in the middle of *-ɲu + nda*, in order to explain its reduction by Rule 2 (2.3.2, 2.3.3).

There is no morphological similarity between nominal purposive *-gu* and verbal purposive *-na*. But comparison with Dya:bugay does suggest that an

earlier stage of the language had a verbal purposive based on *-gu* (with *-na* then being future tense inflection) – 3.8.4.

The three types of subordinate clause have almost identical basic syntax. In each case there are two main subtypes – a majority pattern where the subordinate clause has an NP in common with the main clause, and a minor pattern that provides temporal qualification and does not demand a coreferential NP. We deal in turn with dative and causal clauses below. Since the purposive inflection can occur in a main or in a subordinate clause, this is described in a separate section (4.5).

4.4.1 Dative clauses – coreferential type. About 85 % of subordinate clauses in the writer's corpus are of what we can term the 'coreferential type'. They can in almost every case be translated through a relative clause in English (the exact grammatical status of subordinate clauses in Yidiɲ is discussed at length in 5.3).

Subordinate clauses of this type must satisfy the

COREFERENTIALITY CONSTRAINT: There must be an NP common to main clause and subordinate clause, and it must be in surface S or O function in each clause.

We thus encounter four syntactic possibilities:

[i] Coreferential NP in O function in the main clause and in S function in the subordinate clause (this is the most frequent variety). From

(624) *ɲaɲḍi gaɲa:l bina:ɲal*   We can hear the locust

(625) *gaɲa:l   badiɲ*   The locust is crying

we can form

(626) *ɲaɲḍi gaɲa:l bina:ɲal badiɲunda*   We can hear the locust crying

Other examples are at (116), (181), (278), (285), (368), (490) and (575) above.

[ii] Coreferential NP in O function in both clauses:

(627) *ɲayu wawa:l   miɲa   mugiɲ   biḍu:ŋ*
      I-SA   see-PAST animal-ABS mouse-ABS eaglehawk-ERG
      bugaɲunda
      eat-DAT SUBORD
      I saw the mouse being eaten by the eaglehawk

[iii] Coreferential NP in S function in both clauses. See (256) and

(628) *ɲuɲu buɲa ḍuŋgaŋ maŋgaɲunda*
That woman ran along as she was laughing (literally: That woman who was laughing ran along)

[iv] Coreferential NP in S function in main clause and in O function in subordinate clause:

(629) *dalɲudalɲu dalmba   bunḍi:l   / ŋaɲḍi ɲuŋgu*
ringing-ABS sound-ABS bump-PAST we-SA THERE
　　binaɲalɲu:n
　　hear-DAT SUBORD
The bell rang a peal, which we heard there [in the mission] (cf. text 9 line 27)

(630) *yiɲu   ḍugi   ḍanaŋ   / maḍa   ḍambu:ndu*
THIS-ABS tree-ABS stand-PRES sawdust-ABS grub-ERG
　　baḍalɲunda
　　chew-DAT SUBORD
This tree, which has had sawdust chewed out of it by grubs, is standing [here]

Any sentence may function as main or as subordinate clause. Thus from:

(631) *ŋayu buɲa bunḍa:ɲ*   I hit the woman

(632) *buɲa ḍa:wurga:ɲ*   The woman yawned

we can form either

(633) *ŋayu buɲa bunḍa:ɲ/ ḍa:wurgaɲunda*
I hit the woman who was yawning

or

(634) *buɲa ḍa:wurga:ɲ/ ŋayu bunḍaɲunda*
The woman whom I was hitting yawned

A subordinate clause can show all the complexities that are available to main clauses. It can involve a multi-verb VC, as in (256) and

(635) *ŋayu ɲuniɲ wawa:l   waguḍaŋgu binarɲalɲu:n*
I-SA you-O see-PAST man-ERG   warn-DAT SUBORD
　　buḍiɲunda
　　tell-DAT SUBORD
I saw you being warned by the man

A subordinate clause can take the full range of peripheral constituents – for instance the *-ɲunda* clause in (181) of 3.7.2 includes a locative NP.

A sentence can involve more than one subordinate clause. Thus in

(636) *ŋayu wawa:l   bana   gadaɲunda   / gundu:yɖu*
      I-SA see-PAST water-ABS come-DAT SUBORD brown snake-ERG
      bana   mundalɲunda
      water-ABS pull-DAT SUBORD
    I saw the water coming [into the creek], being drawn up by the
    brown snake

the common NP *bana* 'water' is in O function in the main clause, in
S function in the *gadaɲunda* clause, and again in O function in the final
clause.

If two clauses do involve a common NP, but it is in deep A function
in one or both of them, the antipassive transformation (4.2.3) must be
applied to bring it into surface S function, in order to satisfy the coreferentiality constraint. For instance, if we wanted to have as matrix
clause:

(637) *ŋayu guŋga:mbuɾ wawa:l*   I saw a butterfly

and as constituent clause:

(638) *mayi guŋgambudu maɖa:ɲ*
    The butterfly was sucking nectar [from the flower]

then (638) would have to be put into antipassive form:

(639) *guŋga:mbuɾ maɖa:ɖiɲu mayi:* ⟨= (638)⟩

before it could be attached to (637). We then get:

(640) *ŋayu wawa:l guŋga:mbuɾ maɖa:ɖiɲu:n mayi:*
    I saw the butterfly sucking nectar
    There is another example at (442) in 4.2.3.

An example where the main clause has to be put into -*:ɖi-n* form is:

(641) *ɲuɲu bama ŋanda bunɖa:ɖiɲu/ maŋgaɲunda*
    The man who was laughing hit me

Although pronouns have a single form for S and A functions (and a
different one for O function) the coreferentiality constraint applies to
pronominal just as to nominal NPs. Thus, although *ŋayu* is included in
both

(642) *ŋayu bama wawa:l*   I saw the person

(643) *ŋayu wanda:ɲ*   I fell over

the pronoun is in A function in (642) and in S function in (643); it thus cannot serve as a basis for subordination. The sentence:

(644) *ŋayu bama wawa:l wandaɲunda*

can only mean 'I saw A PERSON fall over'. See also (654–5).

Attempts by the writer to elicit a subordinate clause which has an NP co-referential with the surface A NP in the main clause – along the lines of 'I saw the person as I fell over' – yielded only -*ɖi* clauses. These are discussed in 4.6.2.

Either main or subordinate clause may involve verbal -*ŋa-l* – see (575) and

(645) *ŋayu wawa:l   ɖaɖa   bama:l   binda:*
    I-SA see-PAST baby-ABS person-ERG shoulder-LOC
    maɖindaŋalɲunda
    walk up-COMIT-DAT SUBORD
    I saw the baby being carried uphill by the person, on his shoulder

(583) provided an example where the constituent clause involves a -:*ɖi*+*ŋa-l* sequence, putting an instrumental NP into surface O function in order to satisfy the coreferentiality constraint.

As can be seen from the examples thus far, a -*ɲunda* subordinate clause refers to an event that takes place to the same time as the event referred to by the main clause; the syntactic link is provided by an 'object' that it simultaneously involved in the two events. The choice of which of the two clauses is 'main', and the choice of 'common NP', indicates the orientation of the observer. This can be seen in a story where the narrator relates how:

(646) *ŋayu banɖi:liɲu | gindaɖaŋgu   bulmba*
    I-SA find-GOING-PAST cassowary-ERG camp-ABS
    balgalɲunda
    build-DAT SUBORD
    I went and found a camp that the cassowary was building

with the focus clearly on 'the camp'. The storyteller then has a conversation with the cassowary and helps him clear his site before leaving; the description of the departure places the focus on 'the cassowary':

(647) *ŋayu baɖa:ʈ   ginda:ɖa   bulmba: bilma:ɖiɲu:n*
    I-SA leave-PAST cassowary-ABS camp-LOC clear-:*ɖi*-DAT SUBORD
    I left the cassowary clearing the campsite

More than half the hundred and fifty or so examples of *-ɲunda* clauses
in the writer's corpus involve as matrix verb *wawa-l* 'see, look at' or else
a hyponym such as *baɲḍi-l* 'find'; the next commonest verb is *binaŋa-l*
'hear'. (Four of the five instances of dative subordinate clauses in
texts 2, 9 and 14 involve *wawa-l*!) But the balance of the examples cover
a wide semantic range, and it does seem that ANY verb can feature in a
matrix, as in a subordinate, clause.

4.4.2 Order of constituents. We can now comment on the place
which a relative clause takes in the word order of the complete sentence;
we will discuss first the common NP, and then the verb (and any further
constituents) of the subordinate clause.

It will be seen from the examples above that the NP common to
main and subordinate clauses is normally stated once only, and is sometimes before the verb of the main clause and sometimes after it. In a
survey of 95 subordinate clauses in texts the NP preceded the main verb
in 40 instances, and followed it a further 40 times. In the remaining 15
sentences the NP was split (cf. 4.1.9) with, for example, a generic noun
before the main verb and a specific noun after:

(648) *ŋayu bana   baɲḍi:liɲu   bugun*
     I-SA water-ABS find-GOING-PAST spring-ABS
     bayilɲunda
     come out-DAT SUBORD
     I went and found a spring coming out [of the ground]

or else the head noun first and an adjective following the verb:

(649) *bulmba   wawa:l guriɲbuḍun   wunaɲunda*
     camp-ABS see-PAST good-ABS-STILL lie-DAT SUBORD
     The camp was seen to be lying there alright still

or a deictic first, and a nominal later:

(650) *ŋayu waɲi:ra   wawa:l dungu   bayilɲunda*
     I-SA what kind-ABS see-PAST head-ABS come out-DAT SUBORD
     What kind [of animal] was it whose head I saw pop out [above the
       surface of the water]?

In (630) the main clause included *ḍugi* 'tree' with the subordinate clause
mentioning a part of the tree (something inalienably possessed by it) –
maḍa 'sawdust'.

However, there are some instances (half-a-dozen in the sample) in
which at least part of the common NP occurs twice. Thus in

(651) *ŋayu ŋabul   banḍi:liɲu   bana   ŋabul*
  I-SA noise-ABS find-GOING-PAST water-ABS noise-ABS
  bunḍilɲunda
  burst-DAT SUBORD
  I went and found the water [making a] noise [as its bubbles]
  burst

we get *ŋabul* before the verb and *bana ŋabul* after it. And note the two
occurrences of *bana* in (636).

We use '/' to mark the end of an intonation group – that is, 'sentence
final intonation', on which an utterance could terminate. In some cases –
including (651) – both main and subordinate clauses fall into a single
intonation group; in other examples the two clauses are in separate
intonation groups. This is so with:

(652) *ŋaɲḍi   binaŋalɲu duŋuɽ | duŋuɽ   wunaɲunda*
  we-SA   hear-PAST noise-ABS noise-ABS lie-DAT SUBORD
  We heard a noise, which was lying [over the whole country]

which also features two occurrences of the common NP.

From the fact that, on occasion, both main and subordinate clause
NPs appear to occur, we might suppose that when only one instance of
the common NP is apparent it may belong to either the main or the
subordinate clause. We can thus suggest that either the occurrence of
the common NP in the main clause, or its occurrence in the subordinate
clause may be deleted; or neither may be.

There should be a fourth possibility – that both occurrences are deleted.
Three or four examples of this type have been encountered in texts. For
instance:

(653) *wawa:l   guwa ŋanḍa:da ɲinaɲunda*
  see-PAST west creek-LOC sit-DAT-SUBORD
  [The narrator] saw [something] sitting by the creek over to the west.

We now need to devise a criterion for deciding which clause a single
occurrence of the common NP belongs to. If there are two intonation
groups – as in (652) – then we can say that the NP belongs in the clause
of the verb whose intonation group it shares. But in very many cases
main and subordinate clauses do comprise a single intonation group.
We noted in 4.1.9 that an absolutive NP will normally (but not quite
invariably) precede its verb. This suggests saying that if the NP precedes

the main verb – as in (626) – it belongs to the main clause (and the subordinate clause NP has been deleted); and if it follows the main verb – as in (640) – it belongs to the subordinate clause (with the main clause occurrence being lost). If absolutive nominals occur at two different places in the sentence, then we can say that parts of both NPs are preserved; that these are normally different parts – e.g. in (648) a generic noun in the main clause and a specific term in the subordinate clause – accords with Yidiɲ's preference for alternation – between successive sentences in discourse, or between successive clauses in a sentence – for the sake of stylistic felicity (3.1.3).

The discussion in the last paragraphs – although perhaps not without some theoretical interest – is essentially irrelevant to an understanding of Yidiɲ syntax. It does not appear to make any difference to the meaning or grammatical properties of a sentence WHERE the common NP comes, or which clause we choose to relate it to.

Since the common NP must be in S or O function in both clauses it will – if composed of nominals – have the same case marking in each occurrence (and it is this which gives rise to the difficulties we have tried to resolve above). But a pronoun has different forms for S and O functions (although, as stressed in the discussion of (644), exactly the same coreferentiality condition applies to pronouns as to nouns).

If a pronoun does have S function in one clause and O in another we can, of course, easily distinguish the two occurrences of the common NP. Consider:

(654) *muṛi:du*   *ŋaɲḍi:ɲ baḍa:l | buga:*   *ŋaɲḍi*
     mosquito-ERG we-O   bite-PAST night LOC we-SA
     wunaɲunda
     lie-DAT SUBORD
     Mosquitoes bit us in the night as we were sleeping

and note that either *ŋaɲḍi:ɲ* or *ŋaɲḍi* can be deleted. In fact the inform-ant immediately followed (654) with

(655) *muguy*   *ŋaɲḍi waŋga:ḍiɲu| ŋuḍu wuna:ɲ baḍaḷɲunda*
     all the time we-SA get up-PAST NOT lie-PAST bite-DAT SUBORD
     muguy
     all the time
     We kept getting up all the time, [we] couldn't sleep through being
     bitten all the time

in which the common NP has been deleted from the second main clause (underlying *ŋaɳɖi*) and from the subordinate clause (underlying *ŋaɳɖi:ɲ*). See also (685) below.

This lends support to our suggestion that all or part of the common NP in the main clause, or in the subordinate clause, can be retained; or both can be; or neither.

It remains to consider the place which the remainder of the subordinate clause (the verb, plus ergative and/or peripheral NPs) occupies in the sentence. It will have been noticed that in every one of the examples given so far the subordinate clause (leaving aside common NP) follows the main clause. The writer's corpus does contain four examples of -*ɲunda* subordinate clauses coming first in a sentence. In each of these cases the subordinate clause comprises a distinct intonation group (whereas more than half of postposed subordinate clauses fall in the same intonation group as the main clause). Examples are:

(656) *ŋayu mula:ri   ɲinaɲunda   / ɖambulaŋgu ŋaɲaɲ*
      I-SA initiated man-ABS sit-DAT SUBORD two-ERG   I-O
      ɖili + budil
      eye-put down-PRES
      Two [old people] were looking after me, who was sitting, newly initiated

(657) *muŋgun   gadilala   wunaɲunda / ɲuniɲ*
      wound-ABS small-ABS-NOW lie-DAT SUBORD you-O
      gali:ŋal
      take-COMIT-PRES
      [We'll] take you [out of camp] now that your wound is lying small (i.e. is almost healed)

4.4.3   Dative clauses – non-coreferential type. The 'coreferential NP' type of subordinate clause, that has been dealt with in the last two sections, describes a certain object entering simultaneously into two events: 'I saw the mouse' and 'The eaglehawk was eating the mouse'; or 'The woman ran' and 'The woman laughed'; and so on.

There is another type of -*ɲunda* clause simply describing two events that take place at the same time without being directly related through a common object. In this case there need not, of course, be any co-referential NP:

(658) *mayi*   *ŋayu bugabuga:ɲ* / *ŋuɲu bama*
vegetable food-ABS I-SA eat-REDUP-PAST THAT-S person-ABS
wunaɲunda wurmba
lie-DAT SUBORD asleep-ABS
I ate vegetables while that person slept

(659) *ŋayu wawa:l bulmba* / *maṛun waŋgi gurbilɲunda*
I-SA see-PAST camp-ABS cloud-ABS up get dark-DAT SUBORD
As I looked around the camping place, a cloud up [in the sky] was
getting darker and darker [presaging a volcanic eruption]

Other examples are at (426), (279) and (57) above.

This type of construction can detail two specific co-occurring events,
or it can refer to two things that habitually happen together (sometimes
in a conditional relationship – if X then Y):

(660) *ŋaɲḍi dugu:da wunaŋ bulmba: ḍimurula* / *ḍama*
we-SA house-LOC lie-PRES camp-LOC house-LOC dangerous-ABS
ḍimba:ṛal gadaɲunda
cyclone-ABS come-DAT SUBORD

We stay in a [big low] hut, when [we know] a cyclone is coming

Non-coreferential dative subordinate clauses are outnumbered six
times (in the writer's corpus) by the coreferential type. But there are a
score or so examples attested, enough to establish this as a productive
grammatical device.

There is a close relationship between the two types of *-ɲunda* clause.
In fact in some cases either an NP-relative or a T-relative interpretation
(as Hale 1976b labels these alternatives) could be given. Thus:

(661) *gana ɲundu:ba ŋaɲaɲ wamban* / *wurba:ḍiɲu:n ḍambu:nda*
TRY you all-SA I-O wait-IMP seek-:*ḍi*-DAT SUBORD grub-LOC
You wait for me, who is seeking grubs OR You wait for me, while
I seek grubs

(662) *ɲundu ŋuɲḍu:ɲ baŋga:lda garu bunḍa:na* / *ŋayu*
you-SA THAT-O axe-INST by-and-by hit-PURP I-SA
yaymilɲunda miɲamuḍay
ask-DAT SUBORD meat-COMIT-ABS
You must presently hit that [person], whom I'm asking for meat,
with the axe
OR You must presently hit that [person] with the axe, while I'm
asking him for meat (and distracting him so that he doesn't
notice you creeping up behind him)

Examples (628), (633–4) and (654–5) can also receive either type of interpretation.

A subordinate clause of what we have termed the 'non-coreferential type' (that is, one which does not meet the coreferentiality constraint) CAN – coincidentally as it were – have an NP in common with the main clause; it need not be in S/O function. Isolated examples are known (as against scores of instances of the regular coreferential type) where this NP is in dative case in the main clause:

(663) *ŋayu miɲa wiwi:ɲ ɲuɲḍu:nda maŋgaɲunda*
    I gave the meat to that [person] while the person was laughing

or in ablative or fear inflection:

(664) *ŋayu ḍuŋga:ɲ gaɲaramu (/gaɲarayi:da) ɲabaɲunda*
    I swam quickly away from the crocodile (/for fear of the crocodile) which was bathing (there)

or in locative inflection:

(665) *ŋayu wawa:ḍiɲu   bunbuḍala/   ḍaḍa:n*
    I-SA see-:*ḍi*-PAST top-LOC   child-GEN-ABS
    ḍaralḍaralɲunda
    put standing-REDUP-DAT SUBORD
    I saw the child's top, while the top was being made to spin round

or in genitive form:

(666) *yiɲu   ganda   buɲa:n   / wurmba*
    THIS-ABS yamstick-ABS woman-GEN-ABS asleep-ABS
    wunaɲunda
    lie-DAT SUBORD
    This yamstick belongs to the woman, and the woman is sleeping (over there)

Sentences like these do appear to be related to the majority 'coreferential NP' syntactic pattern. If an NP from the main clause is repeated in the subordinate clause then the latter occurrence can be deleted ONLY IF it is in S or O function in the subordinate clause; this has happened in (663) and (664). Note that in (665) the NP *bunbu:ḍa ḍaḍa:n* 'the top belonging to the child' is split – *bunbuḍa* appears in locative case, appropriate to its function in the main clause, while *ḍaḍa:n* is in absolutive case, qua O function in the subordinate clause. Similarly, in (666) the subject NP is *buɲa wurmba* 'woman sleeping'; *buɲa* has

already occurred with genitive marking in the main clause and just the adjective is stated for the subordinate clause.

Note, though, that a repeated NP cannot be omitted from the subordinate clause if it is NOT in S or O function there. We can have a *-ɲunda* clause of the non-coreferential type:

(667) *ɲaɲaɲ muɻu:yḍu   baḍa:l / ŋayu mayi   gundalɲunda*
      I-O   white bee-ERG bite-PAST I-SA honey-ABS cut-DAT SUBORD
      The white bee bit me as I was cutting honey (out of the bee's nest)

and here *ŋayu* (which is in A function in the subordinate clause) can NOT normally be deleted.

Compare this with a regular coreferential-type subordinate clause:

(668) *ɲaɲaɲ muɻu:yḍu baḍa:l (ŋayu) mayi: gunda:ḍiɲu:n*
      The white bee bit me who was cutting honey (out of its nest)

(668) does satisfy the coreferentiality constraint – with *ɲaɲaɲ* being in O function in the main clause and *ŋayu* in S function in the subordinate clause – and here *ŋayu* can, optionally, be omitted.

4.4.4 Causal NPs. We have already mentioned (3.3.1) that the case inflection *-mu ~ -m* can either have an ablative meaning ('motion from') or a causal sense. In the latter case it indicates a reason for the state or activity referred to by the main verb of the sentence. See (42), (175) and (368).

The inflection *-nim* can indicate past possession (and could then be semantically analysed as genitive-plus-ablative/causal) or it can be used as a causal case marking, alternating with *-mu ~ -m* (3.3.4). Thus we can have (cf. (367)):

(669) *muŋgun wawa* $\left\{\begin{matrix} galam \\ gala:nim \end{matrix}\right\}$ Look at [this] sore, resulting from a spear [wound]!

(670) *yiɲu muŋgun wunaŋ* $\left\{\begin{matrix} biɲḍi:nmu \\ biɲḍi:nim \end{matrix}\right\}$ This sore lying [on my body] was caused by a hornet [stinging me]

(671) *yiɲu maɲḍam wunaŋ* $\left\{\begin{matrix} muŋgu:nmu \\ muŋgu:nim \end{matrix}\right\}$ This mark lying [on my body] is from an [old] sore

The conditions for the alternation between *-mu ~ -m* and *-nim* are unclear. It may possibly be determined by a hierarchy similar to that described in 3.1.2, 4.1.8; but there is no real evidence supporting this.

Although *-nim* and *-mu* ∼ *-m* show considerable overlap, there are still important differences. Thus it seems that *-mu* ∼ *-m* could NOT be used in

(672) *yiɲu   wagu:ḍa   ḍanaŋ   gaḍi   buɲa:nim*
　　　 THIS-S man-ABS stand-PRES long way woman-*nim*
　　　 This man is standing a long way away from the woman

buɲa:nim in (672) implies that the woman used to be the man's girl-friend, but they fell out and he is now behaving stand-offishly towards her.

The nominal affix *-gaṛa:* appears to have a similar meaning to causal *-mu* ∼ *-m* and *-nim*. Compare (669–71) with (97–8) in 3.3.7.

4.4.5 Causal clauses – coreferential type.

Causal subordinate clauses follow the syntactic patterns we have described for dative clauses; the norm variety – making up around 90% of instances recorded – demands that a common NP be in S or O surface function in both main and subordinate clauses.

The main difference between dative and causal clauses is in time reference relative to the main clause. A dative clause will always describe an event that is taking place simultaneously with the event of the main clause; thus 'I saw the woman swimming', 'Mosquitoes bit me whilst I slept', 'He trod on leaves that were lying there', and so on.

A causal clause will describe something that took place prior to the event described by the main clause (and was in fact finished before the main clause event began). A causal clause will explain or comment on the state or position of the referent of the common NP, as it is at the time described by the main clause.

The main clause can be in past tense:

(673) *ŋayu walba   wawa:liɲu   yaŋgi:ɲum*
　　　 I-SA stone-ABS see-GOING-PAST split-CAU SUBORD
　　　 I went and saw the rock that had been split

and the subordinate clause then refers to 'past-in-past'. Or the main clause can be in present or imperative form, with the causal clause referring to something in the immediate past:

(674) *gulugulu   ɲundu:ba buganala   / miɲa   ŋayu*
　　　 black bream-ABS you all-SA eat-IMP-NOW fish-ABS I-SA
　　　 gadaŋalɲum
　　　 come-COMIT-CAU SUBORD

You all eat the black bream, that I've brought [here for you]! (text 14.21)

Alternatively, the main clause can describe a habitual action, which normally follows the event of the subordinate clause:

(675) *ɲaɲḍi bana:*   *ŋabaŋ* / *ɲuŋgum*   *buga:ḍiɲum*
we-SA water-LOC bathe-PRES THERE-ABL eat-:*ḍi*-CAU SUBORD
We (habitually) bathe in the (river) water, after we've eaten

A causal clause can be used to indicate logical or pragmatic consequence. Following soon after (675) in a text about olden-days tribal life came a warning:

(676) *ɲaɲḍi:ɲ gala:*   *bagal*   / *guwa ɲaba:ɲum*   / *ɲaɲḍi:ɲ*
we-O   spear-INST pierce-PRES west bathe-CAU SUBORD we-O
ḍubu:da   *dudal*   / *guwa ɲaba:ɲum*
stone-ERG throw at-PRES west bathe-CAU SUBORD
We'd be pierced by spears if we'd bathed to the west (i.e. upstream from the camp); we'd be pelted with stones if we'd bathed to the west (i.e. any child who bathed upstream from the camping place, and thus polluted the drinking water, would be punished by his elders)

The usefulness of causal clauses in specifying the exact ordering in a series of events is seen in:

(677) *muyŋga*   *gunda:lɲum*   / *waŋga:ḍiɲa:l*   / *dunguḍilŋgu*
cicatrices-ABS cut-CAU SUBORD get up-COMIT-PAST head-DOWN
ɲina:ɲ / *waŋga:ḍiɲa:lɲum*
sit-PAST get up-COMIT-CAU SUBORD
After having had [my] cicatrices cut [I] was lifted up [into a sitting position]; and sat with my head down after having been lifted up

Most of the syntactic possibilities for causal clauses of the coreferential type have already been illustrated: in (673), (674) and (677) the common NP was in O function in the main clause and also in O function in the subordinate clause; in (676) it was in O/S, and in the last part of (677) in S/O. The common NP is in S function in both clauses of (203) and of

(678) *buriburi garu wula:ɲ/ mura:nḍi wuna:ɲum*
By-and-by the old man died, after having lain sick (for a while)

If the common NP is in underlying A function in either clause, an antipassive will have to be formed, as in (623), (675) and:

(679) *ḍambu:l gadigadi: buṟmu   ɲina:ɲ | manḍa*
    two-ABS children-ABS quiet-ABS sit-PAST culprit-ABS
    bunḍa:ḍiɲum
    hit-*:ḍi*-CAU SUBORD
    The two little children sat there quietly (while everyone wondered who had killed the old man), they were the culprits who had murdered [him]

As with -*ɲunda* clauses, an instrumental NP can be brought into surface O function through a -*:ḍi+ŋa l* construction, in order to satisfy the coreferentiality constraint:

(680) *ŋayu yiŋu   bulin   darabaŋal |*
    I-SA THIS-ABS plate-ABS shake-COMIT-PRES
    buga:ḍiŋa:lɲum
    eat-*:ḍi*-COMIT-CAU SUBORD
    I'll clean this plate, which has been used for eating off

Causal clauses are typically used to describe an action that gave rise to some state described by the main clause; for instance:

(681) *ŋayu giramgira:mḍi   ɲinaŋ | bala*
    I-SA cramp-REDUP-COMIT-ABS sit-PRES leg-ABS
    baygaṟmbaygaṟ   yaḍi:lɲum
    be sore-REDUP-PRES   walk about-CAU SUBORD
    I'm sitting [here] with cramps, my legs are feeling sore from walking about [a lot]

Sometimes the main clause may involve just an adjective (with no verb) as 'I'm full from eating' – (99), (193).

The Yidiɲḍi and Guŋgaɲḍi people named places after events that are reported to have taken place there; and explanations of the meanings of names frequently involve a causal subordinate clause (but no verb in the main clause):

(682) *yiŋu   bulmba   bilma | gindaḍaŋgu   bilma:ɲum*
    THIS-ABS place-ABS 'name'-ABS cassowary-ERG clear-CAU SUBORD
    This place is [called] Bilma, since the cassowary cleared it

A main clause can be qualified by both dative and causal subordinates:

(683) *bama:l*   *gaɲa:r*   *baga:liɲu*   /   *munu*
    person-ERG alligator-ABS spear-GOING-PAST inside
      wunaɲunda   /   *ḏabu:*   *bila:ɲum*
      lie-DAT SUBORD ground-LOC go in-CAU SUBORD
    The people went to spear the alligator, who was lying inside [his
      lair] after having gone into [a hole in] the ground

Yidiɲ does also allow iteration with, say, a dative clause qualifying a
causal subordinate clause:

(684) *wuba:yḏu*   *gaɲa:r*   *banḏa:r*   /
    alligator bird-ERG alligator-ABS follow-PAST
      wawa:liɲum   *walŋgalɲunda*   /   *gana ḏadu:l*
      see-GOING-CAU SUBORD float-DAT SUBORD TRY   shade-LOC
      wunaɲunda
      lie-DAT SUBORD
    The alligator bird followed the alligator, after having watched him
      floating [in the water] and trying to lie in the shade

All of our comments (in 4.4.2) about the ordering of dative clauses
apply to causal clauses. Surface structure may retain parts of the
common NP from main or from subordinate clause (or from both, or
from neither). Considerations of stylistic felicity will normally ensure
that there is no exact repetition – as in (674) where the specific noun
gulugulu 'black bream' occurs in the main clause and generic *miɲa* 'meat,
fish' in the causal clause.

    Again, occurrence of the common NP in BOTH clauses is shown most
clearly with a pronoun:

(685) *ɲaɲaɲ ḏugi:ŋ*   *baga:ḏiɲu*   /   *(ɲayu)*
    I-O   stick-ERG pierce-*:ḏi*-PAST I-SA
      gaŋgu + ḏuŋga:ɲum
      take short cut-CAU SUBORD
    The stick pierced my [foot], when I had taken a short cut

(Note that in (685) -*:ḏi-n* marks an inanimate A NP, which does not
'control' the action.)

    Causal clauses normally follow the main clause and can then fall into
the same intonation group or comprise a separate one. They are occasionally encountered preposed – as (623) – and in that position always
constitute a separate intonation group.

4.4.6 Causal clauses and causal NPs. Yidiɲ has two syntactic means of showing the 'cause' of some action. Suppose that a person hits a woman and then, in fright or fear of retribution, runs away. These episodes can be described by simple sentences:

(686) *bama:l buɲa bunḍa:ɲ*   The person hit the woman

(687) *bama ḍuŋga:ɲ*   The person ran away

If we wish to specify in (687) why the person is running away we can simply include a causal NP:

(688) *bama ḍuŋga:ɲ buɲa:nim*
      The person is running away because of (what he has done to) the
      woman

or we could append a causal clause. To satisfy the coreferentiality constraint (686) must first be placed in antipassive form:

(689) *bama bunḍa:ḍinu buɲa:nda*   ⟨= (686)⟩

giving

(690) *bama ḍuŋga:ɲ bunḍa:ḍiɲum buɲa:nda*
      The person is running away after/because he hit the woman

Although (688) and (690) are acceptable Yidiɲ sentences, the most frequent construction is a blend which includes causal marking on NP and on verb:

(691) *bama ḍuŋga:ɲ bunḍa:ḍiɲum buɲa:nim*   ⟨= (690)⟩

Similarly we get (cf. (99), (193)):

(692) *ɲayu galiŋ mayim buga:ḍiɲum*
      I'm going out after eating food

and here **ɲayu galiŋ buga:ḍiɲum mayi:* was judged scarcely acceptable by informants.

We could assign to (691) a deep structure of the type *bama ḍuŋga:ɲ buɲa:nim bunḍa:ḍinu buɲa:nda* (that is, involving both a causal NP and a separate causal clause), and then say that *buɲa:nim* – with causal inflection – takes precedence over dative *buɲa:nda* in the environment of a verb showing causal inflection.

Or we could, alternatively, say that the antipassive transformation marks the underlying O NP as dative or locative EXCEPT within a causal clause when it can instead be in causal case (and except within a

purposive clause when it can be in purposive case – 4.5.4). This suggests a syntactic relation:

dative case : dative clause

:: causal case : causal clause

(:: purposive case : purposive clause)

Within a dative subordinate clause there is no possibility of alternation since the clause marking is the same as the unmarked inflection on an O NP in an antipassive construction. It is only when a subordinate clause has 'to' or 'from' marking, that this can be extended to a constituent peripheral NP.

The latter explanation is perhaps marginally preferable since it simply involves alternative case assignment (causal within a causal clause, etc.). If we took the first alternative it would be necessary precisely to specify the limits of 'precedence' (what case takes precedence over what other case and under what conditions).

'Causal case', in the discussion here, covers the causal senses of *-mu ~ -m* (3.3.2) and of *-nim* (3.3.3), and also the nominal affix *-gaɽa:* – see (99) in 3.3.7.

A textual example similar to (691) but with the main clause referring to an action that is intended to atone for the crime (not escape it) is:

(693) *ɲaɲaɲɲuɽi   ɲundu:ba bunḍaɲadan | ɲayu manḍa |*
      I-O-THIS ONE you all-SA hit-COMING-IMP   I-SA culprit-ABS
      buriburi:nim   bunḍa:ḍiɲum
      old man-CAU hit-:ḍi-CAU SUBORD

      You [fellows] can come and hit me now! I'm the culprit, who killed the old man

A verb of rest will naturally be accompanied by a noun in locative case, indicating the place of rest. There is a typical construction pattern in Yidiɲ which involves a verb of motion in the main clause and a verb of rest in the causal subordinate clause; the noun indicating place of rest may then be in ablative case:

(694) *dama:ri   gali:ɲ | dabu:lmu   ḍana:ɲum*
      'name'-ABS go-PAST beach-ABL stand-CAU SUBORD

      Damari went on, from the beach, after having stood on the beach [for a while]

Here the ablative *dabu:lmu* does double duty – it indicates that Damari went from the beach (in ablative function to *gali-n*) after having stood on the beach (here *dabul* is, in underlying form, in locative relation to *ḍana-n*). Other examples are:

(695) *ḍaruy wala waymbaŋ/ ɲina:ɲum manum*
The bird flew away from the top of the tree, after having sat there

(696) *ŋuɲu garu bama bayil/ ḍugim gaɽbam nila:ɲum*
By-and-by that person came out from behind the tree, after having hidden himself there

Note that this kind of construction can also be used where the NP that is understood in a locative sense in the subordinate clause has causal (not ablative) function in the main clause:

(697) *ŋayu banbaŋ ḍadum ɲina:ɲum*
I'm cold from sitting in the shade

Sentences (694–7) involve an NP that has purely local function in the causal clause and are quite different from (691–3) where the common NP had syntactic function (deep O in an antipassive) within the subordinate clause. It is important to note that causal case can only 'be used in place of' dative – as in (691–3) – or locative – as in (694–7) – never instead of any other case.

The sentence:

(698) *yiɲu   muŋgun   wunaŋ | biɲḍi:nmu/ ŋaɲaɲ baḍa:lɲum*
THIS-ABS sore-ABS lie-PRES hornet-CAU I-O   bite-CAU SUBORD
This sore lying [on my skin] is from a hornet, from having been bitten [by a hornet]

has been recorded. At first sight it might appear to be a blend of (670) and the coreferential causal sentence (where the coreferential NP is *ŋayu muŋgun* 'my wound', involving inalienable possession):

(699) *yiɲu muŋgun wunaŋ/ ŋaɲaɲ biɲḍi:ndu baḍa:lɲum*
This sore, which is from a hornet biting me, is lying [on my skin]

along the lines of (691–3). But note that (698) involves three distinct intonation groups – one for the main clause, one for the causal NP *biɲḍi:nmu*, and one for the causal subordinate clause. It appears that this (isolated) example simply involves a causal NP and a causal clause (from which the ergative NP has been deleted) and does not parallel the productive syntactic patterns exemplified in (691–3) and (694–7).

4.4.7 Causal clauses – non-coreferential type. Again paralleling dative clauses, there are in the writer's corpus just a handful of *-ɲum* clauses which do not involve a common NP with S or O function in each

clause (but they are outnumbered ten times by clauses that do meet the coreferentiality constraint). For instance:

(700) *ŋayu garu   bama   guga:l | burudu:ɽ*
     I-SA by-and-by person-ABS call to-PAST wallaby-ABS
     duga:lɲum
     catch-CAU SUBORD
     I called out to the people that the wallaby had been caught [in the trap]

Note also that (675–8), (681), (683–5) and (694–6) are as it were ambiguous, being each capable of interpretation in terms of a relative clause, or of a 'while' adverbial clause.

There can – coincidentally – be some NP common to the two clauses in this type of construction; as in the case of dative clauses the repeated NP may be omitted in the subordinate position if it is in S or O function there:

(701) *ḍaḍa   gadil   ɲina:ɲ   ɲaru   waŋgulanda*
     child-ABS little-ABS sit-PAST on top of white cockatoo-DAT
     wula:ɲum
     die-DAT SUBORD
     The little child sat on the white cockatoo, after it had died

(702) *bama   ŋabi   gada:ɲ | bulmbam*
     person-ABS many-ABS come-PAST camp-ABL
     ḍari:ɲum
     be submerged-CAU SUBORD
     Many people came [here] from the[ir original] camp, after it had been submerged (by the sea level rising)

Note that we could not take (702) as symptomatic of a further syntactic type in which 'the ablative/causal NP in the main clause is coreferential with the S or O NP in the causal clause'. If this were a general possibility we could in place of (692) say simply:

*(703) *ŋayu galiŋ mayim buga:ɲum*

But (703) is not grammatical; we can here only use (692), which is based on referential identity between the S/O NP in the subordinate clause, and the S/O NP in the main clause.

4.5   Purposive constructions

4.5.1   Purposive NPs. A purposive NP (marked by inflection -*gu*, 3.3.2) refers to something towards which the action described by the sentence is orientated, something that would be expected to be a core participant (S, A or O NP) for a succeeding action. See examples (360–2), (365) in 4.1.6 as well as (137), (498), (406) and

(704)   *burawuŋal bana:gu gali:ɲ*
The Burawuŋal (water sprite woman) went FOR WATER

(705)   *waruwaru   ŋabi   gawal+ḍana:ɲ/ murimuri:ḍiɲu   /*
children-ABS lots-ABS call-stand-PAST scream-REDUP-PAST
    guga:ḍiɲu   bama:gu /   gaɲaraŋgu   bama
    call to-:ḍi-PAST person-PURP alligator-ERG person-ABS
    galiɲalɲu:n   / murba
    go-COMIT-DAT SUBORD   under water
All the children cried out, screamed, and called out TO THE ADULTS, about an alligator taking a person away, under the water

(706)   *gawu: guga   daŋgan   buda:gu*
tree sp.-ABS skin-ABS take off-IMP blanket-PURP
Take the Gawu: bark off [the Gawu: tree] FOR A BLANKET (i.e. to use it as a blanket)

(707)   *ŋayu yiri: walba   mugayŋalɲu*
I-SA slatey stone-ABS stone-ABS grinding stone-CAUS VBLSR-PAST
    mayi:gu   badi:lgu
    vegetable-PURP rickety nut-PURP
I made that piece of Yiriy stone into a Mugay (grinding stone) FOR RICKETY NUT (i.e. to grind rickety nut with it)

In 4.1.6 we contrasted purposive NP – whose referent is likely to play an active role in a succeeding event – with dative NP – which indicates more of a passive participant. The contrast is brought out by:

(708)   *bama ŋanda gaṛbaŋ*
The person is hiding from me (i.e. just so that I will not see him)

(709)   *bama ŋaḍu:ngu gaṛbaŋ*
The person is hiding from me (i.e. with the intention of jumping out and frightening or hurting me)

Dick Moses suggested that the dative (708) could be continued *bama ɲanda gaɽbaŋ wawa:ḍina* 'The person is hiding from me, to watch me (without me knowing I am being observed)' whereas purposive (709) might be part of a dialogue with a second person asking *waɲinbara:* 'What for?' and the first speaker replying *gurbi ɲaɲaŋ bunḍa:na* '[He] might be about to hit me'.

There is in fact a third possible translation of 'The person is hiding from me', involving fear inflection on the pronoun (4.1.6, 4.6.1):

(710) *bama ŋaḍunḍida gaɽbaŋ*
      The person is hiding from me (for fear of me e.g. of what I might do
      to him)

A purposive NP can consist just of an adjective, and will then indicate the attainment of a certain state. Thus:

(711) *bama:l mayi badil muga:yŋḍa bulba:l/ buḍalagu*
      The people ground the rickety nut with a Mugay stone, to [make
      it] fine

It was mentioned in 3.4.1, 3.7.2 that *-gu* can be used to indicate allative case with locational qualifiers and deictics (and occasionally with nouns such as *bulmba* 'camp, place'). This usage is of course grammatically quite distinct from purposive.

-gu can also be used with words that have temporal reference to indicate 'until a certain time' (3.5). But there are also instances of purposive *-gu* being added to a time word:

(712) *ŋayu biya   duguɽ   balgal   / yiwa:ygu*
      I-SA PARTICLE house-ABS build-PRES winter-PURP
      I [haven't yet but] should build a hut for the winter

The central meaning of *yiway* is 'wind'. 'Winter-time' is rendered either by *yiway* or by *yiwa:ɲḍi* (with the comitative affix). Particle *biya* is discussed in 4.10.

4.5.2 Purposive verbs – in main clause.

The purposive inflection *-na* (3.8.4) can occur on a VC in a subordinate clause (parallel to *-ɲunda* and *-ɲum*) or in a main clause (instead of tense or imperative). Within a main clause purposive refers to future time but specifies a particular 'need' – that the actor has to, or tries to, or wants to, or should perform the action; in contrast, the present–future tense inflection (3.8.4) is used for straightforward prediction about the future – see (528), (552), (575), (584), (589b), (657) and (680).

Purposive main verbs often occur with the particle *gana* 'try' (4.10) and then indicate the necessity of making an attempt at something. See (308), (326), (524) and

(713) *gana ŋayu giḍa   gunḍi:na   bama:gu*
     TRY I-SA quick-ABS return-PURP person-PURP
     I must try to hurry back to the people [at the main camp, to warn
     them of the danger which is approaching]

Without *gana*, purposive can indicate necessity:

(714) *ŋaɲḍi garu waraŋaḍi:na*
     We'll all have to shift camp soon (we have exhausted the food
     resources around this camping place)

(715) *ɲundu ŋaḍin wagal/ ŋayu ɲuniɲ galiŋalna wagal/ bulmba:gu*
     You're my wife [now]; I must take you, wife, back to the camp

Other examples are at (94), (228), (312), (324), (352) and (662). Verbal *-na* may sometimes be used in giving instructions:

(716) *ḍilŋgu mayi   wayu   wuna:na bana:*
     down vegetable-ABS long time lie-PURP water-LOC
     [This] vegetable food must [be allowed to] lie in the water for a
     long time [before it is fit to eat] (text 2.50)

A main clause purposive NP may refer to the need for food, water or shelter, to something that must be done in order to escape an enemy or fulfil a social obligation, or just to the desire to continue with a journey:

(717) *ŋayu baḍa:ɽna yiŋu bulmba gaɲḍugaɲḍu*
     I must leave this place Gaɲḍugaɲḍu [and continue my travels]

Purposive can also be employed to stress 'it's MY turn', as in (257) of 3.9.1 'You've eaten, now I must eat'.

The context will often indicate that the agent DID perform the action referred to by a purposive clause (that is, in fact, the unmarked interpretation). But a purposive verb will sometimes be used to indicate that a person intended to do something but for some reason did not carry it through – see (582) in 4.3.6 'the person [raised his stick] intending to hit the woman (but did not bring it down on her)'.

Verbal purposive may also have a 'potential' sense, indicating that something can suitably be involved in a certain action:

(718) *yiŋu bana wuŋa:na*   This water is drinkable

or, in reference to the undistinguished fare served in early mission days:

(719) *miɲa   mulam   guriɲ | buri:nḍi   buga:na*
      meat-ABS stew-ABS good-ABS bread-COMIT-ABS eat-PURP
      Stew is alright, it is eatable [if taken] with bread

See also line 76 of text 2.

4.5.3 Purposive subordinate clauses – coreferential type. Purposive inflection occurs quite frequently on the VC of a main clause (as can be seen from examination of text 2). And, as the inflection in a subordinate clause, it is probably more common than -*ɲunda* (which is, in turn, more frequent than -*ɲum*).

The great majority of -*na* subordinate clauses conform to the syntactic type described in 4.4.1 and 4.4.5: main and subordinate clause must show a 'common NP' which is in S or O function in each clause. If a common NP is in underlying A function, the antipassive transformation has to be employed to bring it into a surface S slot. Pattern S/O is exemplified in (456) of 4.2.4 and O/S in (115) from 3.3.8. O/O and S/S occur in:

(720) *ɲundu:ba bana duga:lin| wuɲa:na*
      You go and get water to be drunk (by us)

(721) *ɲayu bila:ɲ dugu:da| wuna:na*
      I went into the hut to lie down (and sleep there)

Example (109) in 3.3.8 involves a main clause with understood O NP *buɲa ḍina* 'the woman's feet' and a subordinate clause with understood S NP *buɲa* 'woman'. The common head noun is sufficient to satisfy the coreferentiality condition.

The discussion of place of common NP and ordering of clauses, in 4.4.2, carries over to purposive subordinate clauses.

The most usual semantic interpretation is that the event of the main clause is performed IN ORDER THAT the action described by the subordinate clause may be possible. This is the case with the examples referred to above, with (590) in 4.3.7 'the alligator opened its mouth to use it to bite the old man', and with:

(722) *ḍaḍa ḍuḍu:mbu gaṛbagaṛbaɲalɲu| ɲuḍu wawa:lna*
      Auntie hid the [corpse of the] child so that it should not be seen

(723) *ɲayu miɲa gali:ɲal| bama:nda wiwi:na*
      I'm taking some meat, to give it to the people [in the camp]

A variant of this sense is where the main verb is *buḍi-n* 'tell' and the subordinate clause specifies what its object was ordered to do – see (596) and line 104 of text 2.

There is an alternative meaning – the event referred to by the subordinate clause may be A NATURAL RESULT OF that described by the main clause (without any intention being involved). This is the interpretation for (473) in 4.2.5 and for:

(724) *ŋayu burawuɲal duga:l/ ḍinbiḍinbi:lna*
> I grabbed the Burawuɲal (water sprite woman) and as a result she kicked and struggled (trying to escape)

(725) *ŋayu maŋga:ɲ/ bama:l banḍi:ldana/ ŋayu nilaɲunda*
> I laughed, and as a result the people came and found me, who had been hiding (from them)

With a negative subordinate clause, these two interpretations appear to be neutralised. (726), which involves purposive inflection in both main and subordinate clauses, was uttered by a Yidiɲḍi man trying to creep up on a Burawuɲal woman to grab her unawares. He ascertains that the wind is blowing from the south, and remarks:

(726) *ŋayu guŋgaguŋga:ɽ gali:na/ garu   ŋaɲaɲ ŋamu:ray ŋuḍu*
> I-SA north-REDUP go-PURP by-and-by I-O   smell-ABS NOT
> *ɲuma:lna*
> smell-PURP
>
> I must go [round] by the north, so that [she] will not smell me (approaching her)

The actor approaches from the north IN ORDER THAT the Burawuɲal will not smell him AS A NATURAL CONSEQUENCE OF his coming close to her.

4.5.4 Purposive clauses and purposive NPs.
The reason for an action can be indicated either by a purposive NP:

(727) *ŋayu galiŋ miɲa:gu*
> I'm going out for meat (e.g. to spear a wallaby)

or by a purposive subordinate clause:

(728) *ŋayu galiŋ miɲa:(/miɲa:nda) duga:ḍina*
> I'm going out to get some meat

The underlying form of the purposive clause here is:

(729) *ŋayu miɲa duga:lna*   I must get some meat

It is placed in antipassive form – with the deep O *miɲa* taking locative or dative inflection – to satisfy the coreferentiality constraint.

Both (727) and (728) are grammatical sentences, but they are encountered less frequently than:

(730) *ŋayu galiŋ miɲa:gu duga:ḍina*   ⟨ = (728)⟩

in which both noun and verb show purposive inflection. (730) exactly parallels causal (691) in 4.4.6; it suggests modifying the description of antipassive in 4.2.3 to say that a deep O NP takes dative or locative marking in an antipassive construction EXCEPT in a purposive subordinate clause where it can instead be in purposive case (and except within a causal subordinate clause where it can be in causal case – 4.4.6).

The syntactic connection between nominal causal *-m* ∼ *-mu* and verbal causal *-ɲum* is of course supported by morphological similarity. There is no formal resemblance between nominal *-gu* and verbal *-na* (although there is comparative evidence suggesting that *-na* may originally have been a future tense suffix, and that proto-Yidiɲ perhaps had a verbal purposive based on *-gu* – 3.8.4).

Dick Moses once made an error which appeared to reveal a psychological connection between nominal *-gu* and verbal *-na*. When illustrating the nominal affix *-ḍulu:* (3.3.7) he said:

(731) *yiŋu   bana   ɲagi:lḍulu:/ guda:ɽna garu   ḍara*
      THIS-ABS water-ABS hot-*ḍulu:*   cold-*na* by-and-by let stand-IMP
      This water is hot, let it stand to get cold

Here the VERBAL affix was added to ADJECTIVE *gudaɽ* 'cold'. However, Moses immediately corrected himself and said it should be *guda:ɽgu* NOT *guda:ɽna*.

An example similar to (730), but with the common NP in O function in the main clause, is (363) in 4.1.6. We can also just have an adjective (and no verb) in the main clause:

(732) *ŋayu guli bama:gu bunḍa:ḍina*
      I'm angry with the person so that I want to hit him

This syntactic pattern is similar to the 'favourite construction' in Dyirbal (Dixon 1972: 73–7). Important differences are (a) the Dyirbal construction is much more frequent than are sentences like (730), (732) in Yidiɲ; (b) the Dyirbal favourite construction is recursive ('I told the man to fetch the woman to bring you...') whereas no example of iteration has been encountered in Yidiɲ; (c) unlike Dyirbal, Yidiɲ has an exactly analogous construction involving causal NP and causal verb.

This type of construction is found very frequently with -:*ḍi* + *ŋa-l* VCs, for which the instrumental NP is in surface O function:

(733) *gana   biwi   duga   miɲa:gu*
PARTICLE stick knife-ABS get-IMP meat-PURP
gunda:ḍiɲa:lna
cut-:*ḍi*-COMIT-PURP
Pick up the Biwi knife to cut the meat with it!

Except within a purposive subordinate clause the deep O, *miɲa*, of (733) would be – because of the antipassive transformation – in dative or locative case (4.3.6).

Sentences like (733) are frequently used to define the use or function of some plant or implement. See (611) in 4.3.7. and:

(734) *guginarmu   biŋgal   mayi:gu   buga:ḍiɲa:lna*
coconut-ABL spoon-ABS vegetable-PURP eat-:*ḍi*-COMIT-PURP
Spoons made out of coconut shell are for eating vegetable food with

(735) *ḍuluḍulum   baguɽ   gunda / bama:gu*
Johnson hardwood tree-ABL sword-ABS cut-IMP person-PURP
bunḍa:ḍiɲa:lna
hit-:*ḍi*-COMIT-PURP
Cut a sword from the Johnson hardwood tree, to fight people with!

4.5.5 Purposive clauses – non-coreferential type.
As with dative and causal subordinate clauses, the writer's corpus includes a small number of purposive subordinate clauses that do not satisfy the coreferentiality condition. To establish a logical connection between the clauses there will often be some common element, as in (cf. (106)):

(736) *garu bama:l dubur yubi:ɲ/ bana ḍuŋga:na munum dubu:rmu/ waɽi:mari*
By-and-by the people rubbed [the woman's] stomach, so that water would run out from the inside of [her] stomach, through her mouth

where *dubur* is in O function for the main clause, but in ablative case in the purposive clause.

In (364) of 4.1.6 *bugul* 'loya vine' is in O function for the main clause and implicitly in instrumental for the subordinate clause. In lines 2–3 of text 9 *ɲundu* 'you' is in S function in the main clause and in dative case in the subordinate clause.

There are several examples where a peripheral NP in purposive case in a main clause occurs as O NP in a subordinate clause. (233–4) in 3.8.6 provided one instance; others are:

(737) *ɲundu bana   duga:lin | gada:ŋ |*
    you-SA water-ABS get-GOING-IMP come-COMIT-IMP
    mayi:gu | ŋaɲḍi waḍu:lna
    vegetable-PURP we-SA cook-PURP
    You go and get the water, bring it to [soak the] vegetables, then we can cook them

(738) *ŋaɲḍi ŋuyay dugal/ naŋgu:gu wunaɲa:lna*
    We'll get (i.e. pull up) kangaroo grass, for a mattress to sleep on

wunaɲa-l is a *-ɲa-l* derivative of the 'comitative type' (4.3.3); here its O NP is *naŋgu* 'mattress'.

(739) *yiɲu   baḍar   guɲi   wuḍin | miɲa:gu   buga:na*
    THIS-ABS leave-IMP LET BE grow-IMP meat-PURP eat-PURP
    Leave this [chicken] alone, let him grow up! So that [he'll get big enough to be an edible animal] and can be eaten

The implication in (739) is that the chicken is at present too small to be described as *miɲa* 'edible animal' (6.2.1); it should be allowed to go free so that it can grow into *miɲa*, and can then be eaten.

    The recurrence of constructions like (737–9) suggests that this may be a productive syntactic type in Yidiɲ. There are no parallels involving dative or causal clauses (corresponding dative and causal sentences are definitely ungrammatical – for instance *(703) in 4.4.7).

4.6 Apprehensional constructions

There are two ways of indicating that the action described by a sentence is orientated towards avoiding undesirable involvement with some person or thing – the sentence can involve a peripheral NP in 'fear' inflection *-ḍida* ~ *-yida* (3.3.2), or a subordinate clause whose verb is in 'lest' inflection *-ḍi* (3.8.4). We deal with these mechanisms in turn, and then (in 4.6.3) discuss their interrelationship.

4.6.1 'Fear' NPs. Some examples of 'fear' NP were given in 4.1.6; it refers to something that is to be avoided, and the action referred to by the main verb will normally be directed towards this avoidance.

In 3.3.1 we mentioned that *ŋayu galiŋ mayim* is potentially ambiguous. *mayim* can be understood in a causal sense – 'I'm going out after [having eaten] food' – or in ablative – 'I'm going away from the food'. In explaining this ambiguity Dick Moses suggested that there would have to be a reason for anyone to disregard food, and this should be stated; say,

(740) *ŋayu galiŋ mayim/ bamayida*
　　　I'm going away from the food, out of fear of [that] person (who owns the food; he is known to be mean and might harm me if I touch it)

Other examples of 'fear' NPs are at (184), (664), (710) and:

(741) *ŋuŋu   gadaŋ   gaḏigaḏi   / ŋaḏunḏida*
　　　THAT-S come-PRES long way-REDUP I-FEAR
　　　That [person] is coming [by a circuitous route which keeps him always] a long way from me (for fear of me)

(742) *ɲundu:ba waraŋa:ḏin   banayida   gulbulḏida*
　　　you all-SA shift camp-:ḏi-IMP water-FEAR wave-FEAR
　　　ŋalalḏida
　　　big-FEAR
　　　You'd better shift camp, for fear of the very high waves (that threaten to engulf your present camp)

4.6.2 'Lest' subordinate clauses. The types of subordinate clause we have described thus far – marked by verbal inflections *-ɲunda, -ɲum, -na* – have almost identical syntactic behaviour. The fourth variety – with verbal inflection *-ḏi* – shows a number of striking differences (although there is also at least one important similarity).

A 'lest' subordinate clause refers to an undesirable event that some person or thing referred to in the main clause might get involved in; the main clause will describe action that can be taken to try to avoid this:

(743) *ɲundu giyi galin/ wanda:nḏi*
　　　Don't you go [there], you might fall down!

(744) *ɲundu gaḍidagan* / *giyaɽaŋgu*
you-SA long way-INCHO VBLSR-IMP stinging tree-ERG
    guba:nḍi
    burn-LEST-ABS

You keep away, lest you get stung (lit.: 'burnt') by the stinging tree

(745) *yiɲu buɲa*   *waɲḍi:rim wunaŋ* / *gana*   *nulga* /
THIS-S woman-ABS HOW LONG lie-PRES PARTICLE wake-IMP
    wayuwayu   *wuna:nḍi*
    long time-REDUP lie-LEST-ABS

How long has this woman been lying [asleep] for? Better wake
her up, otherwise she might sleep for too long

Note that the (potential) event described by a 'lest' subordinate clause
is ALWAYS something undesirable. Thus the final clause of (745), besides
STATING that if the woman isn't wakened soon she'll have slept for a very
long time, also ASSERTS that this would be a bad thing.

The main clause will, naturally, often be imperative, as in (743–5) and
also (132) and (484) above. But it can be tensed, as in a narrative telling
what would have happened if a certain course of action HAD NOT been
followed:

(746) *gula*   *dandaɽ*   *ɲuniɲ* / *buybuɽ*   / *bunḍuɽ* /
body-ABS rub-PRES you-o blow-PRES fan-PRES
    wira:ŋ-ŋadi   *ḍama:ŋ*   *duga:lḍi*
    thing-ERG-INTENSIFIER dangerous-ERG grab-LEST-ABS

[When you are a newly initiated man] your body is rubbed down,
you are blown on and fanned [with bushes, to drive troubles
away] since otherwise that dangerous thing [the rainbow
serpent] might catch you

or the reason why a certain course WILL NOT be followed:

(747) *ŋayu ḍaḍa*   *ŋuḍu baḍaɽ*   / *bama:l*   *ŋuḍu*
I-SA baby-ABS NOT leave-PRES person-ERG NOT
    ḍili + budi:lḍi
    eye-put down-LEST-ABS

I won't leave the baby in case there's no one to mind it

Note that 'lest', 'might', 'since otherwise', 'in case', used in the translations
of (743–7), could be employed interchangeably for any of these sentences.

A 'lest' construction describes efforts made to avoid involvement in
some undesirable event; note that these may not necessarily be successful. Thus:

(748) *ŋayu nila:ɲ | muḏa:mbu wawa:lḏi   ŋaɲaɲ/ ŋaɲaɲ*
　　　 I-SA hide-PAST mother-ERG see-LEST-ABS I-O　　 I-O
　　　 bidiɲalɲu　　　　　　 wawa:l muguy | ŋaɲaɲ
　　　 properly-CAU VBLSR-PAST see-PAST all the time I-O
　　　 bunḏa:na
　　　 hit-PURP

　　　 I hid lest mother see me; but she kept looking for me very
　　　 thoroughly to spank me (and did find me and spank me)

All the examples given so far satisfy the 'coreferentiality constraint'
which was established for dative, causal and purposive subordinate
clauses – there is a common NP, in S/O function in each clause. The
functions were O in main clause, S in subordinate in the final part of
(745), O/O in (746–7), S/S in (743) and S/O in (744), (748).

In addition to the S/O 'common NP' there may be a further NP repeated
between the two clauses. In (749) it is in locative case in the main clause and
ergative in the subordinate clause:

(749) *giyi   ḏanan   maga:da | ḏigurula | ḏiguruŋgu*
　　　 DON'T stand-IMP outside-LOC thunderstorm-LOC thunderstorm-ERG
　　　 bunḏa:nḏi
　　　 hit-LEST-ABS

　　　 Don't stand outside in a thunderstorm, lest a thunderbolt strike you!

In (750) the NP in ablative case for the main clause is the (implicit) A NP
for the 'lest' clause:

(750) *ɲundu ɲuŋgu   gadan   ḏurinumu/ ɲuniɲ baḏa:lḏi*
　　　 you-SA THERE-LOC come-IMP leech-ABL you-O bite-LEST-ABS
　　　 You come away from the leeches there, or they will bite you

Almost all the examples of 'lest' clauses in the writer's corpus do have
an NP common to main and subordinate clause. And the common NP
must always be in S or O function in the 'lest' clause (this is the point
of similarity with -*ɲunda*, -*ɲum* and -*na* constructions). But the common
NP CAN be in ANY function in the main clause, and the 'lest' verb will
agree – in case inflection – with the common NP in the main clause (here
'lest' clauses depart radically from the patterns described in 4.4–5).

Thus, when illustrating the meaning of adjective *ganan* 'be engaged
in an activity only briefly' Dick Moses gave:

(751) *ŋaɲaɲ bama:l   gana:ndu bunḏaɲada:ɲ   ḏuŋgandiŋgu*
　　　 I-O   person-ERG brief-ERG hit-COMING-PAST run-LEST-ERG
　　　 The person came running up, hit me quickly, and then ran off
　　　 (literally 'the person who was running came and quickly hit me')

The semantic interpretation of 'undesirableness' still holds for (751); this sentence includes the assertion that it is not a good thing to run up, hit someone and run off again (if there is some reason to hit another person it should be a fair fight, with the victim given some warning and allowed a chance to retaliate).

There is an important difference between (743–50) and (751). In the former action was taken to avoid an undesirable event – which then might or might not take place – while (751) describes an ACTUAL event that was undesirable. It may be that we should recognise two subtypes of 'lest' clauses – one where the coreferentiality constraint is satisfied in both clauses, and one where the common NP is not in S/O function in the main clause. But there is certainly a unity to all 'lest' clauses, and it is clear that the semantic common factor is the 'undesirability' of the event referred to by the subordinate clause (and not necessarily the idea of avoidance).

Attempts to obtain a subordinate clause qualifying a noun in A function – for instance *ŋayu* in (642) of 4.4.1 – yielded only *-ḍi* clauses. Thus:

(752) *ŋayu bama   wawa:l   wandandiŋgu*
     I-SA person-ABS see-PAST fall-LEST-ERG
     I saw the person as I was (unfortunately) falling over

is a perfectly acceptable sentence. The interpretation here is helped by the fact that 'falling down' is surely always an undesirable action.

A *-ḍi* verb inflects exactly like a nominal. It is in absolute case (with zero realisation) when the common NP is in S or O function in the main clause, and in ergative case when it it is in surface A function. Ergative *-ŋgu* reduces (by Rule 2 – 2.3.2) when added to an even-syllabled root. Thus:

(753) *ŋaṉaṉ bama:l bunḍa:ṉ* $\begin{Bmatrix} maŋgandiŋgu \\ wiwi:ḍinḍi:ŋ \end{Bmatrix}$ The person hit me whilst he was laughing/giving [things away]

Again, the implication is that laughing/giving things away is not an appropriate action to indulge in whilst one is hitting someone.

An example with the common NP in dative case in the main clause is:

(754) *ŋayu mayi wiwiŋ bama:nda maŋgandinda*
     I'm giving food to the person who is laughing (but it is inappropriate to laugh whilst one is being given food)

'Lest' clauses with the verb in oblique case are not common, and in fact only ergative and dative examples are attested. Note in particular that it has not

been possible to obtain a 'lest' verb in the nominal 'fear' inflection -(*ɖi*)*da*. When asked 'Don't you go, for fear of the person who is walking about' an informant gave:

(755) *ɲundu giyi galin/ bamayida burgiɲunda*

which is of the same syntactic type as (664) in 4.4.3. He would not permit **burgiɳɖida* (or **burgiɳɖiyi:da*) in place of *burgiɲunda* here.

It might be suggested that in (743–54) -*ɖi* actually derives a participle, a deverbal form that functions as an adjective; this would naturally be expected to take nominal inflections. Two arguments can be given against a 'participial' interpretation.

Firstly, the fact that -*ɖi* marks a subordinate CLAUSE can be seen from:

(756) *ɲaɲaɲ bama:l   bunɖa:ɲ wawa:ɖinɖi:ɲ   buɲa:nda*
      I-o   person-ERG hit-PAST see-:*ɖi*-LEST-ERG woman-DAT
      I was hit by a person who was looking at a woman (which he
      shouldn't have been doing whilst he was hitting me)

Here the subject of antipassive *wawa:ɖi-n* is coreferential with *ɲaɲaɲ* (stated only in the main clause); but its O NP, *buɲa:nda*, is clearly included in the subordinate clause.

The second reason against regarding a -*ɖi* verb as an adjective is that in all examples gathered it follows the main verb, whereas an adjective would be expected normally to occur with its head noun, before the verb.

Verbs in 'lest' inflection are less common than -*ɲunda*, -*ɲum* or -*na* forms (although the author has recorded a couple of score instances, and gathered more by elicitation).

We have said that if there is an NP common to a main and a -*ɖi* clause, then the -*ɖi* verb agrees in case with the occurrence of that NP in the main clause. But, as with other types of subordinate clause, there are odd examples where there is NO common NP:

(757) *yiɲu   walɲɖi ɲalal   ɖundaɲ   / ɲundu:ba giyi*
      THIS-ABS cliff-ABS big-ABS hang down-PRES you all-SA DON'T
        bidibidi   galin / waŋga:m   gula:ɖinɖi
      close up-REDUP go-IMP overhang-ABS break-:*ɖi*-LEST-ABS
      There's a big overhang on this cliff. Don't go too near [the edge],
      since it might break off

(758) *yiɲḍu:ŋ ḍabi:l   guma:ndu/ ɲundu giyi   baga*
THIS-ERG tell not to-PAST one-ERG   you-SA DON'T spear-IMP
gala: /   ŋaɲḍi:n   ḍangandaga:nḍi   /   ŋaɲḍi:ɲ
spear-INST we-GEN-ABS bad-INCHO VBLSR-LEST-ABS we-O
buriburi:ŋ   gayɲi:ɲ
old man-ERG warn not to do-PAST

One of these [young newly initiated men] told [the other] not to
do it: 'Don't you spear [anything] with that spear [during our
period of taboo] lest trouble comes to our camp (literally: lest
our [camp] becomes bad). The old people warned us not to do
it (and assured us it would anger the rainbow-serpent, who
would then visit trouble on the whole camp)'

4.6.3 'Lest' clauses and 'fear' NPs. There is a syntactic pattern that
involves a 'fear' NP to the main clause, and a 'lest' subordinate clause.
The referent of the S NP in the main clause is frightened of someone,
lest that person do something to him:

(759) *ŋayu yaɽŋga:ɲ ŋuɲḍunḍida bamayida/ ŋaɲaɲ bunḍa:nḍi*
I'm frightened of that person, lest he should hit me

Or the referent of the A NP does something to the referent of the O NP
for fear of some third party, lest they do something undesirable to the
O referent:

(760) *ŋuɲu   ḍuḍu:mbu   bilayŋgida   bambi:l   / bamayida*
THAT-ABS auntie-ERG blanket-LOC cover-PAST person-FEAR
ŋabiyida   wawa:lḍi
many-FEAR see-LEST-ABS

Auntie covered that [baby's corpse] with a blanket, for fear of all
the people, lest they should see it

Sentences (759–60) are of exactly the same type as (749–50). The
subordinate O NP is coreferential with the main clause S/O NP and
there is a second 'common NP', that is in 'fear' function in the main
clause and in A in the 'lest' clause:

main clause: $NP_{S/O}$...VC + TENSE/IMP   NP + FEAR
subordinate || ||
  clause: NP_O NP_A VC + LEST + ABS

Under these conditions, the ergative NP in the subordinate clause is likely to be omitted.

We can, of course, have a 'fear' NP within the subordinate clause:

(761) *ŋayu ḍaḍa   binda: magilmaŋal | bamayida*
    I-SA   baby-ABS shoulder-LOC climb up-COMIT-PRES person-FEAR
    manŋa:nḍi
    be frightened-LEST-ABS
    I'm carrying the baby on my shoulder as we climb uphill, since he's frightened of that person

This is a quite different syntactic type from (759–60).

The association between 'fear' case and 'lest' verbal inflection is thus substantially different from the interrelation of causal NPs and causal clauses (4.4.6) and of purposive NPs and purposive clauses (4.5.4). There we had an antipassive O NP being marked by causal (/purposive) case within a causal (/purposive) subordinate clause. Here it is the A NP that is deleted when coreferential with a main clause 'fear' constituent.

There are semantic reasons for this difference. Dative, causal and purposive clauses describe SOMEONE DOING SOMETHING at the same time as, or previous to, or as a result of the action described by the main clause (in which he is involved). A 'lest' clause, on the other hand, depicts SOMETHING that might be DONE TO SOMEONE involved in the event of the main clause.

We justified employing the names 'dative', 'causal' and 'purposive' – both for types of NP and for types of subordinate clause – in terms of syntactic, semantic and morphological similarities, and the type of syntactic connection just mentioned. Since this is lacking in the present case it seemed best to use separate names – 'fear' and 'lest' – for the type of NP and of subordinate clause that can be included under the general semantic label 'apprehensional'.

There are morphological similarities between Yidiɲ and Dyirbal qua the marking of apprehension, and its relation to nominal comitative. First note the facts in Dyirbal – 'fear' is one sense of the locative case *-ŋga*; nominal comitative has the form *-bila ~ -ba*; verbal 'lest' involves the affix *-(m)bila ~ -(m)ba*, which can be followed by (at least dative) case inflection (Dixon 1972: 237–8, 222–3, 112–13).

The points of similarity are:

(i) 'Fear' is dealt with by locative case in Dyirbal. It may be that the 'fear' inflection in Yidiɲ originally involved locative added to comitative **-ḍir* (3.3.2, 3.3.4); this remains as *-ḍida* after comitative has reduced to *-ḍi*.

(ii) Verbal 'lest' is identical with nominal comitative in Dyirbal. 'Lest' in Yidiɲ has exactly the same form as nominal comitative (the verbal affix is always preceded by a conjugation marker, so only the 'post-consonantal' allomorph appears).

These similarities may be coincidental. Or they may be indicative of the development of these affixes in the two languages (and perhaps of deep syntactic relationships that are as yet barely glimpsed). For instance, it is perfectly feasible that 'fear' originally involved the addition of locative to comitative in each language; Dyirbal then dropped the comitative while in Yidiɲ the combination came to be recognised as a single affix, through reinterpretation under phonological change. (But it must be stressed that there is NO CLOSE genetic connection evident between Yidiɲ and Dyirbal – that is, they are probably no closer than are any two Australian languages, whatever their geographical placement. And the different forms involved in the two languages, -ɖi(r) and -bila, scotch any idea that these facts could suggest anything about proto-Australian.) Our comments here could at best be taken to refer to an 'areal feature' at some time in the not-too-distant past.

In addition, there may conceivably be some genetic connection between nominal -ɖi(r) and the verbal derivational affix -:ɖi-n (see 3.3.4 and Dixon 1976a); but this is – in our present state of knowledge – even more speculative than the possibility of a connection between nominal comitative and verbal 'lest'.

4.7 Possession

Like most other Australian languages, Yidiɲ distinguishes between two kinds of possession. We can call these by the received names 'alienable' and 'inalienable'; in fact 'inalienable possession' refers only to part–whole relationships, while 'alienable possession' covers all else – material possessions, kin relations and social group membership.

Possession can be shown either by use of the genitive affix, or by simple apposition. The choice between these two methods appears to be governed by a semantic hierarchy, described in 4.7.3.

4.7.1 Alienable possession. Any possession other than whole–part relationship must be marked by the genitive suffix -ni ~ -nu. As mentioned in 3.3.3 this can be thought of as a derivational affix, forming a stem that functions as an adjective and taking the case inflection of the noun it modifies. We can effectively have a full 'genitive NP' embedded within the NP that refers to the thing possessed:

(762) *yiŋu   gala   guran   ŋuɲḍu:n   bama:n*
      THIS-ABS spear-ABS long-ABS THAT-GEN-ABS person-GEN-ABS
      mayaɽani
      initiated man-GEN-ABS
      This long spear belongs to that Maya:ɽ man

Genitive can be followed by any of the case inflections (listed in 3.3.2).
Examples of ergative, locative and dative onto genitive stems are in
3.3.3; purposive case occurs in:

(763) *ŋayu galiŋ dila:gu gambinuni:gu*
      I'm going for the pigeon's feather

   Genitive is used to mark ownership of a material object, and also for
a person or animal's camping place or habitat – someone's house, a
bird's nest or favourite perch – see (163) – or

(764) *yawu: ḍanaŋ galambaɽa:n*
      The grass standing there belongs to the march fly

It is also used to mark ownership of a dog – see (47–9) – for kin relationship, as in (715) and:

(765) *bama:l ŋaḍin muḍam bunḍa:ɲ*   The person hit my mother

and for membership of a local group or tribe. For instance, in line 27
(and succeeding lines) of text 2, Damari and Guyala run off with two
women who are described as *bama:n yiɲu buɲa ḍambu:l* 'these two
women belong[ing] to the people [who live in this place]'. And in an
autobiographical story Dick Moses told how he escaped from the
mission and went to Cairns where:

(766) *ŋaɲḍi banḍi:liɲu bama ŋaɲḍi:n*
      We went to look for one of our own people (i.e. searching for a
      Yidiɲḍi amongst the predominantly white population of
      Cairns)

   A simple statement of possession involves just an NP with embedded
genitive (and does not take any verb) – see (88) in 3.3.6 and

(767) *ŋaḍin yiŋu guda:ga*   This is my dog

Note that (767) is very close in meaning to

(768) *ŋayu yiɲḍu:nḍi gudagayi*   I own this dog

In (767) *gudaga* 'dog' is head noun and *ŋaḍin* 'mine' provides modification to
it. In (768) *ŋayu* 'I' is the head and comitative *yiɲḍunḍi gudagayi* are modifiers;
see also (514–18) in 4.3.1.

Thus, in this particular context (a verbless statement of possession) comitative is effectively the converse of genitive. But note that this relationship between genitive and comitative does not apply when they are within an NP that is in S or A function to a verb. *ɲaḏin guda:ga galiŋ* is 'my dog is going' whereas *ŋayu gudagayi galiŋ* means 'I am going with [my] dog' (see also Dixon 1972: 222).

Australian languages typically have a wideish range of constructions involving verbs of giving (Dixon 1972: 300). In Yidiɲ the 'gift' is normally the O NP, with the 'recipient' being described by a peripheral NP in dative case – as in (352) from 4.1.6. But there is an alternative, in which the recipient is in genitive marking within the O NP:

(769) *ŋayu miɲa   muḏa:mi   wiwi:na*
     I-SA   meat-ABS   mother-GEN-ABS   give-PURP
     I must give meat to mother

The implication here is that I have an obligation to give mother a certain portion of any animal I kill, and she is merely receiving that which she has a right to. With a more general group of recipients, to whom I do not have the same food supplying obligations, dative would most likely be preferred:

(770) *ŋayu miɲa wiwi:na bama:nda*   I must give meat to [those] people

We can of course also have:

(771) *ŋayu miɲa wiwi:ɲ muḏa:mi bama:nda*   I must give the meat belonging to mother (/originally intended for mother) to the [other] person.

4.7.2 -nim. We have already mentioned the genitive-plus-ablative/ causal combination *-nim* (which appears to be moving in the direction of becoming an additional, non-analysable, case inflection – 3.3.3). *-nim* can have a variety of meanings.

Firstly, it can refer to 'past possession' (and in this sense it can be semantically related to 'genitive' plus 'ablative') in contrast with *-ni*, which marks present ownership. See (56) in 3.3.3, (259) in 3.9.1 and

(772) *yiŋu   waŋal   ŋaḏin | bimbi:nim| bimbi:ŋ*
     THIS-ABS   boomerang-ABS   I-GEN-ABS   father-*nim*   father-ERG
     ŋanda wiwi:ɲ |
     I-DAT   give-PAST
     This boomerang is mine; it used to belong to father but he gave it to me.

At least as frequent as the 'past possession' sense is the use of *-nim* simply with 'causal' meaning (and it then appears to be in free variation with *-mu* ~ *-m* – 4.4.4). Causal *-nim* can be used to mark an O NP in an antipassive construction when this constitutes a causal subordinate clause – see 4.4.6 and

(773) *ɲayu ḏira:nḏi banḏabanḏa:ɽḏiɲum ɲuɲḏu:nim*
      I'm tired from following that [person]

Occasionally, *-nim* can have just ablative meaning (again alternating with *-m* ~ *-mu*). Note that a causal/ablative NP may mix these different types of inflection (just as a comitative NP can mingle *-ḏi* ~ *-yi* and *-muḏay* suffixes – 4.3.1); thus in a story concerning an alligator that came and grabbed a sick woman while she was bathing in the river amidst a crowd of children:

(774) *garu   ɲuɲu   duga:ldaɲu | bama:nim   ɲabim*
      by-and-by THAT-S grab-COMING-PAST person-*nim* many-ABL
      Soon [the alligator] came and grabbed that [woman] from amongst
      the crowd of people (= children)

An occurrence of *-nim* may sometimes combine 'ablative' and 'past possession' senses. For instance, a myth describes how a legendary woman Bindam escaped from her husband Gamburguman:

(775) *yiɲu bama buɲa bindam| gali:ɲ| gamburguma:nim ḏuɲga:ɲ*
      This woman Bindam went, ran away from Gamburguman

In (775) *gamburguma:nim* indicates that Bindam ran away FROM Gamburguman who HAD OWNED her (in the sense shown in (765–6)). See also (56) and (672).

Informants indicated that, for felicity of discourse, *-nim* could be alternated with causal or with ablative *-m* ~ *-mu*, within a statement/response framework (3.1.3). Thus, if someone said *ɲayu gada:ɲ waga:lnim* 'I've [just] come from [my] wife', an appropriate reply could be *ɲundu gada:ɲ waga:lmu* '[Oh!] you've come from [your] wife!'.

4.7.3 Inalienable possession. There is a different syntactic process employed for 'inalienable possession' (part–whole relationship). The two nouns are simply placed in apposition within an NP, and take the same inflectional suffixes. Examples were at (307–8) in 4.1.1 and (318) in 4.1.2.

We mentioned (4.1.1, see also 6.2.1) that the 'head' noun in an NP can 'select' a generic modifier. Now in a syntagm of inalienable possession it is the 'possessor' that determines which generic noun can occur in an NP; in view of this we regard 'possessor' as the head, with the 'part' noun having a modifying role. Thus:

(776) *ɲayu wuɲul gambil wawa:l*   I saw the carpet snake's tail

can be expanded to

(777) *ɲayu miɲa wuɲul gambil wawa:l* ⟨= (776)⟩

since *wuɲul* 'carpet snake' falls within the scope of generic *miɲa* 'edible animal'. But *bima* 'death adder' is not classed as *miɲa* and thus

(778) *ɲayu bima gambil wawa:l*   I saw the death adder's tail

cannot be expanded in this way.

There are, in fact, no generic terms corresponding to parts of bodies or of other objects – 6.2.1.

We mentioned that a genitive construction can be regarded as 'an NP embedded within an NP'; a deictic can occur both with the possessor – with genitive marking – and with the 'possessed' head noun, as in (180) of 3.7.2. In contrast, an appositional construction is just a simple NP, with the constituent possibilities listed in 4.1.1, 4.1.2; it can only involve one deictic, for instance.

The central semantic reference of 'whole–part' relationships is obvious enough – 'the man's head', as in (433–4); 'the tree's bark/leaf' as in (706), (308); and so forth. But note that bodily secretions are dealt with in the same way:

(779) *ɲayu ɲuḍu ɲunu:ngu duwu   gadaŋ*
       I-SA NOT you-PURP tears-ABS come-PRES
       I'll have no tears for you (literally: 'my tears will not come [out] for you') (text 14.10)

Inalienable possession also covers smell, as (256) and (726), or – on a more abstract level – a person's name (*guwal waɲa* occurred in (70) from 3.3.6).

The scope of this construction provides interesting insight into the Yidiɲḍi world-view. *bulmba* is used to refer to a 'house', a 'camp', any 'place' that could be used for camping, or 'the world' (as in 'God made the world'). *yigan* 'sky' is regarded as part of *bulmba* – the whole sky is part of the world, or the sky above a particular place is regarded as a part of that place. Thus:

13

(780) *bulmba yigan yiŋu garan-gandaŋ*
  The sky at this place is turning a burning yellow colour

See also (274) in 3.9.2 in which the noise evident at a certain place is regarded as 'part' of the place.

In 4.1.8 and 4.2.3 we discussed the case-marking on an 'appositional NP' when in unmarked peripheral function, or in O function within an antipassive. Although both nouns CAN take dative case, the most normal circumstance is for the 'possessor' head noun to be in dative inflection, and for the 'part' noun to be in locative. Compare (cf. (307), (391)):

(781) *buɲa dungu baygaɹ*   The woman's head is sore

(782) *guli gambaŋ buɲa:nda dungu:*
  A louse is crawling on the woman's head

Inalienable possession is most often realised by an appositional construction. But it can, like alienable possession, be marked by genitive. Thus we can have:

(783) $\left\{\begin{array}{ll}\text{EITHER} & \text{(a) } \textit{ŋaɲaɲ dungu bama:l bunḍa:ɲ}\\ \text{OR} & \text{(b) } \textit{ŋaḍin dungu bama:l bunḍa:ɲ}\end{array}\right\}$ The person hit me on the head

(784) $\left\{\begin{array}{ll}\text{EITHER} & \text{(a) } \textit{ḍugi giɹi ḍundaŋ}\\ \text{OR} & \text{(b) } \textit{ḍugi:n giɹi ḍundaŋ}\end{array}\right\}$ The branch of the tree is hanging down

Similarly, 'the sky at a place' can be described by *bulmba yigan* or by *bulmba:n yigan*. Note also the contrast between (317) and (318) in 4.1.2. Genitive is used to mark inalienable possession in (180) and (283) above, whereas an appositional construction suffices in (477), (536) and (588).

It appears that the choice between the two types of construction is motivated by a hierarchy similar to that described in 3.1.2, 3.7.1 and 4.1.8. Specifically:

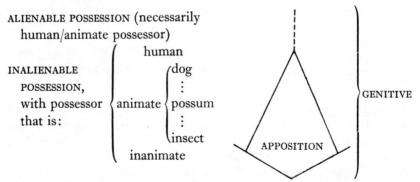

That is, genitive marking CAN be used for any type of possession, alienable or inalienable, whatever the possessor. Apposition is only normally used for inalienable possession, and is most frequently employed when the 'possessor' is inanimate ('the leaf of a tree'), less frequently when it is a non-human animate ('the wing of a bird'), and only occasionally when it is human. As we descend the hierarchy, the chances of encountering apposition increase, and genitive is thus progressively less frequently encountered (although genitive is always POSSIBLE, and always grammatical). The (a) alternative is most likely in the case of (784), but with sentences like (783) (b) is probably as common as (a) in texts (and is preferred when elicitation is directed onto this point).

The hierarchy controlling the choice of possessive constructions has one important difference from that motivating dative/locative and human/inanimate deictics (3.1.2, 3.7.1, 4.1.8). Here apposition can be used even with a human 'inalienable possessor', and is only considered ungrammatical in the case of alienable possession; with dative–locative and deictics one choice was possible with all types of nouns EXCEPT those that have human reference.

The 'past possessive' affix *-nim* can – like unmarked genitive *-ni* – be used on occasion for inalienable possession, and extends even to abstract whole–part relations such as:

(785) *yiŋu guwal ḍa:buga:ynim gurununim*
This word belonged to the Dya:bugay language

An NP can involve both alienable and inalienable possession – the first being realised by genitive marking and the second by apposition:

(786) *ŋayu ŋaḍin   ḍaḍa   ŋumbaɻ wawa:lna*
I-SA I-GEN-ABS child-ABS face-ABS see-PURP
I must look at my child's face

Attempts to elicit an NP which involved genitive marking for both alienable and inalienable possession (with double embedding) failed. The unacceptability of a construction of this type is probably due as much to a wish to contrast these different types of possession as to a desire to avoid syntactic over-complexity.

The alternative ways of expressing inalienable possession are sometimes exploited for stylistic felicity (3.1.3). Thus, a reply to (784a) might be (784b) or vice versa.

There are two kinds of construction in Yidiɲ that it is difficult to know how to classify. With a verb such as *ɲaŋga:ɖi-n* 'talk' the noun describing the language that is being used can occur in absolutive case, apparently within the S NP – see (557) in 4.3.4. And the noun *wabaɽ* 'a walk' commonly functions in the same way with verbs like *gali-n* 'go':

(787) *ɲayu wabaɽ galiŋ*   I'm going out for a walk

In the absence of any reason for treating them in any other way, it seems simplest to suggest that these may be a type of 'inalienable possession', with 'language' and 'walk' being regarded as 'part' of the actor in these cases! It would probably need a native speaker trained as a linguist to decide whether this is in fact a valid assignment.

4.8 Verbalisation

There are four derivational affixes that can be added to non-verbal forms, yielding a verbal stem. We first discuss the fully productive verbalisers – intransitive *-daga-n* and transitive *-ŋa-l*. The less popular and semantically more restrictive suffixes – intransitive *-maɖi-n* and transitive *-luŋa-l* – are dealt with in 4.8.2 and 4.8.3.

4.8.1 Inchoative and causative verbalisers. It appears that any non-verbal stem (excepting pronouns and most deictics) can be verbalised by the addition of

inchoative *-daga-n*, forming an intransitive verbal stem

or   causative *-ŋa-l*, forming a transitive verbal stem

Note that, unlike *-daga-n*, *-ŋa-l* coheres phonologically with the stem to which it is added (2.4), and is reduced by Rule 2 when attached to an even-syllabled stem and followed by the zero imperative inflection (*-ŋa → -:ŋ*, 2.3.3).

Inchoative *-daga-n* indicates a state recently attained (and can be aptly translated into English by 'become'). There is a contrast between a simple adjectival description (cf. 4.1.10):

(788) *yiɲu gumba mura:nɖi*   This girl is sick

and inchoative:

(789) *yiɲu gumba mura:nɖidagaŋ*   This girl has become sick

(788) can be taken as describing a permanent state – the informant suggested extending it to *yiɲu gumba mura:nɖi muguy wunaŋ* 'this girl

lies [here] sick all the time' – whereas (789) implies that the onset of illness was quite recent. (203) in 3.7.8 was given as an extension of (789).

Note also the informant's gloss to

(790) *ŋayu ḍira:nḍidagaŋ*
    I-SA tiredness-COMIT-INCHO VBLSR-PRES
    'All of a sudden I get a cramp'

Here the 'all of a sudden' emphasises the change of state that is realised by inchoative *-daga-n*. See also (758) above.

Causative *-ŋa-l* added to a nominal indicates that someone (A) put something (O) into the state referred to by this nominal. There is an important contrast between:

(791) *ŋayu waŋal balga:l gadil*
    I made a small boomerang (out of a tree-spur)

(792) *ŋayu waŋal balga:l gadilŋalŋu*
    I made a boomerang small (i.e. I made a big boomerang smaller)

In (791) *gadil* 'small' modifies *waŋal* 'boomerang' within the absolutive O NP; but in (792) *gadil + ŋa + l + ŋu* appears in the VC with *balga:l* (a reduction, by Rule 2, from underlying *balga + l + ŋu*), agreeing with it in transitivity and inflection.

Affixed to a number adjective *-ŋa-l* indicates that the action referred to involves that number of objects:

(793) *ŋayu waŋal balga:l ḍambulaŋa:l*   I made two boomerangs

Similarly *ḍambulaŋa-l bunḍa-n* is 'hit two [people]'; and so on.

-daga-n and *-ŋa-l* occur most frequently with adjectives:

(794) *yiŋu bana gaḍu:ldagaŋ*   This water is getting dirty

(795) *ŋaŋḍi:ɲ gula   ŋuɲḍu:ŋ yiŋgilibi:ḍu*
    we-O   body-ABS THAT-ERG English bee-ERG
    guriɲŋalŋu
    good-CAUS VBLSR-PAST
    [Drinking] that English bee [honey dissolved in water] made our
    bodies [feel] good

Note that the A NP in (795) has inanimate reference. Other examples of verbalised adjectives are at (300), (252), (758), (295), line 67 in text 2, and line 6 in text 14.

The two verbalisers also occur quite freely with derived adjectives. Comitatives were exemplified in (789–90); privative occurs in:

(796) *yiŋu bulmba banagimbaldagaŋala*
>   This place is getting to be without water now (i.e. the water supply is drying up)

-daga-n and *-ŋa-l* are encountered less frequently with nouns, but it does seem that ANY noun CAN be verbalised, if this would be semantically plausible:

(797) *guḍuguḍu   muray   ḍura:ḍiɲu*   /
>   rainbow-ABS hair-ABS take off-:ḍi-PAST
>
>   *gunduydaga:ɲ*
>   brown snake-INCHO VBLSR-PAST
>
>   The rainbow shed its hair and turned into a brown snake (the informant later corrected this, and said it should have been a carpet snake)

Dyirbal has a special adjective *wayu* 'turn into' (that does frequently occur with the inchoative verbaliser – Dixon 1972: 391); Yidiɲ has no corresponding lexical item, but must simply use a verbaliser.

(798) *garu bama ḍambu:l ḍuruḍurudaga:ɲ*
>   By-and-by the two [boys] became grown men

In (707) we illustrated *mugay+ŋa-l* 'make [a piece of stone] into a Mugay grinding implement'.

Inchoative occurs quite commonly with locational qualifiers (3.4):

(799) *guŋga:ṛ ŋayu warŋgi:ɲala gali:ɲ ŋiyamanmu/ gali:ɲ guŋga:ṛdaga:ɲ*
>   I went round by the north from Ngiyaman; I went northwards

(800) *gana ŋaɲḍi giḍa/ biridagaŋala gadaŋ*
>   We must be quick, in coming up close [to the island] now

and causative is also possible here (although encountered less frequently):

(801) *ŋayu buɲa galiɲalɲu guŋgaṛiŋa:l*
>   I took the woman to the north

In 3.4.1 we contrasted locational qualifiers *guŋga:ṛ* 'north', *ŋaṛa* 'south' with adjectives *ḍaŋgiṛ* 'northern' and *guɲin* 'southern'. Corresponding to (799), in which *daga-n* is added to *guŋga:ṛ*, there is

(802) *ŋayu gali:ɲ ḍaŋgi:dadaga:ɲ*   I went northwards

in which the inchoative affix is added to the locative form of the adjective.

It is, in fact, possible to form a verbal stem from a local case form of any nominal referring to a place or geographical feature. Illustrating with allative, locative and ablative forms:

(803) *ŋayu galiŋ bulmba:gudagaŋala*
I'm getting close to the camp now

(804) *ɲundu ḍimuruladaga:ɲ*
Did you get to the house?

(805) *ŋayu galiŋ gaba:ymudagaŋ*
I've got off the road as I've gone along

-daga-n has also been encountered following the locative of *guman* 'one':

(806) *ŋuɲu bama guma:ndadagaŋ*
Those people are coming together to make a single [large] group

Time qualifiers can take (at least the inchoative) verbaliser. Either directly on to the root:

(807) *bulmba   guygaguygamdaga:ɲ*
camp-ABS evening-INCHO VBLSR-PAST
[Then] the camp started to get dark (with the onset of twilight)

or following an inflection. Thus:

(808) *ŋayu ŋaḍagura:ngudagaŋ ɲinaŋ*   I'll sit [here] until morning

is an alternative to

(809) *ŋayu ŋaḍagura:ngu ɲinaŋ* ⟨ = (808)⟩

As will be inferred from the examples, a verbalised form can be the sole verb in a sentence, or else it can occur in a VC with a non-derived verb.

-daga-n and *-ŋa-l* can be added to a word belonging to any non-verbal part of speech excepting pronouns (even particles can be verbalised – 4.10). Deictics follow pronouns in not permitting verbalisation, with the exception of the inanimate indefinite stem *waɲin-*. This forms interrogative verbs:

intransitive   *waɲindaga-n*   'do what'
transitive   *waɲinŋa-l*   'do what to [someone/thing]'

These normally constitute a complete VC:

(810) *bama yiɲu waɲindagaŋ*
What are these people doing? (OR: What's wrong with these people?)

(811) *garu ŋayu waɲi:nɲal yiɲu gaɲa:r*
    What shall I do to this alligator [in order to rescue the woman he
       is holding ?]

See also lines 50, 51 of text 2, and line 17 of text 14.

    waɳḍaruɲ 'which direction' (3.7.2) can also be verbalised, and used to
question how some action was performed (the 'how' being understood
in a directional sense). For instance:

(812) *ɲundu ḍugi waɳḍaruɲɲa:l gunda:l*
    Which way did you cut the tree ?

to which a reply could be 'starting at one side and cutting right through
it', or

(813) *ŋayu warŋgiɲalɲu gunda:l*   I cut all around it

employing the adverb *warŋgi-n* 'do all around'.

4.8.2   -maḍi-n. There is a further affix, *-maḍi-n*, which derives an
intransitive verbal stem from a nominal; this is – like all disyllabic
affixes – non-cohering (2.4). It occurs predominantly with number
adjectives and indicates something happening 'so many at a time':

(814) *ɲundu:ba gumanmaḍin galin*   You go out one at a time!

(815) *ŋaɲḍi ḍambu:lmaḍi:na gali:na*   We must go in pairs

(816) *bama ɲinaŋ ŋabimaḍiŋ*
    A whole mob of people sat down together

ḍambu:l + *maḍi-n* appears to have exactly the same semantic effect as the
reduplicated *ḍambuḍambu:l* – see (121) in 3.3.9.

    -maḍi-n has very occasionally been encountered suffixed to a non-
number adjective:

(817) *bama gadilmaḍiŋ galiŋ*
    The [group of] people is getting small as they go along

(817) appears to imply that people must be dropping out 'a few at a
time'. But there are other examples that do not have an 'incremental' or
'decremental' interpretation. In fact, it seems that *-maḍi-n* may sometimes alternate with *-daga-n* simply for the sake of stylistic felicity
(3.1.3) – thus a reply to *ɲuɲu bama ŋalaldagaŋ* 'that fellow is getting big
now' could be *ɲuɲu bama ŋalalmaḍiŋ* '[yes], he certainly is growing up'.

-*maḍi-n* is probably cognate with -*mayi-n*, which Hale (1976a: 239) reports as the (only?) intransitive verbaliser in Dya:bugay.

4.8.3 -**luŋa-l.** The fourth verbaliser has the form -*luŋa-l*; it is non-cohering and derives a transitive stem. Like -*maḍi-n*, -*luŋa-l* is far less frequent than -*daga-n* and -*ŋa-l* and is also restricted in the class of words to which it can be suffixed.

[a] With body-part nouns.

When added to an appropriate body-part noun, -*luŋa-l* indicates that something is 'touched' with this body-part. As would be expected, the most frequent form is *mandi* + -*luŋa-l* 'touch with the hand':

(818) *giyi mandiluŋa ḍugi ḍamuy*
    Don't touch the forbidden tree (it is tabooed since it is sacred to the rainbow-serpent)

We can also get *ḍina* + *luŋa-l* 'touch with the foot', and:

(819) *ŋayu nara binaluŋa:l/ nara ŋanda bina: gunda:ḍiɲu*
    I touched a (prickly) vine with my ear. The vine cut my ear

Notice that *binaluŋa-l* cannot mean 'hear' (referring to the main function of an ear) but only 'touch with the ear'. (And it will be seen that -*luŋa-l* does not distinguish between purposeful and accidental touching.)

-*luŋa-l*, in this sense, is precisely limited to 'touch'. It cannot be added to *mila* 'tongue' simply because to touch with the tongue would normally involve 'tasting', and this is described by *banḍa-l* (which takes *mila* in instrumental case):

(820) *ŋayu bana mila: banḍa:l*   I tasted the water with [my] tongue.

[b] With locatives.

-*luŋa-l* can be added to a noun in locative case, and then indicates that something is put, or is moving, in or on the referent of that noun:

(821) *ŋayu buɲa bulmba:luŋa:l baḍa:ṛna*
    I took the woman to [my] camp to leave [her there]

(822) *ŋayu buɲa gaba:ɲḍaluŋa:l gadaŋalɲu*
    I brought the woman along the road

[c] With datives.

When suffixed to a noun or pronoun in dative case, -*luŋa-l* indicates an action that is performed for the benefit of the referent of that noun or pronoun – the unmarked meaning is 'giving':

(823) *bama:l ɲuɲu miɲa ɲuni:ndaluŋal*
      A person is giving that meat to you

But it seems that a dative form is sometimes ambiguous. It can have the 'giving' sense, or else a 'locative' meaning as described under [b]. Apparently

(824) *bama:l ɲuɲu ŋaḍu:ndaluŋal*

can mean 'the person is giving that to me' or 'the person is bringing that close to me'. In view of this, *ŋaḍunda* could well be taken as having locative in addition to dative function (cf. 3.6.2).

The fact that the last syllable of *-luŋa-l* is identical to regular causative *-ŋa-l* might be thought to suggest a segmentation *-lu+ŋa-l*. There are two arguments against this. Firstly, *-luŋa-l* does not cohere – we get *gaba:ɲḍaluŋa:l* in (822), not *gabaɲḍaluŋalɲu* – suggesting that it is a simple disyllabic affix. Secondly, there is no further occurrence of *-lu-*, that would support the recognition of a morpheme here.

The writer was not able to elicit *-luŋa-l* on to a stem ending in a consonant. Note that this point is of considerable phonotactic interest since *-l-* is never permitted as the second element of a consonant cluster in Yidiɲ (the post-inflectional affix *-la* has allomorph *-ala* following a consonant – 3.9.1. 2.3.9).

4.9   Imperatives

An imperative can be formed from any verbal stem in Yidiɲ. It normally has an explicit or implied second person subject (S or A function):

(825) (*ɲundu*) *guwa galin*   (You) go west!

(826) (*ɲundu:ba*) *buɲa wawa*   (All of you) watch the woman!

See also (107–8) in 3.3.8 and (445–6), (454) in 4.2.3–4.

The subject of an imperative is sometimes a first person non-singular pronoun, as in (143) and line 29 of text 14. It CAN be a first person singular pronoun, in a sentence suggesting an exchange:

(827) *ŋanda wiwin   waŋal   /   ŋayu ɲuni:nda gala*
      I-DAT give-IMP boomerang-ABS I-SA you-DAT spear-ABS
      wiwin   ḍaybaṛ
      give-IMP PARTICLE
      [You] give me [your] boomerang, and I'll give you [my] spear in
      exchange!

(*ḍaybaṛ* 'in turn' is discussed in 4.10). And an imperative with third person subject is attested at line 54 of text 2.

Imperatives frequently occur with the particle *gana* 'try' (4.10).

The inclusion of derivational affix *-:ḍi-n* in the 'continuous action' sense yields a 'continuous imperative' – an exhortation to continue an action that is already in progress – see (498) in 4.1.7.

A negative imperative involves a verb in regular imperative inflection, preceded by the particle 'don't' – this has the form *giyi* in the coastal dialect (as in line 33 of text 2) and *guṇi* in the tablelands dialect (as in line 8 of text 14). See (77), (132), (818) and:

(828) (*ṇundu*) *bulmba giyi wawa*   Don't (you) look around the camp!

Like most other Australian languages, Yidiṇ will often include a positive with a negative imperative; in addition to being told what he should not do, the addressee is also advised about what would be an appropriate course of action to undertake. See line 33 of text 2, and:

(829) *giyi waŋga:ḍin/ ṇinan munubuḍun*
Don't get up! Sit down right inside [the camp]!

(830) *mayi   giyi   wuṇḍay   ḍula / baḍar*
vegetables-ABS DON'T stolen-ABS dig-IMP leave-IMP
Don't dig up vegetables that don't belong to you (literally: 'stolen vegetables')! Leave [them] alone!

One sentence has been recorded with *giyi* but no verb – see (201) in 3.7.8. *ṇinan* 'sit-IMP' is understood here, but has been omitted from the surface form of the sentence.

Positive or negative imperatives are frequently used in the main clause of sentence that has a 'lest' subordinate clause. Examples are in 4.6.2 and at line 32 of text 9.

Note that Yidiṇ uses imperatives to refer to desirable or proscribed actions, but not usually to advise on states or attitudes (differing from English in this regard). Thus, for telling someone to behave himself the appropriate Yidiṇ construction would be:

(831) *ṇundu waṇi:ngu   yaṛuṇdagaŋ*
you-SA what-PURP silly-INCHO VBLSR-PRES
[Literally: 'Why are you being silly?']

which the informant glossed as simply 'Don't be silly!'

4.10 Particles

Yidiɲ has a number of non-inflecting words – that we call 'particles' – which provide logical- or modal-type qualification of a complete sentence.

Particles are set off from the other parts of speech in that they do not inflect for case or for tense. (At least some) particles can, however, be verbalised – details are at the end of this section. The post-inflectional affix -(*a*)*la* can occur with particles.

It appears that the preferred position for all particles is immediately before the verb, although they may occur earlier in the sentence. Some (but probably not all) particles are occasionally encountered following the verb.

[1] *ɲuḍu* 'not, never' is the negative particle in all but imperative sentences.

Examples in which *ɲuḍu* immediately precedes the verb are at (85), (300), (655), (722), (726) and:

(832) *ŋayu ɲuḍula bugaɲ*   I'm not now eating (I've had sufficient)

It occurs sentence-initially in (575) and – unusually – follows the verb in

(833) *ŋayu ḍina budi:liɲu ɲuḍu*

I couldn't go and put my foot [in the water, because the water was too hot]

A sentence whose sole 'comment' is an adjective (i.e. when there is no verb) can be negated quite normally, with *ɲuḍu* usually immediately preceding the adjective. See (534) and

(834) *yiŋu   ḍaḍa   ɲuḍu guriɲ | gaba   mayi*
      THIS-S child-ABS NOT good-ABS feed baby-IMP vegetables-ABS
      ŋabi
      lots-ABS

This child is not [looking too] good. Feed him with lots of vegetables (to make him healthier).

ɲuḍu can also be used to negate a noun 'comment', as in (79), lines 10 and 19 of text 9, and

(835) *ŋayu bama gada:ɲal ɲuḍu miɲa*
      I've brought a person, not an animal

There appears to be a contrast in Yidiɲ between – cf. (73) – *miɲa ɲuḍu* 'there is no meat', and *ŋayu miɲagimbal* 'I've no meat' (see 3.3.6).

In this regard Yidiɲ behaves rather differently from Dyirbal. The negative particle *gulu* in Dyirbal can only normally co-occur with a verb (which it will as a rule immediately precede); in the Mamu dialect *gulu* can negate an adjectival comment, but it MUST then occur sentence-initially (Dixon 1972: 117–18). In Dyirbal only the privative suffix can be used to 'negate' a noun, as in 'there is no meat'.

We have mentioned (3.1.3) that Dyirbal is on the whole far more elliptical that Yidiɲ. In contrast to the general tendency, it appears that negative constructions in Yidiɲ are far more fluid than those in Dyirbal. Note, for instance, (299) above, in which the adjective *wigilwigil* is omitted from *banga ɲuḍu wigil* 'honey is not [so] sweet [as molasses]'; and see the comment in 4.9 on (201) from 3.7.8.

Examples of the post-inflectional affix -(*a*)*la* added to *ɲuḍu* are at (265), (832) and in line 25 of text 14.

ɲuḍu also functions as a negative interjection 'no, no more, nothing' – 4.12.

This is further manifestation of the wide range of use of *ɲuḍu* in Yidiɲ, in contrast with Dyirbal's *gulu*. Dyirbal has a quite separate form for the negative interjection – *yimba* or *maya* (depending on dialect). See Dixon 1972: 124 and 3.1.3 above.

[2] *giyi* 'don't'. This is the negative imperative particle in the coastal dialect – see 4.9. It also serves to negate a tensed sentence involving particle *biya* – see (863) below.

[3] *guɲi*. This particle has negative imperative meaning in the tablelands dialect (corresponding to coastal *giyi*) – see 4.9.

guɲi does occur in the coastal dialect, but with a quite different, positive sense 'let [him] do [it]'. It can occur with an imperative verb, as in (739) and

(836) *ɲayu baḍa:ɽna bama munu guɲi ɲinan*
    I must leave [these] people, and let them sit inside [their cave undisturbed]

or with a verb in tense or purposive inflection – see (102) and

(837) *ɲayu wala   ḍugi   budi:l   gawuɽ   /*
    I-SA PARTICLE stick-ABS put down-PAST crossways-ABS
    guɲila   gubaŋ
    LET-NOW burn-PRES
    I've put down the sticks crossways (i.e. each layer at right-angles to the one below) so that they'll be able to burn now

(838) *ɲundu wiwin guɲi buga:na*
    You give [the food to him] and let [it] be eaten [by him]

[4] *gana* 'try'. This is by far the commonest particle, occurring in texts (pages 513–39) as often as all the other particles put together. Its semantic content is slight and elusive, and is probably best summed up in the informants' gloss 'try'. The preferred position for *gana* appears to be immediately before the verb, but it does often occur sentence-initially.

gana can occur in a sentence with a verb in any inflection; it is frequently found with imperatives (4.9) and especially with purposives (4.5.2) – (143) and (713) are typical examples.

The close association between *gana* and verbal purposive *-na* might be thought to suggest an etymological connection (the suffix being a degenerate form of the particle). But note that such a suggestion would be incompatible with our inference (3.8.4) that *-na* originally had a future meaning, in proto-Yidiɲ–Dya:bugay (with verbal purposive then being based on *-gu*).

There is an adverb (4.1.3) *baɳḍa-l* 'try to do, taste' with more specific conative effect; this often co-occurs with *gana*:

(839) *ŋayu gana ḍugi baɳḍa:lna gunda:lna garu wanda:na*
    I must try to cut the tree, so that by-and-by it falls down

ganawaŋgi 'belly up', involving the homophonous nonce-form *gana*, is mentioned in 3.3.8.

[5] *ganagayuy* 'self'
[6] *ganamaṛbu* 'self'
    These two particles appear to be based on *gana*. There is an adjective *maṛbu* 'one's own' (which can be used to refer to something that is considered an inseparable – but abstract – part of a person: one's conception site, one's wife, or one's language), whereas *gayuy* does not occur elsewhere.

ganagayuy and *ganamaṛbu* have similar meanings, covering both 'reflexive' and 'intensive' functions (very like English 'self'). Reflexive examples are at (453–4) in 4.2.4 and

(840) *bama ɲuɲu* $\begin{Bmatrix} \textit{ganagayuy} \\ \textit{ganamaṛbu} \end{Bmatrix}$ *gunda:ḍiɲu*   That person cut himself

'Intensive' examples are at (64) in 3.3.6 and

(841) *ɲuniɲ ŋuḍu buḍi:ɲ / ganagayuy gali:na*
      you-O NOT tell-PAST SELF   go-PURP
      You hadn't been permitted to go out alone

Compare with post-inflectional affix -di (3.9.2) and particle ŋadi.

[7] ganaŋgar 'do first' appears also to be based on gana (although no explanation can be given for the -ŋgar).

ganaŋgar indicates that the (S or A) subject was the first to perform a certain action – see (437) and

(842) ŋayu gana:ŋgar gali:ɲ/ ŋaɲaɲ ḍaḍa:ŋ gaɽba banḍabanḍa:ɽ gadaŋalɲu
I went first, the child came behind following me

(843) ŋayu gana:ŋgar gunda:l
I was the first person to cut [that tree]

It appears that 'the first time' can also be indicated by the adjective guman 'one' in an appropriate case inflection:

(844) ŋayu yiŋu guma:ndu ḍugi gundagunda:l/ bulmba: yiŋgu
Its the first time I've cut a tree down in this place

ganaŋgar can also be used with a purely locational sense 'in front'; particle ganaŋgar is then the complement of locational qualifier gaɽba 'behind' (3.4.1), as in (842). For instance, in a story about how a sacred woomera was used to calm the raging seas:

(845) baluɽ budi gana:ŋgar   Put the woomera in the prow [of the boat]!

[8] wala 'ceased'. This particle indicates that the (S or A) subject has stopped performing a certain action, for example:

(846) ŋayu buɲa wala bunḍa:ɲ   I've finished hitting the woman

wala can have a perfective meaning with, say, wula-n 'die'. See (316) and another sentence from later in the same text:

(847) ŋayu wala wula:ɲ/ ŋayu galwayala burgiŋ
I really did die; I'm walking about as a spirit now

Note that wala is 'subject-orientated', normally indicating that a certain person has stopped doing something of his own volition. Thus in (534) from 4.3.1 wala buga:ḍiɲu indicates that the subject has stopped eating (even though there is still food left) because he's full. Complementing wala, there is an adverb gaymbi-n (4.1.3); gaymbi-n is 'object orientated', indicating that an action is finished because the set of possible objects is exhausted. Compare (846) with

(848) ŋayu buɲa gaymbi:ɲ bunḍa:ɲ   I've hit all the women

Discussion of 'subject/object orientation', with reference to Dyirbal and English, is in Dixon (1970b).

wala often occurs with an adjective bearing the post-inflectional particle *-di*, and then serves to emphasise the judgement (being best translated as 'really') – 3.9.2. *ɳuɳudi wala* (*guriɳ*) 'it's alright' is a fairly frequent idiom.

[9] *biɽi* 'do again, return'. This particle frequently occurs with *gunḍi-n* 'return, go back' (the sense of particle and verb here overlapping and reinforcing each other); see line 115 of text 2 and

(848) *ɳayu gana gali:na/ biɽi gunḍi:na*
        I tried to go, [that is] to return home

With other verbs *biɽi* makes a more discernible semantic contribution, e.g.

(849) *ɳayu biɽi burwal*
        I've jumped over again (I've already jumped over a log, say, and
        I'll now jump back)

(850) *ɳayu biɽi ɳaŋga:ḍiɳu*   I talked again

(851) *ɳayu biɽi maŋga:ɳ*   I laughed again

(852) *ɳayu miɳa biɽi buga:na*   I must eat some more meat

In sentences like (849–52) *biɽi* indicates that the event is repeated exactly (except that the direction of movement may be reversed). (850) implies talking again TO THE SAME PERSON, (851) is laughing again AT THE SAME THING, and (852) must refer to the actor returning and eating a bit more of a piece of meat that he has already sampled. (849) describes someone jumping over a log that he has already vaulted – he could now be jumping in the other direction (just as (848) refers to someone retracing his path back to the point of origin).

[10] *yurga* 'still' suggests that the subject is engaged in a certain action for a considerable time (up to the 'present'). Thus:

(853) *ɳaɳaɳ bama:l yurga wawa:l*
        [That] person was still looking at me

(854) *yurga wiwiɳ mayi*   [He] gives [me] food all the time

yurga can indicate that someone is still capable of a certain action, at a certain time:

(855) *gala dubu:da/ daŋga:ɳ/ bama yurga burgi:ɳ*
        [There was] a spear in [his] stomach. It was pulled out. [And] he
        could still walk about

but can apparently NOT be used in a general statement of the form 'People still talk Yidiɲ'.

[11] *babaɽ* 'couldn't manage it' indicates that the actor tried to do something but was unable to accomplish it:

(856) *ŋayu gana babaɽ ḍugi gunda:l/ buyal*
I tried to cut the tree but failed – [the wood was too] hard

(857) *waɲḍa ŋayu bunda: magi:lna/ babaɽ ŋayu ɲina:ɲ*
I wanted to climb up the hill at some point, but failed and had to stay [down on the plain]

(858) *ŋayu babaɽ wawa:l waɲa*
I tried to see who that was, but couldn't

As might be expected, *babaɽ* often co-occurs with the particle *gana* 'try', as in (856), and/or with a verb in purposive inflection, as in (857). (Note the occurrence in (857/8) of indefinite/interrogative deictics – *waɲḍa* 'somewhere, where' and *waɲa* 'someone, who'.)

[12] *biya* refers to something that has not been done (or has not happened) but should have been done (or could have happened).

The most frequent sense is to indicate that someone has been remiss in not doing something he should have. See (712) and

(859) *ŋaɲḍi:nda biya gadil baḍar*
[You] should leave a bit [of meat] for us [but you've left nothing]

(860) *ŋayu biya gali:ɲ*   I wish I had gone

If referring to some involuntary action, *biya* can imply that something didn't happen but could well have:

(861) *ɲundu biya wanda:ɲ ḍugim*
You could well have fallen from [that] tree [and are lucky you didn't]

It can also refer to the veracity of some assertion (if X then Y, but not Y, thus not X). Thus, in text 2, Damari had stayed away from a fight but tells his brother Guyala that he was in fact there (sporting false, self-induced wounds as proof). Guyala then says (line 101)

(862) *biya ŋayu ɲuniɲ ŋuḍu wawa:l*
I'd have seen you [if you'd been there] but didn't

Note the occurrence with *biya* in (862) of *ŋuḍu* 'not', emphasising the non-occurrence of the event. To indicate that something was done that

shouldn't have been (the negation of *biya*) *giyi* – and not *ɲuḍu* – is used with *biya*:

(863) *ɲundu miɲa giyi biya wiwi:ɲ ɲuɲḍu:nda*
     You shouldn't have given meat to that [person, since he wasn't behaving properly at the time]

Outside sentences like (863), *giyi* 'don't' only occurs with verbs in imperative inflection.

[13] *wara* 'done the wrong way'. This particle can indicate that a transitive action involved an inappropriate O NP. See (871–2) and:

(864) *ɲundu yiɲḍu:ɲ bama wara buḍi:ɲ*   You told the wrong person

(865) *ɲundu ḍugi wara gunda:l*
     You cut the wrong tree down (you were told to fell a different one)

In other instances *wara* can refer to an inappropriate place:

(866) *ŋayu yiɲḍu:ɲ bama wara galiɲalɲu*
     I took this person to the wrong place

or else just to an inappropriate manner in which an action was performed:

(867) *ɲundu gangu:l wara baga:l*
     You speared the wallaby in the wrong place (i.e. you missed the vital spot, at which you should have aimed)

Some examples could be classified in terms of 'inappropriate place' and/or 'inappropriate manner':

(868) *bama wara biɻi gunḍiŋ*
     He walked home the wrong way (e.g. straying off the path)

   With *ɲaŋga:di-n* 'speak, talk', *wara* forms an idiom-like collocation 'tell a lie'; see, for instance, line 8 in text 14.

Dyirbal has a particle *wara* with similar implications of inappropriacy. There is, however, an important difference of detail – Dyirbal *wara* implies an inappropriate O or S NP, NOT a mistaken place or an ill-advised 'manner'.
   Dyirbal also has a particle *biya*, whose range of meaning may be more restricted than Yidiɲ *biya* – the Dyirbal word can be used in senses similar to (861) and probably also (859–60), but has not been heard in sentences like (862) or (863). See Dixon 1972: 118–19.

[14] *mugu* 'couldn't help it' indicates something that was quite unsatisfactory but which it was impossible to avoid doing (it appears to

coincide exactly in meaning with the particle *mugu* in Dyirbal – Dixon 1972: 118).

(869) *ŋayu mugu maŋga:ɲ*
> I couldn't help laughing (but, say, I shouldn't laugh when someone hurts himself)

(870) *ŋaɲḍi mayi mugu buga:ɲ*
> We had to eat the food (it was not really ripe, but there was nothing else to eat)

See example (292) above, lines 33 and 34 of text 9, and line 2 of text 14.

When the writer was trying to elicit examples of the affix *-ɲa* (3.3.7) with kin terms, he thoughtlessly asked how to say 'I hit my father'. He was given *ŋayu bunḍa:ɲ bimbi:ɲ*, and the informant insisted that anyone hearing such a statement would respond with:

(871) *ɲundu gurbi wara bunḍa:ɲ bimbi*
> You shouldn't have hit your father (he is an inappropriate person for you to hit)

whereupon the original speaker could try to excuse himself by saying:

(872) *mugula/ bunḍa:ɲ/ wara*
> It was impossible to avoid [hitting him] although I know I should not hit [my own father]

[15] *ḍaybaṛ* 'in turn'
[16] *ḍaymbi* 'in turn'

These two particles indicate that something happened to redress a balance – once X has done something to Y, Y should reciprocate towards X. The particle normally accompanies the second, or 'redress' clause. If the subject (A) of the redress clause is the speaker, *ḍaybaṛ* is used; if it is someone other than the speaker, *ḍaymbi* is the appropriate particle. That is:

INITIAL CLAUSE ACTOR	REDRESS CLAUSE ACTOR	PARTICLE IN REDRESS CLAUSE
speaker	someone else	*ḍaymbi*
someone else	speaker	*ḍaybaṛ*

As in:

(873) *ŋayu bama bunḍa:ɲ/ ɲaɲaɲ bama:l ḍaymbi bunḍa:ɲ*
> I hit the person and the person hit me in return

(874) *bama:l ɲaɲaɲ buṇḍa:ɲ/ ɲayu bama ḍaybaṟ buṇḍa:ɲ*
      The person hit me and I hit him in return

or

(875) *ɲayu ɲuni:nda mayi wiwiɲ/ ɲundu ɲanda miɲa ḍaymbi wiwiɲ*
      I'll give you some vegetables and then you can give me some meat
      in exchange

(876) *ɲundu ɲanda miɲa wiwiɲ/ ɲayu ɲuni:nda mayi ḍaybaṟ wiwiɲ*
      You give me some meat and then I'll give you some vegetables in
      exchange

Other examples are (827) in 4.9 and

(877) *ɲayu ɲuɲḍu:nda guru:n wiwi:ɲ/ ɲanda ḍaymbi guru:n buḍi:ɲ
      yiɲḍu:ŋ bama:l*
      I told [this person] a story, and then he, in turn, told me one

(878) *ɲundu ɲanda mayi ḍimir niba/ ɲayu garu ɲuni:nda gangu:l niba:lna/
      ḍaybaṟ*
      You show me where mountain yams [grow] and by-and-by I'll
      show you [some] wallabies, in exchange

If neither of the 'reciprocating actors' is the speaker, *ḍaymbi* may be
included in both clauses:

(879) *ḍaymbi yiɲḍu:ɲ giḍaṟ+gunda:l/ yiɲḍu:ŋ ḍaymbi ɲuɲḍu:ɲ giḍaṟ+
      gunda:l*
      [That person] painted this [one], and this [one] then reciprocated
      by painting that [one]

[17] *ɲadí* 'self'. This particle can bear an intensive or reflexive meaning –
see (746) and

(880) *ɲayu ɲadí baga:ḍiɲu*   I DID spear myself

(881) *bama ɲadí ɲuɲu wawa ɲumbaṟ/ gangu:lɲuṟi ɲumbaṟ*
      Look at that man's face, it is like a wallaby's face

ɲadí is the only word in Yidiɲ with stress on a non-initial syllable that
does not involve a long vowel. It is related to the post-inflectional affix
-di (3.9.2); it is in fact possible that *ɲadí* would be more appropriately
regarded as a clitic, and not a particle.

[18] *ɲulaɲ* 'it's a good job that —' describes an event that is regarded as
quite desirable and satisfactory:

(882) *mayi ɲulaɲ ɲundu gadaɲalɲu*
      It's a good job you brought the food

(883) *ɲulaɲ ɲundu gada:ɲ/ ŋayu ɲuni:ngu wamba:ɖiɲu*
> It's lucky you came, I've been waiting for you

(884) *bama ɲulaɲ gali:ɲ*
> It's a good job [that] person has gone away (he wasn't welcome here)

There are two other forms, *ŋaɖa* and *gurbi*, whose status as particles is in doubt.

[19] *ŋaɖa* 'might be'. This particle has been encountered about a dozen times, always referring to some event that would be unpleasant, and occurring with a verb in 'lest' inflection:

(885) *gana bigu:n dalbal waŋga:ɖiɲa/ bama:l ŋaɖa bunɖa:nɖi*
> Try to hold the shield up high, lest someone might hit you

(886) *ɲundu giyi galin/ ŋaɖa wandaɲali:nɖi*
> Don't you go, you might go and fall down

(887) *ɲundu bambi:ɖin buda:/ garu wumbul wuna:na/ ɲundu ŋaɖa banba:nɖi*
> You wrap yourself in a blanket, so that you can lie down warm, other-wise you might feel cold [in the night]

In explaining these (and other) sentences, the informant glossed *ŋaɖa* as 'might be'. But at other times he remarked that there was only one word *ŋaɖa* in Yidiɲ, the time qualifier 'tomorrow'; and it proved impossible to elicit further examples of the particle.

In view of this difficulty (which was not encountered with any other word!) the status and meaning of *ŋaɖa* must remain in doubt.

[20] *gurbi* 'maybe, perhaps' indicates the possibility of a certain event or a certain state. See (70), (73), (185), (250), (871) and

(888) *yiŋu bama gadaŋ dunguwaŋgi/ wugul gurbi guɳɖi:ɲ*
> This person is coming [holding] his head up – maybe his neck is broken

(889) *garu ŋayu ɖangandagaŋ gurbi*   I think I may die by-and-by

(890) *bulmba gurbi yiŋu bama:n*
> This place may [already] belong to some people

gurbi may be used with each of a sequence of clauses to indicate open disjunction:

(891) *bama gurbi yaluŋunda gadaŋ/ gurbi ŋaɖa gadaŋ*
> [The] person may come today, or he may come tomorrow

(892) *ŋayudi gunduy wawa:ɖiɲu/ gurbi bima*
> I [think I] saw a brown snake, or it may have been a death adder

In examples like (885–9) *gurbi* behaves exactly like a particle. Its behaviour only becomes syntactically anomalous when it is found (unlike any other particle) in ergative case:

(893) *ŋaɲaŋ ŋuɲḍu:ŋ bama:l gurbi:ŋ buɲḍa:ɲ*
It could be that [same] person who hit me [again]

But compare (890) with:

(894) *gurbi yiɲu ḍaban yiŋgu walba: ɲinaŋ bana:*
This might be an eel sitting here in the water by this rock

This suggests recognising two distinct functions of *gurbi*:

[a] as a particle, qualifying a complete sentence – (888–92). In this function *gurbi* cannot decline.

[b] as an adjective, qualifying a noun (or pronoun) – (893–4) and perhaps also (73) above. In this function *gurbi* would be expected to take the full range of nominal inflections.

We have already stressed that the main distinguishing mark of particles is their inability to take inflections of any sort. Some of them can, however, be verbalised by inchoative *-daga-n* (4.8.1):

(895) *ŋayu babaṛdagaŋ miwa:ḍiŋ*
I failed to lift [something, because it was too heavy]

(896) *ŋuɲu baḍar/ guɲidaga:na*
Leave that [person] to let him be [undisturbed]

(897) *ŋayu buɲḍa:ḍiɲu ḍaybaṛdaga:ɲ*
I hit [him], paying him back

(898) *ŋayu biṛidagaŋ gunḍiŋ*   I went back again

And they can also take the causative verbaliser *-ŋa-l*:

(899) *ŋayu ḍugi yurgaŋalɲu gunda:l*   I was still cutting the tree

4.11   Questions

Yidiɲ has a full set of indefinite/interrogative items (these begin with *wa-*, and correspond exactly to 'wh- words' in English) for asking non-polar questions; these were discussed in 3.7.

Polar questions – demanding a yes/no answer – are marked solely by sentence-final rising intonation. There is no word, clitic, affix, or ordering of words to mark polar questions.

Note that Dyirbal does have an interrogative clitic *-ma* (which is added to the first word of a sentence, whatever this is). But this is only used occasionally,

yes/no questions in Dyirbal being normally marked just by intonation, as in Yidiɲ. See Dixon 1972: 122–3.

4.12 Interjections

Interjections have no syntactic function, and most often occur in a separate intonation group at the beginning of an utterance. Those encountered are:

    yiyi 'yes'

    ɲuḍu 'no' (this can be emphasised by the addition of the post-inflectional affix -*di* – 3.9.2)

    ɲuruɲ ~ *ɲuru:* (always with high final rising intonation) 'why'

    ɲara: 'what!'

The use of *ɲundu* as an exclamation or interjection was discussed in 3.1.5.

There is also an exclamation [*yar:*] – with an emphatic long final roll – that is used to indicate displeasure with 'dirty talk' going on in the vicinity.

5 Deep syntax

5.1 Symbolisations for syntactic structure

5.1.1 'Nominative–accusative' versus 'absolutive–ergative' tree structures.
We plainly require some system of syntactic notation as a basis for describing the underlying structure of Yidiɲ sentences, and 'explaining' the various derivational processes detailed in chapter 4.

'Tree structures' have, over the past score or so years, become accepted as a convenient system of explanatory graphs. The most accepted convention for a language like English has been to adopt trees of the form:

(i) NOMINATIVE–ACCUSATIVE-TYPE TREES

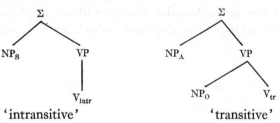

where Σ indicates 'sentence' and subscripts A (transitive subject), S (intransitive subject) and O (transitive object) indicate the underlying functions of NPs. Languages for which trees (i) are appropriate have been said to have a 'nominative–accusative' syntax – S and A are identified for various syntactic operations (and may receive the same morphological marking).

But it has been shown (Dixon 1972: 130–7, and see Hale 1970) that some languages demand basic trees of a different type:

(ii) ABSOLUTIVE–ERGATIVE-TYPE TREES

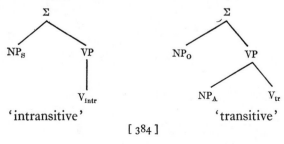

[384]

Note that we are here only contrasting the various hierarchical arrangements of constituents one in another, not their orderings. Thus, we pay no attention

to the difference 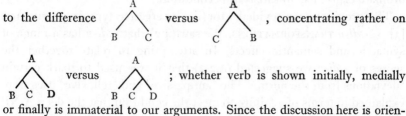 versus , concentrating rather on

versus ; whether verb is shown initially, medially or finally is immaterial to our arguments. Since the discussion here is orientated towards the syntactic description of Yidiɲ, we have utilised the ordering that corresponds most closely to that of Yidiɲ surface structure.

In Dyirbal, for instance, all operations of coordination and subordination identify S and O NPs, treating A NPs in a quite different way; in addition, nouns have one case inflection for S and O functions (absolutive, with zero realisation) whilst 'ergative case' marks A NPs.

Our first task, then, is to decide which of these two possible types of tree structure is most appropriate for Yidiɲ. 'Nominative–accusative trees', (i), claim that NP_O forms a constituent (called VP) with the transitive verb, and that NP_A and NP_S have analogous roles in syntactic operations. In contrast, 'absolutive–ergative trees', (ii), claim that NP_A groups with V_{tr} (as VP) and that NP_O and NP_S have equivalent roles in certain transformations.

The next section assesses the syntactic evidence presented in chapter 4, to decide which syntactic type Yidiɲ falls under.

5.1.2 The Yidiɲ evidence. In assessing whether a language is of grammatical type (i) or (ii) we should plainly take into account data from all areas of the grammar – morphological as well as syntactic. Taking the pieces of evidence one at a time:

[1] – CASE MARKING. We saw (3.6.2) that pronouns have a single form for S and A functions – evidence for (i) – whereas (3.3.1–2) nouns employ one case for S and O functions – evidence for (ii). Deictics can have different forms for all three basic functions, falling between noun and pronoun in terms of the 'grammatical hierarchy' mentioned in 4.1.4.
[2] – SUBORDINATION. It was mentioned in 4.4.1 that about 85 % of subordinate clauses in the corpus have an NP coreferential with one in the main clause; and the coreferential NP must be in S or O function in

each clause. (This was the case for dative, causal and purposive sub-ordinate clauses; for 'lest' clauses only the common NP in the sub-ordinate clause has to satisfy this condition.)

This provides strong evidence for (ii) – an ergative-type deep structure.
[3] – -:*ḍi-n* TRANSFORMATIONS. We saw (4.2) that -:*ḍi-n* has a range of syntactic and semantic effects. In attempting to relate together the senses of -:*ḍi-n* we suggested (4.2.2) that it was used to mark certain 'deviations from the norm'. The 'antipassive' and 'reflexive' uses were explained in terms of a failure to meet the condition that the deep A NP should not occur in surface S function.

In an antipassive construction the deep A NP becomes surface S (and deep O is placed in dative or locative case). In reflexives, deep A and O coincide referentially and there is a single, S, NP in the surface realisation. These two uses of -:*ḍi-n* have in common that deep A is DIFFERENT from, and then BECOMES surface S. There is, however, no evidence relating S to O, or contrasting A with O; we simply have an important distinction between A and S. This could be taken as evidence AGAINST an accusative deep structure, (i) – we plainly do NOT have syntactic identification of A and S functions, which is what (i) implies. But it could hardly be taken as positive evidence in favour of (ii).

[4] – VERBAL DERIVATIONAL AFFIX -*ŋa-l*. The evidence here is quite mixed, and inconclusive. Five of the six senses of -*ŋa-l* distinguished in 4.3.8 – including the most frequently occurring sense, 'comitative' – derive a transitive sentence whose A NP is identical to the original S constituent. But the 'controlling' sense derives a transitive construction whose O NP is equivalent to the S NP of the underlying intransitive sentence.

These sets of facts could be interpreted in various ways. Thus, for the 'controlling' sense we could suggest that
(iii)

effectively becomes the VP of a transitive sentence:
(iv)

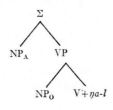

Here (iii) might be *ḍugi guṇḍi:ɲ* 'the stick broke' and (iv) *ŋayu ḍugi guṇḍiɲalɲu* 'I broke the stick' – see (508, 507) in 4.3. This interpretation would plainly support the accusative alternative, (i).

Alternatively, we could maintain that the derivation

$$...NP_S...\Rightarrow...NP_O...$$

indicates a connexion between S and O, providing support for ergative deep structure, (ii).

Similarly, the data from the 'comitative', 'dative' and other senses of *-ŋa-l* could plausibly be interpreted as supporting either type of deep structure. As we have said, the evidence from *-ŋa-l* is, overall, inconclusive.

[5] – IMPERATIVES. Imperative constructions treat S and A NPs alike. The (S or A) subject of an imperative verb is most frequently a second person pronoun, which can be deleted. This constitutes exemplary evidence for the accusative tree, (i).

[6] – PARTICLES. Particles provide modification of the meaning of a sentence. The semantic interpretation of some particles refers to certain sentence constituents. In each of these cases, S appears to be grouped with A.

Thus (4.10) *ganaŋgar* indicates that the referent of the S or A NP was the first to perform a certain action, *babaɽ* that he tried but couldn't manage to achieve some end, and *wala* that the subject stopped doing something of his own volition. Note also the particle *wara*, which can indicate that an action involved an inappropriate O NP referent (NOT S or A referent). These four particles all suggest a grouping of S with A, opposed to O.

The discussion thus far can be summarised:

FOR ACCUSATIVE STRUCTURE (i)	FOR ERGATIVE STRUCTURE, (ii) or AGAINST ACCUSATIVE, (i)
[5] Imperatives	[2] Subordination
[6] Particles	[3] *-:ḍi-n* construction

INCONCLUSIVE

[1] Case marking

[4] Syntax of verbal affix *-ŋa-l*

The deep structures that are set up to relate together instrumental and comitative verbal and nominal constructions could conceivably be taken as additional evidence for an 'accusative' position – see 5.4.5.

The evidence appears thus far to be about equally balanced. But we have not broached the area that, in many languages, provides strongest evidence for the shape of a deep structure: coordination. This is investigated in the next section.

5.1.3   Coordination. There is no overt sentence coordinator in Yidiɲ, along the lines of 'and' in English. Investigation of possible rules of coordination must thus pay attention to:

(a) the conditions under which an NP, that is plainly present in the underlying structures of two successive sentences, is deleted (in all or part) from the surface representation of one sentence (usually the second).

(b) the conditions under which two clauses can occur in a single intonation group.

(b) is encountered relatively rarely; when it is it invariably coincides with an instance of (a) – as in line 5 of text 2.

Yidiɲ's southern neighbour, Dyirbal, has a very strong principle of coordination that is a major factor in assigning Dyirbal an 'ergative' deep structure. A string of a dozen or more clauses may have a 'common NP' that is in surface S or O function for each clause. This 'topic' is normally stated just once, in the first clause of the chain, and is then commented on by each succeeding clause. Yidiɲ has nothing resembling the Dyirbal 'topic-chains'.

Deletion within a Dyirbal sentence is constrained by the principle that each clause must relate to an explicit topic NP. That is, it must either itself involve an NP in surface S or O function, or it must be (directly or indirectly) coordinated to a clause which does. Deletion appears to be freer in Yidiɲ – any (S, A or O) NP is potentially deletable from any Yidiɲ sentence. This again makes it harder to investigate coordination from a formal viewpoint. In fact, recognition of instances of coordination in Yidiɲ has to be partly in terms of the semantic connection between sentences.

There appear to be two main kinds of coordination in Yidiɲ. In each case the two (or more) clauses that are to be joined together involve a 'common NP':

(I) NON-PRONOMINAL NP, MUST BE IN S OR O FUNCTION IN EACH CLAUSE
The common NP will only normally occur in the first clause in this case. Thus (line 110 of text 2):

(900) *dama:ri gada:ɲ/ wurba:ɖiɲu*   Damari came, and searched

and (line 1 of text 14):

(901) *ɖambu:l wagu:ɖa ɖaɖa gaba:l/.../ bambi:l ɖimurula/*

Two male children were born...[they] were covered up [in their cribs] in the big house

In (900) *dama:ri* functions as S NP for both *gada:ɲ* 'came' and *wurba:ɖiɲu* 'searched'; another example of S–S coordination is at line 96 of text 2. In (901) *ɖambu:l wagu:ɖa ɖaɖa* 'two male children' is the O NP for *gaba:l* 'gave birth to' and for *bambi:l* 'covered'; other O–O examples are at (491) above and line 77 of text 2. Coordination involving an S identified with an O NP is in (427) and (476), while O–S sequences are in lines 5 and 121 of text 2.

(II) PRONOMINAL NP, MUST BE IN S OR A FUNCTION IN EACH CLAUSE

Again, the common NP will normally only occur in the first clause. Thus (line 9 of text 2):

(902) *gana ɲaɳɖi gaymbar/ wawa*

Let us sneak up, and have a look [at them]!

Here *ɲaɳɖi* 'we' functions as S NP for intransitive *gaymbar* 'sneak up' and as A NP for transitive *wawa* 'look, see'. Other S–A pronominal sequences are in lines 6 and 26 of text 14, and (989) below.

An example of three coordinated clauses, with the common NP in A function in the first two, and in S for the third, is

(903) *ɲayu guri:li   gala: baga:liɲu   / miɲa*

I-SA wallaby-ABS spear-INST spear-GOING-PAST animal-ABS

baɖa:ʈ   / biʈi   gundi:ɲ   /

leave-PAST PARTICLE return-PAST

I went and speared a wallaby with a spear, [then] left the meat [lying there] and went home

Instances of coordination where the pronominal NP is in S function in both clauses are in lines 2 and 11 of text 9; an A–A sequence is in line 18 of text 9.

Note that the verbs in two coordinated sentences must show identical inflection – that is, they must both be in imperative, in past, or in present (–future) form. (Purposive can occur on the verb in a main clause – 4.5.2; in a non-initial clause purposive is interpreted as marking subordination.) Thus, verbs in both clauses are in imperative inflection

in (902) and (904), in past tense in (900), (901) and (903) and in present tense in line 96 of text 2, for instance.

These 'favourite' schemes of coordination can co-occur, when two clauses have a common pronominal A NP, and also a common nominal O NP, as in line 46 from text 2:

(904) *gana ɲundu:ba   mayi   yiɲu   bana: budi* /
    TRY   you all-SA fruit-ABS this-ABS water-LOC put-IMP
    gurḍi:lna | garu   daŋgan |
    be soaked-PURP by-and-by take out IMP
    You all try to put this food in the water, to let it soak; by-and-by [you] take [it] out!

We mentioned in 4.1.4 that the unmarked role for pronominal referents is 'agent', whereas the unmarked role for nominal referents is more likely to be 'patient'. Sentences like (904) involve a pronoun in the unmarked, nominative, form and a noun in the unmarked, absolutive, form; this type of 'pronominal A–A'/'nominal O–O' coordination is, on several counts, the most natural and typical kind of syntactic sequence.

But suppose that we have a transitive sentence with pronominal A and nominal O, and coordinate this with an intransitive sentence. Suppose further than either O or A NP could plausibly function as intransitive subject. With

(905) *ŋayu bama banḍa:ɽ*   I followed the person

and

(906) *bama wanda:ɲ*   The person fell down

we have a sequence of type (I); the repeated NP can be deleted giving

(907) *ŋayu bama banḍa:ɽ/ wanda:ɲ*

But (905) and

(908) *ŋayu wanda:ɲ*   I fell down

also constitute a valid pair of coordinands, this time of type (II), and the common NP could again be omitted, also yielding (907).

(907) is thus ambiguous between 'I followed the person and he fell down' and 'I followed the person and I fell down'. If it were necessary to resolve this equivocation, *bama* or *ŋayu* could of course simply be retained in the second clause.

S/A coordination, type (II), is definitely restricted to pronominal NPs. Thus, when the writer asked what could be the meaning of

(909) *bimbi:ŋ   guḍuguḍu   wawa:l / biṛi   gunḍi:n*
    father-ERG rainbow-ABS see-PAST PARTICLE return-PAST

he was told it could only mean 'Father saw the rainbow, and the rainbow went back [into its lair in the water]', never *'Father saw the rainbow and then he [father] went home'. That is, coordination is not possible on the basis of the A NP *bimbi:ŋ* and S NP *bimbi*. The informant said that whilst (909) was alright, it would be stylistically better to employ a subordinate clause:

(910) *bimbi:ŋ guḍuguḍu wawa:l/ biṛi gunḍinunda bana:*
    Father saw the rainbow going back into the water

Similarly, no examples of S/O coordination involving pronouns are attested. It appears, in fact, that coordination directly mirrors morphological form. Nouns have one case for S and O functions, and provide a basis for coordination which involves the identification of S and O NPs, while pronouns have a single form for S and A functions and here coordination operates on the principle of S/A coreferentiality.

Yidiɲ syntax here contrasts strongly with that of Dyirbal where – independently of morphological form – coordination depends on a 'common S/O NP' for all parts of speech (Dixon 1972: 130–7).

A deictic would seldom be found making up a complete NP in two successive Yidiɲ clauses. It appears that deictics pattern with nouns qua coordination; it is thus more accurate to talk of 'pronominal' and 'non-pronominal' (rather than 'nominal') NPs.

It will be remarked that the rules we have inferred for coordination in Yidiɲ are quite wide-ranging. In fact, a hearer's interpretation of any coordinated sentence is motivated firstly by considerations of semantic common-sense. A sentence will tend to be understood in such a way that it describes a culturally normal and acceptable event.

Considerations of common-sense can resolve syntactic ambiguities – such as (907) above. And sometimes semantic considerations may overrule syntactic constraints in the interests of providing a culturally plausible interpretation.

This can be illustrated by two sentences which the writer put to a male informant, a week apart. Firstly

(911) *ŋayu buɲa   wawa:l yaṛŋga:n*
    I-SA woman-ABS see-PAST be frightened-PAST

was suggested. The informant confirmed that this was an acceptable Yidiɲ sentence. When asked WHO was frightened he stated emphatically that it was the woman, and that she was scared of the speaker; he repeated the sentence, adding *ŋaḍinḍida* 'I-FEAR'. In fact, on syntactic grounds, *yaɽŋga:ɲ* could have as underlying S NP either *buɲa* – by (I) – or *ŋayu* – by (II). It was, to the informant, unrealistic to think that a man could be frightened of a woman.

The second sentence simply has A and O NPs reversed in the first, transitive clause

(912) *ŋaɲaɲ buna:ŋ   wawa:l   yaɽŋga:ɲ*
    I-O   woman-ERG see-PAST be frightened-PAST

Here the gloss given was 'The woman saw me and she was frightened'. According to the syntactic constraints we have outlined the ONLY interpretation of this coordination should be 'The woman saw me, and I was frightened'. But this interpretation was rejected in favour of a semantically acceptable reading that involved the grammatically odd identification of non-pronominal A and S NPs. (It is the only example of this type in the writer's corpus.) Compare (912) with (909) where an A–S interpretation was firmly rejected (here the O–S reading was, of course, quite plausible).

In view of (912) we should perhaps describe (I) and (II) as 'preferences' rather than rules. The conclusion to be drawn from our study of coordination is that semantic considerations are at least as important as grammatical conventions; and that there is no hard-and-fast syntactic matrix in this area of Yidiɲ grammar.

The principles of coordination we have been able to adduce do not help us one bit in the choice between 'accusative' and 'ergative' deep structure. Coordination appears simply to follow the morphological paradigm – nouns identify S with O and pronouns S with A.

5.1.4   Is there an 'accusative'/'ergative' dichotomy?

It has been suggested (Dixon 1972: 128–37) that every language is either strictly 'nominative–accusative' or else strictly 'absolutive–ergative' in underlying syntax. That is, either S and A are identified, and O can be grouped with V into a VP constituent – as in (i) – or else S and O are identified, with the A NP being grouped with V – as in (ii).

This was put forward as a strong hypothesis, in the hopes that an exhaustive study of a number of languages would reveal whether it

could be maintained, or whether it needed to be modified or weakened in some way.

If we had to push Yidiɲ into one of the structures (i), (ii) it would seem that the ergative alternative, (ii), is slightly more appropriate. The 'S/O coreferentiality' condition on subordination is the most convincing piece of evidence, and could be taken to outweigh the data from imperatives and from particles. But it would be, at best, a 'weak ergative' language, lacking the cumulation of syntactic detail that goes to make Dyirbal such a convincing example of this syntactic type.

The difference between Dyirbal and Yidiɲ is symptomatised by *wara*, a particle indicating the inappropriacy of some aspect of an event, that occurs in both languages. In Dyirbal (Dixon 1972: 118) *wara* specifies an inappropriate person or thing as referent of the S or O NP (this is quite in keeping with the tendency to group together S and O that recurs throughout the grammar of Dyirbal). In Yidiɲ, however, *wara* indicates an inappropriate place or manner or referent of just the O (not the S) NP – see 4.10.

The real conclusion to be drawn is that there is insufficient reason to prefer the accusative or the ergative alternative, in the case of Yidiɲ. The evidence is pretty equally balanced and really resists a procrustean push in either direction. It is clear, too, that Yidiɲ is not alone in this. A 1974 conference symposium (Dixon (ed.) 1976a: 485ff.) addressed to the question of whether individual Australian languages had 'accusative' or 'ergative' deep structures elicited four detailed studies – in each case the evidence seemed pretty evenly balanced. (Indeed, several of the contributors changed their minds in revising their papers for publication – from a 'just ergative' to a 'barely accusative' viewpoint, or vice versa.)

We seem in fact to have a continuum:

<---------------------------------->
S always syntactically   S always syntactically
identified with A   identified with O

The labels for ends of the continuum could be phrased in different ways e.g. 'A (/or O) is, in transitive sentences, the pivot for transformational operations'. Since S is necessarily the pivot in intransitive sentences, this naturally leads to analogous treatment of A(/or O) and S. See Heath 1976.

Some languages fall near enough to one end – English to the left and Dyirbal to the right, for instance – to be untroubled by attempts to replace the scale by a dichotomy. But Yidiɲ and most other Australian

languages lie somewhere in the middle of the range, and the syntactic workings of these languages belie the appropriacy of a strict 'ergative versus accusative deep syntax' dichotomy. In 4.1.4 we summarised Silverstein's (1976) explanation of the occurrence of 'ergative' and 'accusative' cases in terms of a universal hierarchical scale; it now appears likely that a similar scale operates at the syntactic level.

In investigating the syntactic nature of a language linguists have typically assessed each type of transformational operation (whether it identifies S and O, or S and A, etc.) and then totted up the overall balance. Heath (1976) and McKay (1975) suggest an alternative approach – study the operation of a certain type of rule in a wide variety of languages, and see whether it has a constant syntactic effect. It does seem, in fact, that certain rules are likely always to treat S and O in the same way, whereas others will group S and A. That is, certain types of rule have universal (or near universal) syntactic effect, and do not depend on the 'syntactic type' of each language in which they occur.

Thus McKay (1975: 364–7) remarks that noun incorporation appears always to work in terms of S and O (never A) NPs, whereas a rule of jussive complementation (e.g. He told *me to go*, I told *him to spear the fish*) must surely always specify that it is the S or A NP of the complement which must be coreferential with main clause object. He suggests that whenever there is a process of noun incorporation in a language it will involve 'identification of S and O' and whenever there is a jussive complement construction it is likely to involve 'identification of S and A'. (Although it must be pointed out that there can be alternative ways of dealing with jussives. In the case of a sentence like 'I told him to spear the fish' for instance, Dyirbal insists on the constituent sentence 'he speared the fish' being antipassivised before it is embedded, so that the deep A NP is in surface S function. In this way the Dyirbal requirement that the coreferential NP in a complement clause must be in S or O function is satisfied.)

Imperative is perhaps the classical example of a construction which must identify S and A, in every language. That is, a verb in imperative form must always select an (S or A) subject of a certain type – usually second-person pronoun. (But, over and above this, imperatives can also show some 'ergative' characteristics. For instance, Rigsby (1975: 349) mentions that in Nass-Gitksan transitive imperatives will delete the (second person pronominal) A NP while retaining a specification of O NP, but that intransitive imperatives must retain the S element – which is here second person singular nominative pronoun. In this language, although the same selectional restrictions apply to S and A, S behaves like O (and unlike A) is not being subject to deletion.)

5.1.5 Specification in tree structures. The obvious answer to our quandary concerning a choice between tree structures for transitive sentences:

(i) ACCUSATIVE or (ii) ERGATIVE

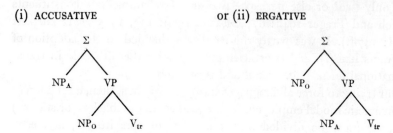

is of course not to group either NP with V_{tr}, that is, simply not to recognise a VP node. This gives us:

(v) in addition to (vi)

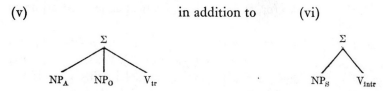

In terms of position on the tree, we can easily refer to NP_A and NP_S by

$\#\#NP\ X\ \#\#$ (indicating the leftmost NP on the tree)

or NP_O and NP_S by

$\#\#(X)NP\ V\ \#\#$ (indicating the NP that comes immediately before V)
Here $\#\#$ indicates sentence boundary and X any (non-null) sequence of constituents.

We could suggest using (i) for English, (ii) for Dyirbal and (v) for Yidiɲ. But if there really is a syntactic continuum linking these types – as the facts from a variety of languages (e.g. Dixon 1976a: 485ff.) indicate there is – then we would get languages on the 'threshold' between the Dyirbal and the Yidiɲ types for which we would not be able to decide between (ii) and (v); and so on. Plainly, one type of deep structure would have to be adopted as the universal base, and this could only be (v).

We have been forced to the conclusion that the question posed in 5.1.1, concerning a 'deep structure' choice between (i) and (ii), was misconceived. This question was formulated within the framework of constituent analysis that was largely begun by the post-Bloomfieldians

and then taken over by Chomsky and incorporated as the base component of transformational generative grammar. Early work on immediate constituent analysis often insisted that a construction would have 'two and only two' or else perhaps 'two or a few' immediate constituents (Bloch and Trager 1942: 67; Gleason 1969: 133, 1965: 141; Hockett 1958: 147ff.). It was partly this tradition that led to the adoption of diagrams like (i), and later attempts to justify the VP node in transformational terms (e.g. Lakoff and Ross 1966).

Our trying to force all languages into (i) or (ii) was, then, a function of the syntactic model employed. This specifies that each (deep or surface) sentence must be divided into a number of constituents, and each constituent then analysed into further constituents, and so on, until the sentence is reduced to its component morphemes. As part of the notion that analysis should be maximally structured – and proceed one step at a time – splits into two (or, at any rate, as few as possible) constituents are preferred.

It now appears that the ternary split of a sentence into NP_A, NP_O and V_{tr}, as in (v), must be substituted for (i) and/or (ii). We should beware, though, of merely amending a theoretical model in this way. If the 'preferred binary' condition was misconceived might there not be other inadequacies in a 'constituency tree' method of syntactic symbolisation? It will surely be worthwhile to examine other aspects of the model, in some detail.

A feature of tree descriptions is that they demand 'total accountability'. Any constituent that is recognised must be connected to SOME higher node. Thus, in the case of a subordinate clause we must decide whether it is immediately dominated by an NP node, or by Σ, or perhaps by VP. This can put us in mind of the discussion of (i) and (ii). We demanded in 5.1.1 that Yidiɲ be described in terms of one type of VP tree or the other, but then found the evidence was pretty equally balanced between (i) and (ii). What if some constituent could equally well be related to any of several nodes on a tree?

There are, in fact, many examples of this nature. There are strong arguments for some constituency groupings – thus in *A dog bit the great big man* all linguists would surely agree in relating together *the*, *great*, *big* and *man* (as an NP). Other groupings will have less strong justification, but will be accepted by a fair number of linguists – the majority of transformational grammars of English (not paying attention to a universal base which would be equally appropriate for languages at any

point on the 'accusative–ergative' continuum – 5.1.4) group *bit* and *the great big man* as a 'verb phrase'. But there are other constituents which it is difficult to know where to place. In a passive sentence *The great big man was bitten by a dog*, there are strong reasons for grouping *by* with *a dog*. There are, however, no really conclusive reasons for attaching *by a dog* to the VP node rather than to the Σ node, or vice versa. Those linguists who would say there is here a VP node, including the verb and also *by a dog*, would be likely to agree that the syntactic connection between verb and *by*-phrase is less strong (and certainly, of a different type) than the connection between verb and direct object in an active sentence. But the 'theory' does not allow us to be non-committal – the *by*-phrase must directly be related to VP, or to Σ, however arbitrary the decision may be.

The 'passive' example is given as a typical and fairly simple illustration of the point being made. Many others could be provided, from English or from other languages.

It could be argued that if there is no reason for attaching a certain constituent to any lower node then it is to be automatically linked to Σ. This can be a helpful convention (for resolving cases of difficulty) but it is not entirely satisfactory in that it would lump together (a) those constituents for which positive reasons can be given for their being dominated by Σ and by nothing else, and (b) those which could be attached at any of several places on the tree. That is, this solution would fail to observe a 'non-committal' category.

The discussion in 5.3.3 of whether subordinate clauses in Yidiɲ are embedded (attached to an NP node) or adjoined (attached to the Σ node) provides a further example of 'evenly balanced' evidence which must lead to an arbitrary decision qua tree structuring. This provides further Yidiɲ evidence against a conventional tree model.

A theoretical model should surely aim at providing maximum explanatory power on the basis of a minimum of internal complexity and specification within the model itself. Our discussion suggests that the 'immediate constituent'/'tree structure' model demands over-specification which sometimes requires arbitrary decisions. Having recognised a number of groupings of forms within any sentence we should surely specify the minimum of hierarchical ordering consistent with providing maximum explanation of those linguistic facts which are to be accounted for. To add further, unmotivated or scarcely motivated, connections between theoretical elements when these add little or nothing to the overall explanation is surely to weaken the theory.

It is important to note that saying 'a *by*-phrase belongs to a certain sentence' but not committing oneself to say whether it is linked to VP or to Σ or whatever is not 'being vague'. It is simply avoiding making an unnecessary and arbitrary decision.

Finally, we can point out that recent work on constituency trees attempts a homogeneous treatment of linguistic relations that are essentially quite different. One can do no better than go back to Sapir for an account of the different sorts of concepts and of grammatical processes that are involved in the synthesis of a simple sentence. Firstly, we can follow Sapir (1921: 24–41) in emphasising the centrality of 'word' (cf. 2.4) and 'sentence' as the main grammatical units of each language. Adapting Sapir's (1921: 82–119) remarks slightly we can then recognise three types of syntactic process. In brief and crude outline:

(a) WORD BUILDING PROCESSES, deriving a word stem from a root. The specification of number on nouns or aspect on verbs are typical examples e.g. the derivation of *horses* from the root *horse* in English or of the word stem *baga:li-n* 'spear-GOING' from root *baga-l* in Yidiɲ. Processes of this type synthesise a 'word' from its component elements (except for inflectional endings – if any – which are added under (c)).

(b) WORD GROUPING PROCESSES, modifying the meaning of a word through the attachment of other words. This maintains the same area of reference, but will provide for more exact specification within it. Examples from English are *fat old horses* from *horses* and *run slowly* from *run*. Processes of this type form a noun phrase (NP) or verb complex (VC) by adding modifier words to a head.

(c) SENTENCE BUILDING PROCESSES, taking groups of words – as synthesised by (b) – and relating them together, to create the description of a complete event. Inflections, clitics/particles, or just word order may be used to mark the type of relation that is involved. An example from English could involve putting the referential elements *fat old horses* and *run slowly* together in that order to form *fat old horses run slowly*. Processes of this type derive a sentence from NPs and VCs.

Plainly these processes are quite different from each other, both formally and semantically. An account of the internal organisation of a language stands to lose a good deal by treating the relation between the components of, say, *boys*, in the same way as that between the constituent words of *men ran*:

(vii-a)   (vii-b)

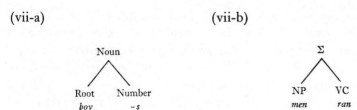

Although the nodes are of course labelled differently, the relations between the elements are dealt with in the same way (qua 'domination', 'constituency', etc.) in standard tree theory. Treating language in this way – as if it were a purely algebraic-type system, with simply distributional properties – obscures the various types of semantic structures, morphophonological rules, and so on, which effectively define 'human language' (and are remarkably recurrent across the whole spectrum of known languages).

5.1.6 Types of grammatical process. In the last section we argued against a homogeneous, distributional 'bricks-and-mortar' view of linguistic structure – that morpheme bricks are put together to make words, word bricks to make phrases and phrase bricks to make sentences (or, the other way round, that a sentence can be divided up into a sequence of phrases, a phrase into a sequence of words, and a word into a sequence of morphemes). Instead, we recognised three different types of semantic process involved in the synthesis of a sentence from the minimal elements of meaning:

(a) WORD BUILDING PROCESSES. These are based on a central formal element, a root. Various processes of semantic specification of the root may be realised by – again following Sapir's (1921: 61ff.) excellent classification – affixation, internal modification, reduplication, or accentual modification.

Processes of affixation in an agglutinative-type language will be likely to be amenable to a 'bricks and mortar' description. But in other types of language it is not always fruitful to attempt to 'segment a word into its component elements'. The proper procedure is to assign a phonological shape to the root, and then to specify how this shape is altered by the various morphological processes, paying attention to the different types of 'boundary' that must be recognised, and the various types of phonological rule (assimilation, apocope etc.) operating within and across them.

Each language will normally have a further word-building process of compounding (or composition) whereby two or more roots are combined together as the basis for a single word. Some languages can also mark semantic specification of a root by clitics, forms that cannot occur by themselves (and do not normally take stress) but are only loosely bound phonologically to a lexical word. The specification of an NP head in English as definite/indefinite – something that is shown by affixation, internal modification etc. in other languages – falls at least in part into this category (and the clitics *the*, *a* are represented as separate words in the orthography).

Word building processes in Yidiɲ have been described quite exhaustively, though informally, in chapter 3. There would be no advantage in repeating this discussion in the present chapter.

(b) WORD GROUPING PROCESSES. This is again an 'endocentric' process, based on noun or verb as 'head' element. Other words are adjoined to this – adjectives or adverbs of various types – and serve to modify the reference of the head. It is important to note that there are fundamental differences between morphological modification, under (a), and syntactic modification, under (b). A word-building process will always operate in terms of closed systems – for instance: singular, dual or plural – whereas in word grouping any one of an open class of adjectives (including, say, any number adjective) may modify a noun. Morphological processes are often (although not invariably) obligatory – thus, every count noun in English must be specified for number and definacy; the modification of a noun by an adjective, or of a verb by an adverb, is in contrast always a matter of choice.

Grouping of words into phrases is often marked simply by their contiguity within a sentence, perhaps in a fixed order (say, modifiers always preceding head) or perhaps in any order so long as all the words occur in one block. But where a sentence building process uses inflectional marking – and the inflection goes on to every word in a phrasal grouping – the words can (in some languages) be freely scatterable, their connection being shown by the recurring inflection.

The grouping of words is always an incremental, agglutinative-type process (the occurrence of external sandhi in some languages is of a quite different order from internal modification). Thus a 'bricks-and-mortar' approach is likely to be most applicable in this area – a phrase can be analysed into its constituent words; or, looked at the other way round, the words can be put together to synthesise a phrase. Internal structuring within a phrase – [old [excitingly fast] trains] as against [[excitingly

fast] white trains] – can adequately be described through hierarchical tree diagramming (but see the comments at the end of 5.6.1).

We return to word grouping processes in Yidiɲ in 5.6.

(c) SENTENCE BUILDING PROCESSES. Taking 'word' and 'sentence' as the fundamental units of any language we have discussed (a) the morphological make-up of words, and (b) the grouping of words into syntactic units. Finally we need to describe the semantic structuring of sentences, in terms of the word-groups synthesised under (b). It is not, however, very useful to say that phrases are 'grouped together' to form sentences, using the terminology that we found appropriate for the grouping of words into phrases. Phrases are endocentric, each modifier being clearly related (directly or indirectly) to the head. Sentences, on the other hand, are exocentric, with each component bearing a relation to the whole (and with relations of government and so on holding between members) but without there being any central pivot.

We shall, in the next sections, consider the network of semantico-syntactic relations that go to make up a sentence, and suggest an appropriate symbolism in terms of which we may discuss the syntactic organisation of Yidiɲ.

5.1.7 A semantico-syntactic symbolism. We first distinguish the obligatory from the optional elements of a sentence. 'Subject', 'object' and 'verb' are regarded as universally obligatory not because they must necessarily occur in the surface structure of every sentence in every language, but because the speaker and hearer must have some understanding of the subject and verb – and object, if the verb is transitive – for the sentence to form a conceptual whole, with the potentiality of referring to some actual, possible or habitual event.

There are a number of apparent exceptions, but these are all quite easily accounted for. Thus, passives can frequently have the agent-phrase deleted; and on hearing *John was hit* one would surely not have any ideas about the deep subject. But there are semantic and syntactic reasons for regarding passives as derived intransitives, with the A NP having been taken out of the core to become a peripheral component (which can freely be deleted – see below). In this semantic view, a passive describes some state of an object; the cause of this state may optionally be specified e.g. *John was hit by Fred*.

A sentence like *It is raining*, which appears to have no semantically perceptible surface subject, can be related to an underlying sentence *Rain is falling* (or, more precisely, *Rain is* VERB-*ing*, where VERB is any item that can typically occur with *rain* as subject).

We can say that these obligatory elements comprise the CORE of the sentence; we will use square brackets to enclose the core. Using the abbreviatory letters for semantico-syntactic functions employed in chapter 4 we can characterise the two universal types of core, which we claim constitute the semantic basis of every human language, by:

(viii) [S V]

(ix) [A O V]

Here V indicates a verb. If it occurs in a core with two NP functives it must be a transitive verb, and in a core with just one functive the verb must be intransitive.

(viii) and (ix) should be regarded not as 'structures' or 'sequences' but simply as 'configurations' of elements. We adopt the convention whereby each position in (viii) and (ix) is associated with a certain element. The choice of convention is inconsequential – we could equally have chosen [A V O] or [O A V] or [V A O] etc. in place of (ix). With the choice shown in (ix) we will always know that, in $[NP_1\ NP_2\ V]$, NP_1 is the subject and NP_2 the object, and that, say, [(the) knife (the) shoot cut] represents the English sentence *The knife cut the shoot*.

What we are trying to represent with (viii) and (ix) is the semantico-syntactic relations between S and an intransitive verb, in the one case, and between A, O and a transitive verb, in the other. Note that in the latter case we do not have to relate A and O each to the verb ('subject-of' and 'object-of' respectively) or indeed attempt any other grouping – we simply note that a transitive sentence has a ternary core, and adopt a convention for representing its components.

A case can be made out for there existing a connection between each pair out of A, O and V. Thus – with, say, a verb of action like 'hit' – it is the referent of A who is responsible for some change in the state of the referent of O; the referent of A initiates an action described by V; the referent of O suffers in an activity referred to by V. (ix) is intended to subsume all of these relationships.

As we have already mentioned, languages employ a number of alternative means of marking the relations between A, O and V (and between S and V). Sometimes the verb involves affixes that cross-reference A, O and S. Or the non-verbal components may be marked by case inflections. Or the syntactic relations can be indicated solely by relative ordering in surface structure. None of these methods of realisation needs to be included in configurations (viii) and (ix); after all syntactic operations have been completed 'marking rules' will assign the appropriate realisations.

Languages can be classified into two types on the basis of the role of word order in their grammars. There are those like English which mark syntactic relations largely by word order; ordering is here quite strict, in keeping with its significant syntactic role. Then there are those languages which make other arrangements for showing syntactic relations; these can sometimes have quite strong word order preferences (as Yidiɲ does – 4.1.1, 4.1.9), but they are always PREFERENCES, of a different nature from the ordering RULES in English.

Since, from the point of view of relational syntax, we can adopt any convention for the arrangement of A, O and V in (ix), we might as well put the elements in a sequence that corresponds most closely to surface word order. A+O+V seems most appropriate for Yidiɲ and we have adopted it here. (Ideally, a universal convention should be adopted, to fit best with the ordering rules/preferences of most languages, taking account of both the types distinguished in the last paragraph.)

In addition to the obligatory core, any sentence may contain any of a number of optional constituents – things like 'dative NP' (or indirect object), locational qualifier, and so on. We refer to these as PERIPHERAL components. Generally speaking, any type of peripheral element may occur with either type of core (which is an additional reason for distinguishing periphery from core), subject of course to selectional restrictions, semantic plausibility, and the like. Thus in English peripheral components like *for Bill* or *to see what I can learn* or *into the Park* can occur equally with an intransitive or with a transitive core – for example, with *I'll go* and *I'll take the book*.

It could be argued that, in some languages at least, we should recognise a third type of core, involving subject (A), object (O) and indirect object, as in *I'll give the book to Mary*. We can argue against this for Yidiɲ by pointing out that whereas ergative (nominal) and accusative (pronominal) NPs occur only in transitive sentences, a dative NP can occur with a 'ditransitive verb' like *wiwi-n* 'give' and also with virtually any transitive or intransitive verb – see (352–6) in 4.1.6. We thus treat *wiwi-n* as a transitive verb, that will often (but need not always) involve a peripheral dative NP, just as we also have some intransitive verbs that display an identical preference (see 4.3.5).

But this is very much an open question. It may be that for some languages (and/or for some linguists) there would be sufficient reason to include one or two further types of core. Further work on a variety of languages will be required in order to resolve this point.

We must distinguish two sorts of peripheral component: syntactic and local. Local elements simply specify the place or direction, and do not add any information about the participants, the purpose or cause of the

activity, and so on. Syntactic elements typically refer to some further participant who is being involved in the chain of events (a beneficiary, for example).

We use ' : ' to introduce syntactic and ' ; ' for local peripheral elements. Thus:

(x) [*I go*]:*Bill*

could, with the appropriate marking conventions, represent *I'll go for Bill*, whereas

(xi) [*I go*];*London*

could indicate *I'll go to London*. We will also adopt the convention that syntactic elements are placed before local ones; thus

(xii) [*I go*]:*Bill*;*London*

could represent *I'll go to London for Bill*.

Subordinate clauses can be regarded as peripheral elements of the syntactic type. *I'll go to see Bill* would be represented by (again under the appropriate realisational conventions):

(xiii) [*I go*]:[*I Bill see*]

Note that under our conventions the leftmost core constituent is always the main clause of a sentence.

Conjunction can be shown simply by ' , '. Thus *I went and I saw Bill* would be

(xiv) [*I go*],[*I Bill see*]

whereas *John and Mary came* would be

(xv) [*John, Mary come*]

Note that we do not employ commas or any other punctuation to separate the basic elements within a core – that is, we write [A O V] and not [A, O, V]. Spaces seem sufficient demarcation here (so that any specific punctuation would be redundant). If there is any danger of confusing an orthographic word space with the spacing between core components, a symbol like ' = ' could be employed to separate the components and/or # to separate orthographic words within a phrase; thus [*snakes = dog#meat = eat*] to indicate *Snakes eat dog meat* (rather than **Snakes dog eat meat*).

Tense specification has been silently omitted from the examples quoted in this section. The treatment of tense in Yidiɲ, in terms of this model, will be found in 5.5.1.

To the basic representation of core and peripheral elements must be added (i) statements of coreferentiality constraints e.g. between main and

subordinate clauses; (ii) syntactic derivations (= transformations) which will remove elements from or put them into the core, or combine two cores into one; (iii) statements of the types of phrase that correspond to each core and peripheral element; (iv) selectional restrictions; and (v) marking conventions – the surface realisations of the syntactic relations (by inflections, word order, prepositions, etc.).

The semantico-syntactic symbolism that we have attempted here to outline, in fairly general terms, is put forward to assist our grammatical discussion of Yidiɲ in the remainder of this chapter. Study of this application of the model should provide some clarification concerning details of its possible organisation and utilisation.

5.1.8 Kinds of syntactic identification. We have suggested:

(viii) [S V]

(ix)   [A O V]

as universal representations of the semantic core for the two kinds of sentence that we believe occur in all human languages. Taken by itself, such a core is the basis for a 'simple sentence' (*John laughed*, or *Mary hit John*).

But speakers do not, of course, simply utter a string of simple sentences, with or without peripheral syntactic and local expansions. Each language has a technique of relating together two or more events – one as the reason for or as the natural result of another, one as happening simultaneously with another, one as sequentially following another, and so on. A speaker will also try to abbreviate the stream of words, cutting out repetitions and redundancies and generally attempting to conform to whatever aesthetic standards of 'style' are current for his language.

These two kinds of consideration give rise to principles of syntactic identification and deletion. For instance, a language may demand that a subordinate clause have an S or A NP that is coreferential with some NP in the main clause. This can be shown (using a, b, c, ... to refer to specific NPs, and X, Y, Z, ... for any non-null sequence of components) by:

(xvi) given [...]:[b X] there must be some a in the leftmost core such that a is coreferential with b.

To take another example, suppose that a language must obligatorily delete an NP in the second sentence of a coordination if it is identical to

an NP with the same syntactic function (S, A or O) in the preceding sentence. This could be shown (with V, W, ... indicating any verb):

(xvii) in [(X) a (Y) V] , [(Z) b (T) W]
        if (1) X and Z are either both present or both absent; and (2) Y and T are either both present or both absent; and (3) a = b, then b → ø

Constraints and rules of these and other types are narrowly syntactic – as opposed to the universal semantico-syntactic configurations (viii) and (ix) – and tend to be language-particular.

Although, as we noted in 5.1.4, Heath (1976) has suggested that an individual rule may have a 'typical form' – presumably determined by the semantic nature of the elements to which the rule refers – in most or all languages in which it occurs. The obvious example of imperative – imposing the same selectional restriction on S and A – has already been mentioned.

Some languages may have a majority of their constraints and rules referring to 'S or O'. This can be specified (cf. 5.1.7 and the discussion at the beginning of 5.1.5):

(xviii) [(X) a V]

that is, 'the NP next to V'. Other languages may make more syntactic reference to 'S or A', that is, 'a' in

(xix)   [a X]

in other words, the leftmost NP in a core configuration.

Languages that have been described as having an 'absolutive–ergative' underlying syntax would simply involve a large number of syntactic specifications of type (xviii) (although it is worth noting that every language of this kind also employs some specifications of type (xix)). Similarly, languages that have been characterised as strongly 'nominative–accusative' in their syntax will make major use of specification (xix). But, as we have already mentioned, there are many languages that lie on a continuum joining these two extremes, identifying S and A in some instances and S and O in others. Yidiɲ is of this type. In the following sections we set out the syntactic derivations, constraints and marking rules of Yidiɲ, working in terms of core-plus-peripheral configurations.

5.2 Basic syntactic configurations for Yidiɲ

5.2.1 Core elements. Working in terms of the symbolism described in 5.1.7, we recognise two universal core configurations:

(viii) [S V]

(ix) [A O V]

Here A refers to the agent of a transitive sentence and O to a transitive patient; S of course refers to an intransitive subject. V is a verb.

The distinction between 'intransitive' and 'transitive' constructions is an important one in Yidiɲ, for both deep and surface syntax (see 4.2.1). Any sentence whose leftmost core involves just two elements (a verb and one NP) is intransitive, while a core involving three elements (a verb and two NPs) is transitive.

Realisation rules differ for pronouns and nouns. For pronouns, the marked function is O, involving the accusative case -:ɲ ~ -ɲ (3.6.2–3). Thus, with X representing any non-null element and M(a) indicating the case marking of a:

(xx) in [X Pronoun V], M(Pronoun) = Accusative

In contrast, the marked nominal case is ergative, for A function:

(xxi) in [Nominal X V], M(Nominal) = Ergative

All other core occurrences of pronouns and nominals receive zero marking ('nominative' and 'absolutive' respectively). If we allow this specification to follow (xx) and (xxi), then, where [...a...] indicates 'any a in the core':

(xxii) in [...Pronoun/Nominal...], M(Pronoun/Nominal) = ø

We noted in 4.1.4 that there is in fact a hierarchy of syntactic marking, the extremes of which are defined by the behaviours of pronouns and nominals. In the middle region, human deictics bear both ergative and accusative marking (zero form being restricted to S function). We can take care of this simply by having BOTH (xx) and (xxi) apply in this case. The conventions then become:

(xx)′ in [X Pronoun/Human Deictic V],

M(Pronoun/Human Deictic) = Accusative

(xxi)′ in [Nominal/Human Deictic X V],

M(Nominal/Human Deictic) = Ergative

The definite inanimate deictic has an accusative form in free variation with the absolutive. This can be handled by extending (xx)′ to cover this

category, but making the convention optional in this case only; if it does not apply an extended version of (xxii) will naturally specify zero marking.

5.2.2   Peripheral elements. Yidiɲ has a symmetric set of peripheral elements: three syntactic functives – purposive, dative and causal – and three corresponding local forms – allative, locative and ablative. We use symbols a, b, c, ... to represent specific NPs and can append superscripts as follows:

+ 'to/in order to' elements – purposive and allative
− 'from/as a result of' elements – causal and ablative
$^{\textit{o}}$ unmarked elements – dative and locative

Generally, $^{\textit{o}}$ can be omitted and the symbol simply left with no superscript in this case. $^{\textit{o}}$ is used when abbreviating reference to several possibilities by means of the disjunctive slash / 'or'. Thus $a^{+/-/\textit{o}}$ indicates 'a^+ or a^- or a' (to use instead $a^{+/-/}$ might prove confusing).

Treating dative and locative as 'unmarked' can be justified both semantically and syntactically (see the discussion throughout chapter 4). The two cases are in fact semantically-conditioned alternants in a wideish range of constructions (4.1.8).

To summarise, the syntactic configuration of a simple sentence in Yidiɲ is:

(xxiii)   CORE   PERIPHERY

$$\left.\begin{array}{l}[\text{a V}]\\ [\text{b c V}]\end{array}\right\} :d^{+/-/\textit{o}};e^{+/-/\textit{o}}$$

where ':' introduces syntactic and ';' local peripheral elements.

It is an integral part of our universal hypothesis (5.1.7) that core elements are obligatory and peripherals optional. We can have both 'marked' local choices (i.e. allative and ablative simultaneously) but we cannot have the unmarked local choice co-occurring with a marked element (that is, we cannot have locative plus allative, **or** locative plus ablative). It is likely that an identical restriction holds between syntactic peripheral elements.

There are only four distinct nominal case markings for these six peripheral functions. Abbreviating by means of / 'or':

(xxiv) a. In $X;a^{+/\textit{o}}$, M(a) = locative(–allative)
       b. In $X:/;a^-$, M(a) = ablative(–causal)
       c. In $X:a^+$, M(a) = purposive
       d. In $X:a$, M(a) = dative $\sim$ locative

Thus, one inflection is used for the local functions 'locative' and 'alla-tive' with nominals (deictics have distinct forms – 3.7.2); and there is one nominal inflection covering both the syntactic function 'causal' and the local 'ablative' (here the inanimate deictics have different forms – 3.7.2).

For the unmarked syntactic peripheral function, either dative or locative case marking can be employed. The choice appears to be basic-ally determined by a hierarchy, as set out in 4.1.8 and 3.1.2. Thus, with nominals locative is both the sole realisation of local function ' ;a', and also an alternative realisation of syntactic function ' :a' (just as one case marking realises both ' :a⁻' and ' ;a⁻'). In the case of deictics, however, locative is restricted to the local function ' ;a' (and pronouns DO NOT HAVE locative – or any other local – case form).

Locative and dative are of course not always interchangeable. For a local function, ' ;a', only locative can be used. And we mentioned (4.1.8) that only dative has been encountered on the beneficiary of a verb of giving, irrespective of animacy, etc. The latter case can be dealt with in terms of the regular dative ~ locative alternation by saying that here the verb (by its semantic nature) demands a dative direct object. We are thus suggesting that the choice between dative and locative, as the realisation of ' :a', depends partly on the nature of the referent of this peripheral element and partly on the verb and its rules of government.

We can exemplify with representations for some of the sentences given in 4.1.7 and 4.1.6. For instance, the locative (= (374)):

(913) *ɲuniɲ bulmba: baḍa:daŋ / buriburi:ŋ*
　　　The old man brings you and leaves you in the camp
is

(xxv) [*buriburi ɲundu baḍa:da-n*]^{PRES}*;bulmba*

whereas a sentence involving ablative and allative NPs (= (375)),

(914) *buɲa ŋuɲu gadaŋ banam bulmba:*
　　　That woman is coming from the river to the camp
would be shown

(xxvi) [*ŋuɲu#buɲa gada-n*]^{PRES}*;bana⁻;bulmba⁺*

An imperative, (362), with deleted subject (see 5.5.1)

(915) *bugul duga:lin bundu:gu*
　　　Go and pull loya vines for dilly-bags!
has underlying

(xxvii) [ɲundu/ɲunduba bugul duga:li-n]^{IMP}:bundu$^+$

whereas a 'giving' construction, (352),

(916) ŋaɲḍi mayi galŋa:nda wiwi:na
     We must give some food to uncle

is simply

(xxviii) [ŋaɲḍi mayi wiwi-n]^{PURP}:galŋa

There is one further peripheral element that we have not so far mentioned – that marked by the syntactic case 'fear' (4.1.6, 4.6.1). This reveals an asymmetry – there is no corresponding local case (although, as mentioned in 3.3.2, the 'fear' inflection may be historically derived from comitative *-ḍir ~ -yir plus the regular locative inflection). The superscript ^{ap} (for 'apprehension') can be employed in this case. The basic configuration is now:

(xxiii)′ $\begin{bmatrix} a & V \\ b & c & V \end{bmatrix}$:d$^{+/-/\theta/\text{ap}}$;e$^{+/-/\theta}$

with an addition to the marking conventions:

(xxiv) e. In X:a^{ap}, M(a) = 'fear'

   Thus, (371) from 4.1.6

(917) yiŋu ḍaḍa yaṟŋgay/ guriliɲḍi:da
     This child is frightened of the wallaby

is represented by

(xxix) [yiŋu≠ḍaḍa yaṟŋga-n]^{PRES}:guriliy^{ap}

There is further discussion of the 'apprehensional' functive, and of the other six peripheral functives, when we come to deal with subordinate clauses in 5.3.

The ordering of words in surface structure is organised in terms of the 'preferences' outlined in 4.1.1–3 and 4.1.9. These specifications should presumably follow the marking conventions. Word order in Yidiɲ is at least partly determined by considerations of style, and ordering specifications should – ideally – relate to a 'stylistic interpretational' component of the grammar.

5.2.3 Antipassive construction. In putting forward the configuration for any antipassive construction we must take account of the following points (4.2.1–3):

(1) although derived from an underlying transitive simple sentence, an antipassive is intransitive;

(2) the deep A NP becomes surface S;

(3) the deep O NP takes dative or locative case (the choice being conditioned by a semantic hierarchy – 5.2.2, 4.1.8, 3.1.2).

We can accommodate these requirements by suggesting that the derivation of an antipassive takes the following form:

(xxx) ANTIPASSIVE DERIVATION (optional)

$$[a\ b\ V] \Rightarrow [a\ V^x]:b$$

where superscript ^{x} indicates that the verb is marked by the affix -:*ɖi-n*.

We are thus simply saying that the antipassive transformation takes the O NP out of the core and places it in the periphery – as the unmarked syntactic peripheral element. The originally ternary (and thus transitive) core loses a term, and is thus recognised as (derived) intransitive. The leftmost core NP (originally A function) is now naturally in S function, and the verb (in its -:*ɖi-n* marking) is identified as intransitive.

Taking specific examples (cf. (420) and (421) in 4.2.2):

(xxxi) [*waguɖa buɲa giba-l*]^{PAST}

(xxxii) [*ŋayu ɲundu giba-l*]^{PAST}

are realised as

(918) *waguɖaŋgu buɲa giba:l*   The man scratched the woman

(919) *ŋayu ɲuniɲ giba:l*   I scratched you

respectively. From (xxxi) and (xxxii) we can derive antipassives:

(xxxiii) [*waguɖa giba-l*^{x}]^{PAST}:*buɲa*

(xxxiv) [*ŋayu giba-l*^{x}]^{PAST}:*ɲundu*

which are realised as

(920) *wagu:ɖa giba:ɖiɲu buɲa:nda*   ⟨= (918)⟩

(921) *ŋayu ɲuni:nda giba:ɖiɲu*   ⟨= (919)⟩

The statement of antipassive in (xxx) perfectly explains all occurrences in main clauses. We shall need, in 5.3.1, to refine the statement of this derivation for 'marked' subordinate clauses.

5.2.4 Reflexives. If in a ternary deep core – involving a transitive verb – the two NP components are simply identical, then one of them is obligatorily deleted and the verb is marked by -:*ɖi-n* (effectively, as a record of this deletion). That is:

(xxxv) REFLEXIVE DERIVATION (obligatory)

$$[a\ a\ V] \Rightarrow [a\ V^x]$$

Again, a binary (intransitive) core is derived from an underlying transitive configuration; 'a' in the derived core thus has S function. (Note that we do not say WHICH of the original occurrences of 'a' is deleted – that in A or that in O function. There is no evidence on which to 'decide' which occurrence goes and which stays; a decision of this nature is totally unnecessary, in terms of the syntactic symbolism that is being employed.)

Thus (cf. (424) and (425) in 4.2.2):

(xxxvi) *[waguḍa waguḍa giba-l]*^{PAST}

(xxxvii) *[ŋayu ŋayu giba-l]*^{PAST}

must be obligatorily reduced to

(xxxviii) *[waguḍa giba-l^x]*^{PAST}

(xxxix) *[ŋayu giba-l^x]*^{PAST}

which are realised as

(922) *wagu:ḍa giba:ḍiɲu*   The man scratched himself (on purpose)

(923) *ŋayu giba:ḍiɲu*   I scratched myself (on purpose)

respectively.

Langacker and Munro (1975: 800) discuss 'a phenomenon found in many languages of the world, namely the extension of a reflexive morpheme to mark passive sense in addition to its basic reflexive use...'. Their explanation differs from ours in detail (including an 'unspecified' A element for passives, whereas we prefer 'movement out of the core' for O in an antipassive) but the facts they quote suggest that 'reflexive = passive' and 'reflexive = antipassive' are different instances of a single universal grammatical tendency. Reflexive – marking A and O as identical – may also be used to indicate that the member of the pair A, O which normally receives 'marked' case inflection is brought into S function, where it will receive unmarked inflection (and will be available as 'pivot' for various syntactic operations).

5.2.5 Sentence coordination. The principles of sentence coordination that we enunciated in 5.1.3 can be summarised (where CR(a, b) indicates that a and b are coreferential):

(xl)   COORDINATION CONDITION, and NP DELETION RULE
    If [...],[...] then it should be the case that

either (1) [a(X) V]^i, [b (Y) W]^j where CR(a,b) and a,b are
pronominal, and i = j
or (2) [(X) a V]^i,[(Y) b V]^j where CR(a,b) and a,b are non-
pronominal, and i = j
and then all or part of b can be deleted

The first condition indicates that the two conjoined clauses have coreferential S/A pronominal NPs, while the next line specifies coreferential S/O nominal NPs. i = j demands that the two clauses make
identical tense/mood choices (see 5.5.1).

It was stressed in 5.1.3 that these principles of coordination are best
regarded as 'preferences' rather than rules. If the conditions of (xl) are
met, then deletion of the NP in the second clause is always possible (so
this much is predictable and 'rule-worthy'). But the rule is not exclusive – the coreferential NP in the first clause could instead be deleted, or
an NP could be deleted – under semantic duress – in quite different
syntactic conditions.

5.2.6 Verb coordination. In 4.1.3 we discussed 'verb complexes',
involving two or more verbs; an overriding condition was that they
should agree in surface transitivity and in final inflection. We will now
deal with the various types in turn, and see whether they might be
derived by reduction of coordinated sentences.

Firstly, verb-plus-adverb combinations should surely not be derived
from coordinated clauses. An adverb does not have any independent
reference, but can only provide modification for a verbal concept
(e.g. 'do quickly,' 'try to do') exactly as an adjective modifies a noun.
We should thus NOT begin with separate sentences, one containing a verb
and one an adverb, and – coincidentally as it were – later conjoin them
(in the same way that we should not derive an adjective–noun syntagm
from two underlying clauses – 5.6.1).

Secondly, we do have occasional but quite grammatical instances of
two lexical verbs appearing together in one clause – for instance
(328–30) in 4.1.3. Here we can surely suggest biclausal origin:

(xli) VERB COORDINATION (optional)

$$[X\ V]^i\ (Y),\ [X\ W]^i\ (Y) \Rightarrow [X\ V\#W]^i\ (Y)$$

We specify that the two clauses make the same choice, i, from the
mood/tense system (that is, they are both imperative, both past tense,

or both present tense – 5.5.1). Note that our requirement that every-thing before the verb be identical across clauses automatically ensures that V and W have the same surface transitivity. The word boundary symbol $\#$ indicates that V and W make up one 'verb complex' that occupies one core position (cf. 5.1.6, 5.6.1).

For example, from (cf. (330))

(xlii) $[\textit{gaŋarA ŋayu baḍa-l}]^{\text{PAST}}$, $[\textit{gaŋarA ŋayu buga-n}]^{\text{PAST}}$

we get

(xliii) $[\textit{gaŋarA ŋayu baḍa-l}\#\textit{buga-n}]^{\text{PAST}}$

realised as

(924) *gaŋaraŋgu ŋaŋaŋ baḍa:l buga:ŋ*
     The alligator bit and ate me

Finally, there are a fair number of clauses which involve either *gali-n* 'go' or *gada-n* 'come' together with some other lexical verb. These should presumably be dealt with in the same way as (xlii). But there is a complication in the case of 'go' and 'come': the other verb will in such cases normally take the appropriate aspectual suffix (see 4.1.3, 3.8.6).

This brings up the whole question of the syntactic treatment of aspects. We believe that historically these morphemes derive from a syntactic association (3.8.6). Then why not treat aspect in this way within a synchronic syntax of Yidiŋ? From

(xliv) $[\text{X } \textit{gali-n/gada-n}]^{\text{i}}$, $[\text{X } \text{V}]^{\text{i}}$

the coordination rule, (xli) derives

(xlv) $[\text{X } \textit{gali-n/gada-n}\#\text{V}]^{\text{i}}$

We would need a rule roughly of the form:

(xlvi) ASPECT INCORPORATION (optional)
     $[...\textit{gali-n/gada-n}\#\text{V}] \Rightarrow [...(\textit{gali-n/gada-n})\#\text{V}^{\text{GO/COME}}]$

where the superscripts indicate a morphological process (5.1.6) applying to V.

Note that the free verb *gali-n/gada-n* would not normally be retained after the aspectual incorporation, although it could be – hence the parentheses in the right-hand side of the rule. And although a verb occurring in the same VC as *gali-n* or *gada-n* will normally receive aspectual specification this is not absolutely necessary – see 3.8.6; to accommodate this (xlvi) must be regarded as optional (although it would NEARLY ALWAYS be applied).

But the aspect incorporation rule, as we have stated it, will only deal with aspect on intransitive verbs (that is, verbs with the same surface transitivity as *gali-n* and *gada-n* themselves). Whereas in fact aspect occurs with all verbs, quite independently of transitivity. This complicates the situation. It seems on balance that a syntactic explanation of aspectual affixes – although according well with diachronic development – is more complex and cumbersome than it is revealing, within a synchronic grammar. We should perhaps leave it at (xlv) and then include an 'agreement rule' ensuring consistency between lexical and affixal specification of 'going' and 'coming' within any VC.

Note that it is POSSIBLE to derive aspect on transitive verbs from underlying *gali-n/gada-n#*V. We must first of all transitivise *gali-n/gada-n*, presumably in terms of the dummy verb INV (see 5.4). Thus

(xlvii) $[a \ gali\text{-}n]^i$ & $[a \ b \ INV]^i \Rightarrow [a \ b \ gali\text{-}n^{INV}]^i$

and then

(xlviii) $[a \ b \ gali\text{-}n^{INV}]^i$, $[a \ b \ V]^i \Rightarrow [a \ b \ gali\text{-}n^{INV}\#V]^i$

An optional INV would have to be specified in the aspect incorporation rule:

(xlvi)' $[\dots gali\text{-}n^{(INV)}/gada\text{-}n^{(INV)}\#V] \Rightarrow [\dots(gali\text{-}n^{(INV)}/gada\text{-}n^{(INV)})\#$
$$V^{GO/COME}]$$

Note that we do in fact need procedures for transitivising and intransitivising verbs in order to deal with coordinations that do not involve *gali-n* and *gada-n* – for instance (328) in 4.1.3.

5.2.7 NP coordination. For sentence coordination we require only one coreferential NP linking the two sentences (together with one of two schemes of syntactic identification). For verbal or nominal coordination everything in the sentence, bar the items to be conjoined, must be identical. Thus for NPs we can specify simply

$$[(X) \ a \ (Y)], \ [(X) \ b \ (Y)].$$

Yidiɲ does have an affix to mark coordination of nominal, pronominal and/or deictic elements – the derivational affix *-ba*; this appears to be restricted to occurrence with words that have human reference (3.3.6). Thus

(xlix) NP COORDINATION (optional)

$$[(X) \ a \ (Y)]^i, \ [(X) \ b \ (Y)]^i, \ \dots \Rightarrow [(X) \ a^{+ba}\# \ b^{+ba}\#\dots \ (Y)]^i$$

For instance, from

(l) [*waguḍa maḍinda-n*]^{PRES}, [*buɲa maḍinda-n*]^{PRES}

is derived the sentence (cf. (74) in 3.3.6):

(925) *waguḍaba buɲa:ba maḍi:ndaŋ*

   The man and the woman (and possibly other people, too) are
   walking uphill

And from (cf. (149) in 3.6.5):

(li) [*ɲundu gali-n*]^{PRES}, [*darŋgidarŋgi gali-n*]^{PRES}

we get

(926) *ɲundu:ba darŋgidarŋgi:ba galiŋ*

   You and the old woman (and possibly other people, too) are
   going

We can, however, run into difficulties with this 'coordination' approach to -*ba*
forms. A Yidiɲ sentence can have an NP which involves just one noun or
pronoun suffixed by -*ba*; for instance:

(927) *waguḍaba (/ɲundu:ba) galiŋ*

   The man (/you) and one or more other people are going

We could suggest an underlying structure of the type:

(lii)   [*waguḍa gali-n*]^{PRES}, [*gali-n*]^{PRES}, ...

that is, a coordination of cores, only the first of which has its S slot specified.
The alternative to using partly-specified cores in this way is to avoid
treating -*ba* in terms of coordination and instead simply say that (926)
corresponds to

(liii)   [SET *gali-n*]^{PRES}

where SET refers to a set of individuals, including the referents of *ɲundu* and
of *darŋgidarŋgi*; and so on. (Cf. Dixon 1972: 212–15.)

5.3 Subordination

5.3.1 Status of subordinate clauses. We can now turn to an examination of the appropriate representation for subordinate clauses. Let us
first consider the three commonest types, marked by verbal inflections
-*ɲu+nda*, -*na* and -*ɲu+m* (4.4–4.5), and then in 5.3.2 extend our
discussion to 'lest' clauses.

There is a three-way correspondence between subordinate clauses and
peripheral syntactic NPs, paralleling the correspondence already

recognised between syntactic and local NPs. This can all be summarised:

	FROM (+) (/as a result of)	UNMARKED (∅) ('at')	TO (−) (/in order to)
local NP	ablative *-mu* ~ *-m*	locative *-la* ~ *-:* ~ *-da*	allative *-la* ~ *-:* ~ *-da*
peripheral syntactic NP	causal *-mu* ~ *-m*	dative *-nda*	purposive *-gu*
subordinate clause	causal *-ɲu + m*	dative *-ɲu + nda*	purposive *-na*

The points of similarity – most of which have already been mentioned in chapters 3 and 4 – can be summarised:

MORPHOLOGICAL. All inflections in the 'from' column involve *-mu* ~ *-m* (in the case of a subordinate clause the second allomorph is added to the subordinate 'foundational' morpheme *-ɲu* – 3.8.4). Similarly, dative case is *-nda* and dative subordinate has *-nda* added to *-ɲu*.

SYNTACTIC. (1) The O NP in an antipassive subordinate clause may be placed in causal or purposive case (in place of the expected dative) if the subordinate clause is of the causal or purposive type, respectively (4.4.6, 4.5.4). With an antipassive dative subordinate clause the O NP must be in dative case.

(2) Dative and locative case are in hierarchically determined alternation, in a variety of constructions (4.1.8, 4.2.3).

(3) With locational qualifiers *-gu* has allative – not purposive – sense. And with some common nouns that have locus-type reference a *-gu* form can function allatively (in addition to the regular purposive use). See 3.4.1.

SEMANTIC. Correspondences of meaning are summarised in the column headings. On the right-hand or 'prospective' side of the table allative refers to motion TO a place, purposive case to action directed TO or FOR some end, and a purposive subordinate clause to an action that is undertaken IN ORDER THAT some further action may result. On the left-hand or 'retrospective' side, ablative refers to motion FROM a place, causal to some state or activity that was CAUSED BY some object, and causal subordinate to a state or activity that FOLLOWED ON FROM some earlier event.

In the middle column, locative indicates 'position AT' (i.e. neither motion to nor from). Dative case marks a 'passive' peripheral participant (in contrast to purposive, which indicates that someone or something is being actively involved in the chain of events – 4.1.6). Dative subordinate marks some action that is simultaneous with that of the main clause, with no temporal or logical connection of 'purpose' or 'cause' holding between them.

In chapter 4 we noted that there are two distinct varieties of each of the three types of subordinate clause. By far the commonest involves an NP that is coreferential with an NP in the main clause; and this 'common NP' must be in surface S or O function in both clauses. The relation between a coreferential subordinate clause and a main clause is similar to that between a peripheral syntactic NP and a main clause. Compare, for example (cf. (727–8)):

(928) purposive NP   (a) *ŋayu galiŋ gangulagu*
                                I'm going for a wallaby
       purposive clause (b) *ŋayu galiŋ gangulanda baga:ḏina*
                                I'm going to spear a wallaby

Just as a peripheral syntactic NP indicates a 'further participant', that is intimately connected with subject or object in the event described by the main clause, so a coreferential subordinate clause specifies an event that concerns one of the core participants (and is logically connected to the event of the main clause).

These similarities can be reflected by extending ' : ' to represent the relation between main and subordinate clauses. Underlying (928-a) we have, as established in 5.2.2,

(liv) $[\textit{ŋayu gali-n}]^{\text{PRES}}\textit{:gangulaA}^{+}$

We are now suggesting, for (928-b):

(lv) $[\textit{ŋayu gali-n}]^{\text{PRES}}\textit{:}[\textit{ŋayu gangulA baga-l}]^{+}$

Subscripts $^{+/-/\emptyset}$ will be applied to subordinate clauses, just as they are to syntactic and local peripheral NPs.

This gives the possible configuration for a Yidiɲ sentence:

(lvi) $[\text{a (b) V}]\text{:c}^{+/-/\emptyset/\text{ap}}\text{:}[\text{d (e) W}]^{+/-/\emptyset}\text{;f}^{+/-/\emptyset}$

Non-coreferential subordinate clauses, on the other hand, are less closely syntactically tied to the main clause. A non-coreferential clause often provides mainly temporal qualification of the event described by

the main clause ('I ate while he slept', 'The people came here after the camp had been submerged' and so on – 4.4.3, 4.4.7, 4.5.5). It has some similarities with local NPs, suggesting that we could employ ';' to represent the relation between a main clause and a non-coreferential subordinate clause. Thus

(lvii) $[\eta a\eta \dot{q}i\ wuna\text{-}n]^{\text{PRES}};bulmba;[\dot{q}imba\underline{r}al\ gada\text{-}n]$

is realised as (cf. (660) in 4.4.3):

(929) $\eta a\eta \dot{q}i\ wuna\eta\ bulmba:/\ \dot{q}imba\text{:}\underline{r}al\ gada\eta unda$
We stay in the house when a cyclone is coming

This enlarges the configurational possibilities to:

(lviii) $[a\ (b)\ V]\text{:}c^{+/-/\emptyset/\text{ap}}\text{:}[d\ (e)\ W]^{+/-/\emptyset}\text{;}f^{+/-/\emptyset}\text{;}[g\ (h)\ U]^{+/-/\emptyset}$

We are here maintaining that ':' (in X:Y) has a constant semantic import, as does ';' (in X;Y). The difference between [...];[...] and [...];a can be explained in terms of the different semantic statuses of 'Y' in each case. An NP refers to some object, that (usually) has a location in space; it is thus natural that ';' in [...];a should indicate locational qualification. In contrast, a clause refers to an event, which is normally of limited temporal extension; and ';' in [...];[...] indicates predominantly temporal qualification. (The same sort of reasoning applies to X:Y. If Y is an NP then ':' indicates a further participant drawn into the main event; whereas when Y is a clause ':' indicates a logical-type connection between two distinct events.)

A main clause must be specified for mood/tense – see the discussion in 5.5.1. Specifications of this sort are not available for subordinate clauses, which instead make a choice from the system $^{+/-/\phi}$ (purposive/causal/dative).

Subordinate clause type is, of course, shown by verbal inflection i.e.

(lix) $\ldots[\text{X V}]^{+/-/\emptyset}\ \ldots\ \Rightarrow\ \ldots[\text{X V}^{+/-/\emptyset}]\ldots$
The realisation rules are then straightforward:

(lx) $M(V^+)$ = purposive; $M(V^-)$ = causal subordinate; $M(V^\emptyset)$ = dative subordinate.

There are no syntactic restrictions on non-coreferential subordinate clauses. Subject to semantic plausibility, any core can occur following ';' in (lviii). A sentence involving a coreferential clause, on the other hand, must satisfy (cf. 4.4.1, 4.4.5, 4.5.3):

(lxi) COREFERENTIALITY CONSTRAINT

In every configuration of the form [...]:[...] there must be a, b such that [(X) a V](Y):[(Z) b W](T)
and CR(a,b)
All or part of a and/or b may then be deleted.

That is, there must be an NP that is in S or O surface function in the main clause, coreferential with an NP in S or O function in the subordinate clause. (lv) does not satisfy this constraint. The subordinate clause must be put into antipassive form (5.2.3):

(lxii) [*ŋayu gali-n*]^{PRES}:[*ŋayu baga-l^x*]$^+$:*gangulA*

This does satisfy (lxi). And, deleting the occurrence of *ŋayu* in the subordinate clause, the marking conventions yield (928-b).

We can now turn to the case marking on the O NP in an antipassive, when this is in a subordinate clause. In an antipassive main clause the O NP must take dative or locative inflection. But – as was mentioned above as proof of the syntactic connection between peripheral NPs and subordinate clauses – in a purposive/causal clause, purposive/causal case can be used in place of dative ∼ locative. Examples were given at (691–3) in 4.4.6 and (730, 732–5) in 4.5.4.

The standard statement of antipassive – (xxx) in 5.2.3 – must be augmented by

(lxiii) ANTIPASSIVE DERIVATION IN SUBORDINATE CLAUSE (optional)
$\quad$ X:[a b V]$^{+/-}$ ⇒ X:[a V^x]$^{+/-}$:b$^{(+/-)}$

This indicates that if the subordinate clause is marked by $^+$ or $^-$, a peripheral NP (extracted from the subordinate core by the antipassive derivation) can have the same marking. The superscripts to b are placed in parentheses since the regular unmarked dative ∼ locative can still be used, as an alternative to purposive/causal.

Thus, applying the transformation (lxiii) to (lv) we obtain:

(lxiv) [*ŋayu gali-n*]^{PRES}:[*ŋayu baga-l^x*]$^+$:*gangulA$^+$*

which is realised as

(930) *ŋayu galiŋ gangulagu baga:ḍina* ⟨= (928-b)⟩

as an alternative to (928-b).

(lxiii) could be written in such a way that it applies equally to dative as well as to purposive and causal clauses. That is:

(lxiii)′ X: [a b V]$^{+/-/\emptyset}$ ⇒ X: [a V^x]$^{+/-/\emptyset}$: b$^{(+/-/\emptyset)}$

In the unmarked dative case the two alternatives simply coincide ($b^o = b$). Whether to write the rule in the maximally general way – applying to ALL types of subordinate clause – as in (lxiii)', or whether to restrict it to non-null applications, as in (lxiii), is a theoretical issue over which it is unnecessary to commit ourselves here.

No sentence has been encountered with all four types of peripheral component allowed by (lviii) – that is, peripheral syntactic NP, local NP, coreferential subordinate clause and non-coreferential subordinate clause. It is likely, though, that such a combination is potentially allowable (there is certainly no obvious restriction that we could impose). A sentence may have both $+$ and $-$ values of any NP category (but, generally, not both ^{o} and $+$ or $-$). This restriction appears not to apply in the case of subordinate clauses – (683) in 4.4.5 involved both dative and causal coreferential subordinate clauses.

Although the extremes of 'syntactic' and 'local' relations are clear enough, there is a considerable middle ground in which it is not always possible to decide whether a relation of type ':' or type ';' is involved. This fuzziness applies equally to peripheral NPs, and to subordinate clauses. Thus in *ŋayu galiŋ bulmba:gu* 'I'm going to the camp', *bulmba* could be intended as an ad hoc place name (merely indicating the focus of movement) or as an indirect object ('I'm going to [build/clear/etc.] the camp'). (See 3.4.1 for the use of *-gu* as an allative marker with nouns like *bulmba*.) Similarly, subordinate clauses can sometimes be amenable either to an NP-relative (i.e. ':'-type) or to a T-relative (';'-type) interpretation – 4.4.3.

5.3.2 'Lest' clauses. Most examples of 'lest' subordinate clauses (4.6) follow exactly the pattern of dative, purposive and causal subordinates. The majority of instances show an NP coreferential with the NP in the main clause; the few 'fear' examples that escape coreferentiality appear to have largely local impact – as (757–8) in 4.6.2. This suggests extending the apprehensional marking [ap] – adopted in 5.2.2 for 'fear' NPs – to cover both types of 'lest' clause. The full configurational pattern is now

(lxv) $[a (b) V]:c^{+/-/o/ap}:[d (e) W]^{+/-/o/ap};f^{+/-/o};[g (h) U]^{+/-/o/ap}$

The only assymetry is that [ap] does not occur in the peripheral local category (';f').

Apprehensional [ap] marks both NPs and subordinate clauses: it has a general sense of 'undesirableness' (something or some event that is likely to affect the status quo in some unwelcome way). Although

syntactically parallel to $+/-/\phi$, ^{ap} is thus semantically quite different from the 'to/from/at' system, involving as it does a value judgement of desirability (and carrying strong emotional overtones).

'Lest' clauses of the coreferential type insist that the common NP be in S or O function in the subordinate clause, but allow wider possibilities in the main clause. Corresponding to (lxi) we can formulate

(lxvi) 'LEST' COREFERENTIALITY CONSTRAINT

> In every configuration involving ...:[...]^{ap} there must be some a,b such that ...a...:[(X) b V]^{ap} and CR(a,b)
> Then all or part of a and/or b can be deleted.

Here ...a... indicates any NP in any part of the core or periphery preceding :[...]^{ap}. The verb of the subordinate clause bears the 'lest' inflection -*nḍi* ~ -*lḍi* ~ -*ṛḍi*, and then a case ending agreeing with the coreferential NP in the main clause ('a'). Thus

(lxvii) 'LEST' MARKING

> If ...a...:[(X) b V]^{ap} and CR(a,b)
> then [(X) b V]^{ap} → [(X) b V$^{ap+M(a)}$]

We mentioned in 4.6.2 that 'lest' subordinate clauses are not common, and that the great majority of examples involve the coreferential NP in S/O function in main as well as in subordinate clauses. Examples where it was in ergative or dative case in the main clause (this inflection then going on to the 'lest' verb) have been encountered spontaneously, and it has been possible to elicit further instances involving these cases. The writer has not, however, been successful in eliciting any other case with 'lest' verbs. Note that ergative and dative are the only non-zero core case, and the 'unmarked' peripheral syntactic case respectively; we should expect them to be the most likely candidates for the marking of subordinate clauses.

There are a number of other common types of main-plus-subordinate combination. But they appear not to involve any significant generalisations and can simply be listed, as frequently-occurring construction types.

Thus, in 4.6.3 we mentioned that a coreferential 'lest' clause will often have a second coreferential NP – this will be in 'fear' function qua the main clause and will fill the A slot in the subordinate clause. That is:

(lxviii) [(X) a V]: b^{ap}: [c d W]^{ap}

> with CR(a, d) and also CR(b, c)
> Then c will frequently be deleted

Another sentence type that must simply be mentioned was described in 4.5.5. Here a purposive clause of the 'non-coreferential type' has O NP identical to a purposive NP in the main clause. That is:

(lxix)   [(X) a V]: b$^+$; [c d W]$^+$
　　　　with CR(b, d)
　　　　Then d will frequently be deleted

These sentence-types illustrate the attraction that exists between NPs and clauses with the same 'value' from the system $^{+/-/\emptyset/\mathrm{ap}}$. The synctactic nature of each individual association depends on the semantic nature of the relationships involved and on extralinguistic plausibility (see the discussion in 4.6.3).

5.3.3 'Embedded' versus 'adjoined' clauses.

Many of the instances of dative and causal subordinate clauses correspond to 'relative clauses' in languages such as English – 'I hit the woman who was yawning', 'I went and saw the rock that had been split', and so on. Purposive subordinates, on the other hand, most often correspond semantically to complement clauses – 'I'm going to spear a wallaby', and so on. But these three types of clause in Yidiɲ do seem to be syntactically parallel, and they demand to be treated and named in the same way.

The solution we have adopted is not to commit ourselves by names such as 'relative clause' or 'complement' (which might be apt for certain types but inappropriate for others) but simply to talk of dative, purposive and causal SUBORDINATE CLAUSES. In terms of our syntactic symbolism a subordinate clause belongs in the periphery of a sentence and bears the same type of syntactic relation to the main core as does a peripheral NP in syntactic case.

In an important recent article Hale (1976b) has discussed the syntactic status of 'relative clauses' in a number of Australian languages (Hale's use of the term 'relative clause' corresponds roughly to 'subordinate clause' in the present discussion); it will be instructive to see how Hale's remarks and criteria apply to Yidiɲ.

Hale distinguishes 'embedded' relative clauses – which are dominated by an NP node, as in (lxx) – from 'adjoined' relative clauses – which are directly related to the main clause Σ, as in (lxxi).

(lxx) 'EMBEDDED' CLAUSES   (lxxi) 'ADJOINED' CLAUSES

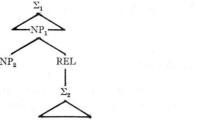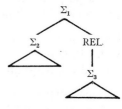

He believes that in Walbiri, for instance, relative clauses are entirely of the adjoined variety, whereas Kaititj could be said to have relative clauses that are adjoined at the level of deep structure but are – through the operation of an 'attraction rule' – embedded in surface structure. Hale suggests that Australian languages may originally have had just adjoined clauses and that the Kaititj attraction rule is a later historical development; he also considers it likely that the process may in some languages have gone further, so that relative clauses are now embedded in deep structure.

Hale indicates a number of criteria which can be used to distinguish the two kinds of relative clause:

(1) POSITION. An embedded clause will often occur mid-way through the main clause, next to the main clause NP which it is qualifying. An adjoined clause, on the other hand, will normally be found on the margins of the sentence 'and it has been widely observed that, in languages which make extensive use of the adjoined relative, when the subordinate clause precedes the main clause, it is terminated with a characteristic falling–rising intonation and followed almost invariably by a pause; but when the main clause precedes the subordinate clause, the intonation over both clauses is more often falling, and the pause between them, if any, is brief' (Hale 1976b: 78).

(2) COREFERENTIALITY AND CASE-MARKING. An embedded clause will always have some NP coreferential with an NP in the main clause (that is, with NP_2 in (lxx)); but adjoined relatives may only sometimes feature a coreferential NP.

The verb of an embedded clause will often show 'case agreement' with the coreferential NP in the main clause; this is less likely to be the case for adjoined relative clauses.

(3) SEMANTIC INTERPRETATION. An embedded clause will normally 'make

more determinate or...supply additional information about an argument [NP] in the main clause' – Hale calls this the 'NP-relative interpretation'. But an adjoined clause may have an NP-relative and/or a
T-relative interpretation, the latter specifying 'the temporal setting of
the event depicted in the main clause, or [making] a subsidiary comment
holding at the time specified in the main clause' (Hale 1976b: 79).

We can now see how the facts of Yidiɲ, as set out in 4.4–6, satisfy
these criteria:

(1) POSITION. Hale's description of the placing of an adjoined relative
clause exactly corresponds to the facts in Yidiɲ. A subordinate clause
never intervenes between main clause constituents. It is sometimes
preposed, and then always constitutes a separate intonation group; it is
most frequently postposed and then can fall into the main clause's
ntonation group, or else form a distinct intonational unit of its own.

(2) COREFERENTIALITY AND CASE MARKING. 85 % or so of subordinate
clauses in Yidiɲ do have an NP coreferential with some element of the main
clause, and there is then a strict 'coreferentiality constraint' – the common
NP must be in S/O function in each clause. This would appear to favour an
'embedded' interpretation in these cases (but it would, presumably,
still be appropriate to treat non-coreferential clauses as 'adjoined').

The question of case concord cannot be answered for Yidiɲ. The coreferential NP must be in S or O function in the main clause, which is
marked by absolutive case. If there were case marking on the subordinate verb, it would have zero realisation.

(3) SEMANTIC INTERPRETATION. All of the coreferential clauses can be
given an NP-relative interpretation, but some can also be understood in
a T-relative sense. Non-coreferential clauses, on the other hand, are all
or almost all restricted to T-relative interpretation.

The evidence appears to be split almost equally between the 'embedded' and 'adjoined' alternatives. 85 % of subordinate clauses behave
syntactically and semantically according to the 'embedded' pattern
(although there is a significant minority of 15 % which do not). But the
positioning of all subordinate clauses suggests an 'adjoined' interpretation. As with the choice between 'accusative' and 'ergative' deep
structures, in 5.1.1–4, the data in Yidiɲ appears pretty equally poised
between these two, quite distinct, syntactic alternatives.

And extending our discussion to cover 'lest' clauses does not help to
resolve things. 'Lest' clauses are mostly coreferential (but again, there is

a significant minority which are not) and they DO agree in case with a coreferential NP in the main clause – new evidence for 'embedded' status. But they must always be positioned on the margins of the sentence – in (751) of 4.6.2 for instance *ḍuŋgaṇḍiŋgu* 'run-LEST-ERG' can NOT be placed next to the ergative A NP, before the main verb.

Plainly, we want to avoid making what would have to be a pretty arbitrary decision between representing subordinate clauses in Yidiɲ according to (lxx) or to (lxxi). Note also Hale's (1976b: 86) remarks that while his discussion implies 'that the distinction between the NP-relative and T-relative interpretations is a discrete and clear-cut one... it is important not to accept this as an established fact'. Often a Yidiɲ sentence could receive either interpretation, and sometimes it seems that there would in effect be no pragmatic difference – cf. (661–2) in 4.4.3.

The necessity of making a choice between (lxx) and (lxxi) is one further argument against a tree-diagram approach to sentence structure. The requirement of maximal hierarchical structuring necessitates a subordinate Σ being attached to NP, if there appear to be syntactic reasons for this. (Further, the implicit requirement that surface ordering should be inferrable from the order of elements in a tree structure necessitates a treatment like (lxx), in the case of a language such as English.)

The syntactic symbolism we have adopted limits itself to a minimal specification of hierarchical inclusion; and it attempts a representation simply of abstract syntactic relations between the components of a sentence, paying no attention at all to word ordering (which is held to be a surface realisational matter, on a level with the specification of allophony). We do not have forced upon us a choice between (lxx) and (lxxi). It is instead likely that every type of subordinate clause (certainly in every Australian language with which the writer is familiar, including Dyirbal, where relative clauses are – in terms of Hale's criteria – clearly of the embedded variety; see Dixon 1972: 99–105, 176–9, 1976a: 3–6) can be adequately represented by a configurational scheme similar to (lxv).

With the symbolism we are using every type of subordinate clause will be shown as an element on the periphery of the main clause. Language-specific constraints will detail coreferential and other restrictions. The semantic commentary that must be provided for each grammar will explain the effect of relations like ':' and ';' in specific instances. Marking conventions will assign inflections, deal with concord and

specify syntactically-significant ordering restrictions. Other types of word order preference will be described in later realisational statements.

There is in Yidiɲ a certain 'fuzziness', with some clauses falling partway between the 'unambiguously NP-relative' and 'plainly T-relative' extremes. But this is treated simply as an alternation between ':' and ';' (rather than between tree structures of markedly different types) and is paralleled by a ':'/';' fuzziness between some types of syntactic and local peripheral NPs.

Dixon (1972: 176–9, 156–60, 112–13) describes a number of types of subordinate clause in Dyirbal: (i) Imperfective and perfective 'relative clauses', whose S/O NP has to be coreferential with some NP in the main clause; the clause was treated as embedded onto this main clause NP node, the subordinate verb agreeing with the NP in case; (ii) 'Purposive' favourite constructions, which must have their S/O NP coreferential with the S/O NP of the main clause; these were treated as complements, attached directly to the main Σ node; (iii) 'Lest' clauses – the syntax of these is not fully understood but it appears that they must have an S/O NP coreferential with some NP in the main clause; a verb in 'lest' inflection can be followed by (at least) the dative case inflection.

As these types of subordinate clause were described, in terms of traditional tree structures, they appear rather different from the subordinate clauses in Yidiɲ. Yet, if we adopt for Dyirbal the configurational symbolism explained in 5.1.7, the differences appear minimal. In both languages – always or almost always in Dyirbal, and in six out of seven instances for Yidiɲ – a subordinate clause must have its S/O NP coreferential with some NP, X, in the main clause. The functions allowed to X can be summarised:

DYIRBAL		YIDIɲ	
TYPE OF SUBORDINATE CLAUSE	FUNCTION OF X IN MAIN CLAUSE	TYPE OF SUBORDINATE CLAUSE	FUNCTION OF X IN MAIN CLAUSE
purposive	S/O	purposive	S/O
imperfective	any	dative	S/O
perfective	any	causal	S/O
'lest'	any(?)	'lest'	any

It may even be that there is a (quasi-universal?) hierarchy involved here (similar to the hierarchy employed by Silverstein to account for the occurrence of ergative and accusative case marking – 4.1.4) with Dyirbal and Yidiɲ differing simply in where the division between 'S/O' and 'any' is drawn on this hierarchy. (Further work would be needed to check whether there is any

basis for this comment, which is here a fairly free speculation from the data of two languages.)

The differences between subordinate clauses in Yidiɲ and Dyirbal are, then, differences of degree rather than of type. There are four kinds of subordinate clause in each language: purposive and 'lest' have apparently identical meanings but causal ('as a result of') differs substantially from 'perfective' ('which HAD happened earlier').

Although both Dyirbal and Yidiɲ show 'preferences' of word order, sequence carries no syntactic load in either language, and deviations from the norm occur quite freely. In Dyirbal texts relative clauses occur about as often in the middle of the main clause – normally, immediately following the co-referential NP – and sentence-finally. Purposive clauses normally occur after the main clause but they can occur before it, or part-way through. Effectively, all possibilities are open in each case in Dyirbal (and there can be at best statistical justification for a division between embedded (imperfective and perfective) as against adjoined (purposive) types.) There is here a significant difference from Yidiɲ, where subordinate clauses must precede or (more often) follow the main clause. But in each language all types of subordinate clause seem pretty comparable, in this as in other respects.

5.4 Comitatives and instrumentals

5.4.1 The dummy verb INV.

Every sentence has an obligatory core, of type (viii) or (ix). In making this claim we are suggesting that every language classifies events into two types: those in which an action involves a single person or thing (as in *The boy runs, The girl cries, The bough breaks*) and those in which something is transmitted from one person or thing to another (as in *The girl slaps the boy, The man hears the woman, The woman tells the man*). But although a rough first division of events into single-argument and double-argument does appear to be a universal feature of human languages, this by no means satisfies all the special semantic demands of particular classes of verbs.

For instance, 'cry, sob, weep' is normally classified as intransitive – that is, it involves a core of type (viii): [S V]. But in the majority of instances there will be a reason for someone crying (there need not, in the same way, be a reason for anyone coughing, or running, or even speaking). Typically, we might say 'the woman is crying over her husband' (he might be ill or unaccountably absent or unfaithful or whatever). Here there is the core [*the woman cry*] and in addition a relation joining 'the woman' and '(her) husband'.

Then there is a set of verbs that describe an actor affecting a patient

through the medium of some tool or weapon (*The man hit the wallaby with a stick*, or *The girl swept the camp with a broom*). Here the core will specify the two obligatory constituents – as in [*the man   the wallaby   hit*] – but the instrument which, although it need not always be obligatorily specified in surface structure, is an integral component of the event, cannot be dealt with within the core. (Nor is it obviously covered by the peripheral relations we have recognised for Yidiɲ.) We have, effectively, a further relation connecting 'the man' and 'a stick'.

There is a semantically natural class of 'affect' verbs which refer to actions that always require an instrument – see 4.2.5 (and also Dixon 1968: 331–45, 1971). But odd verbs from other semantic classes can also take an instrument – the examples given in 4.3.2 included *look with one eye, feed with the breast* and *buy with money*.

As a third example we can mention the case of some core (or peripheral) participant having someone or something with him, which will then necessarily be directly or indirectly involved in the event. Thus, say, *The man went with the girl*. Here, in addition to the core – [*the man   go*] – we have a relation between 'the man' and 'the girl'. (This type of comitative relationship can apply to almost any participant in any type of action.)

Fourthly, we can have a variant on the comitative. Rather than 'X does V with Y', we could have 'X ensures that Y does V': for instance *The man gets the boy up* (i.e. helps him into a standing position). The basic core description of this action is plainly [*the boy   get up*]; but we have also a second participant 'controlling' the actor in this event. There is an additional relation between 'the man' and 'the boy'.

The examples given have dealt with four quite different cases where the core/periphery configuration cannot fully specify all relevant aspects of an event. Yidiɲ appears to treat these through a single syntactic device. We will say that in each case an additional core specification is invoked, with a dummy verb INV[olve]. The full configurations for our sample sentences are then:

(lxxii)
   a. *The woman cried for her husband* – [*the woman   cry*] and [*the woman   (her) husband   INV*]
   b. *The man hit the wallaby with a stick* – [*the man   the wallaby   hit*] and [*the man   a stick   INV*]
   c. *The man went with the girl* – [*the man   go*] and [*the man   the girl   INV*]
   d. *The man gets the boy up* – [*the boy   get up*] and [*the man   the boy   INV*]

Now Yidiɲ does not have, on the surface, any 'purely relational' verbs, like English *have, become, make (cause to do), be* and *do*. Every item that can take verbal inflections has a fairly concrete reference to some actual event (we are here leaving aside the set of five adverbial modifiers – 4.1.3). Corresponding to cases where languages like English employ relational verbs, Yidiɲ – like most Australian languages – uses verbal or nominal derivational affixes, and so on. It is not surprising, in view of this typological characteristic, that INV cannot be realised as a distinct word in surface structure. But the language has a variety of means for syntactically exploiting the INV core, and thus ensuring some sort of morphological–syntactic record of this deep relation. These will be described in the next sections.

The major reason for our recognising INV in this range of uses is to explain the verbal derivational affix *-ŋa-l* ($\sim$ *-maŋa-l*) – 4.3. INV also serves to link together nominal comitative and verbal comitative constructions; verbal and nominal instrumental constructions; the dative sense of *-ŋa-l* and intransitive sentences with a dative NP; and so on. In each case we have two sentences with the same meaning that demand to be related to a single underlying structure: this is achieved by use of INV.

We recognise six distinct subtypes of INV, corresponding exactly to the senses of *-ŋa-l* dealt with in 4.3.3–7. Each is marked by a superscript:

INV^{com} = 'comitative'	INV^{dat} = 'dative'
INV^{inst} = 'instrumental'	INV^{loc} = 'locative'
INV^{fear} = 'fear'	INV^{cont} = 'controlling'

The verbal interpretations are identical, but for INV^{cont}. Nominal realisations are, however, quite different for the two major 'comitative' and 'instrumental' senses, and here we must always be careful to specify the appropriate superscript.

We have not indicated the nature of the relationship between the 'lexical verb core' and the 'INV core' in (lxxii). Presumably we could employ one of the established syntactic means for linking cores – ',' or ':' or even ';'. Alternatively, we could invoke some new symbolism for an INV core. But while there is syntactic reason for recognising a transitive core containing INV – inasmuch as this effectively serves to derive transitive from intransitive lexical-verb configurations – there is no strong reason for choosing any one of these three (or four) linking alternatives over the others. In each case a single

'blended' core is derived from the pair shown in (lxxii), or else the INV core is simply deleted. The coordinate and subordinate coreferentiality constraints do not apply per se to INV cores (it could of course be argued that INV incorporation and deletion PRECEDE the application of these constraints). It would not necessarily be wrong to employ ':' or ',' (or ';'). But, mainly to avoid what would be an arbitrary and unmotivated decision between these, we prefer to use a new symbol, ' & ', to link lexical-verb and INV cores, in each line of (lxxii).

5.4.2   Verbal comitatives. In discussing an event like 'The man went out with the girl' we first recognised a regular intransitive core [*the man go*]^{PAST}, as in 'The man went'. But there is also a relation between 'the man' and 'the girl' and we used the dummy verb INV to represent this within a subsidiary core [*the man   the girl* INV]. In terms of the syntactic symbolism we have been using for Yidiɲ we thus have (reverting now to Yidiɲ lexical forms):

(lxxiii) [*waguḍa gali-n*]^{PAST} & [*waguḍa yabuṟ U* INV]

But INV, representing an abstract relation, cannot be realised as a surface verb in Yidiɲ. There is in fact a syntactic derivation:

(lxxiv) INV INCORPORATION

$$[\text{a V}]^i \ \& \ [\text{a b INV}] \Rightarrow [\text{a b V}^{\text{INV}}]^i$$

where INV bears any superscript excepting ^{cont}

That is, from an intransitive core containing a lexical verb, V, and a transitive core involving INV – where the two cores have the same leftmost argument – is derived a transitive core based on the lexical verb. INV is realised as an affix, *-ŋa-l* ~ *-maŋa-l* (3.8.5) to this V. Note that only the lexical core is specified for tense/mood, here shown by 'i' – see 5.5.1.

Thus from (lxxiii), INV INCORPORATION forms:

(lxxv) [*waguḍa yabuṟ U gali-n*^{INV}]^{PAST}

which is realised, by the marking conventions of 5.2.1, as:

(931) *waguḍaŋgu yabu:ṟ   galiŋalɲu*
       man-ERG   girl-ABS   go-COMIT-PAST
       The man went with the girl (= The man took the girl)

We have thus explained the transitive nature of *-ŋa-l* verbs through a transitive deep core involving the dummy verb INV. The important point to note about INV INCORPORATION is that it demands that the

core containing the lexical verb be intransitive (that is, it must involve just one NP argument). If we have an underlying configuration:

(lxxvi) $[a \; c \; V]^i$ & $[a \; b \; INV]$

whether or not $c = b$, there is no mechanism for deriving a simple core with INV as affix to V. What we must do, in this case, is derive the antipassive form of the transitive lexical-verb core:

(lxxvii) $[a \; V^x]^i{:}c$ & $[a \; b \; INV]$

and INV INCORPORATION can then apply quite normally, giving

(lxxviii) $[a \; b \; V^{x+INV}]^i{:}c$

This was exemplified in (618–19) of 4.3.8. From:

(lxxix) $[bama \; \eta ayu \; wawa\text{-}l]^{PAST}$ & $[bama \; wa\eta al \; INV]$

antipassive derives:

(lxxx) $[bama \; wawa\text{-}l^x]^{PAST}{:}\eta ayu$ & $[bama \; wa\eta al \; INV]$

and then INV INCORPORATION yields:

(lxxxi) $[bama \; wa\eta al \; wawa\text{-}l^{x+INV}]^{PAST}{:}\eta ayu$

which is realised (with the verb being marked by derivational affixes -$:\d{d}i$-n, for ^{x}, and -ηa-l, for ^{INV}):

(932) *bama:l waŋal ŋanda wawa:ḍiŋa:l*
       The person with a boomerang saw me

'b', in [a b INV], is in the critical syntactic function O, which acts as a pivot for nominal coordination and all types of subordination. INV INCORPORATION brings 'b' into this pivotal position in the lexical-verb surface core [a b V^{INV}]. Certainly one of the major reasons for a speaker to choose an underlying configuration like that on the left-hand side of (lxiv), and then apply INV INCORPORATION to it, is to place 'b' in a surface function where it can be the basis for coordination and subordination.

5.4.3   Instrumental sense of -ŋa-l. Similarly, there may be syntactic reasons for placing an instrumental NP into surface S/O function, so that it can be the pivot for operations of coordination or subordination, as in (581) and (583) of 4.3.6 respectively.

An event such as 'the man hit the wallaby with a stick' has underlying representation:

(lxxxii) $[wagu\d{d}a \; gangulA \; bun\d{d}a\text{-}n]^{PAST}$ & $[wagu\d{d}a \; \d{d}ugi \; INV]$

This is treated in exactly the same way as (lxxix). That is, the antipassive transformation acting on the lexical-verb core gives:

(lxxxiii) [*waguḍa bunḍa-n*^{x}]^{PAST}:*gangulA* & [*waguḍa ḍugi* INV]

and INV INCORPORATION now yields:

(lxxxiv) [*waguḍa ḍugi bunḍa-n*$^{x+INV}$]^{PAST}:*gangulA*

which is written out as:

(933) waguḍaŋgu ḍugi   bunḍa:ḍiŋa:l   gangulanda
       man-ERG   stick-ABS   hit-:ḍi-COMIT-PAST   wallaby-DAT
       The man hit the wallaby with a stick

Thus, although (lxxxiii) is actually in terms of INV^{inst}, whereas (lxxiii) and (lxxx) contain INV^{com}, the INV INCORPORATION RULE, (lxxiv), operates identically in each case, blending an intransitive and a transitive core together, and adding the form -*ŋa-l* ~ -*maŋa-l* (as surface realisation of dummy verb INV) to the lexical verb as a derivational affix.

5.4.4 Minor senses of -ŋa-l. We began the discussion of INV (in 5.4.1) with 'the woman is crying over her husband' (cf. 4.3.5). This can be rendered in Yidiɲ by an intransitive sentence with peripheral dative:

(934) buɲa   badiɲ   muŋga:nda
       woman-ABS cry-PRES husband-DAT

Note that a causal NP could not be used to describe a woman crying out of worry for her husband. *buɲa badiɲ muŋgam* would imply that she is crying involuntarily because, say, the husband had hit her.

But 'husband' is here an intrinsic part of the event. While being un-doubtedly less central than the core participant (here *buɲa*) an NP in dative case with a verb like *badi-n* is certainly more important than a run-of-the-mill dative, such as might be encountered with the majority of verbs e.g. that in:

(935) buɲa ɲinaŋ muŋga:nda
       The woman is sitting by [her] husband

It is presumably in view of the special status of dative with a verb of this type – part-way between a core and a peripheral element in its semantic cohesion with the other elements of the sentence, and in its deletability – that Yidiɲ can, as an alternative to (934), represent the relation between *buɲa* and *muŋga* through an INV core. That is:

(lxxxv) [*buɲa badi-n*]^{PRES} & [*buɲa muŋga* INV]

INV INCORPORATION can apply to this configuration, yielding:

(lxxxvi) $[buɲa\ muŋga\ badi\text{-}n^{INV}]^{PRES}$

which is realised as (cf. (567) in 4.3.5):

(936) buɲa:ŋ   muŋga   badi:ɲal
     woman-ERG husband-ABS cry-COMIT-PRES
     The woman is crying over [her] husband $\langle = (934)\rangle$

The subtype of INV occurring in (lxxxv–lxxxvi) is INV^{dat}. Note that, whereas an INV^{com} core can, it seems, co-occur with potentially any lexical verb, and INV^{inst} can occur with any of a largish set of verbs that describe an action which could be assisted by a tool or weapon or body-part etc., INV^{dat} is restricted to a very small class of verbs – those that could be said (in their intransitive usage) to REQUIRE a dative or purposive NP. See 4.3.5.

The 'locative' and 'fear' senses of $-\eta a\text{-}l$ (4.3.4–5) are syntactically very similar to the 'dative' sense. INV^{loc} can only occur with verbs of talking or singing; it relates together the actor and the language or speech/song-style he is employing. Thus, from

(lxxxvii) $[ɲundu\ ɲaŋga:ḍi\text{-}n]^{IMP}$ & $[ɲundu\ yidiɲ\ INV]$

INV INCORPORATION derives:

(lxxxviii) $[ɲundu\ yidiɲ\ ɲaŋga:ḍi\text{-}n^{INV}]^{IMP}$

which the marking conventions realise as (cf. (559)):

(937) ɲundu yidiɲ ɲaŋga:ḍiɲa   You talk in Yidiɲ!

The language or style used can alternatively be shown through a specialised use of the locative case, with an intransitive core, as in (cf. (558) in 4.3.4):

(938) ɲundu ɲaŋga:ḍin yidi:ɲḍa $\langle = (937)\rangle$

A 'fear' NP can be added to a core involving any type of verb; it indicates that the action is performed to avoid undesirable contact with the referent of the NP. We can thus have ɲundu galin 'you go!' or ɲundu galin waguḍayi:da 'you go for fear of [that] man!'. But there are two or three verbs of fearing (all intransitive) that MUST take an NP in 'fear' inflection e.g.

(939) buɲa manɲa:ɲ waguḍayi:da
     The woman was frightened of the man

With a verb from this set, the necessary connection between actor and that which is feared can be rendered by an INV relation:

(lxxxix) [*buɲa manŋa-n*]^{PAST} & [*buɲa waguḍa* INV]

giving, by INV INCORPORATION:

(xc) [*buɲa waguḍa manŋa-n*^{INV}]^{PAST}

which is realised as:

(940) *buɲa:ŋ wagu:ḍa manŋaŋalɲu* ⟨= (939)⟩

'Fear', 'locative' and 'dative' senses of INV each co-occur with just a small set of verbs; these stand out from other verbs by virtually requiring a peripheral NP of the appropriate type, in their regular intransitive usage.

The configurations we have suggested might be taken to imply that we could, in (lxxxv) say, have *muŋga* both as a peripheral constituent to [*buɲa badi-n*], and also as O element in the INV core. We would then get two occurrences of *muŋga* in (936), one in absolutive case and one in dative; similarly for the locative and fear types. Sentences of this nature are not possible in Yidiɲ and could be disallowed simply by specifying that if an NP does occur twice in the surface structure of a single sentence (leaving aside subordinate and co-ordinated clauses) then the core occurrence takes precedence over (and causes the deletion of) a peripheral occurrence.

5.4.5 Nominal instrumentals. We suggested, in 5.4.3, that underlying an event involving 'a man' (*waguḍa*) as actor, 'a stick' (*ḍugi*) as instrument, 'a wallaby' (*gangulA*) as patient, and a 'hitting' action (*bunḍa-n*) were the two transitive cores:

(lxxxii) [*waguḍa gangulA bunḍa-n*]^{PAST} & [*waguḍa ḍugi* INV^{inst}]

Since INV INCORPORATION can only apply to an intransitive lexical-verb core and a transitive INV core we allowed antipassive to apply to the *bunḍa-n* clause. INV INCORPORATION was then applied, producing a structure that was realised as

(933) *waguḍaŋgu ḍugi   bunḍa:ḍiŋa:l   gangulanda*
man-ERG   stick-ABS   hit-:ḍi-COMIT-PAST   wallaby-DAT
The man hit the wallaby with a stick

Now suppose that instead of applying the antipassive derivation to the *bunḍa-n* core in (lxxxii) we form the antipassive of the INV clause. That is:

(xci) [*waguḍa gangulA bunḍa-n*]^{PAST} & [*waguḍa* INV$^{\text{inst+x}}$]:*ḍugi*

Marking conventions applied to (xci) would place the three NPs all in different cases – *waguḍa* in ergative, *gangulA* in absolutive, and *ḍugi* – qua its unmarked peripheral syntactic function – in locative or dative case (according to the hierarchy described in 4.1.8). But what of [*waguḍa* INV^{inst+x}]? Dummy verb INV^{inst} cannot remain as a separate word in surface structure, and the conditions for INV INCORPORATION are plainly not met. The only possibility seems to be simply to delete INV^{inst}. Let us say in fact that we delete the core involving INV^{inst}:

(xcii) INV^{inst} CORE DELETION

$$[a\ b\ V]^{i}X\ \&\ [a\ INV^{inst+x}]{:}d \Rightarrow [a\ b\ V]^{i}{:}d\ X$$

This incorporates a 'condition' that the subject of the lexical verb be the same as the subject of INV. The peripheral NP of the erstwhile INV core is joined on to the lexical-verb core. We now have:

(xciii) [*waguḍa gangulA bunḍa-n*]^{PAST}:*ḍugi*

which will be realised as:

(941) *waguḍaŋgu gangu:l   bunḍa:ɲ ḍugi:*
       man-ERG   wallaby-ABS hit-PAST stick-INST   ⟨= (933)⟩

This is in fact a typical transitive sentence involving an instrumental NP (4.3.2).

We have thus suggested that (941) – involving an instrumental NP – and (933) – involving a -:*ḍi*+*ŋa-l* instrumental construction – can both be derived from the same pair of underlying cores (lxxxii). These sentences do have the same basic meaning, and we should expect them to be related to the same deep structure. They differ in syntactic orientation: in (941) the 'patient NP' (*gangulA*) is in absolutive case and thus available as the pivot for operations of subordination and coordination, whereas in (933) the instrumental NP (*ḍugi*) has this role.

The different surface structures are the results of the varying syntactic operations applied. For (933) the lexical-verb core is antipassivised and INV INCORPORATION then applied; for (941) the INV core is antipassivised and INV^{inst} CORE DELETION then applied.

The derivation of (941) provides an 'explanation' for the identity of instrumental and locative inflections. An instrumental NP is, here, simply the O NP in an antipassive, which has the unmarked peripheral syntactic function, realised by dative ~ locative. In terms of the semantic hierarchy (4.1.8), locative is the predominant choice when the

reference is inanimate (as it must be in the case of an instrument) so it is entirely natural that an instrumental NP MUST BE in locative case.

We cannot, however, dispense with 'instrumental function' and talk just of locative. As the realisation of a syntactic (as against a local) function, locative ALWAYS alternates with dative. But dative could NOT be substituted for locative in (941) (without radical change of meaning, that is). There is thus one additional nuance to the derivation of a transitive sentence with an instrumental NP, as in (941): where the unmarked peripheral syntactic functive originated within an INV^{inst} core, it can only bear locative – never dative – marking. This can be shown by marking the NP with a special feature, perhaps as part of the antipassive derivation (as we already have the special variety of anti-passive for subordinate clauses, transferring the core $+/-$ marking to the extracted peripheral NP – 5.3.1):

(xciv) ANTIPASSIVE OF INV^{inst} CLAUSE (optional)

$$X[a\ b\ INV^{inst}]\ (Y) \Rightarrow X[a\ INV^{inst+x}]:a^{INV^{inst}}\ (Y)$$

And the marking convention must specify:

(xxiv-d)' In $X:a^{INV^{inst}}$, M(a) = locative(–allative–instrumental)

There is other evidence for instrumental as a separate case. The inanimate indefinite deictic has two distinct forms: instrumental *waɲinda* and locative *waɲḍa* – 3.7.2. (Note that the locative forms of deictics can only be used in local function – i.e. only as realisation of ' ;a', not of ' :a'.)

Dyirbal also has both 'nominal' and 'verbal' instrumental constructions. Here the instrumental inflection on an NP is identical in form with ergative case (rather than with locative); there is a simple verbal affix marking a construc-tion in which the instrumental NP is in surface O function (absolutive case) while the deep O NP is in dative case, -*gu*. For Dyirbal the writer put forward exactly the same two deep cores as for Yidiɲ (but called the dummy verb INST rather than INV^{inst} – Dixon 1972: 188) and derived the two surface structures by regular operation of the established syntactic rules of Dyirbal.

In Dyirbal, as in Yidiɲ, the 'instrumental NP' receives the marking appropriate to a deep O NP in an antipassive construction: in Dyirbal this is, in the unmarked case, ergative (quite different from Yidiɲ's dative ~ loca-tive). Thus, if we attempted to generalise from the successful syntactic explanation of the form of 'instrumental inflection' in these two languages, it would be to say that instrumental is related to the surface marking of a deep O NP within an antipassive construction.

(It might be suggested that we could in Yidiɲ simply say that an instrumental NP is the unmarked peripheral syntactic functive – i.e. 'a' in [b c V]:a. Note that this would not do for Dyirbal since there ergative cannot be used to mark a (non-derived) peripheral NP. And even if it could be justified syntactically, it would evade the semantic task, of relating together (933) and (941).)

It is difficult to check for other languages the hypothesis that 'an instrumental NP bears the case marking appropriate to a deep O NP in an antipassive construction' simply because, although morphological details are available for a fair number of Australian languages, very little in the way of adequate syntactic investigation has yet been attempted. But note that H. A. E. Meyer – an acute and insightful early linguist, whose description of the Encounter Bay language has not received the attention it deserves from modern workers – described a transformation of the antipassive type that substitutes nominative for the ergative inflection on a transitive subject, and ergative for the nominative inflection on the object NP (Meyer 1843: 38–9). We would now expect instrumental to coincide with ergative, and this does seem to be the case (Taplin (1880: 8) quotes 'ergative' as having instrumental function, although the data here are not totally clear – locative may sometimes be used to denote an instrument (Meyer 1843: 15).)

But in fact, although we might expect our deep syntactic explanation of why instrumental coincides with ergative in Dyirbal and with locative in Yidiɲ to hold for some other Australian languages, we should not anticipate its applying in every case. (Many Australian languages do have an 'antipassive' transformation, placing a deep A NP in surface S function – often as a secondary sense of the 'reflexive' – but it is unlikely that they all possess this derivational process. And of course the 'antipassive' is an integral part of our Dyirbal/Yidiɲ explanations.)

There is in Dyirbal (Dixon 1972: 196–8) strong evidence for positing two distinct cores to underlie a structure like (933) (and similarly for comitatives like (931)). Basically, a verbal affix -ɖay indicates 'lots' of the referent of the deep S/O NP. If -ɖay is placed between verb root and instrumental suffix it indicates 'many patients' (referring to the deep O of the lexical verb); if -ɖay comes between the instrumental suffix and the final inflection it indicates 'many instruments' (referring now to the deep O of INV[inst]). There is no corresponding affix in Yidiɲ, but the Dyirbal evidence is surely relevant here in view of the fact that applying the rather different syntactic rules of Yidiɲ and Dyirbal to the SAME DEEP STRUCTURES we get in each case the correct surface output (involving quite different case markings in the two languages).

Incidentally, we can note that structures like (lxxiii) and (lxxxii), and the structural description of (lxxiv), involve identification of S and A NPs, and could conceivably be taken as evidence for an 'accusative deep structure', in terms of the debate conducted in 5.1.1–4. In Dyirbal there is overwhelming

evidence from other areas of the syntax for an 'absolutive–ergative deep structure', and the S–A identification was (perhaps not altogether plausibly) 'explained' through a device for linking together topic-chains that identifies A with S/O (and carries verbal marking *-ɲura*). See Dixon 1972: 184–98.

5.4.6 Nominal comitatives.

We can now return to nominal comitatives. It will be recalled that

(lxxiii) $[waguḍa\ gali\text{-}n]^{\text{PAST}}$ & $[waguḍa\ yabuɽ U\ \text{INV}^{\text{com}}]$

was set up as the underlying structure from which, by INV INCOR-PORATION,

(931) *waguḍaŋgu yabu:ɽ galiɲalɲu*   The man went with the girl

was derived.

Suppose that we now repeat the operations applied in the last section, and apply the antipassive derivation to the INV core in (lxxiii). This gives:

(xcv) $[waguḍa\ gali\text{-}n]^{\text{PAST}}$ & $[waguḍa\ \text{INV}^{\text{com+x}}]:yabuɽ U^{\text{INV}^{\text{com}}}$

Here we transfer the feature 'INV^{com}' to *yabuɽ U*, as we had to transfer 'INV^{inst}' in 5.4.5. Deleting the core containing INV^{com} would then yield:

(xcvi) $[waguḍa\ gali\text{-}n]^{\text{PAST}}:yabuɽ U^{\text{INV}^{\text{com}}}$

The sentence we are aiming at here – with the same meaning as (931) – is

(942) *wagu:ḍa gali:ɲ   yabuɽuyi*
    man-ABS go-PAST girl-COMIT-ABS   ⟨= (931)⟩

This suggests a marking convention:

(xxiv-f) In X: $a^{\text{INV}^{\text{com}}}$, M(a) = comitative

There is thus a radical difference between INV^{inst} and INV^{com} as features to NPs. Whereas the former merely selects locative from the locative ∼ dative alternation, INV^{com} demands a quite new suffix – nominal comitative *-ḍi ∼ -yi*.

In 3.3.4 we noted the formal similarity between nominal comitative *-ḍi ∼ -yi* and the verbal derivational affix *-:ḍi-n*, and mentioned that a number of other Australian languages show formal similarity between these two affixes (see Dixon 1976a: 203–309). At our present stage of knowledge it remains an open question whether the similarity of form is coincidental, or is perhaps indicative of some as-yet-unperceived deep grammatical relationship.

There is another, more significant, difference between the nominal constructions corresponding to 'inst' and 'com' varieties of INV. Whereas an INV^{inst} core must have its A NP coreferential to the A NP of the lexical-verb core, an INV^{com} core can have its A NP coreferential with ANY NP in the core or periphery of the main clause, and the comitative NP will then agree in case with that NP. Thus, from

(lxxix) [*bama ŋayu wawa-l*]^{PAST} & [*bama waŋal* INV]

is derived (cf. (512) in 4.3.1):

(943) *ŋaɲaɲ bama:l   wawa:l   waŋaldiŋgu*
       I-o   person-ERG see-PAST boomerang-COMIT-ERG
       The person with a boomerang saw me

whereas from

(xcvii) [*ŋayu bama wawa-l*]^{PAST} & [*bama waŋal* INV]

is derived

(944) *ŋayu bama   wawa:l   waŋa:ldi*
       I-SA person-ABS see-PAST boomerang-COMIT-ABS
       I saw the person with a boomerang

Note here that comitative bears zero case marking when the coreferential NP in the main clause is in O or S function, ergative when it is in A function. With instrumental configurations like (lxxxii) the coreferential NP must be in A function in the main clause, and there is no case ending (beyond the 'instrumental' affix).

Similarly when the coreferential NP is in dative case in the main clause (cf. (57))

(xcviii) [*ŋayu ḍana-n*]^{PAST}:*galŋa* & [*galŋa miɲa* INV^{com}]

will yield:

(945) *ŋayu ḍana:ɲ   galŋa:nda miɲayinda*
       I-SA stand-PAST uncle-DAT meat-COMIT-DAT
       I stood [waiting] for uncle, who has meat (literally '...for uncle, with the meat')

We are now in a position to state the convention that puts an inflection on to a comitative (where ...a... refers to any core or peripheral NP):

(xcix) COMITATIVE NP MARKING CONVENTION

If there is some 'a' such that ...a... & [b c INV^{com}] and CR(a,b), then ...a... & [b c INV]^{com} → ...a... & [b c INV$^{\text{com}+\text{M(a)}}$]

This marking is transferred to the comitative NP through an extension to the special case of antipassive, (xciv):

(xciv)′ ANTIPASSIVE OF INV$^{inst/com+c}$ CLAUSES (optional)

$$X\,[a\ b\ INV^{inst/com+c}]\,(Y) \Rightarrow X\,[a\ INV^{inst+x/com+x+c}]:b^{INV^{inst/com+c}}(Y)$$

(Here 'c' indicates a case marking.) Then rule (xcii) can be extended to cover the deletion of a core containing INV^{com+x}.

The other varieties of INV mentioned above have narrower possibilities of coreference. The A NPs of the two underlying cores must coincide, for INV^{inst} CORE DELETION to apply and a sentence like (941) to result. For 'inst', 'dat', 'loc' and 'fear' (as for 'com') senses, INV INCORPORATION will only apply if A of INV is coreferential with the S NP of the lexical-verb core. If INV cannot be incorporated as an affix, or deleted, through these transformations it will remain in surface structure, and an illicit string will result.

The main reason for our deriving a nominal comitative from an INV core was to provide a common deep origin for (931) and (942). Support for considering a nominal comitative to emanate from a separate clause, rather than being generated within an NP like any normal adjective, comes from its positioning in surface structure. A comitative, even though it agrees in case with an NP preceding the verb, will MOST OFTEN follow the main verb of the sentence – see the examples given in 3.3.4 and 4.3.1 – just as will a subordinate clause. (But note that a comitative NP CAN be interposed within the main clause – as can a peripheral NP – whereas a subordinate clause CANNOT be.)

5.4.7   'Controlling' sense of -ŋa-l. Finally, INV^{cont} can be used to refer to an actor controlling the activity of some person or thing. Thus, for 'the man (*waguḍa*) gets up (intransitive *waŋga:ḍi-n*) the boy (*wuṛgun*)' we have underlying

(c) [*wuṛgun waŋga:ḍi-n*]^{PAST} & [*waguḍa wuṛgun* INV^{cont}]

Incorporation takes the form, for INV^{cont}:

(ci) [a V]^i & [b a INV^{cont}] $\Rightarrow$ [b a V$^{INV^{cont}}$]^i

This will derive, from (c) (cf. (585) in 4.3.7)

(946) *waguḍaŋgu wuṛgun waŋga:ḍiŋa:l*   The man got the boy up

The controlling sense of *-ŋa-l* will be seen to be quite different from the other senses, for all of which INV INCORPORATION takes the form shown in (lxxiv). We are using INV^{cont} – rather than some quite different dummy symbol –

simply because the morphological realisation is -*ŋa-l*. It may be that we should in fact recognise two homonymous -*ŋa-l* suffixes: (i) a verbal affix, covering 'com', 'inst', 'dat', 'loc' and 'fear' senses; and (ii) a suffix covering the 'controlling' sense of verbal -*ŋa-l*, and also the denominal verbaliser -*ŋa-l* (5.4.8).

We can now go through the derivations of the -:*ḍi* + *ŋa-l* forms of *waḍu-l* 'cook, burn' (which selects a human A NP) and *guba-n* 'cook, burn' (demanding an A NP which refers to something actually burning) – see (610) and (614) in 4.3.7. For *waḍu-l*, 'fire' is an instrument:

(cii) [*ŋayu miɲa waḍu-l*]^{PAST} & [*ŋayu buɽi* INV^{inst}]

Applying antipassive to the lexical-verb core we get:

(ciii) [*ŋayu waḍu-l*^{x}]^{PAST}:*miɲa* & [*ŋayu buɽi* INV^{inst}]

to which INV INCORPORATION applies, yielding

(civ) [*ŋayu buɽi waḍu-l*$^{\text{x+INV}}$]^{PAST}:*miɲa*

That is (= (610))

(947) *ŋayu buɽi waḍu:ḍiɲa:l miɲa:*
      I used the fire to cook the meat

With *guba-n*, on the other hand, we must employ INV^{cont}:

(cv) [*buɽi* X *guba-n*]^{PAST} & [*ŋayu buɽi* INV^{cont}]:*miɲa*

Now applying antipassive to the leftmost clause in (cv):

(cvi) [*buɽi guba-n*^{x}]^{PAST}:X & [*ŋayu buɽi* INT^{cont}]:*miɲa*

The unspecified NP, X, is now in peripheral position and may be deleted. INV INCORPORATION, (ci), yields:

(cvii) [*ŋayu buɽi guba-n*$^{\text{x+INV}}$]^{PAST}:*miɲa*

That is (= (614))

(948) *ŋayu buɽi guba:ḍiɲa:l miɲa:*
       I used the [light of] the burning fire to [look at] the meat

Note that *miɲa* in (947) originates as the deep O of *waḍu-l*, whereas *miɲa* in (948) began as a peripheral NP to the INV^{cont} core. Although (947) and (948) appear to be syntactically parallel, and involve verbs that have very similar meanings, they in fact correspond to quite different deep structures – featuring different senses of INV – and have radically different meanings.

We have already indicated, in 4.3, the selectional restrictions on the various senses of *-ŋa-l*. These can best be dealt with by saying that a lexical verb of a certain type can co-occur with a core containing a certain variety of INV. The various types of mutual exclusion summarised in 4.3.7 can be stated in the same way – INV^{cont} cannot normally occur with a verb that takes INV^{dat} or INV^{loc}, and so on. (Most of these are probably best regarded as 'preferences' rather than absolute exclusions. For instance, *wanda+ŋa-l* has been encountered in the 'controlling' sense 'make fall down'; however, when elicitation was directed to this form only the comitative sense 'fall down with' was allowed (this is certainly the central and most frequent sense in texts, but it is not the ONLY sense of *wanda+ŋa-l*).)

5.4.8 Transitive verbaliser.
In 4.1.10 we gave examples of 'minor sentences' which involve no verb, and thus have no tense/mood specification. These consist of just a noun phrase – that is, a grouping of words as described under (b) in 5.1.6. In the case of sentences of this type there is no trace of the third type of grammatical process – putting a series of phrases together in certain syntactico-semantic relationships ((c) from 5.1.6). A minor sentence cannot refer to an activity, but instead describes some state or property of some thing. It will most frequently consist of a specific noun, commented on by a generic noun, or an adjective, or a genitive NP.

We can thus have a sentence with the configuration B $\neq$ C, where B will be a noun (with or without modifiers) and C a noun or adjective. $\#$ represents a word boundary (it is further commented on in 5.6.1). A typical realisation is

(949) *yiŋu bana gaḍu:l*   This water is dirty

Now a single-NP configuration of this type can occur with a core involving INV^{cont}:

(cviii) *yiŋu#bana#gaḍulA* & [*ŋayu yiŋu#bana* INV^{cont}]PAST

and INV^{cont} can then be 'incorporated', as a verbalising suffix *-ŋa-l* to the adjective, giving:

(cix) [*ŋayu yiŋu#bana gaḍulA*^{INV}]PAST

which would be realised as (cf. 4.8.1):

(950) *ŋayu yiŋu bana gaḍulaŋa:l*   I made this water dirty

The general statement of INV^{cont} incorporation onto nominals is:

(cx)   B$\#$C & [a B INV^{cont}]^i $\Rightarrow$ [a B C^{INV}]^i

Note the similarity between (cx) and (ci). In fact the causative denominal verbaliser and the controlling sense of verbal derivational affix *-ŋa-l* also have almost exactly the same semantic effects.

We have here introduced a third type of sentence nucleus, $B \neq C$, consisting just of a number of words joined together in NP-type semantic relations (see 5.6.1). This occurs INSTEAD OF a core of type (viii) or (ix).

We have not put forward $B \neq C$ as a universal – on a par with (viii) and (ix) – since it is by no means clear that this minimal configuration would have to be recognised for all languages. Certainly further work on a variety of languages (not constrained by any desire relentlessly to force all sentences into a 'verbal' pattern) is needed. But it is clear that for Yidiɲ $B \neq C$ must be added to the configurational pattern summarised in (lxv); it can occur with peripheral NPs, with subordinate clauses and, as shown here, with INV cores. (The first sentence of 5.4.1 should thus be amended accordingly.)

5.4.9   Intransitive verbaliser. The inchoative verbaliser *-daga-n* is the intransitive congener of causative *-ŋa-l*, and this is perhaps reason for setting up a similar underlying representation, with dummy verb INCHO. And then an INCHO incorporation rule:

(cxi) $B \neq C$ & $[B \text{ INCHO}]^i \Rightarrow [B \text{ } C^{\text{INCHO}}]^i$

Thus, from underlying

(cxii)   *yiŋu#bana#gaḍulA* & $[yiŋu#bana \text{ INCHO}]^{\text{PRES}}$

is derived

(cxiii) $[yiŋu#bana \text{ } gaḍulA^{\text{INCHO}}]^{\text{PRES}}$

which is realised as (= (794) in 4.8.1):

(951)   *yiŋu bana gaḍu:ldagaŋ*   This water is getting dirty

However, INCHO cannot be supported by the same strength of syntactic evidence as can INV. Whereas INV can occur with a transitive or an intransitive core, or with $B \neq C$, INCHO is restricted to occurrences with $B \neq C$, as on the left-hand side of (cxi).

There are further uses of *-ŋa-l* and *-daga-n*. These suffixes can form verbs from time qualifiers and from particles (5.5.4); and from locational qualifiers or nominals in local cases. For the latter we might appear at first sight to have a derivational process roughly as follows:

(cxiv) $[a \text{ V}]^i \text{ X};b^{+/-/\emptyset} \Rightarrow [a \text{ V}#b^{+/-/\emptyset+\text{INCHO}}]^i \text{ X}$

Thus, corresponding to:

(952) *ŋayu galiŋ gaba:ymu*   I'm going away from the road

there is (= (805) in 4.8.1)

(953) *ŋayu galiŋ gaba:ymudagaŋ*   I've got off the road as I've gone along

But note that these two sentences do not have exactly the same meaning. (952) implies motion away from the road (maybe purposely breaking off passage along the road and setting off, say, at right-angles to it). (953), in contrast, implies that the subject 'became' off the road as he went along it e.g. he just wandered off it. This might cause us to reject (cxiv) and instead include an INCHO core after the local NP, incorporate INCHO as an affix, and then coordinate the two cores, something along the lines of:

(cxv) $[a \ V]^i$; $b^{+/-/\emptyset}$ & $[a \ INCHO] \Rightarrow$
$\quad [a \ V]^i, [a \ b^{+/-/\emptyset + INCHO}] \Rightarrow [a \ V \# b + {}^{/-/\emptyset + INCHO}]^i$

And similarly for *-ŋa-l*.

Minor verbalising affixes *-maḏi-n* and *-luŋa-l* are not well enough understood to justify any attempt at suggesting a 'deep' interpretation for them (the examples quoted in 4.8.2–3 constitute more than half the corpus for these suffixes!).

5.5 Sentence modification

5.5.1 Tense and mood. There are some similarities between locational and temporal qualifications. There is, for instance, semantic iconicity between the ternary locational system 'to/at/from a place' and the ternary temporal system 'until/at/since some time', and there are a number of languages which are like Yidiɲ (3.4.1, 3.5) in having similar or identical inflections for the two series. The connection is sometimes made even more specific – thus in both Chinese and Dyirbal 'past' and 'future' time can be referred to by words for 'uphill' and 'downhill' respectively. And so on.

But the differences are perhaps more significant. Local specifications tend to blur into syntactic ones – it is sometimes not clear whether a particular form is to be given allative or purposive interpretation (or ablative or causal, and so on). We mentioned in 5.3.1 that *ŋayu galiŋ bulmba:gu* 'I'm going to the camp' could be referring to camp simply as a destination, or as an object with which the speaker is about to become involved. Indeed there are many languages which are like English in using a single formal device (preposition 'to') corresponding to the morphologically, syntactically and semantically distinct case endings allative and purposive in Yidiɲ.

Time, on the other hand, is conceptually quite apart from local and syntactic peripheral elements. It is true that *-gu* on to a time word in Yidiɲ can have EITHER temporal 'until' OR purposive interpretation e.g. in (cf. (712) in 4.5.1)

(954) *ɲayu yiwan*   *budil*   *yiŋgu*   *yiwaːygu*
    I-SA   small shelter-ABS   put-PRES   here-LOC   winter-*gu*

yiwaːygu can have a nominal purposive meaning 'I'll put the small shelter here FOR THE WINTER' or else a temporal sense 'I'll put the small shelter here UNTIL THE WINTER'. These two readings are inconsistent one with the other: the first states that the shelter will be put up before winter begins and kept there during that season, whereas the second implies that the shelter will be removed at the onset of winter. There is ambiguity here but no fuzziness, as there was between allative and purposive.

There are two obvious alternatives for dealing with temporal information. We could establish an additional peripheral slot, or specify a 'temporal feature' attached to the sentence as a whole. The existence of temporal qualifiers as separate words (3.5) might be thought to favour the first alternative, while the fact that the main verb of a sentence inflects for tense (3.8.4) could be taken as evidence for the second.

There are, of course, other possible treatments. In fact most traditional grammars have treated sense as a semantic specification of the verb, just as a noun may be specified for number; here semantic relations are plainly being inferred from morphological structure. We prefer to follow Lyons (1968: 305), among others, in considering time/tense to be always essentially a qualification of the event referred to by the complete sentence.

The 'feature' alternative seems marginally more appropriate for Yidiɲ. A tense/mood specification is obligatory for all sentences (other than the minor variety, which do not involve a core – 4.1.10) and the tense/mood feature can thus conveniently be associated with the core. (There is considerable homogeneity amongst peripheral components, shown by the series of semantic similarities between syntactic NPs/local NPs/subordinate clauses – 5.2.2, 5.3.1 – and various mergings and fuzzy areas. As we have already shown, time qualification stands quite apart from this matrix.)

Every Yidiɲ sentence (excepting the 'minimal' non-verbal variety – 4.1.10, 5.4.8) involves just one choice from the system of tense–mood

inflections: {imperative, past, present(–future), purposive}. The inflection goes on to every verb/adverb in the VC of the main clause.

A subordinate clause is specified for $+/-/\emptyset/^{ap}$ instead of tense/mood. In the case of coordination we could either say that each clause must show identical tense/mood specification – as we did in (xl), (xli) and (xlix) – or else say that a tense/mood choice is made only once for any string of clauses conjoined by ',' (and show this on the first clause in sequence). With a verbal core and an INV core joined by '&' there is again just one overall tense/mood specification.

It is natural to suggest, in all these cases, that it is just the main core – which is written on the left in the sentence configuration (before any ':', ';', ',' or '&') – that involves a choice from the tense/mood system. However, this would not cover configurations like (cviii) in 5.4.8 which at the deepest level involve just a noun phrase joined to an INV core by &. The derived sentence, (950), has a tense/mood inflection – whereas a sentence consisting just of an NP, as (949), would not have; this must presumably be associated with the INV core in (cviii).

We are thus led to:

(cxvi) Every sentence that involves a core, [...], makes one choice from the tense/mood system.

We can, rather arbitrarily, write this as a feature on the first core in deep structure – it will thus be on the V core in $[X\ V]^i$ & [Y INV] but on the INV core in X & $[Y\ INV]^i$. The feature is realised on the verb of the leftmost core in surface structure:

(cxvii) $[X\ V]^i\ Z \Rightarrow [X\ V^i]\ Z$
where 'i' is a choice from the system {imperative, past, present, purposive}

Turning now to the breakdown of the tense/mood system, we can first separate off the imperative:

(cxviii) ⎯⎡⎯imperative
              ⎣⎯tense-purposive choice

An imperative sentence has limited selection of S/A, which can be freely deleted; and it takes a different negative particle from tensed sentences (4.9, 4.10).

Amongst the other three inflections, purposive stands out since it can occur on a subordinate as well as on a main clause (4.5.2–3). Allied to

this, we mentioned in 5.1.3 that purposive cannot occur on a series of coordinated clauses.

That is, if purposive occurs in a non-initial clause we interpret it as a subordinate marking – as in (726) from 4.5.3. It may be that we should also allow a sequence of conjoined clauses, all in purposive inflection, and recognize that it is on the surface impossible to tell apart the two types $[...]^{PURP}, [...]^{PURP}$ and $[...]^{PURP}:[...]^{+}$.

Note that it is semantically plausible that, of the two marked inflections on subordinate clauses, only $^{+}$ should also appear on main clauses. One may say that someone needs to do something (without stating the reason) whereas it would scarcely be usual to state a cause without also mentioning the result.

Semantically, purposive is quite different from the two tenses. It indicates necessity or desirability whereas past tense merely refers to something that has already happened, and present(–future) to something already under way or predicted to occur (with no modal overtones).

We can thus organise the system from which each sentence having a core makes one obligatory choice:

(cxix)

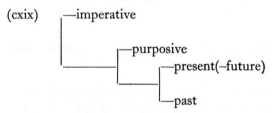

In addition, if 'past' is chosen, a member of the subset of time qualifiers that has past time reference may optionally be added – *guygam* 'yesterday', *girgan* 'last year' or *yurunU* 'a long time ago', and so on. If 'past' is not chosen then a member of the complementary set of non-past qualifiers may be added to the sentence: *garu* 'by-and-by', *ŋaḍa* 'tomorrow' and so on.

5.5.2 'Non-animate agent' and 'chance' senses of -:ḍi-n. The somewhat bewildering array of uses of the verbal derivational affix -*:ḍi-n* were surveyed in 4.2. Those senses which have syntactic effect – antipassive and reflexive – were dealt with in 5.2.3–4. We can now consider uses of -*:ḍi-n* which do not change transitivity, and can only occur with a transitive verb – indicating that the agent of an 'affect' verb is non-animate (4.2.5), or that a certain result was obtained by chance (4.2.6).

For a single affix to indicate sometimes syntactic derivation and sometimes semantic modification is unusual, and something that it is not immediately obvious how to deal with in terms of a standard transformational model (for instance, Chomsky 1965). But -*:ḍi-n* in Yidiɲ is by no means unique. In Arabic, for instance, what is traditionally called the second derived form of the verb involves doubling the middle consonant of the root; it serves (1) to derive a transitive causative from an intransitive verb e.g. 'die' → 'kill', 'walk' → 'make walk', 'be glad' → 'gladden'; (2) to derive a ditransitive causative from a transitive verb e.g. 'understand' → 'explain', 'carry' → 'make carry'; (3) to intensify the meaning of a verb, indicating that something is done with great violence, or continued for a long time e.g. 'break' → 'smash', 'kill' → 'massacre'; (4) to supply an estimative meaning e.g. 'to lie' → 'to think one a liar'; (5) to form a denominative verb e.g. 'leather' → 'to bind', 'soldiers' → 'to levy troops' (Wise 1975: 45–54; Haywood and Nahmad 1962: 159–61). There is no similarity of detail with Yidiɲ – sense (1) is in fact close to the 'controller' sense of verbal -*ŋa-l*, (5) to the causative verbaliser -*ŋa-l*, while (3) shows some similarities to the continuous sense of Yidiɲ -*:ḍi-n*. But this Arabic derivational process would pose similar problems for any grammatical description that attempted rigidly to separate syntactic from semantic considerations.

Now in 4.2.2 we suggested that the use of -*:ḍi-n* could be explained in terms of various types of deviation from a transitive sentence 'norm'. The 'non-animate agent' and 'chance' senses were said to go against the requirement that the deep A NP have 'volitional control' over the action. This suggests establishing a feature system ' ± controlled' as follows:

(a) Verbs in the small set that demand inanimate subjects – e.g. *guba-n* 'burn, cook' (4.1.5) – cannot be marked for ' ± controlled'. All other transitive verbs can be, and the unmarked specification is ' + controlled'.

(b) If the A NP to an 'affect' verb (a well-defined semantic class, listed in the dictionary – 4.2.5) has non-animate reference, then the verb is marked ' − controlled'.

(c) A transitive verb can simply be directly marked ' − controlled' (corresponding to the 'chance' sense).

(d) A verb marked ' − controlled' bears the suffix -*:ḍi-n*.

Note that a ' − controlled' verb cannot occur with imperative inflection (on semantic grounds, the idea of ordering an agent to do something, and an event which the agent does not control, are clearly incompatible). This is probably best stated as a feature co-occurrence

restriction – rather than building 'controlled' into the dependency tree (cxix) just after ' – imperative' – since control specification can apply to subordinate as well as to main clauses.

Our linking the 'inanimate agent' and 'chance' senses of -:*ḍi-n* together through a specification ' – controlled' is not entirely happy. Whereas an affect verb with non-animate subject MUST as a rule receive -:*ḍi-n* marking, this affix is only SOMETIMES used to mark chance events, when there is some compelling reason to draw attention to the accidental nature of the activity (4.2.6).

5.5.3 'Continuous' sense of -:ḍi-n.

The fifth use of -:*ḍi-n* is to mark a transitive or intransitive verb as referring to a 'continuous' action, that cannot be viewed as a whole by looking in either temporal direction from 'the present'. As with the 'chance' sense, -:*ḍi-n* is not obligatory in this use and will only be employed when there is some special reason for drawing attention to the non-discrete nature of the activity.

There is, in fact, little that we can add here to the account in 4.2.7, 4.2.2. No obvious way of linking 'continuous' to the other senses of -:*ḍi-n* presents itself. In a main clause the continuous suffix can be followed by imperative – as in (498), (501) – or present – as in (496) – or past inflection – as in (494). 'Continuous' -:*ḍi-n* has not been encountered in a subordinate clause but this may simply be a gap in the writer's data; it would seem, on a priori grounds, to be possible in a dative subordinate clause (although perhaps not when followed by causal or purposive inflection).

We can simply allow for a verb to be specified ' + continuous' (' – continuous' being taken as the unmarked value). This choice is made independently of ' ± controlled', tense/mood or $+/-/\text{ø}/\text{ap}$ values; but ' – continuous' should perhaps be regarded as incompatible with $^+$ or $^-$.

The syntax of ergative languages has been little studied (and still less understood). Nevertheless, it is possible to perceive some recurrent patterns. First, note that no language is known to be 'wholly ergative' (although there are many examples of 'fully accusative' languages). Even Dyirbal, which is recognised to have a clearly 'ergative syntax', has pronouns inflecting in a nominative–accusative pattern.

A common characteristic is for there to be an 'ergative' construction in past tense e.g. Tibetan (Regamey 1954: 370–3) or in perfective/aorist aspect e.g. Hindi (Allen 1950/1; Kachru 1965) and Georgian (Catford mimeo: 17;

Comrie 1973: 245), and a 'nominative' construction elsewhere. Thus for Georgian the case marking is:

	A	O
Aorist	ERGATIVE	NOMINATIVE
Other	NOMINATIVE	DATIVE–ACCUSATIVE

Here the non-aorist construction appears to be intransitive and to bear the same relation to the transitive 'ergative' construction as an antipassive does to the transitive 'ergative' construction in Yidiɲ (and Dyirbal).

A plausible explanation of this split is suggested by Regamey (1954: 373). For a completed or past action we can focus either on the agent or, as here, on the patient, and describe what has happened to it. But something that has not (yet) occurred can only be viewed with respect to the potentiality of the agent doing it – we can think of a particular person being liable to do an injury (to someone) but not normally, say, of a person being liable to be injured by someone or other. There is thus a semantic reason for having the agent as 'pivot' (in the unmarked case) for uninstantiated events, even though the patient may be pivot for attested events.

(In the North-West Caucasian languages there are two classes of 'semantically double-argument' verbs. The so-called 'transitive' class has ergative A and nominative O NP, while the 'intransitive' class has nominative A and ergative O (pronominal prefixes to the verb are also in reverse sequence). It is worth noting that the 'transitive' class covers mostly verbs referring to some actual event (e.g. 'see', 'write') while members of the 'intransitive' class have potential meanings (e.g. 'look at', 'read') – Catford mimeo: 32–3.)

Yukulta, in north-west Queensland, provides a paradigm example of a tense/aspect-type split. Transitive verbs occur in two constructional patterns, with NP case markings:

	A	O
(i)	ERGATIVE	NOMINATIVE
(ii)	NOMINATIVE	DATIVE

The normal Australian 'ergative' pattern, (i), applies to sentences describing actual past events or future intentions. (ii), which looks like a characteristic antipassive construction, is used in all other cases – with future irrealis (e.g. 'wishing') and past negatives (e.g. 'he didn't do it'). And (ii) must also be used when A is third person and O first or second person OR when A is second person and O first person dual or plural. See Keen 1972 and McConvell 1976.

Now Yidiɲ has an ergative construction in all tenses and aspects; and an antipassive can be derived from it irrespective of time or perfectivity. But note that the antipassive marker -:ḍi-n is also used to indicate that the agent does not control the action (with the ergative construction being retained); we have suggested that in languages like Georgian a nominative construction must be

used when a sentence simply describes some potential action of a possible controller, and that an ergative construction is used for completed events, where the factor of control is to an extent irrelevant.

Yidiɲ -:ɖi-n is also used to mark a 'continuing' non-discrete action; this is reminiscent of the use of an ergative construction in Georgian (and Hindi) ONLY for some completed event. And Catford (mimeo: 42) mentions that in the Caucasian Tsakhur the A NP – normally in ergative case – is placed in nominative when the verb is expressing a DURATIVE action (e.g. 'father is cutting firewood in the yard').

These semantic similarities – such as they are – may be coincidental. Or, on the other hand, they may be amenable to principled explanation in terms of an articulated semantico-syntactic theory of 'ergative constructions', which will hopefully be worked out at some time in the future.

5.5.4   Particles. Finally, there is the set of twenty 'particles' (4.10). These qualify the description of a complete event (rather than, say, specifying the meaning of a VC or an NP) and must be dealt with at the level of sentence syntax. They could be regarded as a special type of peripheral element (the inclusion of a particle is quite optional), or as a heterogeneous system of 'sentence features' (following our treatment of tense/mood).

There appears to be little syntactic or semantic reason for preferring one of these alternatives over the other. Note, however, that particles can occur with 'core-less' minimal sentences, whereas tense/time qualifiers can not. This might be taken as an argument against the 'feature' approach.

The semantic interpretation of particles is sometimes quite complex, often referring the complete event to some property of the S or A (e.g. *ganaŋgar*, *babaɽ*, etc.) or of the O NP (e.g. *wala*); see 5.1.2. Other particles simply supply an aspectual-type comment on the event e.g. *biya* 'it didn't happen but it should or could have done'.

Particles and time qualifiers can be verbalised (4.10, 4.8.1); but, unlike the verbalisation of locational forms (5.4.9) no semantic difference is perceptible between sentences with verbalised and non-verbalised forms. Data on this topic are scanty, and any attempt at 'deep interpretation' would be premature.

5.6   Structure of phrases

5.6.1   Types of semantic relation. We now move on to a second type of grammatical process – (b) in 5.1.6, the grouping of words together to form 'phrases'. We first describe the semantico-syntactic structuring of

phrases, and then describe the relationship between phrases and the core and peripheral elements of the sentence configurations. Possessives are deferred until 5.6.2.

This level of syntax does not lend itself to explanatory generalisation in the way that investigation of sentence structure does. That is, there is at the phrase level nothing as syntactically interesting as the 3×3 matrix of peripheral syntactic NP/local NP/subordinate clauses dealt with in terms of $+/-/^o$, or the modification of the antipassive rules whereby subordinate clause marking $+/-$ is carried over to an extracted peripheral NP.

A phrase simply involves a head word, to which are adjoined specifiers of various types, that serve to delimit or qualify its meaning. But the relation between a head word (specific noun) and a generic noun, or an adjective, or a deictic, are of different semantic types, just as the relations between sentential core and locative NP, or 'lest' clause, or causal NP are semantically different. Just as we employed a syntactic symbolism which would draw attention to the various types of relation between the components of a sentence, so must we adopt an appropriate symbolism to represent the semantic relations which hold between the constituents of a phrase.

That is, we are suggesting that to provide, as the syntactic representation of an NP like *yiŋu bama yabuɽU ŋalal* 'this person girl big' a tree like:

(cxx)

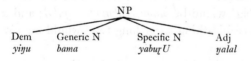

or a labelled diagram like

(cxxi) ₙₚ[*yiŋu bama yabuɽU ŋalal*]ₙₚ

(whether or not any hierarchical grouping is shown) is insufficient basis for a comprehensive account of the overall meaning of a sentence. Individual symbols for each type of inter-phrasal relationship will not be likely to be the basis for any syntactic generalisations or explanations, but they are necessary if our symbolic representation of a sentence is to provide an adequate representation of semantic (rather than solely syntactic) structuring.

STRUCTURE OF NOUN PHRASES

A noun phrase in Yidiɲ (4.1.1) will normally have as head a specific noun, B (i.e. any noun that is not a member of the set of about twenty generic terms listed in 6.2.1). This can contract the following semantic relations:

(a) With a generic noun C – represented by '/' i.e. C/B ('B is a C' or 'C includes B'). There are, as will be illustrated in 6.2.1, two kinds of generic – those based on the 'nature' of an object (e.g. 'a girl is a person', 'a yellow walnut is a tree') and those based on its 'use' (e.g. 'a possum is edible flesh food', 'a yellow walnut is edible non-flesh food'). '/' can be used for either type of relation, but if it is desired to be more specific we can employ:

　// for 'nature' generics e.g. *bama//yabuɽU*, 'person'//'girl'

　$\neq$ for 'use' generics e.g. *miɲa≠gaḍarA*, 'edible flesh food' $\neq$ 'possum'

An NP can involve at most two generics, either two 'nature' terms

D//C//B 'B is by nature a C, and C is by nature a D' e.g. *bama//buɲa// yabuɽU*, 'person'//'woman'//'girl'

or a 'nature' and a 'use' specification:

D≠C//B 'B is by nature a C, and B is by use a D' e.g. *mayi≠ḍugi//gaŋgi*, 'edible non-flesh food'≠'tree'//'yellow walnut'

(b) With an adjective (including numerals) or a logical-type modifier, C – represented by '←' i.e. B ← C. For instance *bama yabuɽU ŋalal* 'person girl big' would be *bama//yabuɽU ← ŋalal*; and *wira gala guran ḍambulA* 'moveable-thing spear long two' would be *wira≠gala←guran ← ḍambulA*.

(c) With an (inalienably possessed) 'part' noun (4.1.1, 4.7.3), C – represented by '⌐' i.e. B⌐C. Thus *miɲa gaḍarA bina* 'edible-flesh-food possum ear' is *miɲa≠gaḍarA ⌐bina*.

(d) With a deictic, C – represented by '{...}' where the braces would normally enclose the whole of the rest of the NP i.e. C{X B Y}. For example *yiɲu bama yabuɽU ŋalal* would be *yiɲu {bama//yaburU ← ŋalal}*.

　A pronoun or proper name, C, may make up a complete NP, or occur with any of the constituents listed above. One way of dealing with this – suggested in 4.1.2 – is to say that we here have two NPs in apposition, making up a 'compound' phrase which will correspond to a single

element of sentence configuration. This can be shown by '↔' i.e. C ↔ XBY. For example, *yiɲu bama buɲa bindam* 'this person woman Bindam' – in (320) of 4.1.2 – will be symbolised as *bindam* ↔ *yiɲu{bama//buɲa//}*.

A noun phrase in Yidiɲ may involve any selection from these constituents (4.1.1–2). None is obligatory; although a specific noun occurs in the majority of NPs, there are plenty of examples involving just a generic noun, or just a deictic, or even just an adjective; and so on. However, from the point of view of semantic structure it is most straightforward to take the 'specific noun slot' as pivot, and when it is not specified simply leave a gap in the pattern, as in the example at the end of the last paragraph, or in *ɲuɲu miɲa gadil* 'that edible-flesh-food small' i.e. *ɲuɲu {miɲa≠ ← gadil}*.

As with sentence structure, we are here interested in representing abstract semantic relations, and can adopt any arbitrary convention for the ordering of elements. Since all else is equal, we follow the preferred surface structure ordering where known (4.1.1, 4.1.2) i.e.

(cxxii) $C \leftrightarrow D\{E//F{\neq}B|\overline{G} \leftarrow H\}$

and, to facilitate comparison of noun phrase structures, we should always state the elements in this order, irrespective of the details of surface structure sequence in any given case. (Note that we gave *bindam* ↔ *yiɲu {bama//buɲa//}* for *yiɲu bama buɲa bindam* since a proper name or pronoun appears (on the slight data available) more often to precede than to follow the apposed NP.)

RELATION BETWEEN NOUN PHRASES AND POSITIONS IN SENTENCE STRUCTURE

A noun phrase can fill the following configurational positions:

(1) non-final element in any core i.e. 'a' such that $[(X) a (Y)]V$
(2) syntactic peripheral element i.e. 'a' such that $X:a^{+/-/\varnothing/ap}(Y)$
(3) local peripheral element i.e. 'a' such that $X;a^{+/-/\varnothing}(Y)$

Exactly the same possibilities for NP expansion apply to (1) and (2). The structure that was indicated in (cxxii) is appropriate here (taking account of the fact that the two generics can both be of the 'nature' type, and that there can be more than one adjective). We could conceivably get a pronoun AND a personal or place name in addition to the nominal components.

A local noun phrase, filling position (3), has slightly different possibilities. A locational qualifier can be included (whereas it cannot occur in

a core or peripheral syntactic NP). We use '.' to indicate the relationship between this and the head noun i.e. C.B (a locational qualifier most often precedes a nominal in local inflection). Thus *dabu:lda ŋaɽa* 'beach-LOC south(-LOC)' in (123) is represented as *ŋaɽa.dabul.*

When a specific-noun-plus-part-noun combination occurs in the periphery, its components receive dative and locative inflections respectively, indicating that it must be a syntactic element (the alternative is for both nouns to be in dative case, an even surer indication of syntactic status – 4.1.8). In view of this we could perhaps tentatively exclude (inalienably possessed) 'part' nouns from the local slot.

This yields the following possibilities for a local NP, (3):

(cxxiii) $C \leftrightarrow D\{J.E//F \not\rightarrow B \leftarrow H\}$

There is one further difference. Whereas 'C' in (cxxii) covers pronoun and both personal and place names, 'C' in (cxxiii) is restricted to place names. Proper nouns and pronouns (the latter not having any locational forms) can only occur on the periphery in syntactic function.

VERB COMPLEXES

The verb complex in an underlying core has very much simpler structure than an NP. It involves a head verb, B, and one (or, conceivably, more) adverbs, C. Adverbs provide the same type of semantic modification for verbs as adjectives do for nouns – compare *waguḍa giḍa* 'man quick' and *giḍa-n gunda-l* 'do-quickly cut'. We can thus use the same symbol i.e. $C \rightarrow B$. (Adverbs seem to prefer a position before the verb, while adjectives most often follow a noun; in each case we write the head of the arrow pointing towards the head of the phrase.)

Verbs and adverbs (V) are strictly subcategorised into two classes – transitive (Vtr) and intransitive (Vintr). Vtr correspond to the final slot in a ternary deep core – [a b V], while Vintr are restricted to binary cores – [a V].

Antipassive and INV incorporation can of course derive a surface verb of different transitivity. And, as was mentioned in 4.3.3, *-ŋa-l* can sometimes be added to an intransitive verb simply to make it agree in transitivity with another verb which is to occur in the same VC. (Note that (553) in 4.3.3 involves two verbs – not a verb and an adverb; we suggested in 5.2.6 that a diverbal VC should arise from sentence coordination. This considerably complicates the treatment of syntactically-motivated *-ŋa-l*.) This type of *-ŋa-l* does NOT satisfy any of the semantic conditions outlined in 5.4; it appears to be no more than a syntactic convenience.

$\#$ is used as a general symbol to indicate any of the types of relation between words listed above (that is, it effectively functions just as a 'word boundary symbol'). '↔', '{', '//', '$\not\diagup$', '$\ulcorner$', '←', '→' and '.' are thus special cases of $\#$.

We noted in 4.1.10 and 5.4.8 the existence of a class of sentences in Yidiɲ which involve no verb. They have the structure of an NP, with the head noun being 'commented on' by the other constituents. These 'nominal sentences' can take peripheral NPs and even subordinate clauses, just like intransitive and transitive cores.

There is no justification, in terms of the grammar of Yidiɲ, for recognising an 'underlying verb', which is then 'deleted'. Instead, we simply allow for a third type of sentence nucleus (a core-like NP): B$\#$C, where B is a noun. (The 'comment' may in fact precede or follow the head in terms of (cxxii); for the purposes of rules (cx) and (cxi) we assume that B is the head noun.)

Cores involving INV and INCHO can be adjoined to B$\#$C, and a verb formed from C by the incorporation of INV or INCHO as an affix – 5.4.8–9.

An important difference between a sentence consisting just of a core-like NP and one involving also an INV core is that the latter involves tense/mood specification. Thus

(955) *yiɲu bama ɲalal*   This person is big

describes a (permanent) state. But the tensed inchoative

(956) *yiɲu bama ɲalaldaga:ɲ*   This person has become big

refers to an activity, with a previous state, a process of change, and a new state.

The syntactic representation of (955) differs in one important way from the structure of, say:

(957) *yiɲu bama ɲalal gadaŋ*   This big person is coming

In (957) *yiɲu* qualifies *bama* ← *ɲalal* i.e.

(cxxiv) [*yiɲu*{*bama* ← *ɲalal*} *gada-n*]^{PRES}

whereas in (955) *yiɲu* qualifies just *bama*, and *ɲalal* is then the comment (providing the 'new information' of the clause). Thus the configuration appropriate to (955) is

(cxxv) *yiɲu*{*bama*} ← *ɲalal*

The semantic difference between (955) and (956) is perfectly brought out by the representations (cxxv) and

(cxxvi) $[yi\eta u\{bama\}$ $\eta alal^{\text{INCHO}}]^{\text{PAST}}$

respectively. (It would be obscured if the underlying structure of (955) were made to involve a verb.)

The difference in semantic organisation between (955) and the NP in (957) cannot adequately be shown in a normal 'tree structure' treatment. (955) plainly is just an NP with *ŋalal* being in the same relationship to $\{yi\eta u\}$ *bama* as it is to *bama* in (957). A tree statement might take *ŋalal* in (955) to be a 'deep verb' (i.e. promoting what is a difference in relationships between phrase components to be a relation between sentence components) but there are strong arguments against this position – for instance, it is impossible to have tense or any temporal qualifier in (955). Or else, if (955) were recognised as just an NP it might be assigned the 'same structure' as the NP in (957), which again is clearly missing a semantic trick (for an example of this treatment see Dixon 1972: 205–8).

5.6.2 Possessives. In chapter 3 we mentioned that comitative and genitive nouns behave like adjectives – that is, they normally co-occur with a noun for which they provide semantic modification and with which they agree in case inflection. An NP can contain all three types of modifier:

(958) *ŋaḍin   yaba   guran gali:ɲ gudagayi*
I-GEN-ABS brother-ABS tall-ABS go-PAST dog-COMIT-ABS
My tall brother went with a dog

(959) *ŋaḍinuŋgu yaba:ŋ   gura:ndu ḍaḍa*
I-GEN-ERG brother-ERG tall-ERG   child-ABS
dimba:ɲ   gudagayi:ŋ
carry on shoulder-PAST dog-COMIT-ERG
My tall brother, who was accompanied by a dog, carried the child on his shoulder

We have not, however, provided similar deep treatment for the two members of this set that have so far been discussed – comitatives and (simple, underived) adjectives. Partly to explain the paraphrase relation that exists between nominal and verbal comitatives, we introduced a core with the dummy verb INV, and then a series of syntactic rules and conventions (5.4). Adjectives, on the other hand, were not related to

sentence structure: the relation of an adjective to its head noun appears to be appropriately described at the level of phrase structure (and facilitates an explanation of the contrast between nominal sentences like (955) and verbal constructions similar to (956)).

If -*ḍi* forms are derived from a subordinate clause, then the same origin should presumably be adopted for -*muḍay* comitatives. But what then of privatives, based on -*gimbal*, and of the various other nominal derivational affixes (3.3.6)? Where to draw the line here is an important grammatical question, but one which the writer does not feel competent to pursue further in the present context.

Adjectives and comitatives do show different ordering preferences. An adjective most frequently comes immediately after the head noun, whereas a comitative will habitually follow the main verb (in the typical position of a subordinate clause, which we suggest as its syntactic origin!). Possessives are different again – a genitive NP normally PRECEDES the head noun it is modifying. (It must be clearly noted that these are only ordering PREFERENCES; in fact each of the three modifiers has been found in all of these positions – 4.1.1.)

Genitive marks a complete NP, as it were embedded within the possessed NP (4.1.1, 4.7.1). This might be taken to suggest an underlying core with a dummy verb 'possess'. That is, for (958):

(cxxvii) [*yaba ← guran gali-n*]^{PAST} & [*ŋayu yaba* POSS] &
$$[yaba\ gudaga\ \text{INV}^{com}]$$

We would have to specify that the O NP of the POSS core must be coreferential with some other NP, and then supply a rule putting genitive marking on to the A NP of the POSS core, plus a case agreeing with that on the coreferential NP in the main clause; finally POSS would have to be deleted.

But this syntactic apparatus would be quite ad hoc and unmotivated. Whereas INV served to explain and relate together a variety of nominal and verbal constructions, a dummy verb POSS would serve merely to complicate the syntax of Yidiɲ. It would not add any measure of explanation or simplification to the grammar as a whole.

There are substantial reasons for deriving possessives in Dyirbal as special cases of relative clauses involving a dummy verb POSS (Dixon 1972: 176–84). This does not carry over to Yidiɲ and constitutes a major grammatical difference between the two languages.

Since there is no syntactic reason to proceed otherwise, we treat possession as a semantic relation between elements OF A PHRASE. The only point of note is that the possessor can itself be an NP. We use ' ⅃ ' to indicate this relation i.e. 'C|B' 'C possesses B'. For example, *yiɲu wuṛu yiŋgu:n gala:n* 'this handle belongs to this spear' – from (180) in 3.7.2 – would be *yiɲu {gala}| yiɲu {wuṛu}*. For inalienable possession either a genitive construction (' ⅃ ') or simple apposition (' ⌐ ') can be employed, the choice being determined by the hierarchy described in 4.7.3. Thus, a paraphrase of *yiɲu wuṛu yiŋgu:n gala:n* could be *yiɲu gala wuṛu* i.e. *yiɲu {gala} |wuṛu*. (And note that whereas 'C' in C| B can be a complete NP, with its own deictic, adjectival etc. modifiers, C in B|C is a single noun.)

Finally, the notation suggested for relationships between components of phrases can be exemplified by the underlying configuration for a reasonably complicated sentence:

(960) *miɲa:ŋ   gaɲaraŋgu   ɲala:ldu ŋaḏin   bama*
   edible animal-ERG alligator-ERG big-ERG I-GEN-ABS person-ABS
      buɲa   wagal   bala   baḏa:l   dira: gura:nda
   woman-ABS wife-ABS shin-ABS bite-PAST teeth-INST long-INST
   A big alligator bit my wife's shin with his long teeth

This is:

(cxxviii) [*miɲa≠gaɲarA←ɲalal ŋayu| bama||buɲa||wagal|bala baḏa-l*]^{PAST}
   & [*miɲa≠gaɲarA ← ɲalal dira←guran* INV^{inst}]

5.7 Summary

We can now usefully summarise the sentence configurations, and the derivations, constraints and marking conventions that have been introduced throughout the chapter. Phrase structure possibilities were stated quite fully in 5.6 and there would be no advantage in repeating them here.

CONFIGURATIONS

The basic sentence configuration for Yidiɲ is:

(α) [a (b) V]^{i}:c$^{+/-/\emptyset/\text{ap}}$;d$^{+/-/\emptyset}$:[e (f) W]$^{+/-/\emptyset/\text{ap}}$;[g (h) U]$^{+/-/\emptyset/\text{ap}}$

[pp. 408, 410, 418, 419, 421]

Here a, b, c, ... refer to elements corresponding to noun phrases, and V, W, U to elements corresponding to verb complexes.

The leftmost [...] is called the MAIN CORE; other cores are referred to as SUBORDINATE. The main core is obligatory; all other elements – including subordinate cores – are referred to as PERIPHERAL and are optional.

i represents a choice from the system {imperative, purposive, present, future}. In addition, the verb in any core can be specified ' – controlled' (5.5.2) and/or ' +continuous' (5.5.3).

To a deep structure configuration (α) can be added a transitive core with INV, giving:

(β) (α) & [j k INV^u]   [pp. 429-31]

where u = 'com', 'loc', 'dat', 'fear', 'inst' or 'cont'. However, a surface structure configuration cannot involve INV as an element in a core (although it may occur as a feature to a verb).

A sentence may involve any number of conjoined (β)'s, separated by ','.

There is one variation on the basic configuration. B$\neq$C may be substituted for the main core in (α); peripheral and INV possibilities remain unchanged, but in this case an INV core will carry a tense/mood choice [i]. Here B represents a noun (with or without modifiers) and C any noun or adjective.

A core B$\neq$C can also be joined by & to [j INCHO]^i.

DERIVATIONS

(γ) ANTIPASSIVE (optional)
    [a b V] $\Rightarrow$ [a V^x]:b   [p. 411]

$(\gamma)'$ ANTIPASSIVE IN SUBORDINATE CLAUSE (optional)
    X:[a b V]$^{+/-}$ $\Rightarrow$ X:[a V^x]$^{+/-}$:b$^{(+/-)}$ [p. 420]

$(\gamma)''$ ANTIPASSIVE OF INV$^{inst/com+c}$ CLAUSES (optional)
    X[a b INV$^{inst/com+c}$](Y) $\Rightarrow$ X[a INV$^{inst+x/com+x+c}$]:b$^{INV^{inst/com+c}}$(Y)
                    [pp. 437, 441]

(δ) REFLEXIVE (obligatory)
    [a a V] $\Rightarrow$ [a V^x]   [p. 412]

(ϵ) INV INCORPORATION
    (i) if u $\neq$ 'cont'
        [a V]^i & [a b INV^u] $\Rightarrow$ [a b V^{INV}]i   [p. 431]
    (ii) if u = 'cont'
        [a V]^i & [b a INV^u] $\Rightarrow$ [b a V^{INV}]^i [p. 441]
    or   B$\neq$C & [a B INV^u]^i $\Rightarrow$ [a B C^{INV}]^i [p. 443]

(ζ) INCHO INCORPORATION

$B \neq C$ & $[B \text{ INCHO}]^i \Rightarrow [B \text{ C}^{\text{INCHO}}]^i$ [p. 444]

(η) INV CORE DELETION

(i) $[a \ b \ V]^i$ & $[a \ \text{INV}^{\text{inst}+x}]:d \Rightarrow [a \ b \ V]^i:d$ [p. 436]

(ii) $(X) \ a \ (Y)$ & $[a \ \text{INV}^{\text{com}+x+c}](Z) \Rightarrow (X) \ a \ (Y) \ (Z)$ [p. 441]

(ϵ), (ζ) and (η) can be regarded as optional rules. If they do not apply INV will remain as an element in surface structure, and an illicit string will result.

(θ) VERB COORDINATION (optional)

$[X \ V]^i \ (Y), [X \ W]^i(Y) \Rightarrow [X \ V \neq W]^i(Y)$ [p. 413]

(ι) NP COORDINATION (optional)

$[(X) \ a \ (Y)]^i, [(X) \ b \ (Y)]^i, \ldots \Rightarrow [(X) \ a^{+ba} \neq b^{+ba} \neq \ldots (Y)]^i$ [p. 415]

CONSTRAINTS

(κ) SENTENCE COORDINATION CONDITION

if $[\ldots], [\ldots]$ and neither (θ) nor (ι) has applied, then it should be the case that

either (1) $[a \ (X) \ V]^i, [b \ (Y) \ W]^i$ where $CR(a,b)$ and a,b are pronominal

or (2) $[(X) \ a \ V]^i, [(Y) \ b \ W]^i$ where $CR(a,b)$ and a,b are nonpronominal

and then all or part of b can be deleted. [pp. 412–13]

(λ) GENERAL SUBORDINATE CLAUSE COREFERENTIALITY CONSTRAINT

in every configuration of the form $[\ldots]:[\ldots]^{+/-/\emptyset}$ there must be a,b such that $[(X) \ a \ V]^i(Y):[(Z) \ b \ W]^{+/-/\emptyset}(T)$

and $CR(a,b)$

All or part of a and/or b may then be deleted. [p. 420]

(μ) 'LEST' CLAUSE COREFERENTIALITY CONSTRAINT

In every configuration involving $\ldots:[\ldots]^{ap}$ there must be some a,b such that $\ldots a \ldots :[(X) \ b \ V]^{ap}$ and $CR(a,b)$

Then all or part of a and/or b can be deleted. [p. 422]

Here $CR(a,b)$ indicates that a and b are coreferential.

MARKING CONVENTIONS

There are two 'case transfer' or agreement rules:

(ν) 'LEST' MARKING

If $\ldots a \ldots [(X) \ b \ V]^{ap}$ and $CR(a,b)$

then $[(X) \ b \ V]^{ap} \rightarrow [(X) \ b \ V^{ap+M(a)}]$

$M(a)$ refers to the case marking on a. [p. 422]

(ξ) COMITATIVE NP MARKING CONVENTION

    If there is some a such that ...a... & [b c INV^{com}] and CR(a,b),
       then [b c INV^{com}] → [b c INV$^{com+M(a)}$]   [p. 440]

Case markings of NPs are given by:

(o) in [X Pronoun/Human-deictic V],
    M(Pronoun/Human-deictic) = Accusative   [p. 407]

This rule should also apply, optionally, for definite inanimate deictics.

(π) in [Nominal/Human-deictic X V],
    M(Nominal/Human-deictic) = Ergative   [p. 407]

(ρ) in [...Pronoun/Nominal/Deictic...],
    M(Pronoun/Nominal/Deictic) = ø   [p. 407]

(σ) a. In X:a$^{+/ø}$,M(a) = locative(–allative–instrumental)
    b. In X:/;a$^-$, M(a) = ablative(–causal)
    c. In X:a$^+$, M(a) = purposive
    d. In X:a, M(a) = dative ~ locative
    e. In X:a^{INVinst}, M(a) = locative
    f. In X:a$^{INVcom+c}$, M(a) = comitative+c
       where c is a case marking assigned by (ξ)
    g. In X:a^{ap}, M(a) = 'fear'   [pp. 408, 437, 439–41, 410]

Syntactic derivational affixes on verbs are assigned by

(τ) V^{INV} → V+*ŋa-l*   [p. 431]

(υ) -*:ḍi-n* ASSIGNMENT RULE
    (1) V^x → V+ *:ḍi-n*   [p. 411]
    (2) In [a b V] if a has non-animate reference, and V belongs to
        the 'affect' class, then V is marked ' – controlled'
    (3) If V is ' – controlled' and/or ' + continuous' then it bears
        the affix -*:ḍi-n*   [pp. 449–50]

Tense/mood and 'subordinate values' are transferred to the verb:

(φ) [X V]$^{i/+/-/ø/ap+c}$ → [X V$^{i/+/-/ø/ap+c}$]   [pp. 447, 419]

and then realised:

(χ) a. In ...V$^+$..., M(V) = purposive
    b. In ...V$^-$..., M(V) = causal subordinate
    c. In ...V^ø..., M(V) = dative subordinate
    d. In ...V^{ap+c}..., M(V) = 'lest'+c
    where c is a case marking assigned by (ν)   [pp. 419, 422]

and similarly for tense/mood specifications.

ORDERING

Generally, derivations should apply before constraints and marking conventions. For instance, it is necessary that (γ), (δ), (ϵ) and (ζ) have applied before, and not after, constraints (λ) and (μ); and (ι) before (κ).

The only extrinsic ordering condition on derivations is that the obligatory reflexive rule (δ) must apply before antipassive (γ); otherwise (γ) could move one of the coreferential NPs out of the core and produce the unacceptable surface configuration *[a V]:a. Since (δ) is the only obligatory rule, this could be formulated in terms of a requirement that 'obligatory rules apply before optional ones' (cf. Ringen 1972).

The examples in 4.3.8 show that antipassive (γ) must be allowed to apply either before or after INV incorporation (ϵ). And so on.

As stated here (ξ) should apply before (γ)". However, this is due to the way in which the rules have been formulated; an alternative statement could be found, which would not require this ordering.

6 *Lexicon*

6.1 Word formation

6.1.1 Compound verbs. Yidiɲ has a type of verb that involves 'noun incorporation' (Sapir 1911: 257). This is formed by prefixing a nominal to a regular verbal root; the resulting compound has the same transitivity as the verbal root. The meaning of a compound verb is not, as a rule, directly inferrable from the meanings of its constituent words (although it does not usually require too great a metaphorical extension). Thus from *ḍili* 'eye' and *budi-l* 'put down' is derived *ḍili + budi-l* 'look after', as in (656) and

(961) *ɲundu ḍambu:l gadan / galiŋalna   / ŋaɲḍi ɲuniɲ*
    you-SA two-ABS come-IMP go-COMIT-PURP we-SA you-O
    ḍili + budi:lna / wugu   burgi:na
    look after-PURP work-ABS walkabout-PURP
    You two come, so that [I can] take you, so that we can look after
    you, and you can work [for us, in Cairns]

The components of *ḍili + budi-l* can, of course, occur as free forms:

(962) *ŋaɲaɲ bama:l   wawa:l ḍili: guma:nda*
    I-O   person-ERG see-PAST eye-INST one-INST
    The person watched me with one eye

(963) *ŋayu ḍaḍa budi:l yawu:*   I put the baby down on the grass

Incorporated nouns (all examples of which are disyllabic) do not cohere phonologically with a following verb root. Thus *ḍili* and *budi:lna* are distinct phonological words (2.4) in (961), just as are *ḍili* and *baygaɽ* in

(964) *ŋaḍin ḍili baygaɽ* My eye is sore

It may thus be asked on what grounds we assert that *ḍili + budi-l* is a compound verb, whereas in (964) *ḍili* is the head noun of the S NP, quite separate from the verb *baygaɽ*. Semantic grounds would not, of course, be sufficient – two words may often have extended meanings in an idiomatic collocation.

[465]

There are two main criteria for recognising compound verbs:
(1) ORDERING. Although there are definite preferences for the ordering of words in Yidiɲ sentences, a given word can – potentially – occur at ANY position (4.1.1, 4.1.9). Thus the words in (964) could be rearranged, with no change in meaning, as *baygaɽ ɲaḍin ḍili, ḍili ɲaḍin baygaɽ, ɲaḍin baygaɽ ḍili*, and so on.

The roots in a compound verb occur in fixed order, and nothing can come between them. The simplest way of testing whether a putative sequence is a compound verb is to negate it – *ɲuḍu* 'not' normally occurs immediately before the verb, as in

(965) *ɲaḍin ḍili ɲuḍu baygaɽ*   My eye is not sore

With *ḍili + budi-l*, *ɲuḍu* MUST precede *ḍili*, as in (747) from 4.6.2.

Note that *wagal* 'wife' is often heard followed by *budi-l* 'put down', this collocation having the meaning 'marry [a woman]'.

(966) *ɲayu yiɲḍu:ɲ wagal budi:lna*   I want to marry this woman

But the elements are separable – *wagal ɲuḍu ɲayu budi:lna* was obtained. We must thus take *wagal* in (966) as making up, with *yiɲḍu:ɲ*, the O NP, and conclude that *wagal* does not form a compound verb with *budi-l*; in this case there is simply an idiom-like noun–verb collocation *wagal budi-l*.

(2) SYNTACTIC FUNCTION. In

(967) *buɲa:ɲ ḍaḍa ḍili + budil*   The woman is looking after the children

the incorporated noun *ḍili* must effectively be referring to the woman's eyes. If it were – with *buɲa* 'woman' – part of the A NP, it should be in ergative case; if it were in instrumental function it should have the case-form *ḍili:*. Since *ḍili* does not show any inflection it would – if it were a separate word in (967) – have to be taken as being in absolutive case, presumably part of the O NP together with *ḍaḍa* 'baby'; but *ḍili* does NOT refer to any part of the baby!

Thus, there is no plausible syntactic interpretation of (967) with *ḍili* taken as a separate word (we cannot have two distinct absolutive NPs). So *ḍili + budi-l* must be a compound verb.

budi-l can involve a dative NP, referring to someone for whose benefit an action was performed. For instance:

(968) *buɲa:ɲ buda budi:l ḍaḍa:nda*
      The woman put a blanket down for the child

Note that we can NOT have the 'object' of *ḍili+budi-l* in dative case (which is what we would expect if *ḍili* were a separate word – presumably O NP):

*(969) *buɲa:ŋ ḍaḍa:nda ḍili+budi:l*

The object of the compound verb MUST be in O function (absolutive case) as in (967) and (961). When the writer tried to elicit *(969) he was given the antipassive version of (967), where the underlying O NP does of course occur with dative inflection:

(970) *buɲa ḍaḍa:nda ḍili+budi:ɟiɲu* ⟨= (967)⟩

There are also intransitive verbs that involve noun incorporation. For instance, the noun *guybil* 'a whistle (noise)' and *ḍana-n* 'to stand' yield *guybil+ḍana-n* 'to whistle'. The criterion of ORDERING applies just as in the case of transitive verbs. For 'Stop whistling!' one must say

(971) *ɲundu giyi guybil+ḍanan*

and not

*(972) *ɲundu guybil giyi ḍanan*

Note that here it is the 'whistling' that is (metaphorically) 'standing', not the whistler himself. There is an important difference between:

(973) *guybil ɲundu ḍanaŋ* You can stand up and whistle

in which *guybil* is part of the S NP ('inalienably possessed' by *ɲundu*); and

(974) *ɲundu guybil+ḍanaŋ* You can whistle

(974), involving the compound verb, does not specify any stance. The informant suggested that, after having issued the instruction in (973), one could a little later on say

(975) *ɲundu guybil+ḍanaŋ wunaŋ*
    [Now] you whistle [the same tune] lying down

emphasising that in (973) *ḍana-n* has its regular lexical meaning.

We can invoke the second criterion, of SYNTACTIC FUNCTION, for intransitives but this takes a somewhat different form from that for transitives. Most of the nouns incorporated into intransitive compounds refer to types of noise. When used outside compounds these are, apparently, regarded as being inalienably possessed by their utterer, this being marked either (a) by the genitive affix, or (b) by simple apposition (4.7.3, and cf. 4.3.4). Thus:

(976) a. *ŋayu bama:n gawal binaŋalŋu*⎱ I heard the person's call
     b. *ŋayu bama gawal binaŋalŋu* ⎰

There is a compound verb *gawal + ḍana-n* 'to call out', involving *gawal* 'a call' and *ḍana-n* 'to stand'. Thus (cf. (705)):

(977) *bama waruwaru ŋabi gawal + ḍanaŋ*
     Lots of children are calling out [as they play]

But note that the word(s) referring to 'the caller' can NOT take the genitive suffix with *gawal + ḍana-n*. That is,

*(978) *bama:n waruwaru:n ŋabi:n gawal + ḍanaŋ*

is not an acceptable Yidiɲ sentence. The head of the O NP in (976) can be either *gawal* or *bama*. But in the case of (977) it must be *bama*, since *gawal* is incorporated as part of the verb. In *(978) there is nothing 'possessed' that *bama:n* could be understood to be qualifying.

It is possible sometimes for a sentence to include a noun both in free form (within the S or O NP) and also as part of a compound verb. While the writer was checking to see whether *gawal + ḍana-n* really was a compound stem, he tried to separate the components with the particle *giyi* 'don't'. When asked whether *ɲundu gawal giyi ḍanan* was possible, the informant responded that it wasn't, but one could say:

(979) *ɲundu gawal giyi gawal + ḍanan*   Don't you call out!

The writer has gathered 25 compound verbs, out of a total corpus of about 320 verbal items (a full list is given below, classified by nominal member). 13 different verb roots are involved, five of them used more than once:

        transitive *ḍara-l* 'set up, put standing' (in 5 compounds)
                     budi-l 'put down' (3)
                     gunda-l 'cut' (2)
   intransitive *ḍana-n* 'stand' (4)
                    wanda-n 'fall down' (3)

while 8 verbs occur each in only one compound:

transitive

bambi-l 'cover'	*baɽa-l* 'kick, punch' (see 4.3.2)
baḍa-l 'bite'	*biya-l* 'blow'
baga-l 'pierce with pointed	*gada-n* (see below)
implement'	*guba-n* 'burn'

intransitive

  ḍuŋga-n 'run'

ŋuyar 'thought' occurs only in intransitive *ŋuyar+wanda-n* 'think' (based on *wanda-n* 'fall down') and transitive *ŋuyar+gada-n*. Each compound verb except *ŋuyar+gada-n* has the same transitivity value as its constituent simple verb, suggesting that we should NOT identify *gada-n* here with the common intransitive root 'to come'. We are thus led to regard *gada-n* as a 'cran' root, occurring only in this compound.

Sixteen nominals are incorporated, six of them in more than one compound. Most of these occur as free forms in NPs, but three appear (on the data available) to be confined to occurrence in compound verbs.

[a] BODY PART NOUNS

(1) *ḏili* 'eye'
    ḏili+budi-l 'look after'
    ḏili+ḏara-l 'stare at'
    ḏili+guba-n 'be jealous concerning'
    ḏili+gunda-l 'stop looking'

(2) *bina* 'ear'
    bina+bambi-l 'forget'
    bina+baṛa-l 'deafen'

(3) *ḏiŋay* 'nostril'
    ḏiŋay+ḏara-l 'sneeze (at)'

Note that although *ḏili* and *ḏara-l* can make up a compound verb, as in

(980) *ŋaṇḏi ŋabi:ŋ wira*   *ḏili+ḏara:l*
    we-SA all-ERG moveable object-ABS stare at-PAST
    We all stared at the aeroplane

ḏili has been encountered in the S NP and *ḏara-l* in the VC of a sentence:

(981) *ŋaḏin   ḏili   bugabuga   ḏara:ḏiṇu*
    I-GEN-ABS eye-ABS darkness-REDUP-ABS put standing-:ḏi-PAST
    My eye has become dark (i.e. I can't see)

There is nothing semantically in common between the syntactic co-occurrence of *ḏili* and *ḏara-l*, in (981), and their inclusion as morphological partners within a verb, in (980).

ḏiŋay+ḏara-l is encountered most frequently in the antipassive, meaning just 'sneeze':

(982) *ŋayu ḏiŋay+ḏara:ḏiŋ*   I sneezed

without any implication of an 'object'. But it can also be used in a transitive sentence:

(983) *bama:l ŋaṇaŋ ḏiŋay+ḏara:l*   The person sneezed at me

[b] CONCRETE NOUNS

(4) *ṇari* 'hole in ground'
    ṇari+baga-l 'dig hole to bury [something] in'
    ṇari+budi-l
    ṇari+ḏara-l } 'put in hole and cover over'

No difference in meaning between *ɲari+budi-l* and *ɲari+ḍara-l* could be ascertained. Both verbs are typically used for the 'kapamari' method of ground cooking.

(5) *giḍaṛ* 'mark, line'
     giḍaṛ+gunda-l 'paint in pattern' – cf. (474–5) in 4.2.5, and (879) in 4.10.

(6) *gaŋgu* 'side of mountain' (also used as body part noun 'waist', and as a locational qualifier – 3.4.1).
     gaŋgu+ḍuŋga-n 'take short cut'

Compare the compound verb in

(984) *ɲayu gaŋgu+ḍuŋga:ɲ gaba:ɲḍa*
     I crossed the road, taking a short-cut

with *gaŋgu* used as a noun (to indicate the manner of motion) in

(985) *ɲayu ḍuŋga:ɲ gaŋgu:y*
     I ran with my waist (i.e. my waist was hurting as I ran)

[c] NOISES AND SONG/DANCE STYLES

(7) *ḍubun* 'squeaky noise made by young animal'
     ḍubun+ḍana-n 'to squeak'

(8) *gawal* 'a call'
     gawal+ḍana-n 'to call'

(9) *guybil* 'a whistle'
     guybil+ḍana-n 'to whistle'

(10) *wulŋgu* 'a female song-style'
     wulŋgu+ḍana-n 'to sing wulŋgu style'

(11) *ɲaṛu* 'shake-a-leg dance style'
     ɲaṛu+wanda-n 'to dance shake-a-leg'

Note that all compound verbs referring to noise-making involve *ḍana-n*. It is NOT the case, though, that any noun referring to noise can be incorporated to *ḍana-n* (it appears that NO others can be). Thus the generic noun *gugu* 'noise' can occur as the subject of *ḍana-n*:

(986) *ḍigirḍigir gugu ḍanaŋ*
     The willy wagtail noise is audible (literally: 'standing') [at that place]

but is not compounded with it, as can be seen from:

(987) *gugu waɲa ḍanaŋ*   Whose noise is it that is audible [here]?

where *waɲa* 'who', the 'inalienable possessor' of *gugu*, intrudes between it and *ḍana-n*.

[d] ABSTRACT NOUNS

(12) *biḍaṛ* 'dream'
     biḍaṛ+wanda-n 'to dream'
     biḍaṛ+baḍa-l 'to dream about'

(13) *ɲuyar* 'thought'
     ɲuyar+wanda-n 'to think'
     ɲuyar+gada-n ' to think about'

biḍaṟ and *ŋuyar* occur only in these compounds. Note that there is in each case a transitive/intransitive pair. What is 'thought/dreamt of' will be marked by peripheral case with the intransitive, and will be the O NP of the transitive verb:

(988) a. *wagu:ḍa ŋuyar+wandaŋ buɲa:gu* ⎫ The man is thinking about the
     b. *waguḍaŋgu buɲa ŋuyar+gadaŋ* ⎭   woman

If one thinks or dreams about an event (rather than just about a person or thing) it is described through a subordinate clause:

(989) *ŋayu wurmba   wuna:ɲ/ biḍaṟ+baḍa:l bama*
       I-SA asleep-ABS lie-PAST dream-PAST   person-ABS
         gadaɲunda   margaɲ   bulmba:gu
         come-DAT SUBORD fighting men-ABS camp-ALL
         I lay asleep, and dreamt that the fighting men were coming home

(14) *ḍirbi* 'promise, promised time'
       ḍirbi+budi-l ⎫
       ḍirbi+ḍara-l ⎬ 'to promise to do something at a certain time'

The object of these verbs can be the person or thing who would be the 'focus' of the promised action:

(990) *ŋaɲaɲ bama:l ḍirbi+budi:l/ garu ŋaɲaɲ wawa:daŋ*
       The person promised to come and see me by-and-by.

(991) *bama:l   ŋanda bindabinda ḍirbi+budi:l*
       person-ERG I-DAT shell-ABS   promise-PAST
       The person promised me we'd have [a ritual exchange of] shells [for
         a dilly-bag]

or it can be, say, the place at which a planned fight will take place:

(992) *ŋaɲḍi ḍirbi+ḍara   bulmba*
       we-SA promise-IMP place-ABS
       We must [fight] at that promised place

No clear difference in meaning could be ascertained between *ḍirbi+budi-l* and *ḍirbi+ḍara-l*, as it could not between *ɲari+budi-l* and *ɲari+ḍara-l* (and note the interchangeability of existentials *wuna-n* and *ḍana-n*, the intransitive correspondents of *budi-l* and *ḍara-l* – 6.2.4).

    ḍirbi occurs as a free form in lines 66, 80, 100 and 102 of text 2, and within a compound in line 15 of text 9.

(15) *buḍu* 'bad luck'
       buḍu+biya-l 'blow on [someone] whilst asleep, to blow away bad
         luck'

buḍu appears only in this single compound verb.

[e] ADJECTIVE
(16) *yaga* 'split in half'
    yaga + ḍara-l 'to split in half'

Although a fairly small number of nouns and verbs enter into compounds of this sort, the process is not productive; it was not, except in isolated cases, possible to elicit new noun-incorporated stems.

Noticing that the corpus contained *ḍili + ḍara-l*, *ḍili + budi-l*; *ḍirbi + ḍara-l*, *ḍirbi + budi-l*; and *ɲari + ḍara-l*, the writer enquired about *ɲari + budi-l* and found that this was a compound stem. But when, on the basis of *biḍaṛ + wanda-n*, *biḍaṛ + baḍa-l* and *ŋuyar + wanda-n* he suggested *ŋuyar + baḍal*, it turned out that this is NOT a possible compound in Yidiɲ.

There are a number of idiomatic collocations (some involving nouns and verbs from these lists) which do not constitute compounds. *wagal budi-l* 'marry' was mentioned at (966) above; and 'to kneel' is expressed through *buŋgu* 'knee' and *ḍara-l* 'put standing' – as in (354) – but here *buŋgu* is simply the object of the verb, and is not morphologically connected to it (one can say, for instance, *buŋgu ḍabu: ḍara* 'kneel on the ground').

(240) in 3.8.7 involves *buŋgu* and the reflexive form *ḍara:ḍi-n* – here 'the actor' and 'his knee' occur together (presumably in a relation of inalienable possession) within the S NP.
  In 4.7.3 we mentioned that constructions like (787) *ŋayu wabaṛ galiŋ* 'I'm going for a walk' do not have any obvious place within our syntactic description. But it is not the case that *wabaṛ gali-n* – or *wugu burgi-n* in (961) – are compound verbs. The components are separable.

There are syntactic and semantic similarities between this class of compound verbs in Yidiɲ and the phenomenon of 'noun incorporation' in a number of Arnhem Land languages. In Tiwi (Osborne 1974: 46–50) and Rembarŋa (McKay 1975: 287–309), for instance, a noun can be included in a verb word, and is placed BETWEEN different classes of prefix. In these languages a noun which is incorporated would be expected to be part of the S or O (never A) NP if it occurred outside the verb. Many examples in Yidiɲ follow this pattern – for instance *bina + bambi-l* 'forget' is literally 'cover ears' (and see the discussion of *guybil + ḍana-n* above) – although in some cases the noun would be expected in instrumental case (as *ḍili + budi-l* 'look after') and in others it is difficult to make any firm judgement.

Other Arnhem Land languages showing noun incorporation include Dalabon (Capell 1962: 101), Gunbalang (Harris 1969: 4, 5, 8), Gunwinggu (Oates 1964: 55) and Nunggubuyu (Hughes and Healey 1971: 54). See also Sapir (1911) for discussion of this phenomenon in American Indian languages.

A main difference is that incorporation appears to be (at least to a degree) productive in languages like Tiwi, whereas in Yidiɲ each compound must, it seems, be learned separately. It may be that we are witnessing, in Yidiɲ, the beginnings of a grammatical process – it would be likely to begin with a few compounds and, once a pattern had been established, these could be generalised to yield a productive process (any nominal of a certain type could, within the limits of semantic plausibility, be incorporated into any one of a certain set of verbal roots).

The writer has a relatively small vocabulary of Yidiɲ (about 1800 words, excluding proper names). A more extensive dictionary would be likely to include a higher proportion of compounds. But the data to hand, and the results of systematic eliciting from them, do clearly show that the process is not at present productive.

6.1.2 Formation of proper names. Proper names of people and places are, in almost every case, based on dictionary items. A place will be named after some object or event which a storytime traveller found there (1.4). A person will be named after something connected with a totem that belongs to his moiety (1.5).

A sample of one hundred proper names (87 of places and 13 of living or recently deceased people) were surveyed:

(a) 42 are identical to a common noun, adjective, locational qualifier or verb root;

(b) 47 involve some addition or phonological alteration to a dictionary root;

(c) 10 are compounds of two dictionary roots (one of which may have undergone phonological alteration);

(d) 1 appears unrelated to any other form.

We now discuss and exemplify these types one at a time.

(a) IDENTICAL TO DICTIONARY ROOT

See the examples quoted in 1.4, *gaɲḍugaɲḍu* in (717), and *bilma* in (682) – the latter is the only item under (a) to involve a verbal root, here *bilma-n* 'clear [ground]'. Also:

(i) A place at the south end of Oombunghi Beach is called *ḍulugunu* 'black myrtle tree' because this species of tree grows there.

(ii) A rock at Cape Grafton Point is called *ɲawuyu* 'salt-water turtle' because when Gulɲḍaṛubay (1.4) first came to this place he saw a turtle's head emerge from the water, and then sink down again.

(iii) One of Tilly Fuller's names was *baḍigal* 'fresh-water turtle', an animal connected with the guramiɲa moiety.

(b) PHONOLOGICAL ADDITION OR ALTERATION

14 of the 47 examples here involve verbs. *ḍariyi*, Dick Moses's name, was discussed in 1.5. Also:

(i) Robert Patterson is called *ɲalmbi* from *ɲarmbi-l* 'to approach but not reach the ground'; this is after a moiety association with the whirlwind, whose passage is appropriately described by this verb.

(ii) A place on the beach just south of Cape Grafton Point is called *giṛiga* since Gulɲḍaṛubay found there a mob of children shouting in play (*giṛi-n*).

There is one name based on a particle:

(iii) Dick Moses's sister, Ida Burnett, is named *ɲuḍun*, after the particle/interjection *ɲuḍu* 'no/not'.

Eight place-names involve a nominal root plus comitative affix *-ḍi* ~ *-yi* (3.3.4, 4.3.1) e.g.

(iv) A place just inland from Cape Grafton Point is called *ḍirgaṛḍi* 'with blady grass' since Gulɲḍaṛubay found lots of blady grass (*ḍirgaṛ*) growing there.

Three names involve the affix *-gaṛa:* 'from' (3.3.6) e.g.

(v) A sandbank just off Fitzroy Island is called *gandagaṛa:*, after *ganda* 'yamstick'.

The remaining names in class (b) involve unexplainable addition or alteration to a nominal or locational root e.g.

(vi) A point in Mission Bay is called *yaɲḍiga* after the noun *ɲaɲḍi* 'body, flesh, meat'.

(vii) The name of Deception Point is *wuŋgu*, after the noun *wuŋgur* referring to ritual shouts '*wɔ́, wɔ́*'. It is said that when the storytime hero Bangilan first landed at Deception Point his group of warriors cut a rock there, which they celebrated with a corroboree, dancing round the rock and singing '*wɔ́, wɔ́*'.

We can now look at the phonological forms of these names. Those that involve an established affix *-ḍi* ~ *-yi* or *gaṛa:* are explainable. Most

of the remainder involve the ADDITION to the root of one or two final segments; these appear quite unmotivated:

root	*ɲuḍu*	name	*ɲuḍun*
	giɽi-n		*giɽiga*
	ḍari-n		*ḍariyi*
	wiḍi		*wiḍiy* (see 2.3.7)

Attempts to elicit an explanation for these accretions met with no success. For instance, there is a place on the side of a hill near Turtle Bay named *ɲiyaman*, after the noun *ɲiya* 'rim of dilly-bag, edge of creek or mountain'. Dick Moses insisted that it was called *ɲiyaman* BECAUSE it is in a *ɲiya* location, the appropriacy of the first two syllables being regarded as an entirely sufficient justification for the form of the complete name.

His discussion of this point had a Socratic flavour. In *Cratylus* (393ff.) Plato suggests that names have a natural basis but can also involve an arbitrary, or conventional, component. For instance, 'beta' as the name of a letter is appropriate by virtue of the initial b (employing the sound of the letter which is being named) and the 'addition of e, t, a gives no offence, and does not prevent the whole name from having the value which the legislator [giver of names] intended – so well did he know how to give the letters names'.

In some cases the final segment of a root has been DELETED to form a name – thus *wuŋgu* (Deception Point), from *wuŋgur*, and *ḍimiḍimi*, a flat spot between Palm Beach and King Beach where there are many *ḍimir* 'mountain yams'.

In other cases the name may involve the SUBSTITUTION of unmotivated segments for part of the root. The place (on White Rock Creek) at which the skin of a storytime cassowary turned soft and dropped off is called *giɽaba*, based on the adjective *giɽaɽ* 'soft (skin)'. And a place at which Gulɲḍaɽubay heard the noise of a spear-fight is *duyuŋu*, from the verb *duyi-l* 'fight with spears'. See also (414) in 4.1.10.

bandi names a place in Mission Bay at which Gulɲḍaɽubay heard people grumbling and groaning; it is based on the root *bani-n* 'to grumble', and could be said to involve INSERTION of *-d-* in the middle of the root. Even with this degree of phonological difference, Dick Moses said that the spot was called *bandi* 'because they *baniŋ* there', again regarding this as entirely sufficient justification for the form.

The 47 names of type (b) involve four cases of more drastic phonological reshaping. They are:

verb root	*ɲarmbi-n*	name	*ɲalmbi*
adjective root	*ɲiwir*		*ɲirwiy*
noun root	*ɲaɲḍi*		*yaɲḍiga*
locational qualifier	*ŋambin*		*mambin*

ɲalmbi and *yaɲḍiga* were discussed above. The place *ɲirwiy* is so called because a storytime boomerang broke up (*ɲiwir*) there – 2.3.7. At *mambin* there is a stone that has fallen belly-up; the name is based on locational qualifier *ŋambin* 'belly down' (3.4.1). (Note the semantic complementarity, correlating – in this instance only – with opposing types of non-coronal nasal!)

In a few cases the form of a name may attest to some historical stage in Yidiɲ. Thus, it may not be a coincidence that a few names based on *-n* conjugation verbs end in *-y* – for instance, *gubay*, the name of a stream running into Mission Bay at *bilma*, that was in storytime days heated by a hot stone (from *guba-n* 'burn'). Note that in most languages of eastern Australia the open intransitive conjugation has marker *-y*, not *-n* (cf. Dixon 1972: 13–16, 54–5).

And there are two instances of a name having three syllables (and not being reducible), where the corresponding common noun is, in absolutive case, reduced by Rule 2 (2.3.4):

absolutive noun	nominal root	place
ḍimu:r	*ḍimurU* 'house'	*ḍimuru* 'a place just above Reeve's Creek'
gaṛba:ṛ	*gaṛbaṛA* 'mangrove tree'	*gaṛbaṛa* 'a place on the beach, just south of the mouth of Badubadu creek'

Note also

gaɲḍi:l	*gaɲḍilA* 'crab'	*gaɲḍiṛa* 'a stoney island in Mission Bay'

in which there is also an *l–ṛ* correspondence.

(c) COMPOUNDS

Five of the ten compound names involve a sequence of two nominals. Either a noun followed by *guman* 'one':

(i) *balaguman* 'shin-one' a place to the west of False Cape where an alligator bit one of Damari's legs off at the knee (line 121 of text 2).

Or a sequence of two nouns:

(ii) George Davis told how his grandfather had two personal *gambunU*, small spirits (said to be rather like 'guiding angels') who told him what was happening elsewhere. One was called *baybagawar* 'squirt blood', from *gawar* 'blood' and *bayba* 'spring (usually of water)'.

There are five nominal-plus-verb compounds, including:

(iii) *ḍubuṛwulay* 'stone-die', a stone near which storytime people are said to have died.
(iv) *waŋalḍuŋgay* 'boomerang-run', the name for Double Island (near Cairns) through which a storytime boomerang travelled fast.
(Note that we have here two more examples of a final *-y* on verbs belonging to the *-n* conjugation – *wula-n* 'die' and *ḍuŋga-n* 'run'; see also 2.3.7.)

Leaving aside the final segment of verbs, there is only one example of a compound showing deviation from the normal forms of roots. Dick Moses's elder brother was called *ḍiliwaŋin* (see line 1 of text 9), based on *ḍili* 'eye' and *yaŋin* 'side of face between eye and ear'. Here *w* corresponds to *y* in the root.

(d) UNEXPLAINABLE FORMS

Only one of our sample of 100 place and contemporary personal names cannot be related to any other word – *muṛubay*, the name of a grassy mound near Gordonvale (that has never sported any trees) which is today called 'Green Hill'.

But, when we look to the names of storytime heroes – such as Gulṇḍaṛubay, Bangilan, Damari and Guyala (1.4, 1.5) – we find that almost all are without explanation. Only Bibiyuwuy, the name of a man who 'began death' (text 14) can be explained – the final part is related to the cry '*wu:y wu:y wu:y...*' that Bibiyuwuy emitted (line 20) on being confronted with his own decayed head.

6.1.3 Root structure. Very little can at present be said about the historical origin of Yidiɲ roots. There are a few obvious similarities across parts of speech:

NOUNS	VERBS	ADJECTIVES
mala 'palm of hand'	*mala-l* 'to feel with the hand'	
bina 'ear'	*binaŋa-l* 'to hear, listen'	*binagal* 'paying attention'
	binarŋa-l 'to tell, warn'	*binabaɲḍa* 'sad, forgetful'
	binagali-n 'to forget'	

binaŋa-l could be the regular causative of *bina* (4.8.1) but no explanation can be put forward for the *-r-* in *binarŋa-l* or for the second elements of *binagal*, *binabaɲḍa*, *bingagali-n*.

And a few other sets of likely cognates, on the lines of:

buga 'night(time)'   *bugamugu* 'daylight'

ḍili 'eye' is, like *bina*, one of the forms most commonly incorporated into verbs (6.1.1). In addition, a number of roots begin with *ḍili*:

ḍilibugabi 'the next day'
ḍilibiɾi 'barramundi'
ḍilibuɾa 'green ant'

but the semantic connection with the body part noun is far from obvious here. And while *buga* 'night' can be recognised in *ḍilibugabi*, there is little semantic reason to associate *ḍilibiɾi* with the particle *biɾi* 'again', or *ḍilibuɾa* with nominal *buɾabuɾa* 'dusty place'.

There are a small number of cognate pairs of verb/adverb and adjective:

giḍa-n 'do quickly'   *giḍa* 'quick'
ŋaŋga-n 'forget'   *ŋaŋga* 'deaf'

and some miscellaneous pairs of other types where there is a possible correlation between semantic and phonological similarities e.g.

buɾmu, Adj. 'quiet'   *buɾmbay*, Noun 'well-behaved person'

A number of roots involve the repetition of a disyllabic unit (see also 3.3.9):

baɾabaɾa '(common) fly'	*bidibidi* 'beetle'
birbibirbi 'small flat fish'	*wabaɾwabaɾ* 'sacred/tabooed object'

There are no roots *baɽa* or *birbi*; and no reasons for connecting the other two forms with the locational qualifier *bidi* 'near' or the abstract noun *wabaɽ* 'a walk'.

Some roots may involve what was once a productive affix; it is difficult to do more than guess about these cases. For instance, four of the thirteen known trisyllabic roots have *-ba-* as the third syllable (3.8.3); note the comment at the very end of 3.8.8 about a possible affix *-ba*.

We can make a few remarks on the historical origin of bound morphemes. For instance, some free forms have certainly developed into (productive or semi-productive) affixes: *ḍamu* is a particle in Dyirbal (Dixon 1972: 120) but functions, with similar meaning, as a derivational affix in Yidiɲ (3.3.6). 'To yawn' is in Yidiɲ *wurga-n* or *ḍa:wurga-n* (*wurga-n* does not have any other meaning); *ḍa:-* here may well relate to the noun *ḍawa* which occurs in many Australian languages with the meaning 'mouth' or 'doorway' (2.4). It is presumably the same *ḍa:-* that is involved in locational forms like *ḍa:guŋga:ɽ* 'northwards' (3.4.3) but here the semantic connection is difficult to discern.

Finally, the number adjective *ḍambulA* 'two' – absolute *ḍambu:l* – may be related to the common Australian root *bula* (Capell 1956: 77–8). The first syllable cannot confidently be explained (one hypothesis could involve *ḍa:-*, with *ḍa:bula* becoming *ḍambula*, but this is highly speculative).

The form in Mbabaram is *mbil*, pretty certainly a development from *ḍambula* ~ *ḍambu:l*. Without the documentation of an intervening stage, in Yidiɲ, it would surely be impossible to relate this to **bula*.

6.1.4 Loan concepts. Many European and Asian artefacts and ideas were described through existing Yidiɲ words. Thus *biŋgal* 'spoon (made from a shell)' was also used for 'chopsticks' (through similarity of function). *ḍama* 'anything dangerous (such as a poisonous snake or a centipede)' was extended to cover 'alcoholic beverages, opium and medicines'. Other examples are given towards the end of 6.2.1.

It is interesting to compare the names given to a certain new concept in different Australian languages. Thus the Yidiɲɖi use the verb *munda-l* 'pull' for rowing a boat whereas the Dyirbalŋan employ *baga-l* 'pierce with a pointed implement'; in the first case it is the effect the rower has on the oar that is described, while in the second it is the action of the oar on the water.

In other cases Yidiɲ introduced a compound name. Thus 'policeman' – *buliman* or *buliḍiman* in most neighbouring languages – is in Yidiɲ

giḏaṛḏi, literally 'with stripes'. This involves the abstract noun *giḏaṛ* 'line, mark' and comitative affix *-ḏi*.

Some English words were taken over as loans, and adapted to conform to the phonological structure of Yidiɲ; all words must begin with a single consonant, must have at least two syllables, and must end in a segment other than a stop or *w*. Thus *yiŋgilibiy* 'English bee', *ḏuwa* 'saw', *biya* 'beer', *bagi* 'bag', *gawuda* 'coat', *gilaḏi* 'glass' and *gabaḏi* 'cabbage'.

The loan-word correspondences between English and Yidiɲ sounds are similar to those described for Dyirbal (Dixon 1972: 326). Also like Dyirbal, loans are almost all nouns or adjectives (the only known exception is *landima-l* 'teach' from English *learn* – see line 3 of text 9).

Dick Moses is careful always to speak pure Yidiɲ. Thus, whereas some recent speakers have muddled together Yidiɲ and Dya:bugay, or Yidiɲ and Guŋgay, Moses is very particular about excluding non-Yidiɲ items (and will correct himself when these do inadvertently intrude). He takes this to the extreme of eliminating loans from English that must – in his youth – have been firmly established in the language (they are retained by all other speakers). In place of *mudaga* 'motor car' and *biligan* 'billy-can' he always used *dundalay* and *gunbu:l* (which Moses says were originally the Dyalŋuy terms for these items – see 1.8).

6.2 Topics in semantics

The Yidiɲ lexicon reveals a number of interesting semantic contrasts and dependencies. These will be fully detailed in a projected dictionary/ thesaurus of the language. In the present chapter we comment on four topics in semantics that have particular relevance for an understanding of the grammar of Yidiɲ.

6.2.1 Noun classification. As already mentioned (4.1.1), an NP in Yidiɲ will typically involve a generic, in addition to a specific, noun. For instance:

(993) *bama:l   yabuṛuŋgu miɲa   gangu:l   wawa:l*
      person-ERG girl-ERG   animal-ABS wallaby-ABS see-PAST
      Literally: 'the person girl saw the animal wallaby'

An early, fairly superficial, examination of this phenomenon revealed the following occurrences of classifiers:

bama, with any noun referring to human beings;

miɲa, with many nouns referring to non-human animates e.g. species of snakes, guanas, frogs, possums, bandicoots, kangaroos, grubs, fishes, birds, etc.;

mayi, with any noun referring to non-flesh food – edible yams, nuts, fruit, ferns, etc.;

bana, with nouns referring to fresh water, salt water, river, swamp, tide, beer, etc.;

buɽi, with nouns referring to fire, sparks, charcoal, a light, etc.;

ḍugi, with nouns referring to types of tree;

wira, with 'inanimate nouns' such as shell, clothes, boomerang, aeroplane, motor car, stick.

It appeared that this set of generics (together with perhaps a few more terms which had not then been uncovered) probably divided up the universe into mutually exclusive areas. It seemed likely that *wira* was defined negatively as 'anything else', after the positive specifications 'human' (*bama*), 'non-human animate' (*miɲa*), 'edible plant' (*mayi*), 'liquid' (*bana*), 'associated with fire' (*buɽi*), and 'tree' (*ḍugi*) had been disposed of.

However, difficulties soon arose with this scheme of interpretation. For instance, it was discovered that *miɲa* did not cover all animals, but only those considered edible. Thus *yalbur*, a grey frog species, is *miɲa*, but a smaller frog, *wiḍi*, is not. The white-tail rat, *durgim*, can be eaten – and is included under *miɲa* – whereas a small rat, referred to by the species name *mugiɲ*, is not. It appeared that *miɲa* refers to 'edible animals', just as *mayi* covers 'edible plants'.

It was also discovered that whereas ANYTHING burning (including even 'hot smoke') is *buɽi*, only certain liquids are describable as *bana*. *bana* applies to waterfall, steam and dew, but not to blood, urine, spittle, snot, semen or sweat. *bana* appeared to be basically 'any drinkable liquid' (although the use of *bana* with *biriɲ* 'salt water' was something of an embarrassment).

A number of new generic terms were uncovered at this stage of the investigation – *maŋgum* refers to ALL frogs (whether edible or not) and *ḍaruy* to ALL birds. *walba* 'stone' is used with specific nouns referring to any type of stone or rock or rocky feature:

> *walba malan* 'flat rock'
> *walba bunda* 'mountain'
> *walba buray* 'cave'
> *walba yiriy* 'type of slatey stone' (as in (707))

And *ḍabu* 'ground, earth, dirt' is used with specific nouns such as mud, sand, white clay, dust, and so on.

bulmba refers to any type of hut or house or windbreak or camp, or even to a potential camping-place. *bulmba* can be used with the proper name of any habitable place, and also with a variety of specific common nouns:

> *bulmba ḍimurU* 'house'
> *bulmba dabul* 'beach'
> *bulmba buluba* 'fighting ground'
> *bulmba buray* 'cave'

Note that *buray* can occur with *walba* or with *bulmba*, suggesting that the generic terms are not strictly exclusive of each other. We could have, in fact, an NP containing *bulmba walba buray* (just as we could also have *miɲa maŋgum yalbur* 'edible-animal frog-genus grey-frog-species').

But the conditions on co-occurrence of these terms appeared, on investigation, not to be straightforward. For instance, we can have *wira walba*, but not *wira bunda. And whereas *ḍugi* can mean 'tree', 'wood' or 'stick', *wira ḍugi* must be referring to a stick, not a growing tree. Similarly, *wira ḍabu* is a possible collocation for describing a handful of dust, but *wira* cannot be used with *ḍabu* when it refers just to 'ground'.

It was obvious, at this stage, that re-appraisal was needed. Generics were found to be of two distinct types.

[I] Those classifying specific nouns according to the INHERENT NATURE of their referents – *bama* 'person', *maŋgum* 'frog', *ḍugi* 'tree', *buɻi* 'fire', *walba* 'stone', *ḍabu* 'solid inanimate matter other than stone or wood', and so on.

[II] Those classifying specific nouns according to the FUNCTION or USE of their referents: edible flesh food (*miɲa*), edible non-flesh food (*mayi*), drinkable liquid (*bana*), habitable place (*bulmba*) or moveable thing (*wira*).

Before discussing each generic in turn we can, in table 6.1, diagram the way in which these two types of classificatory term divide up the universe. The dots at the extreme left refer to specific nouns; 'inherent nature' generics are in the left-hand column, and 'function/use' classifiers on the right. Many–one relations between specific and generic terms are shown schematically (rather than quantitatively – in total over sixty names of bird species are known, all included under *ḍaruy*, for instance). Where there is a natural grouping of species for which there is NO 'inherent nature generic' in Yidiɲ, a dash is shown in the left-hand

TABLE 6.1   *Scope and interrelation of generic nouns*

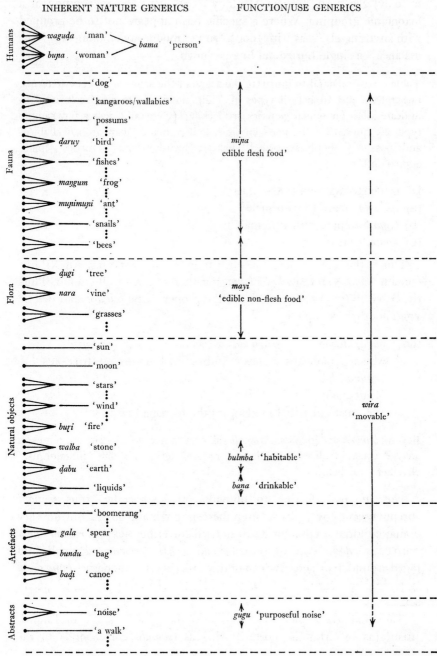

column (for instance 'possums'). Note that in many of these cases there IS (only) a generic term in Dyalŋuy (6.3) justifying recognition of a taxonomic grouping. Where a specific term appears not to be grouped with anything else – as with 'dog', 'sun', 'moon' and 'boomerang' for instance – a single horizontal line is shown.

Table 6.1 is intended to illustrate the scope of the score or so generic terms, rather than just to list all types of Yidiɲ nouns. Dots are freely used to indicate areas for which generics are lacking. (Generally, just a few sample types are quoted for the non-generic sectors – thus to 'kangaroos/wallabies' and 'possums' should be added 'snakes', 'lizards/guanas', 'turtles', 'bats' and so on.)

[I] INHERENT NATURE CLASSIFIERS
(a) *waguḍa* 'man, human male'
(b) *buɲa* 'woman, human female'
(c) *bama* 'person'

This is the only instance of a hierarchy among generics. An NP can contain *bama*, AND *waguḍa* or *buɲa*, together with a specific noun. Thus the S NP in (775) has *bama*, *buɲa*, the proper name *bindam* and deictic *yiɲu*; another example is

(994) *ɲaɲḍi bama   wagu:ḍa wuɽgun   muyŋga*
       we-SA person-ABS man-ABS pubescent boy-ABS cicatrice-ABS
       gunda:lna
       cut-PURP
       We must cut tribal marks [on] the teenage boy

Beyond *bama buɲa* and *bama waguḍa*, all occurrences of two generic nouns in an NP must involve one 'inherent nature' term and one 'function/use' classifier – see below.

Most nouns referring to humans are sex-specific – thus *waɲaɽI* 'prepubescent boy', *gumba* 'prepubescent girl', and so on. But for very young children a common term is used for either sex – *ɲumbubu* 'new born baby', *ḍaḍa* 'crawling or just-walking baby', *waruwaru* 'small child (aged around five)', etc. We can in this case get either generic – *buɲa ḍaḍa* 'girl child' or *waguḍa ḍaḍa* 'boy child' – the classifier serving to specify sex.

Note that *bama* effectively translates the generic sense of English 'man' (as in 'Man is mortal') whereas *waguḍa* corresponds to the

specific 'male' sense. Bilingual speakers of Yidiɲ have institutionalised as translation-equivalents:

bama person

waguḍa man

Note that *bama* occurs much more frequently than 'person'/generic 'man' in English (it may well be the most frequent noun in texts). And it is interesting that the English of young Aborigines at Yarrabah – most of whom know no Yidiɲ beyond a dozen or so simple words – is characterised by a high incidence of 'person'.

These three classifiers can be used with terms referring to stages of life – 'baby', 'adult man', 'old woman' etc.; with kin terms; and with proper names of people. Animals are believed to have once been 'people' and in storytime texts referring to this era the name of an animal can co-occur with *bama*. The names for ghosts and spirits (for anything not living) do not fall within the scope of *bama*.

gaḍa 'spirit of a man' is also used to cover 'white man', and *guyŋgan* 'spirit of a woman' for 'white woman'. But whereas in the spirit senses *gaḍa* and *guyŋgan* can NOT occur with *bama* (and are restricted to the 'use' generic, *wira* – see below), in the 'white person' sense they ARE classified as *bama*.

waguḍa and *buɲa* can be used, in marked circumstances, to specify the sex of an animal – thus *buɲa gangulA* 'female wallaby', *waguḍa gangulA* 'male wallaby' (similarly for 'dog', 'bird' etc.). In these cases *bama* could NOT be included with *waguḍa/buɲa*.

Note that there are no classifiers for body parts (or parts of any other object). A noun like *ḍina* 'foot' will normally be shown as inalienably possessed by some person or animal, and it is the possessor that selects a generic qualifier.

There are only three generic terms for non-human animates in everyday Yidiɲ. Note particularly that there is no term 'fish' (in this Yidiɲ differs from its neighbours, and in fact from most Australian languages); the term *miɲa* is employed, the context usually making it clear that it is AQUATIC edible creatures that are being referred to (for example, line 109 of text 2).

(d) *ḍaruy* 'bird'

This covers all birds except the giant flightless cassowary (emus do not occur in this region). Note that *ḍaruy* does include *ḍaruga* 'scrub-hen', *wawun* 'scrub-turkey' and various birds with distinct mythic roles, which are not included under the generic *dundu* in Dyirbal (Dixon 1972: 303).

(e) *maŋgum* 'frog'

This classifier covers all eight species of frog for which the writer has collected names. (Dick Moses was asked the Yidiɲ term for 'cane toad', a fairly recent invader; he replied that it had not yet been given a Yidiɲ name but that it would certainly be called *maŋgum*.)

(f) *muɲimuɲi* 'ant'

Of the ten or so types of ant (each with its own species name) all but one can be classified by *muɲimuɲi* – thus *muɲimuɲi gaɖu*: 'black tree ant', *muɲimuɲi burbal* 'red ant'. The exception is *ɖilibuɽa* 'green ant'; this insect has a special place in Yidiɲ culture because of its medicinal properties (1.4) and it may be for this reason that it is not regarded as a type of *muɲimuɲi*.

Most plants are included under *ɖugi* 'tree' or *nara* 'vine'. Note that although there are half-a-dozen specific terms for types of grass (and a few more for types of tree-fern, weed and seaweed) there are no classifiers applicable here.

(g) *ɖugi* 'tree'

The semantic extension of this term appears (as far as can be determined) to be about coextensive with the English noun 'tree'. Thus, *ɖugi* covers even fairly low plants such as *ɲulugun* 'small pandamus' (which would not be included within the scope of the generic term *yugu* 'tree' in Dyirbal, for instance – Dixon 1972: 303). Harmful plants – such as the stinging tree *giyaɽA* – are also regarded as a type of *ɖugi* (these are again excluded in Dyirbal).

Note that a single noun will be used to refer to a specific tree, its wood, its fruit, or to a stick broken off it. Similarly, *ɖugi* can be translated in different contexts as 'tree' or 'wood' or 'stick'.

(h) *nara* 'vine'

This classifier is used with more than a dozen species nouns, including the vines of ground vegetables such as yams, and vines growing on trees – for instance, *mudi* 'thick black edible loya vine'.

There are three generics referring to types of natural phenomena. Note that there are no classifiers dealing with celestial objects or meteorological events (*ɖigurU* 'thunderstorm' is discussed below).

(i) *buṟi* 'fire'

As indicated above, anything burning is included within the scope of
buṟi. Thus we can have:

> *buṟi biṟmaṟ* '(hot) charcoal'
> *buṟi mimi* 'a flying spark'
> *buṟi ŋaɲḍal* 'a light (from a burning torch)'

and even *buṟi wuɲḍu* '(hot) smoke'

The class of *buṟi* nouns almost makes up the whole set of possible
subjects for *guba-n* 'burn' (4.1.5). The exception is *buɲan* 'sun' which –
as in (347) – can be the A NP for *guba-n*, although it is not included
under *buṟi*. (Note also that 'lightning' is not regarded as a type of *buṟi*.)

(j) *walba* 'stone'

walba can be used for any moveable rock or pebble, or for a geographical feature made of stone; thus:

> *walba bayŋga* 'a stone heated in the fire and thrust inside a dead
> animal in kapamari cooking'
> *walba ḍaruway* 'a small hill, or island'
> *walba gaṟbi* 'an overhanging mountain ledge'

(k) *ḍabu* 'ground'

This term is complementary to *walba*. Any type of terrain that is not
covered by *walba* is describable as *ḍabu*. Thus *ḍabu* can be used with a
noun describing any type of earth or ground:

> *ḍabu gabuḍu* 'white clay'
> *ḍabu ḍalmbul* 'mud'
> *ḍabu gulgi* 'sand'
> *ḍabu ŋumbun* 'heaps of soft sand'

or a place that is characterised by a particular sort of ground:

> *ḍabu dabul* 'beach'

There are three classifiers referring to types of implement. Note that
these only cover a fraction of the traditional artefacts known to the
Yidiɲḍi. There are no generic terms for woomeras (just two specific
names: *ḍaṟin* 'straight woomera' and *baluṟ* 'curved woomera'), yam-
sticks, axes, knives or traps (quite apart from items like boomerang and
shield, which do not naturally group with anything else).

(l) *gala* 'spear'

There are half-a-dozen types of spear, all with rather specific uses. They include:

> *gala baŋguṟ* 'multi-prong fish-spear'
> *gala biṟḍi* 'small hook spear'

(m) *bundu* 'bag'

This is apparently a generic term for any type of traditional basket. Only two hyponyms are known:

> *bundu dugubil* 'bark bag'
> *bundu ḍuṟbal* '(small) woven grass basket'

But note that *bundu* is used by itself to refer to a dilly-bag plaited from loya-cane (the commonest type of carrier for the olden-times Yidiɲḍi).

bundu does not extend to metal containers, such as *biligan* 'billy can'.

(n) *baḍi* 'canoe'

It seems likely that this was a classifier. It has been encountered with only two specific nouns:

> *baḍi bida* 'bark canoe' or 'bark trough' (for soaking *badil* 'rickety nut' etc. – see the illustration in Roth 1904: Fig. 230)
> *baḍi ginu* 'dug-out canoe'

Dick Moses insisted that *ginu* was NOT a loan from English, the similarity to 'canoe' being quite coincidental. Be that as it may, there is strong anthropological evidence that dug-out canoes were not known in this region before white contact. This would suggest that *baḍi* evolved as a generic term at a very late stage. *baḍi* is complementary to *warḍan*, describing all types of 'raft' (or other 'plank boats').

At one time the informant explained that *wuṟu* meant 'any type of spear handle' (or 'spear stick', as he put it) and named individual types by *wuṟu baṟiɲU* and *wuṟu wuḍigay*. However, *baṟiɲU* ('species with small leaf') and *wuḍigay* ('wild guava') are the names for types of trees, from which spear handles are manufactured. These names are thus of the same type as 'oak table' in English, and there are no grounds for considering *wuṟu* a generic term.

Similar comments apply to *gubu* 'leaf' and *ginga* 'prickle'; they are often accompanied by the name of a tree or vine, indicating the origin of the leaf/prickle.

There are two other terms that might possibly be regarded as 'inherent nature' classifiers – *ḍigurU* 'thunderstorm' and *ḍaŋga* 'hole'.

(o) *ɖigurU* 'thunderstorm'

There are special names for the types of thunderstorm blowing from different compass directions (each characterised by the amount of rain it brings and the intensity of its winds): *guŋga:ɽbara* 'from the north', *ɳaɽabara* 'from the south', *guwabara* 'from the west', and *ɲalabara* 'from the foot of the land-mass, from the east'. They all involve *-bara*, and are discussed under that affix in 3.3.6.

ɖigurU behaves like a generic term in co-occurring with each specific name – thus *ɖigurU ɲalabara*. But it may not properly belong in the set of classifiers since each of the specific names is a derived stem (and its root does not have primary reference to a storm).

(p) *ɖaŋga* 'hole'

Any type of hole is classified under *ɖaŋga*. Thus:

ɖaŋga muygal	'hole dug as a trap (and then disguised by being covered with sticks and leaves)'
ɖaŋga murgu	'hole dug as cooking pit'
ɖaŋga ɖiŋgal	'anus'
ɖaŋga ɖiŋgin	'vagina'

ɖaŋga can also occur with other generics – *ɖabu ɖaŋga* (or *ɖaŋga ɖabu*) 'ground hole' covers *muygal*, *murgu* and also animal burrows. *buɲa ɖaŋga* 'woman hole' would be taken to refer to *ɖiŋgin* (cf. 4.1.8).

It is possible that *ɖaŋga* should be regarded as a rather general 'body part' term, rather than a classifier proper – *ɖabu ɖaŋga* and *buɲa ɖaŋga* would then simply specify inalienable possession (several other body-part terms are extended to aspects of the environment). Or it could be looked upon as the only (body-)part classifier.

[II] FUNCTION/USE CLASSIFIERS

(a) *miɲa* 'edible animal'

This term is used for anything animate that is habitually eaten by the Yidiɳɖi. Some species covered by *muɲimuɲi* 'ant' are eaten, while others are considered inedible; thus *gaɖu:* 'black tree ant' and *burbal* 'red ant' are *miɲa*, but *guɖin* 'bull ant' and *balawa* 'sugar ant with red head and black body' are not. Similarly for *maŋgum* 'frog'. It appears that all birds – included under the 'inherent nature' generic *ɖaruy* – are edible.

An animal may only be describable as *miɲa* when it reaches a size sufficient to warrant killing and eating – see (739) in 4.5.5. Any dish made from meat – for instance, 'stew' in (719) – is also *miɲa*. An egg, *ɖiɲal*, is regarded as a type of flesh food, and is also included within the scope of *miɲa*.

The class of *miɲa* includes all kangaroos/wallabies, possums, bandicoots, bats, turtles, guanas, grubs, eels, most fishes and some snakes,
lizards, frogs, rats, snails as well as echidna (porcupine), platypus and
cow. Note that some (but not all) poisonous snakes are eaten, as is the
potentially harmful gar-fish (but the stone-fish and toad-fish are not
considered edible). The remaining classes of insect – flies, leeches, grass-
hoppers, spiders, worms, cockroaches, etc. – are never eaten. One
potential source of meat, the dog, could never be called *miɲa*; people
in all parts of Australia felt a close relationship to the dog (sometimes
including it within the kinship system) and certainly the Yidiɲɖi would
never have considered eating a dog. (Horses are, perhaps for similar
reasons, also excluded from the class of *miɲa*.)

(b) *mayi* 'edible plant'

This term covers all sorts of non-flesh food. In Yidiɲ the same name
may be applied to, say, a tree and to anything obtained from it – *badil*
is both a rickety nut, and the rickety nut tree. Generally, *ɖugi badil*
would be used to describe the wood of this tree, while *mayi badil* refers
to the fruit (although *ɖugi mayi badil* is perfectly normal – referring to
the tree AND its fruit). *mayi* comprise a subset of *ɖugi* 'tree', a subset of
nara 'vine', and a number of plant species that are not included under
any 'inherent nature' classifier – for instance *ɖalga̠ram* 'flat bottle fern'.

The most interesting aspect of *mayi* (to a speaker of English) is that it
also covers bees and honey. Honey is classed as a non-flesh food, coming
within the scope of *mayi*, and the bees that make the honey fall into the
same category (just as a tree can be referred to as *mayi* – even out of
season – if at some time of the year it bears edible fruit). Thus, among
others:

> *mayi muɼuy* 'white bee'
> *mayi diwu* 'small ground bee'
> *mayi yiŋgilibiy* 'English bee'

ɖumbagi 'tobacco' is not regarded as *mayi*, although it can be chewed as well
as smoked. Yidiɲ here differs from Dyirbal, which does place 'tobacco' in its
'non-flesh food' gender class (Dixon 1972: 312).

(c) *bana* 'drinkable liquid'

bana is used as the unmarked term for referring to 'fresh water' (just
as *miɲa* can, when it occurs without any other noun, often be translated
as 'meat' and *mayi* as 'vegetables', and *buɼi* used alone indicates 'fire');
it is also used as a classifier with a noun referring to a water feature:

spring, creek, lake, rain, dew, steam, and so on. It cannot be used with blood, sweat, urine, spittle or any other type of liquid that is not normally consumed.

The use of *bana* with nouns referring to 'salt water' might be thought to constitute an exception to the 'drinkable' criterion. Note:

> *bana* 'fresh water'
> (*bana*) *biriɲ* 'salt water'

However, study of the meaning and use of the adjective *gilga* sheds some light on this apparent anomaly. *gilga* is used to indicate anything imperfect or inadequate for its purpose – 'soft wood (that will break easily if made into an implement)' or 'a weak (easily breakable) fishing line'. 'Salt water' is characterised as *gilga* – the informant stressed that it is 'soft' just like 'soft wood'. *biriɲ* is thus regarded as 'contaminated or inadequate *bana*'. Just as a soft wood will be described as *ḍugi* – although it could not be used for anything – so salt water is included under *bana* – although it could not be drunk.

Salt water is thus held to belong to the same category as fresh water, but to be an imperfect instance of it. It contrasts with blood, urine, semen etc. which are assigned to a quite different category.

bana is also used with nouns such as *gulbul* 'wave' (which can of course occur on fresh-water lakes as well as on the sea) and *baḍagal* 'tide'.

(d) *bulmba* 'habitable place'

bulmba can be used with a noun referring to a hut or type of structure, e.g.

> *bulmba yiwan* 'shelter for one person'
> *bulmba duguṛ* 'hut holding two or three people'
> *bulmba ḍimurU* 'hut holding from half-a-dozen to ten people'

Or with a description of any geographical feature at which one might camp (some examples were given above). For instance, an informant said that *bulmba walba* only made sense if it were *bulmba walba malan* – one could only camp at a rock (*walba*) if it were a flat rock (*malan*).

bulmba, used without any other noun, can be translated 'place' – it can refer either to an actual camping-site (so that if one says 'I'm going back home to sleep', *bulmba* would be used for 'home') or else to any past or potential camping place. *bulmba* also has a more general meaning:

'the world' (as in 'God made the world') – here 'the world' is effectively identified at the complete set of places at which people can live. ('Sky' is regarded as part of *bulmba* – see 4.7.3.)

Just as *bama* commonly occurs with the names of people, so *bulmba* can be used with place names, as in (414). Similarly, *bana* occurs with the names of lakes, rivers and creeks; and *bunda* 'mountain' or *ḍaruway* 'island, small hill' – both hyponyms of *walba* 'stone' – with the names of rocky features.

(e) *gugu* 'purposeful noise'

Yidiɲ has more than a score of specific nouns for referring to different types of noise – cf. (629), (651–2) above. Some are animal or language noises:

> *gugu gawal* 'a call'
> *gugu gugulu* 'a recitative mourning style used by men'
> *gugu gayagay* 'a whisper'
> *gugu ɲurugu* 'the sound of talking a long way off (when the words cannot quite be made out)'
> *gugu ḍubun* 'squeaky noise made by young animal'

while others are noises of banging or clapping or sawing, and so on:

> *gugu maṛal* 'the noise of a person clapping his hands together'
> *gugu mida* 'the noise of a person clicking his tongue against the roof of his mouth, or the noise of an eel hitting the water'
> *gugu gada* 'the noise of sticks being banged together for dance accompaniment'
> *gugu dalŋudalŋu* 'the noise of a bell ringing'

It appears that *gugu* is used with the name of any sound that results from some person or animal PURPOSEFULLY making a noise. That is, this generic covers all controlled attempts at communication (including, of course, all types of language and para-language activity). It can be used with the NAME of an animal, to describe the noise it makes – for instance, *gugu ḍigirḍigir* 'the call of a willy wagtail' in (986) from 6.1.1.

However, *gugu* does not cover 'involuntary noises', that are side-effects of some other activity. That is, the following nouns are NOT included in the scope of *gugu*:

> *yuyuṛuŋgul* 'the noise ("shshshsh") of a snake sliding through grass'
> *gaŋga* 'the noise of some person approaching e.g. the sound of his feet on leaves or through the grass, or even the sound of a walking-stick being dragged along the ground'

duɲuɽ 'reverberations caused by someone walking over floorboards, or treading heavily over the ground outside'

gugu is also used with the noun *gurunU* 'language'. (Note that in many languages to the north *gugu* means 'language', corresponding to *gurunU* in Yidiɲ. It is often included in the proper name of the language – e.g. Gugu-Yalaɲɖi, Gu:gu-Yimiɖir.)

gurunU (and/or *gugu*) CAN be used with a language name, although it is not a necessary part of its citation form. Thus:

(995) *guru:n yidiɲ ɲaŋga:ɖin*   Talk the Yidiɲ language!

Also attested are *gurunU guŋgay*, *gurunU ɖa:bugay*, *gurunU ɲaɖan* and (referring to the 'mother-in-law' style) *gurunU ɖalɲuy*. But since *gurunU* only occurs with proper names it is not properly regarded as a generic term.

(f) *wira* 'moveable object'

This is perhaps the most difficult and most interesting classifier. It is translated as 'thing' by informants and occurs most frequently with the names of artefacts like 'boomerang', 'shield', 'saddle', and also 'stick', 'stone' – see (513) – and so on. In one enlightening discussion Dick Moses indicated that *wira* could only be used of something moveable – *wira walba* could be a stone, but not a mountain, *wira ɖabu* a handful of soil or sand, but not the ground itself, and *wira ɖugi* a stick but not a tree. It can be used for the sun and moon – see (261) – which certainly move in the sky, and for wind and cloud.

wira cannot be used for anything that is describable as *miɲa*, *mayi* or *bana* (since the Yidiɲɖi did not camp on anything moveable, it is impossible for *wira* and *bulmba* to be applied to the same object). It does thus appear to be defined as, in a way, a residue set – AFTER all other nature/use classifiers have been assigned. Most things that are not included under *miɲa*, *mayi* or *bana* can – if moveable – be classed as *wira*. Thus *wira* covers non-drinkable liquids (like blood) and inedible fruits; and even noises (like *gaŋga*) that are not *gugu*. It can be used for inedible insects and reptiles (although it is not too frequent in this sense) but would not be employed with a noun like *gudaga* 'dog'. *wira* is used with severed body parts, and with excretions (faeces and urine). It occurs with the names of spirits – for instance in (746) *wira* is referring to the rainbow-serpent.

wira also has a quite different use; it is a crude term for referring to female genitalia, with very similar overtones to the English term 'cunt'. It appears that these two senses of *wira* did not cause confusion, the

context indicating whether the speaker was employing a nominal classifier (probably a feature of good style) or whether he was swearing! (The two senses are certainly related – compare with the use of 'thing' for genitalia in colloquial English.)

This account of *wira* applies to the coastal dialect only. It has not been possible exhaustively to investigate the term in tablelands dialects, but it does seem to have had a quite different meaning there, referring effectively to 'dangerous thing' (e.g. a poisonous snake, a stinging tree, or a harmful substance such as opium).

The inclusion of 'moveable' as the criterial condition for *wira* (a frequent and important term in Yidiɲ discourse, and a major indicator of 'world view') is of anthropological interest. One is reminded of Benveniste's (1973: 40–51) discussion of Indo-European **pecu*; this 'originally meant "personal chattels, moveables", and it was only as the result of successive SPECIFICATIONS that it came to mean in certain languages "live-stock", "smaller live-stock" and "sheep"'. It was further specialised to 'wealth in the form of live-stock' and then simply 'money' (Latin *pecunia*). Mulvaney (1975: 238–48) refers to the Australians as 'incipient agriculturalists', and one can but speculate that the semi-nomadic rain-forest dwellers were perhaps further advanced in this direction than groups elsewhere. Certainly the evolution of a term like *wira* could (speculatively) be regarded as a conceptual step on the path towards an agricultural society.

There is one other noun, *ḍama*, that could perhaps be regarded as a function/use classifier.

(g) *ḍama* 'something dangerous or bad'

ḍama in the coastal dialect refers to anything harmful (appearing to correspond to the use of *wira* in tablelands Yidiɲ) – dangerous snakes, centipede, stinging trees, strong drink, opium (or, the writer was told, medicine – presumably classed as *ḍama* because of its unpleasant taste). *ḍama* refers to the rainbow-serpent in (746), and co-occurs with *ḍimbaɽal* 'cyclone' in (660). It is used most often to refer to snakes (sometimes, in fact, *ḍama* seems to be used as a generic term 'snake').

There is a contrast between *ḍama* and *wabaɽwabaɽ*; the latter refers to anything subject to cultural taboo – for instance, the flame tree (which is held to be sacred to the rainbow-serpent) or a young girl (who must remain a virgin up to a certain age).

Some specific nouns can co-occur with two distinct classifiers (there are no examples of occurrence with more than two). Leaving aside *bama buɲa* 'person woman' and *bama waguḍa* 'person man', these cases

always include one 'inherent nature' and one 'function/use' generic. Examples involving animals (*miɲa* plus *maŋgum*, *muɲimuɲi* or *ɖaruy*) and plants (*mayi* plus *ɖugi* or *nara*) have already been quoted, as has *buray* 'cave' with *walba* 'stone' and/or *bulmba* 'habitable place'.

A piece of hot charcoal (*nirgil*), say, can be described as *buɻi* and as *wira*, and a plot of ground both as *ɖabu* and *bulmba*. Some co-occurrences are less predictable: a tree species, *diwiy*, holds water inside its bark (which can be tapped and drunk) yielding *bana diwiy* in addition to *ɖugi diwiy*.

We mentioned in 3.1.3 that, for stylistic felicity, a generic noun may be employed in a statement or question and a specific noun in the reply (or vice versa). Similarly, in a main-plus-subordinate clause construction, a specific term can occur in one clause, and its classifier in the other (4.4.2).

Finally, loan items are sometimes dealt with through unusual combinations of generic and specific nouns. *gulgi* 'sand' normally falls within the scope of *ɖabu* 'ground' – referring to a patch of sand – or of *wira* 'moveable object' – referring to a handful of sand. In recent times 'sugar' has been described as *mayi gulgi* – it looks and feels like sand, but it is edible.

In other cases introduced items may, in the absence of any appropriate specific term, be described simply by a classifier. Dick Moses told the story of the first aeroplane sighted in Cairns; the plane was simply described as *wira* throughout the text. Similarly, in line 3 of text 9 *gurunU* is used to refer to the English language, in the absence of any specific name. And we mentioned earlier that the cane toad could be described only as *maŋgum*.

One criterion for checking whether a word is a generic noun is co-occurrence with *waɲira* 'what kind of'. In 3.7.1 the two levels of inanimate interrogative were detailed: *waɲi* 'what', enquiring as to the genus of an object; or, if the genus is known, *waɲira*, enquiring as to species. Thus *mayi waɲira* 'what sort of food' occurs in lines 40 and 44 of text 2. And in the story of the first aeroplane Yidiɲɖi children keep asking *waɲira wira* 'what sort of moveable object [is this]?'

Corresponding to inanimate *waɲi* there is a human interrogative *waɲa*. In an attempt to discover whether *waɲira* corresponds – at a more specific level – to *waɲa* as well as to *waɲi*, the writer enquired whether it was possible to say *waɲira bama*. He was told that it was, and that this would be equivalent to *waɲɖabara*. Now *waɲɖabara* has the structure of

a local group name (1.2) with *waɲɟa* 'where' in the slot normally reserved for a noun describing a certain type of terrain, and it is plainly enquiring as to local group affiliation. It appears that local group membership (for humans) is regarded as a parallel semantic level to species membership (for animals and plants). Thus:

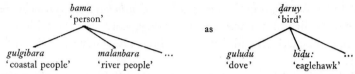

Systems of noun classification similar to that in Yidiɲ have been reported for three languages from the east coast of the Cape York Peninsula – see Thomson (1945: 165–7) on Wik-Moŋkan, Sommer (1972: 74–80) on Oykangand, and Hall (1972: 70–1) on Thaayore. Unfortunately, although these three writers each list a dozen or so classifiers, none has attempted a full semantic investigation of the phenomenon. See also Dixon (1970a) for discussion of how (syntactic) noun classification might be developing into (morphologically marked) noun classes in Olgolo.

Dyirbal has some generic nouns ('tree', 'snake', 'fish', 'bird' etc.) but does not normally include them in an NP with a specific noun. Instead of a system of noun classification, Dyirbal has four noun classes – a noun is normally accompanied by an article-like 'noun marker', agreeing with it in case and showing its class. The semantic basis for the assignment of nouns to these 'gender' classes can be explained, and involves quite detailed knowledge of Dyirbalŋan beliefs and mythology (Dixon 1972: 306–11).

It is worth enquiring whether the Yidiɲ system of noun classification (involving about twenty generic terms) evolved from something like Dyirbal's restricted system of gender classes; or whether the grammatically more complex phenomenon in Dyirbal developed out of multiple syntactic co-occurrence relations, as in modern Yidiɲ. It is, in fact, likely that neither of these alternatives holds. Both the Yidiɲ and Dyirbal systems may well have developed from a proto-organisation of the same type, but this would probably have been simpler than that shown by either modern language. A smallish set of half-a-dozen or so classifiers – used fairly optionally and haphazardly in the first place – may have increased in size and semantic complexity to yield the system described above for Yidiɲ; and it may have moved in quite a different direction in Dyirbal, being here incorporated as an obligatory morphological category.

6.2.2 Logical modifiers. The adjective class in Yidiɲ contains three items which involve logical-type quantification or identification of the reference of the head noun.

(a) *wawur* 'some'

See (319) in 4.1.2 and

(996) *ŋayu ɲuni:nda buɖi:ɲ   wawur   wiwi:na*
     I-SA you-DAT tell-PAST some-ABS give-PURP
     I promised to give you some [food] (Literally: I told you about
     some [food], that I would give some [food] to you)

Note also the double use of *wawur* in Dick Moses's explanation of the
language situation at Yarrabah today:

(997) *bama   yiɲu   wawur   guriɲ   ɲaŋga:ɖiɲ   yidiɲ |*
     person-ABS this-S some-ABS good-ABS speak-PRES Yidiɲ-ABS
     gaɖa:ɲ   duga:lna | bama   yiɲu   wawur
     white man-ERG catch-PURP person-ABS this-S some-ABS
     ɖaguɖagu   ŋaŋgay | ɲuɖu bama:l
     new-chum-ABS can't understand-PRES NOT person-ERG
     buɖi:ɲ   guru:n   ɲaŋga:ɖina
     tell-PAST language-ABS speak-PURP
     Some people here talk good Yidiɲ, for the white man to catch (in
     his tape-recorder and notebook); some others think they know
     a bit but in fact can't understand [or speak] it; they were never
     taught [told] to speak the language by the [old] people

The adjective *ɖaguɖagu* refers to someone who is unable to perform some
task but thinks he can do it. It was always translated by informants through the
colloquial Australian term 'new chum' (originally referring to the over-
confident behaviour of immigrants fresh out from England in the last century).

The quantification 'all' is expressed in Yidiɲ not by a separate word
but by the nominal affix *-ɖamu* (3.3.6).

(b) *bagil* 'another – a further token of the same type'

(c) *gayal* 'another – a token of a different type'

bagil describes another object similar to something already referred to.
In line 17 of text 2, having elicited Damari's name the people ask his
brother *ɲundu waɲa bagil* 'Who are you, other fellow?' Similarly, (330)
from 4.1.3 describes how people left a wounded alligator, saying that
another alligator would come along soon and eat him (using the ergative
case-form of *bagil*). Note also

(998) *ŋaɖin bimbi ɲinaŋ yiŋgu bulmba:| ŋayu galiŋ bulmba: bagi:lda*
     wunaɲaliŋ
     My father is staying in this place; I'm going to sleep in another
     (but similar) place

When explaining to the writer that *waguḍa* 'man' and *buɲa* 'woman' can be used to describe the male and female of animal species, Dick Moses said *yiɲu buɲa gangu:l* 'this is a female wallaby' and *yiɲu bagil wagu:ḍa gangu:l* 'this other wallaby is male'.

gayal indicates something totally novel. In line 34 of text 9 – quoted as (311) in 4.1.1 – *gayal* describes traditional Yidiɲḍi fare, contrasting it with the totally different kind of sustinence offered by the mission. George Davis told a story about the origin of fire; the rainbow had hidden the original fire in a cave and the birds tried one-by-one to snatch it from him, each being in turn repulsed. Finally the satin bird, *baḍin*, tried and:

(999) *guḍuguḍu:ŋ ɲuɲḍu:ɲ ḍimba:na/ ɲuḍu/ ɲuɲu gayal gali:ɲ...*
  The rainbow tried to catch that [satin bird]. But no, he was a
  different sort of bird (i.e. he succeeded) and went (away un-
  scathed, with the fire)...

gayal is appropriately used to describe novel aspects of European culture, including the English language:

(1000) *gaya:lbi   guru:n   gaḍa:n*
  ANOTHER-*bi*-ABS language-ABS white man-GEN-ABS
  The language belonging to white man is a quite different sort of
  thing

Note that both *gayal* – in (70) and (1000) – and *bagil* can occur with the nominal derivational affix -*bi* 'another', the meanings of adjective and affix reinforcing each other.

6.2.3 Semantics of time qualifiers.

Yidiɲ takes 'today' as focal point for its analysis of the temporal continuum. Immediately preceding and following today are:

> *guygam* 'yesterday'
> *ɲaḍa* 'tomorrow'

The unmarked reference of *guygam* is actually to 'yesterday afternoon' and of *ɲaḍa* to 'tomorrow morning' (the parts of those days that are nearest to today). Based on these forms are general terms for parts of a day (whose unmarked reference is to parts of 'today'):

> *guygaguygam* 'afternoon/evening'
> *ɲaḍaguran* 'morning'

(There is an adjective *guran* 'long, tall', but there is no semantic reason to identify it with the second element of *ŋaḍaguran*.)

Members of these pairs can be combined, to give explicit reference to a part of yesterday or tomorrow; for instance:

(1001) *guygaguygam ŋaḍa bana ḍaral* It'll rain tomorrow afternoon

(1002) *bana guygam ḍara:l guygaguygam* It rained yesterday afternoon

Note that, for phonological felicity, *guygam* and *guygaguygam* should be separated by some other word(s), as in (1002).

yaluŋunda was given for 'today' and could be used in this sense when, say, providing disambiguation:

(1003) *bana yaluŋunda ḍara:l ŋaḍaguran* It rained this morning

but normally it has the more general sense 'nowadays':

(1004) *yaluŋunda bama wuŋa:ḍiŋala ḍulugunu:*
        Nowadays people drink [too much] alcohol

Dyirbal organises time in a quite different way, taking the point 'now', rather than 'today', as its focus (cf. Dixon 1972: 114–16). There are terms 'earlier on today', 'now' and 'later on today' whose reference depends on the time of utterance (they are thus 'shifters', of the same semantic type as pronouns and tenses). Dyirbal has no words for 'afternoon' or 'evening' (but would have to use a phrase describing the position of the sun in the sky). Similarly, Yidiɲ has no words for 'earlier on today' or 'now'; and *garu* 'by-and-by, soon' – referring to a time from half-an-hour to a couple of days off – does not correspond to Dyirbal's *gilu* 'later on today'.

It seems that most Australian languages describe time either through the Yidiɲ 'today as focus' model, or the Dyirbal 'now as focus' pattern. Les Hiatt (personal communication) reports a complex arrangement in Gidiŋali (from Arnhem Land) that in effect superimposes these two systems. Gidiŋali has two past tense suffixes – -*ḍa* and -*na* in one conjugation – used as follows:

(a) present: -*ḍa*
(b) time earlier today: -*na*
(c) recent past before today: -*ḍa*
(d) time further in the past: -*na*

We can recognise a contrast -*ḍa* 'now/recently' versus -*na* 'earlier on' that applies both WITHIN today, and in the time span BEFORE today. (See Glasgow 1964; and compare with Hymes 1975.)

There is what appears to be a bound-form classifier used for counting on the fingers; this was employed most frequently for working out the number of days or nights between two events. As the fingers are touched in turn, beginning with the smallest one:

> *waramguman* 'one'
> *waramdjambulA* 'two'
> *waramdagul* 'three'
> *waramɲamugupdi* 'four'
> *warammala* 'five'

Regular number adjectives are added to *waram* for 'one', 'two' and 'three'. There are no Yidiɲ roots for numbers beyond three, so the name of the index finger, *ɲamugupdi*, is used for 'four', and *mala* 'palm of the hand' is utilised for 'five'. Gribble (1900: 135) gives the Guŋgay forms for one,...eleven; eighteen, ..., twenty. *mala* is 'five' here but *waram* is not included. On Gribble's evidence Guŋgay had *mugu* for 'seven' and *muguɲabi* for 'four' (cf. *ɲabi* 'many'). These names were not recognised by present-day Yidiɲ informants and we cannot ascertain whether Gribble's forms relate to the particle *mugu* (4.10) or to some homonym.

The importance of the notion of 'day' to the Yidiɲ system of temporal reference is seen in the interrogative. 'When' involves an affix to *waɲdjirI* 'how many?' – literally, 'how many days [since/until]...?' See 3.7.8 and 3.5.

6.2.4   Existential verbs. We mentioned in 4.1.10 that Yidiɲ does not have any verbal copula. However *wuna-n* 'to lie' can be used in an existential sense (covering a small part of the range of 'to be' in English). See (670–1) in 4.4.4, (387–8) in 4.1.8 and

(1005) *mayi   burin   giyi   budi | muɲimuɲi:ŋ*
      food-ABS bread-ABS DON'T put down-IMP ant-ERG

   buga:ndi | bambi   garu   gurip   wuna:na
   eat-LEST-ABS cover-IMP by-and-by good-ABS lie-PURP

   Don't leave bread [uncovered] lest the ants eat it. Cover it up so that by-and-by it'll [still] be good

(1006) *ɲundu gana   bulin   bana: darabaŋa |*
      you-SA PARTICLE plate-ABS water-LOC shake-COMIT-IMP

   baga   garu   gaṛan   wuna:na/
   wash-IMP by-and-by clean-ABS lie-PURP

   You rinse the plate in water and wash it, so that by-and-by it'll be clean

But note that in each of these cases the referent of the absolutive NP could be said to be 'lying'.

wuna-n is also used for 'live', as in:

(1007) *ŋaḍin muḍam waŋgi wunaŋ gambiṛala*
My mother lives up on the tableland

And it is the unmarked verb for indicating the 'existence' of some geographical feature:

(1008) *yiŋu bulmba wunaŋ yaŋgi:ḍa*
This place is [called] Yaŋgiḍa

However, *ḍana-n* must be used for anything which has greater vertical than horizontal extension – say, a tree or a house:

(1009) *bulmba ḍimu:r ŋalal ḍana:ɲ*
There was a big house standing [there]

An informant spontaneously contrasted *wuna-n* and *ḍana-n* in the context of *ḍaruway* 'island, small hill' and *bunda* 'larger hill, mountain' respectively:

(1010) a. *yiŋu walba ḍaruway wunaŋ*   This is a hill
b. *yiŋu walba bunda ḍanaŋ*   This is a mountain

In Yidiɲ 'lie down' appears to be the unmarked term from the universal 'posture' system {lie; sit; stand}. *wuna-n* is used for 'live' and 'exist' and, for instance, *budi-l* 'put down' – the transitive correspondent of *wuna-n* – is employed for 'marry'; see also 6.1.1. In Dyirbal 'sit' is the unmarked term: *ɲina-y* is used for 'live' and the comitative form *ɲinayma-l* for 'marry' (cf. Dixon 1972: 96).

6.3   Dyalŋuy or 'mother-in-law language'

It appears that each member of the Yidiɲḍi tribe had at his disposal two distinct speech-styles: Yidiɲ (called 'ordinary Yidiɲ' or 'straight-out Yidiɲ') and also an avoidance style called Dyalŋuy which had to be used in the presence of certain taboo relatives (see 1.6). Dyalŋuy has not been in active use for something like fifty years, but the writer was able to elicit a little information from Pompey Langdon and Tilly Fuller, taking care (until the time of Tilly Fuller's death) carefully to cross-check all data obtained. Almost two hundred Dyalŋuy words were painstakingly elicited, over a period of five years. In addition, some text material and sentences were obtained.

Dyalŋuy has exactly the same phonology and grammar as Yidiɲ, but an entirely different lexicon. Pronouns, deictics and all affixes are identical between the two speech-styles, but nouns, adjectives, verbs, locational qualifiers and time qualifiers (that is, all dictionary words) are quite different. For instance, the Dyalŋuy sentence:

(1011) ŋayu ŋulaɲwaŋgi baṛmaŋ/ maygay ŋulaɲḍilŋgu gumbiraŋa:liŋga:liŋ
          I'm going uphill, going to pick up black pine [that is] down [on
          the ground]

corresponds to Yidiɲ:

(1012) ŋayu waŋgi galiɲ/ gubu:m ḍilŋgu gumbi:liŋga:liŋ

These involve the following lexical equivalences:

Dyalŋuy	Yidiɲ	
ŋulaɲwaŋgi	waŋgi	'up'
baṛma-n	gali-n	'go'
maygay	gubumU	'black pine'
ŋulaɲḍilŋgu	ḍilŋgu	'down'
gumbiraŋa-l	gumbi-l	'pick up'

The pronoun ŋayu 'I' is constant, as are the aspectual and tense affixes. It is interesting to note that the 'reduplicated aspectual' suffix -:liŋgali-n 'going' is carried over, even though the lexical item gali-n 'go', on which it is presumed to be historically based (3.8.6), is rendered in Dyalŋuy by baṛma-n.

The formal relationship between corresponding Yidiɲ and Dyalŋuy items can be of several types:

(a) In ninety per cent of the cases the forms are totally dissimilar – as baṛma-n/gali-n and maygay/gubumU.
(b) Sometimes the first syllable of the Dyalŋuy form may coincide with that of the Yidiɲ word – Dyalŋuy birmbiḍa, Yidiɲ biriɲ 'salt water'; similarities of this type can usually be dismissed as 'accidental'. But there are four pairs that involve stronger formal similarity:

Dyalŋuy	Yidiɲ	
ŋalḍan	ŋaɲḍal	'a light'
duwur	dubur	'stomach'
gumbiraŋa-l	gumbi-l	'pick up'
ḍaṛiyiy	ḍaruy	'bird (generic)'

These do not, however, reveal any systematic correspondence. (The members of each pair MAY be distantly GENETICALLY related, the Dyalŋuy term perhaps descending along some other branch of the Australian 'family tree' and being recently taken over from some other language into Yidiɲɖi Dyalŋuy.)

(c) There are a number of cases of a derived stem in Dyalŋuy corresponding to a monomorphemic root in Yidiɲ. Thus Yidiɲ *yaguɲU* 'echidna (porcupine)' is rendered by *biŋgaldamba* – Dyalŋuy *biŋgal* is the correspondent of Yidiɲ *gala* 'spear', and *-damba* is a productive nominal affix 'with a lot of —' (3.3.6); the Dyalŋuy term precisely describes the porcupine's prickly exterior. The nominal affix *-bara* 'belonging to —, pertaining to —' (3.3.6) occurs in a number of Dyalŋuy names. For instance, *gayibara* – based on *gayi* 'ground, soil', the Dyalŋuy equivalent of Yidiɲ *ɖabu*–was given by Pompey Langdon as the name for a number of animals who live on or in the ground: bandicoots, worms, and so on.

There is just one productive way of deriving Dyalŋuy forms from Yidiɲ roots. The major locational qualifiers have – like all other dictionary words – a distinct form in Dyalŋuy. But here the Dyalŋuy term merely involves *ɲulaɲ* prefixed to the Yidiɲ word:

Dyalŋuy	Yidiɲ	
ɲulaɲwaŋgi	*waŋgi*	'up'
ɲulaɲɖilŋgu	*ɖilŋgu*	'down'
ɲulaŋguwa	*guwa*	'west'
ɲulaɲnaga	*naga*	'east'
ɲulaŋguya	*guya*	'across the river'

We mentioned in 3.4.1 that there is both a locational qualifier and an adjective with the meaning 'north', and similarly for 'south'. In these cases Dyalŋuy simply has a *ɲulaɲ* locational qualifier corresponding to both Yidiɲ words:

Dyalŋuy	Yidiɲ	
ɲulaŋguŋgaɽI {	*guŋgaɽI*	'north'
	ɖaŋgiɽ	'northern'
ɲulaɲɲaɽa {	*ɲaɽa*	'south'
	guɲin	'southern'

It is probable that this process does not apply to all locational qualifiers.

When the writer asked Pompey Langdon to translate sentences involving *munu* 'inside' or *ɲaru* 'on top of' into Dyalŋuy, the locational qualifier was simply ignored. Thus:

(1013) a. Yidiɲ: *ŋayu ɲinaŋ ɲaru walba:*
                I'm sitting on top of the stone
       b. Dyalŋuy: *ŋayu ɲiya:rḍiŋ diŋu:nda*
                I'm sitting on the stone

'Prefixing of *ŋulaɲ*' is thus a lexical process which ensures that locational qualifiers – like other lexical items – have distinct form in Dyalŋuy.

In Dyirbal, locational qualification is dealt with by a complex GRAMMATICAL system of noun and verb markers (Dixon 1972: 44–8, 56–7). Like other fully-grammatical words – pronouns and so on – these carry over in the same form into Dyalŋuy. But the northerly dialect Mamu inserts the form *ŋulaɲ* into the middle of a noun or verb marker in Dyalŋuy – e.g. *yaluŋulaɲdayi*, as against *yaludayi* in the everyday style (Dixon 1972: 315). The form *ŋulaɲ* is inexplicable, and seems quite redundant, in Mamu; but it is plainly related to *ŋulaɲ* in Yidiɲḍi Dyalŋuy.

Compound verbs (6.1.1) appear to be translated morpheme-for-morpheme into Dyalŋuy. Thus:

Dyalŋuy *gamaɽ*	Yidiɲ *giḍaɽ* 'mark'
mulbi-n	*gunda-l* 'to cut'
gamaɽ + *mulbi-n*	*giḍaɽ* + *gunda-l* 'to paint in pattern'
gilḍu-l	*baḍa-l* 'to bite'
waruŋu + *gilḍu-l*	*biḍaɽ* + *baḍa-l* 'to dream about'

Some of the examples given already illustrate the one-to-many correspondences that hold between Dyalŋuy and Yidiɲ lexical items. We have mentioned that *gayibara* covers a number of bandicoots, worms etc. (all of whom have specific names in Yidiɲ) and that *ŋulaŋguŋgaɽI* corresponds to *guŋgaɽI* and *ḍaŋgiɽ*. In 4.2.5 we described how the Dyalŋuy verb *maba-l* 'cook, burn' covers both *waḍu-l* and *guba-n* in Yidiɲ (with *maba:ḍi-n* being the specific equivalent of *guba-n*).

It seems clear that Dyalŋuy had a smaller vocabulary than Yidiɲ, often showing just a generic term where Yidiɲ would have a number of species names (and perhaps no generic term). Thus, the Dyalŋuy noun *ḍilmay* 'grass' corresponds to a number of Yidiɲ forms, including *ḍirgaɽ* 'blady grass' and *ŋuyay* 'kangaroo grass'; see also 1.6. In some cases,

important semantic distinctions can be neutralised in Dyalŋuy: Pompey Langdon gave Dyalŋuy *miḍaguran* for *ŋaḍaguran* '(tomorrow) morning' and also for *guygam* 'yesterday' – cf. 6.2.3; tense inflection on the verb would indicate whether past or future reference was intended.

For Dyirbal the writer was able without difficulty to elicit the Dyalŋuy equivalent for almost every word from his 2,500-word dictionary of the 'everyday style', and on the basis of this draw quite detailed conclusions about the semantic organisation of Dyalŋuy, and so on (Dixon 1971). In the case of Yidiɲ, Dyalŋuy equivalents were obtained for less than 20 % of the vocabulary, and in each case a considerable effort of memory on the part of the informants was involved. It is in these circumstances impossible to be certain about many details of the correspondences between Yidiɲ and Dyalŋuy lexicons.

It does appear that Yidiɲɖi Dyalŋuy resembled Dyirbal Dyalŋuy in having no lexical item in common with the everyday style of speech. This contrasts with Guugu-Yimidhir – a hundred or so miles to the north of Yidiɲ – which allows just a few everyday language items to be used in its avoidance (so-called 'brother-in-law') style; see Haviland, mimeo.

Since Yidiɲ intervenes geographically between Guugu-Yimidhir and Dyirbal, it might be expected that its Dyalŋuy would, in terms of complexity, fall part-way between the well-documented avoidance styles of these two languages. There is no evidence that it did.

In searching his memory for Dyalŋuy correspondents Pompey Langdon appeared to be working on the principle that there was in most cases a separate Dyalŋuy correspondent for each separate Yidiɲ word. Thus, he remembered Dyalŋuy *ḍumalA* for Yidiɲ *ḍaṛin* 'straight woomera' but believed there should be another Dyalŋuy term for Yidiɲ *baluṛ* 'curved woomera' (and rejected the writer's tentative suggestion that *ḍumalA* might cover both *ḍaṛin* and *baluṛ*). In some areas of vocabulary Yidiɲ certainly has more one-to-one correspondences than are exhibited by Dyirbal. For instance, Yidiɲɖi Dyalŋuy appears to have a separate term for each wallaby species – *waluṛubara* for Yidiɲ *guriliy* 'black-nose wallaby', *bugi* for Yidiɲ *gangulaA* 'grey wallaby', and so on – whereas Dyirbal Dyalŋuy has just one generic term covering all types of wallaby and kangaroo.

The evidence thus suggests that Yidiɲɖi Dyalŋuy may originally have been – in terms of number of avoidance style items, in proportion to the number of everyday style words – richer than Dyirbal Dyalŋuy, which was in turn richer than the Guugu-Yimidhir avoidance style. There are often one-to-many correspondences between Dyalŋuy and Yidiɲ; but there may have

been less of these, and more one-to-one relationships, than in languages to the north and south.

We are thus suggesting that, in a region characterised by this avoidance language phenomenon, Yidiɲ MAY have been a focus of maximum complexity, with the phenomenon tailing off gradually in surrounding languages. But this is, on the slender data available, very much in the nature of a speculative extrapolation. (It is difficult to know whether a response of a certain type indicates something of the original nature of the organisation of Dyalŋuy, or simply reflects lack of knowledge on the part of the informant.)

One-to-many correspondences have been gathered involving all parts of speech. The Dyalŋuy adjective *yaṛbul* was given for Yidiɲ *ḍangan* 'no good', and *ḍiranḍi* 'tired'. Verb examples include:

Dyalŋuy	Yidiɲ
gumbiraŋa-l	⎰ *gumbi-l* 'pick up' (TR)
	⎱ *maba-l* 'lift' (TR)
	⎱ *waŋga:ḍi+ŋa-l* 'wake up' (TR)
⎰ *dinda-l*	*ḍara-l* 'put standing' (TR)
⎱ *dinda+ :ḍi-n*	*ḍana-n* 'stand' (INTR)
⎰ *baṛma-n*	*gali-n* 'go' (INTR)
⎱ *baṛma+ŋa-l*	*banḍa-ṛ* 'follow' (TR)

In the cases of *dinda-l* and *baṛma-n* we have a single verb in Dyalŋuy corresponding to a transitive/intransitive pair in Yidiɲ. *dinda-l* is transitive, and the antipassive -:*ḍi-n* form is used for *ḍana-n*; *baṛma-n* is intransitive, with the derived 'comitative' form being used in the case of *banḍa-ṛ*.

A third of the Dyalŋuy verb forms have a final syllable -:*ḍi-n* or -*ŋa-l* which must be regarded as part of the root (see 3.8.3). Thus 'sit' – *ɲina-n* in Yidiɲ – is *ɲiya:rḍi-n*, but there is no form *ɲiya-ṛ/r*; and 'pick up' is *gumbiraŋa-l*, but *gumbira-n* does not occur. (Compare with Dyirbal, where many Dyalŋuy verbs appear to be, historically, verbalised adjectives e.g. *maḍirabi-l* for *ɲina-n* 'sit'; see Dixon 1972: 323.)

One verb exists in both -*ŋa-l* and -:*ḍi-n* forms:

Dyalŋuy	*wuyubaŋa-l*	Yidiɲ	*buḍi-n* 'tell' (TR)
	wuyuba:ḍi-n		*ɲaŋga:ḍi-n* 'talk, speak' (INTR)

but there is no verb *wuyuba-n*. This example emphasises that -*ŋa-l* and -:*ḍi-n* are here parts of the root, rather than being instances of the productive derivational suffixes -*ŋa-l* and -:*ḍi-n* (although they are certainly historically related to them). In Yidiɲ -*ŋa-l* can only be added to an intransitive and -:*ḍi-n* to a transitive stem; a given stem can thus only select ONE of the two suffixes.

In some cases a single Dyalŋuy form may be used for two Yidiɲ nouns, according as something is used for a certain purpose:

Dyalŋuy   Yidiɲ

biḍiliɲ $\begin{cases} \textit{baguɽ} & \text{'sword'} \\ \textit{ḍuluḍulu} & \text{'Johnson hardwood tree' (from which swords are} \\ & \text{usually made)} \end{cases}$

or has a certain characteristic:

milgal $\begin{cases} \textit{ḍili} & \text{'eye'} \\ \textit{dawugan} & \text{'silver bream'} \end{cases}$

There is just one 'grammatical word' which has a different form in Dyalŋuy – *muway* corresponds to the Yidiɲ particle/interjection *ɲuḍu* 'not, no'. Other particles appear to occur in the same form in Dyalŋuy.

Dyirbal has separate particle *gulu* 'not' and interjection *yimba* 'no'. The particle occurs in Dyalŋuy but the interjection comes out as *ḍilbu* 'no'.

In Dyirbal those interrogatives which cover lexical classes – 'what', 'do what/do how' – have different forms in Dyalŋuy, whereas those based on grammatical classes – 'who', 'where' – are unchanged. It seems that all deictics – whether definite or indefinite/interrogative – occur in identical form in Yidiɲ and in Yidiɲḍi Dyalŋuy.

Finally, we can note that Dyalŋuy maintains the distinction between 'person', 'man' and 'woman' that characterises Yidiɲ (in contrast to, for instance, Dyirbal and English):

Dyalŋuy *bayabay*   Yidiɲ *bama* 'person'
              bulaɲbay   *waguḍa* 'man'
              mugi:mugi: *buɲa* 'woman'

Appendix Previous work on Yidiɲ

Although there has been close white settlement in the Yidiɲ language area for a hundred years, almost no attempt has been made to record the language. The City of Cairns (with a population of around 30,000) has its Historical and Naturalists' Societies, but these bodies have never initiated any project to study the Aboriginal language or culture.

A few scraps of language were recorded, almost exclusively by visitors to the region. These are listed below under the three main dialects – Guŋgay, Waɲur(u) and Yidiɲ (see 1.2). Nothing at all is recorded of the Maḍay dialect, the last speaker of which died in the late nineteen-sixties (the writer had tried, without success, to contact her in 1964); it is not certain whether Maḍay was another name for Waɲur(u), or a separate linguistic/tribal unit.

[I] *Guŋgay*
(a) Rev. E. R. B. Gribble, missionary at Yarrabah from 1892 to 1909, published a number of short vocabularies and anthropological scraps. Chiefly:

(1) 'By Rev. Mr Gribble, Yarrabah Station, Tribal Dialect of Goon-gan-je', *Australasian Anthropological Journal*, vol. 1, no. 1, p. 13 (1896). About 45 forms – nouns, pronouns and some phrases.
(2) 'C. Grafton dialect of Goonganji tribe, by Rev. E. R. B. G. of Bellendenker Mission', *Australasian Anthropological Journal*, vol. 1, no. 3, pp. 16–17 (1897). About 100 items in a comparative table of vocabularies from a number of languages. (This whole table was reprinted almost in toto in *Science of Man*, vol. 12, pp. 211, 231, 251 (1912).)
(3) 'Class systems' of the 'Goonganji Myarah and Dungarah Tribes, being tribes on Cape Grafton, the Mulgrave River and the Lower Barron River' by Rev. E. R. Gribble. *Australasian Anthropological Journal*, vol. 1, no. 4, p. 84 (1897). Includes some totem names.
(4) 'Three songs of Australian blacks' by Rev. R. B. Gribble. *Science of Man*, vol. 1, no. 1, p. 13 (1898).

(5) 'Linguistics of the Koo-gun-ji Tribe, Chief Camp at Cape Grafton, Queensland' by Rev. E. R. B. Gribble, Bellenden Kerr. *Science of Man.* vol. 3, no. 8, pp. 134–5 (1900). About 100 words – see comments below on Roth.

(6) In Gribble's books *The Problem of the Australian Aboriginal* (Sydney, 1932) and *A Despised Race* (Sydney, 1933) there are odd words and scraps of information. The former has a song with translation on p. 53, and fragments of legends on pp. 56–8.

(b) Dr W. E. Roth, Protector of Aborigines (based at Cooktown), filled in one of the four-page printed vocabulary forms he used, with the heading: 'Kung-gan-ji, occupying the tract of country to the east of the Murray Prior Range, Cape Grafton, etc., see letter book p. 305. Speak Kung-gai. 1898' (in Uncatalogued Manuscript 216, Mitchell Library, Sydney).

Gribble's vocabulary (5) is very close to this list by Roth, following the same order of glosses, and having the same Guŋgay words with similar spellings. There are enough consistent spelling differences to suggest that Gribble and Roth may have taken down the same vocabulary at the same time from the same informant – e.g. Gribble regularly uses 'ar' where Roth has just 'a'. Gribble's transcription is inferior to Roth's (even though he had lived with speakers of Guŋgay for six years). Gribble has ko-la-ga where Roth has ko-da-ga for /gudaga/ 'dog', and koo-roo-la-pa where Roth has ku-ru-pa-pa 'large lizard' (/guɽbaba/ may have been meant), for instance.

Note that the three vocabularies by Gribble – (1), (2) and (5) – are quite dissimilar in spellings, etc., suggesting that they were compiled quite separately (with copies not being retained and referred to).

(c) N. B. Tindale took a vocabulary of 'Koŋkandji' at Yarrabah on 19 September 1938, and also compiled a kinship/section table (the writer is grateful to Dr Tindale for making these manuscript materials available to him). This is on the whole well transcribed, with virtually all segments accurately recorded (including the contrast between long and short vowels).

Other fragments on Guŋgay include a few words by Ursula McConnel (*Oceania* 1: 349, 1930/1) and a short note on the moiety sytem by R. H. Mathews (*Proc. Am. Phil. Soc.* 1900, p. 89). There are quite a lot of anthropological data, with a fair number of words, throughout Roth's *North Queensland Ethnography Bulletins* (1901–10). A duplicated version of a hymn in Guŋgay was produced at Yarrabah (probably in the 1960s);

it is called Gnungin Bimbi – /ɲaɲḍi:n bimbi/ 'our father' was intended – and the transcription is poor throughout.

[II] *Waɲur(u)*

(a) N. B. Tindale took down a vocabulary at Palm Island on 7 November 1938, heading it 'Wanjuru – mouth of Russell River – 2 moiety people in rain forest: Korakulu/Kuraminja'. See comments above.

(b) The microfilm publication *Australian Languages* (Micro-Bibliotheca Anthropos vol. 10, 1953) by H. Nekes and E. A. Worms is generally of a very low linguistic standard. The section on 'The Pygmoid tribes of the South-East of the Cape York Peninsula' (pp. 942ff.) is based on material collected by Worms at Palm Island in the late 'forties. This includes about 130 words attributed to the 'Wundjur tribe'. The standard of transcription is very poor, much worse than Roth and Tindale. Thus, Worms recorded djumbul for 'beard' in place of /ɲumbul/, gulgam for 'yesterday' in place of /guygam/, and so on (although occasional long vowels are marked).

[III] *Yidiɲ*

(a) Archibald Meston led two government-sponsored expeditions to the Bellenden Kerr range, in 1899 and 1904. His papers include vocabularies assigned to three rivers: the Mulgrave, the Russell and the Johnstone. The latter two are entirely Dyirbal but the Mulgrave words begin with some Dyirbal items and end with Yidiɲ words.

In Meston's published account of the first expedition (Queensland government papers CA 95/1889) the Mulgrave vocabulary is published in three columns, on page 10; the first column and the top two-thirds of the middle one are the Ngaḍan or Mamu dialects of Dyirbal, while the remaining column and a third is Yidiɲ.

This vocabulary also occurs in Meston's notebooks (uncatalogued holdings, Oxley library, Brisbane). The published vocabulary is repeated on pages 12–13 of Folio 2, and here a line drawn part-way across the second column separates off the Dyirbal from the Yidiɲ items; some of the Yidiɲ items are also repeated on page 18 of Folio 2, and the whole vocabulary is again given at the front of Folio 4. It is likely that these are NOT field notebooks, but Meston's workbooks into which he copied miscellaneous field notes (the originals appear not to have survived).

(b) Roth's manuscript papers contain two vocabularies identified as Yidiɲ. There is one questionnaire that is almost identical to the Guŋgay listing mentioned above; although it is on separate sheets it appears to

have been taken down at the same time as the Guŋgay vocabulary; and is in fact of Guŋgay, not of Yidiɲ. It is headed 'Yi-din-ji – occupy the valley of the Mulgrave River, along the coast line, Murray Prior Range to Cairns, see letter book p. 305; speak Yi-di. 1898'.

Roth's other Yidiɲ listing is a questionnaire on which both Ngaḍan and Yidiɲ are entered, in parallel columns; the heading reads 'Ngachan – river scrubs of Barron River from Mr Gillett's [?], back of Cairns, up to Tinaroo – mates with Yidin (mob) – Yidin-ji blacks of Cairns. 1898'. The two columns are almost identical, being both Ngaḍan! They were presumably gathered from a single speaker, on the tablelands, just as the Guŋgay/Yidiɲ vocabularies were presumably obtained at Yarrabah.

Roth's two 'Yidiɲ listings' have only about 30% items in common. They are, in fact, neither of them vocabularies of Yidiɲ.

(c) N. B. Tindale gathered a vocabulary of 'Idi:' from Bob Rose, on 4 September 1938 (probably at Mona Mona mission); to this is attached a kinship/section chart. Tindale's journal of his 1938 field trip also includes at least three Yidiɲ texts (the stories of Damari and Guyala, of Gambilguman, and of Danba); the transcription and interlinear glossing are of good quality.

(d) Nekes and Worms's microfilm publication contains about 200 words, four pronouns, and some short phrases attributed to the 'Idin tribe'.

(e) About 1960 Ken Hale spent a day or so at Yarrabah. He worked out the phoneme system, recognised that there were three verbal conjugations, gathered data on pronouns and case affixes, and collected about 300 words. The writer is grateful to Hale for making available his nine-page manuscript grammatical sketch, and field notes.

(f) La Mont West Jnr took down about 150 words at Yarrabah about 1961, and recorded a short text there in 1965.

(g) E. H. Flint recorded and transcribed about 100 words in 1964.

(h) E. F. Aguas visited Yarrabah in 1966 for the Australian Institute of Aboriginal Studies. Her unedited first draft MS 'A partial vocabulary of Idindji' contains notes on phonemes and grammar; it is held in the AIAS library.

(i) Peter Sutton visited Yarrabah for the AIAS in July 1970, and recorded some vocabulary and sentence material in addition to two very short texts and some songs.

(j) Alice Moyle recorded some Guŋgay and Yidiɲ songs at Yarrabah in 1966. These were later issued by AIAS on an LP record; the accompanying booklet contains transcriptions and translations by Moyle.

(k) P. C. Griffin recorded some Guŋgay and Yidiɲ songs in 1968 (issued on the same LP), and also a tape of reminiscences in English, interspersed with the odd Yidiɲ word.

(l) In 1972 the writer asked Tasaku Tsunoda to investigate whether there were any speakers of Guŋgay on Palm Island. Tsunoda recorded a tape which – while still (at the time of writing) catalogued by the AIAS as Guŋgay – contains almost entirely Yidiɲ vocabulary.

(m) In May 1974 a film unit from Sydney, led by Carolyn Strachan, recorded some text material from Dick Moses (making it immediately available to the writer).

Of recent work, only that by Hale and Moyle can be considered fully reliable. Aguas's transcription is extraordinarily poor, and her attempts at analysis quite useless (to take just one example, nominal derivational affix -*bara* 'pertaining to' (3.3.6) is divided up into verb root *ba-* plus aspectual affix -*ra*!). Flint's transcription misses some consonantal segments and contrasts whilst vastly over-differentiating vowels. (Griffin, Tsunoda and Strachan attempted no transcription.)

It is possible to infer the phonemic form of Guŋgay items from comparison of several vocabularies, and knowledge of present-day Yidiɲ. For instance

	'shield'	'two'	'echidna'
Yidiɲ			
Root	/bigunU/	/ḍambulA/	/yaguɲU/
Citation form (absolutive)	/bigu:n/	/ḍambu:l/	/yagu:ɲ/
(c) Tindale	*piku:n*	*tjambu:l*	—
Guŋgay			
(a) Gribble	*pe-koon-no*	$\left\{\begin{array}{l}\textit{jamboola}\\\textit{jhambool}\end{array}\right\}$	*tar-kon-yang*
(b) Roth	*pi-kun-no*	*jam-bu-la*	*ya-kon-yang*
(c) Tindale	*pikuan*	*tjambula*	—
Inferred form	/bigunu/	/ḍambula/	/yaguɲaŋ/

There is corroboration of final -ŋ in Guŋgay with [*molaŋ*] 'father'; Yidiɲ has *bimbi* here (and the '*wuma*' reported for Waɲur(u) may actually be /ŋuma/, as in Dyirbal).

Texts

Tape-recordings of the three texts given below, in addition to recordings and transcriptions of the twenty other Yidiɲ texts collected, have been deposited with the Australian Institute of Aboriginal Studies, P.O. Box 553, Canberra City, A.C.T., 2601, Australia.

Each numbered line constitutes a complete 'sentence' (as defined in chapters 4 and 5). '/' indicates the end of an intonation group (the utterance could finish at such a point).

Text 2

The myth of Damari and Guyala – see 1.5. Guyala was a sensible man, who tried to organise the details of life logically and easily; but his brother Damari was silly and obstructive, often being intent on making things as complex and difficult as he could. Told by Dick Moses in the coastal dialect (recorded at Yarrabah on 15 December 1970; duration 12¼ minutes).

1. *damariŋgu   yaymi:ldaɲu   bulmba* /
   Damari-ERG ask-COMING-PAST place-ABS
   Damari came and asked [his brother] about the place.

Damari and Guyala have come from the north looking for a home. When they reach the Mulgrave region Damari suggests that a likely place may be close by.

2. *gana bulmba   yiŋu   wawa* /
   TRY   place-ABS this-ABS look-IMP
   'Come and have a look at this place!' [Damari says].

3. *gana ŋali   gali:na / gana bulmba   numbin   / ŋaɲḍi*
   TRY   we two-SA go-PURP TRY   camp-ABS look for-IMP we-SA
   gana galin /
   TRY   go-IMP
   'We two should try to go. Let's try to look for a camping-site! We must try to go!' [Damari continued].

The first clause is in purposive inflection ('must do') and the remaining two in imperative with first person non-singular subject ('let's do'); these seem

513]

similar enough to be regarded as a (loose) example of coordination (6 below is similar).

4. *gali:ɲ | wawa:liɲu   bulmba |*
   go-PAST look-GOING-PAST place-ABS
   [They] went, went looking for a [suitable] place.

5. *ɲundú| bama   binaŋ   yiɲu   gugu   ɲinaŋ |*
   hey!   person-ABS hear-PRES this-ABS noise-ABS sit-PRES
   'Hey! [We can] hear this noise [and the noise is coming from some] people sitting around [in the back country somewhere hereabouts]', [Damari said].

6. *gana wawa | gana ŋaɲḍi wawa:lina |*
   TRY look-IMP TRY we-SA look-GOING-PURP
   'Let [us] try to have a look! We should try to go and have a look.'

7. *gali:ɲ | wawa:liɲu | bama   ŋabi   ɲinaɲunda |*
   go-PAST look-GOING-PAST person-ABS many-ABS sit-DAT SUBORD
   bulmba   ḍimu:r |
   camp-ABS house-ABS
   [They] went, went and saw lots of people sitting [there]; [they saw] a large house [there].

8. *bama   yiɲu   ŋabi   ɲinaŋ |*
   person-ABS this-ABS lots-ABS sit-PRES
   'A lot of these people are sitting [there].'

9. *gana ŋaɲḍi gaymbar | wawa |*
   TRY we-SA sneak up-IMP look-IMP
   'Let us sneak up and have a look [at them]!' [continued Damari].

10. *wawa:liɲu |*
    look-GOING-PAST
    [Damari and Guyala] went up and looked [at the people in the camp].

11. *bama:l   wawa:l |*
    person-ERG see-PAST
    The people [in the camp] saw [the brothers, and spoke amongst themselves:]

12. *yiɲu   bama   waɲa   ḍambu:l gada:ɲ |*
    this-ABS person-ABS who-ABS two-ABS come-PAST
    'Who are these two people who have come here?'

13. *gana yaymi |*
    TRY ask-IMP
    'Go on, ask them!' [one of the men said to another of the group].

14. *bama:l   yaymi:l/*
    person-ERG ask-PAST
    [One of the] people asked [the brothers:]

15. *ɲundu waɲa/ guwal   buḍi:ḍiɲu /*
    you-SA who-S name-ABS call-:ḍi-PAST
    'Who are you ? How is your name called ?' (= 'How do you call your name ?')

16. *ŋayu dama:ri /*
    I-SA Damari-ABS
    'I'm Damari.'

17. *ɲundu waɲa bagil   /*
    you-SA who-S another-ABS
    'Who are you, other fellow ?'

18. *ŋayu guya:la /*
    I-SA Guyala-ABS
    'I'm Guyala.'

19. *ɲundu:ba waɲḍa:l   galiŋ /*
    you all-SA where-ALL go-PRES
    'Where are you all going ?' [the people asked Guyala and Damari].

20. *ŋaɲḍi warḍa:nda gada:ɲ   /*
    we-SA raft-LOC   come-PAST
    'We came by raft' [the brothers replied].

21. *bulmba   ḍangan   / gana gali:na   ŋaɲḍi/*
    camp-ABS no good-ABS TRY go-PURP we-SA
    '[Our] camping-place was no good [and] we had to try to go [to find an alternative one].'

22. *ɲundu:ba ḍambu:l wunan/*
    you all-SA two-ABS lie-IMP
    'You two lie down [and sleep here]!' [the people told Guyala and Damari].

23. *ḍambu:l wuna:ɲ/ bulmba: ḍimurula /*
    two-ABS lie-PAST camp-LOC house-LOC
    The two [brothers] lay down [to sleep] in the big house.

24. *dama:ri   waŋga:ḍiɲu buga   / gunaguna   / bulmba*
    Damari-ABS get up-PAST nighttime middle of night camp-ABS
    gunaguna   /
    middle of night
    Damari woke up in the darkness, in the middle of the night. It was the middle of the night in the camp.

25. *ḍiṛi*   / *nulga:l*   /
    daybreak wake up-PAST
    At daybreak [Damari] woke up [his brother Guyala]:

26. *ɲundu gana waŋga:ḍin*/
    you-SA TRY   get up-IMP
    'You try to wake up'

27. *ŋaɲḍi bama:n   yiɲu   buɲa   ḍambu:l*
    we-SA person-GEN-ABS this-ABS woman-ABS two-ABS
    ḍuŋga:riɲa:lna   /
    run-GOING-COMIT-PURP

    'We must run away with these two women who belong to the
    people [that have offered us hospitality]', [Damari suggested to
    his brother].

28. *bama:l   wagal   guman   duga:l   ḍuŋga:riɲa:l*   /
    person-ERG wife-ABS one-ABS grab-PAST run-GOING-COMIT-PAST
    gali:ɲ/
    go-PAST

    [Each] person (i.e. brother) grabbed one woman and ran off with
    her; [they] went off.

29. *bama:n   buɲaḍamu   murimuri:ḍiɲu*   /
    person-GEN-ABS woman-ALL-ABS   scream-REDUP-:*ḍi*-PAST
    All the women belonging to those people really screamed and
    screamed.

30. *ŋaɲaɲ baḍar   / ŋaɲaɲ baḍar   bama:n*
    I-O   leave-IMP I-O   leave-IMP person-GEN-ABS
    guḍu:ga   /
    another person's-ABS

    [The victims cried out:] 'Leave me. Leave me, I belong to these
    other people (i.e. to the local group that had offered hospitality
    to Damari and Guyala).'

guḍuga 'that which belongs to someone else' is opposed to *maṛbu* 'one's
own' – used to refer to something that is considered an inseparable – but
abstract – part of a person e.g. wife, or conception site.

31. *ɲundu gadan   ŋaḍin   wagal / ŋayu ɲuniɲ*
    you-SA come-IMP I-GEN-ABS wife-ABS I-SA you-O
    galiɲalna   / *garu   ŋayu ḍulbun ḍara:ḍiŋ*   /
    go-COMIT-PURP   by-and-by I-SA fight-ABS put standing-:*ḍi*-PRES
    ŋayu galiɲalɲu   /
    I-SA go-COMIT-PAST

[Damari told the woman he had abducted:] 'You come on, you're my wife [now]! I must take you off. Soon I'll be prepared to fight over you. [Now] I'm taking [you off].'

Adjective *ḍulbun* describes a man who is ready to fight over his recognised wife. It must be distinguished from *gunugunu* which describes a man offering his body as a target for spear-throwing, to expiate some crime he has committed; and from *guli* 'wild, angry, ready to fight' which lacks the 'wife-defending' sense of *ḍulbun* and the retributional overtones of *gunugunu*.

32. *damariŋgu   yaymi:l/*
    Damari-ERG ask-PAST
    Damari asked [his brother]:

33. *ŋaḍin   waɲḍa   guman / ɲundu ḍambu:l giyi   budi*
    I-GEN-ABS where-LOC one-ABS you-SA two-ABS DON'T marry-IMP
    wagal / ɲundu ŋanda wiwin   guman /
    wife-ABS you-SA I-DAT give-IMP one-ABS
    'Where's my one [woman]? You mustn't marry two wives! You give one to me!'

34. *ɲundu gadan   / ŋayu garu   ɲunda   wiwiɲaliŋ   /*
    you-SA come-IMP I-SA by-and-by you-DAT give-GOING-PRES
    bulmba: /
    camp-LOC
    You come on! I'll give [a wife] to you by-and-by, when we reach the camp', [said Guyala].

It appears that during the flight Guyala took charge of both women, and began behaving as if they were both his wives. Dick Moses later said that although Guyala here promises that he will eventually give one to Damari, his understanding is that he never did.

35. *ŋaɲḍi bulmba:gu galiɲalna   / bayi:lina   bama:nda /*
    we-SA camp-ALL go-COMIT-PURP emerge-GOING-PURP person-DAT
    'We must take [the women] to the camp; we must go so that we emerge [from the bush] at the people['s camp]', [Guyala said, and then added:]

36. *waɲḍa   bulmba /*
    where-LOC camp-ABS
    'Where is the camp?'

37. *bulmba   ŋanda buḍiŋ   yiŋgu:ɲ ŋaṛa waɲḍa   /*
    camp-ABS I-DAT tell-PRES this-ACC south somewhere-LOC
    waŋgi/
    up

'I was told this camp was somewhere to the south, uphill', [Damari replied]

38. *gali:ɲ | waŋgi gali:ɲ | bama   banḍi:liɲu |*
    go-PAST up   go-PAST person-ABS find-GOING-PAST
    [They] went, [they] went uphill, went and found [another group of] people [sitting in their camp].

39. *ɲundu:ba yiɲu   ɲinaŋ |*
    you all-SA this-ABS sit-PRES
    [The people welcomed the brothers:] 'You can sit [here with us].'

The S NP here involves pronoun *ɲunduba* and deictic *yiɲu* – literally 'you, these [people], can sit...'.

40. *mayi   waɲi:ra   garu   ŋaɲḍi bugaŋ | mayi*
    fruit-ABS what kind-ABS by-and-by we-SA eat-PRES fruit-ABS
    banga   gunda:l| yiŋgilibi: mayi   gunda:l|
    native bee-ABS cut-PAST English bee-ABS fruit-ABS cut-PAST
    ḍarḍi   ḍara:l | muygal   budi:l |
    net-trap-ABS set-PAST hole-trap-ABS put-PAST
    [Guyala asked:] 'What sort of food shall we eat by-and-by? Native bee has been cut down. English bee has been cut down. Nets have been set (to catch, say, turkeys), and holes have been dug (for wallabies or cassowaries).'

Guyala is commenting on an apparent dearth of food. Supplies of honey have been exhausted and although traps have been prepared they may not yield much. Very shortly, Guyala will demonstrate a number of new vegetable foodstuffs.

41. *bulmba: guma:nda wuna:ɲ ḍimur[ula] bama   ŋabi |*
    camp-LOC one-LOC   lie-PAST house-LOC person-ABS many-ABS
    'Lots of people are sleeping in this one big house.'

42. *ɲundu:ba ḍambu:l wunaŋadan   yiŋgu | ŋaɲḍi ɲina:na*
    you all-SA two-ABS lie-COMING-IMP here-LOC we-SA sit-PURP
    guma:nda|
    one-LOC
    'You two come and sleep here! Then we can all settle down together (i.e. all in one group).'

43. *mayi | mayi   bama:l   guwal   buḍi:ɲ |*
    fruit-ABS fruit-ABS person-ERG name-ABS tell-PAST
    The people told [Guyala and Damari] the names of the fruits [they were eating; and then enquired of Guyala what it was he was consuming:]

44. *waɲi:ra   mayi   bugaŋ |*
    what kind-ABS fruit-ABS eat-PRES
    'What kind of fruit or vegetable are [you] eating?'

45. *waɲḍa   guyalaŋgu buḍi:ɲ |*
    where-LOC Guyala-ERG tell-PAST
    Guyala told [them] where [the food he was eating came from, and
        where it had to be prepared, to render it edible:]

46. *gana ɲundu:ba mayi   yiɲu   bana: budi |*
    TRY   you all-SA fruit-ABS this-ABS water-LOC put-IMP
        gurḍi:lna | garu | daŋgan |
        be soaked-PURP by-and-by take out-IMP
    'You all try to put this food in the water, to let it soak; by-and-by
        [you] take [it] out!'

47. *damariŋgu   buḍi:ɲ |*
    Damari-ERG tell-PAST
    [Then] Damari told the people:

48. *bana: giyi gurḍi | mayi   gurḍi:lna |*
    water-LOC DON'T be soaked-IMP fruit-ABS be soaked-PURP
        budi | waɲḍa   guygaguygam mayi   daŋgan |
        put-IMP sometime evening   fruit-ABS take out-IMP
        mamba |
        sour-ABS
    'Don't let [it] be soaked in the water [for too short a time!] Put
        the fruit to soak, and then take it out sometime in the evening.
        It'll be sour [if not soaked for a considerable time].'

This is the first of a number of arguments between the two brothers. Guyala is
trying to arrange it so that this fruit (which is never named in the narrative)
will be fresh and ready to eat after just a few minutes soaking in water. But
Damari wants to make it very sour, so that it will require a full day's soaking
to get rid of the bitter flavour and render it edible.

49. *guyalaŋgu   buḍi:ɲ | mayi   guriɲ   budi | bana*
    Guyala-ERG tell-PAST fruit-ABS good-ABS put-IMP water-ABS
        ḍiga | daŋgan | mayi   buyal | mayi
        pour water on-IMP take out-IMP fruit-ABS hard-ABS fruit-ABS
        garu   buga:na gabun |
        by-and-by eat-PURP fresh-ABS
    Guyala told [them all]: '[Just] put the fruit into water and it'll be
        good. Pour some water on it, and take it out – it'll be hard. By-
        and-by the fruit will be fresh and ready to eat.'

50. *ɲundu waɲi:nɲal*   *ŋuɲu | ɖilŋgu mayi   wayu*
    you-SA what-TR VBLSR-PRES that-ABS down fruit-ABS long time
    wuna:na bana: | guygaguygam daŋgan |
    lie-PURP water-LOC evening   take out-IMP
    [Damari responded:] 'Why are you doing that to that [fruit]? The
    fruit must [be allowed to] lie down in the water for a long time
    [before it is fit to eat]. Take it out in the evening!'

51. *ɲundu waɲi:nɲal   ŋuɲa:riɲ | mayi*
    you-SA what-TR VBLSR-PRES that sort of thing-ABS fruit-ABS
    wayula   wala | wambawamba:nɖi   bama |
    long time-NOW PARTICLE wait-REDUP-LEST-ABS person-ABS
    [Guyala said to him:] 'Why do you want to do that sort of thing?
    The fruit [has to lie in the water] for a long time now – and the
    people will unfortunately have to wait [a long time for their food.]'

52. *garu   bama:l   mayi   buga:na/ giɖa:na*
    by-and-by person-ERG fruit-ABS eat-PURP do quickly-PURP
    daŋga:na   banam |
    take out-PURP water-ABL
    'People should be able to eat it soon. It should be able to be taken
    out of the water quickly [and eaten straightway]' [Guyala
    continued.]

Damari, through sheer stubborn persistence, won this round. Dick Moses
affirmed that this fruit does require lengthy soaking before it can be eaten.
The brothers then turned to a different type of food: yams.

53. *gana mayi   ɖimir   ɖula:lin | munda   nara |*
    TRY fruit-ABS yam-ABS dig-GOING-IMP pull-IMP vine-ABS
    [Guyala said:] 'Go and try to dig some yams up. [Just] pull on the
    vine [and the yams will come out of the ground]!'

54. *damariŋgu buɖi:ɲ | mayi   ɖimir   bilan | ɖilŋgu/*
    Damari-ERG tell-PAST fruit-ABS yam-ABS enter-IMP down
    ɖabu: | murgu: ɲina:na ɖurgu:nda/ garu
    ground-LOC hole-LOC sit-PURP deep-LOC   by-and-by
    ganda: ɖula:lna/
    yamstick-INST dig-PURP
    [Then] Damari told [him]: 'The yam must go down into the
    ground. It must sit at [the bottom of] a deep hole. By-and-by it
    will have to be dug up with a [long pointed] yamstick (i.e. it is
    set too deep to be just pulled up by the vine).'

55. *guyalaŋgu   buḍi:ɲ / garu   mayi   muygun*
    Guyala-ERG tell-PAST by-and-by fruit-ABS yam-vine-ABS
    mundu:ŋ munda / muygun   munda / garu   mayi
    ease-ERG pull-IMP yam-vine-ABS pull-IMP by-and-by fruit-ABS
    bayi:lna   / gabun   garu   bayi:lna   /
    emerge-PURP fresh-ABS by-and-by emerge-PURP
    [But] Guyala told [him]: 'By-and-by [just] easily pull the vine,
    pull on the vine, and by-and-by the fruit will emerge; it will
    come out fresh [and ready to eat].'

56. *damariŋgu   buḍi:ɲ / mayi   garu   ḍilŋgu ḍurgu:nda*
    Damari-ERG tell-PAST fruit-ABS by-and-by down   deep-LOC
    wayu   ɲina:na/
    long time sit-PURP
    Damari told [him]: '[This] fruit must sit deep under the ground
    for a long time.'

57. *waɲi:ngu   ɲundu   ŋuɲa:riɲ   bila:ŋal*
    what-PURP you-SA that sort of thing-ABS enter-COMIT-PRES
    ḍilŋgubuḍun ḍurgu:nda/ garu   ganda: ḍula:lna/
    down-STILL deep-LOC   by-and-by yamstick-INST dig-PURP
    wayuwayu:ɲa   ḍula:lna/ mayi   muygun   mundu
    long time-REDUP-ɲa dig-PURP fruit-ABS yam-vine-ABS ease-ABS
    munda   /
    pull-IMP
    [Guyala remonstrated with him:] 'What did you put that sort of
    food so deep down for? By-and-by it'll have to be dug up with a
    yamstick. It'll take a long time to dig. It's easier just to pull up
    the fruit by the vine.'

Damari got his way again – the mountain yam known as *ḍimir* does grow at a
fair depth and requires some solid digging.

58. *garu   ŋuŋgum   gali:ɲ/*
    by-and-by there-ABL go-PAST
    By-and-by [Guyala and Damari] went on from there.

59. *ḍabu   –   ḍabu   ḍula:l / ḍabu   ḍula:l*
    ground-ABS ground-ABS dig-PAST ground-ABS dig-PAST
    muygal   budi:l / bambi:l /
    hole-trap-ABS put-PAST cover-PAST
    [They] dug the ground. [They] dug the ground and made a trap in
    the form of a hole, and covered it over [with bushes, to hide the
    entrance].

60. *miɲa   ginda:ɖa   gangu:l | wanda:ɲ muyga:lda |*
    animal-ABS cassowary-ABS wallaby-ABS fall-PAST hole-trap-LOC
       miɲa   duga:l   muyga:lmu|
       animal-ABS take-PAST trap-ABS

    Animals – cassowaries and wallabies – dropped into the hole. The
    animals were taken out of the trap [to be eaten].

61. *ɖarɖi: | miɲa   wawun   ɖarɖi: duga:l |*
    net-trap-INST animal-ABS turkey-ABS net-trap-INST catch-PAST
       ɖarɖim |
       net-trap-ABL

    Turkeys were caught in a net, and [taken] out of the net [to be
    eaten].

62. *gaɲu:n   ɖara:l | miɲa   mani:ɲ   ɖarɖi: |*
    bush-trap-ABS set-PAST animal-ABS catch-PAST trap-INST

    Bushes were set up (in a cone-shaped pattern, and animals chased
    into the trap so that they could be speared as they came through
    the narrow apex). Animals were caught in the traps.

63. *ɲuŋgum | guwal   ɖara:l   galiɲalɲu | bulmba |*
    there-ABL name-ABS assign-PAST go-COMIT-PAST place-ABS

    And then [Guyala] gave names to all the places as he went along.

64. *ɲundu waɲi:ngu guwal   ɖaral   gali:ɲal |*
    you-SA what-PURP name-ABS assign-PRES go-COMIT-PRES

    'Why are you giving out all these names as we go along?' [asked
    Damari].

65. *bama:n   guwal   ɖaral   gali:ɲal | garu*
    person-GEN-ABS name-ABS assign-PRES go-COMIT-PRES by-and-by
       binaɲalna   bulmba   waɲɖa   galiŋ | bulmba
       listen-PURP place-ABS where-LOC go-PRES place-ABS
       biribiri   ɖara | gaɖi   ɖaral |
       close together-REDUP assign-IMP long way apart assign-PRES
       wurba:nɖi |
       search for-LEST-ABS

    [Guyala replied]: 'People's names must be given to places all along
    the way. So that by-and-by [people] can listen to [and remember
    the sequence of place-names along a route and know] where the
    places are going to. Names must be given to places close
    together. If names were [only] assigned [to places] a long way
    apart, people might have to search [around a lot for them, and
    get lost].'

Damari was suggesting that place names be given out sparingly, a mile or two apart. But Guyala insisted that names be allocated quite generously, so that people could learn a route by a sequence of place-names; and each place could be easily accessible from the previous one. Guyala got his own way in this instance.

66. *gana galin | ḍirbi | bulmba |*
    TRY go-IMP promised time camp-ABS
    '[We must] try to go on [now]. [We] promised [to be at a certain] place [at a certain] time.'

67. *badil | mundi:may | damariŋgu*
    rickety nut-ABS vegetable sp.-ABS Damari-ERG
    mambaŋalɲu |
    bitter-TR VBLSR-PAST
    [Then] Damari made rickety nuts and Mundimay (a long yam-like vegetable found on the beach) sour (i.e. so that they would require lengthy preparation).

68. *mayi mamba | ḍiga | buŋa:nda waṇḍa*
    fruit-ABS bitter-ABS pour water on-IMP sun-LOC somewhere
    yiɲu waŋgi dungu: ɲinaŋ buŋan | mayi daŋgan |
    this-s up head-LOC sit-PRES sun-ABS fruit-ABS take out-IMP
    [Damari said]: 'The fruit is bitter. Pour water on it! [Until] the sun is where? – [until] the sun is sitting high [in the sky] (literally: at the head of the sky). Take the fruit out [of the water then, after it has soaked for half-a-day].'

69. *guyalaŋgu buḍi:ɲ | mayi waṇḍa bana: budi |*
    Guyala-ERG tell-PAST fruit-ABS somewhere water-LOC put-IMP
    daŋgan | garu gabun buga:na|
    take out-IMP by-and-by fresh-ABS eat-PURP
    Guyala told [Damari]: '[Just] put the fruit somewhere in the water, and take it out [again after a couple of minites] – it'll be fresh and ready to eat.'

Guyala wanted to make these vegetables only mildly bitter, so that they would only require a few minutes immersion to wash out the poisonous overtones. Damari – who again got his own way – insisted that they be made really bitter and require lengthy preparation.

70. *damariŋgu buḍi:ɲ | mayi mamba | wayu wuna:na*
    Damari-ERG tell-PAST fruit-ABS sour-ABS long time lie-PURP
    bana: |
    water-LOC

Damari told [him]: 'The fruit is sour! It must lie in the water for a long time.'

71. *guyalaŋgu   baḍa:ɻ   /*
    Guyala-ERG leave-PAST
    Guyala left [it i.e. gave in to Damari's persistence].

72. *gali:ɲ   /*
    go-PAST
    [The two brothers] went on.

73. *gubu:m   / gubu:m   duga:l   /*
    black pine-ABS black pine-ABS pick up-PAST
    [They] picked up black pine nuts.

74. *guyalaŋgu buḍi:ɲ / yiɲu   mayi   gabun   / gubu:m   /*
    Guyala-ERG tell-PAST this-ABS fruit-ABS fresh-ABS black pine-ABS
    Guyala told [his brother]: 'This fruit is [always] fresh, the black pine.'

75. *damariŋgu   buḍi:ɲ / bana: budi   / ḍiga   /*
    Damari-ERG tell-PAST water-LOC put-IMP pour water on-IMP
    mamba /
    sour-ABS
    [Then] Damari told [him]: 'Put it in the water, pour water on it, it's bitter!'

76. *guyalaŋgu buḍi:ɲ / garu   bana: – buɻi: waḍu   /*
    Guyala-ERG tell-PAST by-and-by water-LOC fire-INST heat-IMP
    ḍuŋgun   buga:na/ gabun   / bana:
    half-cooked black pine-ABS eat-PURP fresh-ABS water-LOC
    ḍiga   / garu   banam   buga:na/
    pour water on-IMP by-and-by water-ABL eat-PURP
    Guyala told [Damari]: 'Heat it in the fire [for a few minutes] and the Dyuŋgun (the name for lightly roasted Gubu:m) can be eaten – it's fresh. Pour water on it [for a very short time] and it can be eaten straight from the water.'

77. *guyalaŋgu – damariŋgu   buḍi:ɲ / ɲuɲudi   wala*
    Guyala-ERG Damari-ERG   tell-PAST that-ABS-INTENS PARTICLE
    guriɲ   / mayi   guriɲ   bana:
    good-ABS fruit-ABS good-ABS water-LOC
    ḍigaḍamu   buɻi: waḍu   /
    pour water on-IMP-JUST fire-INST heat-IMP
    ḍuŋgun   bunḍan / buga:na/
    half-cooked black pine-ABS beat-IMP eat-PURP

Guyala – I mean, Damari told [his brother]: 'That's all right then. The food'll be good if it's just soaked in water [briefly], [quickly] heated in the fire, then the Dyuŋgun can be hammered [with a stone] and eaten.'

Damari gives in to Guyala. In fact black pine needs only a few minutes preparation – as described here by Damari. It can even be eaten raw (whereas rickety nuts (*badil*) are poisonous when raw).

78. *dama:ri   gali:ɲ | gali:ɲ   bulubagu |*
   Damari-ABS go-PAST go-PAST fighting ground-ALL
   Damari went, he went to the fighting ground (to arrange a fight with an inland local group).

79. *ɲundu gadan | bulubagu |*
   you-SA come-IMP fighting ground-ALL
   [On his return he told Guyala] 'You come, to the fighting ground!'

80. *guyalaŋgu   buḍi:ɲ   waɳḍaɲunda ḍirbi |*
   Guyala-ERG tell-PAST what time   promised time
   Guyala asked: 'When have we promised [to fight]?'

81. *ḍilibuga:bi|*
   next day
   'Tomorrow'

82. *garu   bugamugu waŋga:ḍin|*
   by-and-by daybreak get up-IMP
   'We must get up at daybreak.'

83. *guyalaŋgu   buḍi:ɲ | binabina: wunan| garu*
   Guyala-ERG tell-PAST ear-REDUP-LOC lie-IMP by-and-by
   nulga:ldaŋ |
   wake-COMING-PRES
   Guyala told [his brother]: 'Lie with your ears alert! I'll come and wake [you] by-and-by.'

Damari was intent on avoiding the fight; he got up and sneaked out of the camp before his brother was awake. Guyala imagined that Damari had already set off for the fighting ground and followed (as he imagined) in the same direction. But Damari had gone the other way – he ran up against a Bougainvillea tree, piercing himself on the tree's prickles to simulate spear wounds. Damari eventually appeared at the fighting ground after the battle was over.

In 85 and 86 the storyteller says 'Guyala', when 'Damari' was intended.

84. *guya:la   waŋga:ḍiɲu bugamugu | ḍiɽi |*
   Guyala-ABS get up-PAST early morning daybreak
   Guyala got up in the early morning, at daybreak.

85. *ɲundu   guya:la   waɲḍa:ruɲ gali:ɲ* /
    you-SA Guyala-ABS which way go-PAST
    'You, [Damari], which way did you go?' [Guyala called
    out].

86. *wala   gali:ɲ / guya:l   gali:ɲ* /
    PARTICLE go-PAST Guyala-ABS go-PAST
    'He'd completely gone, [Damari] had gone.'

87. *wagal   ḍambu:l galiɲalɲu   /
    wife-ABS two-ABS go-COMIT-PAST
    [Guyala] took the two women with him:

88. *ɲunda:ba ḍambu:l gadan   / ɲayu galiɲalna   /
    you all-SA two-ABS come-IMP I-SA   go-COMIT-PURP
    'You two come! I must take [you].'

89. *dama:ri   waɲḍa   /
    Damari-ABS where-LOC
    'Where's Damari?'

90. *dama:ri   gurbi   ɲinaɲ* /
    Damari-ABS MIGHT BE sit-PRES
    'Damari might be stopping back.'

91. *wala   gali:ɲ / gana:ŋgar/*
    PARTICLE go-PAST PARTICLE
    '[Or he may] have gone already; [he may have been] the first
    to [go].'

92. *banḍa:ɽ* /
    follow-PAST
    [Guyala] followed [Damari, as he thought].

93. *dama:ri   gali:ɲ / ŋambu / danba   /*
    Damari-ABS go-PAST part-way Bougainvillea tree-ABS
         danba   wawa:l /
         Bougainvillea tree-ABS see-PAST
    Damari had gone only part-way [along a route from the camp], and
    saw a Bougainvillea tree.

94. *danba   yiɲu   ḍanaɲ* /
    Bougainvillea tree-ABS this-ABS stand-PRES
    'Here's a Bougainvillea tree standing' [Damari said to
    himself].

95. *ɲayu yiŋgu   ḍuŋgaḍuŋgaɲ* /
    I-SA here-LOC run-REDUP-PRES
    'I'll run up and down here.'

96. *bunḍil* / *ḍugi:l* *bunḍi:liŋ* *danba:* /
    bump-PRES tree-LOC bump-GOING-PRES Bougainvillea tree-LOC
    gula *baga:ḍiŋ* /
    body-ABS pierce-:-ḍi-PRES

    [Damari runs up and] bumps [into the tree; he] goes and collides
    with the Bougainvillea tree; and spears his body [on its prickles].

97. *ŋayu ḍuŋga:na*/ *ŋaɲaɲ gula* *baga:ḍina* /
    I-SA run-PURP I-O body-ABS pierce-:-ḍi-PURP

    'I had to run [in the fight], and as a result my body got speared'.

98. *garu* *ŋaɲaɲ yaymi:lna*/
    by-and-by I-O ask-PURP

    [I'll tell this to Guyala when] by-and-by [he] asks me [where I was
    in the battle, Damari thought to himself.]

Damari uses verbal derivational affix -*:ḍi-n* in the 'inanimate agent' sense, so
that the verb *baga:ḍi-n* in 97 is still transitive (this is clearly shown by the O
pronominal form *ŋaɲaɲ*); he is thus implying that his wounds were caused
accidentally. In fact they were self-inflicted, and he should have used the
'reflexive' sense of -*:ḍi-n*, deriving an intransitive stem, and said *ŋayu gula
baga:ḍi-n*. See 4.2.5.

99. *ɲundu waɲḍam* /
    you-SA where-ABL

    [When Damari eventually did turn up at the fighting ground,
    Guyala asked him:] 'Where have you [come] from?'

100. *ŋayu ḍirbi* *ḍana:ɲ* / *muŋgun* *yiŋa:riɲ* *wawal* /
     I-SA promised stand-PAST wound-ABS this sort of-ABS see-PRES
     galam /
     spear-CAU

     [Damari replied]: 'I've been standing [fighting] as promised; [you
     can] see all these sorts of wounds, caused by spears.'

101. *guyalaŋgu* / *biya* *ŋayu ɲuniɲ ɲuḍu wawa:l* / *ɲundu*
     Guyala-ERG PARTICLE I-SA you-O NOT see-PAST you-SA
     waɲḍam *gada:ɲ* /
     where-ABL come-PAST

     Guyala [said]: 'I'd have seen you [in the fight if you'd been there]
     but didn't. Where did you come from?'

102. *ŋayu ḍirbi* *guman bayi:l* /
     I-SA promised one-ABS emerge-PAST

     'I'm the one who came out of the promised [fight]', [Damari
     insisted].

103. *ɲundu ŋaɲaɲ ŋuḏu wawa:l ḏanaɲunda   ḏiwa:*   /
    you-SA I-O   NOT see-PAST stand-DAT SUBORD middle-LOC
    bigunuyi   /
    shield-COMIT-ABS
    'Didn't you see me standing in the middle [of the fight], with [my]
    shield?'

104. *waɲḏu   buḏi:ɲ   ɲundu ḏana:na   ŋuŋgu*   /
    who-ERG   tell-PAST you-SA stand-PURP there-LOC
    'Who told you [where] to stand there [in the fighting ground]?'
    [asked Guyala].

105. *ŋayu ɲunda   wurba:ḏiɲu*   /
    I-SA   you-DAT look for-:ḏi-PAST
    'I've been looking for you.'

106. *ŋayu gada:ɲ   / gada:ɲ   / gada:ɲ   / ŋayu wawa:l*
    I-SA   come-PAST come-PAST come-PAST I-SA see-PAST
    ŋaḏin   yaba   guya:la   /
    I-GEN-ABS brother-ABS Guyala-ABS
    'I came, I certainly came, and saw my brother Guyala there'
    [Damari said].

107. *ɲundu ŋuŋgu   ḏanan   / ŋayu galiŋala   bulmba:gu/*
    you-SA there-LOC stand-IMP I-SA go-PRES-NOW camp-ALL
    'You stand there! I'll go at once to the camp' [Damari now said to
    Guyala].

108. *ḏuŋga:ɲ / dama:ri   ḏuŋga:ɲ/*
    run-PAST Damari-ABS run-PAST
    [He] ran away, Damari ran away.

109. *ŋayudi   yuŋgu   ḏilŋgu galiŋ / biri:ɲḏa   /*
    I-SA-INTENSIF yonder-LOC down   go-PRES salt-water-LOC
    miɲa:gu   /
    animals-PURP
    'I'm going myself a fair way down to the saltwater, for fish'
    [Damari called out].

110. *dama:ri   gada:ɲ   / wurba:ḏiɲu*   /
    Damari-ABS come-PAST look for-:ḏi-PAST
    [Eventually] Damari came [back], searching:

111. *waɲḏa   ŋaḏin   yaba*   /
    where-LOC I-GEN-ABS brother-ABS
    'Where's my brother?'

112. *yaba   gali:ɲ   ḏilŋgu/ biri:ɲḏa   /*
brother-ABS go-PAST down   salt-water-LOC
[His] brother [Guyala] had gone down to the salt-water [too].

113. *guya:la   gada:ɲ   /*
Guyala-ABS come-PAST
Guyala came back [after a while, and Damari said to him:]

114. *ɲundu galin / guɲi:nda / ɲundu guɲi:nda   galin/*
you-SA go-IMP south-LOC you-SA south-LOC go-IMP
'You go, to the south. You go to the south!'

115. *ŋayu guŋga:ɻ biɻi   gunḏiŋ   / bulmba:gu/ ŋayu warḏan*
I-SA north   PARTICLE return-PRES camp-ALL I-SA raft-ABS
     daybil   gali:ŋal   / guŋaɻigu/ biri:ɲḏa
     take-PRES go-COMIT-PRES north-ALL salt-water-ALL
     biɻi   gunḏiŋ   /
     PARTICLE return-PRES
[But Guyala told him:] 'I'm going back north to the camp [we came from]. I'll take the boat, to the north, returning [home] by sea.'

The brothers split up at this stage of the story. Guyala returns north, and dies in that region some time later. The storyteller follows Damari, to the south.

116. *dama:ri   gada:ɲ   /*
Damari-ABS come-PAST
Damari came.

117. *ŋayu guman / gana ŋayu gali:na/*
I-SA one-ABS TRY I-SA go-PURP
'I'm on my own [now]' [said Damari,] 'I must try to go [along by myself].'

118. *waɲḏa   yiŋu   wuɻu: /*
where-LOC this-ABS river-ABS
'Where is the big river?' [Damari said to himself].

119. *yuŋa:ɲ   bana: / ḏala: wuḏaŋada:ɲ   /*
cross river-PAST water-LOC shallow-LOC cross-COMING-PAST
     gada:ɲ /
     come-PAST
He crossed the river, came across into shallower water.

120. *ŋanḏar   banḏa:ɻ   galiŋalɲu   guwa:gu/*
creek-ABS follow-PAST go-COMIT-PAST west-ALL
[He] went following a small creek up to the west.

121. *bana:*   *yuŋa:ɲ*   / *gaɲaraŋgu*   *bala*   *baḍa:l* /
     water-LOC cross river-PAST alligator-ERG shin-ABS bite-PAST
     bala   *baḍa:ɼ* / *bala*   *gulga*   *gali:ɲ* /
     shin-ABS leave-PAST shin-ABS short-ABS go-PAST
     [He] was crossing the creek [when] an alligator bit one shin off.
     [He] left [the bitten] limb and went on with one leg short.

122. *ŋayu gana gamba:na* / *gali:na* / *yagalḍida:*   *wuna:na*/
     I-SA TRY crawl-PURP go-PURP Yagalḍida-LOC lie-PURP
     yagalḍida: *ŋayu wulaŋaliŋ*   *ŋuŋgu* /
     Yagalḍida-LOC I-SA die-GOING-PRES there-LOC
     'I must try to go on by crawling, in order to lie down at Yagaldyida
     [my home]. I'm going to die there in Yagaldyida.'

123. *guya:la*   *ŋaḍin*   *guŋga:ɼ yaba*   *gali:ɲ* / *bulmba:* /
     Guyala-ABS I-GEN-ABS north   brother-ABS go-PAST camp-ALL
     murgu: / *ḍaruwayɲḍa ɲinaŋaliŋ* /
     Murgu-ALL hill-LOC   sit-GOING-PRES
     'My brother Guyala has gone north, to a place [called]
     Murgu, gone to settle down [and eventually die] on that hill
     [Murgu].'

124. *ŋayu yiŋu   wula:ɲ* /
     I-SA this-s die-PAST
     'I'm dying here.'

Dick Moses later mentioned that Damari died near by the present-day site of
Yarrabah mission.

Text 9

Autobiographical reminiscence by Dick Moses of his early life soon after
being brought into the mission. Told in the coastal dialect (recorded at
Yarrabah on 30 December 1971; duration 7½ minutes).

1. *ŋaɲaɲ gadaŋalɲu*/ *yaba:ŋ*/ *ḍiliwaɲi:ndu*/
   My brother, Dyiliwaŋin, brought me [into the mission, when I was
   about nine years old].

2. *ɲundu gadan miḍi:nda*/ *ɲinaŋadan*/
   'You come into the mission! Come and settle down [here]!'

3. *gaḍa:ŋ garu ɲuni:nda guru:n buḍi:na*/ *niba:lna*/ *waɲḍa ŋaŋga:ḍin*
   ɲundu/ *landimalna*/ *buḍi:na guru:n ɲuni:nda*/ *bama:l ɲaŋga:-*
   ḍiŋa:lna guru:n/

'So that by-and-by the white man can tell you stories, and show you
things. [Show you] where to speak, and teach you things. He'll
tell you stories, the [white] people will talk to you in
[English] language.'

4. *ɲundu:ba gadigadi:/ ŋayu gada:ɲ/*

'All you little children, I've come' [Moses shouted out to the
Yidiɲɖi children already at the mission].

5. *banɖi:ldaɲu bama ɲabi/ gadigadi:/*

[I] came and found lots of people [at the mission, lots of] children.

6. *ɲundu bama ɲabi yiɲu waruwaru ɲinaŋ/ gana ŋaɲɖi mugu bama:nda
maga/ burgi:na/ ŋaɲɖi dundi:ɲ waruwaru bama:nda/ ŋabi waruwaru/
bama gadigadi:/*

'All you children sitting [there]. It doesn't matter [being in the
mission] since we're all together, and can go walkabout [together].
All us little children can play together in a mob. All the children –
the little ones.'

7. *ŋaɲɖi:ɲ bama:l guga:l mayi:gu* dinner time now – *mayi:gu/ buga:ɖina/*

A man called us all to eat vegetable food.

8. *ɲundu:ba gadan/ mayi:gu/ buɲan waŋgila/ mayi bugaŋadan/*

'You all come, for food. The sun is high now (i.e. it is noon), come
and eat some food.'

9. *ŋaɲɖi yaymi:l/ miɲa guriɲ/ miɲa guriɲ/*

We asked: 'Is the meat good?' 'Yes, the meat is good.'

10. *ŋaɲɖi buga:ɲ/ muɽu:ɖum/ ɖinil/ maɽa baŋga:mu/ gubu bamu:gin/
ŋuɲa:riɲ/ ɖiwa bilaɲalɲu miɲa: mula:mba/ ɖulmbu:ran/ ŋuɲa:riɲ
miɲa ŋaɲɖi buga:ɲ/ burin ɲuɖu/ damba ŋaɲɖi buga:ɲ/*

We ate stingaree, and whip-tail stingaree, potato tops and pumpkin
leaves – that sort of thing. All mixed into a meat soup. And
dugong – we ate that sort of meat. There was no bread; but we
did eat damper.

11. *ŋaɲɖi mayim galiɲ/ yaɖil waruwaru/ burgiɲ/ bama:nda ŋabi:nda
ɖiwadaga:ɲ/ ŋaɲɖi bandu burgi:na/ ŋaɲɖi gayal muyubara/ bama
ŋabi yiɲu ɲinaŋ/*

After having [eaten] food, all of us children went out walkabout. We
all got into one mob and travelled together. I was the new fellow
amongst us. This group [of us] all sat down together.

12. *mayi galiɲa:ɖin/ ɲinaŋali:na/ waɳɖa wabaɽ ɲinaŋaliɲ/ wunaŋaliɲ
bulmba:/*

[The white man said to us:] 'Take this food with you, for when you

rest after having gone along [for a while]. Wherever you rest on the walk, when you go and sleep in a camp (i.e. make a temporary one-night camp in the bush during walkabout).'

13. *mala:ḍi galiŋalɲu/ ŋuɲu mayi damba:gu galiŋalɲu mala:ḍi/*

[We] took molasses with us. Took those molasses for damper (i.e. to spread the molasses on damper we cooked, like jam).

14. *ŋaɲḍi gunḍi:ɲ/ ɲundu:ba ɲina:ɲ guriɲ/ ŋaɲḍi guriɲ ɲina:ɲ/*

We returned home [and asked the people who had remained at the mission:] 'Have you been alright sitting [here]?' 'Yes, we've been sitting [here] alright.'

15. *gana ɲundu:ba gada:ɲ guygaguygam/ bimbi: ŋaɲḍi:nda/ ḍirbi + budil ɲundu:ba guygaguygam/ yalmbin ḍanan/ wurmba:gu/ ŋaɲḍi buḍi:ḍinu yiyi/ garu ŋaɲḍi yalmbin ḍanaŋ bulmba: wurmba:gu/ guygaguygam/ ŋaɲḍi ɲina:ɲ/*

You promised to come [to church] in the evening, for Our Father – you promised to come in the evening. 'Stand in line [after church before returning home] to sleep!' We said 'yes'. By-and-by we stand in line [before going back] to sleep in the camp, in the evening. We sat down [waiting].

16. *ŋaɲḍi burgi:ɲ/ ŋaɲḍi burgi:ɲ/ gaḍa:nda burgi:na/*

We went walkabout – we worked for the white man.

17. *buḍi:n/ɲundu:ba burgin/ ŋaɲḍi ɲundubanda garu/ gambi muṟay wiwi:na/ mayi garu wiwi:na/*

[He] told [us]: 'You all work! So that by-and-by we can give you clothes, and by-and-by give you food.'

18. *ŋaɲḍi ḍirgaṟ munda:l/ yawu: munda:liɲu/ dugu:ṟgu/ duguṟ balga:l ḍirga:da/ ḍugi burmbuṟ gunda:l/*

We pulled up blady grass; [we] went and pulled up shorter grass, for a house. [We] made [= thatched] a house with blady grass. [And we] cut a palm tree down [for the floor].

19. *bini:r ŋuḍu/ biba giḍaṟ ŋaɲḍi:nda bini:r wiwi:ɲ/*

[We were given] no money. We were given paper with a mark on (i.e. an ad hoc mission docket) [in place of] money.

20. *ŋaɲḍi ŋuŋgu/ gambi duga:l/ giḍa:da biba:/*

We bought clothes there [at the mission store] with the docket.

21. *garu ŋuŋgum ŋaɲḍi yaymi:l/ bama ŋabi/ bini:r ŋuḍu/*

By-and-by we asked all the [other Yidiɲḍi] people 'Is there no money?'

22. *ɲuɲudi bini:r ɲuni:nda wiwi:ɲ giḏaṟ/ biba gunda:l/*

'That IS money you've been given – paper with lines drawn on it' [they answered].

23. *ŋaɲḏi buḏi:ɲ/ ɲuɲudi wala/ ɲuɲu guriɲ/*

We told [them then]: 'Oh, that's alright. That's good [then].'

24. *ŋaɲḏi burgi:ɲ/ gadigadi:/ bama:l ŋaɲḏi:nda buḏi:ɲ/ ɲundu:ba burgin/ mayi:gu/*

All of us little children went for walkabout. Someone asked us: 'Are you coming on walkabout, for food?'

25. *ŋaɲḏi gali:ɲ yiŋariɲḏal/ bama ŋabi waruwaru galiɲ/ yiŋariɲḏal ḏimuḏimurula/ dugu:da ŋabi bandu galiɲ/ giḏaṟ + gunda:ḏina biba:/ ɲuŋa:riɲ ŋaɲḏi:n wugu/*

We went to this sort of place. All of us children went to this sort of big house (i.e. schoolhouse). We all went together in a group to the house, to make lines on paper (i.e. to learn to read and write). That was our sort of work.

26. *garu yuŋgudi ŋala:lda bimbi:nda gali:ɲ/ dugu:da bilaŋali:ɲ ɲuŋgu/ wurmba:gu/*

By-and-by we went yonder there to the big father (i.e. the missionary); we went and entered the house [church] to [attend evening service before] sleep.

27. *waɲḏa yiɲu dalɲudalɲu/ dalmba bunḏil/ ŋaɲḏi ɲuŋgu binaŋalɲu:n/ garu ŋaɲḏi galiɲunda ɲuŋgu dalɲudalɲu waɲḏa/ dalmba bunḏil/ ŋabi ŋaɲḏi yalmbin galiɲunda/ guranguran/ ɲuŋgu:gu dugu:ṟgu bila:na/*

Where is the bell ringing? – the sound is banging out, and we heard it. By-and-by we go when the bell rings there – the clapper hits. We all go in a long line, to enter the building [church] there.

28. *ŋaɲḏi ɲuŋgu bimbi:nda/ buŋgu ḏara:liɲu/ ɲina:ɲ/ garu yuŋgum bayi:l ŋaɲḏi guygaguygam/ bayi:l gali:ɲ dugu:da/*

We all went and knelt there [in Church] for the [Heavenly] Father. [Then we] sat. By-and-by in the evening [we] came out [of the church] and went to [our own] huts.

29. *garu dugu:ṟmu/ gaḏa:ŋ ŋaɲḏi:nda buḏi:ɲ/ ɲundu:ba garu wawa yiɲu giḏaṟ wunaɲunda/ yiɲu garu maɲḏam wunaŋadaŋ/ ɲundu:ba binabinaŋ/ bulmba: wurmba:gu/ wuna:na buga/ ɲuɲudi wala/*

By-and-by [in the morning we came] out of the house (i.e. came out of the dormitory and went across to the schoolhouse). The white man told us: 'You see these lines lying [on the page]!' [He

continued:] 'By-and-by this mark [the hand of the clock] will come and lie [at this position]. You people listen [to the prayers I tell you] so that [when you're] at home [you can say them to yourselves] before sleep, when you lie [in bed] at night. That's right!'

30. *ɲaɲḍi ŋuŋgum/ ɲina:ɲ/ ɲaɲḍi ɲina:ɲ/*

Then we sat down, we settled down [there].

31. *ɲaɲḍi:nda gaḍa:ŋ wiwi:ɲ/ ɲundu:ba yiŋa:riɲ bugan/ yiŋa:riɲ nuba bugan ḍadam/*

The white man gave us [food]: 'You eat this sort of thing! Eat these ripe wild bananas!'

32. *ɲundu:ba wuɲḍay giyi bugan/ ɲundu:baɲ gaḍa:ŋ ḍangaɲyalḍi/ yiŋa:riɲ/ yiŋa:riɲ mayi diradira/ giyi duga/ gaḍa:ŋ ɲundu:baɲ ḍangaɲyalḍi/ ɲaɲḍi baḍa:ɽ/*

'Don't you eat stolen [food], or the white man might punish you. Don't take this sort of thing, this kind of corn [planted here] or the white man might punish you.' We left [it alone].

33. *garu ŋuŋgum/ ɲaɲḍi gaḍa:ɲ mayi:gu/ mayi binaŋ guriɲɲuɽi/ mayi ḍangan/ ɲaɲḍi mayi mugu buga:ɲ/ miɲa wuda/ miɲa muɽu:ḍum/ miɲa ḍidin/ maɽa budidaɲḍa/ gabaḍila/ waḍu:l mulam/ ɲaɲḍi mugu buga:na/*

Then we came for food. We thought the food was good – but it was no good. We had to eat it anyway – shark, and stingaree, and periwinkles, and leaves, in a potato and cabbage [stew]. Cooked up in a stew. We ate it anyway (i.e. the food was poor and we didn't like it, but there was nothing else).

Dick Moses is here regretting that they were fed on scraps of European-type food, instead of on traditional Yidiɲḍi fare. They had to wait until they were old enough to go foraging for themselves, before they could obtain the sort of food they wanted.

34. *ɲaɲḍi gayal mugu ŋaŋga:ɲ/ ɲaɲḍi ŋuḍu binaɲalɲu/ waɲḍa mayi guriɲ/ garu ɲaɲḍi:nda bama:l buḍi:ɲ/ waɲḍa ŋalalŋalalala/ ɲaɲḍidi binaɲalɲu/ ŋuŋa:riɲ ɲaɲḍi mayi buga:ɲ/ ɲaɲḍi walnḍa:l/ mayi ɲaɲḍi buga:na guriɲ/ ŋuŋa:riɲ/*

We'd had to forget the other things. We didn't listen to [the old] people [of the tribe] telling us where good food [was to be found]. When we got to be big men, then we listened. And we ate that kind of [traditional] food. We picked over the food [in the bush] and ate the good stuff, that kind of thing.

35. *ɲuɲumbuḍun/ ŋaɲḍi bimbi:nda gada:ɲ/ ŋaɲḍi:ɲ gadaɲalɲu/ giḍaɾ +
gunda:lna/ ŋaɲḍi:ɲ gadaɲalɲu/ buŋgu ḍara:ḍina ḍabu:/ yiɲḍu:nda
waŋgi bimbi:nda/ ŋaɲḍi:ɲ gadaɲalɲu/ milbadaga:na/ yiŋgu bimbi:-
nda waŋgi/ waɲḍa giḍaɾ budi:lna/*

And then the same thing. We came to the father; he brought us
[to school] to write. He brought us to kneel on the ground 'To
Our Father on high'. He brought us, to make us clever
'For Our Father on high'. When he'll write our names (i.e. at
a certain educational stage, the missionary would baptise us,
and write our names in the register).

Text 14

The myth of Bibiyuwuy, a man who was killed by his brother and –
returning as a spirit – set eyes on his own skull. Bibiyuwuy then went off
to the land of spirits, calling all his people to follow him in due course –
this was the origin of 'death'. Told by Tilly Fuller in the tablelands
dialect (recorded at Kairi on 3 November 1972; duration 5½ minutes).

1. *ḍambu:l wagu:ḍa ḍaḍa gaba:l/ yiŋgu dugu:da/ ḍimu:r duguɾ/ guygi/
guygi: bambi:l ḍimurula/*

Two male children were born, in this house. [It was] a large house,
of loya vine. [They] were covered over [in their cribs] in the big
loya vine house.

2. *ḍaḍa ḍambu:l wagu:ḍa/ ŋalalala/ guman buɲamuḍay/ guman mugu/
ɲina:ɲ/*

The two male children were now big (i.e. grown-up). One had [two]
wives, but the other had no option but to sit [in front of the fire
alone, since he had no wives].

3. *guman baḍa:ɾ bulmba:/ ḍambu:l gali:ɲ/ ḍambu:ngu/ ḍambu:ngu
daga:ḍina/ ḍambun daga:l/*

One [man – the unmarried brother] was left at the camp. Two
[people – the married brother and one wife] went for grubs. To
cut out grubs. [They] cut grubs [from the rotten wood in which
they burrow].

4. *guman gunda:ḍiɲu/ galba:nda/ banḍa:l/*

One [the married brother] cut [an ash tree] with an axe. [He cut out
a grub, and] tasted [it. He found it tasted of semen, and knew
that his brother was misbehaving with his other wife, back at the
camp.]

5. *ŋaḏin wagal/ ḏurmaŋ/ ŋaṇḏaguma:ndu/ ḏambu:nda ŋayu yiŋu/ miɲa
    bunḏal/*

  'My wife is being swived (= made love to) by my brother. I've
  [tasted] a bad slimey animal taste in this grub' [the man said to
  himself].

6. *ŋayu gana gunḏiŋ bulmba:gu/ ŋaḏin wagal wawa:liŋga:liŋ /ḏaḏa/
    ḏanga:nɲal ŋaḏin/ bulmba:/ gana gunḏiŋ/ wawa:ldaŋga:daŋ/*

  'I must return to the camp, go right up and have a look at my wife,
  and my child. Something bad has been done to my [folks] in the
  camp. I must return – come close and have a look.'

7. *ɲundu ḏurma:ɲ ŋaḏin wagal/ ŋuḏu/*

  'You've been swiving my wife' [the married man challenged his
  brother, getting the reply] 'No'.

8. *guɲi wara ɲaŋga:ḏin/ ɲundu ḏurma:ɲ/ ŋayu ɲuniɲ garu bunḏaŋ/*

  'Don't tell lies! You swived [her]. By-and-by I'm going to hit [and
  kill] you.'

9. and he *bunḏa:ɲ/ gurga:mari/*

  And he hit him across the [back of the] neck [and killed him].

10. *ɲundu wulaŋala/ ŋayu ŋuḏu ɲunu:ngu duwu gaḏaŋ/ ŋayu bumba
    ɲinaŋ/ ɲundú/ ŋuḏu duwu bayil ŋanda/ bunḏa:ɲ/ wula:ɲ/*

  'Now you're dead. My tears will not come [into my eyes] for you.
  I'm sitting here dry[-eyed]. Hey! No tears will come to my eyes.
  [You] were hit [by me] and [you're] dead.'

11. *gula ɲari + baga:l/ dungu guga: budi:l/*

  [He] dug a hole [to bury] the body. And put the head [which had
  been cut off] into a bark [container].

12. *gali:ɲ bana: ŋabaŋali:ɲ/ biri:ɲḏa/ malu:way/ gana gada:ɲ gulugulu:y/
    gulugulu gadaŋalɲu gabulula/*

  [The spirit of the murdered man] went to the water, went and bathed
  in the salt-water. The spirit came with a black bream [for all the
  people to eat]. He brought the black bream on a small stick
  (*gabu:l*).

13. *ɲundu waɲa/ ŋayuɲa/ ɲundu ŋaɲaɲ bunḏa:ɲ/ ŋayu gana gunḏi:ɲ/*

  'Who are you?' [all the people in the camp ask the returning spirit].
  'It's me alright.' 'You killed me' [he tells his brother in front of
  all the other people] 'but I've come back.'

14. *waɲi:ngu ɲundu gaḏaŋ/ ŋayu gaḏa:ɲdi wawa:ḏina bulmba:gu/*

  [The people ask him]: 'What are you coming [here] for?' [and he
  replies] 'I've come to have a look at the camp.'

On playback Tilly Fuller said that although *ŋayu gada:ɲdi* is grammatical, *ŋayudi gada:ɲ* would really be better here.

15. *ɲundu:ba guriɲ ɲinaŋ/ ɯ̃ɯ̃ ŋaɲḍi guriɲ ɲinaŋ/*

'Are you all alright sitting [here]?' [he asks them] 'Yes, we're alright sitting [here].'

16. *waɲi bulu guḍil/ ŋaɲḍi ḍubuɲ/ ŋuru:/*

'What's the stink [I can] smell?' [the spirit asked]. We were all silent [not answering him]. Why?

17. *ŋaɲḍi waɲi:nŋal yiŋu dungu/ ŋuɲḍu:ŋ dungu ɲuma:l/*

'What shall we do with this head? That [spirit] smelt [his own] head' [the people spoke amongst themselves].

18. *ŋayudi manŋalala/ ɲari+baga:lna/ ŋayu buḍi:ɲ/ ŋuriḍulu:/ ɲari+ baga:lna/*

'I'm really frightened. We'll have to dig a hole [and bury the head]' [the dead boy's mother said] 'I told you some time ago, to dig a hole [and bury the head].'

19. *ŋayu garu buḍiŋ/ ɲuniɲ ŋuŋu dungu ŋayu gunda:l/ wula:ɲ/ ŋaḍin ŋumbaɾ wawawawa:lna/ dungula baba:l/*

'I'll have to tell [him] soon' [Mother says, and when the spirit of her son next returns she says to him:] 'I cut off your head [after you'd] died. I wanted to gaze on the face of my dead child – on his skull.'

20. *ŋayu gundiŋala/ ŋayu ɲundu:baɲ yiŋu baḍaɾala/ ŋayu galiŋala/ [wu:y] [wu:y] [wu:y] [wu:y] [wu:y]/ ŋayu ḍugimari ḍaḍa:maŋ/ guman ḍaḍamaŋal/ guma:nbi ḍaḍamaŋal/ ŋayu guma:nbi/ ŋayu bana: biri:ɲḍa galiŋ/*

[The spirit said] '[Having seen my own skull], I'm returning now [to my spirit-home in the water]. I'm leaving you all now. I'm going away now.' [And as he went he called out] 'Wuy, wuy, wuy, wuy, wuy...' [being known as Bibiyuwuy from then on]. [He continued:] 'I'm jumping through the trees; I jump over one [stick], I jump over another [stick], then I [jump over] a third one. I go into the salt-water.'

21. *gulugulu ɲundu:ba buganala/ miɲa ŋayu gadaŋalɲum/*

'Now you can all eat the black bream, the seafood that I brought [for you]!'

22. *ŋayu gana gundiŋ/ ŋayu ɲuniɲ wawal ḍambulamay/ ḍambulamay gadan/*

'I'm returning [to the water]. I'll see you in two [days]. Come in two [days]!'

23. *ŋayu gana:ŋgar galiŋ/ badiŋ/*
    'I'm the first to go [to heaven] crying as I go.'

Having seen his own head, Bibiyuwuy has to go to the land of spirits and remain there (effectively, dying). He tells the other people that they will in time follow him. The reference to 'in two days' here is obscure. On replay Tilly Fuller mentioned that she should have said 'in three days'. In fact, Bibiyuwuy is supposed – in other versions of this myth that the writer has heard – to have returned on each of the three days after his death, to have seen his head on the third day and then 'gone to heaven'.

    The remainder of the story given by Tilly Fuller (below) is essentially irrelevant to the main theme.

24. *buɲaḍamu muḍam badi:ɲ/ bimbi/ ŋaɲḍaguman badi:ɲala bunḍa:ḍiɲum/*
    [First], just the women, including mother, are crying. Then father [joins in]. And now brother cries because he had killed him.

25. *ŋayudi waga:lgu biɽmbi:rḍidagaŋ/ wagal ŋaḍin ḍangan/ ŋayu ŋaɲḍaguman ŋayu waɲi:ngu bunḍa:ɲ/ ŋayu bunḍa:ɲ ŋaḍin ŋaɲḍaguman/ ŋaḍin guyi:gu/ guyi:gu/mundu biɲḍula/ ŋuḍula/ ŋuḍula badi:na/ wula:ɲala/*
    [The murdering brother said]: 'I was jealous over my wife. But it was my wife who was no good [and seduced my brother]. Why did I kill my brother? I killed my [own] brother. My heart is broken [because of my deed]. I'm spiritless, sad and depressed. But no more now. No more crying now [because] he's dead and gone [and nothing can bring him back].'

26. *ŋaɲḍi yiŋgu ɲinaŋala/ bulmba wawa:ḍiŋ/ wawa:ḍiŋ/ bulmba ŋali:nala/*
    'We all sit about here now, looking around the camp, gazing about the camp. The camp [just] belongs to you and I now' [the murdering brother tells his son].

27. *bama badiŋ bulmba:/ ŋaḍin wagu:da ḍaḍa/ ŋayu gumanala/ bimbi badiŋ/ galŋa/ ḍuḍum/ ŋaɲḍaguman/ ḍaŋgul/ badiŋ/ wuŋga ŋuŋgu:gu guma:ngu/ waguḍagu/*
    The people cried and prayed in the camp. 'There's [only] my boy child, I'm on my own' father cries. And uncle, auntie, brother, and sister [all] cry, pray for that one dead man.

28. *guriɲ/ bulmba:gu ŋuŋgu buɽi:gu daga:ḍina/ bana:gu duga:ḍina/ buŋa:ndu/*
    [He was a] good [man]. [He] would cut wood for the fire at the camp there, and [he] would fetch water, in the daytime.

On playback, Tilly Fuller said that the last word should be *buɲa:nḍi*, rather than *buɲa:ndu*.

29. *ɲaɲḍi ɲuŋgum galinala/ duguɽ yuŋgula ḍara:lna/ yiɲu ɲamu:ray/ dungu ɲari + bagal/ ɲaɲḍi ɲumbaɽ/ ɲumbaɽ wawa:l yiŋgu/ bulmba:/*

    'We must go [from here] now, to build a camp in another place, some way off. This place [smells] stale. [First] we'll bury the head. We've been seeing his face all the time here in this camp.'

30. *ɲaɲḍi galiŋ yuŋgu/ ḍalabiɲala ɲina:na/*

    'We'll go far away, to settle on the other side [of the creek].'

31. *ɲayu ɲuḍula ɲaḍin dungu/ ɲumbaɽ wayba:ḍiɲala/ dungu/ ɲaḍin ɲuḍula/*

    [Mother said]: 'I feel like nothing. My head – my face and head are going round (i.e. feeling dizzy). There's nothing for me (i.e. nothing left in life for me).'

32. *bama ḍaɲḍi:ɲ ɲuŋgum bulmbam/ gali:ɲ/*

    The people shifted camp from that place, and went away.

33. *ḍuga:bal ḍara:l/ bulmbabiɲala/*

    [They] set up house-frames, at another place.

34. *yiɲu guriɲ/ gadaŋ/ ɲumbaɽ/ wawa:l burgiɲunda/*

    This [mother] felt better [when she] came [to the new camp]. Her head [felt alright now], and she could be seen walking about.

References

Allen, W. S. (1950/1). 'A study in the analysis of Hindi sentence structure', *Acta Linguistica* [*Hafniensia*], 6, 68–86.

Benveniste, E. (1973). *Indo-European language and society*. (London: Faber and Faber.)

Biskup, P. (1973). *Not slaves, not citizens: the Aboriginal problem in Western Australia, 1898–1954*. (Brisbane: University of Queensland Press.)

Blake, B. J. (1969). *The Kalkatungu language: a brief description*. (Canberra: Australian Institute of Aboriginal Studies.)

Blake, B. J. and Breen, J. G. (1971). *The Pitta-pitta dialects* (= *Linguistic Communications 4*). (Melbourne: Monash University.)

Bloch, B. and Trager, G. L. (1942). *Outline of linguistic analysis*. (Baltimore: Linguistic Society of America.)

Bolton, G. C. (1963). *A thousand miles away: a history of North Queensland to 1920*. (Canberra: ANU Press.)

Capell, A. (1956). *A new approach to Australian linguistics*. (Sydney: Oceania Linguistic Monographs.)

(1962). *Some linguistic types in Australia*. (Sydney: Oceania Linguistic Monographs.)

Catford, J. C. (mimeo). 'Ergativity in Caucasian languages.' (University of Michigan.)

Chadwick, N. (1975). *A descriptive study of the Djingili language*. (Canberra: Australian Institute of Aboriginal Studies.)

Chomsky, N. (1965). *Aspects of the theory of syntax*. (Cambridge, Mass: MIT Press.)

Comrie, B. (1973). 'The ergative: variations on a theme', *Lingua* 32, 239–53.

Crowley, T. M. (forthcoming). *The Middle Clarence dialects of Bandjalang*.

Dixon, R. M. W. (1968). *The Dyirbal language of North Queensland*. Ph.D. thesis (University of London).

(1970a). 'Olgolo syllable structure and what they are doing about it', *Linguistic Inquiry* 1, 273–6.

(1970b). 'Syntactic orientation as a semantic property', pp. 1–22 of *Mathematical linguistics and automatic translation*, Report NSF-24. (Cambridge, Mass: Harvard University Computation Laboratory.)

(1970c). 'Proto-Australian laminals', *Oceania Linguistics* 9, 79–103.

(1971). 'A method of semantic description', pp. 436–71 of *Semantics, an interdisciplinary reader in philosophy, linguistics and psychology*, edited by D. D. Steinberg and L. A. Jakobovits. (Cambridge: Cambridge University Press.)

(1972). *The Dyirbal language of North Queensland*. (Cambridge: Cambridge University Press.)

(1976a). Editor of *Grammatical categories in Australian languages, Proceedings of the 1974 AIAS Conference*. (Canberra: Australian Institute of Aboriginal Studies.)

(1976b). 'Tribes, languages and other boundaries in north-east Queensland', pp. 207–38 of *Tribes and boundaries in Australia*, edited by Nicholas Peterson. (Canberra: Australian Institute of Aboriginal Studies.)

(1977). 'Some phonological rules in Yidin^y', *Linguistic Inquiry* 8.

(forthcoming-a). *A grammar of Wargamay*.

(forthcoming-b). *A grammar of Mbabaram*.

Douglas, W. H. (1964). *An introduction to the Western Desert language*, revised edition. (Sydney: Oceania Linguistic Monographs.)

Geytenbeek, Brian and Helen (1971). *Gidabal grammar and dictionary*. (Canberra: Australian Institute of Aboriginal Studies.)

Glasgow, Katherine (1964). 'Frame of reference for two Burera tenses', p. 118 of *Papers on the languages of the Australian Aborigines*, edited by Richard Pittman and Harland Kerr. (Canberra: Australian Institute of Aboriginal Studies.)

Glass, A. and Hackett, D. (1970). *Pitjantjatjara grammar*. (Canberra: Australian Institute of Aboriginal Studies.)

Gleason, H. A. (1965). *Linguistics and English grammar*. (New York: Holt.)

(1969). *Introduction to descriptive linguistics*, revised edition. (New York: Holt.)

Gribble, E. R. B. (1897a). 'Linguistics – C. Grafton dialect of Goonganji tribe', *Australasian Anthropological Journal* 1, 1, 16–17.

(1897b). 'Class systems', *Australasian Anthropological Journal* 1, 4, 84.

(1900). 'Linguistics of the Koo-gun-ji tribe', *Science of Man* 3, 8, 134–5.

(1930). *Forty years with the Aborigines*. (Sydney: Angus and Robertson.)

(1932). *The problem of the Australian Aboriginal*. (Sydney: Angus and Robertson.)

(1933). *A despised race: the vanishing Aboriginals of Australia*. (Sydney: Australian Board of Missions.)

Hale, Kenneth L. (1970). 'The passive and ergative in language change: the Australian case', pp. 757–81 of *Pacific linguistics studies in honour of Arthur Capell*, edited by S. A. Wurm and D. C. Laycock. (Canberra: Pacific Linguistics.)

(1973). 'Deep-surface canonical disparities in relation to analysis and change: an Australian example', pp. 401–58 of *Current trends in linguistics*, vol. 11, edited by T. A. Sebeok. (The Hague: Mouton.)

(1976a). 'Tʸa:pukay', pp. 236–42 of *The languages of Cape York*, edited by Peter Sutton. (Canberra: Australian Institute of Aboriginal Studies.)

(1976b). 'The adjoined relative clause in Australia', pp. 78–105 of Dixon (1976a).

Hall, A. H. (1972). *A study of the Thaayorre language*. PhD thesis (University of Queensland).

Harris, Joy Kinslow (1969). 'Preliminary grammar of Gunbalang', pp. 1–49 of *Papers in Australian Linguistics* No. 4. (Canberra: Pacific Linguistics.)

Haviland, J. B. (1972). *Guugu-Yimidhirr word list*, mimeo. (Canberra: Department of Linguistics, SGS, ANU.)

(mimeo). 'Guugu-Yimidhirr brother-in-law-language'.

(forthcoming). 'A grammar of Guugu-Yimidhirr'.

Haywood, J. A. and Nahmad, H. M. (1962). *A new Arabic grammar of the written language*. (London: Percy Lund, Humphries.)

Heath, Jeffrey (1976). '"Ergative/Accusative" typologies in morphology and syntax', pp. 599–611 of Dixon (1976a).

Hershberger, Ruth (1964). 'Personal pronouns in Gugu-Yalanji', pp. 55–68 of *Papers on the languages of the Australian Aborigines*, edited by Richard Pittman and Harland Kerr. (Canberra: Australian Institute of Aboriginal Studies.)

Hockett, C. F. (1958). *A course in modern linguistics*. (New York: Macmillan.)

Householder, F. W. (1971). *Linguistic speculations*. (Cambridge: Cambridge University Press.)

Hughes, E. J. and Healey, Alan (1971). 'The Nunggubuyu language, part one – the Nunggubuyu verb', pp. 46–57 of *Papers on the languages of Australian Aborigines* by B. J. Blake et al. (Canberra: Australian Institute of Aboriginal Studies.)

Hymes, Dell (1975). 'From space to time in tenses in Kiksht', *International Journal of American Linguistics*, 41, 313–29.

Kachru, Yamuna (1965). *A transformational treatment of Hindi verbal syntax*. PhD thesis (University of London).

Keen, Sandra (1972). *A description of the Yukulta language*. MA thesis (Monash University).

Lakoff, George (1971). 'On generative semantics', pp. 232–96 of *Semantics, an interdisciplinary reader in philosophy, linguistics and psychology*, edited by D. D. Steinberg and L. A. Jakobovits. (Cambridge: Cambridge University Press.)

Lakoff, George and Ross, J. R. (1966). 'A criterion for VP constituency' in *Linguistics and automatic translation*, Report NSF-17. (Cambridge, Mass: Harvard University Computation Laboratory.)

Langacker, R. W. and Munro, P. (1975). 'Passives and their meaning', *Language* 51, 789–830.

Lehiste, I. (1965). 'The function of quantity in Finnish and Estonian', *Language* 41, 447–56.

(1970). *Suprasegmentals*. (Cambridge, Mass: MIT Press.)

Lightner, T. M. (1973). 'Remarks on universals in phonology', pp. 13–49 of *The formal analysis of natural languages*, edited by Maurice Gross, Morris Halle and Marcel-Paul Schutzenberger. (The Hague: Mouton.)

Lyons, John (1968). *Introduction to theoretical linguistics*. (Cambridge: Cambridge University Press.)

Mathew, John (1910). *Two representative tribes of Queensland*. (London: T. Fisher Unwin.)

McCawley, J. D. (1968). 'Lexical insertion in a transformational grammar without deep structure', pp. 71–80 of *Papers from the Fourth Regional Meeting of the Chicago Linguistic Society*, edited by B. J. Darden et al. (Chicago.)

McConnel, U. H. (1939–40). 'Social organisation of the tribes of the Cape York Peninsula, North Queensland', *Oceania* 10, 54–72, 434–55.

McConvell, Patrick (1976). 'Nominal hierarchies in Yukulta', pp. 191–200 of Dixon (1976a).

McKay, G. R. (1975). *Rembarnga – a language of central Arnhem Land*. PhD thesis (Australian National University).

Meyer, H. A. E. (1843). *Vocabulary of the language spoken by the aborigines of the southern and eastern portions of the settled districts of South Australia... preceded by a grammar*. (Adelaide: James Allen.)

Mulvaney, D. J. (1975). *The prehistory of Australia*, revised edition. (Melbourne: Penguin.)

Oates, L. F. (1964). *A tentative description of the Gunwinggu language (of western Arnhem Land)*. (Sydney: Oceania Linguistic Monographs.)

O'Grady, G. N. (1960). 'More on lexicostatistics', *Current Anthropology* 1, 338–9.

Osborne, C. R. (1974). *The Tiwi language*. (Canberra: Australian Institute of Aboriginal Studies.)

Pike, K. L. (1964). 'Stress trains in Auca', pp. 425–31 of *In honour of Daniel Jones*, edited by David Abercrombie et al. (London: Longmans.)

Plato, *Cratylus*.

Pope, M. K. (1934). *From Latin to modern French*. (Manchester: Manchester University Press.)

Regamey, C. (1954). 'A propos de la "construction ergative" en indo-aryen moderne', pp. 363–84 of *Sprachgeschichte und Wortbedeutung, Festschrift Albert Debrunner*. (Bern: Francke.)

Ringen, C. (1972). 'On arguments for rule ordering', *Foundations of Language* 8, 266–73.

Rigsby, Bruce (1975). 'Nass-Gitksan: an analytical ergative syntax', *International Journal of American Linguistics*, 41, 346–54.

Roth, W. E. (1901a). *The structure of the Koko-Yimidir language* (= North Queensland Ethnography, Bulletin no. 2). (Brisbane.)

(1901b). *Food: its search, capture and preparation* (= NQE, Bull. 3). (Brisbane.)

(1903). *Superstition, magic and medicine* (= NQE, Bull. 5). (Brisbane.)

(1904). *Domestic implements, arts and manufactures* (= NQE, Bull. 7). (Brisbane.)

(1908). 'Miscellaneous papers (= NQE, Bull. 11)', *Records of the Australian Museum* 7, 74–107.

(1909). 'Fighting weapons (= NQE, Bull. 13)', *Rec. Aust. Mus.* 7, 189–211.

(1910a). 'Transport and trade (= NQE, Bull. 14)', *Rec. Aust. Mus.* 8, 1–19.

(1910b). 'Social and individual nomenclature (= NQE, Bull. 18)', *Rec. Aust. Mus.* 8, 79–106.

Rowland, E. C. (1960). *The tropics for Christ, being a history of the Diocese of North Queensland*. (Townsville: Diocese of North Queensland.)

Sapir, E. (1911). 'The problem of noun incorporation in American languages', *American Anthropologist* 13, 250–82.

(1921). *Language*. (New York: Harcourt Brace.)

(1949). *Selected writings of Edward Sapir in language, culture and personality*, edited by D. G. Mandelbaum. (Berkeley and Los Angeles: University of California Press.)

Schmidt, P. W. (1912). 'Personal pronomina in den Australischen Sprachen', *Anthropos*.

Sharp, R. L. (1939). 'Tribes and totemism in north-east Australia', *Oceania* 9, 254–75, 439–61.

Silverstein, Michael (1976). 'Hierarchy of features and ergativity', pp. 112–71 of Dixon (1976a).

Sommer, B. A. (1972). *Kunjen syntax – a generative view*. (Canberra: Australian Institute of Aboriginal Studies.)

Strehlow, T. G. H. (1944). *Aranda phonetics and grammar*. (Sydney: Oceania monographs.)

Taplin, G. (1880). 'Grammar of the Narrinyeri tribe of Australian aborigines', addendum to *The folklore, manners, customs and languages of the South Australian aborigines*, edited by G. Taplin. (Adelaide.)

Thomson, D. F. (1945). 'Names and naming in the Wik Moŋkan tribe', *Journal of the Royal Anthropological Institute* 75, 157-68.

Tindale, N. B. (1940). 'Distribution of Australian Aboriginal tribes: a field survey', *Transactions of the Royal Society of South Australia* 64, 140–231.

(1974). *Aboriginal tribes of Australia.* (Berkeley and Los Angeles: University of California Press.)

Tindale, N. B. and Birdsell, J. B. (1941). 'Tasmanoid tribes in North Queensland', *Records of the South Australian Museum* 7, 1–9.

Trubetzkoy, N. S. (1969). *Principles of Phonology*, translated by C. A. M. Baltaxe (Berkeley and Los Angeles: University of California Press.)

Tsunoda, Tasaku (1976). 'The derivational affix "having" in Warungu', pp. 214–25 of Dixon (1976a).

Wise, Hilary (1975). *A transformational grammar of spoken Egyptian Arabic.* (Oxford: Blackwell.)

Vocabulary

Only words occurring in the discussion, examples and texts of this book are listed here; proper names are not included. Each root is specified for part of speech, and also transitivity (in the case of verbs and adverbs) and whether generic or not (in the case of nouns - 6.2.1). Verbal conjugation membership is shown by a final -*n*, -*l*, or -*ṛ*. The following abbreviations are used:

N gen	generic noun	Vint	intransitive verb
N	other nouns	Vtr	transitive verb
Adj	adjective	Adint	intransitive adverb
Loc	locational qualifier	Adtr	transitive adverb
Time	time qualifier	Part	particle

Although particles are listed, no attempt has been made to cross-reference other 'grammatical words' – pronouns and deictics; however, some initial segments of roots are identified.

All roots given occur in the unmarked 'everyday' variety of Yidiɲ, unless Dyalŋuy is specifically indicated. Where a root is known to occur in only one dialect the letter 'C' (coastal) or 'T' (tablelands) is included. All loan words are clearly identified.

Since this vocabulary is intended mainly to facilitate understanding of the grammatical examples and texts, it has not been thought appropriate to give a full statement of the 'meaning' of each item. Instead, entries are mostly confined to one or two English words that give some indication of the most central meanings of the Yidiɲ word. The writer hopes soon to complete a dictionary/thesaurus of Yidiɲ which will attempt comprehensive statements of meaning, with citations etc.

The alphabetical order followed is:

a, b, d, ḍ, g, i, l, m, n, ɲ, ŋ, r, ṛ, u, w, y

baba, Adj: deaf, half-witted
babalA, N: bone
babaṛ, Part: couldn't manage it
badil, N: rickety nut
badi-n, Vint: cry, sob, weep, mourn
baḍa, N: grassy plain
baḍagal, N: king tide
baḍa-l, Vtr: bite

baḍa-ṛ, Vtr: leave
baḍi, N gen: canoe
baḍigal, N: fresh-water turtle
baḍin T, *baḍinḍi* C, N: sutton bird
baga-l, Vtr: piece with pointed implement, spear
bagi, LOAN, N: bag
bagil, Adj: another (see 6.2.2)

bagiram T, N: tea-tree sp.

baguɽ, N: sword

bala, N: shin

bala-n, Vint: open out, become wide

balawa, N: black and red sugar ant

balbaɽA T, N: crane

balbun, N: tree species

balga-l, Vtr: make, build

balmbiɲ, N: grasshopper

balŋga-ɽ, Vtr: hit with a stick

baluɽ, N: curved woomera

bama, N gen: person

bambaɽa-n, Vint: be frightened, nervous

bambi-l, Vtr: cover

bamugin, LOAN, N: pumpkin

bana, N & N gen: fresh water, drinkable liquid

banba-n, Vint: be cold

banbaɽA C, N: crane

banbi, N: eyebrow, river bank

bandu, Adj: all together in a mob

banḍa-l, Adtr: try to do, taste

banḍa-ɽ, Vtr: follow

banḍaɽA, N: madness in head

banḍi-l, Vtr: find

banga, N: small native bee and its honey

bani:ḍi-n, Vint: grumble

baŋgal, N: large stone axe

baŋgamu, N: English potato

baŋga-n, Vtr: pass by

baŋguɽ, N: multi-prong fish-spear

baŋuḍulu: T, Time: a few months ago

barganda-n, Vtr: pass by

barŋga-n, Vtr: praise

baɽabaɽa, N: common fly

baɽa-l, Vtr: deliver short, sharp blow with rounded implement, e.g. kick, punch

baɽgu, N: cane knife

baɽiɲU, N: small-leafed tree, used for spear handles

baɽma-n Dyalŋuy, Vint: go

baɽumbar, N: wattle tree grub

bawu:, N: backbone

bayabay Dyalŋuy, N: person

bayba, N: spring (of water)

bayga-ɽ, Vint: feel sore, have pain

bayi-l, Vint: come out, emerge

bayŋga, N: hot stone used in cooking

biba, LOAN, N: paper, docket

biba-n, Vtr: look back at

bibiya, N: coconut tree

bida, N: bark canoe, bark trough

bidi, Loc: near (and Time: just now)

bidibidi, N: beetle species

biḍaɽ + baḍa-l, Vtr: dream about

biḍaɽ + wanda-n, Vint: dream

biḍi, Adj: proper, properly

biḍiliɲ Dyalŋuy, N: sword, and Johnson hardwood tree

biḍir, N: loya cane sp.

biḍu:, N: eaglehawk

bigunU, N: shield

biguɲ, N: finger- and toe-nail, claw

bila-n, Vint: enter, go in

bilayŋgir, LOAN, N: blanket

bilgilI, N: spur wood tree

biligan, LOAN, N: billy-can

biliybiliy, N: small hickory tree

bilma-l, Vtr: clear the ground (for a camp)

bilɲḍi-n, Vint: jump down

bima, N: death adder

bimbi, N: father, and father's brother

bina, N: ear

bina + bambi-l, Vtr: forget

binabaɲḍa, Adj: sad, forgetful

bina + baɽa-l, Vtr: deafen

binagal, Adj: paying attention

binagali-n, Vtr: forget

bina-n, Vtr: hear, think

binaɲa-l, Vtr: listen to, hear

binarɲa-l, Vtr: tell, warn

binda, N: shoulder, top of tree, top of waterfall

bindabinda, N: type of shell

binduba, N: crayfish, small fig tree

binirI, N: shell, money

biɲḍin, N: hornet

biɲḍu, Adj: weak, innocuous, useless, tired

biŋgal C, N: spoon, chopsticks

biŋgal T Dyalŋuy, N: spear, yamstick

birbibirbi, N: small flat fish

birgalA, N: night hawk

birgil, Time: for a short while

biri, Loc: very near

biriɲ, N: salt-water

birmbiḍa Dyalŋuy, N: salt-water

birmi-n, Vtr: wait for

biṟḍi, N: small hook spear

biṟi, Part: do again, return

biṟmaṟ, N: charcoal

biṟmbir, N: jealousy

biṟɲḍali-n Dyalŋuy, Vint: run

biwi, N: stick knife

biwuṟ, N: fish spear

biya, Part: could have happened

biya, LOAN, N: beer

biyal, N: ripple on water

biya-l, Vtr: (wind) blows, pushes

buda, N: blanket

budidaɲ, LOAN(?), N: potato

budi-l, Vtr: put down, marry

buḍalA, Adj: fine, finely ground

buḍibiɲ, N: a black and red pigeon

buḍi-n, Vtr: tell, call (a name)

buḍu+biya-l, Vtr: blow off bad luck

buga, N: a night, nighttime, darkness

bugal, Adj: black

bugamugu, N: daylight, daybreak

buga-n, Vtr: eat

bugi Dyalŋuy, N: grey wallaby

bugul, N: small loya vine

bugun, N: spring (of water)

bulaɲbay Dyalŋuy, N: man

bulba-l, Vtr: grind (food), rub

bulguṟU, N: swamp

bulin, LOAN, N: plate

buliyiṟ, N: chicken hawk

bulmba, N gen: habitable place, camp

bulna, Adj: impure, poorly defined

bulu, Adj: rotten, stinking

buluba, N: fighting ground

buluṟU, N: storytime person, thing or place

bumba T, Adj: dry

bunbuḍa, N: (spinning) top

bunda, N: mountain, big hill

bundu, N: plaited loya-cane dilly-bag; & N gen: bag

bunḍal, N: bad taste or smell

bunḍa-n, Vtr: strike, beat, hit, kill

bunḍi-l, Vint: burst, explode, bump, collide

bunḍu-ṟ, Vtr: (doctor) fans to wipe off pain

buɲa, N gen: woman, female human

buɲan, N: sun

buŋgu, N: knee

buray, N: cave

burawuɲal, N: female mythic people who live in streams

burbal, N: red ant

burga-l, Vtr: pull out

burganbaɲa-l Dyalŋuy, Vtr: dig

burgi-n, Vint: walk about

buriburi, N: old people

burin, LOAN(?), N: bread

burmbuṟ, N: palm tree sp.

burɲa, N: heart

burɲḍi-n, Adtr: finish off, make die out

burŋga-l, Vint: snore

buruɖuɽ, N: pademelon (wallaby sp.)

burwa-l, Vint: jump

buɽabuɽa, N: dusty place

buɽi, N & N gen: fire, anything burning

buɽimbuɽim, N: small red bird

buɽmbay, N: well-behaved person

buɽmu, Adj: quiet

buɽuɽ U Dyalŋuy, N: cloud

buwum C, N: a vine

buyal, Adj: hard, solid, strong, brave

buybu-ɽ, Vtr: blow, spit at

dabul, N: beach

dabuy, N: a brown bird

daɖu-ɽ T, Vtr: put blanket out

daga-l, Vtr: cut, chop, sever

dagul, Adj: three

dalbal, Adj: on high, reaching up

daliy(i), N/Adj: hunger/hungry

dalmba, N: noise of cutting or ringing

dalŋudalŋu, N: sound of bell ringing

dalu, N: forehead

damari, Adj: silly(person), cf. *damari*, name of mythic character (text 2)

damba, LOAN, N: damper

danba, N: Bougainvillea tree (prickle pine)

dandaba-n, Vint: dance about, feeling lively and pugnacious

dandada-n, Vtr: (doctor) rubs

danda-ɽ, Vtr: rub

dangil, N: bank of creek

daɳɖiri-n, Vint: feel frisky

daŋga-n, Vtr: take out

daraba-n, Vint: shake, rinse mouth

darŋgidarŋgi, N: old woman

daɽba-n, Vint: slip, slide

dawugan, N: silver bream (in freshwater)

daybi-l, Vtr: pick up and take

digara, N: coast, beach

digil, N: Mulgrave walnut

digir, N: nose

dila, N: long feather

dimba-n, Vtr: carry on shoulder

dinda-l Dyalŋuy, Vtr: put standing, set up, erect

diɲal, N: egg

diɲun Dyalŋuy, N gen: stone

dira, N: tooth, cutting edge of axe

diradira, N: corn, maize

dirgul, N/Adj: fat

diwiy, N: tree species

diwu, N: small ground bee

dubur, N: stomach

duda-l, Vtr: throw (sticks or stones) at

duga-l, Vtr: catch, grab, pick up, fetch, buy, get

dugubil, N: bark bag

duguldugul, N: tree with large blue leaves

duguɽ, N: house

dulnbilay, N: white cedar

dumbul, N: blue-tongue lizard

dumbun U, N: scorpion

dundalay Dyalŋuy (?), N: motor car

dunɖi-n, Vint: feel happy, lively; (children) play

dungu, N: head, top of mountain

duŋgul, N: stone fish-yard (i.e. trap)

duɳuɽ, N: reverberating noise

durgim, N: white-tail rat

durgu:, N: mopoke owl

duɽwu Dyalŋuy, N: leaf

duwu T, N: tears

duwur Dyalŋuy, N: stomach

duyi-l, Vtr: fight with spears

ɖa:-, a prefix: see 3.4.3

ɖaban, N: large freshwater eel

ɖabi-l, Vtr: tell not to do, stop

ḍabiṟ, N: flat rock

ḍabu, N gen: ground, earth; solid inanimate matter other than stone or wood

ḍa:bugay, Proper: name of language; ḍa:bugaṇḍi: name of tribe

ḍadam, N: wild banana

ḍadu, N: shade

ḍadu-l, Vtr: put blanket out

ḍaḍa, N: small child

ḍaḍa-l, Vtr: (sacred water) turns against (some person who has broken a taboo)

ḍaḍama-n, Vint: jump over

ḍaḍirI, N: seven sisters (stars); a trap

ḍaguḍagu, Adj: can't do some task (but thinks he can)

ḍala, Adj: shallow

ḍalabi, Loc: on the other side of a creek

ḍalamU, Adj: fresh, young (e.g. leaf)

ḍalga, N: small snail sp.

ḍalgaṟam, N: flat bottle fern

ḍalmbul, N: mud

ḍalŋga-l, Vtr: chop, cut into pieces

ḍalŋgan, N: small black bird

ḍalŋuy, N: avoidance language style

ḍama, N gen (?): anything dangerous, e.g. snake, strong drink, opium

ḍambulA, Adj: two

ḍambun, N: grub sp. (on candlenut and pine trees)

ḍamuy, Adj: sacred, forbidden

ḍana-n, Vint: stand

ḍangan, Adj: no good, bad

ḍangi-l, Vint: get caught, snagged, bogged

ḍaṇḍi-n T, Vint: shift camp

ḍaŋa, N gen (?): hole

ḍaŋa-l, Vtr: grumble at, jealously growl at

ḍaŋgiṟ, Adj: north, northern

ḍaŋgul, N: sister

ḍaŋguy, N: black and white possum

ḍaraga, N: step(-relative)

ḍara-l, Vtr: put standing, set up, erect, assign (name), rain

ḍarḍi, N: net trap, spider web

ḍargi-n, Vtr: embed (e.g. spear-point in handle, meat in ashes)

ḍari-n, Vint: be submerged, sink down, disappear, become lost, fall asleep

ḍaruga, N: scrub hen

ḍaruway, N: small hill, island

ḍaruy, N gen: bird

ḍaṟin, N: straight woomera

ḍaṟiyiy Dyalŋuy, N gen: bird

ḍawaḍawa, N: scrub magpie

ḍa:wurga-n ~ wurga-n, Vint: yawn

ḍaybaṟ, Part: in turn

ḍaymbi, Part: in turn

ḍayŋgaṟ T, N: rapids in river

ḍiba, N: liver, front of shield

ḍibi, Guŋgay and Waṇur only, N: hair

ḍibin, N: navel

ḍibuḍibu, Adj: fancying oneself to know more than one does

ḍidin, N: periwinkle sp.

ḍiga-l, Vtr: pour water on

ḍigirḍigir, N: willy wagtail

ḍigurU, N: thunderstorm

ḍilaṟiy Dyalŋuy, N: black guana

ḍili, N: eye

ḍilibiṟi, N: barramundi

ḍili+budi-l, Vtr: look after

ḍilibugabi, Time: next day

ḍilibuṟa, N: green ant

ḍili+ḍara-l, Vtr: stare at

ḍili+guba-n, Vtr: be jealous concerning

ḍili+gunda-l, Vtr: stop looking

ḍilmay Dyalŋuy, N: grass

ḍilŋaṛ, N: diamond-shaped shell
ḍilŋgu, Loc: down
ḍimba-n, Vtr: catch (something that is in a trajectory)
ḍimbaṛal, N: cyclone
ḍimir, N: a mountain yam
ḍimurU, N: a large house
ḍina, N: foot
ḍinaṛA, N: root
ḍinbi-l, Vint: wriggle, struggle
ḍinḍalam, N: grasshopper sp.
ḍinil, N: whip-tail stingaree
ḍiŋay, N: nostril
ḍiŋay+ḍara-l, Vtr: sneeze at
ḍiŋgal, N: anus
ḍiŋgin, N: vagina
ḍira, N: dry twigs
ḍiran, N: tiredness
ḍirbi, N(?): promise, promised time
ḍirbi+budi-l, Vtr: promise to do something at a certain time
ḍirbi+ḍara-l, Vtr: promise to do something at a certain time
ḍirgaṛ, N: blady grass
ḍiṛi, Time: daybreak
ḍiṛmbi-n, Vint: play up, misbehave
ḍiwa, Adj: middle (of some geographical feature)
ḍiyuya, N: catbird
ḍubu, N: walking stick
ḍubun, N: squeaky noise made by young animal
ḍubun+ḍana-n, Vint: squeak
ḍubuṇ, Adj: quiet
ḍubuṛ, N: stone
ḍuda-n, Vint: go down
ḍudulu, N: brown pigeon
ḍuḍum, N: father's sister
ḍugabal, N: house frame
ḍugarba-n, Vint: have unsettled mind
ḍugi, N gen: tree, stick, wood
ḍula-l, Vtr: dig

ḍulbun, Adj: ready to fight over woman
ḍulmburan, N: dugong
ḍulŋulU, N: waterfall
ḍuluḍulu, N: Johnson hardwood tree
ḍulugunu, N: black myrtle tree (used for fish poison); alcoholic drink
ḍumalA Dyalŋuy, N: straight woomera
ḍumbagi, LOAN, N: tobacco
ḍumba-l C, Vtr: swive (= copulate with)
ḍumbaṛiy, N: grandchild
ḍunda-n, Vint: hang down
ḍundu, N: stump
ḍungi, N: freshwater shrimp
ḍuṇḍa-ṛ, Vint: wade across stream
ḍuŋa-n, Vint: run, move quickly
ḍuŋgumU, N: worm
ḍuŋgun, N: half-cooked gubumA
ḍura:ḍi-n, Vint: shed hair, skin
ḍurgun, Adj: deep
ḍurinU, N: leech
ḍurma-n T, Vtr: swive (= copulate with)
ḍuruḍuru, N: adult man
ḍuṛbal, N: small woven grass basket
ḍuṛi, Adj: sharp, pointed
ḍuwa, LOAN, N: saw
ḍuwi-n, Vint: swim
ḍuwarA, N: wattle tree
ḍuyu-n, Vint: (long thing, e.g. snake) wriggles

gabaḍi, LOAN, N: cabbage
gaba-l, Vtr: give birth to, feed (baby)
gabanU, N: rain
gabaṛ, N: lower arm
gabay, N: road, track, pad
gabuḍu, N: white clay
gabulU, N: stick for carrying fish
gabun, Adj: fresh

gada, N: noise of sticks being banged together for dance accompaniment

gada-n, Vint: come

gadigadiy, N: very small children

gadil, Adj: very small

gaḍa, N: spirit of a man, white man

gaḍarA, N: brown possum

gaḍi, Loc: long way

gaḍu:, N: black tree ant

gaḍulA ~ U, Adj: dirty (e.g. water)

gagal, Adj: light (in weight)

gala, N: gen spear

galambaṟa:, N: march fly

galban, N: small stone axe

galbin, N: son

galbiy, N: catfish

galgali, N: curlew

gali-n, Vint: go

galŋa, N: mother's brother

galŋgiṟ, N: sister

galway, N: spirit, shadow, reflection

gama-n, Vint: vomit

gamaṟ Dyalŋuy, N: line, mark

gamaṟ + mulbi-n Dyalŋuy, Vtr: paint in pattern

gamba-n, Vint: crawl

gambi, N: clothes; & Adj: flat

gambil, N: tail; mountain spur

gambinU, N: top-knot pigeon

gambiṟA, N: tablelands

gambunU, N: a type of spirit

gambuṟ, N: white clay (for face painting etc.)

gamim, N: father's father

gamu, N: flower, blossom

gana, Part: try

ganagayuy, Part: 'self'

ganamaṟbu, Part: 'self'

ganan, Adj: be doing briefly

ganaŋgar, Part: do first

ganawaŋgi, Adj: belly up

ganayir, Loc: underneath

ganba, Loc: very long way

ganda, N: yamstick

gangulA, N: grey wallaby

gani, Loc: way outside the camp

gaṇalA, N: black scrub locust

gaṇarA, N: alligator

gaṇḍilA, N: crab

gaṇḍugaṇḍu, N: tree with small black fruit

gaṇaṟA, N: European-type axe

gaŋa, N: noise of a person nearing

gaŋgi, N: yellow walnut

gaŋgu, N: side of mountain, waist

gaŋgu + ḍuŋga-n, Vint: take short cut

gaŋunA, N: bushes arranged as animal trap

garanganda-n, Vint: (sky) glows burning yellow

garaway, N: brown snail

garu, Time: by-and-by

gaṟan, Adj: clean

gaṟana T, N: black cockatoo

gaṟaŋgal, N: vine with white inedible fruit

gaṟba, Loc: behind

gaṟba-n, Vint: hide

gaṟbaṟA, N: mangrove tree

gaṟbi, N: overhanging mountain ledge

gaṟna C, N: black cockatoo

gawal, N: a call, shout

gawal + ḍana-n, Vint: call out

gawam, N: broken bank

gawanday, N: spirit of a dead person

gawar, N: blood

gawirI, Adj: crescent shaped

gawu:, N: tree sp.

gawuda, LOAN, N: coat

gawulA (~ U?), N: blue gum tree

gawuṟ, Adj: crossways

gayagay, N: whisper

gayal, Adj: another (see 6.2.2)

gayba-ṟ, Vtr: make body feel good

gayi Dyalŋuy, N gen: ground, earth; solid inanimate matter other than stone or wood

gaymba-ṟ, Vtr: follow, sneak up on

gaymbi-n, Adtr: do to all of a set of objects

gayŋi-n, Vtr: warn not to do

giba-l, Vtr: scrape, scratch

gidi, N: tea-tree torch

gidigidiy, N: small children

gidil, Adj: small

giḍa, Adj: quick

giḍa-n, Adtr: do quickly

giḍaṟ, N: line, mark

giḍaṟḍi, N: policeman

giḍaṟ+gunda-l, Vtr: paint in pattern

gilaḍi, LOAN, N: glass

gilbay, N: guana sp.

gilbi-l, Vtr: throw, chuck away

gilḍu-l Dyalŋuy, Vtr: bite

gilga, Adj: imperfect, 'soft'

gimalA, N: tree from which firedrills are made

gindaḍa, N: cassowary

gindalba, N: small lizard sp.

gindanU, N: moon

ginga, N: prickle

gini, N: penis

ginu, N: (dug-out) canoe

giŋa, N: fever

giŋa:, N: vine sp.

giraguṇḍiy, N: green frog sp.

giramgiram, N: cramp

girgan, Time: last year

giṟaṟ, Adj: soft (skin)

giṟi, N: branch, fork of tree

giṟi-n, Vint: (children) shout in play

giwa-n, Vint: be stirred up

giyaṟA, N: stinging nettle tree

giyi C, Part: don't

guba-n, Vtr: burn, cook

guban, N: big butterfly

gubi, N(?): 'storytime' (see 1.4)

gubu, N: leaf

gubumA, N: black pine

gudaga, N: dog

gudaṟ, Adj: cold

gudubuṟ, N: stinking rat sp.

guḍal, Adj: pregnant

guḍara, N: broom-like implement made of weed

guḍi-l, Vtr: smell

guḍin, N: bull ant

guḍuga, Adj: belonging to someone else

guḍuguḍu, N: rainbow

guḍun, N: bottom (anat.)

guḍunU, N: wind

guga, N: skin, bark

guga-l, Vtr: call out to

gugal, N: fire drill

gugaṟ, N: large guana

guginar, LOAN, N: coconut

gugiŋU, N: flying fox

gugu, N gen: language or other controlled noise

gugulu, N: recitative mourning style used by men

gula, N: body

gula-l, Vtr: break, break up

gulanU, N: walnut tree

gulaṟI, N: big-leafed fig tree

gulbul, N: wave

gulga, Adj: short

gulgi, N: sand, sugar

guli, Adj: wild, ready to fight

guli, N: louse

guludu, N: dove

gulugulu, N: small freshwater black bream

guman, Adj: one, alone

gumaṟi, Adj: red (normally applied to mineral-coloured water)

gumba, N: prepubescent girl

gumbalA, N: a stage in the development of grubs

gumbi-l, Vtr: pick up

gumbiraŋa-l, Dyalŋuy, Vtr: pick up

gunaguna, Time(?): middle of the night

gunbulA ~ U Dyalŋuy(?), N: billy-can

gunda-l, Vtr: cut

gunduy, N: brown snake

gunḏi-n, Vint: return

gunugunu, Adj: ready to fight to expiate crime

guṇḏilbay, N: short tiger snake

guṇḏi-n, Vint: break

guɲi, Part: T don't, C let do

guɲin, Adj: south, southern

guŋgambuṟ, N: small butterfly sp.

guŋgaṟI, Loc: north

guŋgay, Proper: name of language; *guŋgaɲḏi*: name of tribe

guralŋgan, N: curlew

guran, Adj: long, tall

gurbi, Part: maybe, perhaps

gurbi-l, Vint: (sky) darkens

gurḏi-l, Vint: be soaked

gurga, N: neck

gurgiya, N: fresh-water khaki bream

guriliy, N: black nose wallaby

guriɲ, Adj: good

gurŋga C, N: kookaburra

gurunU, N: language, story, news

guruŋga T, N: kookaburra

guṟabay, N: small lizard sp.

guṟbaba, N: lizard sp.

guṟbanU, N: crow

guṟi, N: waist

guṟuŋga, N: a scrub insect

guwa, Loc: west

guwal, N: name

guya ~ guyabay, Loc: across (the river)

guyalA, N: fish hawk cf. *guyala*, name of mythic character (text 2)

guybil, N: a whistle (noise)

guybil+ḏana-n, Vint: whistle

guygaguygam, Time: afternoon/evening

guygal, N: long-nose bandicoot; large salt-water eel

guygam, Time: yesterday

guygi, N: leafy loya vine

guyi, Adj(?): heart-broken (?)

guyirI, Adj: calm (water)

guyŋgan, N: spirit of a woman, white woman; grasshopper sp.

guyŋgilbi, N: Moreton Bay tree

guyu, N: tree vine sp.

guyuṟU, N: storm

landima-l, LOAN, Vtr: teach

lululumba-l, Vtr: rock baby to sleep

maba-l C, Vtr: light torch, fire

maba-l, T Dyalŋuy, Vtr: burn, cook

maba-l, Vtr: lift up

mabi, N: tree-climbing kangaroo

mada, Adj: soft

maḏa, N: sawdust

maḏalA, N: tree fern

maḏa-n, Vtr: suck, chew

maḏinda-n, Vint: walk up

maḏur, N: small frog sp.

maga, Adj(?): in company

magaṟ, Adj: outside (house)

magi-l, Vint: climb up

magu, N: chest (& lap ?)

magulA(~ U ?), N: a root vegetable

mala, N: palm of hand

malaḏi, LOAN, N: molasses

mala-l, Vtr: feel with hand

malan, N: flat rock

malanU, N: right hand

malaṟA, N: spider web

malgay, N: small freshwater fish sp.

maluway T, N: spirit, shadow

malway C, N: spirit, shadow

mamba, Adj: sour, salty, bitter

mandi, N: hand

manḍa, N: culprit

manḍa-n, Vtr: fill up any part of body

manḍalA Dyalŋuy, N: water

mani-n, Vtr: catch (e.g. in trap)

manya-n, Vint: be frightened

manu, N: top of tree

maɳḍam, N: mark (e.g. from wound, writing)

maŋga, N: (bird's) nest

maŋga-n, Vint: laugh, smile

maŋgum, N gen: frog

maŋgumbar, N: leaf grub

margaɲ, N: fighting men

margu, N: grey possum sp.

maɽa, N: leaf

maɽal, N: noise of hand-clapping

maɽbu, Adj: one's own (part of oneself)

maɽun, N: cloud

mayaɽA, N: young initiated man of the *gurabana* moiety

maygay Dyalŋuy, N: black pine

mayi, N gen: non-flesh food

mida, N: clicking noise

miḍaguran Dyalŋuy, Time: yesterday, tomorrow

miḍi-l, Vtr: block (e.g. road)

miḍin, LOAN, N: mission

mila, N: tongue

milba, Adj: clever

milgal Dyalŋuy, N: eye; silver bream

milirI, N: cramp, pins and needles

milma-l, Vtr: tie up

mimi, N: flying spark

mindil, N: tick

mindirI, N: salt-water centipede

miɲa, N gen: edible animal, meat

mirimbal, N: yellow cockatoo feather

miwa-l, Vtr: pick up, lift (anything heavy)

miwuɽ, Adj: gathered up

miyiɽ, N: wind connected with thunderstorm

mudaga, N: pencil cedar tree

mudaga, LOAN, N: motor car

mudalA, N: black mangrove tree; garfish

mudi, N: thick black edible loya vine

muḍam, N: mother, and mother's sister

mugaɽu, N: fish net

mugay, N: upper grinding stone

mugiɲ, N: small rat

mugiɽV, N: small mussels

mugiymugiy Dyalŋuy, N: woman

mugu, Part: couldn't help it

muguy, Time: all the time

mulam, N: stew, soup, meat gravy

mulari, N: initiated man

mulbi-n Dyalŋuy, Vtr: cut

mulɲari Dyalŋuy, N: blanket

munda-l, Vtr: pull

mundimay, N: vegetable sp.

mundu, N: wind (in lungs), spirit, temper, desire, ease

munil, N: wait-a-while vine sp.

munu, Loc: inside

muɳḍuɽU, Adj: plenty

muɲimuɲi, N gen: ant

muɲaɽA Dyalŋuy, N: scrub turkey

muŋga, N: husband

muŋgun, N: wound

muran, N: sickness

muray, N: headhair

murba, Loc: under water

murgan, N: quandong tree

murgu, N: hole in ground, cooking pit

muri:ḍi-n, Vint: scream

murŋgal, N: short feather

muɽay, N: snake skin that has been shed; clothes

muɽinU, N: ashes

muɽiɽ, N: mosquito

muɽuḍum, N: stingaree

muɽuy, N: white bee

muway Dyalŋuy, Part/Interjection: not/no

muygal, N: hole dug as animal trap

muygun, N: yam vine

muyŋga, N: cicatrices (tribal marks)

muyŋgin, Adj: cooked

muyubara, Adj: strange, foreign, new

nada-l, Vtr: peel skin off

naga, Loc: east

nambi-l, Vtr: hold, hold down

nani-l, Vtr: growl, swear at

naŋgu, N: grass mattress

nara, N gen: vine

nayŋu-ɽ Dyalŋuy, Vtr: throw

niba-l, Vtr: show

nila-n, Vint: hide

nirgil, N: hot charcoal, hot coals

nuba, Adj: ripe

nulga-l, Vtr: wake up

numa-n, Vint: move about (e.g. eyes blink, adam's apple moves up and down)

numbi-n, Vtr: look around for

ɲagilI(~ *A* ?), Adj: warm

ɲala, N: butt of tree; coast

ɲalaɲ, Adj: unfamiliar, strange (place)

ɲambi-n, Vtr: paint

ɲaɲḍi, N: body, flesh, meat

ɲaŋga:ḍi-n, Vint: talk, speak

ɲari, N: hole in ground

ɲari+baga-l, Vtr: dig hole (to bury something in)

ɲari+budi-l, Vtr: put in hole and cover over

ɲari+ḍara-l, Vtr: put in hole and cover over

ɲarmbi-l, Vint: approach (but not quite reach) the ground

ɲaru, Loc: on top of

ɲiban, Adj: stubborn

ɲina-n, Vint: sit

ɲirḍa-ɽ, Vtr: put sitting down

ɲiriɲi ~ *ɲirɲi*, N: long peppery fruit

ɲiwir, Adj: broken up

ɲiya:rḍi-n Dyalŋuy, Vint: sit

ɲulaɲ, Part: it's a good job that—

ɲuma-l, Vtr: smell

ɲumbul, N: beard

ɲundu, 2 sg pronoun

ɲunduba, 2 n-sg pronoun

ɲuni-, 2 sg pronoun oblique root

ɲunmul Dyalŋuy, Adj: one

ɲuɲḍu-ɽ Dyalŋuy, Vtr: smell

ɲuɲga-ɽ Dyalŋuy, Vtr: smell

ɲuŋgulU, N: Torres Straits pigeon

ɲurugu, N: sound of talking a long way off (when the words cannot quite be made out)

ŋaba-n, Vint: bathe

ŋabi, Adj: many, a lot of

ŋabul, N: a clicking noise

ŋabuŋga, N: wattle tree sp.

ŋadi, Part: 'self'

ŋaḍa, Part(?): 'might be'(?)

ŋaḍa, Time: tomorrow

ŋaḍaguran, Time: morning

ŋaḍan, Proper: name of language; *ŋaḍanḍi*: name of tribe

ŋaḍu-, I sg pronoun oblique root

ŋalal, Adj: big

ŋalḍan Dyalŋuy, N: a light

ŋali, I du pronoun

ŋambin, Loc: belly down

ŋambu, Adj(?): part-way

ŋamuguɳḍi, N: index finger

ŋamuray, N: a smell

ŋanḍar, N: creek

ŋaɳḍaguman, N: brother

ŋaɳḍal, N: a light

ŋaɳḍi, ı n-sg pronoun

ŋaŋga, Adj: deaf

ŋaŋga-n, Vtr: forget

ŋara:, Interjection: 'what'

ŋaɽa, Loc: south

ŋaɽu, N: shake-a-leg dance style; &
   Adj: between legs

ŋaɽu+wanda-n, Vint: dance shake-
   a-leg style

ŋawuyu, N: salt-water turtle

ŋayu, ı sg pronoun

ɲiḍubaɲ, N: small salt-water mussel

ɲiɽa-l, Vtr: hang up

ɲiya, N: rim of dilly-bag, side of
   creek or hill

ɲu-, deictic root 'that'

ɲubirbiɲ, N: leech

ɲuḍu, Part/Interjection: not/no

ɲulaɲ-, prefix to Loc in Dyalŋuy (see
   6.3)

ɲulugun, N: small pandamus tree

ɲumbaɽ, N: face

ɲumbubu, N: new-born baby

ɲumbun, N: heaps of soft sand

ɲunaŋgara, N: whale

ɲunɲun Dyalŋuy, N: breast

ɲuɲurU, N: initiated man

ɲuɲariɲ, deictic 'that kind of thing'

ɲuɲudi wala, IDIOM: that's alright

ɲura-l, Vtr: show by lifting up

ɲuriḍulu: T, Time: a few days ago

ɲuruɲ ~ ɲuru:, Interjection: 'why'

ɲuɽil T, Time: just now

ɲuɽulU, N: shade (of a bushy plant)

ɲuyar+gada-n, Vtr: think about

ɲuyar+wanda-n, Vint: think

ɲuyay, N: kangaroo grass

ŋuygunU, N: whispered talk

wabaɽ, N: a walk

wabaɽwabaɽ, N(?): anything subject
   to cultural taboo

wadir, N: serrations (e.g. cicatrices,
   ribs, washboard, on grinding stone)

waḍu-l, Vtr: cook, burn

wagal, N: wife

wagaɽI ~ A, Adj: wide

waguḍa, N gen: man, male human

wala, Part: ceased

walba, N gen: stone

walmbay, N: waterfall

walmbir, Adj(?): beside – see 3.4.2

walnḍa-l, Vtr: select best of anything

walɲḍi, N: cliff

walŋa-l, Vint: float (in water), glide
   (through air)

walŋgu-ɽ, Vtr: peep in/around at

walu, N: side of head above ear, side
   of hill

waluɽubara Dyalŋuy, N: black nose
   wallaby

wamba-n, Vtr: wait for

wanda-n, Vint: fall down, drop

wangamU, N: kidney

waɲa, 'who', human indefinite/in-
   terrogative

waɳḍa, 'where', indefinite/interro-
   gative locational root

waɳḍariɲ, deictic 'what kind of'

waɳḍaɲunda, Time: when

waɳḍirI, Adj: how many

waɳḍirim, Time: how long

waɳḍirimay, Time: when

waɳḍu-, 'who' human indefinite/in-
   terrogative oblique root

waɳḍuluy, deictic 'how/which way'

waɲi, 'what', non-animate indefinite/
   interrogative

waɲinbara:, 'what's the matter'

waɲira, 'what kind of'

waŋal, N: boomerang

waɲaɼI, N: prepubescent boy

waŋga:ɖi-n, Vint: wake up, get up

waŋgamU, N: overhanging cliff

waŋgi, Loc: up

waŋgulay, N: white cockatoo

wara, Part: done the wrong way

warabal, N: flying squirrel

waram-, Classifier for counting days – see 6.2.3

wara-n, Vint: shift camp

warɖan, N: raft, plank boat

wargin, N: forest

wari-n, Vint: jump (e.g. animal jumps, or person jumps away in fright)

waɼŋgi-n, Adtr: do all around, turn around

waruɲu+gilɖu-l Dyalŋuy, Vtr: dream about

waruwaru, N: small child

waɼaba, N: wide creek

waɼa:buga, N: white apple tree

waɼi, N: mouth

waɼil, N: doorway of house, mouth of trap

wawa-l, Vtr: see, look at

wawun, N: scrub turkey

wawur, Adj: some – see 6.2.2

wayba-n, Vint: go round

wayilI, N: red bream

waymbala-n, Vint: roll

waymba-n, Vint: fly

wayu, Time: for a long time

wiɖi, N: small frog sp.

wigi-l, Vtr: (rich food) makes (a person) feel satiated and sick

wigilwigil, Adj: sweet

winaɼA Dyalŋuy, N: foot

wira, N gen: movable object; N: 'cunt'

wiɼa-n, Vint: be bent, twisted

wiɼulU, N: shell fish sp.

wiwi-n, Vtr: give

wubay, N: alligator bird

wubulV, Adj: lucky (at hunting, etc.)

wuda, N: shark

wuɖa-n, Vint: cross river

wuɖar, N: dew, frost

wuɖigay, N: wild guava

wuɖi-n, Vint: grow up

wugamU, N: firefly

wugu, LOAN, N/Adj: work(ing)

wugul, N: nape

wula-n, Vint: die

wulmbuɼU, N: leafy broom

wulŋga-n, Vint: covered by water, drowned

wulŋgu, N: a female song-style

wulŋgu+ɖana-n, Vint: sing *wulŋgu* style

wumbul, Adj: hot

wuna-n, Vint: lie down, sleep; exist

wuɲday, N: stolen article

wuɲɖu, N: smoke

wuɲaba-n, Vtr: look for meat, hunt

wuɲa-n, Vtr: drink, swallow

wuŋga, N: mourning song style used by women

wuŋgur, N: shouts of 'wɔ wɔ' during dance

wuɲul, N: carpet snake

wurba-n, Vtr: look for, search, seek

wurga-n ~ ɖa:wurga-n, Vint: yawn

wurgulV, N: pelican

wurmba, Adj: asleep (& N: a sleep?)

wuɼgun, N: postpubescent boy

wuɼu, N: spear handle

wuɼu:, N: large river; small slatey-coloured snake

wuɼuɲ Dyalŋuy, N: shrimp, crayfish

wuwuy T, N: small bean tree

wuyuba:ḍi-n Dyalŋuy, Vint: speak, talk

wuyubaŋa-l Dyalŋuy, Vtr: tell, call (a name)

yaba, N: brother

yabi, N: grey possum

yabulam, N: an edible loya vine

yabuṟU, N: postpubescent girl

yaḍi-l, Vint: walk about

yaga, Adj: split in half

yaga+ḍara-l, Vtr: split in half

yaga-ṟ, Vtr: hunt away

yaguɲU, N: echidna, porcupine

yalbur, N: grey frog sp.

yalmbin, Adj: in line

yaluga, Loc: (motion to) close up

yaluɲunda, Time: today, nowadays

yangaṟA, Adj: straight

yaŋgi-n, Vtr: split, rip, tear, slice

yaɲin, N: side of face between eye and ear

yaraman, LOAN, N: horse

yarga, Adj: nothing, none

yaṟbul Dyalŋuy, Adj: no good, bad

yaṟŋga-n, Vint: be frightened

yaṟuɲ, Adj: silly, stupid (person)

yawu:, N: grass sp.

yaymi-l, Vtr: ask

yi-, deictic root 'this'

yibu:, N(?): miming in dance routine

yidiɲ, Proper: language name; *yidiɲḍi*: tribal name

yigan, N: sky

yilari-n, Vint: be scattered, spread about

yiŋariɲ, deictic 'this sort of thing'

yiŋgilibiy LOAN C, N: English bee

yiɲiliman LOAN T, N: English bee

yiraba:ḍi-n Dyalŋuy, Vint: bathe

yiriy, N: type of slatey stone

yiwan, N: small shelter

yiway, N: wind

yiway ~ *yiwaɲḍi*, Time: wintertime

yiyi, Interjection: yes

yu-, deictic root 'that' (C: far distant; T: not visible)

yubi-n, Vtr: rub

yulba-l, Vint: sneak up

yulu:, N: flat-tail stingaree

yumba-ṟ, Vtr: send message to

yuɲa-n, Vint: cross river

yuɲariɲ, deictic 'that other sort of thing'

yuŋga-l, Vtr: grind

yurga, Part: still

yurunU, Time: a long time ago

yuṟiya, N: saltwater snake sp.

yuyuṟuŋgul, N: noise of snake sliding through grass

List of affixes

All allomorphs of grammatical affixes are listed below, together with the section(s) containing major discussion of their morphological occurrence and conditioning.

C indicates an affix that is cohering (2.4) but is not reduced by Rule 2 (2.3.2–3). CR denotes an affix that is cohering and does reduce. N indicates non-coherence (and therefore non-reduction).

-(a)la N 'now' – 2.3.9, 3.9.1
-(a)m C durational time – 3.7.8
-(a)may C point time – 3.7.8

-ba C locative – 3.3.2
-ba C one of a group – 3.3.6, 3.6.5, 3.7.5, 5.2.7
-baɲ C juxtapositional – 3.4.2
-bara N 'belonging to' – 3.3.6
-bi C 'another' – 3.3.6
-biḍi-n N dispersed activity – 3.8.8
-bu C ergative – 3.3.2
-buḍun N 'still' – 3.9.5

-da C locative – 3.3.2
-(n)da C dative – 3.3.2, 3.6.2–3
-daga-n N inchoative verbaliser – 2.4, 3.7.2–3, 4.8.1
-:da-n C coming – 2.3.5, 3.8.6–7
-:daŋgada-n reduplicated coming – 3.8.6
-damba N 'with a lot of' – 3.3.6
-di N 'self' – 3.9.2
-du C ergative – 3.3.2, 3.7.2–3

ḍa:- N 'towards' – 2.4, 3.4.3, 3.8.1
-ḍamu N 'only, all' – 3.3.6, 3.9.7
-ḍa C locative – 3.3.2

-ḍi C comitative – 2.4, 3.3.4, 3.6.2–3, 3.6.5, 3.7.2–3, 4.3.1
-ḍi C 'lest' – 3.8.4, 4.6.2–3
-ḍi+da C 'fear' – 3.3.2, 3.6.2–3, 3.7.2–3, 4.6.1, 4.6.3
-ḍilŋgu N 'down' – 3.3.8
-:ḍi-n C antipassive etc. – 2.3.5–6, 2.6.4, 3.8.5, 3.8.7, 4.2, 4.3.8, 5.2.3–4, 5.5.2–3
-ḍu C ergative – 3.3.2
:ḍulu: N durative – 3.3.7, 3.5

-gaɽa: N 'from' – 3.3.7
-gimbal N privative – 2.4, 3.3.6, 3.7.2–3, 4.3.1
-gu C purposive – 3.3.2, 3.6.2–3, 3.7.2–3, 4.5.1, 4.5.4
-gu C allative – 3.4.1, 3.7.2–3
-gu C 'until' – 3.5, 3.7.8
-guwa N 'west' – 3.3.8

-l- C conjugation marker – 3.8.3
-l C present tense – 3.8.4
-:l C irregular ergative – 3.3.2
-:l C irregular locative – 3.3.2
-:l C allative – 3.7.2–3
-la CR(?) locative – 2.3.3, 3.3.2
-la N 'now' – 2.3.9, 3.9.1

-:*li-n* C going – 2.3.5–6, 2.5.1,3.8.6–7

-:*liŋgali-n* reduplicated going – 3.8.6

-*l(n)da* C irregular dative – 3.3.2

-*luŋa-l* N transitive verbaliser – 4.8.3

-*m* C durational time – 3.7.8

-*m* C ablative-causal – 2.3.3, 3.3.2, 3.4.1

-*m* C 'since' – 3.5, 3.7.8

-*maḍi-n* N incremental verbaliser – 4.8.2

-*maŋa-l* N verbal comitative – 3.8.5, 3.8.7, 4.3, 5.4

-*mari* N 'along' – 3.3.7, 3.9.7

-*may* C point time – 3.7.8

-*mu* CR(?) ablative-causal – 2.3.3, 3.3.2, 3.4.1, 3.7.2–3, 4.4.4, 4.4.6

-*mu* CR(?) 'since' – 3.5, 3.7.8

-*muḍay* N comitative – 2.4, 3.3.6, 3.7.2–3, 4.3.1

-*muŋgal* N 'lots, all' – 3.3.6

-*n*- C conjugation marker – 3.8.3

-*n* C imperative – 3.8.4

-*na* C verbal purposive – 3.8.4, 4.5.2–5

-*naga* N 'east' – 3.3.8

-:*nbiḍi-n* N dispersed activity – 3.8.8

-*nda* C dative – 3.3.2, 3.6.2–3, 3.7.2–3

-*ni* ~ -:*n* CR genitive – 2.3.2, 3.3.3, 3.6.2–3, 3.7.2–3, 4.7

-*nim* C causal/past possessive – 3.3.3, 3.6.2–3, 3.7.2–3, 4.4.4, 4.4.6, 4.7.2

-*ɲa* ~ -:*ɲ* CR accusative – 3.3.7, 3.6.2–3, 3.7.2–3

-*ɲa* N emphatic – 3.3.7, 3.9.7

-*ɲḍa* C locative – 3.3.2

-*ɲḍi* C comitative – 3.3.4

-(*ɲ*)*ḍu* C ergative – 3.3.2

-*ɲu* ~ -:*ɲ* CR past tense – 2.3.2, 3.8.4

-*ɲu+nda* ~ -*ɲu:+n* CR dative subordinate – 2.3.2, 3.8.4, 4.4.1–4

-*ɲu+m* C causal subordinate – 3.8.4, 4.4.5–6

-*ŋ* C present tense – 2.6.3, 3.8.4

-*ŋada-n* N coming – 2.3.5, 3.8.6–7

-*ŋadaŋgada-n* reduplicated coming – 3.8.6

-*ŋa-l* CR verbal comitative – 2.4, 2.6.4, 3.8.5, 3.8.7, 4.3, 5.4

-*ŋa-l* CR causative verbaliser – 2.4, 3.7.2–3, 4.8.1

-*ŋali-n* N going – 2.3.5, 2.4, 2.5.1, 3.8.6–7

-*ŋaliŋgali-n* reduplicated going – 3.8.6

-*ŋgu* ~ -:*ŋ* CR ergative – 2.3.2, 3.3.2, 3.7.2–3

-*ŋuɻi* N 'this—, like—' – 3.9.3

-*ŋuɻu* N 'for another thing' – 3.9.4

-*r* C imperative – 3.8.4

-:*ri-n* C going – 2.3.5–6, 2.5.1,3.8.6–7

-*ruɲ* C allative of direction – 3.7.2–3

-*ɻ*- C conjugation marker – 3.8.3

-*ɻ* C present tense – 3.8.4

-:*ɻi-n* C aspect – 2.3.5–6, 2.5.1,3.8.6–7

-:*ɻiŋgali-n* reduplicated going – 3.8.6

-*waḍan* N comparative – 3.9.6

-*waŋgi* N 'up' – 3.3.8

-*yi* ~ -:*y* CR comitative – 2.3.3, 2.3.9, 2.4, 3.3.4, 3.7.2–3, 4.3.1

-*yi+da* C 'fear' – 3.3.2, 3.7.2–3, 4.6.1, 4.6.3

-: C locative – 2.3.3, 3.3.2

Index of Australian languages and tribes